Reel Portrayals

The Lives of 640 Historical Persons on Film, 1929 through 2001

Michael G. Stevens

Edited by R. THOMPSON

McFarland & Company, Inc., Publishers
Jefferson, North Carolina, and London

LIBRARY OF CONGRESS CATALOGUING-IN-PUBLICATION DATA

Stevens, Michael G., 1955–1997
    Reel portrayals: the lives of 640 historical persons on film, 1929
through 2001 / Michael G. Stevens ; edited by R. Thompson.
        p.   cm.
    Includes bibliographical references and index.

    ISBN 0-7864-1461-8 (softcover : 50# alkaline paper)

    1. Biographical films — Catalogs.   I. Thompson, Rita M.,
1937– II. Title.
    PN1995.9.B55S74   2003
    016.79143'658 — dc21   2003005731

British Library cataloguing data are available

On the cover: Ben Franklin (*Art Today*) and Howard Da Silva in the
musical *1776* playing Franklin (*Museum of Modern Art Film Stills Archive*)

Manufactured in the United States of America

McFarland & Company, Inc., Publishers
    Box 611, Jefferson, North Carolina 28640
        www.mcfarlandpub.com

For Peg

Acknowledgments

A talented entertainer and dedicated film buff, Michael Stevens was in the process of writing this film reference book when he died on June 10, 1997. The work was intended for film lovers, students, and anyone with an interest in or curiosity about the subject. The goal was to include all characters meeting the criteria in films released from the advent of "talkies" through the millennium. Unfortunately, the work stopped at the end of 1996, leaving the manuscript incomplete.

His friends felt that the work should be made available to the people for whom it was intended. We have completed it to include releases from 1997 through 2001. The royalties from the sale of this book are assigned to the Michael Stevens Memorial Scholarship for Theater Arts at Northern Essex Community College in Haverhill, Massachusetts.

A sincere thank you to the special people without whose help this task could not have been accomplished: Michael Sljaka, Vincent Sljaka, Lisa O'Hearn, Mark Brady, and Kate Korbey.

A special thank you to Terry Geesken and Mary Corlis of the Museum of Modern Art Film Stills Archive in New York City.

R. Thompson
April 2003

Contents

Introduction

There was a time when I would laugh when I heard about authors who spent ten years working on a book. That was before I read Roy Pickard's *Who Played Who in the Movies*. That was before I became inspired to write my own book of film portrayals. That was 11 years ago.

In that time other books concentrating on film depictions have been published, but none has tried to cover nonfictional portrayals as comprehensively as I have done with this book.

My selection criteria for characters to be included have been fairly simple: (1) the character must be non-fictional; (2) the character must have some historical or social importance; and (3) the character must have been portrayed at least twice in feature films (self-depictions not counting).

I know that arguments could be made on each of these points. Was Barabbas a real person? (I've given the benefit of any doubt to Biblical characters. Call it hedging my bets.) How historically/socially important is Robert Roy MacGregor, or Sam Phillips, or Richard Sutherland? (I guess that depends on whether you're a student of Scotland, rock 'n' roll or military history.)

Why require two portrayals? What about Alexander the Great, or Lon Chaney, or Julius Reuter? (See Roy Pickard's *Who Played Who on the Screen* or Eileen Karsten's *From Real Life to Reel Life* for these and many other single portrayal listings.)

Because of the volume of research required and the need for a limitation in order to get the book finished, my concentration has been primarily on films produced in the United States and Great Britain.

Michael G. Stevens
October 20, 1996

1

The Portrayals

Adams, John *see* 570

Adams, John Quincy *see* 573

1 Adamson, George (1906–1989)

British (Indian born) game warden, Adamson, along with his wife **Joy**, devoted his life to the preservation of wildlife in Kenya. He was killed by poachers in 1989. He played himself in the short film *The Lion at the End of the World* (74) and in the feature version of it: *Christian the Lion* (76).

Bill Travers. *Born Free* (GB/1966/95m/C) D: James Hill. B/on the book by Joy Adamson. C: Virginia McKenna, Geoffrey Keen, Peter Lukoye, Omar Chambati.

Nigel Davenport. *Living Free* (GB/1972/90m/C) D: Jack Couffer. B/on books by Joy Adamson. C: Susan Hampshire, Geoffrey Keen, Edward Judd, Peter Lukoye, Shane De Louvres, Robert Beaumont.

Richard Harris. *To Walk with Lions* (Canada/1999/108m/C) D: Carl Schultz. C: John Michie, Ian Bannen, Kerry Fox, Hugh Quarshi, Honor Blackman, Geraldine Chaplin, David Mulwa, Ng'ang'a Kirumburu.

2 Adamson, Joy (1910–1980)

(Joy Friederike Victoria Gessner) Austrian born writer and wildlife conservationist, Adamson's experiences raising Elsa the lioness were the basis for her books *Born Free* and *Living Free*. She was murdered (by an employee) in 1980 at the Shaba Game preserve in Kenya.

Virginia McKenna. *Born Free* (GB/1966/95m/C) D: James Hill. B/on the book by Joy Adamson. C: Bill Travers, Geoffrey Keen, Peter Lukoye, Omar Chambati.

Susan Hampshire. *Living Free* (GB/1972/90m/C) D: Jack Couffer. B/on books by Joy Adamson. C: Nigel Davenport, Geoffrey Keen, Edward Judd, Peter Lukoye, Shane De Louvres, Robert Beaumont.

Honor Blackman. *To Walk with Lions* (Canada/1999/108m/C) D: Carl Schultz.

C: Richard Harris, John Michie, Ian Bannen, Kerry Fox, Hugh Quarshi, Geraldine Chaplin, David Mulwa, Ng'ang'a Kirumburu.

3 Aguirre, Lope de (1508?–1561)

A Spanish adventurer who tried to establish his own kingdom in South America, Aguirre was captured and killed by the Spanish army.

Klaus Kinski. *Aguirre, the Wrath of God* (Germany/1972/94m/C) D: Werner Herzog. C: Ruy Gueirra, Del Negro, Helena Rojo, Cecilia Rivera, Peter Berling, Danny Ades.

Omero Antonutti. *El Dorado* (Spain-France-Italy/1988/151m/C) D: Carlos Saura. C: Eusebio Poncela, Lambert Wilson, Gabriela Roel, José Sancho, Fédor Atkine, Patxi Bisquert, Francisco Algora, Francisco Merino, Abel Víton, Mariono Gonzáles, Inés Sastre, Gladys Catania, Alfredo Catania, Gustavo Rojas.

4 Albert, Prince (1819–1861)

(Albert Francis Charles Augustus Emmanuel of Saxe-Coburg-Gotha) German born cousin and husband to **Queen Victoria**, Albert was her beloved confidante and most trusted advisor until his death from typhoid fever at the age of 42. In the British TV mini-series *Edward VII* (75), he was portrayed by Robert Hardy, and in the mini-series *Victoria and Albert* (2001) by Jonathan Firth.

Eugene Leahy. *Balaclava* (aka *Jaws of Hell*) (GB/1930/94m/BW) D: Maurice Elvey & Milton Rosmer. B/on *The Charge of the Light Brigade* by Alfred Lord Tennyson. Made as a silent in 1928, with sound added in 1930. C: Benita Hume, Cyril McLaglen, J. Fisher White, Bos Ranevsky, Wallace Bosco, Marian Drada.

Heinz von Cleve. *Waltz Time in Vienna* (aka *Walzerkrieg*) (Germany/1933/80m/BW) D: Ludwig Berger. C: Adolf Wohlbruck (Anton Walbrook), Hanna Waag, Willy Fritsch.

Friedrich Benfer. *Mädchenjahre Einer Königin* (Germany/1936/BW) D: Erich Engel. C: Jennie Jugo, Otto Tressler, Olga Limburg, Paul Henckels, Ernst Schiffner, Renee Stobrawa.

Anton Walbrook. *Victoria the Great* (GB/1937/110m/C) D: Herbert Wilcox. B/on the play *Victoria Regina* by Laurence Housman. C: Anna Neagle, H.B. Warner, James Dale, Charles Carson, Hubert Harben, Felix Aylmer, Arthur Young, Derrick De Marney, Hugh Miller, Percy Parsons, Henry Hallatt, Gordon McLeod, Wyndham Goldie.

Anton Walbrook. *Sixty Glorious Years* (aka *Queen of Destiny*) (GB/1938/90m/C) D: Herbert Wilcox. C: Anna Neagle, C. Aubrey Smith, Charles Carson, Felix Aylmer, Pamela Standish, Gordon McLeod, Henry Hallatt, Wyndham Goldie, Malcolm Keen, Derrick De Marney, Joyce Bland, Harvey Braban, Aubrey Dexter, Laidman Browne.

Jacques Catelain. *Entente Cordiale* (France/1938/95m/BW) D: Marcel L'Herbier. B/on *Edward VII and His Times* by Andre Maurois. C: Victor Francen, Gaby Morlay, Andre Lefaur, Marcelle Praince, Jeanine Darcey, Arlette Marchal, Jean Galland, Andre Roanne, Jean Toulot, Jacques Baumer, Jean d'Yd, Jean Perrier.

David Read. *Alice in Wonderland* (GB-France/1951/83m/C) D: Dallas Bower. B/on stories by Lewis Carroll. C: Stephen Murray, Pamela Brown, Carol Marsh.

Peter Graves. *The Lady with a Lamp* (aka *The Lady with the Lamp*) (GB/1951/ 112m/BW) D: Herbert Wilcox. B/on the play *The Lady with the Lamp* by Reginald Berkeley. C: Anna Neagle, Michael Wilding, Felix Aylmer, Arthur Young, Helena Pickard.

Peter Graves. *Let's Make Up* (aka *Lilacs in the Spring*) (GB/1954/94m/C) D: Herbert Wilcox. B/on the play *The Glorious Days* by Harold Purcell. C: Anna Neagle, Errol Flynn, David Farrar, Kathleen Harrison, Sean Connery.

Adrian Hoven. *The Story of Vickie* (aka *Young Victoria*) (aka *Dover Interlude*) (aka *Girl Days of a Queen*). (aka *Mädchenjahre Einer Königin*) (Austria/1955/ 108–90m/C) D: Ernst Marischka. B/on the diaries of Queen Victoria. C: Romy Schneider, Magda Schneider, Karl Ludwig Diehl, Christl Mardayn, Paul Horbiger, Alfred Neugebauer, Otto Tressler, Rudolf Lenz, Fred Liewehr, Eduard Strauss, Peter Weck.

Julian Chagrin. *The Great McGonagall* (GB/1975/95m/C) D: Joseph McGrath. C: Spike Milligan, Peter Sellers, Julia Foster, Victor Spinetti, John Bluthal, Valentine Dyall.

Alexander I *see* 637

Alexander II *see* 639

5 Alexandria, Czarina (1872–1918)

(Aleksandra Fyodorovna) The last Czarina of Russia, Alexandra dominated her husband (**Nicholas II**) and virtually ruled the Empire while he was off fighting in the First World War. Following the Russian Revolution she and her family were executed by the Bolsheviks. She was portrayed by Claire Bloom in the TV film *Anastasia: The Mystery of Anna* (86). (See **Rasputin**)

Lucie Hoeflich. *1914: The Last Days Before the War* (Germany/1931/110m/BW) D: Richard Oswald. C: Albert Basserman, Wolfgang von Schwind, Heinrich Schroth, Reinhold Schunzel, Ferdinand Hart, Oskar Homolka, Theodor Loos, Alfred Abel, Paul Mederow, Heinrich George, Varl Goetz, Paul Bildt.

Ethel Barrymore. *Rasputin and the Empress* (aka *Rasputin the Mad Monk*) (US/1932/132m/BW) D: Richard Boleslawsky. Original screenplay by Charles MacArthur. C: John Barrymore, Lionel Barrymore, Ralph Morgan, Diana Wynyard, Tad Alexander, C. Henry Gordon, Edward Arnold.

Hermine Sterler. *Rasputin* (Germany/1932/82m/BW) D: Adolf Trotz. C: Conrad Veidt, Paul Otto, Kenny Rieve, Alexandra Sorina, Brigitte Horney, Bernhard Goetzke.

Lisa D'Esterre. *Knight Without Armour* (GB/1937/107m/BW) D: Jacques Feyder. B/on the novel *Without Armour* by James Hilton. C: Marlene Dietrich, Robert Donat, Irene Vanbrugh, Herbert Lomas, Austin Trevor, Basil Gill, Miles Malleson, David Tree.

Marcelle Chantal. *Rasputin* (France/1939/93m/BW) D: Marcel L'Herbler.

B/on the novel *Tragedie Imperiale* by Alfred Neumann. C: Harry Baur, Jean Worms, Denis d'Ines.

Isa Miranda. *Raspoutine* (France/1954/105m/C) D: Georges Combret. C: Pierre Brasseur, Rene Faure, Jacques Berthier, Micheline Francey.

Gianna Maria Canale. *The Night They Killed Rasputin* (aka *The Nights of Rasputin*) (France-Italy/1960/95m/BW) D: Pierre Chenal. C: Edmund Purdom, Jany Clair, Ugo Sasso.

Renee Asherson. *Rasputin—The Mad Monk* (GB/1966/92m/C) D: Don Sharp. C: Christopher Lee, Barbara Shelley, Richard Pasco, Francis Matthews, Suzan Farmer, Joss Ackland.

Pamela Abbott. *Oh! What a Lovely War* (GB/1969/144m/C) D: Richard Attenborough. B/on the musical play by Joan Littlewood and the play *The Long, Long Trail* by Charles Chilton. Best English Language Foreign Film (GG), and the United Nations Award (BFA). C: Jack Hawkins, Laurence Olivier, Ralph Richardson, John Mills, John Gabriel, Paul Daneman, Dirk Bogarde, Vanessa Redgrave, Kenneth More, Michael Redgrave, Ian Holm, Wensley Pithey, Frank Forsyth, John Gielgud, Maggie Smith, Guy Middleton.

Janet Suzman. *Nicholas and Alexandra* (GB/1971/183m/C) D: Franklin J. Schaffner. B/on the book by Robert K. Massie. C: Michael Jayston, Roderic Noble, Fiona Fullerton, Harry Andrews, Irene Worth, Tom Baker, Ralph Truman, Alexander Knox, John McEnery, Michael Bryant, James Hazeldine, Brian Cox, Ian Holm, Roy Dotrice, Martin Potter.

Velta Linie. *Agony* (aka *Rasputin*) (USSR/1975/148–107m/C) D: Elem Klimov. C: Alexei Petrenko, Anatoly Romashin, Alisa Freindtlich.

Alfred the Great *see* 591

6 Ali, Muhammad (1942–)

(Cassius Marcellus Clay, Jr.) American boxer, 1960 Olympic Gold Medal Winner; World Heavyweight Champion in 1964, 1974, and 1978; whose motto was "Float like a butterfly, sting like a bee." Cassuis Clay became Muhammad Ali upon his conversion to Islam in 1964. Ali was portrayed by David Ramsey in the TV mini-series *Ali: an American Hero* (2000).

Muhammad Ali (Himself). Chip McAllister (Young Cassius Clay). *The Greatest* (US-GB/1977/101m/C) D: Tom Gries. B/on the book *The Greatest: My Own Story* by Muhammad Ali. C: Ernest Borgnine, Lloyd Haynes, John Marley, Robert Duvall, James Earl Jones, Dina Merrill, Ben Johnson.

Will Smith. Maestro Harrell (Young Cassius Clay). *Ali* (US/2001/158m/C) D: Michael Mann. C: Jamie Foxx, Jon Voight, Mario Van Peebles, Ron Silver, Jeffrey Wright, Mykelti Williamson, Vincent De Paul, Jon A. Barnes, Michael Bentt, Malick Bowens, Candy Ann Brown, LeVar Burton, David Cubitt, Lee Cummings, James Currie, Rufus Dorsey, Martha Edgerton, Giancarlo Esposito, Sheldon Fogel, Themba Gasa, Nona M. Gaye, Ross Haines, Michael Michele, Joe Morton, Patrick New, Al Quinn, Paul Rodriguez, Gailard Sartain, Charles Shufford, Jada Pinkett Smith, James Toney, Jack Truman, William Utay, Wade Williams.

Will Smith received an Academy Award nomination for his vivid portrayal of Muhammad Ali in *Ali* (2001). The actor worked on perfecting his characterization for almost a year before actual production. (Photo by Frank Connor. Courtesy of Columbia Pictures and Allied Advertising, Boston)

7 Allenby, Edmund Henry Hynman (1861–1936)

(1st Viscount Allenby) British Field Marshal Allenby was commander of the Allied offensive against the Turks in Palestine during the first World War.

Jack Hawkins. *Lawrence of Arabia* (GB/1962/222m/C) D: David Lean. B/on the book *The Seven Pillars of Wisdom* by T.E. Lawrence. Best Picture (AA), Best Director (AA), Best Film — Any Source (BFA), Best British Film (BFA). C: Peter O'Toole, Alec Guinness, Anthony Quinn, Jose Ferrer, Anthony Quayle, Omar Sharif, Claude Rains.

Anthony Hawkins. *The Lighthorsemen* (Australia/1987/128–115m/C) D: Simon Wincer. C: Jon Blake, Peter Phelps, Tony Bonner, Bill Kerr, Sigrid Thornton.

8 Amherst, Jeffrey Amherst, 1st Baron (1717–1797)

British soldier, Amherst was commander-in-chief of British North America during the French and Indian Wars.

Lumsden Hare. *Northwest Passage* (US/1940/125m/C) D: King Vidor. B/on the novel by Kenneth Roberts. C: Spencer Tracy, Robert Young, Walter Brennan, Ruth Hussey.

Ramsey Hill. *The Battles of Chief Pontiac* (US/1952/71m/BW) D: Felix Feist. C: Lon Chaney, Jr.

Trainer Bundini Brown (Jamie Foxx) giving Ali (Will Smith) a victorious embrace, looking on (left to right) are Luis Sarria (Laurence Mason), Howard Bingham (Jeffrey Wright), and Dr. Freddie Pacheco (Paul Rodriguiz). This match took place when Ali was still known as Cassius Clay. *Ali* (2001). (Photo by Frank Connor. Courtesy of Columbia Pictures and Allied Advertising, Boston)

Lester Matthews. *Fort Ti* (US/1953/73m/C) D: William Castle. C: George Montgomery, Joan Vohs, Irving Bacon, James Seay, Howard Petrie.

9 Amin (Dada), Idi (1925–)

Ugandan soldier and dictator (1971–79), Amin's regime was infamous for its brutality with Amin being responsible for the deaths of more than a quarter million of his fellow countrymen.

Julius Harris. *Victory at Entebbe* (US/1976/150m/C) D: Marvin J. Chomsky. C: Kirk Douglas, Burt Lancaster, Theodore Bikel, Richard Dreyfuss, Linda Blair, Harris Yulin.

Yaphet Kotto. *Raid on Entebbe* (US/1977/115m/C) D: Irvin Kershner. Made for US television, released theatrically in Europe. C: Peter Finch, Charles Bronson, Martin Balsam, Horst Bucholz, John Saxon, Sylvia Sidney, Tige Andrews, David Opatoshu.

Joseph Olita. *Amin—The Rise and Fall* (aka *The Rise and Fall of Idi Amin*) (Kenya/1982/101m/C) D: Sharad Patel. C: Geoffrey Kenya.

Joseph Olita. *Mississippi Masala* (US-GB/1992/118m/C) D: Mira Nair. C:

Denzel Washington, Sarita Choudhury, Roshan Seth, Charles S. Dutton, Sharmila Tagore.

Themba Gasa. *Ali* (US/2001/158m/C) D: Michael Mann. C: Will Smith, Jamie Foxx, Jon Voight, Mario Van Peebles, Ron Silver, Jeffrey Wright, Mykelti Williamson, Vincent De Paul, Jon A. Barnes, Michael Bentt, Malick Bowens, Candy Ann Brown, LeVar Burton, David Cubitt, Lee Cummings, James Currie, Rufus Dorsey, Martha Edgerton, Giancarlo Esposito, Sheldon Fogel, Nona M. Gaye, Ross Haines, Maestro Harrell, Michael Michele, Joe Morton, Patrick New, Al Quinn, Paul Rodriguez, Gailard Sartain, Charles Shufford, Jada Pinkett Smith, James Toney, Jack Truman, William Utay, Wade Williams.

10 Amundsen, Roald (1872–1928)
Norwegian Arctic/Antarctic explorer, Amundsen was the first man to reach the South Pole.

Joachim Calmeyer. *Only One Life—The Story of Fridtjof Nansen* (aka *Bare Et Liv—Historien Om Fridtjof Nansen*) (Norway-USSR/1968/90m) D: Sergei Mikaelyan. C: Knut Wigart, Veslemoy Haslund.

Sean Connery. *The Red Tent* (aka *La Tenda Rossa*) (Italy-USSR/1971/121m/C) D: Mikhail Kalatozov. C: Claudia Cardinale, Hardy Kruger, Peter Finch, Massimo Girotti.

11 Anastasia, Albert (1902–1957)
(Umberto Anastasia) The head of "Murder, Incorporated," the notorious underworld assassination syndicate, Anastasia was himself gunned down in 1957 while sitting in a barber's chair waiting for a quick trim.

Howard I. Smith. *Murder, Inc.*(US/1960/103m/BW) D: Burt Balaban & Stuart Rosenberg. B/on the book by Burton Turkus & Sid Feder. C: Stuart Whitman, May Britt, Henry Morgan, Peter Falk, David J. Stewart, Simon Oakland, Vincent Gardenia.

Fausto Tozzi. *The Valachi Papers* (Italy-France/1972/125m/C) D: Terence Young. B/on the book by Peter Maas. C: Charles Bronson, Lino Ventura, Jill Ireland, Angelo Infante, Giancomino De Michelis, Joseph Wiseman, Walter Chiari.

Richard Conte. *My Brother Anastasia* (Italy/1973/95m/C) D: Stefano Vanzina. B/on the book by Salvatore Anastasia. C: Alberto Sordi, Eddy Fay.

Gianni Russo. *Lepke* (US/1975/110–98m/C) D: Menahem Golan. C: Tony Curtis, Anjanette Comer, Michael Callan, Warren Berlinger, Vic Tayback, Milton Berle, Erwin Fuller, Jack Ackerman, Vaughn Meader, Zitto Kazan, John Durren.

12 Andersen, Hans Christian (1805–1875)
Denmark's famous creator of children's stories, Anderson wrote more than 160 tales including "The Red Shoes" and "The Emperor's New Clothes."

Joachim Gottschalk. *Die Schwedische Nachtigall* (Germany/1940/BW) D: Peter Paul Brauer. C: Ilse Werner, Karl Diehl, Bernhard Goetzke, Karl Tiedtke.

Ashley Glynne. *Mr. H.C. Andersen* (GB/1950/62m/BW) D: Ronald Haines.

B/on the book *The True Story of My Life* by Hans Christian Anderson. C: Constance Lewis, Terence Noble, Stuart Sanders, June Elvin, Edward Sullivan, Victor Rietty.

Danny Kaye. *Hans Christian Andersen* (US/1952/120m/C) D: Charles Vidor. C: Farley Granger, (Zizi) Jeanmaire, John Qualen, Roland Petit, Joey Walsh, Philip Tonge.

Paul O'Keefe. *The Daydreamer* (US/1966/101m/C) D: Jules Bass. B/on stories by Hans Christian Andersen. C: Jack Gilford, Ray Bolger, Margaret Hamilton. The voices of: Cyril Ritchard, Hayley Mills, Burl Ives, Tallulah Bankhead, Terry-Thomas.

Richard Wordsworth. *Song of Norway* (US/1970/142m/C) D: Andrew L. Stone. B/on the musical play by Milton Lazarus, Robert Wright & George Forrest. C: Toralv Maurstad, Edward G. Robinson, Florence Henderson, Robert Morley, Henry Gilbert.

Murray Melvin. *Stories from a Flying Trunk* (GB/1979/88m/C) D: Christine Edzard. B/on stories by Hans Christian Andersen. C: Ann Firbank, Tasneem Maqsood, John Tordoff.

Jesper Klein. *Hans Christian Andersen in Italy* (aka *H. C. Andersen I Italien*) (Denmark-Italy/1979/70m/C) D: Fernando Cavaterra. C: Sune Schmidt, Maude Berthelsen, Palle Schmidt.

13 Andrew, Saint

The first-called of **Jesus Christ**'s Apostles, Andrew was **Peter**'s brother and according to tradition was crucified in Greece on an "X" shaped cross. TV portrayals of Saint Andrew have been by Tony Vogel in the mini-series *Jesus of Nazareth* (77), and Gilly Gilchrist in the TV film *Jesus* (99).

Harold Minjir. *The Great Commandment* (US/1941/78m/BW) D: Irving Pichel. C: John Beal, Marjorie Cooley, Albert Dekker, Marc Lobell, Olaf Hytten, Maurice Moscovich.

Michael Connors. *Day of Triumph* (US/1954/110m/C) D: Irving Pichel & John T. Coyle. C: Lee J. Cobb, Robert Wilson, Ralph Freud, Tyler McVey, Joanne Dru, James Griffith, Lowell Gilmore, Anthony Warde, Peter Whitney, Everett Glass.

Rhodes Reason. *The Big Fisherman* (US/1959/180m/C) D: Frank Borzage. B/on the novel by Lloyd C. Douglas. C: Howard Keel, Susan Kohner, John Saxon, Martha Hyer, Herbert Lom, Alexander Scourby, Jay Barney, Brian Hutton, Thomas Troupe, Herbert Rudley.

Tino Barrero. *King of Kings* (US/1961/168m/C) D: Nicholas Ray. C: Jeffrey Hunter, Siobhan McKenna, Hurd Hatfield, Viveca Lindfors, Rita Gam, Carmen Sevilla, Rip Torn, Brigid Bazlen, Harry Guardino, Frank Thring, Guy Rolfe, Maurice Marsac, Gregoire Aslan, Royal Dano, Robert Ryan, Gerard Tichy, Michael Wager, Jose Antonio, Orson Welles (Narrator).

Alfonso Gatto. *The Gospel According to St. Matthew* (France-Italy/1964/142m/BW) D: Pier Paolo Pasolini. B/on the *New Testament book of Matthew*. C: Enrique Irazoqui, Susanna Pasolini, Mario Socrate, Marcello Morante, Rodolfo Wilcock, Francesco Leonetti, Amerigo Bevilacqua, Otello Sestilli, Settimio Di Porto, Ferruccio Nuzzo, Alessandro Tosca, Paolo Tedesco, Franca Cupane, Giacomo Morante, Rosario Migale.

Burt Brinckerhoff. *The Greatest Story Ever Told* (US/1965/141m/C) D: George Stevens. B/on the book by Fulton Oursler. C: Max von Sydow, Dorothy McGuire, Robert Loggia, Claude Rains, Jose Ferrer, Charlton Heston, Donald Pleasence, David McCallum, Gary Raymond, Robert Blake, John Considine, David Hedison, Joanna Dunham, Sal Mineo, Van Heflin, Ed Wynn, Martin Landau, Telly Savalas, Sidney Poitier, Roddy McDowell, Angela Lansbury, Richard Conte, Carroll Baker, Janet Margolin, Tom Reese.

Christian van Cau. *The Milky Way* (France-Italy/1969/105m/C) D: Luis Bunuel. C: Paul Frankeur, Laurent Terzieff, Alain Cuny, Bernard Verley, Edith Scob, Michel Piccoli, Jean Clarieux, Pierre Clementi, Georges Marchal, Delphine Seyrig.

Lyle Nicholson. *The Gospel Road* (US/1973/93m/C) D: Robert Elfstrom. C: Robert Elfstrom, June Carter Cash, Larry Lee, Paul Smith, Alan Dater, John Paul Kay, Gelles LaBlanc, Robert Elfstrom, Jr., Terrance W. Mannock, Thomas Levanthal, Sean Armstrong, Steven Chernoff, Jonathan Sanders, Ulf Pollack.

Dan Ades. *The Passover Plot* (Israel/1976/108m/C) D: Michael Campus. B/on the book by Hugh Schonfield. C: Harry Andrews, Hugh Griffith, Zalman King, Donald Pleasence, Scott Wilson, Michael Baselon, Lewis van Bergen, William Burns, Dan Hedaya, Kevin O'Connor, Robert Walker.

Gadi Rol. *Jesus* (US/1979/117m/C) D: Peter Sykes & John Kirsh. B/on the *New Testament book of Luke*. C: Brian Deacon, Rivka Noiman, Yossef Shiloah, Niko Nitai, Richard Peterson, Eli Cohen, Shmuel Tal, Kobi Assaf, Talia Shapira, Eli Danker, Mosko Alkalai, Nisim Gerama, Leonid Weinstein, Peter Frye, David Goldberg.

Gary Basaraba. *The Last Temptation of Christ* (US/1988/164m/C) D: Martin Scorsese. B/on the novel by Nikos Kazantzakis. C: Willem Dafoe, Harvey Keitel, Paul Greco, Verna Bloom, Barbara Hershey, Victor Argo, Michael Been, John Lurie, Harry Dean Stanton, David Bowie, Nehemiah Persoff, Leo Burmester, Irvin Kershner, Andre Gregory, Tomas Arana, Juliette Caton, Roberts Blossom, Barry Miller, Alan Rosenberg.

Anne *see* 607

14 Anne of Austria (1601–1666)

The daughter of Philip III of Spain, Anne became the Queen of France when she married **Louis XIII** in 1615. After his death she served as regent for her son **Louis XIV** from 1643–1661. In TV productions she has been portrayed by Amy Irving in *Panache* (76) and by Brenda Bruce in *The Man in the Iron Mask* (77).

Belle Bennett. *The Iron Mask* (US/1929/95m/BW) D: Allan Dwan. B/on *The Three Musketeers* and *The Viscount of Bragelonne* by Alexandre Dumas. C: Douglas Fairbanks, Dorothy Revier, William Bakewell, Rolfe Sedan, Nigel De Brulier.

Andree Lafayette. *The Three Musketeers* (France/1932/128m/BW) D: Henri Diamant-Berger. B/on the novel by Alexandre Dumas. C: Aime Simon-Girard, Edith Mera, Samson Fainsilber, Harry Baur, Edith Mera, Maurice Escande, Fernand Francell.

Andree Lafayette. *Milady* (France/1933/120m/BW) D: Henri Diamant-Berger.

C: Aime Simon-Girard, Samson Fainsilber, Harry Baur, Blanche Montel, Fernand Francell, Edith Mera, Louis Allibert, Tommy Bourdelle, Henri Rollan, Maurice Escande.

Katherine Alexander. *Cardinal Richelieu* (US/1935/83m/BW) D: Rowland V. Lee. B/on the play *Richelieu* by Edward Bulwer-Lytton. C: George Arliss, Edward Arnold.

Rosamond Pinchot. *The Three Musketeers* (US/1935/97m/BW) D: Rowland V. Lee. B/on the novel by Alexandre Dumas. C: Walter Abel, Paul Lukas, Margot Grahame, Heather Angel, Ian Keith, Onslow Stevens, Ralph Forbes, Nigel De Brulier, Miles Mander.

Doris Kenyon. *The Man in the Iron Mask* (US/1939/110m/BW) D: James Whale. B/on the novel by Alexandre Dumas. C: Louis Hayward, Joan Bennett, Warren William, Joseph Schildkraut, Alan Hale, Miles Mander, Walter Kingsford, Albert Dekker, Nigel De Brulier.

Gloria Stuart. *The Three Musketeers* (aka *The Singing Musketeer*) (US/1939/73m/BW) D: Allan Dwan. B/on the novel by Alexandre Dumas. C: Don Ameche, The Ritz Brothers, Binnie Barnes, Lionel Atwill, Pauline Moore, Joseph Schildkraut, Miles Mander, John Carradine, Douglas Dumbrille, John King, Lester Matthews.

Consuelo Frank. *The Three Musketeers* (aka *Tres Mosqueteros*) (Mexico/1942/139m/BW) D: Miguel M. Delgado. B/on the novel by Alexandre Dumas. C: Cantinflas, Angel Garasa, Raquel Rojas, Andres Soler, Julio Villarreal, Jorge Reyes.

Germaine Dermoz. *Monsieur Vincent* (France/1947/73m/BW) D: Maurice Cloche. Special Academy Award as the most outstanding foreign film of 1948. C: Pierre Fresnay, Lisa Delamare, Aime Clarimond, Jean Debucourt, Gabrielle Dorziat, Yvonne Godeau.

Angela Lansbury. *The Three Musketeers* (US/1948/126m/C) D: George Sidney. B/on the novel by Alexandre Dumas. C: Lana Turner, Gene Kelly, June Allyson, Van Heflin, Frank Morgan, Vincent Price, Kennan Wynn, John Sutton, Gig Young, Robert Coote.

Gladys Cooper. *At Sword's Point* (aka *Sons of the Musketeers*) (US/1951/81m/C) D: Lewis Allen. C: Cornel Wilde, Maureen O'Hara, Robert Douglas, Peter Miles.

Marjorie Lord. *Blades of the Musketeers* (aka *The Sword of D'Artagnan*) (US/1953/54m/BW) D: Budd Boetticher. B/on the novel *The Three Musketeers* by Alexandre Dumas. C: Robert Clarke, John Hubbard, Mel Archer, Paul Cavanagh, Don Beddoe, Charles Lang.

Françoise Christophe. *The Three Musketeers* (France/1961/100m/C) D: Bernard Borderie. B/on the novel by Alexandre Dumas. C: Gerard Barry, Georges Descrieres, Bernard Woringer, Jacques Toja, Daniel Sorano, Mylene Demongeot, Henri Nassiet.

Katherina Renn. *The Rise of Louis XIV* (France/1966/100m/BW) D: Roberto Rossellini. C: Jean-Marie Patte, Raymond Jourdan, Silvagni, Dominique Vincent, Pierre Barrat.

Catherine Jourdan. *The Four Charlots Musketeers* (France/1974/110m/C) D: Andre Hunnebelle. B/on the novel *The Three Musketeers* by Alexandre Dumas. C: The Charlots, Gerard Rinaldi, Josephine Chaplin, Daniel Ceccaldi, Bernard Haller.

Geraldine Chaplin. *The Three Musketeers* (GB-US-Panama/1974/105m/C) D: Richard Lester. B/on the novel by Alexandre Dumas. C: Oliver Reed, Richard Chamberlain, Michael York, Frank Finlay, Jean-Pierre Cassel, Simon Ward, Charlton Heston.

Geraldine Chaplin. *The Four Musketeers* (aka *The Revenge of Milady*) (GB-US/1975/108m/C) D: Richard Lester. B/on the novel *The Three Musketeers* by Alexandre Dumas. C: Michael York, Charlton Heston, Oliver Reed, Richard Chamberlain, Christopher Lee, Frank Finlay, Raquel Welch, Jean-Pierre Cassel, Simon Ward.

Olivia de Havilland. *The Fifth Musketeer* (aka *Behind the Iron Mask*) (Austria/1979/103–90m/C) D: Ken Annakin. B/on the novel *The Man in the Iron Mask* by Alexandre Dumas. C: Beau Bridges, Sylvia Kristel, Ursula Andress, Cornel Wilde, Ian McShane, Alan Hale, Jr., Helmut Dantine, Jose Ferrer, Rex Harrison.

Geraldine Chaplin. *The Return of the Musketeers* (GB-France-Spain/1989/101m/C) D: Richard Lester. B/on the novel *Twenty Years Later* by Alexandre Dumas. Shown on US cable in 1991, released theatrically elsewhere. C: Michael York, Oliver Reed, Frank Finlay, Richard Chamberlain, C. Thomas Howell, Philippe Noiret, Roy Kinnear.

Gabrielle Anwar. *The Three Musketeers* (US/1993/105m/C) D: Stephen Herek. B/on the novel by Alexandre Dumas. C: Charlie Sheen, Kiefer Sutherland, Chris O'Donnell, Oliver Platt, Tim Curry, Rebecca DeMornay, Michael Wincott, Hugh O'Connor.

Anne Parillaud. *Man in the Iron Mask* (US-GB/1998/132m/C) D: Randall Wallace. B/on the novel by Alexandre Dumas. C: Leonardo DiCaprio, Jeremy Irons, John Malkovich, Gérard Depardieu, Gabriel Byrne, Judith Godrèche, Edward Atterton, Peter Sarsgaard, Hugh Laurie, David Lowe, Brigitte Boucher, Karine Belly, Emmanuel Guttierez.

Meg Foster. *The Man in the Iron Mask* (US/1998/85m/C) D: William Richert. B/on the novel by Alexandre Dumas. C: Edward Albert, Dana Barron, Timothy Bottoms, Brigid Conley Walsh, Fannie Brett, James Gammon, Dennis Hayden, William Richert, Nick Richert, Rex Ryon, Brenda James, R.G. Armstrong, Robert Tena, Daniel J. Coplan.

Catherine Deneuve. *The Musketeer* (Germany-Luxemburg/2001/US/105m/C) D: Peter Hyams. B/on the novel by Alexandre Dumas. C: Mena Suvari, Stephen Rea, Tim Roth, Justin Chambers, Bill Treacher, Daniel Mesguich, David Schofield, Nick Moran, Steven Spiers, Jan Gregor Kremp, Jeremy Clyde, Michael Byrne, Jean-Pierre Castaldi, Tsilla Chelton, Bertrand Witt.

15 Anne of Cleves (1515–1557)

Henry VIII's fourth wife (in a marriage made for political reasons), Anne was to spend six months as his queen before he had the marriage annulled.

Elsa Lanchester. *The Private Life of Henry VIII* (GB/1933/97m/BW) D: Alexander Korda. C: Charles Laughton, Robert Donat, Binnie Barnes, Merle Oberon, Wendy Barrie, Everley Gregg, Franklyn Dyall, Miles Mander, Claude Allister, John Loder, Lawrence Hanray.

Jenny Bos. *The Six Wives of Henry VIII* (aka *Henry VIII and His Six Wives*) (GB/1972/125m/C) D: Waris Hussein. C: Keith Michell, Frances Cuka, Charlotte Rampling, Jane Asher, Lynne Frederick, Barbara Leigh-Hunt, Donald Pleasence, Simon Henderson, Annette Crosbie, John Bryans, Michael Goodliffe, Bernard Hepton, Dorothy Tutin.

16 Antony, Marc (83?–30 BC)

A would-be successor to **Julius Caesar**, Antony became locked in a power struggle with Caesar's heir, Octavian (**Augustus Caesar**). He gained control of the Western empire where he met and fell in love with **Cleopatra**, which eventually led to his defeat and suicide. Antony was portrayed by Billy Zane in the TV movie *Cleopatra* (99).

Henry Wilcoxon. *Cleopatra* (US/1934/102m/BW) D: Cecil B. DeMille. C: Claudette Colbert, Warren William, Gertrude Michael, Joseph Schildkraut, Ian Keith, Ian Maclaren, Arthur Hohl, Claudia Dell, Robert Warwick, Charles Morris.

Charlton Heston. *Julius Caesar* (US/1950/BW) D: David Bradley. B/on the play by Wm. Shakespeare. C: Robert Holt, David Bradley, Harold Tasker, Grosvenor Glenn, William Russell, Helen Ross.

Marlon Brando * Best Foreign Actor (BFA). *Julius Caesar* (US/1953/120m/BW) D: Joseph L. Mankiewicz. B/on the play by Wm. Shakespeare. C: James Mason, Louis Calhern, John Gielgud, Edmond O'Brien, Greer Garson, Deborah Kerr, Alan Napier, Douglas Watson.

Raymond Burr. *Serpent of the Nile* (US/1953/81m/C) D: William Castle. C: Rhonda Fleming, William Lundigan, Michael Ansara, Jean Byron, Michael Fox, Robert Griffin.

Ettore Manni. *Two Nights with Cleopatra* (Italy/1953/80m/BW) D: Mario Mattoli. C: Sophia Loren, Alberto Sordi, Paul Muller, Alberto Talegalli, Rolf Tasna, Gianni Cavalieri.

Helmut Dantine. *The Story of Mankind* (US/1957/100m/C) D: Irwin Allen. B/on the book by Hendrik van Loon. C: Ronald Colman, Hedy Lamarr, Virginia Mayo, Agnes Moorehead, Peter Lorre, Dennis Hopper, Marie Wilson, Edward Everett Horton, Reginald Gardiner, Marie Windsor, Francis X. Bushman, Anthony Dexter, Austin Green, Jim Ameche, Harpo Marx, Bobby Watson, Reginald Sheffield, Cedric Hardwicke, Cesar Romero.

Georges Marchal. *Legions of the Nile* (Italy/1959/87m/C) D: Vittorio Cottafavi. C: Linda Cristal, Ettore Manni, Maria Mahor, Alfredo Mayo, Daniela Rocca.

Bruno Tocci. *Caesar the Conqueror* (Italy/1962/103m/C) D: Amerigo Anton. C: Cameron Mitchell, Rick Battaglia, Dominique Wilms, Nerio Bernardi, Carlo Tamberlani, Carla Calo.

Richard Burton. *Cleopatra* (US/1963/243m/C) D: Joseph L. Mankiewicz. B/on works by Plutarch, Appian, and Seutonius, and the novel *The Life and Times of Cleopatra* by Carlo M. Franzero. C: Elizabeth Taylor, Rex Harrison, Pamela Brown, Jean Marsh, Kenneth Haig, Roddy McDowall, Francesca Annis, John Hoyt, Gwen Watford, Martin Landau, Michael Hordern, Douglas Wilmer, Carroll O'Connor, Finlay Currie.

Sidney James. *Carry on Cleo* (GB/1964/92m/C) D: Gerald Thomas. C: Kenneth Williams, Charles Hawtrey, Joan Sims, Amanda Barrie, Julie Stevens, Brian Oulton, Jim Dale.

Charlton Heston. *Julius Caesar* (GB/1970/117m/C) D: Stuart Burge. B/on the play by Wm. Shakespeare. C: John Gielgud, Jason Robards, Richard Johnson, Robert Vaughn, Richard Chamberlain, Diana Rigg, Jill Bennett, Christopher Lee, David Dodimead, Peter Eyre, Andre Morrell, Christopher Cazenove.

Johnny Rocco. *The Notorious Cleopatra* (US/1970/88m/C) D: A.P. Stootsberry. C: Sonora, Jay Edwards, Woody Lee, Dixie Donovan, Tom Huron, Michael Cheal.

Charlton Heston. *Antony and Cleopatra* (GB/1973/160m/C) D: Charlton Heston. B/on the play by Wm. Shakespeare. C: Hildegard Neil, Eric Porter, John Castle, Fernando Rey.

17 Arbuckle, Roscoe Conkling "Fatty" (1887–1933)

Hollywood star of silent comedies, Arbuckle's career ended when he was charged with the death of a woman who died at a party he had given. His story is considered the basis for the 1975 film *The Wild Party*, with James Coco. In the video release *Forever* (94), he was played by Captain Haggerty.

William Hootkins. *Valentino* (GB/1977/132m/C) D: Ken Russell. B/on the story *Valentino, An Intimate Expose of the Sheik* by Brad Steiger & Chaw Mank. C: Rudolf Nureyev, Leslie Caron, Michelle Phillips, Carol Kane, Felicity Kendal, Peter Vaughan, Huntz Hall, David De Keyser, Anthony Dowell, Anton Diffring.

Glenn Shadix. *Sunset* (US/1988/107m/C) D: Blake Edwards. C: Bruce Willis, James Garner, Malcolm McDowell, Patricia Hodge, Rod McCary, John Fountain.

18 Arnold, Benedict (1741–1801)

Traitorous American general of the Revolutionary War, Arnold's plans were uncovered and he fled to the British side.

John Davidson. *Where Do We Go from Here?* (US/1945/77m/C) D: Gregory Ratoff. C: Fred MacMurray, Joan Leslie, June Haver, Anthony Quinn, Alan Mowbray, Fortunio Bonanova.

Robert Douglas. *The Scarlet Coat* (US/1955/101m/C) D: John Sturges. C: Cornel Wilde, Michael Wilding, George Sanders, Anne Francis, John McIntire, Rhys Williams, John Dehner.

Arthur, Chester A. *see* 582

19 Astor, John Jacob (1763–1848)

German born, American fur trader and financier, Astor arrived in the U.S. penniless but was the wealthiest man in the country when he died 64 years later. His great-grandson, John Jacob Astor IV, who died in the sinking of the Titanic, was portrayed by William Johnstone in *Titanic* (53), by David Janssen in *S.O.S. Titanic* (80), and by Eric Braeden in *Titanic* (97).

Harry Stubbs. *Sutter's Gold* (US/1936/69m/BW) D: James Cruze. B/on the novel *L'Or* by Blaise Cendrars. C: Edward Arnold, Lee Tracy, Binnie Barnes, Katherine Alexander, Addison Richards, Harry Carey, Montagu Love, John Miljan, Robert Warwick.

Roger Imhof. *Little Old New York* (US/1940/99m/BW) D: Henry King. B/on the play by Rida Johnson Young. C: Alice Faye, Richard Greene, Fred Mac-Murray, Brenda Joyce, Theodore von Eltz, Robert Middlemass, Andy Devine.

Sig Rumann. *This Woman Is Mine* (US/1941/91m/BW) D: Frank Lloyd. B/on the novel *I, James Lewis* by Gilbert W. Gabriel. C: Franchot Tone, John Carroll, Carol Bruce.

Astor, John Jacob, IV *see* Astor, John Jacob

20 Attila the Hun (406?–453)

Leader of the nomadic Huns who overran much of Europe in the fifth century, Attila extorted tribute from both the Eastern and Western Roman Empires. Gerard Butler portrayed the Hun in the TV movie *Attila* (2000).

Anthony Quinn. *Attila the Hun* (aka *Attila*) (Italy/1954/87m/C) D: Pietro Francisci. C: Sophia Loren, Henri Vidal, Irene Papas, Ettore Manni.

Jack Palance. *Sign of the Pagan* (US/1954/91m/C) D: Douglas Sirk. C: Jeff Chandler, Ludmilla Tcherina, Rita Gam, Jeff Morrow, Alexander Scourby, Eduard Franz, George Dolenz, Walter Coy, Moroni Olsen, Leo Gordon.

Josef Madaras. *Young Attila* (Italy/1971/90m/C) D: Miklos Jancso. C: Anna Zinneman.

21 Augustus Caesar (63 BC–AD 14)

(Gaius Julius Caesar Octavius known as Octavian) The great nephew, adopted son, and heir of **Julius Caesar**, Octavian needed an army to defeat the forces of **Brutus, Cassius, Antony** and **Cleopatra** before becoming the first Emperor of Rome in 29 BC. He was later given the title of Augustus by the Roman Senate (27 BC).

Ian Keith. *Cleopatra* (US/1934/102m/BW) D: Cecil B. DeMille. C: Claudette Colbert, Warren William, Henry Wilcoxon, Gertrude Michael, Joseph Schildkraut, Ian Maclaren, Arthur Hohl, Claudia Dell, Robert Warwick, Charles Morris.

Robert Holt. *Julius Caesar* (US/1950/BW) D: David Bradley. B/on the play by Wm. Shakespeare. C: Charlton Heston, David Bradley, Harold Tasker, Grosvenor Glenn, William Russell, Helen Ross.

Memo Benassi. *The Affairs of Messalina* (aka *Messalina*) (Italy/1951/120m/BW) D: Carmine Gallone. C: Maria Felix, Georges Marchal, Jean Tissier.

Michael Fox. *Serpent of the Nile* (US/1953/81m/C) D: William Castle. C: Rhonda Fleming, William Lundigan, Raymond Burr, Michael Ansara, Jean Byron, Robert Griffin.

Douglas Watson. *Julius Caesar* (US/1953/120m/BW) D: Joseph L. Mankiewicz. B/on the play by Wm. Shakespeare. C: James Mason, Marlon

Brando, Louis Calhern, John Gielgud, Edmond O'Brien, Greer Garson, Deborah Kerr, Alan Napier.

Alfredo Mayo. *Legions of the Nile* (Italy/1959/87m/C) D: Vittorio Cottafavi. C: Linda Cristal, Ettore Manni, Georges Marchal, Maria Mahor, Daniela Rocca.

Massimo Girotti. *Herod the Great* (Italy/1959/93m/C) D: Arnaldo Genoino. C: Edmund Purdom, Sylvia Lopez, Sandra Milo, Alberto Lupo.

Roddy McDowall. *Cleopatra* (US/1963/243m/C) D: Joseph L. Mankiewicz. B/on works by Plutarch, Appian, and Seutonius, and the novel *The Life and Times of Cleopatra* by Carlo M. Franzero. C: Elizabeth Taylor, Richard Burton, Rex Harrison, Pamela Brown, Jean Marsh, Kenneth Haig, Francesca Annis, John Hoyt, Gwen Watford, Martin Landau, Michael Hordern, Douglas Wilmer, Carroll O'Connor, Finlay Currie.

Richard Chamberlain. *Julius Caesar* (GB/1970/117m/C) D: Stuart Burge. B/on the play by Wm. Shakespeare. C: Charlton Heston, John Gielgud, Jason Robards, Richard Johnson, Robert Vaughn, Diana Rigg, Jill Bennett, Christopher Lee, David Dodimead, Peter Eyre, Andre Morrell, Christopher Cazenove.

John Castle. *Antony and Cleopatra* (GB/1973/160m/C) D: Charlton Heston. B/on the play by Wm. Shakespeare. C: Charlton Heston, Hildegard Neil, Eric Porter, Fernando Rey.

22 Austin, Stephen (1793–1836)

Known as the "Father of Texas," Austin along with **Sam Houston** was one of the early leaders in the fight for Texas' independence from Mexico. Austin was portrayed by James Stephens in the TV movie *Houston: The Legend of Texas* (86) and by Patrick Duffy in the mini-series *Texas* (94).

Earle Hodgins. *Heroes of the Alamo* (aka *Remember the Alamo*) (US/1937/80m/BW) D: Harry Fraser. C: Lane Chandler, Roger Williams, Rex Lease, Edward Piel, Julian Rivero, Lee Valianos, Ruth Findlay, Jack Smith, Tex Cooper.

Ralph Morgan. *Man of Conquest* (US/1939/97m/BW) D: George Nichols, Jr. C: Richard Dix, Edward Ellis, Victor Jory, Robert Barrat, Robert Armstrong, C. Henry Gordon, George "Gabby" Hayes, Gail Patrick, Joan Fontaine, Max Terhune, Lane Chandler.

Otto Kruger. *The Last Command* (US/1955/110m/C) D: Frank Lloyd. B/on the story *The Last Command* by Sy Bartlett. C: Sterling Hayden, Richard Carlson, Arthur Hunnicutt, J. Carroll Naish, Hugh Sanders, Don Kennedy, Anna Maria Alberghetti, Ernest Borgnine, Ben Cooper, Virginia Grey, John Russell, Edward Colmans, Jim Davis.

Dayton Lummis. *The First Texan* (US/1956/82m/C) D: Byron Haskin. C: Joel McCrea, Jeff Morrow, William Hopper, David Silva, James Griffith, Carl Benton Reid, Felicia Farr, Wallace Ford, Chubby Johnson, Jody McCrea, Abraham Sofaer.

23 Balfour, Arthur James, 1st Earl of Balfour (1848–1930)

British statesman and Prime Minister (1902–05), Balfour was Foreign Secretary (under **Lloyd George**) when he issued the Balfour Declaration which pledged British support for a Jewish national home in Palestine.

Wyndham Goldie. *Sixty Glorious Years* (aka *Queen of Destiny*) (GB/1938/90m/C) D: Herbert Wilcox. C: Anna Neagle, Anton Walbrook, C. Aubrey Smith, Charles Carson, Felix Aylmer, Pamela Standish, Gordon McLeod, Henry Hallatt, Malcolm Keen, Derrick De Marney, Joyce Bland, Harvey Braban, Aubrey Dexter, Laidman Browne.

Andre Roanne. *Entente Cordiale* (France/1938/95m/BW) D: Marcel L'Herbier. B/on *Edward VII and His Times* by Andre Maurois. C: Victor Francen, Gaby Morlay, Andre Lefaur, Marcelle Praince, Jeanine Darcey, Arlette Marchal, Jean Galland, Jacques Catelain, Jean Toulot, Jacques Baumer, Jean D'Yd, Jean Perrier.

William Dexter. *Young Winston* (GB/1972/145m/C) D: Richard Attenborough. B/on the book *My Early Life: A Roving Commission* by Winston Churchill. Best English-Language Foreign Film (GG). C: Simon Ward, Peter Cellier, Ronald Hines, John Mills, Anne Bancroft, Robert Shaw, Laurence Naismith, Basil Dignam, Reginald Marsh, Anthony Hopkins, Robert Hardy, Colin Blakely, Michael Auderson, Jack Hawkins.

24 Barabbas

Barabbas was the New Testament rebel/bandit whom the Passover crowds shouted to have released instead of **Jesus Christ**. Other than in the Gospels, there is no historical mention of Barabbas' existence. He was played by Stacy Keach in the TV mini-series *Jesus of Nazareth* (77), and by Claudio Amendola in the TV film *Jesus* (99).

Ulf Palme. *Barabbas* (Sweden/1952) D: Alf Sjöberg. B/on the novel by Pär Lagerkvist.

Anthony Warde. *Day of Triumph* (US/1954/110m/C) D: Irving Pichel & John T. Coyle. C: Lee J. Cobb, Robert Wilson, Ralph Freud, Tyler McVey, Michael Connors, Joanne Dru, James Griffith, Lowell Gilmore, Peter Whitney, Everett Glass.

Harry Guardino. *King of Kings* (US/1961/168m/C) D: Nicholas Ray. C: Jeffrey Hunter, Siobhan McKenna, Hurd Hatfield, Viveca Lindfors, Rita Gam, Carmen Sevilla, Rip Torn, Brigid Bazlen, Frank Thring, Guy Rolfe, Maurice Marsac, Gregoire Aslan, Royal Dano, Robert Ryan, Gerard Tichy, Michael Wager, Tino Barrero, Jose Antonio, Orson Welles (Narrator).

Anthony Quinn. *Barabbas* (Italy/1962/144m/C) D: Richard Fleischer. B/on the novel by Pär Lagerkvist. C: Silvana Mangano, Arthur Kennedy, Katy Jurado, Harry Andrews, Roy Mangano, Ivan Triesault, Michael Gwynn, Arnold Foa.

Livio Lorenzon. *Pontius Pilate* (Italy-France/1962/100m/C) D: Irving Rapper. C: Jean Marais, Jeanne Crain, Basil Rathbone, Leticia Roman, John Drew Barrymore.

Richard Conte. *The Greatest Story Ever Told* (US/1965/141m/C) D: George Stevens. B/on the book by Fulton Oursler. C: Max von Sydow, Dorothy McGuire, Robert Loggia, Claude Rains, Jose Ferrer, Charlton Heston, Donald Pleasence, David McCallum, Gary Raymond, Robert Blake, John Considine, David Hedison, Joanna Dunham, Sal Mineo, Van Heflin, Ed Wynn, Martin Landau, Telly Savalas, Sidney Poitier, Roddy McDowell, Angela Lansbury, Carroll Baker, Janet Margolin, Burt Brinckerhoff, Tom Reese.

25 Barker, Ma (1872–1935)

(Arizona Donnie Clark) Matriarchal leader of the "Bloody Barker Gang," Kate Barker directed her three sons in kidnapping, robbery and murder throughout the midwest in the late twenties and early thirties until gunned down by federal authorities. Ma Barker's story was loosely the basis for several other films including: *Queen of the Mob* (40), *Machine Gun Mama* (44), *The Grissom Gang* (71), *Big Bad Mama* (74) and *Big Bad Mama II* (87).

Jean Harvey. *Guns Don't Argue* (US/1955/92m/BW) D: Bill Karn & Richard Kahn. Feature film edited from the TV series *Gangbusters*. C: Myron Healey, Lyle Talbot, Paul Dubov, Sam Edwards, Richard Crane, Tamar Cooper, Baynes Barron, Doug Wilson.

Lurene Tuttle. *Ma Barker's Killer Brood* (US/1960/82m/BW) D: Bill Karn. C: Tris Coffin, Paul Dubov, Robert Kendall, Vic Lundin, Don Grady, Eric Sinclair, Ronald Foster.

Shelley Winters. *Bloody Mama* (US/1970/90m/C) D: Roger Corman. C: Pat Hingle, Don Stroud, Diane Varsi, Bruce Dern, Robert Walden. Robert De Niro.

Barnacle, Nora *see* Joyce, James

26 Barnum, P.T. (1810–1891)

(Phineas Taylor Barnum) The ultimate con man/impresario/entrepreneur, Barnum's "Greatest Show on Earth" is still playing as Ringling Bros., Barnum and Bailey's Circus. He was portrayed by Burt Lancaster in the 1986 TV mini-series *Barnum*. In the 1999 mini-series *P.T. Barnum*, Beau Bridges played the adult Barnum, and Bridges' son Jordan played the young Barnum.

Wallace Beery. *A Lady's Morals* (aka *Jenny Lind*) (aka *The Soul Kiss*) (US/1930/86m/BW) D: Sidney Franklin. C: Grace Moore, Reginald Denny, Gus Shy, Jobyna Howland.

Wallace Beery. *The Mighty Barnum* (US/1934/87m/BW) D: Walter Lang. C: Adolphe Menjou, Virginia Bruce, Janet Beecher, Herman Bing, Davison Clark, George MacQuarrie.

Raymond Brown. *High, Wide and Handsome* (US/1937/112m/BW) D: Rouben Mamoulian. C: Irene Dunne, Randolph Scott, Dorothy Lamour, Charles Bickford, Elizabeth Patterson.

Gustav Partos. *Semmelweis* (Hungary/1939/80m/BW) D: Andre De Toth. C: Theodore Uray, Arthur Somlay, Lajos Vertes, Julia Ligeti, Elizabeth Simor.

Burl Ives. *Those Fantastic Flying Fools* (aka *Jules Verne's Rocket to the Moon*) (aka *Blast-Off*) (GB/1967/95m/C) D: Don Sharp. B/on the novel *Rocket to the Moon* by Jules Verne. C: Joan Sterndale-Bennett, Troy Donahue, Gert Frobe.

27 Barrow, Clyde (1910–1934)

Glorified in 1967's *Bonnie and Clyde*, Barrow was actually a 5'3" psychotic who, with his wife **Bonnie Parker**, killed more than a dozen people during their notorious criminal career. Also loosely based on their story were: *You Only Live Once*

(37), *Persons in Hiding* (39), *Gun Crazy* (49), *They Live By Night* (49) and *Thieves Like Us* (74).

Baynes Barron. *Guns Don't Argue* (US/1955/92m/BW) D: Bill Karn & Richard Kahn. Feature film edited from the TV series *Gangbusters*. C: Myron Healey, Lyle Talbot, Jean Harvey, Paul Dubov, Sam Edwards, Richard Crane, Tamar Cooper, Doug Wilson.

Jack Hogan (as Guy Darrow). *The Bonnie Parker Story* (US/1958/79m/BW) D: William Witney. C: Dorothy Provine, Richard Bakalyan, Joseph Turkel, William Stevens, Ken Lynch.

Warren Beatty. *Bonnie and Clyde* (US/1967/111m/C) D: Arthur Penn. C: Faye Dunaway, Gene Hackman, Michael J. Pollard, Estelle Parsons, Denver Pyle, Gene Wilder.

Lucky Mosley. *The Other Side of Bonnie and Clyde* (US/1968/75m/BW) D: Larry Buchanan. C: Joe Enterentree, Frank Hamer, Jr., Burl Ives (Narrator).

28 Barrymore, John (1882–1942)

(John Blythe) The most famous actor of the early 20th century, the film depictions of Barrymore have concentrated more on his drinking than on his acting. In the TV film *My Wicked, Wicked Ways* (85) he was played by Barrie Ingham.

Errol Flynn. *Too Much, Too Soon* (US/1958/121m/BW) D: Art Napoleon. B/on the book by Diana Barrymore & Gerold Frank. C: Dorothy Malone, Efrem Zimbalist, Jr., Ray Danton.

Jack Cassidy. *W.C. Fields and Me* (US/1976/111m/C) D: Arthur Hiller. B/on the book by Carlotta Monti & Cy Rice. C: Rod Steiger, Valerie Perrine, Paul Stewart, Dana Elcar.

29 Bass, Sam (1851–1878)

A Western train and bank robber, Sam Bass was killed by Texas Rangers on July 21, 1878 — his twenty-seventh birthday.

Charles Grapewin. *Wild Horse Mesa* (US/1932/61m/BW) D: Henry Hathaway. B/on the novel by Zane Grey. C: Randolph Scott, Sally Blane, Fred Kohler, Sr., Lucille LaVerne.

Trevor Bardette. *Wild Bill Hickok Rides* (US/1942/81m/BW) D: Ray Enright. C: Bruce Cabot, Constance Bennett, Warren William, Betty Brewer, Walter Catlett, Ward Bond, Ray Teal.

Nestor Paiva. *Badman's Territory* (US/1946/98m/BW) D: Tim Whelan. C: Randolph Scott, Ann Richards, George "Gabby" Hayes, Chief Thundercloud, Lawrence Tierney, Tom Tyler, Steve Brodie, Phil Warren, William Moss, Isabell Jewell, Emory Parnell.

Jim Davis. *The Fabulous Texan* (US/1947/97m/BW) D: Edward Ludwig. C: William Elliott, John Carroll, Catherine McLeod, Albert Dekker, Andy Devine, John Hamilton.

Howard Duff. *Calamity Jane and Sam Bass* (US/1949/85m/C) D: George Sherman. C: Yvonne De Carlo, Dorothy Hart, Willard Parker, Norman Lloyd, Lloyd Bridges, Milburn Stone.

William Bishop. *The Texas Rangers* (US/1951/68m/C) D: Phil Karlson. C: George Montgomery, Gale Storm, Noah Beery, Jr., John Dehner, Ian MacDonald, John Doucette.

Leonard Penn. *Outlaw Women* (US/1952/76m/C) D: Sam Newfield & Ron Ormond. C: Marie Windsor, Richard Rober, Alan Nixon, Carla Balenda, Jackie Coogan.

Rex Marlow. *Deadwood '76* (US/1965/94m/C) D: James Landis. C: Arch Hall, Jr., Melissa Morgan, Jack Lester, Robert Dix.

Cliff Alexander. *Ride a Wild Stud* (aka *Ride the Wild Stud*) (US/1969) D: Revilo Ekard. C: Tex Gates, Frenchy LeBoyd, William Fosterwick, Bill Ferrill.

30 Bean, "Judge" Roy (1825?–1903)

The "Law West of the Pecos," Bean is remembered for his bizarre sentencing and for his obsession with British singer/actress **Lillie Langtry.**

Walter Brennan * Best Supporting Actor (AA). *The Westerner* (US/1940/ 100m/BW) D: William Wyler. C: Gary Cooper, Doris Davenport, Fred Stone, Forrest Tucker, Dana Andrews, Lillian Bond.

Victor Jory. *A Time for Dying* (US/1969/87m/C) D: Budd Boetticher. C: Richard Lapp, Anne Randall, Audie Murphy, Beatrice Kay, Burt Mustin.

Robert Hossein. *Judge Roy Bean* (aka *Trouble in Sacramento*) (aka *All'Ovest Di Sacramento*) (France/1970/C) D: Richard Owens. C: Silva Monti, Xavier Gelin, Pierre Perret, Anne-Marie Balin.

Paul Newman. *The Life and Times of Judge Roy Bean* (US/1972/120m/C) D: John Huston. C: Ava Gardner, John Huston, Jacqueline Bisset, Tab Hunter, Victoria Principal, Stacy Keach.

31 Becket, Saint Thomas (1118–1170)

Archbishop of Canterbury to **Henry II,** Becket and the king divided over the rights and privileges of the church. After exile in France, Becket returned to Canterbury where he was murdered by partisans of the king.

Father John Groser. *Murder in the Cathedral* (GB/1951/140m/BW) D: George Hoellering. B/on the play by T.S. Eliot. C: Alexander Gauge, David Ward, T.S. Eliot, Michael Aldridge.

Richard Burton. *Becket* (GB/1964/148m/C) D: Peter Glenville. B/on the play by Jean Anouilh. Best Picture (GG). C: Peter O'Toole, Donald Wolfit, John Gielgud, Martita Hunt, Pamela Brown, Sian Phillips, Paolo Stoppa, Felix Aylmer.

32 Beethoven, Ludwig von (1770–1827)

Though recognized by many as the greatest composer of all time, Beethoven has only recently been given the full Hollywood biopic treatment as **Chopin, Liszt, Mozart** and others had been previously.

Harry Baur. *The Life and Loves of Beethoven* (aka *Beethoven's Great Love*) (France/1936/135–80m/BW) D: Abel Gance. C: Annie Ducaux, Jany Holt, Jean Debucourt, Jean-Louis Barrault.

Auguste Boverio. *Schubert's Serenade* (aka *Serenade*) (France/1940/90m/BW)

D: Jean Boyer. C: Bernard Lancret, Lilian Harvey, Louis Jouvet, Marcel Vallee, Jelix Oudart.

Albert Basserman. *New Wine* (aka *The Great Awakening*) (aka *The Melody Master*) (US/1941/84m/BW) D: Reinhold Schunzel. C: Ilona Massey, Alan Curtis, Binnie Barnes, Billy Gilbert, Sterling Holloway, John Qualen, Forrest Tucker.

Rene Deltgen. *The Mozart Story* (aka *Whom the Gods Love*) (aka *Mozart*) (aka *Wenn Die Gotter Lieben*) (Germany/1942/91m/C) D: Karl Hartl. C: Hans Holt, Winnie Markus, Irene von Meyendorf, Edward Vedder, Wilton Graff, Curt Jurgens, Carol Forman, Walther Jansson, Paul Hoerbiger.

Memo Benassi. *Rossini* (Italy/1946/90m/BW) D: Mario Bonnard. C: Nino Bessozi, Paolo Barbara, Camillo Pilotto, Armando Falconi, Greta Gonda.

Ewald Balser. *Eroica* (Austria/1949/90m/BW) D: Walter Kolm-Veltee & Karl Hartl. C: Marianna Schoenaper, Judith Holzmeister, Oskar Werner, Dagny Servaes, Ivan Petrovich.

Erich von Stroheim. *Napoleon* (France/1954/190m/C) D: Sacha Guitry. C: Jean-Pierre Aumont, Gianna Maria Canale, Jeanne Boitel, Pierre Brasseur, Daniel Gelin, Sacha Guitry, O.W. Fisher, Raymond Pellegrin, Danielle Darrieux, Lana Marconi, Michele Morgan, Dany Roby, Henri Vidal, Clement Duhour, Serge Regianni, Maria Schell.

Ewald Balser. *The House of the Three Girls* (Austria/1958/102m/C) D: Ernst Marischka. B/on the novel *Schwammer* by Rudolf Bascht. C: Karl Boehm, Gustav Knuth, Magda Schneider.

Karl Boehm. *The Magnificent Rebel* (US/1961/94m/C) D: Georg Tressler. C: Ernst Nadhering, Giulia Rubini, Ivan Desny, Gabriele Porks, Peter Arens.

Larry Bishop. *Shanks* (US/1974/93m/C) D: William Castle. C: Marcel Marceau, Tsilla Chelton, Philippe Clay, Cindy Eilbacher, Helena Kallianiotes, Don Calfa, Mondo, Phil Adams, William Castle.

Donatas Banionis. *Beethoven—Tage Aus Einem Leben* (East Germany/1976/110m/C) D: Horst Seeman. C: Stefan Lisewski, Hans Teuscher, Renate Richter.

Wolfgang Reichmann. *Beethoven's Nephew* (France/1985/105m/C) D: Paul Morrissey. B/on a novel by Luigi Magnani. C: Dietmar Prinz, Jane Birkin, Nathalie Baye.

Clifford David. *Bill and Ted's Excellent Adventure* (US/1989/90m/C) D: Stephen Herek. C: Keanu Reeves, Alex Winter, George Carlin, Amy Stock-Poynton, Terry Camilleri, Dan Shor, Rod Loomis, Al Leong, Jane Wiedlin, Robert V. Barron, Tony Steedman, Fee Waybill.

Neil Munro. *Beethoven Lives Upstairs* (Canada/1992/52m/C) D: David Devine. C: Illya Woloshyn, Fiona Reid, Paul Soles, Albert Schultz, Sheila McCarthy.

Gary Oldman. *Immortal Beloved* (US/1994/123m/C) D: Bernard Rose. C: Isabella Rosselini, Valeria Golino, Jeroen Krabbe, Barry Humphries, Gerard Horan.

33 Bell, Alexander Graham (1847–1922)
Famous as the inventor of the telephone, Bell was also a respected teacher of the deaf and a co-founder of the National Geographic Society. In TV movies he has

been portrayed by John Randolph in *The Winds of Kittyhawk* (78) and by Don Robinson in *Cook and Peary: The Race to the Pole* (83).

Don Ameche. *The Story of Alexander Graham Bell* (aka *The Modern Miracle*) (US/1939/97m/BW) D: Irving Cummings. C: Loretta Young, Henry Fonda, Charles Coburn, Beryl Mercer, Sally Blaine.

Jim Ameche. *The Story of Mankind* (US/1957/100m/C) D: Irwin Allen. B/on the book by Hendrik van Loon. C: Ronald Colman, Hedy Lamarr, Virginia Mayo, Agnes Moorehead, Peter Lorre, Dennis Hopper, Marie Wilson, Helmut Dantine, Edward Everett Horton, Reginald Gardiner, Marie Windsor, Francis X. Bushman, Anthony Dexter, Austin Green, Harpo Marx, Bobby Watson, Reginald Sheffield, Cedric Hardwicke, Cesar Romero.

34 Bellini, Vincenzo (1801–1835)

Italian composer, Bellini's operas include "La Sonnambula" and "Norma."

Phillips Holmes. *The Divine Spark* (aka *Casta Diva*) (Italy-GB/1935/100–81m/ BW) D: Carmine Gallone. C: Martha Eggerth, Benita Hume, Edmund Breon, Hugh Miller.

Maurice Ronet. *Casa Ricordi* (aka *House of Ricordi*) (France-Italy/1954/ 130–112m/C) D: Carmine Gallone. C: Roland Alexandre, Fosco Giachetti, Miriam Bru.

35 Berlioz, Louis-Hector (1803–1869)

A prime force in the development of modern orchestration, Berlioz is remembered for his "Symphonie Fantastique," "Romeo and Juliet" and "Harold in Italy" among other works.

Jean-Louis Barrault. *Symphonie Fantastique* (France/1942/85m/BW) D: Christian-Jaque. C: Renee Saint-Cyr, Lise Delamare, Jules Berry, Bernard Blier.

Murray Melvin. *Lisztomania* (GB/1975/105m/C) D: Ken Russell. C: Roger Daltrey, Sara Kestelman, Paul Nicholas, Fiona Lewis, Veronica Qilligan, Ken Colley, Andrew Reilly, Otto Diamant, Anulka Dziubinska, Imogen Claire, Ken Parry.

36 Bernadette, Saint (1844–1879)

(Marie-Bernarde Soubirous) A miller's daughter who in 1858 had visions of the Virgin Mary in a cave near Lourdes in France.

Jennifer Jones * Best Actress (AA,GG). *The Song of Bernadette* (US/1943/156m/BW) D: Henry King. B/on the novel by Franz Werfel. Best Picture (GG). C: William Eythe, Charles Bickford, Vincent Price, Lee J. Cobb, Anne Revere, Jerome Cowan, Patricia Morison, Gladys Cooper.

Daniele Ajoret. *Bernadette of Lourdes* (France/1960/90m/BW) D: Robert Darene. C: Nadine Alari, Robert Arnoux, Blanchette Brunoy, Jean Clarieux, Lise Delamare, Jean-Jaques Delbo.

Sydney Penney. *Bernadette* (France/1988/118m/C) D: Jean Delannoy. C: Jean-Marc Bory, Roland Lesaffre, Michele Simonnet, Michel Duchaussoy, Bernard Dheran.

37 Bernhardt, Sarah (1844–1923)

(Henriette Rosine Bernard) Undoubtedly, the most famous actress to have ever portrayed Hamlet, "The Divine Sarah" (as she billed herself) is probably the most famous actress to have ever lived.

Colette Regis. *Three Waltzes* (France/1938/96m/BW) D: Ludwig Berger. C: Yvonne Printemps, Pierre Fresnay, Henri Guisol, Jean Perier.

Jeanne Boitel. *If Paris Were Told to Us* (France/1955/135m/C) D: Sacha Guitry. C: Danielle Darrieux, Jean Marais, Robert Lamoureaux, Sacha Guitry, Michelle Morgan, Lana Marconi, Gilbert Boka, Renee Saint-Cyr, Gerard Philipe.

Glenda Jackson. *The Incredible Sarah* (GB/1976/105m/C) D: Richard Fleischer. C: Daniel Massey, Yvonne Mitchell, Douglas Wilmer, David Langton, Simon Williams.

Bernstein, Carl *see* Woodward, Bob

38 Bierce, Ambrose (1842–1914?)

American author and journalist, known for his wit and satirical writings, and his obsession with horror and death. Bierce served in the Union Army during the Civil War, and used his wartime experiences as the basis for some of his finest short stories. Among his best known works are *The Devil's Dictionary* and *Can such Things Be?* In 1913 Bierce went to Mexico, his fate unknown. He was portrayed by Michael Parks in the 2000 video release *From Dusk to Dawn 3: The Hangman's Daughter*.

Gregory Peck. *Old Gringo* (US/1989/119m/C) D: Luis Puenzo. B/on the novel *Gringo Viejo* by Carlos Fuentes. C: Jane Fonda, Jimmy Smits, Pedro Armendariz, Jr.

Jim Beaver. *Ah! Silenciosa* (Mexico-US/1999/C) D: Marcos Cline-Márquez. C: Ana Sobero, Alberto Tejada, Carlos Roberto Majul, Ricardo Cárdenas, Lourdes Castillo, Chico Hernandez.

39 Billy the Kid (1859–1881)

(Patrick Henry McCarty known as William H. Bonney) The most notorious and most filmed gunman of the Old West, Billy is often portrayed as a victim of circumstance rather than as the psychopathic killer he actually was. He claimed one murder for every year of his life until gunned down by Sheriff **Pat Garrett**. In the TV film *Gore Vidal's Billy the Kid* (89) he was played by Val Kilmer and by Donnie Wahlberg in *Purgatory* (99). Note: Dean Stockwell played the part of an actor portraying Billy the Kid in Dennis Hopper's *The Last Movie* (1971). (See Appendix F for the PRC "**Billy the Kid**" series.)

Johnny Mack Brown. *Billy the Kid* (aka *The Highwayman Rides*) (US/1930/95m/BW) D: King Vidor. B/on the novel *The Saga of Billy the Kid* by Walter Noble Burns. C: Wallace Beery, Karl Dane, Wyndham Standing, Russell Simpson, Blanche Frederici.

Roy Rogers. *Billy the Kid Returns* (US/1938/51m/BW) D: Joseph Kane. C: Smiley Burnette, Lynne Roberts, Morgan Wallace, Fred Kohler, Wade Boteler, Joseph Crehan.

Robert Taylor. *Billy the Kid* (US/1941/94m/C) D: David Miller. B/on the novel *The Saga of Billy the Kid* by Walter Noble Burns. C: Brian Donlevy, Ian Hunter.

Jack Buetel. *The Outlaw* (US/1943/126m/BW) D: Howard Hughes. C: Jane Russell, Thomas Mitchell, Walter Huston, Mimi Aguglia, Joe Sawyer, Dickie Jones.

Dean White. *Return of the Bad Men* (US/1948/90m/BW) D: Ray Enright. C: Randolh Scott, George "Gabby" Hayes, Robert Ryan, Anne Jeffreys, Steve Brodie, Richard Powers, Robert Bray, Lex Barker, Walter Reed, Michael Harvey, Robert Armstrong.

George Baxter. William Perrott (plays Billy in a flashback sequence). *Son of Billy the Kid* (US/1949/65m/BW) D: Ray Taylor. C: Lash La Rue, Al St. John, June Carr, Clarke Stevens.

Don Barry. *I Shot Billy the Kid* (US/1950/57m/BW) D: William Berke. C: Robert Lowery, Wally Vernon, Tom Neal, Wendy Lee, Claude Stroude, Richard Farmer.

Audie Murphy. *The Kid from Texas* (aka *Texas Kid, Outlaw*) (US/1950/78m/C) D: Kurt Neumann. C: Gale Storm, Shepperd Strudwick, Will Geer, Robert Barrat, Frank Wilcox.

Scott Brady. *The Law vs. Billy the Kid* (US/1954/72m/C) D: William Castle. C: Betta St. John, James Griffith, Alan Hale, Jr., Paul Cavanagh, Bill Phillips, Otis Garth, Robert Griffin.

Tyler MacDuff. *The Boy from Oklahoma* (US/1954/87m/C) D: Michael Curtiz. C: Will Rogers, Jr., Nancy Olson, Lon Chaney, Jr., Anthony Caruso, Sheb Wooley, Slim Pickens.

Nick Adams. *Strange Lady in Town* (US/1955/112m/C) D: Mervyn LeRoy. C: Greer Garson, Dana Andrews, Lois Smith, Cameron Mitchell, Walter Hampden, Ralph Moody.

Anthony Dexter. *The Parson and the Outlaw* (US/1957/71m/C) D: Oliver Drake. C: Buddy Rogers, Jean Parker, Sonny Tufts, Robert Lowery, Marie Windsor, Bob Steele.

Paul Newman. *The Left-Handed Gun* (US/1958/102m/BW) D: Arthur Penn. B/on the teleplay *The Death of Billy the Kid* by Gore Vidal. C: Lita Milan, John Dehner, Hurd Hatfield, James Congdon, Colin Keith-Johnston, John Dierkes, Denver Pyle.

Jack Taylor. *Billy the Kid* (Spain/1962/C) D: Leon Klimovsky.

Gaston Sands (Santos). *A Bullet for Billy the Kid* (Mexico/1963/63m/C) D: Rafael Baledon. C: Steve Brodie, Lloyd Nelson, Marla Blaine, Richard McIntyre, Rita Mace.

Johnny Ginger. *The Outlaws Is Coming* (US/1965/88m/BW) D: Norman Maurer. C: Larry Fine, Moe Howard, Joe De Rita, Nancy Kovack, Murray Alper, Joe Bolton, Bill Camfield, Hal Fryar, Wayne Mack, Ed McDonnell, Bruce Sedley, Paul Shannon, Sally Starr.

Chuck Courtenay. *Billy the Kid vs. Dracula* (US/1966/73m/C) D: William

Beaudine. C: John Carradine, Melinda Plowman, Virginia Christine, Roy Barcroft, Harey Carey, Jr.

Peter Lee Lawrence. *The Man Who Killed Billy the Kid* (aka *For a Few Bullets More*) (Spain-Italy/1967/90m/C) D: Julio Buchs. C: Fausto Tozzi, Diane Zura, Gloria Milland.

Geoffrey Deuel. *Chisum* (US/1970/110m/C) D: Andrew McLaglen. C: John Wayne, Forrest Tucker, Christopher George, Ben Johnson, Glenn Corbett, Andrew Prine, Patric Knowles, Lynda Day, John Agar, Robert Donner, Ray Teal, Ron Soble.

Jean-Pierre Leaud. *A Girl Is a Gun* (France/1971/80m/C) D: Luc Moullet. C: Rachel Kesterber, Jean Valmont, Bruno Kresoja, Michel Minaud.

Michael J. Pollard. *Dirty Little Billy* (US/1972/100m/C) D: Stan Dragoti. C: Lee Purcell, Richard Evans, Charles Aidman, Gary Busey, Dran Hamilton, Dick Van Patten, Ed Lauter.

Kris Kristofferson. *Pat Garrett and Billy the Kid* (US/1973/122–106m/C) D: Sam Peckinpah. C: James Coburn, Bob Dylan, Jason Robards, Richard Jaeckel, Katy Jurado, Barry Sullivan.

Emilio Estevez. *Young Guns* (US/1988/97m/C) D: Chris Cain. C: Kiefer Sutherland, Lou Diamond Phillips, Charlie Sheen, Casey Siemaszko, Terence Stamp, Patrick Wayne.

Dan Shor. *Bill and Ted's Excellent Adventure* (US/1989/90m/C) D: Stephen Herek. C: Keanu Reeves, Alex Winter, George Carlin, Amy Stock-Poynton, Terry Camilleri, Clifford David, Rod Loomis, Al Leong, Jane Wiedlin, Robert V. Barron, Tony Steedman, Fee Waybill.

Emilio Estevez. *Young Guns II* (US/1990/105m/C) D: Geoff Murphy. C: Kiefer Sutherland, Lou Diamond Phillips, Christian Slater, William Petersen, James Coburn, Balthazar Getty, Scott Wilson, Chief Buddy Redbow, Alan Ruck, R.D. Call, Jack Kehoe.

40 Bismarck, Otto von (1815–1898)

Known as the "Iron Chancellor," Bismarck was the man who unified Germany while serving as Prussia's Prime Minister during its successful wars against Denmark, Austria and France in the mid–nineteenth century.

Lyn Harding. *Spy of Napoleon* (GB/1936/98m/BW) D: Maurice Elvey. B/on the novel by the Baroness Orczy. C: Richard Barthelmess, Dolly Haas, Frank Vosper, Joyce Bland.

Friedrich Otto Fischer. *Robert Koch* (Germany/1939/BW) D: Hans Steinhoff. C: Elisabeth Flickenschildt, Paul Dahlke, Bernhard Goetzke, Emil Jannings, Rudolf Klein-Rogge.

Paul Hartmann. *Bismarck* (Germany/1940/BW) D: Wolfgang Liebeneiner. C: Lil Dagover, Otto Gebuhr, Bernhard Goetzke, Kathe Haack.

Lyn Harding. *The Prime Minister* (GB/1940/94m/BW) D: Thorold Dickinson. C: John Gielgud, Diana Wynyard, Will Fyfe, Stephen Murray, Owen Nares, Fay Compton, Leslie Perrins, Vera Bogetti, Frederick Leister, Nicolas Hannan, Kynaston Reeves, Gordon McLeod.

Friedrich Otto Fischer. *Carl Peters* (Germany/1941) D: Herbert Selpin. C: Hans Albers.

Emil Jannings. *Die Entlassung* (aka *The Dismissal*) (Germany/1942/BW) D: Wolfgang Liebeneiner. C: Karl Diehl, Otto Hasse, Werner Hinz, Fritz Kampers, Werner Krauss, Theodor Loos.

Kurt Katch. *Salome, Where She Danced* (US/1945/90m/C) D: Charles Lamont. C: Yvonne De Carlo, Rod Cameron, David Bruce, Walter Slezak, Albert Dekker, John Litel, Nestor Paiva.

Friedrich Domin. *Ludwig II* (Germany/1955) D: Helmut Kautner. C: O.W. Fischer, Paul Bildt, Klaus Kinski, Marianne Koch, Ruth Leuwerik.

Oliver Reed. *Royal Flash* (GB/1975/98m/C) D: Richard Lester. B/on the novel by George MacDonald Fraser. C: Malcolm McDowell, Alan Bates, Florinda Balkan.

41 Black Beard (1680?–1718)

(Edward Teach or Thatch) An English born pirate, Blackbeard sailed his ship, the "Queen Anne's Revenge," out of North Carolina where he had a loot-sharing deal with the governor. He was finally captured and beheaded by a British Naval Force.

Louis Bacigalupi. *Double Crossbones* (US/1950/75m) D: Charles Barton. C: Donald O'Connor, Helena Carter, Will Geer, John Emery, Hope Emerson, Alan Napier, Robert Barrat.

Thomas Gomez. *Anne of the Indies* (US/1951/81m/C) D: Jacques Tourneur. C: Jean Peters, Louis Jourdan, Debra Paget, Herbert Marshall, James Robertson Justice, Olaf Hytten.

Robert Newton. *Blackbeard the Pirate* (US/1952/98m/C) D: Raoul Walsh. C: Linda Darnell, William Bendix, Torin Thatcher, Irene Ryan, Alan Mowbray, Richard Egan.

Murvyn Vye. *The Boy and the Pirates* (US/1960/84m/C) D: Bert I. Gordon. C: Charles Herbert, Susan Gordon, Timothy Carey, Paul Guilfoyle, Joseph Turkel, Archie Duncan.

Peter Ustinov. *Blackbeard's Ghost* (US/1967/106m/C) D: Robert Stevenson. B/on the novel by Ben Stahl. C: Dean Jones, Suzanne Pleshette, Elsa Lanchester, Joby Baker.

42 Bligh, William (1754–1817)

It's often said that Captain Bligh has been portrayed unfairly as too harsh and cruel in films of the Bounty mutiny yet when he was later made a governor in New South Wales, Australia, the men rebelled against him again and locked him up for two years. Just coincidence?

Mayne Lynton. *In the Wake of the Bounty* (Australia/1933/66m/BW) D: Charles Chauvel. C: Errol Flynn, John Warwick, Victor Gouriet.

Charles Laughton * Best Actor (NYC). *Mutiny on the Bounty* (US/1935/132m/BW) D: Frank Lloyd. B/on the novels *Mutiny on the Bounty, Men Against the Sea,* and *Pitcairn's Island* by Charles Nordhoff & James Norman Hall. Best Picture (AA). C: Clark Gable, Franchot Tone, David Torrence, Eddie Quillan, Dudley Digges, Donald Crisp, Francis Lister, Ian Wolfe.

Trevor Howard. *Mutiny on the Bounty* (US/1962/179m/C) D: Lewis Milestone. B/on the novel by Charles Nordhoff & James Norman Hall. C: Marlon Brando, Richard Harris, Hugh Griffith, Richard Haydn, Tarita, Gordon Jackson, Noel Purcell.

Anthony Hopkins. *The Bounty* (US/1984/132m/C) D: Roger Donaldson. B/on the novel *Captain Bligh and Mr. Christian* by Richard Hough. C: Mel Gibson, Laurence Olivier, Edward Fox, Daniel Day-Lewis, Liam Neeson, Bernard Hill.

43 Boleyn, Anne (1505–1536)

Second wife of **Henry VIII** and mother of **Elizabeth I**, Anne Boleyn was beheaded for (allegedly) sleeping with her brother.

Merle Oberon. *The Private Life of Henry VIII* (GB/1933/97m/BW) D: Alexander Korda. C: Charles Laughton, Robert Donat, Binnie Barnes, Elsa Lanchester, Wendy Barrie, Everley Gregg, Franklyn Dyall, Miles Mander, Claude Allister, John Loder, Lawrence Hanray.

Barbara Shaw. *The Pearls of the Crown* (France/1937/120–100m/BW) D: Sacha Guitry & Christian-Jaque. C: Sacha Guitry, Jacqueline Delubac, Lyn Harding, Ermete Zacconi, Marguerite Moreno, Yvette Plenne, Catalano, Arletty, Percy Marmont, Derrick De Marney, Simone Renant, Jean Louis Barrault, Emile Drain, Enrico Glori, Renee Saint-Cyr, Pizani, Claude Dauphin, Aime-Simon Gerard.

Elaine Stewart. *Young Bess* (US/1953/112m/C) D: George Sidney. B/on the novel by Margaret Irwin. C: Jean Simmons, Stewart Granger, Deborah Kerr, Charles Laughton, Kay Walsh, Cecil Kellaway, Rex Thompson, Dawn Addams, Lumsden Hare.

Vanessa Redgrave. *A Man for All Seasons* (GB/1966/120m/C) D: Fred Zinnemann. B/on the play by Robert Bolt. Best Picture Awards: (AA, NBR, GG, NYC, BFA Any Source and Best British Film), Best Director Awards: (AA, NBR, GG, NYC, DGA). C: Paul Scofield, Wendy Hiller, Leo McKern, Robert Shaw, Orson Welles, Susannah York, Nigel Davenport, Cyril Luckham.

Genevieve Bujold. *Anne of the Thousand Days* (GB/1969/145m/C) D: Charles Jarrott. B/on the play by Maxwell Anderson. C: Richard Burton, Irene Papas, Anthony Quayle, John Colicos, Michael Hordern, Katharine Blake, William Squire, Lesley Patterson, Nicola Pagett.

Charlotte Rampling. *The Six Wives of Henry VIII* (aka *Henry VIII and His Six Wives*) (GB/1972/125m/C) D: Waris Hussein. C: Keith Michell, Frances Cuka, Jane Asher, Jenny Bos, Lynne Frederick, Barbara Leigh-Hunt, Donald Pleasence, Simon Henderson, Annette Crosbie, John Bryans, Michael Goodliffe, Bernard Hepton, Dorothy Tutin.

44 Bonaparte, (Marie-) Pauline (1780–1825)

Napoleon's wild (and favorite) sister, Pauline, who had been expelled from his court in 1810, accompanied her brother on his exile to Elba in 1814.

Simone Genevois. *Napoleon Bonaparte* (France/1934/140m/BW) D: Abel Gance. Three-dimensional sound version of Gance's 1927 epic *Napoléon*. C: Albert Dieudonné, Edmond von Daele, Alexandre Koubitsky, Antonin Artaud,

Boudreau, Alberty, Jack Rye, Favière, Gina Manès, Suzanne Blanchetti, Marguerite Gance, Genica Missirio.

Gladys Holland. *Lydia Bailey* (US/1952/89m/C) D: Jean Negulesco. B/on the novel by Kenneth Roberts. C: Dale Robertson, Anne Francis, William Marshall, Luis Van Rooten, Charles Korvin, Juanita Moore.

Gianna Maria Canale. *Napoleon* (France/1954/190m/C) D: Sacha Guitry. C: Jean-Pierre Aumont, Jeanne Boitel, Pierre Brasseur, Daniel Gelin, Sacha Guitry, O.W. Fisher, Raymond Pellegrin, Danielle Darrieux, Lana Marconi, Michele Morgan, Erich von Stroheim, Dany Roby, Henri Vidal, Clement Duhour, Serge Regianni, Maria Schell.

Claudia Cardinale. *Austerlitz* (aka *The Battle of Austerlitz*) (France-Italy-Yugoslavia/1959/166m/C) D: Abel Gance. C: Pierre Mondy, Jean Mercure, Martine Carol, Jack Palance, Orson Welles, Georges Marchal, Roland Bartrop, Anthony Stuart, Jean Marais, Vittorio De Sica, Ettore Manni.

Laura Valenzuela. *Madame* (aka *Madame Sans-Gene*) (France-Italy-Spain/1961/104m/C) D: Christian-Jaque. B/on the play *Madame Sans Gene* by Emile Moreau & Victorien Sardou. C: Sophia Loren, Robert Hossein, Julien Bertheau, Renaud Mary, Marina Berti, Carlo Giuffere, Gabriella Pallotta, Annalis Gade.

Gina Lolobrigida. *Imperial Venus* (Italy-France/1962/140m/C) D: Jean Delannoy. C: Stephen Boyd, Gabrielle Ferzetti, Raymond Pellegrin, Micheline Presle.

45 Bonney, Anne (??)

The illegitimate daughter of a wealthy Irish lawyer, Anne Bonney grew to become the most famous female pirate on the Spanish Main. Captured off the coast of Jamaica in 1720, she escaped the hangman's noose by feigning pregnancy.

Binnie Barnes. *The Spanish Main* (US/1945/100m/C) D: Frank Borzage. C: Paul Henried, Maureen O'Hara, Walter Slezak, John Emery, Barton MacLane, Ian Keith.

Hope Emerson. *Double Crossbones* (US/1950/75m) D: Charles Barton. C: Donald O'Connor, Helena Carter, Will Geer, John Emery, Alan Napier, Robert Barrat, Louis Bacigalupi.

Jean Peters (as Anne Providence). *Anne of the Indies* (US/1951/81m/C) D: Jacques Tourneur. C: Louis Jourdan, Debra Paget, Herbert Marshall, Thomas Gomez, James Robertson Justice, Olaf Hytten.

Hillary Brooke. *Abbott and Costello Meet Captain Kidd* (US/1952/70m/C) D: Charles Lamont. C: Bud Abbott, Lou Costello, Charles Laughton, Fran Warren, Leif Erickson, Rex Lease.

46 Boone, Daniel (1734–1820)

American soldier and pioneer, Boone fought in the French and Indian War and established the first permanent settlement in Kentucky at the modestly named Boonesborough. In *The Return of Daniel Boone* (41) Bill Elliott played his namesake grandson. His most remembered depiction was by Fess Parker in the TV series *Daniel Boone* of which two episodes were edited and released theatrically as *Daniel Boone, Frontier Trail Rider* (67).

George O'Brien. *Daniel Boone* (US/1936/75m/BW) D: David Howard. C: Heather Angel, John Carradine, Ralph Forbes, Clarence Muse, George Regas, Dickie Jones.

David Bruce. *Young Daniel Boone* (US/1950/71m/C) D: Reginald LeBorg. C: Kristine Miller, Damian O'Flynn, Don Beddoe, Mary Treen, John Mylong, Nipo T. Strongheart.

Bruce Bennett. *Daniel Boone, Trailblazer* (US/1956/76m/C) D: Albert C. Gannaway & Ismael Rodriguez. C: Lon Chaney, Jr., Faron Young, Kem Dibbs, Damian O'Flynn.

47 Booth, John Wilkes (1838–1865)

Following in the footsteps of his famous father, Junius (Raymond Massey in *Prince of Players*) and brother, Edwin (Richard Burton in that film), Booth was also a Shakespearean actor. His most famous performance came on April 14, 1865, at Ford's Theatre in Washington, D.C., when he shot and killed **Abraham Lincoln**. TV portrayals include Bill Gribble's in *The Ordeal of Dr. Mudd,* (80) and Glenn Faigen's in *Gore Vidal's Lincoln* (89).

Ian Keith. *Abraham Lincoln* (US/1930/97m/BW) D: D.W. Griffith. C: Walter Huston, Una Merkel, Kay Hammond, E. Alyn Warren, Edgar Deering, Hobart Bosworth, Fred Warren, Frank Campeau, Francis Ford, Oscar Apfel, Cameron Prud'Homme.

Francis McDonald. *The Prisoner of Shark Island* (US/1936/95m/BW) D: John Ford. C: Warner Baxter, Gloria Stuart, Joyce Kay, Claude Gillenwater, Frank McGlynn, Leila McIntyre, Harry Carey, Paul Fix, John Carradine, Arthur Byron, Ernest Whitman.

Harry Worth. *Tennessee Johnson* (aka *The Man on America's Conscience*) (US/1942/103m/BW) D: William Dieterle. C: Van Heflin, Ruth Hussey, Lionel Barrymore, Marjorie Main, Regis Toomey, Montagu Love, Porter Hall, Morris Ankrum, Ed O'Neill, Harrison Greene, Charles Dingle, Grant Withers, Lynne Carver, Noah Beery, Sr.

John Derek. *Prince of Players* (US/1955/102m/BW) D: Philip Dunne. B/on the book by Eleanor Ruggles. C: Richard Burton, Raymond Massey, Stanley Hall, Sarah Padden.

Bradford Dillman. *The Lincoln Conspiracy.* (US/1977/90m/C) D: James L. Conway. B/on the book by David Balsiger & Charles E. Sellier, Jr. C: John Anderson, Frances Fordham, Robert Middleton, E.J. Andre, Wallace K. Wilkinson, John Dehner, Whit Bissell.

48 Borgia, Cesare (1475–1507)

The model for Machiavelli's "The Prince," Borgia was one of the most calculating, ruthless and brutal of the major princes of the Italian Renaissance. His personal motto: "Either Caesar or Nothing."

Gabriel Gabrio. *Lucrezia Borgia* (France/1935/80m/BW) D: Abel Gance. C: Edwige Feuillere, Aime Clariond, Roger Karl.

Orson Welles. *Prince of Foxes* (US/1949/107m/BW) D: Henry King. B/on the

The always devious Prince, Cesare Borgia (Orson Wells, left) and sister Lucretia (Marina Berti) break bread with Don Esteban (Leslie Bradley) in this banquet scene from *Prince of Foxes* (1949). (Museum of Modern Art Film Stills Archive)

novel by Samuel Shellabarger. C: Tyrone Power, Wanda Hendrix, Everett Sloane, Marina Berti.

Macdonald Carey. *Bride of Vengeance* (US/1949/92m/BW) D: Mitchell Leisen. C: Paulette Goddard, John Lund, Albert Dekker, John Sutton, Raymond Burr, Fritz Leiber, Rose Hobart.

Pedro Armendariz. *Lucrece Borgia* (aka *Sins of the Borgias*) (aka *Lucrezia Borgia*) (Italy-France/1953/95m/C) D: Christian-Jaque. C: Martine Carol, Massimo Serrato.

Franco Fabrizi. *The Nights of Lucretia Borgia* (Italy/1960/108m/C) D: Sergio Grieco. C: Belinda Lee.

Cameron Mitchell. *The Black Duke* (Italy/1962/C) D: Pino Mercanti.

Edmund Purdom. *The Man Who Laughs* (aka *The Man with the Golden Mask*) (aka *L'Uomo Che Ride*) (Italy/1965/94m/C) D: Sergio Corbucci. C: Lisa Gastoni, Jean Sorel, Ilaria Occhini, Linda Sini.

Lou Castel. *Lucrezia* (Italy-Austria/1968/102m/C) D: Osvaldo Civirani. C: Olinka Berova, Leon Askin, Gianni Garko, Giancarlo Del Duca.

Lorenzo Berinizi. *Immoral Tales* (France/1974/105m/C) D: Walerian Borowczyk. C: Florence Bellamy, Jacopo Berinzini, Lise Danvers.

49 Borgia, Lucretia (1480–1519)

In films Lucretia Borgia has generally been depicted as an opportunistic poisoner and while she was no stranger to political intrigue, she was more often a victim of the machinations of her brother, **Cesare Borgia**.

Edwige Feuillere. *Lucrezia Borgia* (France/1935/80m/BW) D: Abel Gance. C: Gabriel Gabrio, Aime Clariond, Roger Karl.

Leone Lane. *Dante's Inferno* (US/1935/88m/BW) D: Harry Lachman. C: Spencer Tracy, Claire Trevor, Henry B. Walthall, Scotty Becket, Lorna Lowe, Andre Johnsen, Juana Sutton.

Marina Berti (as Amanda). *Prince of Foxes* (US/1949/107m/BW) D: Henry King. B/on the novel by Samuel Shellabarger. C: Tyrone Power, Orson Welles, Wanda Hendrix, Everett Sloane.

Paulette Goddard. *Bride of Vengeance* (US/1949/92m/BW) D: Mitchell Leisen. C: Macdonald Carey, John Lund, Albert Dekker, John Sutton, Raymond Burr, Fritz Leiber, Rose Hobart.

Martine Carol. *Lucrece Borgia* (aka *Sins of the Borgias*) (aka *Lucrezia Borgia*) (Italy-France/1953/95m/C) D: Christian-Jaque. C: Pedro Armandariz, Massimo Serrato.

Belinda Lee. *The Nights of Lucretia Borgia* (Italy/1960/108m/C) D: Sergio Grieco. C: Franco Fabrizi.

Lisa Gastoni. *The Man Who Laughs.* (aka *The Man with the Golden Mask*) (aka *L'Uomo Che Ride*) (Italy/1965/94m/C) D: Sergio Corbucci. C: Edmund Purdom, Jean Sorel, Ilaria Occhini, Linda Sini.

Olinka Berova. *Lucrezia* (Italy-Austria/1968/102m/C) D: Osvaldo Civirani. C: Lou Castel, Leon Askin, Gianni Garko, Giancarlo Del Duca.

Florence Bellamy. *Immoral Tales* (France/1974/105m/C) D: Walerian Borowczyk. C: Lorenzo Berinizi, Jacopo Berinzini, Lise Danvers.

Boris Godunov *see* 633

50 Bormann, Martin (1900–1945?)

Deputy Fuhrer to **Adolf Hitler**, Bormann disappeared after the war and though declared legally dead by the German government the rumor persists that he survived and is living in Paraguay.

Robert Berkeley. *Eyes That Kill* (GB/1947/55m/BW) D: Richard M. Grey. C: Sandra Dorne.

Kurt Eilers. *The Last Ten Days* (aka *Ten Days to Die*) (aka *Last Ten Days of Adolf Hitler*) (aka *Der Letzte Akt*) (aka *The Last Act*) (Germany/1955/115m/BW) D: G.W. Pabst. B/on the novel *Ten Days to Die* by M.A. Mussanno. C: Albin Skoda, Oskar Werner, Lotte Tobisch, Willy Krause, Erich Stuckmann, Edmund Erlandsen, Helga Dohrn, Leopold Hainisch, Otto Schmoele.

G. Stanley Jones. *Hitler* (aka *Women of Nazi Germany*) (US/1962/107m/BW) D: Stuart Heisler. C: Richard Basehart, Cordula Trantow, Maria Emo, Martin Kosleck, John Banner, Martin Brandt, William Sargent, Gregory Gay, Theodore Marcuse, Rick Traeger, John Mitchum, Walter Kohler, Carl Esmond, Berry Kroeger.

Henry Brandon. *The Search for the Evil One* (US/1967/C) D: Joseph Kane. C: Lee Patterson, Lisa Pera, James Dobson, Pitt Herbert, Anna Lisa, H.M. Wynant.

Mark Kingston. *Hitler: The Last Ten Days* (GB–Italy/1973/106m/C) D: Ennio De Concini. B/on the book *The Last Days of the Chancellery* by Gerhardt Boldt. C: Alec Guinness, Simon Ward, Gabriele Ferzetti, Doris Kunstmann, John Bennett, Philip Stone.

51 Boswell, James (1740–1795)

Scottish writer, Boswell's fame rests on his friendship with **Dr. Samuel Johnson** and his work *The Life of Samuel Johnson, LL.D.*

William Wagner. *Lloyds of London* (US/1936/115m/BW) D: Henry King. C: Freddie Bartholomew, Madeleine Carroll, Sir Guy Standing, Tyrone Power, George Sanders, C. Aubrey Smith, John Burton, Hugh Huntley, Thomas Pogue, Yorke Sherwood.

Alexander McCrindle. *I'll Never Forget You* (aka *The House in the Square*) (US/1951/89m/C) D: Roy Baker. B/on the play *Berkeley Square* by John L. Balderston. C: Tyrone Power, Ann Blyth, Michael Rennie, Ronald Simpson, Robert Atkins.

52 Bothwell, Lord (1535–1578)

(James Hepburn, 4th Earl of Bothwell) **Mary, Queen of Scots**' third husband, Bothwell was acquitted of the murder of her second husband, **Lord Darnley**, and was married to her briefly before she was deposed in 1567.

Fredric March. *Mary of Scotland* (US/1936/123m/BW) D: John Ford. B/on the play by Maxwell Anderson. C: Katharine Hepburn, Florence Eldridge, Douglas Walton, John Carradine, Robert Barrat, Gavin Muir, Ian Keith, Ralph Forbes, Alan Mowbray, Walter Byron.

Nigel Davenport. *Mary, Queen of Scots* (GB/1971/128m/C) D: Charles Jarrot. C: Vanessa Redgrave, Glenda Jackson, Patrick McGoohan, Timothy Dalton, Trevor Howard, Daniel Massey, Ian Holm, Andrew Keir, Katherine Kath, Robert James, Richard Denning, Rick Warner.

53 Bowie, Jim (1796?–1836)

Smuggler, gambler, slave trader, pirate (with **Jean LaFitte**) and supposed designer of the Bowie knife, Bowie became a hero when dying along with **Crockett** and **Travis** at the Alamo. Bowie was portrayed by Hal Taliafero in the 1937 serial *Painted Stallion*.

Roger Williams. *Heroes of the Alamo* (aka *Remember the Alamo*) (US/1937/80m/BW) D: Harry Fraser. C: Earl Hodgins, Lane Chandler, Rex Lease, Edward Piel, Julian Rivero, Lee Valianos, Ruth Findlay, Jack Smith, Tex Cooper.

Robert Armstrong. *Man of Conquest* (US/1939/97m/BW) D: George Nichols, Jr. C: Richard Dix, Edward Ellis, Victor Jory, Robert Barrat, Ralph Morgan, C. Henry Gordon, George "Gabby" Hayes, Gail Patrick, Joan Fontaine, Max Terhune, Lane Chandler.

Macdonald Carey. *Comanche Territory* (US/1950/76m/C) D: George Sherman. C: Maureen O'Hara, Will Geer, Charles Drake, Ian MacDonald, Pedro De Cordoba, James Best.

Alan Ladd. *The Iron Mistress* (US/1952/110m/C) D: Gordon Douglas. C: Virginia Mayo, Joseph Calleia, Phyllis Kirk, Alf Kjellin, George Voskovec, Anthony Caruso.

Stuart Randall. *The Man from the Alamo* (US/1953/79m/C) D: Budd Boetticher. C: Glenn Ford, Julia Adams, Chill Wills, Victor Jory, Trevor Bardette, Ward Negley, Arthur Space.

Sterling Hayden. *The Last Command* (US/1955/110m/C) D: Frank Lloyd. B/on the story *The Last Command* by Sy Bartlett. C: Richard Carlson, Arthur Hunnicutt, J. Carroll Naish, Otto Kruger, Hugh Sanders, Don Kennedy, Anna Maria Alberghetti, Ernest Borgnine, Ben Cooper, Virginia Grey, John Russell, Edward Colmans, Jim Davis.

Kenneth Tobey. *Davy Crockett, King of the Wild Frontier* (US/1955/90m/C) D: Norman Foster. C: Fess Parker, Buddy Ebsen, Basil Ruysdael, Hans Conried, Pat Hogan, Helene Stanley, Don Megowan.

Jeff Morrow. *The First Texan* (US/1956/82m/C) D: Byron Haskin. C: Joel McCrea, Dayton Lummis, William Hopper, David Silva, James Griffith, Carl Benton Reid, Felicia Farr, Wallace Ford, Chubby Johnson, Jody McCrea, Abraham Sofaer.

Richard Widmark. *The Alamo* (US/1960/192m/C) D: John Wayne. C: John Wayne, Laurence Harvey, Patrick Wayne, Ruben Padilla, Joseph Calleia, Richard Boone.

54 Bradley, Omar (1893–1981)

Leader of the U.S. 1st Army in the invasion of Normandy, Bradley was subsequently made commander of the million-soldier U.S. 12th Army and was instrumental in the German defeat in World War II.

Nicholas Stuart. *The Longest Day* (US/1962/180m/BW) D: Andrew Marton, Ken Annakin & Bernherd Wicki. B/on the novel by Cornelius Ryan. Best English Language Picture (NBR). C: John Wayne, Robert Mitchum, Henry Fonda, Robert Ryan, Rod Steiger, Robert Wagner, Sal Mineo, Roddy McDowall, Curt Jurgens, Paul Hartman, Henry Grace, Wolfgang Lukschy, Werner Hinz, Trevor Reid, Alexander Knox.

Glenn Ford. *Is Paris Burning?* (US-France/1966/173m/C) D: Rene Clement. C: Jean-Paul Belmondo, Charles Boyer, Leslie Caron, Jean-Pierre Casal, George Chakiris, Claude Dauphin, Alain Delon, Kirk Douglas, Gert Frobe, Daniel Gelin, Orson Welles, E.G. Marshall, Simone Signoret, Billy Frick, Hannes Messemer, Robert Stack.

Karl Malden. *Patton* (aka *Patton—Lust for Glory*) (US/1970/170m/C) D: Franklin J. Schaffner. B/on *Patton: Ordeal and Triumph* by Ladislas Farago and *A Soldier's Story* by Omar Bradley. Best Picture, Best Direction (AA). Best English-Language Picture (NBR). Best Director (DGA). C: George C. Scott, Michael Bates, Edward Binns, Lawrence Dobkin, John Doucette, Stephen Young, Michael Strong, Frank Latimore, James Edwards, Richard Meunch, Karl Michael Vogler.

Fred Stuthman. *MacArthur* (US/1977/128m/C) D: Joseph Sargent. C: Gregory Peck, Ed Flanders, Dan O'Herlihy, Ivan Bonar, Ward Costello, Nicholas Coster, Art Fleming, Addison Powell, Marj Dusay, Kenneth Tobey, John Fujioka, Sandy Kenyon.

55 Brady, Diamond Jim (1856–1917)

(James Buchanan Brady) Known for his diamond jewelry, his wealth and his size, Brady was the toast of New York society around the turn of the century.

Edward Arnold. *Diamond Jim* (US/1935/93m/BW) D: Edward Sutherland. B/on the book *Diamond Jim Brady* by Parker Morell. C: Jean Arthur, Binnie Barnes, Bill Hoolahan.

Charles Wilson. *The Gentleman from Louisiana* (US/1936/67m/BW) D: Irving Pichel. C: Edward Quillan, Chic Sale, Charlotte Henry, John Kelly, Matt McHugh, Ruth Gillette, Holmes Herbert.

Edward Arnold. *Lillian Russell* (US/1940/127m/BW) D: Irving Cummings. C: Alice Faye, Don Ameche, Henry Fonda, Warren William, Claud Allister, Nigel Bruce, Eddie Foy, Jr., William B. Davidson, Leo Carillo, Milburn Stone.

Robert Hall. *Diamond Stud* (US/1970/82m/C) D: Greg Corarito. C: John Alserman, Monika Henreid, Victoria Carbe, Michael Greer, Ann Dee.

56 Bramante, Donato (1444–1514)

Italian Renaissance architect, Bramante designed St. Peter's Basilica in Rome.

A. Bromley Davenport. *The Cardinal* (GB/1936/70m/BW) D: Sinclair Hill. B/on the play by Louis N. Parker. C: Matheson Lang, Eric Portman, Wilfred Fletcher, F.B.J. Sharpe, Robert Atkins.

Harry Andrews. *The Agony and the Ecstasy* (US/1965/136m/C) D: Carol Reed. B/on the novel by Irving Stone. C: Charlton Heston, Rex Harrison, Diane Cilento, Tomas Milian.

57 Braun, Eva (1912–1945)

Hitler's mistress (from 1936) and wife (for one day), film portrayals of Eva Braun generally concentrate on her last few days spent in a Berlin bunker. She was played by Susan Blakely in the TV movie *The Bunker* (81) and by Renee Soutendijk in the mini-series *Inside the Third Reich* (82).

M. Novakova. *The Fall of Berlin* (USSR/1949/124m/C) D: Mikhail Chiaureli. C: Mikhail Gelovani, Oleg Froelich, V. Savelyev, Victor Stanitsin, Y. Verikh, M. Petrunkin.

Patricia Knight. *The Magic Face* (Austria/1951/88m/BW) D: Frank Tuttle. C: Luther Adler, William L. Shirer, Ilka Windish, Sukman, Herman Ehrhardt, Hans Sheel.

Lotte Tobisch. *The Last Ten Days* (aka *Ten Days to Die*) (aka *Last Ten Days of Adolf Hitler*) (aka *Der Letzte Akt*) (aka *The Last Act*) (Germany/1955/115m/BW) D: G.W. Pabst. B/on the novel *Ten Days to Die* by M.A. Mussanno. C: Albin Skoda, Oskar Werner, Willy Krause, Erich Stuckmann, Edmund Erlandsen, Kurt Eilers, Helga Dohrn, Leopold Hainisch, Otto Schmoele.

Maria Emo. *Hitler* (aka *Women of Nazi Germany*) (US/1962/107m/BW) D: Stuart Heisler. C: Richard Basehart, Cordula Trantow, Martin Kosleck, John Banner, Martin Brandt, William Sargent, Gregory Gay, Theodore Marcuse, Rick Traeger, John Mitchum, G. Stanley Jones, Walter Kohler, Carl Esmond, Berry Kroeger.

Doris Kunstmann. *Hitler: The Last Ten Days* (GB-Italy/1973/106m/C) D: Ennio De Concini. B/on the book *The Last Days of the Chancellery* by Gerhardt Boldt. C: Alec Guinness, Simon Ward, Gabriele Ferzetti, John Bennett, Philip Stone, Mark Kingston.

Alice Sapritch. *The Fuhrer Runs Amok* (France/1974/95m/C) D: Philippe Clair. C: Henri Tisot, Luis Rego, Maurice Risch, Michel Galabru.

Ila von Hasperg. *Adolf and Marlene* (Germany/1976/92m/C) D: Ulli Lommel. C: Kurt Raab, Margit Carstensen, Harry Baer, Ulli Lommel, Andrea Schober.

Margaret Klenck. *Loose Cannons* (US/1990/94m/C) D: Bob Clark. C: Gene Hackman, Dan Aykroyd, Dom Deluise, Ronny Cox, Nancy Travis, Ira Lewis, Robert Prosky.

Camilla Søeberg. *The Empty Mirror* (US/1997/129m/C) D: Barry J. Hershey. C: Norman Rodway, Peter Michael Goetz, Doug McKeon, Glenn Shadix, Joel Grey, Hope Allen, Lori Scott, Raul Kobrinsky, Randy Zielinski, Shannon Yowell, Courtney Dale, Elizabeth Hershey, Christopher Levitus, Chip Marks.

58 Braun, Wernher von (1912–1977)

German born scientist, and developer of the liquid fuel rocket, came to the United States in 1945 to work on the space program. Under his leadership the Saturn V rocket was developed for the Apollo space capsule.

Curt Jürgens. Gunther Mruwka (Young Wernher). *I Aim at the Stars* (US/1960/106m/BW) D: J. Lee Thompson. C: Victoria Shaw, Herbert Lom, Gia Scala, Eric Zuckmann, Adrian Hoven.

Joey Gaetano. *October Sky* (aka *Rocket Boys*) (US/1999/108m/C) D: Joe Johnston. B/on the book by Homer H. Hickam, Jr. C: Jake Gyllenhaal, Chris Cooper, Laura Dern, Chris Owen, William Lee Scott, Chad Lindberg, Natalie Canerday, Scott Miles, Randy Stripling, Chris Ellis, Elya Baskin, Courtney Fendley, David Dwyer, Terry Loughlin, Kailie Hollister.

59 Brice, Fanny (1891–1951)

(Fannie Borach) A comic singer-actress who headlined in the **Ziegfeld** Follies at the age of 20, Fanny was also known to millions of radio listeners as "Baby Snooks." In *The Rose of Washington Square* (39), Alice Faye portrayed a singer whose life was uncomfortably similar to Brice's. Fanny sued Fox Studios for invasion of privacy, settling out of court for $25,000. She was portrayed by Catherine Jacoby in the TV film *Ziegfeld: The Man and His Women* (78).

Fanny Brice. *The Great Ziegfeld* (US/1936/170m/BW) D: Robert Z. Leonard. Best Picture (AA). C: William Powell, Luise Rainer, Myrna Loy, Frank Morgan, Reginald Owen, Ray Bolger, A.A. Trimble, Buddy Doyle, Rosina Lawrence, Ruth Gillette.

Barbra Streisand * Best Actress (AA,GG). *Funny Girl* (US/1968/151m/C) D: William Wyler. B/on the musical play by Jule Styne, Bob Merrill & Isobel Lennart. C: Omar Sharif, Kay Medford, Anne Francis, Walter Pidgeon, Lee Allen, Gerald Mohr, Frank Faylen.

Barbra Streisand. *Funny Lady* (US/1975/136m/C) D: Herbert Ross. C: James Caan, Omar Sharif, Roddy McDowall, Ben Vereen, Larry Gates, Heidi O'Rourke.

Rosalind Harris. *The Cotton Club* (US/1984/127m/C) D: Francis Ford Coppola. C: Richard Gere, Gregory Hines, Diane Lane, Lonette McKee, Bob Hoskins, James Remar, Nicolas Cage, Fred Gwynne, Gregory Rozakis, Joe Dallesandro, Maurice Hines, Gwen Verdon, Lisa Jane Persky, Woody Strode, Zane Mark, Larry Marshall.

60 Bridger, Jim (1804–1881)

The first white man to see the Great Salt Lake, Bridger is (along with **Kit Carson**) one of the most famous of the early explorers of the old West.

Tully Marshall. *Fighting Caravans* (aka *Blazing Arrows*) (US/1931/91m/BW) D: Otto Brower & David Burton. B/on the novel by Zane Grey. C: Gary Cooper, Lily Damita, Ernest Torrence, Fred Kohler, Eugene Pallette, Jane Darwell.

Raymond Hatton. *Kit Carson* (US/1940/97m/BW) D: George B. Seitz. C: Jon Hall, Lynn Bari, Dana Andrews, Edwin Maxwell, Harold Huber.

Will Wright. *Along the Oregon Trail* (US/1947/64m/BW) D: R.G. Springsteen. C: Monte Hale, Adrian Booth, Roy Barcroft, LeRoy Mason, Forrest Taylor, Kermit Maynard.

Van Heflin. *Tomahawk* (aka *Battle of Powder River*) (US/1951/82m/C) D: George Sherman. C: Yvonne De Carlo, Preston Foster, Rock Hudson, John War Eagle, Ann Doran.

Porter Hall. *Pony Express* (US/1953/101m/C) D: Jerry Hopper. C: Charlton Heston, Rhonda Fleming, Jan Sterling, Forrest Tucker, Michael Moore, Pat Hogan.

Dennis Morgan. *The Gun That Won the West* (US/1955/69m/C) D: William Castle. C: Paula Raymond, Richard Cutting, Richard Denning, Robert Bice, Howard Wright, Roy Gordon.

Brontë, Anne *see* Brontë, Charlotte

61 Brontë, Charlotte (1816–1855)

The author of *Jane Eyre*, Charlotte has been portrayed twice in films about her literary family and once in the solo piece starring Julie Harris. Emily Brontë (1818–1848), author of *Wuthering Heights*, was played by Ida Lupino in *Devotion* and by Isabelle Adjani in *The Brontë Sisters*. Anne Brontë (1820–1849) was played by Nancy Coleman in *Devotion* and by Isabelle Hupert in *The Brontë Sisters*.

Olivia de Havilland. *Devotion* (US/1946/108m/BW) D: Curtis Bernhardt. C: Ida Lupino, Nancy Coleman, Paul Henried, Sydney Greenstreet, Arthur Kennedy, Dame May Whitty, Montagu Love, Reginald Sheffield, Brandon Hurst, Victor Francen.

Marie-France Pisier. *The Brontë Sisters* (France/1979/115m/C) D: Andre Techine. Isabelle Adjani, Isabelle Huppert, Pascal Gregory, Patrick Magee, Helen Surgere.

Julie Harris. *Brontë* (US-Ireland/1983/88m/C) D: Delbert Mann. B/on the radio play by William Luce from the writings of Charlotte Brontë.

Brontë, Emily *see* Brontë, Charlotte

62 Brown, John (1800–1859)

Radical, abolitionist, martyr, Brown was hanged after his failed raid on the federal arsenal at Harper's Ferry, Virginia. Portrayals of Brown on television include Sterling Hayden in *The Blue and The Gray* (82) and Johnny Cash in *North and South* (85).

Raymond Massey. *Santa Fe Trail* (US/1940/110m/BW) D: Michael Curtiz. C: Errol Flynn, Ronald Reagan, Olivia de Havilland, Alan Hale, Guinn Williams, Van Heflin, Moroni Olsen, Charles Middleton, Erville Alderson, David Bruce, Frank Wilcox.

Raymond Massey. *Seven Angry Men* (US/1955/90m/BW) D: Charles Marquis Warren. C: Debra Paget, Jeffrey Hunter, Larry Pennell, Leo Gordon, Dennis Weaver, Robert Osterloh.

Royal Dano. *Skin Game* (US/1971/102m/C) D: Paul Bogart. C: James Garner, Lou Gossett, Susan Clark, Brenda Sykes, Edward Asner, Andrew Duggan, Henry Jones.

63 Brown, John (?–1883)

Scottish servant of **Queen Victoria**, Brown's outspoken manner gained him quite a bit of notoriety during her reign.

Gordon McLeod. *Victoria the Great* (GB/1937/110m/C) D: Herbert Wilcox. B/on the play *Victoria Regina* by Laurence Housman. C: Anna Neagle, Anton Walbrook, H.B. Warner, James Dale, Charles Carson, Hubert Harben, Felix Aylmer, Arthur Young, Derrick De Marney, Hugh Miller, Percy Parsons, Henry Hallatt, Wyndham Goldie.

Gordon McLeod. *Sixty Glorious Years* (aka *Queen of Destiny*) (GB/1938/90m/C) D: Herbert Wilcox. C: Anna Neagle, Anton Walbrook, C. Aubrey Smith, Charles Carson, Felix Aylmer, Pamela Standish, Henry Hallatt, Wyndham Goldie, Malcolm Keen, Derrick De Marney, Joyce Bland, Harvey Braban, Aubrey Dexter, Laidman Browne.

Gordon McLeod. *The Prime Minister* (GB/1940/94m/BW) D: Thorold Dickinson. C: John Gielgud, Diana Wynyard, Will Fyfe, Stephen Murray, Owen Nares, Fay Compton, Lyn Harding, Leslie Perrins, Vera Bogetti, Frederick Leister, Nicolas Hannan, Kynaston Reeves.

Finlay Currie. *The Mudlark* (GB/1950/98m/BW) D: Jean Negulesco. B/on the novel by Theodore Bonnet. C: Irene Dunne, Alec Guinness, Andrew Ray, Beatrice Campbell, Anthony Steel, Wilfrid Hyde-White, Robin Stevens, Kynaston Reeves, Vi Stevens.

Valentine Dyall. *The Great McGonagall* (GB/1975/95m/C) D: Joseph McGrath. C: Spike Milligan, Peter Sellers, Julia Foster, Julian Chagrin, Victor Spinetti, John Bluthal.

Billy Connoly. *Mrs. Brown* (GB-Ireland-US/1997/103m/C) D: John Madden. C: Judi Dench, Geoffry Palmer, Antony Sher, Gerald Butler, Richard Pasco, David Westhead.

64 Brown, Molly (1873?–1932)

(Margaret Tobin Brown) "The Unsinkable Molly Brown" not only survived the sinking of the Titanic, but rowed a boatload of people to safety following the tragic crash.

Tucker McGuire. *A Night to Remember* (GB/1958/91m/BW) D: Roy Baker. B/on the book by Walter Lord. C: Kenneth More, David McCallum, Jill Dixon, Laurence Naismith.

Debbie Reynolds. *The Unsinkable Molly Brown* (US/1964/128m/C) D: Charles Walters. B/on the musical play by Meredith Wilson & Richard Morris. C: Harve Presnell, Ed Begley.

Cloris Leachman. *S.O.S. Titanic* (GB-US/1980/105m/C) D: Billy Hale. C: David Janssen, Susan Saint James, Harry Andrews, Helen Mirren, David Warner, Ian Holm.

Kathy Bates. *Titanic* (US/1997/193mc) D: James Cameron. 11 Oscars, including: Best Picture, Director, Visual Effects, Music, Song, Cinematography, Sound, and Costumes. GG Best Film (drama), Best Director, Best Original Score, Best Original Song. C: Leonardo DeCaprio, Kate Winslet, Bily Zane, Frances Fisher, Gloria Stuart, Bill Paxton, Bernard Hill, David Warner, Victor Garber, Jonathan Hyde, Suzy Amis, Lewis Abernathy, Nicholas Cascone, Dr. Anatoly Sagalevitch, Danny Nucci, Jason Barry, Ewan Stewart, Ioan Gruffudd, Johnny Phillips, Mark Lindsay Chapman, Richard Graham, Paul Brightwell, Ron Danachie, Eric Braeden, Charlotte Chatton, Bernard Fox.

65 Browning, Elizabeth Barrett (1806–1861)

English poet ("Poems," "Sonnets from the Portuguese"), Elizabeth's marriage to Robert Browning created one of the greatest literary romances of all time. Robert (1812–1889) was played by Fredric March (34) and Bill Travers (57).

Norma Shearer. *The Barretts of Wimpole Street* (aka *Forbidden Alliance*) (US/1934/110m/BW) D: Sidney Franklin. B/on the play by Rudolph Besier. C: Fredric March, Charles Laughton, Maureen O'Sullivan, Katherine Alexander, Una O'Connor, Ian Wolfe.

Jennifer Jones. *The Barretts of Wimpole Street* (US/1957/105m/C) D: Sidney Franklin. B/on the play by Rudolph Besier. C: John Gielgud, Bill Travers, Virginia McKenna, Susan Stephen.

Suzanne Hunt. *The Best House in London* (GB/1969/97m/C) D: Philip Savile. C: David Hemmings, Joanna Pettet, Arnold Diamond, John DeMarco, Neal Arden, George Reynolds.

Browning, Robert *see* Browning, Elizabeth

66 Bruce, Lenny (1925–1966)
(Leonard Alfred Schneider) Ground-breaking standup comic remembered for his incisive (and frequently vulgar) commentaries, Lenny died of a drug overdose at the age of 42.

Bernie Travis. *Dirtymouth* (US/1970/102m/C) D: Herbert S. Altman. C: Courtney Sherman, Wynn Irwin, Harry Spillman, Miss Sam Teardrop, Peter Clune.

Dustin Hoffman. *Lenny* (US/1974/112m/BW) D: Bob Fosse. B/on the play by Julian Barry. C: Valerie Perrine, Jan Miner, Stanley Beck, Clarence Thomas.

67 Brummell, George Bryan "Beau" (1778–1840)
English dandy and friend of the Prince of Wales (**George IV**), Brummell set the standard for men's dress and manners in the eighteenth century.

Barry Morse. *Mrs. Fitzherbert* (GB/1947/99m/BW) D: Montgomery Tully. B/on the novel *Princess Fitz* by Winifred Carter. C: Peter Graves, Joyce Howard, Leslie Banks, Margaretta Scott, Wanda Rotha, Mary Clare, Frederick Valk, Ralph Truman, John Stuart, Henry Oscar, Arthur Dulay, Moira Lister, Julian Dallas, Lily Kann.

Stewart Granger. *Beau Brummell* (US-GB/1954/111m/C) D: Curtis Bernhardt. B/on the play by Clyde Fitch. C: Elizabeth Taylor, Peter Ustinov, Robert Morley, James Donald, James Hayter, Rosemary Harris, Paul Rogers, Noel Willman, Peter Bull.

68 Brutus (85–42 BC)
(Lucius Junius Brutus) A leader in the assassination of **Julius Caesar**, Brutus' army then battled for control of Rome. After defeat by **Marc Antony** and **Augustus**, he did the Roman thing and fell on his sword.

Arthur Hohl. *Cleopatra* (US/1934/102m/BW) D: Cecil B. DeMille. C: Claudette Colbert, Warren William, Henry Wilcoxon, Gertrude Michael, Joseph Schildkraut, Ian Keith, Ian Maclaren, Claudia Dell, Robert Warwick, Charles Morris.

David Bradley. *Julius Caesar* (US/1950/BW) D: David Bradley. B/on the play by Wm. Shakespeare. C: Charlton Heston, Robert Holt, Harold Tasker, Grosvenor Glenn, William Russell, Helen Ross.

James Mason. *Julius Caesar* (US/1953/120m/BW) D: Joseph L. Mankiewicz. B/on the play by Wm. Shakespeare. C: Marlon Brando, Louis Calhern, John Gielgud, Edmond O'Brien, Greer Garson, Deborah Kerr, Alan Napier, Douglas Watson.

Robert Griffin. *Serpent of the Nile* (US/1953/81m/C) D: William Castle. C: Rhonda Fleming, William Lundigan, Raymond Burr, Michael Ansara, Jean Byron, Michael Fox.

Kenneth Haig. *Cleopatra* (US/1963/243m/C) D: Joseph L. Mankiewicz. B/on works by Plutarch, Appian, and Seutonius, and the novel *The Life and Times of*

Cleopatra by Carlo M. Franzero. C: Elizabeth Taylor, Richard Burton, Rex Harrison, Pamela Brown, Jean Marsh, Roddy McDowall, Francesca Annis, John Hoyt, Gwen Watford, Martin Landau, Michael Hordern, Douglas Wilmer, Carroll O'Connor, Finlay Currie.

Brian Oulton. *Carry on Cleo* (GB/1964/92m/C) D: Gerald Thomas. C: Sidney James, Kenneth Williams, Charles Hawtrey, Joan Sims, Amanda Barrie, Julie Stevens, Jim Dale.

Jason Robards. *Julius Caesar* (GB/1970/117m/C) D: Stuart Burge. B/on the play by Wm. Shakespeare. C: Charlton Heston, John Gielgud, Richard Johnson, Robert Vaughn, Richard Chamberlain, Diana Rigg, Jill Bennett, Christopher Lee, David Dodimead, Peter Eyre, Andre Morrell, Christopher Cazenove.

Tom Huron. *The Notorious Cleopatra* (US/1970/88m/C) D: A.P. Stootsberry. C: Sonora, Johnny Rocco, Jay Edwards, Woody Lee, Dixie Donovan, Michael Cheal.

69 Bryan, William Jennings (1860–1925)

A famous orator, politician and three-time loser in Presidential elections (1896, 1900 and 1908), Bryan died within a week after the famous "Scopes monkey trial" for which he was an associate prosecutor. TV portrayals have been by Jason Robards in *Inherit the Wind* (88), and George C. Scott (as Matthew Harrison Brady) in *Inherit the Wind* (99).

Niles Welch. *Silver Dollar* (US/1932/84m/BW) D: Alfred E. Green. B/on the book *Silver Dollar; The Story of the Tobors* by David Karsner. C: Edward G. Robinson, Bebe Daniels, Emmett Corrigan, Walter Rogers, Aline MacMahon, DeWitt Jennings.

Edwin Maxwell. *Wilson* (US/1944/154m/C) D: Henry King. C: Alexander Knox, Charles Coburn, Geraldine Fitzgerald, Cedric Hardwicke, Vincent Price, Sidney Blackmer, Eddie Foy, Jr., Marcel Dalio, Francis X. Bushman, Clifford Brooke.

Fredric March (as Matthew Harrison Brady). *Inherit the Wind* (US/1960/127m/BW) D: Stanley Kramer. B/on the play by Jerome Lawrence & Robert E. Lee. C: Spencer Tracy, Gene Kelly, Florence Eldridge, Dick York, Donna Anderson, Harry Morgan, Claude Akins.

70 Bryant, Louise (1885–1936)

American journalist and the wife of **John Reed**, Bryant traveled with him to Russia to cover the Revolution which she recounted in her book *Six Red Months in Russia*.

Galina Vodyanitskaya. *In the October Days* (USSR/1958/116m/C) D: Sergei Vasiliev. C: V. Chestnokov, V. Brener, A. Kobaladze, A. Fyodorinov.

Diane Keaton. *Reds* (US/1981/200m/C) D: Warren Beatty. Best Picture (NYC), Best Director (AA,DGA). C: Warren Beatty, Edward Herrmann, Jerzy Kosinski, Jack Nicholson, Paul Sorvino, Maureen Stapleton, Roger Sloman, Stuart Richman.

Sydne Rome. *Red Bells* (aka *Red Bells: I've Seen the Birth of the New World*) (aka *Ten Days That Shook the World*) (USSR-Mexico-Italy/1982/137m/C) D: Sergei Bondarchuk. C: Franco Nero, Anatoly Ustiuzhaninov.

71 Buchalter, Louis "Lepke" (1897–1944)

The only leading member of American organized crime to die in the electric chair, Lepke was **Lucky Lucaino's** partner in Murder, Inc.

David J. Stewart. *Murder, Inc.*(US/1960/103m/BW) D: Burt Balaban & Stuart Rosenberg. B/on the book by Burton Turkus & Sid Feder. C: Stuart Whitman, May Britt, Henry Morgan, Peter Falk, Howard I. Smith, Simon Oakland, Vincent Gardenia.

Tony Curtis. *Lepke* (US/1975/110–98m/C) D: Menahem Golan. C: Anjanette Comer, Michael Callan, Warren Berlinger, Gianni Russo, Vic Tayback, Milton Berle, Erwin Fuller, Jack Ackerman, Vaughn Meader, Zitto Kazan, John Durren.

Gordon Zimmerman. *The Private Files of J. Edgar Hoover* (US/1978/112m/C) D: Larry Cohen. C: Broderick Crawford, Jose Ferrer, Michael Parks, Ronee Blakely, Michael Sacks, Raymond St. Jacques, Andrew Duggan, Howard Da Silva, James Wainwright, Brad Dexter, William Jordan, Richard M. Dixon, Lloyd Nolan, June Havoc, Dan Dailey, John Marley, Lloyd Gough.

72 Buckingham, Duke of (1592–1628)

(George Villeirs) A close friend of **Charles II**, Buckingham's cinematic life is due to his alleged affair with **Anne of Austria**, which was a sub-plot of Dumas' *The Three Musketeers*.

Maurice Escande. *The Three Musketeers* (France/1932/128m/BW) D: Henri Diamant-Berger. B/on the novel by Alexandre Dumas. C: Aime Simon-Girard, Edith Mera, Samson Fainsilber, Harry Baur, Edith Mera, Andree Lafayette, Fernand Francell.

Maurice Escande. *Milady* (France/1933/120m/BW) D: Henri Diamant-Berger. C: Aime Simon-Girard, Samson Fainsilber, Harry Baur, Blanche Montel, Andree Lafayette, Fernand Francell, Edith Mera, Louis Allibert, Tommy Bourdelle, Henri Rollan.

Ralph Forbes. *The Three Musketeers* (US/1935/97m/BW) D: Rowland V. Lee. B/on the novel by Alexandre Dumas. C: Walter Abel, Paul Lukas, Margot Grahame, Heather Angel, Ian Keith, Onslow Stevens, Rosamond Pinchot, Nigel De Brulier, Miles Mander.

Lester Matthews. *The Three Musketeers* . (aka *The Singing Musketeer*) (US/1939/73m/BW) D: Allan Dwan. B/on the novel by Alexandre DumasC: Don Ameche, The Ritz Brothers, Binnie Barnes, Lionel Atwill, Gloria Stuart, Pauline Moore, Joseph Schildkraut, Miles Mander, John Carradine, Douglas Dumbrille, John King.

Jorge Reyes. *The Three Musketeers* (aka *Tres Mosqueteros*) (Mexico/1942/139m/BW) D: Miguel M. Delgado. B/on the novel by Alexandre Dumas. C: Cantinflas, Angel Garasa, Raquel Rojas, Consuelo Frank, Andres Soler, Julio Villarreal.

John Sutton. *The Three Musketeers* (US/1948/126m/C) D: George Sidney. B/on the novel by Alexandre Dumas. C: Lana Turner, Gene Kelly, June Allyson, Van Heflin, Angela Lansbury, Frank Morgan, Vincent Price, Kennan Wynn, Gig Young, Robert Coote.

Charles Lang. *Blades of the Musketeers* (aka *The Sword of D'Artagnan*) (US/1953/54m/BW) D: Budd Boetticher. B/on the novel *The Three Musketeers* by Alexandre Dumas. C: Robert Clarke, John Hubbard, Mel Archer, Paul Cavanagh, Don Beddoe, Marjorie Lord.

Bernard Haller. *The Four Charlots Musketeers* (France/1974/110m/C) D: Andre Hunnebelle. B/on the novel *The Three Musketeers* by Alexandre Dumas. C: The Charlots, Gerard Rinaldi, Josephine Chaplin, Daniel Ceccaldi, Catherine Jourdan.

Simon Ward. *The Three Musketeers* (GB-US-Panama/1974/105m/C) D: Richard Lester. B/on the novel by Alexandre Dumas. C: Oliver Reed, Richard Chamberlain, Michael York, Frank Finlay, Jean-Pierre Cassel, Geraldine Chaplin, Charlton Heston.

Simon Ward. *The Four Musketeers* (aka *The Revenge of Milady*) (GB-US/1975/108m/C) D: Richard Lester. B/on the novel *The Three Musketeers* by Alexandre Dumas. C: Michael York, Charlton Heston, Oliver Reed, Richard Chamberlain, Christopher Lee, Frank Finlay, Geraldine Chaplin, Raquel Welch, Jean-Pierre Cassel.

Jeremy Clyde. *The Musketeer* (Germany-Luxemburg/2001/US/105m/C) D: Peter Hyams. B/on the novel by Alexandre Dumas. C: Catherine Deneuve, Mena Suvari, Stephen Rea, Tim Roth, Justin Chambers, Bill Treacher, Daniel Mesguich, David Schofield, Nick Moran, Steven Spiers, Jan Gregor Kremp, Michael Byrne, Jean-Pierre Castaldi, Tsilla Chelton, Bertrand Witt.

73 Buffalo Bill (1846–1917)

(William Frederick Cody) Originally a buffalo hunter and Indian scout, Buffalo Bill became a master showman and toured for more than thirty years with his "Wild West Show." Depictions in TV films include: Peter Coyote in *Buffalo Girls* (95), Jeffrey Jones in *Kenny Rogers As the Gambler; Part 3* (87), Ken Kercheval in *Calamity Jane* (83), R.L. Tolbert in *The Legend of the Golden Gun* (79), Buff Brady in *The Last Ride of the Dalton Gang* (79), John Hansen in *The Incredible Rocky Mountain Race* (77), and Matt Clark in *This Is the West That Was* (74).

Douglas Dumbrille. *The World Changes* (US/1933/90m/BW) D: Mervyn LeRoy. B/on the story *America Kneels* by Sheridan Gibney. C: Paul Muni, Aline MacMahon, Mary Astor, Donald Cook, Patricia Jean Muir, Alan Mowbray.

Moroni Olsen. *Annie Oakley* (US/1935/79m/BW) D: George Stevens. C: Barbara Stanwyck, Preston Foster, Melvyn Douglas, Chief Thundercloud, Dick Elliott.

James Ellison. *The Plainsman* (US/1936/115m/BW) D: Cecil B. DeMille. B/on the novel *Wild Bill Hickok* by Frank J. Wilstach. C: Gary Cooper, Jean Arthur, Porter Hall, John Miljan, Frank McGlynn, Edwin Maxwell, Leila McIntyre, Charles H. Herzinger.

Carlyle Moore, Jr. *Outlaw Express* (US/1938/56m/BW) D: George Waggner. C: Bob Baker, Cecilia Callejo, Don Barclay, LeRoy Mason, Carleton Young.

Roy Rogers. *Young Buffalo Bill* (US/1940/59m/BW) D: Joseph Kane. C: George "Gabby" Hayes, Pauline Moore, Hugh Sothern, Chief Thundercloud, Trevor Bardette.

Joel McCrea. *Buffalo Bill* (US/1944/90m/C) D: William Wellman. C: Maureen O'Hara, Linda Darnell, Thomas Mitchell, Edgar Buchanan, Anthony Quinn, Moroni Olsen, Chief Thundercloud, John Dilson, Sidney Blackmer, Evelyn Beresford.

Richard Arlen. *Buffalo Bill Rides Again* (US/1947/70m/BW) D: Bernard B. Ray. C: Jennifer Holt, Lee Schumway, Edward Cassidy, Charles Stevens, Shooting Star, Many Treaties.

Monte Hale. *Law of the Golden West* (US/1949/60m/BW) D: Philip Ford. C: Paul Hurst, Gail Davis, Roy Barcroft, John Holland, Lane Bradford.

Tex Cooper. *King of the Bullwhip* (US/1950/59m/BW) D: Ron Ormond. C: Lash LaRue, Al St. John, Jack Holt, Tom Neal, Anne Gwynne, Jimmie Martin.

Louis Calhern. *Annie Get Your Gun* (US/1950/107m/C) D: George Sidney. B/on the musical play, book by Herbert and Dorothy Fields. C: Betty Hutton, Howard Keel, J. Carrol Naish, Chief Yowlachie, Evelyn Beresford, John Mylong, Nino Pipitone.

Clayton Moore. *Buffalo Bill in Tomahawk Territory* (US/1952/66m/BW) D: Bernard B. Ray. C: Slim Andrews, Rod Redwing, Sharon Dexter, Eddie Phillips, Chief Yowlachie, Chief Thundercloud.

Charlton Heston. *Pony Express* (US/1953/101m/C) D: Jerry Hopper. C: Rhonda Fleming, Jan Sterling, Forrest Tucker, Porter Hall, Michael Moore, Pat Hogan.

Malcolm Atterbury. *Badman's Country* (US/1958/85m/BW) D: Fred F. Sears. C: George Montgomery, Buster Crabbe, Neville Brand, Karin Booth, Gregory Wolcott, Russell Johnson, Richard Devon, Morris Ankrum.

Gordon Scott. *Buffalo Bill* (aka *Buffalo Bill, Hero of the Far West*) (Italy-Germany-France/1962/93m/C) D: John W. Fordson (Mario Costa). C: Jan Hendriks.

James McMullen. *The Raiders* (US/1964/75m/C) D: Herschel Daugherty. C: Robert Culp, Brian Keith, Judi Meredith, Alfred Ryder, Simon Oakland, Ben Cooper.

Rick van Nutter. *Seven Hours of Gunfire* (Italy-Germany-Spain/1964/C) D: Joaquim Marchent. C: Gloria Milland, Adrian Hoven.

Guy Stockwell. *The Plainsman* (US/1966/92m/C) D: David Lowell Rich. C: Don Murray, Abby Dalton, Brad Dillman, Leslie Nielsen, Simon Oakland, Emily Banks.

Michel Piccoli. *Do Not Touch the White Woman* (aka *Touche Pas La Femme Blanche*) (aka *Don't Touch White Women!*) (France/1974/108m/C) D: Marco Ferreri. C: Marcello Mastroianni, Catherine Deneuve, Philippe Noiret, Ugo Tognazzi, Alain Cuny.

Paul Newman. *Buffalo Bill and the Indians, Or Sitting Bull's History Lesson* (aka *Buffalo Bill and the Indians*) (US/1976/120m/C) D: Robert Altman. B/on the play *Indians* by Arthur Kopit. C: Paul Newman, Burt Lancaster, Joel Grey, Harvey Keitel, Geraldine Chaplin, Frank Kaquitts, Will Sampsen, Pat McCormick.

Ted Flicker. *The Legend of the Lone Ranger* (US/1981/98m/C) D: William A. Fraker. C: Klinton Spilsbury, Michael Horse, Jason Robards, Richard Farnsworth, Lincoln Tate.

Keith Carradine. *Wild Bill* (US/1995/98m/C) D: Walter Hill. B/on the novel *Deadwood* by Pete Dexter and the play *Fathers and Sons* by Thomas Babe. C: Jeff Bridges, Ellen Barkin, John Hurt, Diane Lane, Susannah Moore, David Arquette.

74 Bülow, Hans Guido von (1830–1894)

A noted 19th century German pianist and conductor, von Bülow studied with **Franz Liszt** and married his daughter, Cosima (1857), who left him for **Richard Wagner** in 1869. (See **Wagner, Cosima**)

Eric Schumann. *Magic Fire* (US/1956/94m/C) D: William Dieterle. B/on the novel by Bertita Harding. C: Yvonne De Carlo, Carlos Thompson, Rita Gam, Valentina Cortesa, Alan Badel, Peter Cushing, Gerhard Riedmann, Frederick Valk.

Mark Burns. *Ludwig* (Italy-Germany-France/1973/186m/C) D: Luchino Visconti. C: Helmut Berger, Romy Schneider, Trevor Howard, Silvana Mangano.

Andrew Reilly. *Lisztomania* (GB/1975/105m/C) D: Ken Russell. C: Roger Daltrey, Sara Kestelman, Paul Nicholas, Fiona Lewis, Veronica Qilligan, Ken Colley, Murray Melvin, Otto Diamant, Anulka Dziubinska, Imogen Claire, Ken Parry.

Miguel Herz-Kestranek. *Wagner* (GB-Austria-Hungary/1983/540–300m/C) D: Tony Palmer. C: Richard Burton, Vanessa Redgrave, Gemma Craven, Laszlo Galffi, John Gielgud, Ralph Richardson, Laurence Olivier, Ekkerhard Schall, Ronald Pickup, Marthe Keller, Gwyneth Jones, Franco Nero.

75 Buntline, Ned (1823–1886)

(Edward Zane Carroll Judson) The originator of the "dime novel" and the creator of **Buffalo Bill's** legend, Buntline's life included such episodes as his dishonorable discharge during the Civil War (for drunkenness) and his trial for the murder of his mistress' husband.

Dick Elliott. *Annie Oakley* (US/1935/79m/BW) D: George Stevens. C: Barbara Stanwyck, Preston Foster, Melvyn Douglas, Moroni Olsen, Chief Thundercloud.

Thomas Mitchell. *Buffalo Bill* (US/1944/90m/C) D: William Wellman. C: Joel McCrea, Maureen O'Hara, Linda Darnell, Edgar Buchanan, Anthony Quinn, Moroni Olsen, Chief Thundercloud, John Dilson, Sidney Blackmer, Evelyn Beresford.

Burt Lancaster. *Buffalo Bill and the Indians, Or Sitting Bull's History Lesson* (aka *Buffalo Bill and the Indians*) (US/1976/120m/C) D: Robert Altman. B/on the play *Indians* by Arthur Kopit. C: Paul Newman, Joel Grey, Harvey Keitel, Geraldine Chaplin, Frank Kaquitts, Will Sampsen, Pat McCormick.

76 Burns, Robert (1759–1796)

Scottish poet depicted in several British films, Burns is best remembered for his songs including "Auld Lang Syne" and "Comin" Thro' the Rye."

Joseph Hislop. *The Loves of Robert Burns* (GB/1930/100m/BW) D: Herbert Wilcox. C: Dorothy Seacombe, Eve Gray, Nancy Price, C.V. France.
Andrew Cruickshank. *Auld Lang Syne* (GB/1937/72m/BW) D: James A. Fitzpatrick. C: Christine Adrian, Richard Ross, Marian Spencer, Malcolm Graham. Terence Alexander. *Comin' Thro' the Rye* (GB/1947/55m/BW) D: Walter C. Mycroft. C: Patricia Burleigh, Beryl Bowen, Olivia Barley, Sylvia Abbott.

Burr, Aaron *see* Hamilton, Alexander

77 Burroughs, William S. (1914–1999)
American writer and Harvard graduate, whose forays into drug addiction and homosexuality led to his extraordinary, nightmarish, satirical, and often humorous, writings. His best known work is *Naked Lunch,* published in Paris in 1959. (See **Ginsberg, Allen** and **Kerouac, Jack**)
Peter Weller (as William Lee). *Naked Lunch* (Canada-GB/1991/115m/C) D: David Cronenberg. B/on the novel by William S. Burroughs. C: Judy Davis, Ian Holm, Julian Sands, Roy Scheider, Monique Mercure, Nicholas Campbell, Michael Zelniker, Robert A. Silverman, Joseph Scorsiani, Claude Afalo, Peter Boretsky, Deirdre Bowen, Michael Caruana, Yuval Daniel, Joseph di Mambro, John Friesen, Laurent Hazout, Howard Jerome, Justin Louis, Sean McCann, Kurt Reis, Julian Riching, Jim Yip.
Dennis Hopper. *The Source* (US/1999/88m/BW/C) D: Chuck Workman C: Johnny Depp, John Turturro.
Kiefer Sutherland. *Beat* (US/2000/89m/C) D: Gary Walkow. C: Courtney Love, Norman Reedus, Ron Livingston, Daniel Martínez, Kyle Secor, Sam Trammell, Lisa Sheridan, Rene Rubio, Georgiana Sîrbu, Tommy Perna, Alec Von Bargen, Steve Hedden, Patricia De Llaca, Luis Felipe Tovar, Luisa Huertas, Darren Ross, Serafina De Lorca.

Bush, George *see* 590

78 Byron, Lord (1788–1824)
(George Gordon Noel Byron) Portrayed in recent films more for his flamboyant lifestyle and his friendship with **Mary** and **Percy Shelley** than for his fame as a writer, Byron, the romantic poet, is remembered for "Don Juan" and "Childe Harold's Pilgrimage" among other works.
Gavin Gordon. *The Bride of Frankenstein* (US/1935/80m/BW) D: James Whale. B/on the novel *Frankenstein, or the Modern Prometheus* by Mary Shelley. C: Boris Karloff, Colin Clive, Valerie Hobson, Elsa Lanchester, Una O'Connor, Douglas Walton.
Malcolm Graham. *The Last Rose of Summer* (GB/1937/60m/BW) D: James Fitzpatrick. C: John Garrick, Kathleen Gibson, Marian Spencer, Cecil Ramage.
Dennis Price. *The Bad Lord Byron* (GB/1949/83m/BW) D: David MacDonald. C: Mai Zetterling, Joan Greenwood, Linden Travers, Sonia Holm, Nora Swinburne, Irene Browne.

Noel Willman. *Beau Brummell* (US-GB/1954/111m/C) D: Curtis Bernhardt. B/on the play by Clyde Fitch. C: Stewart Granger, Elizabeth Taylor, Peter Ustinov, Robert Morley, James Donald, James Hayter, Rosemary Harris, Paul Rogers, Peter Bull.

Richard Chamberlain. *Lady Caroline Lamb* (GB/1972/122m/C) D: Robert Bolt. C: Sarah Miles, Jon Finch, John Mills, Margaret Leighton, Ralph Richardson, Laurence Olivier.

Gabriel Byrne. *Gothic* (GB/1987/90m/C) D: Ken Russell. C: Julian Sands, Natasha Richardson, Myriam Cyr, Timothy Spall, Andreas Wisniewski.

Philip Anglim. *Haunted Summer* (US/1988/115m/C) D: Ivan Passer. B/on the novel by Anne Edwards. C: Laura Dern, Alice Krige, Eric Stolz, Alex Winter.

Hugh Grant. *Rowing With the Wind* (Spain/1988/96m/C) D: Gonzalo Suarez. C: Lizzy McInnerny, Valentine Pelka, Elizabeth Hurley, Jose Luis Gomez, Bibi Andersson.

Jason Patric. *Frankenstein Unbound* (aka *Roger Corman's Frankenstein Unbound*) (US/1990/85m/C) D: Roger Corman. B/on the novel by Brian Aldiss. C: John Hurt, Raul Julia, Bridget Fonda, Michael Hutchence, Nick Brimble, Catherine Rabett.

Michael Oosterom. Charles Pinion (CD ROM character). *Conceiving Ada* (aka *Leidenschaftliche Berechnung*) (Germany-US/1997/85m/C) D: Lynn Hershman-Leeson. B/on *Ada, the Enchantress of Numbers, A Selection of the Letters of Lord Byron's Daughter and Her Description of the First Computer* by Betty A. Toole. C: Tilda Swinton, Francesca Faridany, Timothy Leary, Karen Black, John O'Keefe, John Perry Barlow, J.D. Wolfe, Owen Murphy, David Brooks, Esther Mulligan, Ellen Sebastian, Mark Capri, Joe Wemple, Chris von Sneidern, David Eppel, R.U. Sirius, Kashka Peck, Rose Lockwood, Jesse Talman Boss, Lillian L. Malmberg, Cyrus Mare, Pollyanna Jacobs, CD-ROM characters,/voices: Bruce Sterling, Dave Nelson, Henry S. Rosenthal, Melissa Howden, Josh Rosen, Roger Shaw, Lynn Hershman-Leeson.

Guy Lankester. *Pandaemonium* (GB/2000/124m/C) D: Julien Temple. C: Linus Roache, John Hannah, Samantha Morton, Emily Woof, Emma Fielding, Andy Serkis, Samuel West, Michael N. Harbour, William Scott-Masson, Clive Merrison, Dexter Fletcher.

79 Caesar, Julius (100–44 BC)

(Gaius Julius Caesar) Considered one of the greatest military leaders ever; Caesar's Roman armies conquered Gaul, Briton and Spain after which he was made dictator for life. Caesar ruled wisely but his power didn't sit well with **Cassius** and **Brutus** and they murdered him on the Ides of March. He was portrayed by Timothy Dalton in the TV movie *Cleopatra* (99).

Warren William. *Cleopatra* (US/1934/102m/BW) D: Cecil B. DeMille. C: Claudette Colbert, Henry Wilcoxon, Gertrude Michael, Joseph Schildkraut, Ian Keith, Ian Maclaren, Arthur Hohl, Claudia Dell, Robert Warwick, Charles Morris.

Harry Burkhart. *Are We Civilized?* (US/1934/70m/BW) D: Edwin Carewe. C: Frank McGlynn, Alin Cavin, Charles Requa, Bert Lindley, Aaron Edwards, William Humphrey.

Claude Rains. *Caesar and Cleopatra* (GB/1946/138m/C) D: Gabriel Pascal. B/on the play by George Bernard Shaw. C: Vivien Leigh, Stewart Granger, Flora Robson, Basil Sydney.

Harold Tasker. *Julius Caesar* (US/1950/BW) D: David Bradley. B/on the play by Wm. Shakespeare. C: Charlton Heston, Robert Holt, David Bradley, Grosvenor Glenn, William Russell, Helen Ross.

Louis Calhern. *Julius Caesar* (US/1953/120m/BW) D: Joseph L. Mankiewicz. B/on the play by Wm. Shakespeare. C: James Mason, Marlon Brando, John Gielgud, Edmond O'Brien, Greer Garson, Deborah Kerr, Alan Napier, Douglas Watson.

Reginald Sheffield. *The Story of Mankind* (US/1957/100m/C) D: Irwin Allen. B/on the book by Hendrik van Loon. C: Ronald Colman, Hedy Lamarr, Virginia Mayo, Agnes Moorehead, Peter Lorre, Dennis Hopper, Marie Wilson, Helmut Dantine, Edward Everett Horton, Reginald Gardiner, Marie Windsor, Francis X. Bushman, Anthony Dexter, Austin Green, Jim Ameche, Harpo Marx, Bobby Watson, Cedric Hardwicke, Cesar Romero.

John Gavin. *Spartacus* (US/1960/196m/C) D: Stanley Kubrick. B/on the novel by Howard Fast. Best Motion Picture — Drama (GG). C: Kirk Douglas, Laurence Olivier, Tony Curtis, Jean Simmons, Charles Laughton, Peter Ustinov, Nina Foch.

Conrado Sanmartin. *Legions of the Nile* (Italy/1959/87m/C) D: Vittorio Cottafavi. C: Linda Cristal, Ettore Manni, Georges Marchal, Maria Mahor, Alfredo Mayo, Daniela Rocca.

Cameron Mitchell. *Caesar the Conqueror* (Italy/1962/103m/C) D: Amerigo Anton. C: Rick Battaglia, Dominique Wilms, Nerio Bernardi, Carlo Tamberlani, Bruno Tocci, Carla Calo.

Ivo Garrani. *The Slave* (aka *The Son of Spartacus*) (Italy/1962/102–90m/C) D: Sergio Corbucci. C: Steve Reeves, Jacques Sernas, Gianna Maria Canale, Claudio Gora.

Gianni Solaro. *The Centurion* (aka *Conqueror of Corinth*) (Italy-France/1962/-77m/C) D: Mario Costa. C: Jacques Sernas, John Drew Barrymore, Gianna Maria Canale.

Giorgio Ardisson. *A Queen for Caesar* (Italy-France/1963/C) D: Victor Tourjansky & Piero Pierotti. C: Pascale Petit.

Rex Harrison. *Cleopatra* (US/1963/243m/C) D: Joseph L. Mankiewicz. B/on works by Plutarch, Appian, and Seutonius, and the novel *The Life and Times of Cleopatra* by Carlo M. Franzero. C: Elizabeth Taylor, Richard Burton, Pamela Brown, Jean Marsh, Kenneth Haig, Roddy McDowall, Francesca Annis, John Hoyt, Gwen Watford, Martin Landau, Michael Hordern, Douglas Wilmer, Carroll O'Connor, Finlay Currie.

Kenneth Williams. *Carry on Cleo* (GB/1964/92m/C) D: Gerald Thomas. C: Sidney James, Charles Hawtrey, Joan Sims, Amanda Barrie, Julie Stevens, Brian Oulton, Jim Dale.

John Gielgud. *Julius Caesar* (GB/1970/117m/C) D: Stuart Burge. B/on the play by Wm. Shakespeare. C: Charlton Heston, Jason Robards, Richard Johnson, Robert Vaughn, Richard Chamberlain, Diana Rigg, Jill Bennett, Christopher Lee, David Dodimead, Peter Eyre, Andre Morrell, Christopher Cazenove.

Jay Edwards. *The Notorious Cleopatra* (US/1970/88m/C) D: A.P. Stootsberry. C: Sonora, Johnny Rocco, Woody Lee, Dixie Donovan, Tom Huron, Michael Cheal.

80 Cagliostro, Count (1743–1795)

(Giuseppe Balsamo) A successful con man, the Count (self-proclaimed) traveled the courts of eighteenth century Europe selling his services (fortune telling, hypnosis, youth serums, etc.) until imprisoned by the Inquisition.

Paul Otto. *Barberina* (Germany/1932/78m/BW) D: Friedrich Zelnik. C: Otto Gebuehr, Lil Dagover, Rosa Valetti, Hans Stuewe, Hans Junkermann.

Mihalesco. *Francis The First* (aka *François Ier*) (France/1937/BW) D: Christian-Jaque. C: Fernandel, Mona Goya, Alexandre Rignault, Henri Bosc, Sinoel, Aime-Simon Girard.

Zero Mostel. *Du Barry Was a Lady* (US/1943/96m/C) D: Roy Del Ruth. B/on the play by B.G. De Sylva & Herbert Fields. C: Lucille Ball, Red Skelton, Gene Kelly, Rags Ragland.

Ferdinand Marian. *Münchhausen* (aka *The Adventures of Baron Munchaussen*) (aka *Baron Muenchhausen*) (Germany/1943/134–100m/C) D: Josef von Baky. C: Hans Albers, Wilhelm Bendow, Michael Bohnen, Brigette Horney, Gustav Waldau.

Orson Welles. *Black Magic* (US/1949/105m/BW) D: Gregory Ratoff. B/on the novel *Joseph Balsamo* by Alexandre Dumas. C: Nancy Guild, Akim Tamiroff, Raymond Burr, Margot Grahame, Berry Kroeger, Charles Goldner, Lee Kresel, Robert Atkins.

Gino Cervi. *Royal Affairs in Versailles* (aka *Versailles*) (aka *Affairs in Versailles*) (aka *If Versailles Were Told to Me*) (aka *Si Versailles M'Était Couté*) (France/1953/180–152m/C) D: Sacha Guitry. C: Sacha Guitry, Claudette Colbert, Orson Welles, Gerard Phillippe, Micheline Presle, Jean Marais, Georges Marchal, Gilbert Boka, Lana Marconi, Fernand Gravet, Louis Arbessier, Jacques Berthier, Samson Fainsilber, Gilbert Gil, Emile Drain, Jacques de Feraudy, Gaston Rey, Philippe Richard.

Bekim Fehmiu. *Cagliostro* (Italy/1975/103m/C) D: Daniele Pettinari. C: Curt Jurgens, Massimo Girotti, Robert Alda, Rosanna Schiaffino, Ida Galli.

81 Caiaphas

Jewish rabbi appointed by the Romans as the High Priest in Jerusalem, Caiaphas was the interrogator in the trial of **Jesus Christ**. He has been played by Anthony Quinn in the TV mini-series *Jesus of Nazareth* (77), Colin Blakely in the TV film *The Day Christ Died* (80), and by Christian Kohlund in *Jesus* (99).

Charles Granval. *Golgotha* (France/1935/97m/BW) D: Julien Duvivier. C: Harry Baur, Robert Le Vigan, Jean Gabin, Andre Bacque, Hubert Prelier, Lucas Gridoux, Edwige Feuillere, Juliette Verneuil, Vana Yami, Van Daele.

Ralph Freud. *Day of Triumph* (US/1954/110m/C) D: Irving Pichel & John T. Coyle. C: Lee J. Cobb, Robert Wilson, Tyler McVey, Michael Connors, Joanne Dru, James Griffith, Lowell Gilmore, Anthony Warde, Peter Whitney, Everett Glass.

Felix Acaso. *The Redeemer* (Spain/1959/93m/C) D: Joseph Breen. C: Luis Alvarez, Maruchi Fresno, Manuel Monroy, Antonio Vilar, Virgilio Teixeira, Carlos Casaravilla, Sebastian Cabot (Narrator).

Guy Rolfe. *King of Kings* (US/1961/168m/C) D: Nicholas Ray. C: Jeffrey Hunter, Siobhan McKenna, Hurd Hatfield, Viveca Lindfors, Rita Gam, Carmen Sevilla, Rip Torn, Brigid Bazlen, Harry Guardino, Frank Thring, Maurice Marsac, Gregoire Aslan, Royal Dano, Robert Ryan, Gerard Tichy, Michael Wager, Tino Barrero, Jose Antonio, Orson Welles (Narrator).

Basil Rathbone. *Pontius Pilate* (Italy-France/1962/100m/C) D: Irving Rapper. C: Jean Marais, Jeanne Crain, Leticia Roman, John Drew Barrymore, Livio Lorenzon.

Rodolfo Wilcock. *The Gospel According to St. Matthew* (France-Italy/1964/142m/BW) D: Pier Paolo Pasolini. B/on the *New Testament book of Matthew*. C: Enrique Irazoqui, Susanna Pasolini, Mario Socrate, Marcello Morante, Alfonso Gatto, Francesco Leonetti, Amerigo Bevilacqua, Otello Sestilli, Settimio Di Porto, Ferruccio Nuzzo, Alessandro Tosca, Paolo Tedesco, Franca Cupane, Giacomo Morante, Rosario Migale.

Martin Landau. *The Greatest Story Ever Told* (US/1965/141m/C) D: George Stevens. B/on the book by Fulton Oursler. C: Max von Sydow, Dorothy McGuire, Robert Loggia, Claude Rains, Jose Ferrer, Charlton Heston, Donald Pleasence, David McCallum, Gary Raymond, Robert Blake, John Considine, David Hedison, Joanna Dunham, Sal Mineo, Van Heflin, Ed Wynn, Telly Savalas, Sidney Poitier, Roddy McDowell, Angela Lansbury, Richard Conte, Carroll Baker, Janet Margolin, Burt Brinckerhoff, Tom Reese.

Bob Bingham. *Jesus Christ, Superstar* (US/1973/107m/C) D: Norman Jewison. B/on the rock opera by Tim Rice & Andrew Lloyd Webber. C: Ted Neeley, Carl Anderson, Yvonne Elliman, Barry Dennen, Larry T. Marshall, Joshua Mostel, Philip Toubus.

Hugh Griffith. *The Passover Plot* (Israel/1976/108m/C) D: Michael Campus. B/on the book by Hugh Schonfield. C: Harry Andrews, Zalman King, Donald Pleasence, Scott Wilson, Dan Ades, Michael Baselon, Lewis van Bergen, William Burns, Dan Hedaya, Kevin O'Connor, Robert Walker.

John Anderson. *In Search of Historic Jesus* (US/1979/91m/C) D: Henning Schellerup. B/on the book by Lee Roddy & Charles E. Seller. C: John Rubinstein, Nehemiah Persoff, Andrew Bloch, Morgan Brittany, Walter Brooke, Annette Charles, Royal Dano, Anthony DeLongis, Lawrence Dobkin, David Opatoshu, John Hoyt, Jeffrey Druce.

82 Calamity Jane (1852?–1903)

(Martha Jane Cannary) So much of Calamity Jane's life was ballyhoo that it is hard to separate the fact from legend. This much is known: she dressed in men's clothing, she did know **Wild Bill Hickok** (briefly) and she wasn't one tenth as pretty as the least attractive actress who ever portrayed her.

Louise Dresser. *Caught* (US/1931/62m/BW) D: Edward Sloman. C: Richard Arlen.

Jean Arthur. *The Plainsman* (US/1936/115m/BW) D: Cecil B. DeMille. B/on the novel *Wild Bill Hickok* by Frank J. Wilstach. C: Gary Cooper, James Ellison, Porter Hall, John Miljan, Frank McGlynn, Edwin Maxwell, Leila McIntyre, Charles H. Herzinger.

Sally Payne. *Young Bill Hickok* (US/1940/59m/BW) D: Joseph Kane. C: Roy Rogers, George "Gabby" Hayes, Jacqueline Wells (Julie Bishop), John Miljan, Monte Blue.

Frances Farmer. *Badlands of Dakota* (US/1941/74m/BW) D: Alfred E. Green. C: Robert Stack, Richard Dix, Ann Rutherford, Andy Devine, Lon Chaney, Jr., Addison Richards.

Jane Russell. *The Paleface* (US/1948/91m/C) D: Norman Z. McLeod. C: Bob Hope, Robert Armstrong, Iris Adrian, Bobby Watson, Jack Searle, Joseph Vitale.

Yvonne DeCarlo. *Calamity Jane and Sam Bass* (US/1949/85m/C) D: George Sherman. C: Howard Duff, Dorothy Hart, Willard Parker, Norman Lloyd, Lloyd Bridges, Milburn Stone.

Evelyn Ankers. *The Texan Meets Calamity Jane* (US/1950/71m/C) D: Andre Lamb. C: James Ellison, Lee "Lasses" White, Jack Ingram, Ruth Whitney.

Doris Day. *Calamity Jane* (US/1953/100m/C) D: David Butler. C: Howard Keel, Allyn McLerie, Philip Carey, Dick Wesson, Paul Harvey, Chubby Johnson.

Barbara Mansell. *Young Guns of Texas* (US/1962/78m/C) D: Maury Dexter. C: James Mitchum, Alana Ladd, Jody McCrea, Chill Wills, Robert Lowery, Gary Conway.

Judi Meredith. *The Raiders* (US/1964/75m/C) D: Herschel Daugherty. C: Robert Culp, Brian Keith, James McMullan, Alfred Ryder, Simon Oakland, Ben Cooper.

Gloria Milland. *Seven Hours of Gunfire* (Italy-Germany-Spain/1964/C) D: Joaquim Marchent. C: Rick van Nutter, Adrian Hoven.

Abby Dalton. *The Plainsman* (US/1966/92m/C) D: David Lowell Rich. C: Don Murray, Guy Stockwell, Brad Dillman, Leslie Nielsen, Simon Oakland, Emily Banks.

Catherine O'Hara. *Tall Tale: the Unbelievable Adventures of Pecos Bill* (aka *Tall Tale: the Incredible Adventure*) (US/1995/98m/C) D: Jeremiah Chechik. C: Patrick Swayze, Oliver Platt, Scott Glenn.

Ellen Barkin. *Wild Bill* (US/1995/98m/C) D: Walter Hill. B/on the novel *Deadwood* by Pete Dexter and the play *Fathers and Sons* by Thomas Babe. C: Jeff Bridges, John Hurt, Diane Lane, Susannah Moore, David Arquette, Keith Carradine.

83 Caligula (AD 12–41)

(Gaius Julius Caesar Germanicus) Insane Roman Emperor remembered for a series of atrocious acts of debauched sex, torture and murder, Caligula was assassinated after ruling for less than four years.

Jay Robinson. *The Robe* (US/1953/135m/C) D: Henry Koster. B/on the novel by Lloyd C. Douglas. Best Picture — Drama (GG). C: Richard Burton, Jean Simmons, Victor Mature, Michael Rennie, Dean Jagger, Torin Thatcher, Richard Boone, Ernest Thesiger, Michael Ansara, Cameron Mitchell (the voice of Jesus Christ).

Jay Robinson. *Demetrius and the Gladiators* (US/1954/101m/C) D: Delmer Daves. C: Victor Mature, Susan Hayward, Michael Rennie, Debra Paget, Anne Bancroft, Barry Jones.

Carlo Colombo. *Caligula's Hot Nights* (Italy/1977/C) D: Roberto B. Montero. C: Gastone Pescucci.

Malcolm McDowell. *Caligula* (US-Italy/1980/156m/C) D: Tinto Brass. C: Peter O'Toole, Teresa Ann Savoy, Helen Mirren, John Gielgud, Anneka DiLorenzo.

David Cain Haughton. *The Emperor Caligula—The Untold Story* (Italy/1981/C) D: David Hills. C: David Cain, Laura Gemser, Oliver Finch, Fabiola Toledo, Sasha D'Arc.

John Turner. *Caligula and Messalina* (France/1982/C) D: Antonio Passalia. C: Betty Roland.

84 Calpurnia

Third wife of **Julius Caesar**, Calpurnia received no visitors following the assassination of her husband save for **Marc Antony** who came to claim Caesar's papers and loose cash.

Gertrude Michael. *Cleopatra* (US/1934/102m/BW) D: Cecil B. DeMille. C: Claudette Colbert, Warren William, Henry Wilcoxon, Joseph Schildkraut, Ian Keith, Ian Maclaren, Arthur Hohl, Claudia Dell, Robert Warwick, Charles Morris.

Helen Ross. *Julius Caesar* (US/1950/BW) D: David Bradley. B/on the play by Wm. Shakespeare. C: Charlton Heston, Robert Holt, David Bradley, Harold Tasker, Grosvenor Glenn, William Russell.

Greer Garson. *Julius Caesar* (US/1953/120m/BW) D: Joseph L. Mankiewicz. B/on the play by Wm. Shakespeare. C: James Mason, Marlon Brando, Louis Calhern, John Gielgud, Edmond O'Brien, Deborah Kerr, Alan Napier, Douglas Watson.

Carla Calo. *Caesar the Conqueror* (Italy/1962/103m/C) D: Amerigo Anton. C: Cameron Mitchell, Rick Battaglia, Dominique Wilms, Nerio Bernardi, Carlo Tamberlani, Bruno Tocci.

Gwen Watford. *Cleopatra* (US/1963/243m/C) D: Joseph L. Mankiewicz. B/on works by Plutarch, Appian, and Seutonius, and the novel *The Life and Times of Cleopatra* by Carlo M. Franzero. C: Elizabeth Taylor, Richard Burton, Rex Harrison, Pamela Brown, Jean Marsh, Kenneth Haig, Roddy McDowall, Francesca Annis, John Hoyt, Martin Landau, Michael Hordern, Douglas Wilmer, Carroll O'Connor, Finlay Currie.

Joan Sims. *Carry on Cleo* (GB/1964/92m/C) D: Gerald Thomas. C: Sidney James, Kenneth Williams, Charles Hawtrey, Amanda Barrie, Julie Stevens, Brian Oulton, Jim Dale.

Jill Bennett. *Julius Caesar* (GB/1970/117m/C) D: Stuart Burge. B/on the play by Wm. Shakespeare. C: Charlton Heston, John Gielgud, Jason Robards, Richard Johnson, Robert Vaughn, Richard Chamberlain, Diana Rigg, Christopher Lee, David Dodimead, Peter Eyre, Andre Morrell, Christopher Cazenove.

85 Canaris, (Adm.) Wilhelm (1887–1945)

The head of German military intelligence during WWII, Admiral Canaris was hanged for his involvement in the 1944 attempt to assassinate **Hitler**. Canaris was portrayed by Anton Diffring in the European TV mini-series *Jane Horney* (85).

O.E. Hasse. *Canaris* (Germany/1954/113m/BW) D: Alfred Weldenmann. C: Adrian Hovan, Barbara Ruetting, Martin Held, Wolfgang Priess, Charles Regnier.

Wolf Frees. *The Man Who Never Was* (GB/1956/103m/C) D: Ronald Neame. B/on the novel by Ewen Montagu. C: Clifton Webb, Gloria Grahame, Robert Flemyng, Stephen Boyd, Peter Williams, Michael Hordern. Cyril Cusack, Peter Sellers (voice of Churchill).

Walter Hudd. *The Two-Headed Spy* (GB/1959/93m/BW) D: Andre De Toth. C: Jack Hawkins, Gia Scala, Erik Schumann, Alexander Knox, Felix Aylmer, Laurence Naismith, Kenneth Griffith, Richard Grey, Donald Pleasence, Michael Caine, Bernard Fox.

Harry Studt. *The Assault* (aka *Atentát*) (Czechoslovakia/1964/BW) D: Jirí Sequens. C: Radoslav Brzobohaty, Vladimír Hlavaty, Jirí Holy, Rudolph Jelínek, Jirí Kodet, Ludek Munzar, Josef Vinklár, Siegfried Loyda, Pavel Bartl.

Anthony Quayle. *The Eagle Has Landed* (GB/1976/134m/C) D: John Sturges. B/on the novel by Jack Higgins. C: Michael Caine, Donald Sutherland, Robert Duvall, Jenny Agutter, Donald Pleasence, Leigh Dilley, Jean Marsh, Judy Geeson, Larry Hagman.

Denholm Elliott. *Voyage of the Damned* (GB/1976/155m/C) D: Stuart Rosenberg. B/on the book by Max Morgan-Witts & Gordon Thomas. C: Faye Dunaway, Max von Sydow, Oskar Werner, Malcolm MacDowell, Orson Welles, James Mason, Lee Grant.

86 Cantor, Eddie (1892–1964)

(Edward Israel Iskowitz) Popular American singer and actor, Cantor headlined the **Ziegfeld** Follies and starred in such films as *Whoopee* (30) and *Roman Scandals* (33).

Buddy Doyle. *The Great Ziegfeld* (US/1936/170m/BW) D: Robert Z. Leonard. Best Picture (AA). C: William Powell, Luise Rainer, Myrna Loy, Frank Morgan, Reginald Owen, Fannie Brice, Ray Bolger, A.A. Trimble, Rosina Lawrence, Ruth Gillette.

Keefe Brasselle. *The Eddie Cantor Story* (US/1953/115m/C) D: Alfred E. Green. C: Marilyn Erskine, Aline MacMahon, Arthur Franz, William Forrest, Will Rogers, Jr., Jackie Barnett.

87 Capone, Al (1899–1947)

(Alfonso Capone) The most famous American gangster, Capone was the "King of Chicago" during the 1920s. Convicted of tax evasion in 1931 he went to prison for eight years and died in Florida, a syphilitic cripple. Paul Muni's role (Tony Camonte) in *Scarface* (32) was fashioned after Capone.

Rod Steiger. *Al Capone* (US/1959/105m/BW) D: Richard Wilson. C: Fay Spain, Murvyn Vye, Lewis Charles, Nehemiah Persoff, James Gregory, Martin Balsam, Robert Gist.

Neville Brand. *The George Raft Story* (aka *Spin of a Coin*) (US/1961/105m/BW) D: Joseph M. Newman. C: Ray Danton, Jayne Mansfield, Julie London, Barrie Chase, Frank Gorshin, Barbara Nichols, Brad Dexter, Robert Strauss, Herschel Bernardi.

Neville Brand. *The Scarface Mob* (US/1962/105m/BW) D: Phil Karlson. B/on the book *The Untouchables* by Eliot Ness & Oscar Fraley. C: Robert Stack, Bruce Gordon, Keenan Wynn, Barbara Nichols, Bill Williams, Pat Crowley, Walter Winchell (Narrator).

Jason Robards. *The St. Valentine's Day Massacre* (US/1967/100m/C) D: Roger Corman. C: George Segal, Ralph Meeker, Jean Hale, Clint Ritchie, Frank Silvera, Joseph Campanella, Harold J. Stone, Bruce Dern, John Agar, Reed Hadley, Rico Cattani, Jack Nicholson.

Ben Gazzara. *Capone* (US/1975/101m/C) D: Steve Carver. C: Susan Blakely, Harry Guardino, John Cassavetes, Sylvester Stallone, Robert Phillips, John D. Chandler, John Orchard.

Robert De Niro. *The Untouchables* (US/1987/119m/C) D: Brian De Palma. C: Kevin Costner, Sean Connery, Charles Martin Smith, Andy Garcia, Billy Drago, Richard Bradford.

Thomas G. Waites. *Verne Miller* (US/1987/95m/C) D: Rod Hewitt. C: Scott Glenn, Barbara Stock, Lucinda Jenney, Diane Salinger, Andrew Robinson, Sean Moran.

Titus Welliver. *Mobsters* (US/1991/104m/C) D: Michael Karbelnikoff. C: Christian Slater, Patrick Dempsey, Richard Grieco, Costas Mandylor, F. Murray Abraham, Anthony Quinn, Michael Gambon, Lara Flynn Boyle, Nicholas Sadler.

Bernie Gigliotti. *The Babe* (US/1992/115m/C) D: Arthur Hiller. C: John Goodman, Kelly McGillis, Trini Alvarado, Bruce Boxleitner, Joe Ragno, Michael McGrady, Randy Steinmeyer, Michael Nicolasi, Bernard Kates, Harry Hutchinson, Guy Barile.

F. Murray Abraham. *Dillinger and Capone* (US/1995/95m/C) D: Jon Purdy. C: Martin Sheen, Stephen Davies, Catherine Hicks, Don Stroud, Christopher Kriesa, Debi A. Monahan.

88 Capote, Truman (1924–1984)

American author born in New Orleans, Capote was the darling of the Jet Set and often quoted in the media. He wrote many autobiographical novels, some of which were adapted for the screen. One of them was *The Grass Harp* (95) with Piper Laurie and Sissy Spacek playing the aunts who raised him, Edward Furlong as Colin Fenwick (Capote) and Grayson Fricke as the young Collin.

Louis Negin. *Studio 54* (aka *54*) (US/1998/89m/C) D: Mark Christopher. C: Ryan Phillippe, Salma Hayek, Neve Campbell, Mike Myers, Sela Ward, Breckin Meyer, Sherry Stringfield, Ellen Albertini Dow, Cameron Mathison, Michelle Risi, Noam Jenkins, Jay Goede, Patrick Taylor, Heather Matarazzo, Skipp Sudduth, Aemilia Robinson, Sean Sullivan, Lauren Hutton, Thelma Houston.

Sam Street. *Isn't She Great* (US/2000/93m/C) D: Andrew Bergman. C: Bette Midler, Nathan Lane, Daniel Cosgrove, Stockard Channing, David Hyde Pierce,

Amanda Peet, John Cleese, Jason Fuchs, John Larroquette, Richard McConomy, Rebekah Mintzer, Sarah Jessica Parker, Frank Vincent.

89 Cardigan, Lord (1797–1868)

(James Thomas Brudenell, 7th Earl of Cardigan) British soldier, Cardigan led and survivied the Charge of the Light Brigade at Balaclava during the Crimean War. (See **Raglan, Lord**)

Charles Croker King. *Charge of the Light Brigade* (US/1936/115m/BW) D: Michael Curtiz. C: Errol Flynn, Patric Knowles, Olivia de Havilland, David Niven, Brandon Hurst, Nigel Bruce.

Trevor Howard. *Charge of the Light Brigade* (GB/1968/145–130m/C) D: Tony Richardson. C: Vanessa Redgrave, John Gielgud, Harry Andrews, David Hemmings, Peter Bowles.

90 Carroll, Lewis (1832–1898)

(Charles Lutwidge Dodgson) English mathematician and author, Carroll is remembered for *Alice's Adventures in Wonderland* and *Through the Looking Glass.* Alice Liddell, for whom those books were written, was played by Amelia Shankley (as a child) and Coral Browne in *Dreamchild.*

Stephen Murray. *Alice in Wonderland* (GB-France/1951/83m/C) D: Dallas Bower. B/on stories by Lewis Carroll. C: Pamela Brown, Carol Marsh, David Read.

Ian Holm. *Dreamchild* (GB/1985/94m/C) D: Gavin Millar. C: Coral Browne, Amelia Shankley, Jane Asher, Peter Gallagher, Caris Corfman, Nicola Cowper.

91 Carson, Christopher "Kit" (1809–1868)

Early American hunter and explorer, Carson served as **John Fremont's** scout on excursions to California from 1842–1846. Carson was portrayed by Sammy McKim in the 1937 serial *Painted Stallion.*

Harry Carey. *Sutter's Gold* (US/1936/69m/BW) D: James Cruze. B/on the novel *L'Or* by Blaise Cendrars. C: Edward Arnold, Lee Tracy, Binnie Barnes, Katherine Alexander, Addison Richards, Montagu Love, Harry Stubbs, John Miljan, Robert Warwick.

Richard Lane. *Mutiny on the Blackhawk* (US/1939/67m/BW) D: Christy Cabanne. C: Richard Arlen, Andy Devine, Constance Moore, Noah Beery, Sr., Charles Trowbridge.

Jon Hall. *Kit Carson* (US/1940/97m/BW) D: George B. Seitz. C: Lynn Bari, Dana Andrews, Raymond Hatton, Edwin Maxwell, Harold Huber.

Allan Lane. *Trail of Kit Carson* (US/1945/57m/BW) D: Lesley Selander. C: Helen Talbot, Tom London, Twinkle Watts, Roy Barcroft, Jack Kirk.

Forrest Taylor. *Along the Oregon Trail* (US/1947/64m/BW) D: R.G. Springsteen. C: Monte Hale, Adrian Booth, Roy Barcroft, LeRoy Mason, Will Wright, Kermit Maynard.

Dean Smith. *Seven Alone* (aka *House Without Windows*) (US/1975/96m/C) D:

Earl Bellamy. B/on the novel *On to Oregon* by Honore Morrow. C: Dewey Martin, Aldo Ray, Anne Collings, James Griffith, Stewart Petersen, Dehl Berti.

Carter, Jimmy *see* 588

92 Caruso, Enrico (1873–1921)

A powerful Italian tenor, Caruso became famous world-wide with the aid of the new medium of phonograph records. He is still remembered as one of the greatest singers of the century for his performance of "I Pagliacci."

Ermanno Randi. *Enrico Caruso — Legend of a Voice* (aka *The Young Caruso*) (Italy/1951/108–78m/BW) D: Giacomo Gentilomo. B/on the novel *Neapolitanische Legende* by Frank Theiss. C: Gina Lollobrigida, Mario del Monaco, Maurizio di Nardo.

Mario Lanza. *The Great Caruso* (US/1951/109m/C) D: Richard Thorpe. C: Ann Blyth, Dorothy Kirsten, Jarmila Novotna, Richard Hageman, Carl Benton Reid, Nestor Paiva.

Howard Caine. (David Poleri, Voice of Enrico Caruso). *Pay Or Die* (US/1960/111m/BW) D: Richard Wilson. C: Ernest Borgnine, Zohra Lampert, Alan Austin, Renata Vanni.

Milan Karpisek. *The Divine Emma* (Czechoslovakia/1979/105m/C) D: Jiri Krejcik. C: Bozidara Turzonovova, Juraj Kukura, Milos Kopecky.

93 Carver, George Washington (1864?–1943)

Born a slave, Carver was a brilliant agriculturalist who dedicated his life to improving the status of black Americans. He portrayed himself in *George Washington Carver*.

George Washington Carver (Himself). Milton Sprague (Carver as a young man). *George Washington Carver* (US/1940/69m/BW) D: Ben Parker. C: Booker T. Washington III, Ralph Edwards, Tim Campbell, Raye Gilbert.

Ed Cambridge. *Bill and Ted's Bogus Journey* (US/1991/95m/C) D: Pete Hewitt. C: Keanu Reeves, Alex Winter, George Carlin, William Sadler, Amy Stock-Poynton, Joss Ackland, John Ehrin, Don Forney, Tad Horino.

94 Casanova, Giovanni Giacomo (1725–1798)

Kicked out of a seminary at sixteen, Casnova went on to be a soldier, gambler, alchemist, spy and director of the Paris lottery. In retirement he worked as a librarian and wrote his memoirs (12 volumes) recounting his adventures and many love affairs. Casnova was portrayed by Richard Chamberlain in the 1987 TV movie *Casanova*.

Gustav Waldau. *Münchhausen* (aka *The Adventures of Baron Munchaussen*) (aka *Baron Muenchhausen*) (Germany/1943/134–100m/C) D: Josef von Baky. C: Hans Albers, Wilhelm Bendow, Michael Bohnen, Brigette Horney, Ferdinand Marian.

Georges Guetary. *Loves of Casanova* (aka *Les Aventures de Casanova*) (France/

1947/101m/BW) D: Jean Boyer. C: Aime Clariond, Helene Dassonville, Noelle Norman.

Arturo de Cordova. *Adventures of Casanova* (US/1948/83m/BW) D: Roberto Gavaldon. C: Lucille Bremer, Turhan Bey, John Sutton, George Tobias.

Vincent Price. *Casanova's Big Night* (US/1954/85m/C) D: Norman McLeod. C: Bob Hope, Joan Fontaine, Audrey Dalton, Basil Rathbone, Hugh Marlowe, Arnold Moss, John Carradine.

Gabriele Ferzetti. *Casanova* (Italy-France/1954) D: Stefano Vanzina.

Felix Le Breux. *Les Dernieres Roses de Casanova* (aka *Posledni Ruze Od Casnovi*) (Czechoslovakia/1966) D: Vaclav Krska.

Leonard Whiting. *Youth, Vocation and Early Experiences of Casanova* (aka *Infanzia, Vocazione e Prime Esperienze di Giacomo Casanova Veneziano*) (Italy/1969/119m/C) D: Luigi Comencini. C: Claudio De Kunert, Senta Berger, Maria Grazia Buccella, Lionel Stander, Tina Aumont.

Massimo Girotti. *Cagliostro* (Italy/1975/103m/C) D: Daniele Pettinari. C: Bekim Fehmiu, Curt Jurgens, Robert Alda, Rosanna Schiaffino, Ida Galli.

Donald Sutherland. *Fellini's Casanova* (aka *Casanova*) (Italy/1976/166m/C) D: Federico Fellini. C: Tina Aumont, Cicely Browne, Olimpia Carlisi, Adele Angela Lojodice.

Tony Curtis. *Casanova & Company* (aka *Some Like It Cool*) (aka *The Rise and Rise of Casanova*) (aka *Sex on the Run*) (Austria-Italy-France-Germany/1976/100–88m/C) D: François Legrand (Franz Antel). C: Marisa Berenson, Hugh Griffith, Britt Ekland.

Giulio Boseti. *The Return of Casanova* (Italy/1978/C) D: Pasquale Festa Campanile.

Marcello Mastroianni. *La Nuit de Varennes* (France-Italy/1983/150–133m/C) D: Ettore Scola. C: Jean-Louis Barrault, Hanna Schygulla, Harvey Keitel, Jean-Claude Brialy, Jean-Louis Trintignant, Michel Piccoli, Eleonore Hirt, Daniel Gelin.

95 Cassidy, Butch (1866–1908?)

(Robert Leroy Parker) Leader of the infamous Hole-in-the-Wall gang, Butch and his partner, the **Sundance Kid**, robbed banks and trains throughout the West before heading to South America where they continued their outlaw careers. Most sources say he was killed in Bolivia in 1908 though some members of his family claim that he survived and died in Nevada in 1937.

John Doucette. *The Texas Rangers* (US/1951/68m/C) D: Phil Karlson. C: George Montgomery, Gale Storm, Noah Beery, Jr., William Bishop, John Dehner, Ian MacDonald.

Howard Petrie. *The Maverick Queen* (US/1955/92m/C) D: Joseph Kane. B/on the novel by Zane Grey. C: Barbara Stanwyck, Barry Sullivan, Scott Brady, Mary Murphy.

Gene Evans. *Wyoming Renegades* (US/1955/73m/C) D: Fred Sears. C: Phil Carey, Martha Hyer, William Bishop, Douglas Kennedy, Roy Roberts, George Keymas, A. Guy Teague, Aaron Spelling, John (Bob) Cason, Don Beddoe.

Neville Brand. *The Three Outlaws* (US/1956/74m/BW) D: Sam Newfield. C: Alan Hale, Jr., Bruce Bennett, Jose Gonzalez, Jeanne Carmen, Stanley Andrews.

Neville Brand. *Badman's Country* (US/1958/85m/BW) D: Fred F. Sears. C: George Montgomery, Buster Crabbe, Karin Booth, Gregory Wolcott, Malcolm Atterbury, Russell Johnson, Richard Devon, Morris Ankrum.

Arthur Hunnicutt. *Cat Ballou* (US/1965/97m/C) D: Eliot Silverstein. B/on the novel by Roy Chanslor. C: Jane Fonda, Lee Marvin, Michael Callan, Dwayne Hickman.

John Crawford. *Return of the Gunfighter* (US/1967/100m/C) D: James Neilson. Made for U.S. TV, released theatrically in Europe. C: Robert Taylor, Ana Martin, Chad Everett, John David Chandler, Lyle Bettger, Mort Mills, Michael Pate.

Paul Newman. *Butch Cassidy and the Sundance Kid* (US/1969/112m/C) D: George Roy Hill. Best Film, Best Director (BFA-1970). C: Robert Redford, Katherine Ross, Strother Martin, Jeff Corey, Henry Jones, Ted Cassidy, Charles Dierkop, Cloris Leachman, Sam Elliott.

Tex Gates. *Ride a Wild Stud* (aka *Ride the Wild Stud*) (US/1969) D: Revilo Ekard. C: Cliff Alexander, Frenchy LeBoyd, William Fosterwick, Bill Ferrill.

Tom Berenger. *Butch and Sundance: the Early Days* (US/1979/110m/C) D: Richard Lester. C: William Katt, Jill Eikenberry, John Schuck, Brian Dennehy, Paul Plunkett, Jeff Corey, Peter Weller.

96 Cassius (?–42 BC)

(Gaius Cassius Longinus) After lending a hand in **Julius Caesar's** murder, Cassius joined **Brutus** in the war against **Augustus** but committed suicide after the first battle.

Ian Maclaren. *Cleopatra* (US/1934/102m/BW) D: Cecil B. DeMille. C: Claudette Colbert, Warren William, Henry Wilcoxon, Gertrude Michael, Joseph Schildkraut, Ian Keith, Arthur Hohl, Claudia Dell, Robert Warwick, Charles Morris.

Grosvenor Glenn. *Julius Caesar* (US/1950/BW) D: David Bradley. B/on the play by Wm. Shakespeare. C: Charlton Heston, Robert Holt, David Bradley, Harold Tasker, William Russell, Helen Ross.

John Gielgud * Best British Actor (BFA). *Julius Caesar* (US/1953/120m/BW) D: Joseph L. Mankiewicz. B/on the play by Wm. Shakespeare. C: James Mason, Marlon Brando, Louis Calhern, Edmond O'Brien, Greer Garson, Deborah Kerr, Alan Napier, Douglas Watson.

John Hoyt. *Cleopatra* (US/1963/243m/C) D: Joseph L. Mankiewicz. B/on works by Plutarch, Appian, and Seutonius, and the novel *The Life and Times of Cleopatra* by Carlo M. Franzero. C: Elizabeth Taylor, Richard Burton, Rex Harrison, Pamela Brown, Jean Marsh, Kenneth Haig, Roddy McDowall, Francesca Annis, Gwen Watford, Martin Landau, Michael Hordern, Douglas Wilmer, Carroll O'Connor, Finlay Currie.

Richard Johnson. *Julius Caesar* (GB/1970/117m/C) D: Stuart Burge. B/on the play by Wm. Shakespeare. C: Charlton Heston, John Gielgud, Jason Robards, Robert Vaughn, Richard Chamberlain, Diana Rigg, Jill Bennett, Christopher Lee, David Dodimead, Peter Eyre, Andre Morrell, Christopher Cazenove.

Woody Lee. *The Notorious Cleopatra* (US/1970/88m/C) D: A.P. Stootsberry. C: Sonora, Johnny Rocco, Jay Edwards, Dixie Donovan, Tom Huron, Michael Cheal.

97 Castro, Fidel (1927–)

World famous as the Cuban revolutionary and dictator, Castro was once a Hollywood extra and appeared in *Holiday in Mexico* (46).

Jack Palance. *Che!* (US/1969/96m/C) D: Richard Fleischer. C: Omar Sharif, Cesare Danova, Robert Loggia, Woody Strode, Barbara Luna, Frank Silvera.

Jacobo Morales. *Up the Sandbox* (US/1972/97m/C) D: Irvin Kershner. B/on the novel by Anne Richardson Roiphe. C: Barbra Streisand, David Selby, Jane Hoffman.

Anthony LaPaglia. *Company Man* (France-GB-US/2000/86m/C) D: Peter Askin, Douglas McGrath. C: Paul Guilfoyle, Jeffrey Jones, Reathel Bean, Harriet Koppel, Douglas McGrath, Sigourney Weaver, Terry Beaver, Sean Dugan, Grant Walden, Nathan Dean, Nathan Bean, John Randolph Jones, Ryan Phillippe, Kim Merrill, Merwin Goldsmith, Meredith Patterson, Tuck Milligan.

98 Catherine de Medici (1519–1589)

The Queen of France as the wife of **Henri II**, Catherine was the mother of three of France's kings: **François II**, **Charles IX**, and **Henri III**. She served as Regent for her two eldest sons and continued to exert enormos political power as the Queen Mother. (See Appendix C)

Juana Sutton. *Dante's Inferno* (US/1935/88m/BW) D: Harry Lachman. C: Spencer Tracy, Claire Trevor, Henry B. Walthall, Scotty Becket, Lorna Lowe, Andre Johnsen, Leone Lane.

Marguerite Moreno. *The Pearls of the Crown* (France/1937/120–100m/BW) D: Sacha Guitry & Christian-Jaque. C: Sacha Guitry, Jacqueline Delubac, Lyn Harding, Ermete Zacconi, Yvette Plenne, Catalano, Arletty, Percy Marmont, Derrick De Marney, Barbara Shaw, Simone Renant, Jean Louis Barrault, Emile Drain, Enrico Glori, Renee Saint-Cyr, Pizani, Claude Dauphin, Aime-Simon Gerard.

Françoise Rosay. *La Reine Margot* (France-Italy/1954/125m/C) D: Jean Dreville. B/on a novel by Alexandre Dumas. C: Jeanne Moreau, Armando Francioli, Henri Genes, Robert Porte, Andre Versini, Danile Ceccaldi, Nicole Riche.

Marisa Pavan. *Diane* (US/1955/110m/C) D: David Miller. B/on the novel *Diane de Poitier* by John Erskine. C: Lana Turner, Pedro Armendariz, Roger Moore, Cedric Hardwicke, Ronald Green, Torin Thatcher, Henry Daniell, Basil Ruysdael.

Lia Padovani. *La Princesse de Cléves* (France/1961/115m/C) D: Jean Delannoy. B/on the novel by Madame De La Fayette. C: Jean Marais, Annie Ducaux, Raymond Gerome.

Katherine Kath. *Mary, Queen of Scots* (GB/1971/128m/C) D: Charles Jarrot. C: Vanessa Redgrave, Glenda Jackson, Patrick McGoohan, Timothy Dalton, Nigel Davenport, Trevor Howard, Daniel Massey, Ian Holm, Andrew Keir, Robert James, Richard Denning, Rick Warner.

Amanda Plummer. *Nostradamus* (GB-Germany/1994/118m/C) D: Roger Christian. C: Tcheky Karyo, F. Murray Abraham, Rutger Hauer, Anthony Higgins, Diana Quick.

Virna Lisi. *Queen Margot* (aka *La Reine Margot*) (France-Germany-Italy/1994/159–143m/C) D: Patrice Chareau. B/on the novel by Alexandre Dumas. C:

Isabelle Adjani, Vincent Perez, Jean-Hugues Anglade, Daniel Auteuil, Pascal Greggory.

99 Catherine the Great (1729–1796)

A Prussian born princess, Catherine married into the Russian royalty and became the Empress of all the Russias upon the murder of her husband, which she helped engineer. She is remembered today for her vociferous appetite for men and, if rumor is correct, other creatures as well. In the TV production *Young Catherine* (91) she was portrayed by Julia Ormond, and by Catherine Zeta-Jones in *Catherine the Great* (2000).

Elisabeth Bergner. *Catherine the Great* (aka *The Rise of Catherine the Great*) (GB/1934/94m/BW) D: Paul Czinner. B/on the play *The Czarina* by Melchior Lengyel & Lajos Biro. C: Douglas Fairbanks, Jr., Flora Robson, Gerald du Maurier.

Marlene Dietrich. *The Scarlet Empress* (US/1934/110m/BW) D: Josef Von Sternberg. C: John Lodge, Sam Jaffe, Louise Dresser, Maria Sieber, Ruthelma Stevens, Gavin Gordon.

Suzy Prim. *Betrayal* (France/1937/85m/BW) D: Fedor Ozep. B/on the novel *The Princess Tarakova* by G.P. Danilevski. C: Annie Vernay, Pierre-Richard Willm.

Françoise Rosay. *The Devil Is An Empress* (aka *The Chess Player*) (aka *The Checker Player*) (France/1938/90/70m/BW) D: Jean Dreville. B/on the story *The Chess Player of Vilna* by H. Dupuy-Mazuel. C: Conrad Veidt, Micheline Francey, Jacques Gretillat.

Brigitte Horney. *Münchhausen* (aka *The Adventures of Baron Munchaussen*) (aka *Baron Muenchhausen*) (Germany/1943/134–100m/C) D: Josef von Baky. C: Hans Albers, Wilhelm Bendow, Michael Bohnen, Ferdinand Marian, Gustav Waldau.

Olga Zhizneva. *Christmas Slippers* (USSR/1944/BW) D: E. Shapiro & N. Kosheverova.

Tallulah Bankhead. *A Royal Scandal* (aka *Czarina*) (US/1945/94m/BW) D: Otto Preminger. B/on the play *The Czarina* by Melchior Lengyel & Lajos Biro. C: Charles Coburn, Anne Baxter, William Eythe, Vincent Price, Mischa Auer, Sig Rumann.

Binnie Barnes. *Shadow of the Eagle* (GB/1950/93m/BW) D: Sidney Salkow. C: Richard Greene, Valentina Cortesa, Greta Gynt, Charles Goldner, Walter Rilla, Hugh French.

Olga Zhizneva. *Admiral Ushakov* (USSR/1953/C) D: Mikhail Romm. C: Ivan Pereverzev, Boris Livanov, V. Vasyliev, N. Volkov, I. Solovyov.

Viveca Lindfors. *Tempest* (Italy-France-Yugoslavia/1958/125m/C) D: Alberto Lattuada. B/on the novel *The Captain's Daughter* by Alexander Pushkin. C: Silvana Mangano, Van Heflin, Geoffrey Horne, Robert Keith, Agnes Moorehead.

Bette Davis. *John Paul Jones* (US/1959/126m/C) D: John Farrow. B/on the story *Nor'wester* by Clements Ripley. C: Robert Stack, Marisa Pavan, Charles Coburn, Jean-Pierre Aumont, Macdonald Carey, Susana Canales, John Crawford, Eric Pohlmann.

Hildegarde Neff. *Catherine of Russia* (Italy-France/1962) D: Umberto Lenzi.

Jeanne Moreau. *Great Catherine* (GB/1968/98m/C) D: Gordon Flemyng. B/on the play *Great Catherine Whom Glory Still Adores* by George Bernard Shaw. C:

Peter O'Toole, Zero Mostel, Jack Hawkins, Akim Tamiroff, Marie Lohr, Marie Kean.

100 Cattle Annie (1876–?)

(Annie McDougal) Briefly a member of the **Doolin-Dalton** gang, Annie spent two years in prison after which little was heard of her.

Dona Drake. *The Doolins of Oklahoma* (aka *The Great Manhunt*) (US/1949/90m/BW) D: Gordon Douglas. C: Randolph Scott, George Macready, Louise Albritton, John Ireland, Virginia Huston, Noah Beery, Jr., Robert Barrat, Frank Fenton.

Amanda Plummer. *Cattle Annie and Little Britches* (US/1980/97m/C) D: Lamont Johnson. B/on the novel by Robert Ward. C: Burt Lancaster, Rod Steiger, John Savage, Diane Lane, Scott Glenn.

101 Cellini, Benvenuto (1500–1571)

Versatile artist of the Italian High Renaissance, Cellini recounted his dramatic life in his *Autobiography*, which became the basis for several films.

Fredric March. *Affairs of Cellini* (US/1934/90–80 m/BW) D: Gregory La Cava. B/on the play *The Firebrand* by Edwin Justus Mayer. C: Constance Bennett, Frank Morgan.

Raimondo van Riel. *Magnificent Rogue* (aka *Lorenzino de Medici*) (Italy/1936/89m/BW) D: Guido Brignoni. C: Alessandro Moissi, Camillo Pilotto, Germana Paolieri.

Brett Halsey. *The Magnificent Adventurer* (aka *Il Magnifico Avventuriero*) (France-Italy-Spain-/1963/93m/C) D: Riccardo Freda. Cast: Carmelo Artale, Bernard Blier, Andrea Bosic, Carla Caló, Rossella Como, Umberto D'Orsi, Félix Dafauce, Sandro Dori, Françoise Fabian, Félix Fernández, Rafael Ibáñez, Giampiero Littera, Diego Michelotti, Claudia Mori, José Nieto, Elio Pandolfo, Dany París, Nazzareno Piana, Jancito San Emeterio, Bruno Scipioni, Mirko Valentin.

102 Cerdan, Marcel (?–1949)

Once boxing's Middleweight Champion, Cerdan was engaged to singer **Edith Piaf** at the time of his early death in a plane crash.

Louis Raftis. *Raging Bull* (US/1980/128m/BW) D: Martin Scorsese. B/on the book by Jake LaMotta with Joseph Carter & Peter Savage. C: Robert De Niro, Cathy Moriarty, Joe Pesci, Frank Vincent, Nicholas Colasanto, Theresa Saldana, Johnny Barnes.

Marcel Cerdan, Jr. *Edith and Marcel* (France/1983/162–104m/C) D: Claude Lelouch. C: Evelyne Bouix, Charles Aznavour, Jacques Villeret, Jean-Claude Brialy.

103 Cervantes (1547–1616)

(Miguel de Cervantes Saavedra) Spanish author and playwright, Cervantes is remembered for his masterpiece *Don Quixote*. He died on April 23, 1616, the same day as **William Shakespeare**.

Horst Bucholz. *The Young Rebel* (aka *Cervantes*) (Spain-Italy-France/1967/ 111m/C) D: Vincent Sherman. B/on the book *Cervantes* by Bruno Frank. C: Francisco Rabal, Gina Lollobrigida, Jose Ferrer, Louis Jourdan, Fernando Rey, Soledad Miranda.

Peter O'Toole. *Man of La Mancha* (US/1972/135m/C) D: Arthur Hiller. B/on the play by Dale Wasserman. C: Sophia Loren, James Coco, Harry Andrews, John Castle.

104 Chaliapin, Feodor Ivanovich (1873–1938)

Noted Russian bass singer, Chaliapin also starred in several films including G.W. Pabst's *Don Quixote* (33).

Nikolai Okhlopkov. *Yakov Sverdlov* (USSR/1940/128m/BW) D: Sergei Yutkevich. B/on the play by B. Levin & Pyotr Pavlenko. C: Pavel Kadochnikov, Maxim Strauch.

A. Ognivtsev. *Rimsky-Korsakov* (USSR/1952/88m/C) D: Grigori Roshal. C: Grigori Belov, Nikolai Cherkasov, L. Griasenko, L. Sukharevskaya.

Ezio Pinza. *Tonight We Sing* (US/1953/109m/C) D: Mitchell Leisen. B/on the book *Impressario* by Sol Hurok & Ruth Goode. C: David Wayne, Tamara Toumanova.

105 Chamberlain, Joseph (1836–1914)

British politician, Chamberlain, as a member of the Liberal and leader of the Liberal Unionist parties, served in many government posts from 1876–1906.

Henry Hallatt. *Victoria the Great* (GB/1937/110m/C) D: Herbert Wilcox. B/on the play *Victoria Regina* by Laurence Housman. C: Anna Neagle, Anton Walbrook, H.B. Warner, James Dale, Charles Carson, Hubert Harben, Felix Aylmer, Arthur Young, Derrick De Marney, Hugh Miller, Percy Parsons, Gordon McLeod, Wyndham Goldie.

Jean d'Yd. *Entente Cordiale* (France/1938/95m/BW) D: Marcel L'Herbier. B/on *Edward VII and His Times* by Andre Maurois. C: Victor Francen, Gaby Morlay, Andre Lefaur, Marcelle Praince, Jeanine Darcey, Arlette Marchal, Jean Galland, Andre Roanne, Jacques Catelain, Jean Toulot, Jacques Baumer, Jean Perrier.

Henry Hallatt. *Sixty Glorious Years* (aka *Queen of Destiny*) (GB/1938/90m/C) D: Herbert Wilcox. C: Anna Neagle, Anton Walbrook, C. Aubrey Smith, Charles Carson, Felix Aylmer, Pamela Standish, Gordon McLeod, Wyndham Goldie, Malcolm Keen, Derrick De Marney, Joyce Bland, Harvey Braban, Aubrey Dexter, Laidman Browne.

Basil Dignam. *Young Winston* (GB/1972/145m/C) D: Richard Attenborough. B/on the book *My Early Life: A Roving Commission* by Winston Churchill. Best English-Language Foreign Film (GG). C: Simon Ward, Peter Cellier, Ronald Hines, John Mills, Anne Bancroft, Robert Shaw, Laurence Naismith, William Dexter, Reginald Marsh, Anthony Hopkins, Robert Hardy, Colin Blakely, Michael Audreson, Jack Hawkins.

106 Chaplin, Charlie (1889–1977)

(Charles Spencer Chaplin) Called "the greatest screen clown of all time"; Chaplin's films include: *The Gold Rush* (25), *Modern Times* (36), *The Great Dictator*

(40), and *Limelight* (52). In TV movies he has been portrayed by Clive Revill in *Moviola: The Scarlett O'Hara War* (80) and by Lorne Kennedy in *The Hearst and Davies Affair* (85).

Gregory Rozakis. *The Cotton Club* (US/1984/127m/C) D: Francis Coppola. C: Richard Gere, Gregory Hines, Diane Lane, Lonette McKee, Bob Hoskins, James Remar, Nicolas Cage, Rosalind Harris, Fred Gwynne, Joe Dallesandro, Maurice Hines, Gwen Verdon, Lisa Jane Persky, Woody Strode, Zane Mark, Larry Marshall.

Robert Downey, Jr. *Chaplin* (US/1992/144m/C) D: Richard Attenborough. B/on the books *Chaplin:His Life & Art* by David Robinson and *My Autobiography* by Charlie Chaplin. C: Kevin Kline, Kevin Dunn, Moira Kelly, Geraldine Chaplin, John Thaw.

Brian Mulligan. *Cobb* (US/1994/128m/C) D: Ron Shelton. B/on the book *Cobb: A Biography* by Al Stump. C: Tommie Lee Jones, Robert Wuhl, Lolita Davidovitch.

Eddie Izzard. *The Cat's Meow* (Canada-Germany-GB/2001/110m/BW/C) D: Peter Bogdanovich. C: Kirsten Dunst, Cary Elwes, Edward Herrmann, Joanna Lumley, Victor Slezak, Jennifer Tilly, James Laurenson, Ronan Vibert, Chiara Schoras, Ingrid Lacey, John C. Vennema, Claudia Harrison, Claudie Blakley.

107 Charles I (1600–1649)

Called England's "martyr king" by some and insensitive and stupid by many more, Charles' struggles with Parliament led to the English Civil War and eventually his own execution. (See **Cromwell, Oliver**)

Hugh Miller. *The Vicar of Bray* (GB/1937/66m/BW) D: Henry Edwards. C: Stanley Holloway, K. Hamilton Price, Felix Aylmer, George Merritt, Esmond Knight.

Robert Rietty. *The Crimson Blade* (aka *The Scarlet Blade*) (GB/1963/83m/C) D: John Gilling. C: Lionel Jeffries, Oliver Reed, Jack Hedley, June Thorburn, Michael Ripper.

Alec Guinness. *Cromwell* (GB/1970/139m/C) D: Ken Hughes. C: Richard Harris, Robert Morley, Dorothy Tutin, Frank Finlay, Timothy Dalton, Robin Stewart.

108 Charles II (1630–1685)

After years in exile Charles was restored to the English throne and ruled over what is considered the most licentious and immoral court in England's history, which must explain why he has been portrayed so many more times than his father, **Charles I.**

Cedric Hardwicke. *Nell Gwyn* (GB/1934/75m/BW) D: Herbert Wilcox. B/on diaries of Samuel Pepys, Charles II and Nell Gwyn. C: Anna Neagle, Muriel George, Esme Percy.

Allan Jeayes. *Colonel Blood* (GB/1934/98m/BW) D: W.P. Lipscomb. C: Frank Cellier, Anne Gray, Arthur Chesney, Mary Lawson, Stella Arbenina, Hilda Trevelyan.

K. Hamilton Price. *The Vicar of Bray* (GB/1937/66m/BW) D: Henry Edwards. C: Stanley Holloway, Hugh Miller, Felix Aylmer, George Merritt, Esmond Knight.

Vincent Price. *Hudson's Bay* (US/1940/95m/BW) D: Irving Pichel. C: Paul Muni, Gene Tierney, Laird Cregar, John Sutton, Nigel Bruce, Chief Thundercloud.

Dennis Arundell. *The Courageous Mr. Penn* (aka *Penn of Pennsylvania*) (GB/1941/78m/BW) D: Lance Comfort. B/on the book *William Penn* by C.E. Vulliamy. C: Clifford Evans, Deborah Kerr, Aubrey Mallalieu, Henry Oscar, O.B. Clarence.

Douglas Fairbanks, Jr. *The Exile* (US/1947/94m/BW) D: Max Ophuls. B/on the novel *His Majesty, the King* by Cosmo Hamilton. C: Maria Montez, Paula Croset, Henry Daniell, Nigel Bruce, Robert Coote, Otto Waldis, Charles Stevens.

George Sanders. *Forever Amber* (US/1947/140m/C) D: Otto Preminger. B/on the novel by Kathleen Winsor. C: Linda Darnell, Cornel Wilde, Richard Greene.

Anthony Hulme. *The Cardboard Cavalier* (GB/1949/97m/BW) D: Walter Forde. C: Sid Field, Margaret Lockwood, Edmund Willard, Mary Clare.

Curt Bois. *Fortunes of Captain Blood* (US/1950/90m/BW) D: Gordon Douglas. B/on a novel by Rafael Sabatini. C: Louis Hayward, Patricia Medina, George Macready, Alfonso Bedoya.

Lester Matthews. *Lorna Doone* (US/1951/88m/C) D: Phil Karlson. B/on the novel by Richard D. Blackmore. C: Barbara Hale, Richard Greene, William Bishop, Ron Randell.

David Farrar. *Let's Make Up* (aka *Lilacs in the Spring*) (GB/1954/94m/C) D: Herbert Wilcox. B/on the play *The Glorious Days* by Harold Purcell. C: Anna Neagle, Errol Flynn, Kathleen Harrison, Peter Graves, Sean Connery.

George Sanders. *The King's Thief* (US/1955/78m/C) D: Robert Z. Leonard. C: Ann Blyth, Edmund Purdom, David Niven, Roger Moore, John Dehner, Alan Mowbray.

Gary Raymond. *The Moonraker* (GB/1958/82m/C) D: David MacDonald. B/on the play by Arthur Watkyn. C: George Baker, Sylvia Syms, Peter Arne, John Le Mesurier.

Robin Stewart. *Cromwell* (GB/1970/139m/C) D: Ken Hughes. C: Alec Guinness, Richard Harris, Robert Morley, Dorothy Tutin, Frank Finlay, Timothy Dalton.

Mark Burns. *The Wicked Lady* (GB/1983/99m/C) D: Michael Winner. B/on the novel *The Life and Death of the Wicked Lady Skelton* by Magdalen King-Hall. C: Faye Dunaway, Alan Bates, John Gielgud, Denholm Elliott, Prunella Scales, Teresa Codling.

Sam Neill. *Restoration* (GB/1995/113m/C) D: Michael Hoffman. B/on the novel by Rose Tremain. C: Robert Downey, Jr., Hugh Grant, Polly Walker, Meg Ryan.

Charles VI *see* 616

Charles VII *see* 617

Charles IX *see* 623

Charles X *see* 630

109 Charlotte, Queen (1744–1818)

(Charlotte Sophia of Mecklenburg-Strelitz) The wife of **George III**, Charlotte bore him 15 children including the future kings **George IV** and **William IV**. The cities of Charlotte, North Carolina, and Charlottesville, Virginia (USA), and Charlottetown, PEI (Canada), are named for her.

Agnes Laughlin. *The Young Mr. Pitt* (GB/1942/118m/BW) D: Carol Reed. C: Robert Donat, Robert Morley, Phyllis Calvert, Raymond Lovell, Max Adrian, Felix Aylmer, Albert Lieven, Stephen Haggard, Geoffrey Atkins, John Mills, Herbert Lom.

Lily Kann. *Mrs. Fitzherbert* (GB/1947/99m/BW) D: Montgomery Tully. B/on the novel *Princess Fitz* by Winifred Carter. C: Peter Graves, Joyce Howard, Leslie Banks, Margaretta Scott, Wanda Rotha, Mary Clare, Frederick Valk, Ralph Truman, John Stuart, Barry Morse, Henry Oscar, Arthur Dulay, Moira Lister, Julian Dallas.

Frances Waring. *The First Gentleman* (aka *The Affairs of a Rogue*) (GB/1948/111–95m/BW) D: Alberto Cavalcanti. B/on the play by Norman Ginsbury. C: Jean-Pierre Aumont, Joan Hopkins, Cecil Parker, Margaretta Scott, Hugh Griffith, Tom Gil, Jack Livesy.

Helen Mirren. *The Madness of King George* (aka *The Madness of George III*) (GB/1994/107m/C) D: Nicholas Hytner. Best Art Direction (AA). B/on the play by Alan Bennett. C: Nigel Hawthorne, Rupert Everett, Amanda Donohoe, Julian Wadham, Caroline Harker, Ian Holm, Rupert Graves, Geoffrey Palmer, Barry Stanton, Jim Carter, Peter Bride-Kirk, Cyril Shaps.

110 Chaucer, Geoffrey (1340?–1400)

Major English poet, the first to write in iambic pentameter. His greatest work is the unfinished *Canterbury Tales*, stories about a group of pilgrims on their way to the Shrine of **Thomas Becket** at Canterbury. The tales give a vivid account of medieval society and its attitudes on love, marriage, and religion.

Pier Paolo Pasolini. *I Racconti di Canterbury* (aka *The Canterbury Tales*) (aka *Les Contes de Canterbury*) (Italy-France/1971/109m/C) D: Pier Paolo Pasolini. B/on the novel by Geoffrey Chaucer. C: Hugh Griffith, Laura Betti, Ninetto Davoli, Franco Citti, Josephine Chaplin, Alan Webb, J.P. Van Dyne, Vernon Dobtcheff, Adrian Street, Derek Deadman, Nicholas Smith, George Bethell, Dan Thomas, Michael Balfour.

Paolo Casella. *Novelle licenziose di vergini vogliose* (aka *Le Mille e una notte di Boccaccio a Canterbury*) (Italy/1972/C) D: Joe D'Amato. C: Gabriella Giorgelli, Rose Margaret Keil, Enza Sbordone, Antonio Spaccatini, Mimmo Poli, Marco Mariani, Ewelin Melcherich, Attilio Dottesio, Antonio Aschi, Enzo Pulcrano, Stefano Oppedisano, Fausto Di Bella, Lucia Modugno, Rino Cassano.

Paul Bettany. *A Knight's Tale* (US/2001/132m/C) D: Brian Helgeland. C:

Heath Ledger, Rufus Sewell, Shannyn Sossamon, Laura Fraser, Mark Addy, Alan Tudyk, Bérénice Bejo, Scott Handy, James Purefoy, Leagh Conwell, Christopher Cazenove, Steve O'Donnel, Jonathan Slinger, Nick Brimble.

111 Chisum, John Simpson (1824–1884)

New Mexico cattle baron, Chisum allegedly hired **Billy the Kid** to fight in the Lincoln County War of 1878–1884.

Roy Roberts. *San Antone* (US/1953/90m/BW) D: Joseph Kane. B/on the novel *The Golden Herd* by Curt Carroll. C: Rod Cameron, Arleen Whelan, Richard Hale, Bob Steele.

John Wayne. *Chisum* (US/1970/110m/C) D: Andrew McLaglen. C: Forrest Tucker, Christopher George, Ben Johnson, Glenn Corbett, Geoffrey Deuel, Andrew Prine, Patric Knowles, Lynda Day, John Agar, Robert Donner, Ray Teal, Ron Soble.

Barry Sullivan *Video and TV versions only. *Pat Garrett and Billy the Kid* (US/1973/122–106m/C) D: Sam Peckinpah. C: Kris Kristofferson, James Coburn, Bob Dylan, Jason Robards, Richard Jaeckel, Katy Jurado.

James Coburn. *Young Guns II* (US/1990/105m/C) D: Geoff Murphy. C: Emilio Estevez, Kiefer Sutherland, Lou Diamond Phillips, Christian Slater, William Petersen, Balthazar Getty, Scott Wilson, Chief Buddy Redbow, Alan Ruck, R.D. Call, Jack Kehoe.

112 Chopin, Frédéric François (1810–1849)

Polish/French composer whose music established the piano as a solo concert instrument and was a strong influence on **Liszt** and **Wagner** among countless others. (See **Sand, George**)

Wolfgang Liebeneiner. *Abschiedswalzer* (Germany/1934/BW) D: Geza von Bolvary.

Cornell Wilde. *A Song to Remember* (US/1945/113m/C) D: Charles Vidor. C: Merle Oberon, Paul Muni, Stephen Bekassy, Nina Foch, George Coulouris, George Macready, Roxy Roth.

Vaclav Vosca. *Bohemian Rapture* (Czechoslovakia/1948/88m/BW) D: Vaclav Krska. C: Jaromir Spol, Karel Dostal, Vlasia Fabianova, Libuse Zemkova.

Czeslaw Wollejko. *Young Chopin* (Poland/1951/97m/BW) D: Aleksander Ford.

Alex Davion. *Song Without End* (US/1960/145m/C) D: George Cukor & Charles Vidor. C: Dirk Bogarde, Capucine, Genevieve Page, Patricia Morison, Ivan Desny, Martita Hunt, Lou Jacobi, Lyndon Brook, E. Erlandsen, Hans Unterkirchner, Katherine Squire.

Christopher Sandford. *Jutrzenka: A Winter in Majorca* (Spain/1971/105m/C) D: Jaime Camino. C: Lucia Bose, Henri Serre, Maurice Dudevant, Solange Dudevant.

Ken Colley. *Lisztomania* (GB/1975/105m/C) D: Ken Russell. C: Roger Daltrey, Sara Kestelman, Paul Nicholas, Fiona Lewis, Veronica Qilligan, Andrew Reilly, Murray Melvin, Otto Diamant, Anulka Dziubinska, Imogen Claire, Ken Parry.

Hugh Grant. *Impromptu* (GB/1990/107m/C) D: James Lapine. C: Judy Davis, Mandy Patinkin, Bernadette Peters, Julian Sands, Ralph Brown, Emma Thompson.

113 Christian, Fletcher (?–1790?)

Leader of the mutiny on the *Bounty*, Christian was killed by the natives on Pitcairn Island where the mutineers finally settled. (See **Bligh, William**)

Errol Flynn. *In the Wake of the Bounty* (Australia/1933/66m/BW) D: Charles Chauvel. C: Mayne Lynton, John Warwick, Victor Gouriet.

Clark Gable. *Mutiny on the Bounty* (US/1935/132m/BW) D: Frank Lloyd. B/on the novels *Mutiny on the Bounty*, *Men Against the Sea*, and *Pitcairn's Island* by Charles Nordhoff & James Norman Hall. Best Picture (AA). C: Charles Laughton, Franchot Tone, David Torrence, Eddie Quillan, Dudley Digges, Donald Crisp, Francis Lister, Ian Wolfe.

Marlon Brando. *Mutiny on the Bounty* (US/1962/179m/C) D: Lewis Milestone. B/on the novel by Charles Nordhoff & James Norman Hall. C: Trevor Howard, Richard Harris, Hugh Griffith, Richard Haydn, Tarita, Gordon Jackson, Noel Purcell.

Mel Gibson. *The Bounty* (US/1984/132m/C) D: Roger Donaldson. B/on the novel *Captain Bligh and Mr. Christian* by Richard Hough. C: Anthony Hopkins, Laurence Olivier, Edward Fox, Daniel Day-Lewis, Liam Neeson, Bernard Hill.

114 Christina, Queen (1626–1689)

Queen of Sweden from 1632–1654, Christina abdicated her throne to become a Roman Catholic.

Greta Garbo. *Queen Christina* (US/1933/97m/BW) D: Rouben Mamoulian. C: John Gilbert, Ian Keith, Lewis Stone, C. Aubrey Smith, Elizabeth Young, Reginald Owen.

Edith Evans. *Upon This Rock* (US/1970/90m/C) D: Harry Rosky. C: Orson Welles, Dirk Bogarde, Ralph Richardson.

Liv Ullmann. *The Abdication* (GB/1974/103m/C) D: Anthony Harvey. B/on the play by Ruth Wolff. C: Peter Finch, Cyril Cusack, Graham Crowden, Michael Dunn.

115 Christy, Edwin P. (1815–1862)

Creator of the minstrel show (where white players blackened their faces to perform), Christy's Minstrels helped popularize the songs of **Stephen Foster**.

William Frawley. *Harmony Lane* (US/1935/85m/BW) D: Joseph Santley. C: Douglass Montgomery, Evelyn Venable, Adrienne Ames, Joseph Cawthorn, Clarence Muse.

Al Jolson. *Swanee River* (US/1939/84m/C) D: Sidney Lanfield. C: Don Ameche, Andrea Leeds, Felix Bressart, Chick Chandler, Russell Hicks, George Reed, Charles Trowbridge.

Ray Middleton. *I Dream of Jeannie* (US/1952/90m/C) D: Allan Dwan. C: Bill Shirley, Muriel Lawrence, Christy, Lynn Bari, Louise Beavers, Rex Allen.

116 Churchill, Winston Leonard Spencer (1874–1965)

British statesman and Prime Minister (1940–45, 1951–55) whose stirring oratory and courageous leadership inspired Great Britain (and all Allied countries) throughout the Second World War.

    C.M. Hallard. *Regal Cavalcade* (aka *Royal Cavalcade*) (GB/1935/100m/BW) D: Thomas Bentley, Herbert Brenton, Norman Lee, Walter Summers, Will Kellino & Marcel Varnel. C: Marie Lohr, Esme Percy, Pearl Argyle, Frank Vosper, Austin Trevor, Harry Brunning, John Mills, H. Saxon-Snell, Patric Knowles, Matheson Lang, Athene Seyler.

    Dudley Field Malone. *Mission to Moscow* (US/1943/123m/BW) D: Michael Curtiz. B/on the book by Joseph E. Davies. C: Walter Huston, Ann Harding, Oscar Homolka, George Tobias, Gene Lockhart, Frieda Inescourt, Eleanor Parker, Richard Travis, Henry Daniell, Manart Kippen, Charles Trowbridge, Georges Renavent, Clive Morgan, Captain Jack Young, Leigh Whipper, Doris Lloyd, Olaf Hytten, Moroni Olsen.

    Victor Stanitsin. *The Fall of Berlin* (USSR/1949/124m/C) D: Mikhail Chiaureli. C: Mikhail Gelovani, Oleg Froelich, V. Savelyev, M. Novakova, Y. Verikh, M. Petrunkin.

Simon Ward as the youthful Winston Churchill, a preview of the strong leader to come, in this portrait from *Young Winston* (1972). (Museum of Modern Art Film Stills Archive)

Victor Stanitsin. *The First Front* (USSR/1949/81m/BW) D: Vladimir Petrov. Part I of *Battle of Stalingrad* (50). C: Alexei Diki, Y. Shumsky, V. Merkuryev, B. Livanov, Nikolai Cherkasov, M. Astangov, K. Mikhailov, N. Simono.

Victor Stanitsin. *The Unforgettable Year: 1919* (USSR/1952/C) D: Mikhail Chiaureli. B/on the play by Vsevold Vishnevsky. C: I. Molchanov, Mikhail Gelovani, Boris Andreyev, M. Kovaleva, Yevgeni Samoilov, V. Koltsov, Gnat Yura, L. Korsakov, Sergei Lukyanov.

Peter Sellers (voice only). *The Man Who Never Was* (GB/1956/103m/C) D: Ronald Neame. B/on the novel by Ewen Montagu. C: Clifton Webb, Gloria Grahame, Robert Flemyng, Stephen Boyd, Peter Williams, Wolf Frees, Michael Hordern. Cyril Cusack.

Jimmy Sangster. *The Siege of Sidney Street* (aka *The Siege of Hell Street*) (GB/1960/93m/BW) D: Robert S. Baker. C: Donald Sinden, Nicole Berger, Kieron Moore, Peter Wyngarde.

Patrick Wymark. *Operation Crossbow* (aka *The Great Spy Mission*) (GB-US-Italy/1965/118m/C) D: Michael Anderson. C: Sophia Loren, George Peppard, Trevor Howard.

Yuri Durov. *The Great Battle* (aka *Liberation*) (USSR-Poland-Yugoslavia-Italy/1969/118m/C) D: Yuri Ozerov. C: Buhuti Zakariadze, Stanislav Yaskevich, Ivo Garani, Fritz Diez.

Simon Ward. *Young Winston* (GB/1972/145m/C) D: Richard Attenborough. B/on the book *My Early Life: A Roving Commission* by Winston Churchill. Best English-Language Foreign Film (GG). C: Peter Cellier, Ronald Hines, John Mills, Anne Bancroft, Robert Shaw, Laurence Naismith, William Dexter, Basil Dignam, Reginald Marsh, Anthony Hopkins, Robert Hardy, Colin Blakely, Michael Audreson, Jack Hawkins.

Leigh Dilley. *The Eagle Has Landed* (GB/1976/134m/C) D: John Sturges. B/on the novel by Jack Higgins. C: Michael Caine, Donald Sutherland, Robert Duvall, Jenny Agutter, Donald Pleasence, Anthony Quayle, Jean Marsh, Judy Geeson, Larry Hagman.

Georgi Menglet. *Victory* (aka *Pobeda*) (USSR/1984/160m/C) D: Yevgeni Matveyev. B/on the novel by Aleksandr Chakovsky. C: Aleksandr Mikhajlov, Andrei Mironov, Klaus-Peter Thiele, Ramaz Chkhikvadze, Algimantas Masiulis, Mikhail Ulyanov, Viktor Ilyichyov, Nikolai Zasukhim.

Richard Huggett. *Jane and the Lost City* (GB/1987/94m/C) D: Terry Marcel. B/on the cartoon strip *Jane*. C: Kristen Hughes, Maud Adams, Sam Jones.

117 Cicero, Marcus Tullius (106–43 BC)

Roman orator, politician and author, Cicero opposed **Julius Caesar** and later spoke against **Marc Antony** on whose orders he was executed.

Charles Morris. *Cleopatra* (US/1934/102m/BW) D: Cecil B. DeMille. C: Claudette Colbert, Warren William, Henry Wilcoxon, Gertrude Michael, Joseph Schildkraut, Ian Keith, Ian Maclaren, Arthur Hohl, Claudia Dell, Robert Warwick.

Alan Napier. *Julius Caesar* (US/1953/120m/BW) D: Joseph L. Mankiewicz. B/on the play by Wm. Shakespeare. C: James Mason, Marlon Brando, Louis Calhern, John Gielgud, Edmond O'Brien, Greer Garson, Deborah Kerr, Douglas Watson.

Nerio Bernardi. *Caesar the Conqueror* (Italy/1962/103m/C) D: Amerigo Anton. C: Cameron Mitchell, Rick Battaglia, Dominique Wilms, Carlo Tamberlani, Bruno Tocci, Carla Calo.

Michael Hordern. *Cleopatra* (US/1963/243m/C) D: Joseph L. Mankiewicz. B/on works by Plutarch, Appian, and Seutonius, and the novel *The Life and Times of Cleopatra* by Carlo M. Franzero. C: Elizabeth Taylor, Richard Burton, Rex Harrison, Pamela Brown, Jean Marsh, Kenneth Haig, Roddy McDowall, Francesca Annis, John Hoyt, Gwen Watford, Martin Landau, Douglas Wilmer, Carroll O'Connor, Finlay Currie.

Andre Morrell. *Julius Caesar* (GB/1970/117m/C) D: Stuart Burge. B/on the play by Wm. Shakespeare. C: Charlton Heston, John Gielgud, Jason Robards, Richard Johnson, Robert Vaughn, Richard Chamberlain, Diana Rigg, Jill Bennett, Christopher Lee, David Dodimead, Peter Eyre, Christopher Cazenove.

Michael Cheal. *The Notorious Cleopatra* (US/1970/88m/C) D: A.P. Stootsberry. C: Sonora, Johnny Rocco, Jay Edwards, Woody Lee, Dixie Donovan, Tom Huron.

118 Cid, El (1040?–1099)

(Rodrigo Diaz de Vivar) Unlike the many legends, El Cid (The Lord) was not a champion of the Christians against the Moors, but fought all comers in 11th century Spain.

Charlton Heston. *El Cid* (US/1961/180m/C) D: Anthony Mann. C: Sophia Loren, John Fraser, Raf Vallone, Genevieve Page, Gary Raymond, Ralph Truman.

Sandro Moretti. *The Sword of El Cid* (aka *La Spada Del Cid*) (Italy-Spain/1962/C) D: Miguel Iglesias Bonns.

119 Clanton, Joseph Isaac "Ike" (?–1887)

A small-time cattle rustler and gambler, Clanton lead the outlaws who faced **Wyatt Earp** and **Doc Holliday** in the shootout at the O.K. Corral.

Victor Jory. *Tombstone, The Town Too Tough to Die* (US/1942/79m/BW) D: William McGann. B/on the book *Tombstone, The Toughest Town in Arizona* by Walter Noble Burns. C: Richard Dix, Kent Taylor, Edgar Buchanan, Frances Clifford, Don Castle, Rex Bell, Dick Curtis.

Grant Withers. *My Darling Clementine* (US/1946/97m/BW) D: John Ford. B/on the novel *Wyatt Earp, Frontier Marshal* by Stuart N. Lake. C: Henry Fonda, Linda Darnell, Victor Mature, Walter Brennan, Tim Holt, Ward Bond, Don Garner, John Ireland, Cathy Downs, Alan Mowbray, Roy Roberts, Jane Darwell, J. Farrell MacDonald.

William Bishop. *Gun Belt* (US/1953/77m/C) D: Ray Nazarro. C: George Montgomery, Tab Hunter, Helen Westcott, John Dehner, Douglas Kennedy, James Millican, Bruce Cowling, William Philips, Jack Elam, Boyd Morgan, Boyd Stockman.

Lyle Bettger. *Gunfight at the O.K. Corral* (US/1957/122m/C) D: John Sturges. B/on the story *The Killer* by George Scullin. C: Burt Lancaster, Kirk Douglas,

Rhonda Fleming, Jo Van Fleet, John Ireland, Frank Faylen, Earl Holliman, Whit Bissell, DeForrest Kelley, Martin Milner, Kenneth Tobey, Lee Van Cleef, Jack Elam, Bing Russell.

Gerald Milton. *Toughest Gun in Tombstone* (US/1958/72m/BW) D: Earl Bellamy. C: George Montgomery, Beverly Tyler, Don Beddoe, Jim Davis, Hank Worden, Lane Bradford.

Robert Ryan. *Hour of the Gun* (aka *The Law and Tombstone*) (US/1967/101m/C) D: John Sturges. B/on the novel *Tombstone's Epitaph* by Douglas D. Martin. C: James Garner, Jason Robards, Albert Salmi, Charles Aidman, Frank Converse, Larry Gates.

James Craig. *Arizona Bushwackers* (US/1968/87m/C) D: Lesley Selander. C: Howard Keel, Yvonne De Carlo, John Ireland, Marilyn Maxwell, Scott Brady.

Mike Witney. *Doc* (US/1971/95m/C) D: Frank Perry. C: Stacy Keach, Faye Dunaway, Harris Yulin, Dan Greenburg, Bruce M. Fischer, Ferdinand Zogbaum, Fred Dennis.

Stephen Lang. *Tombstone* (US/1993/128m/C) D: George Pan Kosmatos. C: Kurt Russell, Val Kilmer, Michael Biehn, Powers Booth, Robert Blake, Dana Delaney, Sam Elliott, Terry O'Quinn, Joanna Pacula, Bill Paxton, Jason Priestley, Michael Rooker.

Jeff Fahey. *Wyatt Earp* (US/1994/195m/C) D: Lawrence Kasdan. C: Kevin Costner, Dennis Quaid, Gene Hackman, David Andrews, Linden Ashby, Mark Harmon, Michael Madsen, Catherine O'Hara, Bill Pullman, Isabella Rossellini, Tom Sizemore, JoBeth Williams, Norman Howell, Mare Winningham, Rex Linn, Randle Mell.

120 Claudia Procula

The wife of **Pontius Pilate**, Claudia, who is depicted in the Gospels as sympathetic to **Jesus Christ**, is a Saint in the Greek Orthodox and Ethiopian Orthodox Churches. She was played by Hope Lange in the TV movie *The Day Christ Died* (80).

Edwige Feuillere. *Golgotha* (France/1935/97m/BW) D: Julien Duvivier. C: Harry Baur, Robert Le Vigan, Jean Gabin, Charles Granval, Andre Bacque, Hubert Prelier, Lucas Gridoux, Juliette Verneuil, Vana Yami, Van Daele.

Viveca Lindfors. *King of Kings* (US/1961/168m/C) D: Nicholas Ray. C: Jeffrey Hunter, Siobhan McKenna, Hurd Hatfield, Rita Gam, Carmen Sevilla, Rip Torn, Brigid Bazlen, Harry Guardino, Frank Thring, Guy Rolfe, Maurice Marsac, Gregoire Aslan, Royal Dano, Robert Ryan, Gerard Tichy, Michael Wager, Tino Barrero, Jose Antonio, Orson Welles (Narrator).

Jeanne Crain. *Pontius Pilate* (Italy-France/1962/100m/C) D: Irving Rapper. C: Jean Marais, Basil Rathbone, Leticia Roman, John Drew Barrymore, Livio Lorenzon.

Angela Lansbury. *The Greatest Story Ever Told* (US/1965/141m/C) D: George Stevens. B/on the book by Fulton Oursler. C: Max von Sydow, Dorothy McGuire, Robert Loggia, Claude Rains, Jose Ferrer, Charlton Heston, Donald Pleasence, David McCallum, Gary Raymond, Robert Blake, John Considine, David Hedison, Joanna Dunham, Sal Mineo, Van Heflin, Ed Wynn, Martin Landau, Telly

Savalas, Sidney Poitier, Roddy McDowell, Richard Conte, Carroll Baker, Janet Margolin, Burt Brinckerhoff, Tom Reese.

John Case. *Monty Python's Life of Brian* (aka *Life of Brian*) (GB/1979/93m/C) D: Terry Jones. C: Graham Chapman, Eric Idle, Michael Palin, John Cleese, Terry Gilliam, Terry Jones, Ken Colley.

Phyllis Logan. *The Inquiry* (aka *L'Inchiesta*) (aka *The Investigation*) (aka *The Inquest*) (Italy/1986/107m/C) D: Damiano Damiani. C: Keith Carradine, Harvey Keitel, Lina Sastri, Angelo Infanti, Sylvan.

121 Claudius (10 BC–AD 54)

Ignored most of his life due to a slight paralysis, Claudius was made Roman Emperor upon the murder of his nephew **Caligula**. He was portrayed by Derek Jacobi in the British series *I, Claudius* (77) and by Richard Kiley in the miniseries *A.D.* (84). In the unfinished film *I, Claudius* (37) he was portrayed by Charles Laughton.

Barry Jones. *Demetrius and the Gladiators* (US/1954/101m/C) D: Delmer Daves. C: Victor Mature, Susan Hayward, Michael Rennie, Debra Paget, Anne Bancroft, Jay Robinson.

Vittorio Caprioli. *Messalina, Messalina* (Italy/1977/81m/C) D: Bruno Corbucci. C: Anneka DiLorenzo, Giancarlo Prete, Lory Kay Wagner, Tomas Milian.

122 Clemenceau, Georges Benjamin (1841–1929)

French journalist, politician and Premier of France (1906–09, 1917–20), during the **Alfred Dreyfus** Affair, Clemenceau and his newspaper "L'Aurore" were staunch supporters of the wrongly convicted soldier.

Paul Bildt. *The Dreyfus Case* (aka *Dreyfus*) (Germany/1930/BW) D: Richard Oswald. C: Fritz Kortner, Grete Moshelm, Albert Basserman, Oscar Homolka, Heinrich George, Ferdinand Hart.

Leonard Shephard. *Dreyfus* (aka *The Dreyfus Case*) (GB/1931/90m/BW) D: F.W. Kraemer. B/on the play *The Dreyfus Case* by Herzog and Rehfisch. C: Cedric Hardwicke, Charles Carson, George Merritt, Sam Livesey, Beatrix Thomson, Garry Marsh.

Grant Mitchell. *The Life of Emile Zola* (US/1937/123m/BW) D: William Dieterle. Best Picture (AA,NYC). C: Paul Muni, Gale Sondergaard, Joseph Schildkraut, Gloria Holden, Donald Crisp, Morris Carnovsky, Louis Calhern, Ralph Morgan, Vladimir Sokoloff.

Jacques Baumer. *Entente Cordiale* (France/1938/95m/BW) D: Marcel L'Herbier. B/on *Edward VII and His Times* by Andre Maurois. C: Victor Francen, Gaby Morlay, Andre Lefaur, Marcelle Praince, Jeanine Darcey, Arlette Marchal, Jean Galland, Andre Roanne, Jacques Catelain, Jean Toulot, Jean d'Yd, Jean Perrier.

Marcel Dalio. *Wilson* (US/1944/154m/C) D: Henry King. C: Alexander Knox, Charles Coburn, Geraldine Fitzgerald, Cedric Hardwicke, Vincent Price, Sidney Blackmer, Eddie Foy, Jr., Edwin Maxwell, Francis X. Bushman, Clifford Brooke.

Gnat Yura. *The Unforgettable Year: 1919* (USSR/1952/C) D: Mikhail Chiaureli. B/on the play by Vsevold Vishnevsky. C: I. Molchanov, Mikhail Gelovani, Boris Andreyev, M. Kovaleva, Yevgeni Samoilov, Victor Stanitsine, V. Koltsov, L. Korsakov, Sergei Lukyanov.

Peter Illing. *I Accuse!* (GB/1958/99m/BW) D: Jose Ferrer. B/on the book *Captain Dreyfus — A Story of Mass Hysteria* by Nicholas Halasz. C: Jose Ferrer, Viveca Lindfors, Anton Walbrook, Leo Genn, Emlyn Williams, David Farrar, Donald Wolfit.

Raymond Queneau. *Landru* (aka *Bluebeard*) (France/1963/114m/C) D: Claude Chabrol. C: Charles Denner, Michele Morgan, Danielle Darrieux, Hildegard Neff.

123 Cleopatra (69–30 BC)

Queen of Egypt and lover of **Julius Caesar** and **Marc Antony**, Cleopatra also tried to seduce **Augustus** after his military victory over Antony. Failing in this she commited suicide by holding an asp to her breast. The Queen was portrayed by Leonor Varela in the TV movie *Cleopatra* (99).

Claudette Colbert. *Cleopatra* (US/1934/102m/BW) D: Cecil B. DeMille. C: Warren William, Henry Wilcoxon, Gertrude Michael, Joseph Schildkraut, Ian Keith, Ian Maclaren, Arthur Hohl, Claudia Dell, Robert Warwick, Charles Morris.

Lorna Lowe. *Dante's Inferno* (US/1935/88m/BW) D: Harry Lachman. C: Spencer Tracy, Claire Trevor, Henry B. Walthall, Scotty Becket, Andre Johnsen, Leone Lane, Juana Sutton.

Vivien Leigh. *Caesar and Cleopatra* (GB/1946/138m/C) D: Gabriel Pascal. B/on the play by George Bernard Shaw. C: Claude Rains, Stewart Granger, Flora Robson, Basil Sydney.

Rhonda Fleming. *Serpent of the Nile* (US/1953/81m/C) D: William Castle. C: William Lundigan, Raymond Burr, Michael Ansara, Jean Byron, Michael Fox, Robert Griffin.

Sophia Loren. *Two Nights With Cleopatra* (Italy/1953/80m/BW) D: Mario Mattoli. C: Ettore Manni, Alberto Sordi, Paul Muller, Alberto Talegalli, Rolf Tasna, Gianni Cavalieri.

Virginia Mayo. *The Story of Mankind* (US/1957/100m/C) D: Irwin Allen. B/on the book by Hendrik van Loon. C: Ronald Colman, Hedy Lamarr, Agnes Moorehead, Peter Lorre, Dennis Hopper, Marie Wilson, Helmut Dantine, Edward Everett Horton, Reginald Gardiner, Marie Windsor, Francis X. Bushman, Anthony Dexter, Austin Green, Jim Ameche, Harpo Marx, Bobby Watson, Reginald Sheffield, Cedric Hardwicke, Cesar Romero.

Linda Cristal. *Legions of the Nile* (Italy/1959/87m/C) D: Vittorio Cottafavi. C: Ettore Manni, Georges Marchal, Maria Mahor, Alfredo Mayo, Daniela Rocca.

Elizabeth Taylor. *Cleopatra* (US/1963/243m/C) D: Joseph L. Mankiewicz. B/on works by Plutarch, Appian, and Seutonius, and the novel *The Life and Times of Cleopatra* by Carlo M. Franzero. C: Richard Burton, Rex Harrison, Pamela Brown, Jean Marsh, Kenneth Haig, Roddy McDowall, Francesca Annis, John Hoyt, Gwen Watford, Martin Landau, Michael Hordern, Douglas Wilmer, Carroll O'Connor, Finlay Currie.

Pascale Petit. *A Queen for Caesar* (Italy-France/1963/C) D: Victor Tourjansky & Piero Pierotti. C: Giorgio Ardisson.

Antony (Henry Wilcoxon) and Cleopatra (Claudette Colbert), ancient lovers through the eyes of 1930's Hollywood in *Cleopatra* (1934). (Museum of Modern Art Film Stills Archive)

Amanda Barrie. *Carry on Cleo* (GB/1964/92m/C) D: Gerald Thomas. C: Sidney James, Kenneth Williams, Charles Hawtrey, Joan Sims, Julie Stevens, Brian Oulton, Jim Dale.

Sonora. *The Notorious Cleopatra* (US/1970/88m/C) D: A.P. Stootsberry. C: Johnny Rocco, Jay Edwards, Woody Lee, Dixie Donovan, Tom Huron, Michael Cheal.

Hildegard Neil. *Antony and Cleopatra* (GB/1973/160m/C) D: Charlton Heston. B/on the play by Wm. Shakespeare. C: Charlton Heston, Eric Porter, John Castle, Fernando Rey.

Cleveland, Grover *see* 583

124 Cline, Patsy (1932–1963)

(Virginia Patterson Hensley) Popular Country and Western singer whose career was cut short when she was killed in a plane crash.

Beverly D'Angelo. *Coal Miner's Daughter* (US/1980/125m/C) D: Michael Apted. B/on the book by Loretta Lynn and George Vescey. C: Sissy Spacek, Tommy Lee Jones.

Jessica Lange. *Sweet Dreams* (US/1985/115m/C) D: Karel Reisz. C: Ed Harris, AnnWedgeworth, David Clennon, James Staley, Gary Basaraba, John Goodman.

Alice Krige. *Baja Oklahoma* (US/1988/105m/C) D: Bobby Roth. B/on the novel by Dan Jenkins. C: Lesley Ann Warren, Peter Coyote, Swoosie Kurtz, Anthony Zerbe.

125 Clive, Robert, 1st Baron Clive of Plassey (1725–1774)

English soldier and administrator, Clive helped establish Great Britain's dominance in India in the eighteenth century.

Ronald Colman. *Clive of India* (US/1935/92m/BW) D: Richard Boleslawski. B/on the play *Clive* by W.P. Lipscomb & R.J. Minne. C: Loretta Young, Colin Clive, Francis Lister, Ian Wolfe, Leonard Mudie, Vernon Downing.

Paul Cavanagh. *Flame of Calcutta* (US/1953/70m/C) D: Seymour Friedman. C: Denise Darcel, Patric Knowles, George Keymas, Joseph Mell, Ted Thorpe.

126 Clum, John Philip (1851–1932)

An Indian agent during the Apache wars in Arizona, Clum was later the mayor of Tombstone and the editor of its paper, The Tombstone Epitaph.

Audie Murphy. *Walk the Proud Land* (US/1956/88m/C) D: Jesse Hibbs. B/on the book *Apache Agent* by Woodworth Clum. C: Anne Bancroft, Pat Crowley, Charles Drake, Eugene Iglesias, Jay Silverheels, Robert Warwick, Anthony Caruso, Addison Richards.

Whit Bissell. *Gunfight at the O.K. Corral* (US/1957/122m/C) D: John Sturges. B/on the story *The Killer* by George Scullin. C: Burt Lancaster, Kirk Douglas, Rhonda Fleming, Jo Van Fleet, John Ireland, Lyle Bettger, Frank Faylen, Earl Holliman, DeForrest Kelley, Martin Milner, Kenneth Tobey, Lee Van Cleef, Jack Elam, Bing Russell.

Larry Gates. *Hour of the Gun* (aka *The Law and Tombstone*) (US/1967/101m/C) D: John Sturges. B/on the novel *Tombstone's Epitaph* by Douglas D. Martin. C: James Garner, Jason Robards, Robert Ryan, Albert Salmi, Charles Aidman, Frank Converse.

Dan Greenburg. *Doc* (US/1971/95m/C) D: Frank Perry. C: Stacy Keach, Faye Dunaway, Harris Yulin, Mike Witney, Bruce M. Fischer, Ferdinand Zogbaum, Fred Dennis.

Terry O'Quinn. *Tombstone* (US/1993/128m/C) D: George Pan Kosmatos. C: Kurt Russell, Val Kilmer, Michael Biehn, Powers Booth, Robert Blake, Dana Delaney, Sam Elliott, Stephen Lang, Joanna Pacula, Bill Paxton, Jason Priestley, Michael Rooker.

Randle Mell. *Wyatt Earp* (US/1994/195m/C) D: Lawrence Kasdan. C: Kevin Costner, Dennis Quaid, Gene Hackman, David Andrews, Linden Ashby, Jeff Fahey, Mark Harmon, Michael Madsen, Catherine O'Hara, Bill Pullman, Isabella Rossellini, Tom Sizemore, JoBeth Williams, Norman Howell, Mare Winningham, Rex Linn.

127 Cobb, Tyrus Raymond "Ty" (1886–1961)

One of the greatest baseball players of all time, Cobb was the first man elected to the Baseball Hall of Fame.

Randy Steinmeyer. *The Babe* (US/1992/115m/C) D: Arthur Hiller. C: John Goodman, Kelly McGillis, Trini Alvarado, Bruce Boxleitner, Joe Ragno, Michael McGrady, Bernie Gigliotti, Michael Nicolasi, Bernard Kates, Harry Hutchinson, Guy Barile.

Tommie Lee Jones. *Cobb* (US/1994/128m/C) D: Ron Shelton. B/on the book *Cobb: A Biography* by Al Stump. C: Robert Wuhl, Lolita Davidovitch, Brian Mulligan.

128 Cochise (1815?–1874)

Apache chief who led his tribe in brilliantly executed raids against white settlers in Arizona for ten years before finally surrendering in 1871.

Antonio Moreno. *Valley of the Sun* (US/1942/84m/BW) D: George Marshall. B/on the book by Clarence Budington Kelland. C: Lucille Ball, James Craig, Cedric Hardwicke, Dean Jagger, Billy Gilbert, Tom Tyler, George Cleveland, Stanley Andrews.

Miguel Inclan. *Fort Apache* (US/1948/127m/BW) D: John Ford. B/on the story *Massacre* by James Warner Bellah. C: Henry Fonda, John Wayne, Shirley Temple, Ward Bond, John Agar, George O'Brien, Victor McLaglen, Anna Lee.

Jeff Chandler. *Broken Arrow* (US/1950/93m/C) D: Delmer Daves. B/on the novel *Blood Brother* by Elliott Arnold. C: James Stewart, Debra Paget, Jay Silverheels.

Chief Yowlachie. *The Last Outpost* (US/1951/88m/C) D: Lewis R. Foster. C: Ronald Reagan, Rhonda Fleming, Bruce Bennett, Bill Williams, Noah Beery, Jr., John War Eagle.

Jeff Chandler. *The Battle at Apache Pass* (US/1952/85m/C) D: George Sherman. C: John Lund, Beverly Tyler, Bruce Cowling, Jay Silverheels, Hugh O'Brian, Jack Elam.

John Hodiak. *Conquest of Cochise* (US/1953/70m/C) D: William Castle. C: Robert Stack, Joy Page, Rico Alaniz, Guy Edward Hearn, Alex Montoya.

Jeff Chandler. *Taza, Son of Cochise* (US/1954/79m/C) D: Douglas Sirk. C: Rock Hudson, Barbara Rush, Gregg Palmer, Morris Ankrum, Ian MacDonald, Eugene Iglesias.

Michael Keep. *40 Guns to Apache Pass* (US/1967/95m/C) D: William Witney. C: Audie Murphy, Michael Burns, Kenneth Tobey, Laraine Stephens, Robert Brubaker.

Cody, William F. *see* Buffalo Bill

129 Cohan, George Michael (1878–1942)

American theatrical writer/producer/performer remembered for his rousing shows and such songs as "Over There" and "I'm a Yankee Doodle Dandy."

James Cagney * Best Actor (AA,NYC). *Yankee Doodle Dandy* (US/1942/

126m/BW) D: Michael Curtiz. C: Joan Leslie, Walter Huston, George Tobias, Eddie Foy, Jr., Captain Jack Young, Wallis Clark.

James Cagney. *The Seven Little Foys* (US/1955/95m/C) D: Melville Shavelson. C: Bob Hope, Milly Vatale, George Tobias, Angela Clark, Herbert Heyes, Billy Gray.

Mark Baker. *After the Ball* (GB/1957/89m/C) D: Compton Bennett. B/on *Recollections of Vesta Tilley* by Lady de Frece. C: Pat Kirkwood, Laurence Harvey, Peter Carlisle.

130 Coll, Vincent "Mad Dog" (1909–1932)

New York gangster of the early Thirties, Coll received the nickname "Mad Dog" after killing a child in an attempted hit of a rival mobster. He was later gunned down by members of **Dutch Schultz's** gang.

Richard Gardner. *The Rise and Fall of Legs Diamond* (US/1960/101m/BW) D: Budd Boetticher. C: Ray Danton, Karen Steele, Elaine Stewart, Jesse White, Robert Lowery, Sid Melton.

John Chandler. *Mad Dog Coll* (US/1961/88m/BW) D: Burt Balaban. C: Vincent Gardenia, Neil Nephew, Brooke Hayward, Joy Harmon, Jerry Orbach, Telly Savalas, Gene Hackman.

Evan McCord. *Portrait of a Mobster* (US/1961/108m/BW) D: Joseph Pevney. B/on the book by Harry Grey. C: Vic Morrow, Leslie Parrish, Peter Breck, Ray Danton.

Nicholas Sadler. *Mobsters* (US/1991/104m/C) D: Michael Karbelnikoff. C: Christian Slater, Patrick Dempsey, Richard Grieco, Costas Mandylor, F. Murray Abraham, Anthony Quinn, Michael Gambon, Lara Flynn Boyle, Titus Welliver.

Christopher Bradley. *Hit the Dutchman* (US-Russia/1993/116m/C) D: Menahem Golan. C: Bruce Nozick, Eddie Bowz, Will Kempe, Sally Kirkland, Jeff Griggs, Jennifer Miller, Jack Conley, Matt Servitto, Menahem Golan.

Christopher Bradley. *Mad Dog Coll* (aka *Killer Instinct*) (US-Russia/1993/101m/C) D: Greydon Clark & Ken Stein. C: Bruce Nozick, Rachel York, Jeff Griggs, Thomas McHugh, Eddie Bowz, Jack Conley, Matt Servitto, Will Kempe, Dennis Predovic.

131 Columbus, Christopher (1451–1506)

Italian explorer credited with discovering America, Columbus was portrayed by Gabriel Byrne in the TV film *Christopher Columbus* (85).

Bert Lindley. *Are We Civilized?* (US/1934/70m/BW) D: Edwin Carewe. C: Frank McGlynn, Alin Cavin, Harry Burkhart, Charles Requa, Aaron Edwards, William Humphrey.

Fortunio Bonanova. *Where Do We Go from Here?* (US/1945/77m/C) D: Gregory Ratoff. C: Fred MacMurray, Joan Leslie, June Haver, Anthony Quinn, Alan Mowbray, John Davidson.

Fredric March. *Christopher Columbus* (GB/1949/104m/C) D: David MacDonald. C: Florence Eldridge, Francis L. Sullivan, Kathleen Ryan, Francis Lister, Derek Bond.

Anthony Dexter. *The Story of Mankind* (US/1957/100m/C) D: Irwin Allen.

B/on the book by Hendrik van Loon. C: Ronald Colman, Hedy Lamarr, Virginia Mayo, Agnes Moorehead, Peter Lorre, Dennis Hopper, Marie Wilson, Helmut Dantine, Edward Everett Horton, Reginald Gardiner, Marie Windsor, Francis X. Bushman, Austin Green, Jim Ameche, Harpo Marx, Bobby Watson, Reginald Sheffield, Cedric Hardwicke, Cesar Romero.

    Carl Sturmer. *Stuck on You* (US/1983/88m/C) D: Samuel Weil & Michael Herz. C: Irwin Corey, Daniel Harris, Robin Burroughs, Julie Newdow, Barbie Kielian.

    George Corraface. *Christopher Columbus: The Discovery* (US-Spain/1992/122m/C) D: John Glen. C: Rachel Ward, Tom Selleck, Marlon Brando, Robert Davi, Catherine Zeta-Jones.

    Jim Dale. *Carry on Columbus* (GB/1992/91m/C) D: Gerald Thomas. C: Bernard Cribbins, Maureen Lipman, Rik Mayall, Alexei Sayle, Larry Miller, Leslie Phillips, June Whitfield.

    Gérard Depardieu. *1492: Conquest of Paradise* (US-GB-France-Spain/1992/145m/C) D: Ridley Scott. C: Sigourney Weaver, Armand Assante, Frank Langella, Loren Dean, Angela Molina, Fernando Rimida, Fernando Rey, Michael Wincott, Tcheky Karyo.

Conan Doyle, Sir Arthur *see* Doyle, Sir Arthur Conan

Coolidge, Calvin *see* 586

132 Corbett, James John (1866–1933)
After defeating **John L. Sullivan** for the heavyweight boxing crown, "Gentleman Jim" Corbett went on to a career in vaudeville and silent films.

    Erroll Flynn. *Gentleman Jim* (US/1942/104m/BW) D: Raoul Walsh. B/on the book *The Roar of the Crowd* by James J. Corbett. C: Alexis Smith, Jack Carson, Ward Bond, Alan Hale, John Loder, William Frawley, Minor Watson, Rhys Williams.

    Rory Calhoun. *The Great John L.* (aka *A Man Called Sullivan*) (US/1945/96m/BW) D: Frank Tuttle. C: Greg McClure, Linda Darnell, Barbara Britton, Lee Sullivan, Otto Kruger.

    George Turner. *Vigilantes of Boomtown* (US/1947/56m/BW) D: R.G. Springsteen. C: Allan Lane, Bobby Blake, Martha Wentworth, Roscoe Karns, Peggy Stewart, John Dehner.

    John Day. *City of Bad Men* (US/1953/81m/C) D: Harmon Jones. C: Jeanne Crain, Dale Robertson, Richard Boone, Lloyd Bridges, Carole Mathews, Carl Betz, Gil Perkins.

    Steve Oliver. *Tom Horn* (US/1980/98m/C) D: William Wiard. B/on *Life of Tom Horn, Government Scout and Interpreter* by Tom Horn. C: Steve McQueen, Linda Evans, Richard Farnsworth, Billy Green Bush, Slim Pickens, Elisha Cook, Jr.

133 Corday, Charlotte (1768–1793)
(Marie Anne Charlotte Corday d'Armont) French revolutionary assassin, Corday murdered **Jean Paul Marat** on July 13, 1793. She was guillotined four days later.

Marguerite Gance. *Napoleon Bonaparte* (France/1934/140m/BW) D: Abel Gance. Three-dimensional sound version of Gance's 1927 epic *Napoléon*. C: Albert Dieudonné, Edmond von Daele, Alexandre Koubitsky, Antonin Artaud, Boudreau, Alberty, Jack Rye, Favière, Gina Manès, Suzanne Blanchetti, Simone Genevois, Genica Missirio.

Glenda Jackson. *Marat/Sade* (aka *The Persecution and Assasination of Jean-Paul Marat As Performed By the Inmates of Charenton Under the Direction of the Marquis de Sade*) (GB/1966/115m/C) D: Peter Brook. B/on the play by Peter Weiss. C: Patrick Magee, Clifford Rose, Ian Richardson, John Harwood, Brenda Kempner, Ruth Baker, Michael Williams, Freddie Jones, Henry Woolf.

134 Cranmer, Thomas (1489–1556)

The first Protestant Archbishop of Canterbuty, Cranmer was instrumental in helping **Henry VIII** dissolve several of his marriages. Not so popular with Henry's eldest daughter, he was executed (burned at the stake) by **Mary I**.

Lawrence Hanray. *The Private Life of Henry VIII* (GB/1933/97m/BW) D: Alexander Korda. C: Charles Laughton, Robert Donat, Binnie Barnes, Elsa Lanchester, Merle Oberon, Wendy Barrie, Everley Gregg, Franklyn Dyall, Miles Mander, Claude Allister, John Loder.

Halliwell Hobbes. *The Prince and the Pauper* (US/1937/120m/BW) D: William Keighley. B/on the novel by Mark Twain and the play by Catherine C. Cushing. C: Errol Flynn, Claude Rains, Henry Stephenson, Billy Mauch, Bobby Mauch, Montagu Love, Alan Hale, Robert Warwick, Helen Valkis, Ann Howard, Barton MacLane.

Lumsden Hare. *Young Bess* (US/1953/112m/C) D: George Sidney. B/on the novel by Margaret Irwin. C: Jean Simmons, Stewart Granger, Deborah Kerr, Charles Laughton, Kay Walsh, Cecil Kellaway, Rex Thompson, Elaine Stewart, Dawn Addams.

Cyril Luckham. *A Man for All Seasons* (GB/1966/120m/C) D: Fred Zinnemann. B/on the play by Robert Bolt. Best Picture Awards: (AA, NBR, GG, NYC, BFA (Any Source and Best British Film), Best Director Awards: (AA, NBR, GG, NYC, DGA). C: Paul Scofield, Wendy Hiller, Leo McKern, Robert Shaw, Orson Welles, Susannah York, Nigel Davenport, Vanessa Redgrave.

Bernard Hepton. *The Six Wives of Henry VIII* (aka *Henry VIII and His Six Wives*) (GB/1972/125m/C) D: Waris Hussein. C: Keith Michell, Frances Cuka, Charlotte Rampling, Jane Asher, Jenny Bos, Lynne Frederick, Barbara Leigh-Hunt, Donald Pleasence, Simon Henderson, Annette Crosbie, John Bryans, Michael Goodliffe, Dorothy Tutin.

David Waller. *Lady Jane* (GB/1986/144m/C) D: Trevor Nunn. C: Helena Bonham Carter, Cary Elwes, John Wood, Michael Hordern, Jane Laportaire, Warren Saire.

135 Crazy Horse (1842?–1877)

Along with **Sitting Bull**, Crazy Horse led the Sioux and Cheyenne tribes in the defeat of **Custer** at the Little Big Horn. Forced to surrender the following year, he was murdered while in the custody of the U.S. Army.

Anthony Quinn. *They Died With Their Boots On* (US/1941/140m/BW) D: Raoul Walsh. C: Errol Flynn, Olivia de Havilland, Arthur Kennedy, Charles Grapewin, Gene Lockhart, John Litel, Stanley Ridges, Sydney Greenstreet, Regis Toomey, Hattie McDaniel, Joseph Crehan.

Chief Thundercloud. *Buffalo Bill* (US/1944/90m/C) D: William Wellman. C: Joel McCrea, Maureen O'Hara, Linda Darnell, Thomas Mitchell, Edgar Buchanan, Anthony Quinn, Moroni Olsen, John Dilson, Sidney Blackmer, Evelyn Beresford.

Iron Eyes Cody. *Sitting Bull* (US/1954/105m/C) D: Sidney Salkow. C: J. Carrol Naish, Dale Robertson, Mary Murphy, John Litel, Douglas Kennedy, John Hamilton.

Victor Mature. *Chief Crazy Horse* (aka *Valley of Fury*) (US/1954/86m/C) D: George Sherman. C: Suzan Ball, John Lund, Ray Danton, Keith Larsen, Morris Ankrum.

Iron Eyes Cody. *The Great Sioux Massacre* (aka *Custer Massacre*) (aka *The Massacre at the Rosebud*) (US/1965/92m/C) D: Sidney Salkow. C: Joseph Cotten, Darren McGavin, Philip Carey, Julie Sommars, Nancy Kovack, Michael Pate, Don Haggerty.

Murray Alper. *The Outlaws Is Coming* (US/1965/88m/BW) D: Norman Maurer. C: Larry Fine, Moe Howard, Joe De Rita, Nancy Kovack, Joe Bolton, Bill Camfield, Hal Fryar, Johnny Ginger, Wayne Mack, Ed McDonnell, Bruce Sedley, Paul Shannon, Sally Starr

Will Sampson. *The White Buffalo* (aka *Hunt to Kill*) (US/1977/97m/C) D: J. Lee Thompson. B/on the novel by Richard Sale. C: Charles Bronson, Jack Warden, Kim Novak, Clint Walker, Stuart Whitman, Slim Pickens, John Carradine, Martin Kove.

136 Crockett, David "Davy" (1786–1836)

Famed Tennessee frontiersman and Indian fighter, Crockett was later elected to Congress where he spent several terms. In 1835 he went to Texas where along with **Jim Bowie**, he met his death at the Alamo. Crockett was portrayed by Jack Perrin in the 1937 serial *Painted Stallion* and in *Davy Crockett, Indian Scout* (50) George Montgomery played Crockett's namesake nephew.

Lane Chandler. *Heroes of the Alamo* (aka *Remember the Alamo*) (US/1937/80m/BW) D: Harry Fraser. C: Earl Hodgins, Roger Williams, Rex Lease, Edward Piel, Julian Rivero, Lee Valianos, Ruth Findlay, Jack Smith, Tex Cooper.

Robert Barrat. *Man of Conquest* (US/1939/97m/BW) D: George Nichols, Jr. C: Richard Dix, Edward Ellis, Victor Jory, Ralph Morgan, Robert Armstrong, C. Henry Gordon, George "Gabby" Hayes, Gail Patrick, Joan Fontaine, Max Terhune, Lane Chandler.

Trevor Bardette. *The Man from the Alamo* (US/1953/79m/C) D: Budd Boetticher. C: Glenn Ford, Julia Adams, Chill Wills, Victor Jory, Stuart Randall, Ward Negley, Arthur Space.

Arthur Hunnicutt. *The Last Command* (US/1955/110m/C) D: Frank Lloyd. B/on the story *The Last Command* by Sy Bartlett. C: Sterling Hayden, Richard Carlson, J. Carroll Naish, Otto Kruger, Hugh Sanders, Don Kennedy, Anna Maria

Alberghetti, Ernest Borgnine, Ben Cooper, Virginia Grey, John Russell, Edward Colmans, Jim Davis.

Fess Parker. *Davy Crockett, King of the Wild Frontier* (US/1955/90m/C) D: Norman Foster. C: Buddy Ebsen, Basil Ruysdael, Hans Conried, Kenneth Tobey, Pat Hogan, Helene Stanley, Don Megowan.

Fess Parker. *Davy Crockett and the River Pirates* (US/1956/81m/C) D: Norman Foster. C: Buddy Ebsen, Jeff York, Irvin Ashkenazy, Kenneth Tobey, Clem Bevans, Douglas Dumbrille.

James Griffith. *The First Texan* (US/1956/82m/C) D: Byron Haskin. C: Joel McCrea, Jeff Morrow, Dayton Lummis, William Hopper, David Silva, Carl Benton Reid, Felicia Farr, Wallace Ford, Chubby Johnson, Jody McCrea, Abraham Sofaer.

Fess Parker. *Alias Jesse James* (US/1959/92m/C) D: Norman McLeod. C: Bob Hope, Rhonda Fleming, Wendell Corey, Jim Davis, Hugh O'Brian, James Arness, Gail Davis.

John Wayne. *The Alamo* (US/1960/192m/C) D: John Wayne. C: Richard Widmark, Laurence Harvey, Patrick Wayne, Ruben Padilla, Joseph Calleia, Richard Boone.

137 Cromwell, Oliver (1599–1658)

Commander of the armies that dethroned **Charles I** during the English Civil War, Cromwell ruled England himself as the Lord Protector (1653–58).

George Merritt. *The Vicar of Bray* (GB/1937/66m/BW) D: Henry Edwards. C: Stanley Holloway, Hugh Miller, K. Hamilton Price, Felix Aylmer, Esmond Knight.

Edmund Willard. *The Cardboard Cavalier* (GB/1949/97m/BW) D: Walter Forde. C: Sid Field, Margaret Lockwood, Anthony Hulme, Mary Clare.

John Le Mesurier. *The Moonraker* (GB/1958/82m/C) D: David Macdonald. B/on the play by Arthur Watkyn. C: George Baker, Sylvia Syms, Peter Arne, Gary Raymond.

Patrick Wymark. *The Conqueror Worm* (aka *Witchfinder General*) (GB/1968/87m/C) D: Michael Reeves. B/on the novel *Witchfinder General* by Ronald Bassett. C: Vincent Price, Ian Oglivy, Rupert Davies, Hilary Dwyer, Robert Russell, Wilfrid Brambell.

Richard Harris. *Cromwell* (GB/1970/139m/C) D: Ken Hughes. C: Alec Guinness, Robert Morley, Dorothy Tutin, Frank Finlay, Timothy Dalton, Robin Stewart.

138 Cromwell, Thomas (1485?–1540)

Principal minister to **Henry VIII** and instrumental in the king's marriage to **Anne of Cleves**, Cromwell lost the king's favor and was beheaded.

Franklyn Dyall. *The Private Life of Henry VIII* (GB/1933/97m/BW) D: Alexander Korda. C: Charles Laughton, Robert Donat, Binnie Barnes, Elsa Lanchester, Merle Oberon, Wendy Barrie, Everley Gregg, Miles Mander, Claude Allister, John Loder, Lawrence Hanray.

Leo McKern. *A Man for All Seasons* (GB/1966/120m/C) D: Fred Zinnemann.

B/on the play by Robert Bolt. Best Picture Awards: (AA, NBR, GG, NYC, BFA Any Source and Best British Film), Best Director Awards: (AA, NBR, GG, NYC, DGA). C: Paul Scofield, Wendy Hiller, Robert Shaw, Orson Welles, Susannah York, Nigel Davenport, Vanessa Redgrave, Cyril Luckham.

John Colicos. *Anne of the Thousand Days* (GB/1969/145m/C) D: Charles Jarrott. B/on the play by Maxwell Anderson. C: Richard Burton, Genevieve Bujold, Irene Papas, Anthony Quayle, Michael Hordern, Katharine Blake, William Squire, Lesley Patterson, Nicola Pagett.

Kenneth Williams. *Carry on Henry VIII* (GB/1970/89m/C) D: Gerald Thomas. C: Sidney James, Joan Sims, Charles Hawtrey, Terry Scott, Peter Gilmore, Monica Dietrich, Patsy Rowlands.

Donald Pleasance. *The Six Wives of Henry VIII* (aka *Henry VIII and His Six Wives*) (GB/1972/125m/C) D: Waris Hussein. C: Keith Michell, Frances Cuka, Charlotte Rampling, Jane Asher, Jenny Bos, Lynne Frederick, Barbara Leigh-Hunt, Simon Henderson, Annette Crosbie, John Bryans, Michael Goodliffe, Bernard Hepton, Dorothy Tutin.

139 Curie, Madame (1867–1934)

(Marie Sklodowska Curie) Continuing the work of her husband Pierre (1859–1906), Marie Curie was famous for her studies in radioactivity. She died of pernicious anemia caused by overexposure to radiation.

Greer Garson. *Madame Curie* (US/1943/124m/BW) D: Mervyn LeRoy. B/on the book by Eve Curie. C: Walter Pidgeon, Robert Walker, Wyndham Standing.

Ruth Maleczech. *Dead End Kids* (aka *Dead End Kids: A Story of Nuclear Power*) (US/1986/90m/C) D: JoAnne Akalaitis. B/on the play by Mabou Mines. C: Ellen McElduff, George Bartenieff, David Brisbin, John Schofield, Terry O'Reilly.

Odile Le Clezio. *Young Einstein* (Australia/1988/91m/C) D: Yahoo Serious. C: Yahoo Serious, Pee Wee Wilson, Basil Clarke, Tim McKew, Ian James Tait, Nick Conroy.

Curry, Kid *see* Logan, Harvey

140 Custer, George Armstrong (1839–1876)

Controversial U.S. Army officer (who was once court-martialed and suspended from duty for harsh treatment of his troops), Custer's 7th Cavalry was destroyed at the Battle of the Little Big Horn. Henry Fonda's role as Lt. Col. Thursday in *Fort Apache* (48) is based on Custer. (See **Crazy Horse** and **Sitting Bull**)

Clay Clement. *The World Changes* (US/1933/90m/BW) D: Mervyn LeRoy. B/on the story *America Kneels* by Sheridan Gibney. C: Paul Muni, Aline MacMahon, Mary Astor, Donald Cook, Patricia Ellis, Douglas Dumbrille, Jean Muir, Alan Mowbray.

John Miljan. *The Plainsman* (US/1936/115m/BW) D: Cecil B. DeMille. B/on the novel *Wild Bill Hickok* by Frank J. Wilstach. C: Gary Cooper, Jean Arthur, James Ellison, Porter Hall, Frank McGlynn, Edwin Maxwell, Leila McIntyre, Charles H. Herzinger.

Paul Kelly. *Wyoming* (aka *Bad Man of Wyoming*) (US/1940/89m/BW) D: Richard Thorpe. C: Wallace Beery, Leo Carillo, Ann Rutherford, Lee Bowman, Joseph Calleia, Bobby Watson, William Tannen, Chill Wills, Addison Richards, Chief Thundercloud, Glenn Strange.

Ronald Reagan. *Santa Fe Trail* (US/1940/110m/BW) D: Michael Curtiz. C: Errol Flynn, Olivia de Havilland, Raymond Massey, Alan Hale, Guinn Williams, Van Heflin, Moroni Olsen, Charles Middleton, Erville Alderson, David Bruce, Frank Wilcox.

Addison Richards. *Badlands of Dakota* (US/1941/74m/BW) D: Alfred E. Green. C: Robert Stack, Richard Dix, Ann Rutherford, Frances Farmer, Andy Devine, Lon Chaney, Jr.

Errol Flynn. *They Died With Their Boots On* (US/1941/140m/BW) D: Raoul Walsh. C: Olivia de Havilland, Arthur Kennedy, Charles Grapewin, Gene Lockhart, Anthony Quinn, John Litel, Stanley Ridges, Sydney Greenstreet, Regis Toomey, Hattie McDaniel, Joseph Crehan.

James Millican. *Warpath* (US/1951/95m/C) D: Byron Haskin. C: Edmond O'Brien, Dean Jagger, Charles Stevens, Forrest Tucker, Harry Carey, Jr., Polly Bergen, Paul Fix.

Sheb Wooley. *Bugles in the Afternoon* (US/1952/85m/C) D: Roy Rowland. B/on the novel by Ernest Haycox. C: Ray Milland, Helena Carter, Hugh Marlowe, Forrest Tucker.

Douglas Kennedy. *Sitting Bull* (US/1954/105m/C) D: Sidney Salkow. C: J. Carrol Naish, Dale Robertson, Mary Murphy, Iron Eyes Cody, John Litel, John Hamilton.

Britt Lomond. *Tonka* (aka *A Horse Named Comanche*) (US/1958/97m/C) D: Lewis R. Foster. B/on the novel *Comanche* by David Appel. C: Sal Mineo, Philip Carey, Jerome Courtland, Rafael Campos, John War Eagle, Herbert Rudley.

Philip Carey. *The Great Sioux Massacre* (aka *Custer Massacre*) (aka *The Massacre at the Rosebud*) (US/1965/92m/C) D: Sidney Salkow. C: Joseph Cotten, Darren McGavin, Julie Sommars, Nancy Kovack, Michael Pate, Don Haggerty, Iron Eyes Cody.

Leslie Nielsen. *The Plainsman* (US/1966/92m/C) D: David Lowell Rich. C: Don Murray, Guy Stockwell, Abby Dalton, Brad Dillman, Simon Oakland, Emily Banks.

Robert Shaw. *Custer of the West* (US-Spain/1967/143m/C) D: Robert Siodmark & Irving Lern. C: Mary Ure, Jeffrey Hunter, Ty Hardin, Charles Stalnaker, Robert Hall, Lawrence Tierney, Kieron Moore, Robert Ryan, Marc Lawrence.

Richard Mulligan. *Little Big Man* (US/1970/147m/C) D: Arthur Penn. B/on the novel by Thomas Berger. C: Dustin Hoffman, Faye Dunaway, Martin Balsam, Jeff Corey.

Marcello Mastroianni. *Do Not Touch the White Woman* (aka *Touche Pas La Femme Blanche*) (aka *Don't Touch White Women!*) (France/1974/108m/C) D: Marco Ferreri. C: Catherine Deneuve, Michel Piccoli, Philippe Noiret, Ugo Tognazzi, Alain Cuny.

Lincoln Tate. *The Legend of the Lone Ranger* (US/1981/98m/C) D: William A. Fraker. C: Klinton Spilsbury, Michael Horse, Jason Robards, Ted Flicker, Richard Farnsworth.

141 Dalai Lama, The 14th (1935–   )

(Birth name, Lhamo Donhup; name given upon becoming the Dalai Lama, Getsul Ngawang Lobsang Tenzin Gyatso Sisunwangyal Tsungpa Mapai Dephal Sangpo) The Dalai Lama is the spiritual and political leader of Tibet and has been living in exile in India since the 1959 Chinese invasion. In 1989 he was awarded the Nobel Peace Prize. *Seven Years in Tibet* was based on the book by Heinrich Harrer; in the film, Harrer was portrayed by Brad Pitt.

Jamyand JamshoWangchuck (Age 14). Ama Ashe Dongste (Age 8). Soman Wangchuck (Age 4). *Seven Years in Tibet* (US/1997/136m/C) D: Jean-Jacques Annaud. B/on the book by Heinrich Harrer. C: Brad Pitt, David Thewlis, B.D.Wong, Mako, Danny Denzongpa, Victor Wong.

Tenzin Thuthob Tsarong (Adult). Gyurme Tethong (Age 12). Tulku Jamyaang Kunga Tenzin (Age 5). Tenzin Yeshi Paichang (Age 2). *Kundun* (US/1997/134m/C) D: Martin Scorsese. C: Tencho Gyalpe, Tenzin Topjar, Tsewang Migyur Khangsar, Tenzin Lhamo, Geshi Yeshi Gyatso, Soman Phuntsok, Gytaso Lukhand.

The Dalton Brothers

One-time lawmen in Arkansas, the Dalton boys switched sides and gained infamy robbing banks and trains until their ill-fated attempt to rob two banks at the same time in Coffeyville, Kansas. Bob and Grat were killed in the robbery attempt and Emmett was captured and sent to prison. Bill, who wasn't riding with them that day, later joined the **Bill Doolin** gang and was eventually gunned down by lawmen as well.

142 Dalton, Bill (William [aka Ben] Dalton) (1873–1893)

Stuart Erwin. *When the Daltons Rode* (US/1940/80m/BW) D: George Marshall. B/on the book by Emmett Dalton & Jack Jungmeyer. C: Randolph Scott, Kay Francis, Brian Donlevy, Broderick Crawford, Frank Albertson, George Bancroft, Andy Devine, Sally Payne.

Noah Beery, Jr. *The Daltons Ride Again* (US/1945/72m/BW) D: Ray Taylor. C: Alan Curtis, Kent Taylor, Lon Chaney, Jr., Martha O'Driscoll, Jess Barker, Milburn Stone, Douglas Dumbrille.

William Moss. *Badman's Territory* (US/1946/98m/BW) D: Tim Whelan. C: Randolph Scott, Ann Richards, George "Gabby" Hayes, Chief Thundercloud, Lawrence Tierney, Tom Tyler, Steve Brodie, Phil Warren, Nestor Paiva, Isabell Jewell, Emory Parnell.

William Reynolds. *The Cimarron Kid* (US/1951/84m/C) D: Budd Boetticher. C: Audie Murphy, Yvette Dugay, Beverly Tyler, Leif Erickson, Noah Beery, Palmer Lee, Rand Brooks.

Holly Bane. *Montana Belle* (US/1952/81m/BW) D: Allan Dwan. C: Jane Russell, George Brent, Scott Brady, Forrest Tucker, Andy Devine, Ray Teal, Rory Mallinson.

Bill Phipps. *Jesse James versus the Daltons* (US/1954/65m/C) D: William Castle.

Despite the title, Jesse James is not depicted in the film. C: Brett King, Barbara Lawrence, James Griffith, John Cliff, Rory Mallinson, William Tannen.

Scott Glenn. *Cattle Annie and Little Britches* (US/1980/97m/C) D: Lamont Johnson. B/on the novel by Robert Ward. C: Burt Lancaster, Rod Steiger, John Savage, Diane Lane, Amanda Plummer.

143 Dalton, Bob (Robert Dalton) (1867–1892)

Broderick Crawford. *When the Daltons Rode* (US/1940/80m/BW) D: George Marshall. B/on the book by Emmett Dalton & Jack Jungmeyer. C: Randolph Scott, Kay Francis, Brian Donlevy, Stuart Erwin, Frank Albertson, George Bancroft, Andy Devine, Sally Payne.

Kent Taylor. *The Daltons Ride Again* (US/1945/72m/BW) D: Ray Taylor. C: Alan Curtis, Lon Chaney, Jr., Noah Beery, Jr., Martha O'Driscoll, Jess Barker, Milburn Stone, Douglas Dumbrille.

Steve Brodie. *Badman's Territory* (US/1946/98m/BW) D: Tim Whelan. C: Randolph Scott, Ann Richards, George "Gabby" Hayes, Chief Thundercloud, Lawrence Tierney, Tom Tyler, Phil Warren, William Moss, Nestor Paiva, Isabell Jewell, Emory Parnell.

Walter Reed. *Return of the Bad Men* (US/1948/90m/BW) D: Ray Enright. C: Randolh Scott, George "Gabby" Hayes, Robert Ryan, Anne Jeffreys, Steve Brodie, Richard Powers, Robert Bray, Lex Barker, Michael Harvey, Dean White, Robert Armstrong.

Noah Beery, Jr. *The Cimarron Kid* (US/1951/84m/C) D: Budd Boetticher. C: Audie Murphy, Yvette Dugay, Beverly Tyler, Leif Erickson, Palmer Lee, Rand Brooks, William Reynolds.

Scott Brady. *Montana Belle* (US/1952/81m/BW) D: Allan Dwan. C: Jane Russell, George Brent, Forrest Tucker, Andy Devine, Ray Teal, Rory Mallinson, Holly Bane.

James Griffith. *Jesse James versus the Daltons* (US/1954/65m/C) D: William Castle. Despite the title, Jesse James is not depicted in the film. C: Brett King, Barbara Lawrence, Bill Phipps, John Cliff, Rory Mallinson, William Tannen.

Joe Bolton. *The Outlaws Is Coming* (US/1965/88m/BW) D: Norman Maurer. C: Larry Fine, Moe Howard, Joe De Rita, Nancy Kovack, Murray Alper, Bill Camfield, Hal Fryar, Johnny Ginger, Wayne Mack, Ed McDonnell, Bruce Sedley, Paul Shannon, Sally Starr.

144 Dalton, Emmett (1871–1937)

Frank Albertson. *When the Daltons Rode* (US/1940/80m/BW) D: George Marshall. B/on the book by Emmett Dalton & Jack Jungmeyer. C: Randolph Scott, Kay Francis, Brian Donlevy, Broderick Crawford, Stuart Erwin, George Bancroft, Andy Devine, Sally Payne.

Alan Curtis. *The Daltons Ride Again* (US/1945/72m/BW) D: Ray Taylor. C: Kent Taylor, Lon Chaney, Jr., Noah Beery, Jr., Martha O'Driscoll, Jess Barker, Milburn Stone, Douglas Dumbrille.

Lex Barker. *Return of the Bad Men* (US/1948/90m/BW) D: Ray Enright. C: Randolh Scott, George "Gabby" Hayes, Robert Ryan, Anne Jeffreys, Steve Brodie,

Richard Powers, Robert Bray, Walter Reed, Michael Harvey, Dean White, Robert Armstrong.

Rand Brooks. *The Cimarron Kid* (US/1951/84m/C) D: Budd Boetticher. C: Audie Murphy, Yvette Dugay, Beverly Tyler, Leif Erickson, Noah Beery, Palmer Lee, William Reynolds.

Ray Teal. *Montana Belle* (US/1952/81m/BW) D: Allan Dwan. C: Jane Russell, George Brent, Scott Brady, Forrest Tucker, Andy Devine, Rory Mallinson, Holly Bane.

William Tannen. *Jesse James versus the Daltons* (US/1954/65m/C) D: William Castle. Despite the title, Jesse James is not depicted in the film. C: Brett King, Barbara Lawrence, James Griffith, Bill Phipps, John Cliff, Rory Mallinson.

Touch (Michael) Connors. *The Dalton That Got Away* (US-Mexico/1960/69m/C) D: Jaime Salvador. C: Elsie Cardenas, Carlos Rivas, Felix Moreno, Zachary Milton.

145 Dalton, Grat (Grattan Dalton) (1862–1892)

Brian Donlevy. *When the Daltons Rode* (US/1940/80m/BW) D: George Marshall. B/on the book by Emmett Dalton & Jack Jungmeyer. C: Randolph Scott, Kay Francis, Broderick Crawford, Stuart Erwin, Frank Albertson, George Bancroft, Andy Devine, Sally Payne.

Lon Chaney, Jr. *The Daltons Ride Again* (US/1945/72m/BW) D: Ray Taylor. C: Alan Curtis, Kent Taylor, Noah Beery, Jr., Martha O'Driscoll, Jess Barker, Milburn Stone, Douglas Dumbrille.

Phil Warren. *Badman's Territory* (US/1946/98m/BW) D: Tim Whelan. C: Randolph Scott, Ann Richards, George "Gabby" Hayes, Chief Thundercloud, Lawrence Tierney, Tom Tyler, Steve Brodie, William Moss, Nestor Paiva, Isabell Jewell, Emory Parnell.

Michael Harvey. *Return of the Bad Men* (US/1948/90m/BW) D: Ray Enright. C: Randolh Scott, George "Gabby" Hayes, Robert Ryan, Anne Jeffreys, Steve Brodie, Richard Powers, Robert Bray, Lex Barker, Walter Reed, Dean White, Robert Armstrong.

Palmer Lee. *The Cimarron Kid* (US/1951/84m/C) D: Budd Boetticher. C: Audie Murphy, Yvette Dugay, Beverly Tyler, Leif Erickson, Noah Beery, Rand Brooks, William Reynolds.

Rory Mallinson. *Montana Belle* (US/1952/81m/BW) D: Allan Dwan. C: Jane Russell, George Brent, Scott Brady, Forrest Tucker, Andy Devine, Ray Teal, Holly Bane.

John Cliff. *Jesse James versus the Daltons* (US/1954/65m/C) D: William Castle. Despite the title, Jesse James is not depicted in the film. C: Brett King, Barbara Lawrence, James Griffith, Bill Phipps, Rory Mallinson, William Tannen.

146 Danton, Georges Jacques (1759–1794)

French Revolutionary leader, Danton's opposition to **Robespierre** led to his own denouncement and death at the guillotine.

Richard Cramer. *Captain of the Guard* (US/1930/85m/BW) D: John S. Robertson. C: John Boles, Laura La Plante, Sam De Grasse, George Hackathorne, Evelyn Hall, Stuart Holmes.

Fritz Kortner. *Danton* (Germany/1931/94m/BW) D: Hans Behrendt. B/on the book by Hans Rehfisch. C: Gustaf Gründgens, Lucie Mannheim, Alexander Granach, Ernst Stahl-Nachbaur, Walter Werner, Gustav von Wangenheim.

Alexandre Koubitsky. *Napoleon Bonaparte* (France/1934/140m/BW) D: Abel Gance. Three-dimensional sound version of Gance's 1927 epic *Napoléon*. C: Albert Dieudonné, Edmond von Daele, Antonin Artaud, Boudreau, Alberty, Jack Rye, Favière, Gina Manès, Suzanne Blanchetti, Marguerite Gance, Simone Genevois, Genica Missirio.

Wade Crosby. *Marie Antoinette* (US/1938/160m/BW) D: W.S. Van Dyke II. B/on the book by Stefan Zweig. C: Norma Shearer, Tyrone Power, John Barrymore, Gladys George, Robert Morley, Anita Louise, Joseph Schildkraut, Albert Dekker, Scotty Becket, Alma Kruger, George Meeker, Anthony Warde, Walter Walker, John Burton.

Wade Crosby. *The Black Book* (aka *Reign of Terror*) (US/1949/89m/BW) D: Anthony Mann. C: Robert Cummings, Arlene Dahl, Richard Hart, Arnold Moss, Richard Basehart, Jess Barker, Wilton Graff, Norman Lloyd, John Doucette.

William Sabatier. *Valmy* (France/1967/C) D: Abel Gance. C: Jacques Castelot, Bernard Dhéran, Marc Eyraud, Serge Gainsbourg.

Gerard Depardieu. *Danton* (France-Poland/1982/136m/C) D: Andrzej Wajda. B/on the play *The Danton Affair* by Stanislawa Przybyszewska. C: Wojciech Pszoniak, Patrice Chereau, Angela Winkler, Boguslaw Linda, Roland Blanche.

Oliver de Kersauzon. *Liberty, Equality and Sauerkraut* (aka *Liberte, Egalite, Choucroute*) (France/1985/C) D: Jean Yanne. C: Ursula Andress, Roland Giraud.

147 Darnley, Henry Stewart, Lord (1545–1567)

The second husband of **Mary**, **Queen of Scots** and the father of **James I**, Darnley was murdered in a plot devised by her third husband, **Lord Bothwell**.

Douglas Walton. *Mary of Scotland* (US/1936/123m/BW) D: John Ford. B/on the play by Maxwell Anderson. C: Katharine Hepburn, Fredric March, Florence Eldridge, John Carradine, Robert Barrat, Gavin Muir, Ian Keith, Ralph Forbes, Alan Mowbray, Walter Byron.

Derrick De Marney. *The Pearls of the Crown* (France/1937/120–100m/BW) D: Sacha Guitry & Christian-Jaque. C: Sacha Guitry, Jacqueline Delubac, Lyn Harding, Ermete Zacconi, Marguerite Moreno, Yvette Plenne, Catalano, Arletty, Percy Marmont, Barbara Shaw, Simone Renant, Jean Louis Barrault, Emile Drain, Enrico Glori, Renee Saint-Cyr, Pizani, Claude Dauphin, Aime-Simon Gerard.

Timothy Dalton. *Mary, Queen of Scots* (GB/1971/128m/C) D: Charles Jarrot. C: Vanessa Redgrave, Glenda Jackson, Patrick McGoohan, Nigel Davenport, Trevor Howard, Daniel Massey, Ian Holm, Andrew Keir, Katherine Kath, Robert James, Richard Denning, Rick Warner.

148 Darrow, Clarence Seward (1857–1938)

Renowned American defense lawyer, Darrow's most famous case was the 1925 Scopes Trial in which he argued that **Darwin**'s theories of evolution should be allowed to be taught in public schools. His adversary in that case was **William Jennings Bryan**. TV portrayals have been by Kirk Douglas in *Inherit the Wind* (88), and Jack Lemmon (as Henry Drummond) in *Inherit the Wind* (99).

Orson Welles (as Jonathan Wilk). *Compulsion* (US/1959/103m/BW) D: Richard Fleischer. B/on the novel by Meyer Levin. C: Diane Varsi, Dean Stockwell, Bradford Dillman, E.G. Marshall.

Spencer Tracy (as Matthew Drummond). *Inherit the Wind* (US/1960/127m/ BW) D: Stanley Kramer. B/on the play by Jerome Lawrence & Robert E. Lee. C: Fredric March, Gene Kelly, Florence Eldridge, Dick York, Donna Anderson, Harry Morgan, Claude Akins.

Robert Read. *Swoon* (US/1992/90m/C) D: Tom Kalin. C: Daniel Schlachet, Craig Chester, Paul Connor, Ron Vawter, Michael Kirby, Michael Stumm, Valda Drabla.

149 Darwin, Charles Robert (1809–1882)

English naturalist; Darwin's work firmly established the theory of evolution.

Nicholas Clay. *The Darwin Adventure* (GB/1972/91m/C) D: Jack Couffer. C: Susan Macready, Ian Richardson, Robert Flemyng, Aubrey Woods.

Basil Clarke. *Young Einstein* (Australia/1988/91m/C) D: Yahoo Serious. C: Yahoo Serious, Odile Le Clezio, Pee Wee Wilson, Tim McKew, Ian James Tait, Nick Conroy.

150 David (1012?–972? BC)

Warrior king of ancient Israel whose story is told in the books of Samuel, Kings and Chroncles of the Old Testament.

Gregory Peck. *David and Bathsheba* (US/1951/116m/C) D: Henry King. B/on *The Second Book of Samuel*. C: Susan Hayward, Raymond Massey, Francis X. Bushman.

Finlay Currie. *Solomon and Sheba* (US/1959/139–120m/C) D: King Vidor. C: Yul Brynner, Gina Lollobrigida, George Sanders, David Farrar, Marisa Pavan, John Crawford.

Jeff Chandler. *A Story of David* (GB/1960/104m/C) D: Bob McNaught. C: Basil Sydney, Peter Arne, David Knight, Barbara Shelley, Donald Pleasence, Robert Brown.

Ivo Payer. *David and Goliath* (Italy/1961/95m/C) D: Richard Pottier & Ferdinando Baldi. C: Orson Welles, Edward Hilton, Eleonora Rossi-Drago, Kronos, Massimo Serato.

Gianni Garko. *Saul and David* (Italy-Spain/1965/105m/C) D: Marcello Baldi. C: Norman Wooland, Elisa Cegani, Stefy Lang, Luz Marquez.

Richard Gere. *King David* (US/1985/114m/C) D: Bruce Beresford. C: Alice Krige, Edward Woodward, Denis Quiley, Cherie Lunghi, Hurd Hatfield, Jason Carter.

151 Davies, Marion (1897–1961)

Hollywood actress who is now more remembered for her affair with **William Randolph Hearst** than her films. Davies made her screen debut in *Runaway Romany*

(1917) and her last picture was *Ever since Eve* (37). Hearst took control of her career and lost millions of dollars on lavish productions starring Davies in unsuitable roles. In the TV film *The Hearst and Davies Affair* (85) she was portrayed by Virginia Madsen, and in *RKO 281* (99) she was portrayed by Melanie Griffith.

Dorothy Comingore (as Susan Alexander). *Citizen Kane* (US/1941/119m/BW) D: Orson Welles. AA Best Screenplay, Orson Welles and Herman Mankiewicz. NYF: Best Picture. C: Orson Welles, Joseph Cotton, Everett Sloan, Agnes Moorehead, Ray Collins, George Coulouris, Ruth Warrick, William Alland, Paul Stewart, Erskine Sanford.

Gretchen Moll. *Cradle Will Rock* (US/1999/109m/C) D: Tim Robbins. C: Hank Azaria, Rubén Blades, Joan Cusack, John Cusack, Cary Elwes, Philip Baker Hall, Cherry Jones, Angus MacFadyen, Bill Murray, Vanessa Redgrave, Susan Sarandon, John Turturro, Barnard Hughes, John Carpenter, Corina Katt.

Kirsten Dunst. *The Cat's Meow* (Canada-Germany-GB/2001/110m/BW/C) D: Peter Bogdanovich. C: Cary Elwes, Edward Herrmann, Eddie Izzard, Joanna Lumley, Victor Slezak, Jennifer Tilly, James Laurenson, Ronan Vibert, Chiara Schoras, Ingrid Lacey, John C. Vennema, Claudia Harrison, Claudie Blakley.

Da Vinci, Leonardo *see* Leonardo da Vinci

152 Davis, Jefferson (1808–1889)

President of the Confederate States of America during the American Civil War (1861–1865).

Roy Watson. *Carolina* (aka *House of Connelly*) (US/1934/83m/BW) D: Henry King. B/on the play *House of Connelly* by Paul Green. C: Janet Gaynor, Lionel Barrymore, Robert Young, Richard Cromwell, John Elliott, Stepin Fetchit.

Erville Alderson. *Hearts in Bondage* US/1936/72m/BW) D: Lew Ayres. C: James Dunn, Mae Clark, Charlotte Henry, David Manners, Frank McGlynn, Douglas Wood.

Erville Alderson. *Santa Fe Trail* (US/1940/110m/BW) D: Michael Curtiz. C: Errol Flynn, Ronald Reagan, Olivia de Havilland, Raymond Massey, Alan Hale, Guinn Williams, Van Heflin, Moroni Olsen, Charles Middleton, David Bruce, Frank Wilcox.

Charles Middleton. *Virginia City* (US/1940/121m/BW) D: Michael Curtiz. C: Errol Flynn, Miriam Hopkins, Randolph Scott, Humphrey Bogart, Thurston Hall, Victor Kilian.

Morris Ankrum. *Tennessee Johnson* (aka *The Man on America's Conscience*) (US/1942/103m/BW) D: William Dieterle. C: Van Heflin, Ruth Hussey, Lionel Barrymore, Marjorie Main, Regis Toomey, Montagu Love, Porter Hall, Harry Worth, Ed O'Neill, Harrison Greene, Charles Dingle, Grant Withers, Lynne Carver, Noah Beery, Sr.

153 De Sylva, George Gard "Buddy" (1896–1950)

Lyricist and film producer whose songwriting career, along with partners Lew Brown (played by Ernest Borgnine) and Ray Henderson (played by Dan Dailey), was depicted in *The Best Things in Life Are Free*.

Eddie Marr. *Rhapsody in Blue* (US/1945/139m/BW) D: Irving Rapper. C: Robert Alda, Joan Leslie, Alexis Smith, Charles Coburn, Julie Bishop, Oscar Levant, Herbert Rudley.

Gordon MacRae. *The Best Things in Life Are Free* (US/1956/104m/C) D: Michael Curtiz. C: Dan Dailey, Ernest Borgnine, Norman Brooks, Sheree North, Larry Keating, Tommy Noonan.

154 Diaghilev, Sergei Pavlovich (1872–1929)

Russian impresario and founder of the Ballet Russes, Diaghilev worked with such artists as **Chaliapin, Pavlova, Nijinsky** and **Picasso.**

Alan Bates. *Nijinsky* (GB/1980/129m/C) D: Herbert Ross. B/on The Diary of Vaslav Nijinsky and *Nijinsky* by Romola Nijinsky. C: George De La Pena, Leslie Browne, Alan Badel, Colin Blakely, Ronald Pickup, Jeremy Irons, Janet Suzman.

Vsevolod Larianov. *Pavlova* (aka *Pavlova — A Woman for All Time*) (GB-USSR/1984/133m/C) D: Emil Lotianou. C: Galina Beliaeva, James Fox, Serge Shakourov, Michael Kradunin, Martin Scorsese, Bruce Forsyth, Roy Kinnear, Lina Boultakova.

155 Diamond, John Thomas "Legs" (1896–1931)

Ambitious New York gangster of the 1920s, he was called "Legs" for his talent at running from the police, not for dancing as has been reported. In the 1993 video release *The Outfit* he was played by Josh Mosby.

Ray Danton. *The Rise and Fall of Legs Diamond* (US/1960/101m/BW) D: Budd Boetticher. C: Karen Steele, Elaine Stewart, Jesse White, Robert Lowery, Richard Gardner, Sid Melton.

Ray Danton. *Portrait of a Mobster* (US/1961/108m/BW) D: Joseph Pevney. B/on the book by Harry Grey. C: Vic Morrow, Leslie Parrish, Peter Breck, Evan McCord.

Will Kempe. *Hit the Dutchman* (US-Russia/1993/116m/C) D: Menahem Golan. C: Bruce Nozick, Christopher Bradley, Eddie Bowz, Sally Kirkland, Jeff Griggs, Jennifer Miller, Jack Conley, Matt Servitto, Menahem Golan.

Will Kempe. *Mad Dog Coll* (aka *Killer Instinct*) (US-Russia/1993/101m/C) D: Greydon Clark & Ken Stein. C: Christopher Bradley, Bruce Nozick, Rachel York, Jeff Griggs, Thomas McHugh, Eddie Bowz, Jack Conley, Matt Servitto, Dennis Predovic.

156 Diane de Poitiers (1499–1566)

Mistress of **Henri II**, Diane remained friendly with his wife, **Catherine de Medici,** while retaining more influence over the French king.

Lana Turner. *Diane* (US/1955/110m/C) D: David Miller. B/on the novel *Diane de Poitier* by John Erskine. C: Pedro Armendariz, Roger Moore, Marisa Pavan, Cedric Hardwicke, Ronald Green, Torin Thatcher, Henry Daniell, Basil Ruysdael.

Annie Ducaux. *La Princesse de Cléves* (France/1961/115m/C) D: Jean Delannoy.

As the dumb waiter rises, Legs Diamond (Ray Danton, left) has a surprise. *The Rise and Fall of Legs Diamond* (1960). (Museum of Modern Art Film Stills Archive)

B/on the novel by Madame de La Fayette. C: Jean Marais, Lea Padovani, Raymond Gerome.

Diana Quick. *Nostradamus* (GB-Germany/1994/118m/C) D: Roger Christian. C: Tcheky Karyo, Amanda Plummer, F. Murray Abraham, Rutger Hauer, Anthony Higgins.

157 Diaz, Porfirio (1830–1915)

Mexican soldier and dictator, Diaz ruled Mexico for more than 30 years until his overthrow by **Francisco Madero**.

John Garfield. *Juarez* (US/1939/132m/BW) D: William Dieterle. B/on the novel *The Phantom Crown* by Bertita Harding and the play *Juarez and Maximillian* by Franz Werfel. C: Paul Muni, Bette Davis, Brian Aherne, Claude Rains, Donald Crisp, Walter Kingsford, Harry Davenport, Gale Sondergaard, Joseph Calleia.

Earl Gunn. *The Mad Empress* (aka *Juarez and Maximillian*) (Mexico-US /1939 /72m/BW) D: Miguel Contreras Torres. C: Medea Novara, Lionel Atwill, Conrad Nagel, Guy Bates Post, Evelyn Brent, Jason Robards, Sr., Frank McGlynn, Duncan Renaldo.

Fay Roope. *Viva Zapata!* (US/1952/113m/BW) D: Elia Kazan. B/on the book

Zapata the Unconquerable by Edgcumb Pinchon. C: Marlon Brando, Anthony Quinn, Jean Peters, Alan Reed, Harold Gordon, Margo, Frank Silvera, Frank De Kova, Joseph Wiseman, Lou Gilbert.

Carlos Rivas. *The Undefeated* (US/1969/119m/C) D: Andrew McLaglen. C: John Wayne, Rock Hudson, Tony Aguilar, Roman Gabriel, Bruce Cabot, Lee Meriwether.

158 Dickens, Charles John Huffam (1812–1870)

English novelist famous for creating such classics as *Oliver Twist, A Tale of Two Cities,* and *David Copperfield.*

Morton Lowry. *The Loves of Edgar Allan Poe* (US/1942/67m/BW) D: Harry Lachman. C: Linda Darnell, John Sheppard, Virginia Gilmore, Jane Darwell, Mary Howard, Gilbert Emery.

Reginald Sheffield. *Devotion* (US/1946/108m/BW) D: Curtis Bernhardt. C: Ida Lupino, Olivia de Havilland, Nancy Coleman, Paul Henried, Sydney Greenstreet, Arthur Kennedy, Dame May Whitty, Montagu Love, Brandon Hurst, Victor Francen.

Edward Sullivan. *Mr. H.C. Andersen* (GB/1950/62m/BW) D: Ronald Haines. B/on the book *The True Story of My Life* by Hans Christian Anderson. C: Asley Glynne, Constance Lewis, Terence Noble, Stuart Sanders, June Elvin, Victor Rietty.

Arnold Diamond. *The Best House in London* (GB/1969/97m/C) D: Philip Savile. C: David Hemmings, Joanna Pettet, John DeMarco, Neal Arden, George Reynolds, Suzanne Hunt.

159 Dietrich, Marlene (1901–1992)

(Maria Magdalena Dietrich von Losch) The epitome of the sultry, sensual Hollywood star, Dietrich's films include *The Blue Angel* (30), *The Devil Is a Woman* (35), and *Witness For the Prosecution* (57). She was the subject of Maximilian Schell's 1984 documentary *Marlene,* for which she provided narration, though she refused to appear on screen.

Margit Carstensen. *Adolf and Marlene* (Germany/1976/92m/C) D: Ulli Lommel. C: Kurt Raab, Ila von Hasperg, Harry Baer, Ulli Lommel, Andrea Schober.

Ksenia Prohaska. *Bugsy* (US/1991/135m/C) D: Barry Levinson. B/on the book *We Only Kill Each Other: The Life and Bad Times of Bugsy Siegel* by Dean Jennings. C: Warren Beatty, Annette Bening, Harvey Keitel, Ben Kingsley, Joe Mantegna, Elliott Gould, Wendy Phillips, Bill Graham, Don Carrara, Carmine Caridi.

Katja Flint. *Marlene* (Germany-Italy/2000/125m/C) D: Joseph Vilsmaier. C: Herbert Knaup, Heino Ferch, Hans Werner Meyer, Christiane Paul, Suzanne von Borsody, Armin Rohde, Josefina Vilsmaier, Theresa Vilsmaier, Janina Vilsmaier, Monika Bleibtreu, Cosma Shiva Hagen, Katharina Müller-Elmau, Oliver Elias, Sandy Martin.

160 Dillinger, John Herbert (1903?–1934)

Notorious Depression era bank robber, Dillinger was reportedly gunned down in front of a Chicago theatre by Federal agents, although some insist that they shot the wrong man and that Dillinger was never there at all.

Lawrence Tierney. *Dillinger* (US/1945/70m/BW) D: Max Nosseck. C: Anne Jeffreys, Edmund Lowe, Eduardo Cianelli, Marc Lawrence, Elisha Cook, Jr., Lee White.

Myron Healey. *Guns Don't Argue* (US/1955/92m/BW) D: Bill Karn & Richard Kahn. Feature film edited from the TV series *Gangbusters*. C: Lyle Talbot, Jean Harvey, Paul Dubov, Sam Edwards, Richard Crane, Tamar Cooper, Baynes Barron, Doug Wilson.

Leo Gordon. *Baby Face Nelson* (US/1957/85m/BW) D: Don Siegel. C: Mickey Rooney, Carolyn Jones, Cedric Hardwicke, Elisha Cook, Jr., Ted De Corsia, Dan Terranova, Jack Elam.

Scott Peters. *The FBI Story* (US/1959/149m/C) D: Mervyn LeRoy. B/on the book by Don Whitehead. C: James Stewart, Vera Miles, Murray Hamilton, Larry Pennell, Nick Adams, William Phipps, Jean Willes, Diane Jergens.

Eric Sinclair. *Ma Barker's Killer Brood* (US/1960/82m/BW) D: Bill Karn. C: Lurene Tuttle, Tris Coffin, Paul Dubov, Robert Kendall, Vic Lundin, Don Grady, Ronald Foster.

Nick Adams. *Young Dillinger* (US/1965/102m/BW) D: Terry Morse. C: Robert Conrad, John Ashley, Dan Terranova, Mary Ann Mobley, Victor Buono, John Hoyt, Reed Hadley.

Warren Oates. *Dillinger* (US/1973/107m/C) D: John Milius. C: Michelle Phillips, Ben Johnson, Harry Dean Stanton, Geoffrey Lewis, Richard Dreyfuss, Steve Kanaly.

Robert Conrad. *The Lady in Red* (aka *Guns, Sin and Bathtub Gin*) (US/1979/93m/C) D: Lewis Teague. C: Pamela Sue Martin, Louise Fletcher, Robert Hogan, Laurie Heineman, Phillip R. Allen, Robert Forster, Alan Vint.

Martin Sheen. *Dillinger and Capone* (US/1995/95m/C) D: Jon Purdy. C: F. Murray Abraham, Stephen Davies, Catherine Hicks, Don Stroud, Christopher Kriesa, Debi A. Monahan.

161 Disraeli, Benjamin, 1st Earl of Beaconsfield (1804–1881)

English author and politician, Disraeli served as Prime Minister twice, in 1868, and 1874–1880.

George Arliss * Best Actor (AA). *Disraeli* (US/1929/90m/BW) D: Alfred E. Green. B/on the play by Louis N. Parker. C: Joan Bennett, Florence Arliss, Margaret Mann, Anthony Bushell.

Derrick De Marney (the Younger Disraeli). Hugh Miller (the Older Disraeli). *Victoria the Great* (GB/1937/110m/C) D: Herbert Wilcox. B/on the play *Victoria Regina* by Laurence Housman. C: Anna Neagle, Anton Walbrook, H.B. Warner, James Dale, Charles Carson, Hubert Harben, Felix Aylmer, Arthur Young, Percy Parsons, Henry Hallatt, Gordon McLeod, Wyndham Goldie.

Miles Mander. *Suez* (US/1938/104m/BW) D: Allan Dwan. C: Tyrone Power, Loretta Young, Annabella, George Zucco, Leon Ames, Victor Varconi, Brandon Hurst.

Derrick De Marney. *Sixty Glorious Years* (aka *Queen of Destiny*) (GB/1938/90m/C) D: Herbert Wilcox. C: Anna Neagle, Anton Walbrook, C. Aubrey Smith, Charles Carson, Felix Aylmer, Pamela Standish, Gordon McLeod, Henry Hallatt,

Wyndham Goldie, Malcolm Keen, Joyce Bland, Harvey Braban, Aubrey Dexter, Laidman Browne.

John Gielgud. *The Prime Minister* (GB/1940/94m/BW) D: Thorold Dickinson. C: Diana Wynyard, Will Fyfe, Stephen Murray, Owen Nares, Fay Compton, Lyn Harding, Leslie Perrins, Vera Bogetti, Frederick Leister, Nicolas Hannan, Kynaston Reeves, Gordon McLeod.

Abraham Sofaer. *The Ghosts of Berkeley Square* (GB/1947/85m/BW) D: Vernon Sewell. B/on the novel *No Nightingales* by Caryl Brahms & S.J. Simon. C: Robert Morley, Felix Aylmer, Yvonne Arnaud, Robert Beaumont, Martita Hunt, Wilfrid Hyde-White.

Alec Guinness. *The Mudlark* (GB/1950/98m/BW) D: Jean Negulesco. B/on the novel by Theodore Bonnet. C: Irene Dunne, Andrew Ray, Beatrice Campbell, Finlay Currie, Anthony Steel, Wilfrid Hyde-White, Robin Stevens, Kynaston Reeves, Vi Stevens.

Antony Sher. *Mrs. Brown* (GB-Ireland-US/1997/103m/C) D: John Madden. C: Judi Dench, Billy Connolly, Geoffry Palmer, Gerald Butler, Richard Pasco, David Westhead.

162 Doolin, Bill (1863–1896)

Once a member of the **Dalton Brothers** gang, Doolin was the leader of the Doolin gang, one of the last of the Western outlaw bands.

Robert Armstrong. *Return of the Bad Men* (US/1948/90m/BW) D: Ray Enright. C: Randolph Scott, George "Gabby" Hayes, Robert Ryan, Anne Jeffreys, Steve Brodie, Richard Powers, Robert Bray, Lex Barker, Walter Reed, Michael Harvey, Dean White.

Randolph Scott. *The Doolins of Oklahoma* (aka *The Great Manhunt*) (US/1949/90m/BW) D: Gordon Douglas. C: George Macready, Louise Albritton, John Ireland, Virginia Huston, Noah Beery, Jr., Dona Drake, Robert Barrat, Frank Fenton.

Frenchy LeBoyd. *Ride a Wild Stud* (aka *Ride the Wild Stud*) (US/1969) D: Revilo Ekard. C: Cliff Alexander, Tex Gates, William Fosterwick, Bill Ferrill.

Burt Lancaster. *Cattle Annie and Little Britches* (US/1980/97m/C) D: Lamont Johnson. B/on the novel by Robert Ward. C: Rod Steiger, John Savage, Diane Lane, Scott Glenn, Amanda Plummer.

163 Dorsey, Tommy (1905–1956)

Trombonist Dorsey and his brother Jimmy led popular dance bands from the 1930s through the 1950s. They played themselves in *The Fabulous Dorseys* (47) and Jimmy was played by Ray Anthony in *The Five Pennies* (59).

Bobby Troup. *The Gene Krupa Story* (aka *Drum Crazy*) (US/1959/102m/BW) D: Don Weis. C: Sal Mineo, Susan Kohner, James Darren, Susan Oliver, Yvonne Craig.

William Tole. *New York, New York* (US/1977/164–153m/C) D: Martin Scorsese. C: Robert De Niro, Liza Minnelli, Lionel Stander, Mary Kay Place, Barry Primus.

164 Dostoyevsky, Fyodor Mikhailovich (1821–1881)

Influential Russian novelist, Dostoyevsky's works include *Crime and Punishment,*
Notes from the Underground, and *The Brothers Karamazov.* Gregory Peck starred
in *The Great Sinner* (49) which was based on Dostoyevsky's semi-autobiographical story *The Gambler.*

    Nikolai Khmelyov. *House of Death* (aka *The House of the Dead*) (USSR/1932/
73m/BW) D: V. Fyodorov. B/on the novel by Fyodor Dostoyevsky. C: N. Podgorn, N. Viteftof.

    Anatoly Solinitsin. *Twenty-Six Days in the Life of Dostoevsky* (USSR/1981/
87m/C) D: Alexander Zarkhi. C: Evgenia Simonova, Eva Szykulska.

    Michael Gambon. *The Gambler* (GB-Netherlands-France-Hungary/1997/
97m/C) D: Karoly Makk. B/on a story by Dostoyevsky. C: Jodhi May, Luise
Rainer, Polly Walker, Dominic West, John Wood, William Houston.

165 Douglas, Lord Alfred Bruce "Bosie" (1870–1945)

A minor poet remembered for his relationship with **Oscar Wilde** and the scandal that occurred when Douglas' father accused Wilde of homosexuality.

    John Fraser. *The Trials of Oscar Wilde* (aka *The Man With the Green Carna-
tion*) (aka *The Green Carnation*) (GB/1960/123m/C) D: Ken Hughes. B/on the
book by Montgomery Hyde and the play *The Stringed Lute* by John Furnell. Best
English-Language Foreign Film (GG). C: Peter Finch, Yvonne Mitchell, Lionel
Jeffries, Nigel Patrick, James Mason, Emrys Jones, Laurence Naismith, Naomi
Chance, Sonia Dresdel.

    John Neville. *Oscar Wilde* (GB/1960/96m/BW) D: Gregory Ratoff. B/on the
play by Leslie and Sewell Stokes. C: Robert Morley, Phyllis Calvert, Ralph
Richardson, Dennis Price, Alexander Knox, Edward Chapman, Leonard
Sachs.

    George Reynolds. *The Best House in London* (GB/1969/97m/C) D: Philip Sav-
ile. C: David Hemmings, Joanna Pettet, Arnold Diamond, John DeMarco, Neal
Arden, Suzanne Hunt.

    Douglas Hodge. *Salome's Last Dance* (GB/1988/89m/C) D: Ken Russell. B/on
the play *Salome* by Oscar Wilde. C: Nickolas Grace, Glenda Jackson, Stratford
Johns, Imogen Millais-Scott, Denis Ull, Ken Russell, Imogen Claire.

    Jude Law. *Wilde* (GB/1998/115m/C) D: Brian Gilbert. C: Stephen Fry, Tom
Wilkinson, Vanessa Redgrave, Jennifer Ehle, Gemma Jones, Judy Parfitt, Zoe
Wannamaker, Michael Sheen.

166 Douglas, Stephen Arnold (1813–1861)

U.S. Senator (1847–61), Douglas' debates with **Abraham Lincoln** have been
depicted in several films about Lincoln's early career.

    E. Alyn Warren. *Abraham Lincoln* (US/1930/97m/BW) D: D.W. Griffith. C:
Walter Huston, Una Merkel, Kay Hammond, Edgar Deering, Hobart Bosworth,
Fred Warren, Frank Campeau, Francis Ford, Ian Keith, Oscar Apfel, Cameron
Prud'Homme.

    Milburn Stone. *Young Mr. Lincoln* (US/1939/100m/BW) D: John Ford. C:

Henry Fonda, Alice Brady, Marjorie Weaver, Arlene Whelan, Richard Cromwell, Pauline Moore.

Gene Lockhart. *Abe Lincoln in Illinois* (aka *Spirit of The People*) (US/1940/110m/BW) D: John Cromwell. B/on the play by Robert E. Sherwood. C: Raymond Massey, Ruth Gordon, Mary Howard, Dorothy Tree, Harvey Stephens, Howard Da Silva.

167 Doyle, Sir Arthur Conan (1859–1930)

British novelist and creator of Sherlock Holmes. In later life Conan Doyle developed an intense interest in spiritualism. Among the many TV portrayals, some produced for British television, are two by Nigel Davenport, *Conan Doyle* (72) and *The Edwardians* (72); Peter Cushing in *The Great Houdini* (76), Roy Dotrice in *Young Harry Houdini* (87), David Warner in *Houdini* (98), and by Robin Laing in *Murder Rooms* (2000).

Paul Bildt. *Der Mann, der Sherlock Holmes war* (aka *The Man Who Was Sherlock Holmes*) (aka *Two Merry Adventurers*) (aka *Zwei lustige Abenteurer*) (Germany/1937/112m/BW) D: Karl Hartl. C: Hans Albers, Heinz Rühmann, Marieluise Claudius, Hansi Knoteck, Hilde Weissner, Günther Ballier, Ernst Behmer, Horst Birr, Gerhard Dammann, Erich Dunskus, Angelo Ferrari, Lothar Geist, Aribert Grimmer, Harry Hardt.

Peter O'Toole. *Fairy Tale: A True Story* (US-GB/1997/99m) D: Charles Sturridge. C: Florence Hoath, Elizabeth Earl, Paul McGann, Phoebe Nicholls, Harvey Keitel, Jason Salkey, Lara Morgan, Adam Franks, Guy Wichter, Joseph May, John Bradley, Anna Chancellor, Leonard Kavanagh, Anton Lesser, Bob Peck, Lynn Farleigh, Sarah Marsden, Tara Marie, Alannah McGahan, Bill Nighy, Tim McInnerny, Peter Mullan, John Wiggins, David Calder, Anthony Calf, Mel Gibson (cameo role).

Edward Hardwicke. *Photographing Fairies* (aka *Apparition*) (GB/1997/106m/C) D: Nick Willing. C: Toby Stephens, Emily Woof, Ben Kingsley, Frances Barber, Philip Davis, Hannah Bould, Miriam Grant, Rachel Shelley, Clive Merrison, Stephen Churchett, Mary Healey, Maggie Wells, Richenda Carey, Jeremy Young.

168 Drake, Sir Francis (1540?–1596)

English sea captain famous for his circumnavigation of the globe and his part in the defeat of the Spanish Armada.

Matheson Lang. *Drake the Pirate* (aka *Drake of England*) (aka *Elizabeth of England*) (GB/1935/96m/BW) D: Arthur Woods. B/on a play by Louis N. Parker. C: Athene Seyler, Jane Baxter, Henry Mollison, Ben Webster, Donald Wolfit.

Rod Taylor. *Seven Seas to Calais* (Italy/1962/99m/C) D: Rudolph Mate & Primo Zeglio. C: Irene Worth, Keith Michell, Anthony Dawson, Esmerelda Ruspoli, Umberto Raho, Basil Dignam.

Philip Stearns. *Winstanley* (GB/1975/96m/BW) D: Kevin Brownlow & Andrew Mollo. B/on the novel *Comrade Jacob* by David Caute. C: Miles Halliwell, Jerome Willis, Terry Higgins, Phil Oliver, Flora Skrine, David Bramley.

169 Dreyfus, Alfred (1859–1935)

Jewish officer of the French army whose false conviction on spying charges (primarily due to anti–Semitism), imprisonment on Devil's Island and ultimate exoneration has provided the basis for several films.

Fritz Kortner. *The Dreyfus Case* (aka *Dreyfus*) (Germany/1930/BW) D: Richard Oswald. C: Grete Moshelm, Albert Basserman, Oscar Homolka, Heinrich George, Paul Bildt, Ferdinand Hart.

Cedric Hardwicke. *Dreyfus* (aka *The Dreyfus Case*) (GB/1931/90m/BW) D: F.W. Kraemer. B/on the play *The Dreyfus Case* by Herzog and Rehfisch. C: Charles Carson, George Merritt, Sam Livesey, Beatrix Thomson, Garry Marsh, Leonard Shepherd.

Joseph Schildkraut. *The Life of Emile Zola* (US/1937/123m/BW) D: William Dieterle. Best Picture (AA,NYC). C: Paul Muni, Gale Sondergaard, Gloria Holden, Donald Crisp, Morris Carnovsky, Louis Calhern, Ralph Morgan, Grant Mitchell, Vladimir Sokoloff.

Jose Ferrer. *I Accuse!* (GB/1958/99m/BW) D: Jose Ferrer. B/on the book *Captain Dreyfus—A Story of Mass Hysteria* by Nicholas Halasz. C: Viveca Lindfors, Anton Walbrook, Leo Genn, Emlyn Williams, David Farrar, Donald Wolfit, Peter Illing.

170 Du Barry, Madame (1743–1793)

(Countess Jeanne Bécu du Barry) Mistress of **Louis XV** of France, during the French Revolution she was tried for treason and guillotined.

Norma Talmadge. *Du Barry, Woman of Passion* (US/1930/88m/BW) D: Sam Taylor. B/on the play by David Belasco. C: William Farnum, Hobart Bosworth, Conrad Nagel.

Dolores Del Rio. *Madame du Barry* (US/1934/79m/BW) D: William Dieterle. C: Reginald Owen, Victor Jory, Osgood Perkins, Verree Teasdale, Anita Louise, Maynard Holmes.

Gitta Alpar. *I Give My Heart* (aka *The Loves of Madame du Barry*) (aka *Give Me Your Heart*) (GB/1935/90m/BW) D: Marcel Varnel. B/on the opera "The Dubarry" by Paul Knepler & J.M. Welleminsky. C: Patrick Waddington, Owen Nares, Arthur Margeston, Hugh Miller, Hay Petrie.

Simone Renant. *The Pearls of the Crown* (France/1937/120–100m/BW) D: Sacha Guitry & Christian-Jaque. C: Sacha Guitry, Jacqueline Delubac, Lyn Harding, Ermete Zacconi, Marguerite Moreno, Yvette Plenne, Catalano, Arletty, Percy Marmont, Derrick De Marney, Barbara Shaw, Jean Louis Barrault, Emile Drain, Enrico Glori, Renee Saint-Cyr, Pizani, Claude Dauphin, Aime-Simon Gerard.

Gladys George. *Marie Antoinette* (US/1938/160m/BW) D: W.S. Van Dyke II. B/on the book by Stefan Zweig. C: Norma Shearer, Tyrone Power, John Barrymore, Robert Morley, Anita Louise, Joseph Schildkraut, Albert Dekker, Scotty Becket, Alma Kruger, George Meeker, Wade Crosby, Anthony Warde, Walter Walker, John Burton.

Liane Pathe. *Champs-Elysées* (aka *Remontons Les Champs-Elysées*) (France/1938/100m/BW) D: Sacha Guitry. C: Sacha Guitry, Lucien Baroux, Jacqueline Delubac,

Germaine Dermoz, Jeanne Boitel, Raymonde Allain, Jean Davy, Emile Drain, Jacques Erwin, Rene Fauchois, Robert Pizani, Claude Martin, Raymond Galle, Andre Laurent.

Lucille Ball. *Du Barry Was a Lady* (US/1943/96m/C) D: Roy Del Ruth. B/on the play by B.G. De Sylva & Herbert Fields. C: Red Skelton, Gene Kelly, Zero Mostel, Rags Ragland.

Margot Grahame. *Black Magic* (US/1949/105m/BW) D: Gregory Ratoff. B/on the novel *Joseph Balsamo* by Alexandre Dumas. C: Orson Welles, Nancy Guild, Akim Tamiroff, Raymond Burr, Berry Kroeger, Charles Goldner, Lee Kresel, Robert Atkins.

Martine Carol. *Madame du Barry* (aka *Mistress du Barry*) (France-Italy/1954/110m/C) D: Christian-Jaque. C: Andre Luguet, Daniel Ivernel, Isabelle Pia, Dennis Gianna, Maria Canale, Massimo Serato, Denis d'Ines, Jean Paredes.

171 Earp, Wyatt Berry Stapp (1848–1929)

Legendary lawman of the American West, Earp served in Dodge City, Deadwood and finally in Tombstone where he participated in the gunfight at the O.K. Corral. Other films loosely based on Wyatt's story include: *Law and Order* (32, Walter Huston as Frame Johnson), *Frontier Marshal* (34, George O'Brien as Michael Wyatt), *Law and Order* (40, Johnny Mack Brown as Bill Ralston) and *Law and Order* (53, Ronald Reagan as Frame Johnson). TV movie portrayals include: Bruce Boxleitner in *I Married Wyatt Earp* (83), Fred Ward in *Four Eyes and Six-Guns* (92), and Hugh O'Brian reprising the role for which he is best known in *Wyatt Earp: Return to Tombstone* (94).

Randolph Scott. *Frontier Marshal* (US/1939/71m/BW) D: Allan Dwan. B/on the novel *Wyatt Earp, Frontier Marshal* by Stuart N. Lake. C: Nancy Kelly, Cesar Romero, Binnie Barnes, John Carradine, Edward Norris, Eddie Foy, Jr., Joe Sawyer, Charles Stevens.

Richard Dix. *Tombstone, The Town Too Tough to Die* (US/1942/79m/BW) D: William McGann. B/on the book *Tombstone, The Toughest Town in Arizona* by Walter Noble Burns. C: Kent Taylor, Edgar Buchanan, Frances Clifford, Don Castle, Victor Jory, Rex Bell, Dick Curtis.

Henry Fonda. *My Darling Clementine* (US/1946/97m/BW) D: John Ford. B/on the novel *Wyatt Earp, Frontier Marshal* by Stuart N. Lake. C: Linda Darnell, Victor Mature, Walter Brennan, Tim Holt, Ward Bond, Don Garner, John Ireland, Grant Withers, Cathy Downs, Alan Mowbray, Roy Roberts, Jane Darwell, J. Farrell MacDonald.

Will Geer. *Winchester '73* (US/1950/92m/BW) D: Anthony Mann. B/on the story by Stuart N. Lake. C: James Stewart, Shelley Winters, Dan Duryea, Steve Darrell.

James Millican. *Gun Belt* (US/1953/77m/C) D: Ray Nazarro. C: George Montgomery, Tab Hunter, Helen Westcott, John Dehner, William Bishop, Douglas Kennedy, Bruce Cowling, William Philips, Jack Elam, Boyd Morgan, Boyd Stockman.

Bruce Cowling. *Masterson of Kansas* (US/1954/72m/C) D: William Castle. C:

Tombstone Marshall Wyatt Earp (Henry Fonda, left) and his friend, Doc Holliday (Victor Mature) on a peace keeping operation in John Ford's classic Western, *My Darling Clementine* (1946). (Museum of Modern Art Film Stills Archive)

George Montgomery, Nancy Gates, James Griffith, Jean Willes, Benny Rubin, Donald Murphy.

Joel McCrea. *Wichita* (US/1955/81m/C) D: Jacques Tourneur. C: Vera Miles, Lloyd Bridges, Wallace Ford, Edgar Buchanan, Peter Graves, Keith Larsen, John Smith.

Burt Lancaster. *Gunfight at the O.K. Corral* (US/1957/122m/C) D: John Sturges. B/on the story *The Killer* by George Scullin. C: Kirk Douglas, Rhonda Fleming, Jo Van Fleet, John Ireland, Lyle Bettger, Frank Faylen, Earl Holliman, Whit Bissell, DeForrest Kelley, Martin Milner, Kenneth Tobey, Lee Van Cleef, Jack Elam, Bing Russell.

Buster Crabbe. *Badman's Country* (US/1958/85m/BW) D: Fred F. Sears. C: George Montgomery, Neville Brand, Karin Booth, Gregory Wolcott, Malcolm Atterbury, Russell Johnson, Richard Devon, Morris Ankrum.

Hugh O'Brian. *Alias Jesse James* (US/1959/92m/C) D: Norman McLeod. C: Bob Hope, Rhonda Fleming, Wendell Corey, Jim Davis, James Arness, Fess Parker, Gail Davis.

James Stewart. *Cheyenne Autumn* (US/1964/159m/C) D: John Ford. B/on the novel by Mari Sandoz. C: Richard Widmark, Carroll Baker, Karl Malden, Arthur Kennedy.

Guy Madison. *Gunmen of the Rio Grande* (aka *Duel at Rio Bravo*) (France-Italy-Spain/1965/86m/C) D: Tullo DeMicheli. C: Madeleine Lebeau, Gerard Tichy, Fernando Sancho.

Bill Camfield. *The Outlaws Is Coming* (US/1965/88m/BW) D: Norman Maurer. C: Larry Fine, Moe Howard, Joe De Rita, Nancy Kovack, Murray Alper, Joe Bolton, Hal Fryar, Johnny Ginger, Wayne Mack, Ed McDonnell, Bruce Sedley, Paul Shannon, Sally Starr.

James Garner. *Hour of the Gun* (aka *The Law and Tombstone*) (US/1967/101m/ C) D: John Sturges. B/on the novel *Tombstone's Epitaph* by Douglas D. Martin. C: Jason Robards, Robert Ryan, Albert Salmi, Charles Aidman, Frank Converse, Larry Gates.

Harris Yulin. *Doc* (US/1971/95m/C) D: Frank Perry. C: Stacy Keach, Faye Dunaway, Mike Witney, Dan Greenburg, Bruce M. Fischer, Ferdinand Zogbaum, Fred Dennis.

James Garner. *Sunset* (US/1988/107m/C) D: Blake Edwards. C: Bruce Willis, Malcolm McDowell, Patricia Hodge, Glenn Shadix, Rod McCary, John Fountain.

Kurt Russell. *Tombstone* (US/1993/128m/C) D: George Pan Kosmatos. C: Val Kilmer, Michael Biehn, Powers Booth, Robert Blake, Dana Delaney, Sam Elliott, Stephen Lang, Terry O'Quinn, Joanna Pacula, Bill Paxton, Jason Priestley, Michael Rooker.

Kevin Costner. *Wyatt Earp* (US/1994/195m/C) D: Lawrence Kasdan. C: Dennis Quaid, Gene Hackman, David Andrews, Linden Ashby, Jeff Fahey, Mark Harmon, Michael Madsen, Catherine O'Hara, Bill Pullman, Isabella Rossellini, Tom Sizemore, JoBeth Williams, Norman Howell, Mare Winningham, Rex Linn, Randle Mell.

172 Edison, Thomas Alva (1847–1931)

With virtually no formal schooling (three months) Edison became America's greatest inventor. The electric light bulb, a phonograph recording device and the motion picture projector were among his more than 1300 patents.

Spencer Tracy. *Edison, the Man* (US/1940/104m/BW) D: Clarence Brown. C: Rita Johnson, Lynne Overman, Charles Coburn, Gene Lockhart, Henry Travers, Felix Bressart.

Mickey Rooney. *Young Tom Edison* (US/1940/85m/BW) D: Norman Taurog. C: Fay Bainter, George Bancroft, Virginia Weidler, Eugene Pallette, Victor Kilian, Bobby Jordan.

Dennis Patrick. *The Secret of Nikola Tesla* (aka *Tesla*) (Yugoslavia/1980/120m/C) D: Krsto Papic. C: Peter Bozovic, Orson Welles, Strother Martin, Oja Kodar, Ana Karic.

Ian James Tait. *Young Einstein* (Australia/1988/91m/C) D: Yahoo Serious. C: Yahoo Serious, Odile Le Clezio, Pee Wee Wilson, Basil Clarke, Tim McKew, Nick Conroy.

Peter Andorai. *My 20th Century* (Hungary/1990/92m/BW) D: Ildiko Enyedi. C: Dorotha Segda, Oleg Jankowski, Paulus Manker, Gabor Mate, Gyula Keri.

Edward the Confessor *see* 592

Edward I *see* 594

Edward II *see* 595

Edward III *see* 596

Edward IV *see* 599

Edward V *see* 600

173 Edward VI (1537–1553)

The only son of **Henry VIII**, Edward ascended the throne at the age of nine (with the actual governing in the hands of a Lord Protector). Prior to his death (of tuberculosis) he left a will naming **Lady Jane Grey** as his successor, to the exclusion of his sisters **Mary I** and **Elizabeth I**.

Desmond Tester. *Tudor Rose* (aka *Lady Jane Grey*) (aka *Nine Days a Queen*) (GB/1936/78m/BW) D: Robert Stevenson. C: Cedric Hardwicke, John Mills, Felix Aylmer, Frank Cellier, Nova Pilbeam, Gwen Frangcon-Davies, Sybil Thorndike.

Bobby Mauch. *The Prince and the Pauper* (US/1937/120m/BW) D: William Keighley. B/on the novel by Mark Twain and the play by Catherine C. Cushing. C: Errol Flynn, Claude Rains, Henry Stephenson, Billy Mauch, Montagu Love, Alan Hale, Robert Warwick, Helen Valkis, Ann Howard, Halliwell Hobbes, Barton MacLane.

Rex Thompson. *Young Bess* (US/1953/112m/C) D: George Sidney. B/on the novel by Margaret Irwin. C: Jean Simmons, Stewart Granger, Deborah Kerr, Charles Laughton, Kay Walsh, Cecil Kellaway, Elaine Stewart, Dawn Addams, Lumsden Hare.

Sean Scully. *The Prince and the Pauper* (GB/1962/93m/C) D: Don Chaffey. B/on the novel by Mark Twain. C: Jane Asher, Paul Rogers, Guy Williams, Laurence Naismith.

Simon Henderson. *The Six Wives of Henry VIII* (aka *Henry VIII and His Six Wives*) (GB/1972/125m/C) D: Waris Hussein. C: Keith Michell, Frances Cuka, Charlotte Rampling, Jane Asher, Jenny Bos, Lynne Frederick, Barbara Leigh-Hunt, Donald Pleasence, Annette Crosbie, John Bryans, Michael Goodliffe, Bernard Hepton, Dorothy Tutin.

Mark Lester. *Crossed Swords* (aka *The Prince and the Pauper*) (US/1977/121m/C) D: Richard Fleischer. B/on the novel *The Prince and the Pauper* by Mark Twain. C: Oliver Reed, Raquel Welch, Ernest Borgnine, Charlton Heston, Lalla Ward, Felicity Dean, George C. Scott, Rex Harrison, Harry Andrews, David Hemmings.

Warren Saire. *Lady Jane* (GB/1986/144m/C) D: Trevor Nunn. C: Helena Bonham Carter, Cary Elwes, John Wood, Michael Hordern, Jane Laportaire, David Waller.

174 Edward VII (1841–1910)

The eldest son of **Queen Victoria**, Edward was the Prince of Wales for sixty years and was famous for his interests in wine, women (See **Langtry, Lillie**) and gambling. A popular king (from 1901) his reign lasted a brief nine years before his death in 1910.

Aubrey Dexter. *Sixty Glorious Years* (aka *Queen of Destiny*) (GB/1938/90m/C) D: Herbert Wilcox. C: Anna Neagle, Anton Walbrook, C. Aubrey Smith, Charles Carson, Felix Aylmer, Pamela Standish, Gordon McLeod, Henry Hallatt, Wyndham Goldie, Malcolm Keen, Derrick De Marney, Joyce Bland, Harvey Braban, Laidman Browne.

Victor Francen. *Entente Cordiale* (France/1938/95m/BW) D: Marcel L'Herbier. B/on *Edward VII and His Times* by Andre Maurois. C: Gaby Morlay, Andre Lefaur, Marcelle Praince, Jeanine Darcey, Arlette Marchal, Jean Galland, Andre Roanne, Jacques Catelain, Jean Toulot, Jacques Baumer, Jean d'Yd, Jean Perrier.

Edwin Maxwell. *Holy Matrimony* (US/1943/87m/BW) D: John Stahl. B/on the novel *Buried Alive* by Arnold Bennett. C: Monty Wooly, Gracie Fields, Laird Cregar, Una O'Connor.

Cecil Kellaway. *Mrs. Parkington* (US/1944/124m/BW) D: Tay Garnett. B/on the novel by Louis Bromfield. C: Greer Garson, Walter Pidgeon, Edward Arnold, Lee Patrick.

Ian Murray. *The First Traveling Saleslady* (US/1956/92m/C) D: Arthur Lubin. C: Ginger Rogers, Barry Nelson, Carol Channing, David Brian, James Arness, Clint Eastwood, Edward Cassidy.

Laurence Naismith. *The Trials of Oscar Wilde* (aka *The Man With the Green Carnation*) (aka *The Green Carnation*) (GB/1960/123m/C) D: Ken Hughes. B/on the book by Montgomery Hyde and the play *The Stringed Lute* by John Furnell. Best English-Language Foreign Film (GG). C: Peter Finch, John Fraser, Yvonne Mitchell, Lionel Jeffries, Nigel Patrick, James Mason, Emrys Jones, Naomi Chance, Sonia Dresdel.

James Robertson Justice. *Mayerling* (GB/1968/140m/C) D: Terence Young. B/on the novel *Mayerling* by Claude Anet and on the novel *The Archduke* by Michael Arnold. C: Omar Sharif, Catherine Deneuve, James Mason, Ava Gardner, Genevieve Page.

Reginald Marsh. *Young Winston* (GB/1972/145m/C) D: Richard Attenborough. B/on the book *My Early Life: A Roving Commission* by Winston Churchill. Best English-Language Foreign Film (GG). C: Simon Ward, Peter Cellier, Ronald Hines, John Mills, Anne Bancroft, Robert Shaw, Laurence Naismith, William Dexter, Basil Dignam, Anthony Hopkins, Robert Hardy, Colin Blakely, Michael Audreson, Jack Hawkins.

Victor Langley. *Murder By Decree* (GB-Canada/1979/121m/C) D: Bob Clark. B/on characters created by A. Conan Doyle and the book *The Ripper File* by John Lloyd & Elwyn Jones. C: Christopher Plummer, James Mason, John Gielgud, Frank Finlay.

John Standing. *The Young Visitors* (GB/1984/93m/C) D: James Hill. B/on a story by Daisy Ashford. C: Alec McCowan, Carina Radford, Tracey Ullman, Kenny Ireland.

David Westhead. *Mrs. Brown* (GB-Ireland-US/1997/103m/C) D: John Madden. C: Judi Dench, Billy Connolly, Geoffry Palmer, Antony Sher, Gerald Butler, Richard Pasco.

Mark Dexter (actor also portrays Edward Sickert). *From Hell* (Czech Republic-US/2001/121m/C) D: Albert and Allen Hughes. C: Johnny Depp, Heather Graham, Ian Holm, Jason Flemyng, Robbie Coltran, Lesley Sharp, Susan Lynch, Terence Harvey, Katrin Cartlidge, Estelle Skornik, Paul Rhys, Nicholas McGaughey, Ian Richardson, Annabelle Apsion, Joanna Page, Liz Moscrop.

Edward VIII *see* 611

175 Eichmann, Karl Adolph (1906–1962)

The head of the Nazi's Jewish Extermination Department, Eichmann escaped after the war until tracked down by Israeli agents while living in Argentina. He was brought to Jerusalem, tried, and executed for his crimes against humanity. *The Man in the Glass Booth* (75) features Maximillian Schell in a role somewhat based on Eichmann.

Werner Klemperer. *Operation Eichmann* (US/1961/92m/BW) D: R.G. Springsteen. C: Ruta Lee, Donald Buka, Barbara Turner, John Banner, Luis van Rooten, Hans Gudegast.

Walter Czaschke. *Death Is My Trade* (Germany/1977/145m/C) D: Theodor Kotulla. B/on the novel *La Mort est Mon Metier* by Robert Merle. C: Goetz George, Elisabeth Schwarz, Kurt Hubner, Hans Korte, Kai Taschner, Sigurd Fitzek.

Alfred Burke. *The House on Garibaldi Street* (US/1979/96m/C) D: Peter Collinson. B/on the book by Isser Harel. C: Nick Mancuso, (Chaim) Topol, Martin Balsam, Janet Suzman.

Gerd Bockmann. *The Wannsee Conference* (Germany-Austria/1987/87m/C) D: Heinz Schirk. C: Robert Artzorn, Friedrich Beckhaus, Dietrich Mattausch, Jochen Busse.

Laszlo Soos. *Good Evening, Mr. Wallenberg* (Sweden/1993/115m/C) D: Kjell Grede. C: Stellan Skarsgard, Katharina Thalbach, Karoly Eperjes, Miklos Szekely, Jesper Christensen.

176 Einstein, Albert (1879–1955)

German-American physicist, Einstein, developer of the Theories of Relativity, is considered to be the greatest theoretical physicist of all time. In the TV film *A Man Called Intrepid* (79) he was portrayed by Joseph Golland.

Ludwig Stossel. *The Beginning Or the End* (US/1947/110m/BW) D: Norman Taurog. C: Brian Donlevy, Beverly Tyler, Hume Cronyn, Godfrey Tearle, Barry Nelson, Art Baker.

Petr Cepek. *I Killed Einstein* (aka *Zabil Jsem Einsteina, Panove*) (Czechoslovakia/1969/95m/C) D: Oldrich Lipsky. C: Jiri Sovak, Jana Brejchova, Lubomir Lipsky.

Don Calfa. *Shanks* (US/1974/93m/C) D: William Castle. C: Marcel Marceau,

Tsilla Chelton, Philippe Clay, Cindy Eilbacher, Helena Kallianiotes, Larry Bishop, Mondo, Phil Adams, William Castle.

Yahoo Serious. *Young Einstein* (Australia/1988/91m/C) D: Yahoo Serious. C: Odile Le Clezio, Pee Wee Wilson, Basil Clarke, Tim McKew, Ian James Tait, Nick Conroy.

John Ehrin. *Bill and Ted's Bogus Journey* (US/1991/95m/C) D: Pete Hewitt. C: Keanu Reeves, Alex Winter, George Carlin, William Sadler, Amy Stock-Poynton, Joss Ackland, Don Forney, Ed Cambridge, Tad Horino.

Walter Matthau. *I.Q.* (US/1994/96m/C) D: Fred Schepisi. C: Tim Robbins, Meg Ryan, Lou Jacobi, Gene Saks, Joseph Maher, Charles Durning, Stephen Fry, Keene Curtis.

177 Eisenhower, Dwight David (1890–1969)

Supreme Commander of the Allied Forces during World War II, Eisenhower was rewarded by the American people with election as President in 1952.

Harry Carey, Jr. *The Long Gray Line* (US/1955/138m/C) D: John Ford. B/on the novel *Bringing Up the Brass* by Marty Maher & Nardi Reeder. C: Tyrone Power, Maureen O'Hara, Robert Francis, Donald Crisp, Milburn Stone, Elbert Steele, James Sears.

Henry Grace. *The Longest Day* (US/1962/180m/BW) D: Andrew Marton, Ken Annakin & Bernherd Wicki. B/on the novel by Cornelius Ryan. Best English Language Picture (NBR). C: John Wayne, Robert Mitchum, Henry Fonda, Robert Ryan, Rod Steiger, Robert Wagner, Sal Mineo, Roddy McDowall, Curt Jurgens, Paul Hartman, Nicholas Stuart, Wolfgang Lukschy, Werner Hinz, Trevor Reid, Alexander Knox.

Robert Beer. *The Right Stuff* (US/1983/192m/C) D: Philip Kaufman. B/on the book by Tom Wolfe. C: Sam Shepard, Scott Glenn, Ed Harris, Dennis Quaid, Fred Ward, Barbara Hershey, Kim Stanley, Veronica Cartwright, Donald Moffat.

Keene Curtis. *I.Q.* (US/1994/96m/C) D: Fred Schepisi. C: Walter Matthau, Tim Robbins, Meg Ryan, Lou Jacobi, Gene Saks, Joseph Maher, Charles Durning, Stephen Fry.

178 Eleanor of Aquitaine (1122?–1204)

The wife of two kings (**Louis VII** of France and **Henry II** of England) and the mother of two more (**Richard I** and **John**), she was imprisoned by Henry for twelve years after supporting their sons' revolt against him. She was played by Janet Suzman in the TV movie *The Zany Adventures of Robin Hood* (84).

Martita Hunt. *The Story of Robin Hood* (aka *The Story of Robin Hood and His Merrie Men*) (GB/1952/84m/C) D: Ken Annakin. C: Richard Todd, Joan Rice, Peter Finch, James Hayter, James Robertson Justice, Hubert Gregg, Patrick Barr, Antony Eustrel.

Pamela Brown. *Becket* (GB/1964/148m/C) D: Peter Glenville. B/on the play by Jean Anouilh. Best Picture (GG). C: Richard Burton, Peter O'Toole, Donald Wolfit, John Gielgud, Martita Hunt, Sian Phillips, Paolo Stoppa, Felix Aylmer.

Katherine Hepburn * Best Actress AA, BFA. *The Lion in Winter* (GB/1968/

134m/C) D: Anthony Harvey. B/on the play by James Goldman. Best Picture
(GG [Drama], NYC). Best Director (DGA). C: Peter O'Toole, Jane Merrow,
John Castle, Anthony Hopkins, Timothy Dalton, Nigel Terry, Nigel Stock, Ken-
neth Griffith.

179 Elisabeth, Empress of Austria (1837–1898)

The wife of **Franz Josef**, Elisabeth was assassinated in Switzerland by an Italian anarchist.

Lil Dagover. *Elisabeth of Austria* (Germany/1931/110–74m/BW) D: Adolf
Trotz. C: Paul Otto, Maria Solveg, Ekkehard Arend, Gert Pilary, Ida Perry, Ludwig Stoessel.

Gabrielle Dorziat. *Mayerling* (France/1935/96m/BW) D: Anatole Litvak. B/on
the novel *Idyl's End* by Claude Anet. C: Charles Boyer, Danielle Darrieux, Suzy
Prim, Jean Dax, Jean Debucourt, Vladimir Sokoloff.

Carola Hoehn. *The Royal Waltz* (Germany/1935/80m/BW) D: Herbert
Maisch. C: Paul Hoerbiger, Curt Jurgens, Anton Pointer, Willi Forst.

Grace Moore. *The King Steps Out* (US/1936/85m/BW) D: Josef von Sternberg. B/on the play *Cissy* by Gustav Hohn & Ernest Decsey and the operetta by
Ernst & Hubert Marischka. C: Franchot Tone, Walter Connolly, Raymond Walburn.

Romy Schneider. *Forever My Love* (Austria/1962/147m/C) D: Ernst Marischka.
U.S. theatrical release edited from three Austrian films: *Sissi* (55), *Sissi Die Junge
Kaiserin* (56), and *Sissi-Schicksalsjare Einer Kaiserin* (57). C: Karl Boehm, Magda
Schneider, Vilma Degischer, Gustav Knuth, Uta Franz.

Ava Gardner. *Mayerling* (GB/1968/140m/C) D: Terence Young. B/on the novel
Mayerling by Claude Anet and on the novel *The Archduke* by Michael Arnold.
C: Omar Sharif, Catherine Deneuve, James Mason, Genevieve Page, James
Robertson Justice.

Elizabeth *see* 634

180 Elizabeth I (1533–1603)

The daughter of **Henry VIII** and **Anne Boleyn**, Elizabeth, "the Virgin Queen,"
ruled England for 55 years.

Athene Seyler. *Drake the Pirate* (aka *Drake of England*) (aka *Elizabeth of
England*) (GB/1935/96m/BW) D: Arthur Woods. B/on a play by Louis N. Parker.
C: Matheson Lang, Jane Baxter, Henry Mollison, Ben Webster, Donald Wolfit.

Athene Seyler. (scene taken from Drake the Pirate) *Regal Cavalcade* (aka *Royal
Cavalcade*) (GB/1935/100m/BW) D: Thomas Bentley, Herbert Brenton, Nor-
man Lee, Walter Summers, Will Kellino & Marcel Varnel. C: Marie Lohr, Esme
Percy, Pearl Argyle, Frank Vosper, Austin Trevor, Harry Brunning, John Mills,
C.M. Hallard, H. Saxon-Snell, Patric Knowles, Matheson Lang.

Florence Eldridge. *Mary of Scotland* (US/1936/123m/BW) D: John Ford. B/on
the play by Maxwell Anderson. C: Katharine Hepburn, Fredric March, Douglas
Walton, John Carradine, Robert Barrat, Gavin Muir, Ian Keith, Ralph Forbes,
Alan Mowbray, Walter Byron.

Flora Robson. *Fire Over England* (GB/1937/92m/BW) D: William K. Howard. B/on the novel by A.E.W. Mason. C: Laurence Olivier, Leslie Banks, Raymond Massey, Vivien Leigh, Tamara Desni, Robert Newton, Lyn Harding, James Mason.

Yvette Plenne. *The Pearls of the Crown* (France/1937/120–100m/BW) D: Sacha Guitry & Christian-Jaque. C: Sacha Guitry, Jacqueline Delubac, Lyn Harding, Ermete Zacconi, Marguerite Moreno, Catalano, Arletty, Percy Marmont, Derrick De Marney, Barbara Shaw, Simone Renant, Jean Louis Barrault, Emile Drain, Enrico Glori, Renee Saint-Cyr, Pizani, Claude Dauphin, Aime-Simon Gerard.

Bette Davis. *The Private Lives of Elizabeth and Essex* (aka *Elizabeth the Queen*) (US/1939/106m/C) D: Michael Curtiz. B/on the play *Elizabeth the Queen* by Maxwell Anderson. C: Errol Flynn, Olivia de Havilland, Donald Crisp, Alan Hale, Vincent Price, Robert Warwick.

Flora Robson. *The Sea Hawk* (US/1940/126m/BW) D: Michael Curtiz. C: Errol Flynn, Brenda Marshall, Claude Rains, Donald Crisp, Henry Daniell, Alan Hale, Montagu Love, Henry David.

Maria Koppenhofer. *Heart of a Queen* (aka *Das Herz Einer Königin*) (Germany/1940/BW) D: Carl Froelich. C: Zarah Leander, Axel von Ambesser, Willy Bergel, Erich Ponto.

Olga Lindo. *Time Flies* (GB/1944/88m/BW) D: Walter Forde. C: Tommy Handley, Evelyn Dall, George Moon, John Salew, Leslie Bradley, Roy Emerson, Iris Lang.

Jean Simmons. *Young Bess* (US/1953/112m/C) D: George Sidney. B/on the novel by Margaret Irwin. C: Stewart Granger, Deborah Kerr, Charles Laughton, Kay Walsh, Cecil Kellaway, Rex Thompson, Elaine Stewart, Dawn Addams, Lumsden Hare.

Bette Davis. *The Virgin Queen* (US/1955/92m/C) D: Henry Koster. C: Richard Todd, Joan Collins, Jay Robinson, Herbert Marshall, Dan O'Herlihy, Robert Douglas.

Agnes Moorehead. *The Story of Mankind* (US/1957/100m/C) D: Irwin Allen. B/on the book by Hendrik van Loon. C: Ronald Colman, Hedy Lamarr, Virginia Mayo, Peter Lorre, Dennis Hopper, Marie Wilson, Helmut Dantine, Edward Everett Horton, Reginald Gardiner, Marie Windsor, Francis X. Bushman, Anthony Dexter, Austin Green, Jim Ameche, Harpo Marx, Bobby Watson, Reginald Sheffield, Cedric Hardwicke, Cesar Romero.

Irene Worth. *Seven Seas to Calais* (Italy/1962/99m/C) D: Rudolph Mate & Primo Zeglio. C: Rod Taylor, Keith Michell, Anthony Dawson, Esmerelda Ruspoli, Umberto Raho, Basil Dignam.

Catherine Lacey. *The Fighting Prince of Donegal* (GB/1966/112m/C) D: Michael O'Herlihy. B/on the novel *Red Hugh, Prince of Donega'* by Robert T. Reilly. C: Peter McEnery, Susan Hampshire, Tom Adams, Gordon Jackson, Andrew Keir, Peter Jeffrey.

Glenda Jackson. *Mary, Queen of Scots* (GB/1971/128m/C) D: Charles Jarrot. C: Vanessa Redgrave, Patrick McGoohan, Timothy Dalton, Nigel Davenport, Trevor Howard, Daniel Massey, Ian Holm, Andrew Keir, Katherine Kath, Robert James, Richard Denning, Rick Warner.

Lalla Ward. *Crossed Swords* (aka *The Prince and the Pauper*) (US/1977/121m/C)

D: Richard Fleischer. B/on the novel *The Prince and the Pauper* by Mark Twain. C: Oliver Reed, Raquel Welch, Mark Lester, Ernest Borgnine, Charlton Heston, Felicity Dean, George C. Scott, Rex Harrison, Harry Andrews, David Hemmings.

Jenny Runacre. *Jubilee* (GB/1977/103m/C) D: Derek Jarman. C: Little Nell, Linda Spurrier, Jordan, Ian Charleson, Adam Ant.

Quentin Crisp. *Orlando* (GB/1993/92m/C) D: Sally Potter. B/on the novel by Virginia Woolf. C: Tilda Swinton, Billy Zane, Lothaire Bluteau, Charlotte Valandrey, Peter Eyre, Thom Hoffman, Dudley Sutton, Sarah Crowden, Roger Hammond.

Cate Blanchette *Best Actress (GG). *Elizabeth* (US/1998/124m/C) D: Shekar Kapur. AA Best makeup. C: Joseph Fiennes, Fanny Ardant, James Frain, Richard Attenborough, Christopher Eccleston, Vincent Cassel, George Yiasoumi, Geoffrey Rush, Kathy Burke.

Judi Dench *Best Supporting Actress (AA). *Shakespeare in Love* (GB/1998/ 153m/C) D: John Madden. Best Picture, Best Actress, Best Original Screenplay, Original Musical Score, Art Direction, Costume Design (AA). Best Picture (Comedy), Best Actress, Best Screenplay (GG). C: Gwyneth Paltrow, Joseph Fiennes, Ben Affleck, Colin Firth, Geoffrey Rush, Antony Sher, Tom Wilkinson, Simon Callow, Steven O'Donnell, Tim McMullen, Rupert Everett (as Christopher Marlowe) uncredited.

Elizabeth II *see* 612

181 Epstein, Brian (1934–1967)

A record shop owner who became the manager of The Beatles, Epstein died of a drug overdose shortly after the band assumed their own management. In TV films he's been played by Brian Jameson in *The Birth of the Beatles* (79), by Richard Morant in *John and Yoko: A Love Story* (85), and by Julian Glover *In His Life: The John Lennon Story* (2000).

David Cardy. *Prick Up Your Ears* (GB/1987/111m/C) D: Stephen Frears. B/on the book by John Lahr. C: Gary Oldman, Alfred Molina, Vanessa Redgrave, Wallace Shawn.

David Angus. *The Hours and Times* (US/1992/60m/BW) D: Christopher Munch. C: Ian Hart, Stephanie Pack, Robin McDonald, Sergio Moreno, Unity Grimwood.

182 Esterhazy, Ferdinand Walsin (1847–1923)

The actual culprit in the **Dreyfus** Affair, Esterhazy was tried and acquitted in 1897, after which he moved to England where he became a grocer.

Oscar Homolka. *The Dreyfus Case* (aka *Dreyfus*) (Germany/1930/BW) D: Richard Oswald. C: Fritz Kortner, Grete Moshelm, Albert Basserman, Heinrich George, Paul Bildt, Ferdinand Hart.

Garry Marsh. *Dreyfus* (aka *The Dreyfus Case*) (GB/1931/90m/BW) D: F.W. Kraemer. B/on the play *The Dreyfus Case* by Herzog & Rehfisch. C: Cedric Hardwicke, Charles Carson, George Merritt, Sam Livesey, Beatrix Thomson, Leonard Shepherd.

Robert Barrat. *The Life of Emile Zola* (US/1937/123m/BW) D: William Dieterle. Best Picture (AA,NYC). C: Paul Muni, Gale Sondergaard, Joseph Schildkraut, Gloria Holden, Donald Crisp, Morris Carnovsky, Louis Calhern, Ralph Morgan, Grant Mitchell, Vladimir Sokoloff.

Anton Walbrook. *I Accuse!* (GB/1958/99m/BW) D: Jose Ferrer. B/on the book *Captain Dreyfus — A Story of Mass Hysteria* by Nicholas Halasz. C: Jose Ferrer, Viveca Lindfors, Leo Genn, Emlyn Williams, David Farrar, Donald Wolfit, Peter Illing.

183 Eugenie, Empress (1826–1920)

(Eugenia Maria de Montijo de Guzman) Eugenie, the daughter of a Spanish count, became the Empress of France upon marrying **Napoleon III**. She took an active interest in government, supporting France's ill-fated actions in Mexico (See **Maximillian**) and in the Franco-Prussian War. In 1870 her husband was deposed and they were exiled to England where she remained for the rest of her life.

Mady Christians. *Ich Und Die Kaiserin* (Germany/1933/84m/BW) D: Friedrich Hollander. C: Conrad Veidt, Lilian Harvey, Friedel Schuster, Heinz Ruchmann, Julius Falkenstein.

Mady Christians. *The Only Girl* (aka *Heart Song*) (GB-Germany/1933/84m/BW) D: Friedrich Hollaender. English language version of the German film *Ich Und Die Kaiserin* (33). C: Lilian Harvey, Charles Boyer, Ernest Thesiger, Julius Falkenstein.

Joyce Bland. *Spy of Napoleon* (GB/1936/98m/BW) D: Maurice Elvey. B/on the novel by the Baroness Orczy. C: Richard Barthelmess, Dolly Haas, Frank Vosper, Lyn Harding.

Iphigenie Castiglioni. *The Story of Louis Pasteur* (US/1936/85m/BW) D: William Dieterle. C: Paul Muni, Josephine Hutchinson, Anita Louise, Donald Woods, Walter Kingsford.

Iphigenie Castiglioni. *Maytime* (US/1937/132m/BW) D: Robert Z. Leonard. B/on the operetta by Rida Johnson Young & Sigmund Romberg. C: Jeanette MacDonald, Nelson Eddy, John Barrymore, Herman Bing, Tom Brown, Guy Bates Post.

Margeruite Margeno. *The Pearls of the Crown* (France/1937/120–100m/BW) D: Sacha Guitry & Christian-Jaque. C: Sacha Guitry, Jacqueline Delubac, Lyn Harding, Ermete Zacconi, Yvette Plenne, Catalano, Arletty, Percy Marmont, Derrick De Marney, Barbara Shaw, Simone Renant, Jean Louis Barrault, Emile Drain, Enrico Glori, Renee Saint-Cyr, Pizani, Claude Dauphin, Aime-Simon Gerard.

Loretta Young. *Suez* (US/1938/104m/BW) D: Allan Dwan. C: Tyrone Power, Miles Mander, Annabella, George Zucco, Leon Ames, Victor Varconi, Brandon Hurst.

Gale Sondergaard. *Juarez* (US/1939/132m/BW) D: William Dieterle. B/on the novel *The Phantom Crown* by Bertita Harding and the play *Juarez and Max-*

imillian by Franz Werfel. C: Paul Muni, Bette Davis, Brian Aherne, Claude Rains, John Garfield, Donald Crisp, Walter Kingsford, Harry Davenport, Joseph Calleia.

Evelyn Brent. *The Mad Empress* (aka *Juarez and Maximillian*) (Mexico-US/ 1939/72m/BW) D: Miguel Contreras Torres. C: Medea Novara, Lionel Atwill, Conrad Nagel, Guy Bates Post, Earl Gunn, Jason Robards, Sr., Frank McGlynn, Duncan Renaldo.

Patricia Morison. *The Song of Bernadette* (US/1943/156m/BW) D: Henry King. B/on the novel by Franz Werfel. Best Picture (GG). C: Jennifer Jones, William Eythe, Charles Bickford, Vincent Price, Lee J. Cobb, Anne Revere, Jerome Cowan, Gladys Cooper.

Margaretta Scott. *Idol of Paris* (GB/1948/106m/BW) D: Leslie Arliss. B/on the novel *Paiva, Queen of Love* by Alfred Shirkauer. C: Michael Rennie, Beryl Baxter, Christine Norden, Miles Malleson, Kenneth Kent.

Espanita Cortez. *The Amazing Monsieur Fabre* (aka *Monsieur Fabre*) (France/ 1952/90–78m/BW) D: Henri Diamond-Berger. C: Pierre Fresnay, Andre Randall, Georges Tabet, Pierre Bertin.

184 Farmer, Frances (1910 [1913, or 1914]–1970)

Broadway/Hollywood actress of the 1930s and 40s, Farmer's problems with alcohol and mental illness ended her film career in 1942. In the TV movie *Will There Really Be a Morning?* (83) she was played by Susan Blakely.

Jessica Lange. *Frances* (US/1982/140m/C) D: Graeme Clifford. C: Sam Shepard, Kim Stanley, Jeffrey DeMunn, Jordan Charney, Donald Craig, Bart Burns.

Sheila McLaughlin. *Committed* (US/1984/77m/BW) D: Sheila McLaughlin & Lynne Tillman. C: Victoria Boothby, Lee Breuer, John Erdman, Heinz Emigholz.

185 Farragut, David Glasgow (1801–1870)

American naval hero of the Civil War, Farragut was the first admiral of the U.S. Navy.

Douglas Wood. *Hearts in Bondage* US/1936/72m/BW) D: Lew Ayres. C: James Dunn, Mae Clark, Charlotte Henry, David Manners, Frank McGlynn, Erville Alderson.

Scott Brady. *Yankee Buccaneer* (US/1952/86m/C) D: Frederick De Cordova. C: Jeff Chandler, Suzan Ball, Joseph Calleia, Rodolfo Acosta, David Janssen, Jay Silverheels, Michael Ansara.

186 Ferdinand V (1452–1516)

King of Aragon, Castille, Leon, Sicily and Naples, Ferdinand, with his wife **Isabella**, not only financed **Columbus** and completed the unification of Spain, but also found time to institute the Spanish Inquisition. In the mini-series *Christopher Columbus* (85) he was played by Nicol Williamson.

Francis Lister. *Christopher Columbus* (GB/1949/104m/C) D: David MacDonald. C: Fredric March, Florence Eldridge, Francis L. Sullivan, Kathleen Ryan, Derek Bond.

Fernando Rimada. *1492: Conquest of Paradise* (US-GB-France-Spain/1992/ 145m/C) D: Ridley Scott. C: Gérard Depardieu, Sigourney Weaver, Armand Assante, Frank Langella, Loren Dean, Angela Molina, Fernando Rey, Michael Wincott, Tcheky Karyo.

Leslie Phillips. *Carry on Columbus* (GB/1992/91m/C) D: Gerald Thomas. C: Jim Dale, Bernard Cribbins, Maureen Lipman, Rik Mayall, Alexei Sayle, Larry Miller, June Whitfield.

Tom Selleck. *Christopher Columbus: The Discovery* (US-Spain/1992/122m/C) D: John Glen. C: George Corraface, Rachel Ward, Marlon Brando, Robert Davi, Catherine Zeta-Jones.

187 Fields, W.C. (1880–1946)

(William Claude Dukenfield) American actor-screenwriter with a unique, misanthropic, comic style, Fields starred in such films as *David Copperfield* (35) and *My Little Chickadee* (40). He was played by Chuck McCann in the TV movie *Mae West* (82).

Rod Steiger. *W.C. Fields and Me* (US/1976/111m/C) D: Arthur Hiller. B/on the book by Carlotta Monti & Cy Rice. C: Valerie Perrine, Jack Cassidy, Paul Stewart, Dana Elcar.

Bob Leeman. *The Rocketeer* (US/1991/108m/C) D: Joe Johnston. B/on the book by Dave Stevens. C: Bill Campbell, Jennifer Connelly, Alan Arkin, Timothy Dalton, Paul Sorvino, Terry O'Quinn, Gene Daily, James Handy.

188 Fitzgerald, Francis Scott Key (1896–1940)

The author of *The Great Gatsby* and *Tender Is the Night*, Fitzgerald also wrote for Hollywood and worked on the screenplays to *Three Comrades* (38) and (uncredited) *Gone With the Wind* (39). Several of his short stories about the ne'er do well screenwriter Pat Hobby have been dramatized for television starring Christopher Lloyd in the wickedly funny, autobiographical role. TV portrayals include Richard Chamberlain in *F. Scott Fitzgerald and "The Last of the Belles"* (74) and Jason Miller in *F. Scott Fitzgerald in Hollywood* (76).

Gregory Peck. *Beloved Infidel* (US/1959/123m/C) D: Henry King. B/on the book by Sheilah Graham. C: Deborah Kerr, Eddie Albert, Herbert Rudley, Philip Ober.

Malcolm Gets. *Mrs. Parker and the Viscous Circle* (US/1994/125m/C) D: Alan Rudolph. C: Jennifer Jason Leigh, Campbell Scott, Matthew Broderick, Peter Gallagher, Tom McGowan, Lili Taylor, Keith Carradine, Nick Cassavetes, David Thornton, Gwyneth Paltrow.

189 Fitzherbert, Maria (1756–1837)

(Maria Anne Smythe) The first wife of **George IV**, and though the widow Fitzherbert's 1785 marriage to the future king was ruled illegal, she remained his mistress for nearly 20 years.

Nora Swinburne. *The Man in Grey* (GB/1943/93m/BW) D: Leslie Arliss. B/on the novel by Lady Eleanor Smith. C: James Mason, Margaret Lockwood, Phyllis Calvert, Stewart Granger, Raymond Lovell, Martita Hunt, Helen Haye.

Joyce Howard. *Mrs. Fitzherbert* (GB/1947/99m/BW) D: Montgomery Tully. B/on the novel *Princess Fitz* by Winifred Carter. C: Peter Graves, Leslie Banks, Margaretta Scott, Wanda Rotha, Mary Clare, Frederick Valk, Ralph Truman, John Stuart, Barry Morse, Henry Oscar, Arthur Dulay, Moira Lister, Julian Dallas, Lily Kann.

Rosemary Harris. *Beau Brummell* (US-GB/1954/111m/C) D: Curtis Bernhardt. B/on the play by Clyde Fitch. C: Stewart Granger, Elizabeth Taylor, Peter Ustinov, Robert Morley, James Donald, James Hayter, Paul Rogers, Noel Willman, Peter Bull.

Pamela Brown. *On a Clear Day You Can See Forever* (US/1970/129m/C) D: Vincente Minnelli. B/on the musical play by Alan Jay Lerner & Burton Lane. C: Barbra Streisand, Yves Montand, Bob Newhart, Roy Kinnear, Larry Blyden, Simon Oakland, Jack Nicholson.

Caroline Harker. *The Madness of King George* (aka *The Madness of George III*) (GB/1994/107m/C) D: Nicholas Hytner. B/on the play by Alan Bennett. C: Nigel Hawthorne, Helen Mirren, Rupert Everett, Amanda Donohoe, Julian Wadham, Ian Holm, Rupert Graves, Geoffrey Palmer, Barry Stanton, Jim Carter, Peter Bride-Kirk, Cyril Shaps.

190 Floyd, Pretty Boy (1901–1934)

(Charles Arthur Floyd) Depression era bankrobber and one-time member of **John Dillinger's** gang, Floyd was finally shot down in an Ohio field by FBI agent **Melvin Purvis**. In TV movies he's been played by Martin Sheen in *The Story of Pretty Boy Floyd* (74) and by Bo Hopkins in *The Kansas City Massacre* (75).

Doug Wilson. *Guns Don't Argue* (US/1955/92m/BW) D: Bill Karn & Richard Kahn. Feature film edited from the TV series *Gangbusters*. C: Myron Healey, Lyle Talbot, Jean Harvey, Paul Dubov, Sam Edwards, Richard Crane, Tamar Cooper, Baynes Barron.

John Ericson. *Pretty Boy Floyd* (US/1959/96m/BW) D: Herbert J. Leder. C: Barry Newman, Joan Harvey, Herbert Evers, Carl York, Peter Falk, Roy Fant, Shirley Smith, Al Lewis.

Robert Conrad. *Young Dillinger* (US/1965/102m/BW) D: Terry Morse. C: Nick Adams, John Ashley, Dan Terranova, Mary Ann Mobley, Victor Buono, John Hoyt, Reed Hadley.

Fabian Forte. *A Bullet for Pretty Boy* (US/1970/88m/C) D: Larry Buchanan. C: Jocelyn Lane, Astrid Warner, Michael Haynes, Adam Roarke.

Steve Kanaly. *Dillinger* (US/1973/107m/C) D: John Milius. C: Warren Oates, Michelle Phillips, Ben Johnson, Harry Dean Stanton, Geoffrey Lewis, Richard Dreyfuss.

Andrew Robinson. *Verne Miller* (US/1987/95m/C) D: Rod Hewitt. C: Scott Glenn, Barbara Stock, Thomas G. Waites, Lucinda Jenney, Diane Salinger, Sean Moran.

191 Ford, Bob (1861–1892)

Remembered as the man who shot **Jesse James** in the back, Ford was eventually shot and killed himself, though not by a member of the James Gang, as has often been portrayed. In TV productions he has been portrayed by Darrel Wilks in *The Last Days of Frank and Jesse James* (86) and by Jim Flowers in *Frank and Jesse* (94).

John Carradine. *Jesse James* (US/1939/105m/C) D: Henry King. C: Tyrone Power, Henry Fonda, Nancy Kelly, Randolph Scott, Henry Hull, Jane Darwell, Charles Tannen.

John Carradine. *The Return of Frank James* (US/1940/92m/C) D: Fritz Lang. C: Henry Fonda, Gene Tierney, Jackie Cooper, Henry Hull, Donald Meek, Charles Tannen, Eddie Collins.

John Ireland. *I Shot Jesse James* (US/1949/81m/BW) D: Samuel Fuller. C: Preston Foster, Barbara Britton, Reed Hadley, Barbara Woodell, Tom Tyler, Tom Noonan.

Clifton Young. *The Return of Jesse James* (US/1950/75m/BW) D: Arthur Hilton. C: John Ireland, Ann Dvorak, Henry Hull, Reed Hadley, Tom Noonan, Hugh O'Brian, Sid Melton.

Roger Anderson. *Gunfire* (US/1950/59m/BW) D: William Berke. C: Don Barry, Robert Lowery, Wally Vernon, Pamela Blake, Claude Stroud, Gaylord Pendleton.

Whit Bissell. *The Great Missouri Raid* (US/1950/84m/C) D: Gordon Douglas. C: Wendell Corey, MacDonald Carey, Ward Bond, Ellen Drew, Bruce Bennett, Bill Williams, Anne Revere, Edgar Buchanan, Louis Jean Heydt, Lois Chartrand, James Millican.

Jim Bannon. *The Great Jesse James Raid* (US/1953/73m/BW) D: Reginald Le Borg. C: Willard Parker, Barbara Payton, Tom Neal, Wallace Ford, Barbara Woodell, Earl Hodgins, Tom Walker.

Rory Mallinson. *Jesse James versus the Daltons* (US/1954/65m/C) D: William Castle. Despite the title, Jesse James is not depicted in the film. C: Brett King, Barbara Lawrence, James Griffith, Bill Phipps, John Cliff, William Tannen.

Carl Thayler. *The True Story of Jesse James* (aka *The James Brothers*) (US/1957/92m/C) D: Nicholas Ray. C: Robert Wagner, Jeffrey Hunter, Hope Lange, Agnes Moorehead, Alan Hale, Jr.

Robert Vaughn. *Hell's Crossroads* (US/1957/73m/C) D: Franklin Andreon. C: Stephen McNally, Peggie Castle, Harry Shannon, Henry Brandon, Myron Healy, Douglas Kennedy.

Nicholas Guest. *The Long Riders* (US/1980/99m/C) D: Walter Hill. C: David Carradine, Keith Carradine, Robert Carradine, James Keach, Stacy Keach, Dennis Quaid, Randy Quaid, Kevin Brophy, Christopher Guest, Pamela Reed, James Remar, Fran Ryan, Savannah Smith, Harry Carey, Jr., James Whitmore, Jr., Shelby Leverington.

Ford, Gerald *see* 587

113   Fouché / 193

192 Foster, Stephen Collins (1826–1864)

American minstrel songwriter, Foster composed such songs as "My Old Kentucky Home" and "Oh, Susannah" among many others.

Douglass Montgomery. *Harmony Lane* (US/1935/85m/BW) D: Joseph Santley. C: Evelyn Venable, Adrienne Ames, Joseph Cawthorn, William Frawley, Clarence Muse.

Don Ameche. *Swanee River* (US/1939/84m/C) D: Sidney Lanfield. C: Andrea Leeds, Al Jolson, Felix Bressart, Chick Chandler, Russell Hicks, George Reed, Charles Trowbridge.

Bill Shirley. *I Dream of Jeannie* (US/1952/90m/C) D: Allan Dwan. C: Ray Middleton, Muriel Lawrence, Christy, Lynn Bari, Louise Beavers, Rex Allen.

193 Fouché, Joseph (1759–1820)

French statesman, Fouché, a consummate career opportunist, managed to serve in every government (notably as **Napoleon's** minister of police) from the French Revolution through the Bourbon Restoration.

Faviere. *Napoleon Bonaparte* (France/1934/140m/BW) D: Abel Gance. Three-dimensional sound version of Gance's 1927 epic *Napoléon*. C: Albert Dieudonné, Edmond von Daele, Alexandre Koubitsky, Antonin Artaud, Boudreau, Alberty, Jack Rye, Gina Manès, Suzanne Blanchetti, Marguerite Gance, Simone Genevois, Genica Missirio.

Enzo Biliotti. *Campo di Maggio* (aka *100 Days of Napoleon*) (Italy/1936/100m/BW) D: Giovacchino Forzano. C: Corrado Racca, Emilia Varini, Pino Locchi, Rosa Stradner, Lamberto Picasso, Augusto Marcacci, Ernseto Marini.

Homero Carpena. *Madame Sans Gene* (Argentina/1945/BW) D: Luis Cesar Amadori. B/on the play by Victorien Sardou. C: Nina Marshall, Eduardo Cuitino, Adrien Cuneo, Luis A. Otero, Herminia Franco.

Arnold Moss. *The Black Book* (aka *Reign of Terror*) (US/1949/89m/BW) D: Anthony Mann. C: Robert Cummings, Arlene Dahl, Richard Hart, Richard Basehart, Wade Crosby, Jess Barker, Wilton Graff, Norman Lloyd, John Doucette.

Jacques Brunius. *Sea Devils* (GB/1953/91m/C) D: Raoul Walsh. B/on *The Toilers of the Sea* by Victor Hugo. C: Yvonne De Carlo, Rock Hudson, Gerard Oury.

Sam Gilman. *Désirée* (US/1954/110m/C) D: Henry Koster. B/on the novel by Annemarie Selinko. C: Marlon Brando, Jean Simmons, Merle Oberon, Michael Rennie, John Hoyt, Elizabeth Sellars, Cameron Mitchell, Cathleen Nesbitt, Alan Napier.

Renaud Mary. *Madame* (aka *Madame Sans-Gene*) (France-Italy-Spain/1961/104m/C) D: Christian-Jaque. B/on the play *Madame Sans Gene* by Emile Moreau & Victorien Sardou. C: Sophia Loren, Robert Hossein, Julien Bertheau, Marina Berti, Carlo Giuffere, Gabriella Pallotta, Annalis Gade, Laura Valenzuela.

Rodolfo Lodi. *Waterloo* (Italy-USSR/1970/123m/C) D: Sergei Bondarchuk. C: Rod Steiger, Orson Welles, Virginia McKenna, Michael Wilding, Donal Donnelly, Christopher Plummer, Jack Hawkins, Dan O'Herlihy, Rupert Davies, Aldo Cecconi.

Albert Finney. *The Duellists* (GB/1977/95m/C) D: Ridley Scott. B/on the story *The Duel* by Joseph Conrad. C: Keith Carradine, Harvey Keitel, Edward Fox, Diana Quick.

194 Fouquet, Nicolas (1615–1680)

French politician, Fouquet sought to succeed **Cardinal Mazarin** in **Louis XIV's** court, but he lost favor with the king and was imprisoned for life from 1661.

Clarence Wilson. *The Count of Monte Cristo* (US/1934/113m/BW) D: Rowland V. Lee. B/on the novel by Alexandre Dumas. C: Robert Donat, Elissa Landi, Louis Calhern, Paul Irving, Ferdinand Munier, Sidney Blackmer, Luis Alberni.

Joseph Schildkraut. *The Man in the Iron Mask* (US/1939/110m/BW) D: James Whale. B/on the novel by Alexandre Dumas. C: Louis Hayward, Joan Bennett, Warren William, Alan Hale, Miles Mander, Walter Kingsford, Albert Dekker, Doris Kenyon, Nigel De Brulier.

Pierre Barrat. *The Rise of Louis XIV* (France/1966/100m/BW) D: Roberto Rossellini. C: Jean-Marie Patte, Raymond Jourdan, Silvagni, Katherina Renn, Dominique Vincent.

Ian McShane. *The Fifth Musketeer* (aka *Behind the Iron Mask*) (Austria/1979/103–90m/C) D: Ken Annakin. B/on the novel *The Man in the Iron Mask* by Alexandre Dumas. C: Beau Bridges, Sylvia Kristel, Ursula Andress, Cornel Wilde, Olivia de Havilland, Alan Hale, Jr., Helmut Dantine, Jose Ferrer, Rex Harrison.

Timothy Bottoms. *The Man in the Iron Mask* (US/1998/85m/C) D: William Richert. B/on the novel by Alexandre Dumas. C: Edward Albert, Dana Barron, Brigid Conley Walsh, Fannie Brett, Meg Foster, James Gammon, Dennis Hayden, William Richert, Nick Richert, Rex Ryon, Brenda James, R.G. Armstrong, Robert Tena, Daniel J. Coplan.

195 Fox, Charles James (1749–1806)

British politician and orator, Fox, a political enemy of **George III** and **William Pitt,** served in Parliament from the age of 19 and was working for the abolition of the slave trade at the time of his death.

Robert Morley. *The Young Mr. Pitt* (GB/1942/118m/BW) D: Carol Reed. C: Robert Donat, Phyllis Calvert, Raymond Lovell, Max Adrian, Felix Aylmer, Albert Lieven, Stephen Haggard, Geoffrey Atkins, John Mills, Herbert Lom, Agnes Laughlan.

Leslie Banks. *Mrs. Fitzherbert* (GB/1947/99m/BW) D: Montgomery Tully. B/on the novel *Princess Fitz* by Winifred Carter. C: Peter Graves, Joyce Howard, Margaretta Scott, Wanda Rotha, Mary Clare, Frederick Valk, Ralph Truman, John Stuart, Barry Morse, Henry Oscar, Arthur Dulay, Moira Lister, Julian Dallas, Lily Kann.

Peter Bull. *Beau Brummell* (US-GB/1954/111m/C) D: Curtis Bernhardt. B/on the play by Clyde Fitch. C: Stewart Granger, Elizabeth Taylor, Peter Ustinov, Robert Morley, James Donald, James Hayter, Rosemary Harris, Paul Rogers, Noel Willman.

Jim Carter. *The Madness of King George* (aka *The Madness of George III*) (GB/1994/107m/C) D: Nicholas Hytner. B/on the play by Alan Bennett. C: Nigel Hawthorne, Helen Mirren, Rupert Everett, Amanda Donohoe, Julian Wadham,

Caroline Harker, Ian Holm, Rupert Graves, Geoffrey Palmer, Barry Stanton, Peter Bride-Kirk, Cyril Shaps.

196 Foy, Edward Fitzgerald "Eddie" (1857–1928)

Foy, a vaudevillian actor who has shown up as a small character in several period films, was given the full Hollywood bio-pic treatment in 1955.

Eddie Foy, Jr. *Frontier Marshal* (US/1939/71m/BW) D: Allan Dwan. B/on the novel *Wyatt Earp, Frontier Marshal* by Stuart N. Lake. C: Randolph Scott, Nancy Kelly, Cesar Romero, Binnie Barnes, John Carradine, Edward Norris, Joe Sawyer, Charles Stevens.

Eddie Foy, Jr. *Lillian Russell* (US/1940/127m/BW) D: Irving Cummings. C: Alice Faye, Edward Arnold, Don Ameche, Henry Fonda, Warren William, Claud Allister, Nigel Bruce, William B. Davidson, Leo Carillo, Milburn Stone.

Eddie Foy, Jr. *Yankee Doodle Dandy* (US/1942/126m/BW) D: Michael Curtiz. C: James Cagney, Joan Leslie, Walter Huston, George Tobias, Captain Jack Young, Wallis Clark.

Charley Foy. *The Woman of the Town* (US/1943/90m/BW) D: George Archainbaud. C: Claire Trevor, Albert Dekker, Barry Sullivan, Henry Hull, Marion Martin, Porter Hall, Beryl Wallace.

Eddie Foy, Jr. *Wilson* (US/1944/154m/C) D: Henry King. C: Alexander Knox, Charles Coburn, Geraldine Fitzgerald, Cedric Hardwicke, Vincent Price, Sidney Blackmer, Marcel Dalio, Edwin Maxwell, Francis X. Bushman, Clifford Brooke.

Bob Hope. *The Seven Little Foys* (US/1955/95m/C) D: Melville Shavelson. C: Milly Vitale, George Tobias, Angela Clark, Herbert Heyes, James Cagney, Billy Gray.

197 Francis of Assisi (1182–1226)

Italian friar and founder of the Franciscan order, Francis was the first person known to receive the stigmata. He was canonized in 1228.

Jose Luiz Jiminez. *St. Francis of Assisi* (aka *San Francisco de Asis*) (Mexico/1943/BW) D: Alberto Gout.

Bradford Dillman. *Francis of Assisi* (US/1961/105m/C) D: Michael Curtiz. B/on the novel *The Joyful Beggar* by Louis De Wohl. C: Dolores Hart, Stuart Whitman, Pedro Armendariz, Cecil Kellaway, Finlay Currie, Eduard Franz, Mervyn Johns, Feodor Chaliapin.

Lou Castel. *Francis of Assisi* (Italy/1966/C) D: Liliana Cavani. Made for Italian TV, released theatrically in other markets.

Graham Faulkner. *Brother Sun, Sister Moon* (GB-Italy/1972/121m/C) D: Franco Zeffirelli. C: Judi Bowker, Alec Guinness, Leigh Lawson, Valentina Cortese, Lee Montague.

Mickey Rourke. *Francesco* (Italy-Germany/1989/155–115m/C) D: Liliana Cavani. B/on the novel *Francis of Assisi* by Herman Hesse. C: Helena Bonham Carter, Paolo Bonacelli, Hans Zischler, Mario Adorf, Peter Berling.

François I *see* 620

François II *see* 622

198 Franklin, Benjamin (1706–1790)

American scientist, writer and statesman, Franklin's involvement in the Revolutionary War has been portrayed several times in films. Television portrayals have been by Robert Symonds in the mini-series *The Adams Chronicles* (76), Tom Bosley in *The Bastard* (78), by Bosley again in *The Rebels* (79), Philip Bosco in *Liberty, the American Revolution* (97), and by Hal Holbrook in *Founding Fathers* (2000).

Thomas Pogue. *Lloyds of London* (US/1936/115m/BW) D: Henry King. C: Freddie Bartholomew, Madeleine Carroll, Sir Guy Standing, Tyrone Power, George Sanders, C. Aubrey Smith, John Burton, Hugh Huntley, Yorke Sherwood, William Wagner.

Walter Walker. *Marie Antoinette* (US/1938/160m/BW) D: W.S. Van Dyke II. B/on the book by Stefan Zweig. C: Norma Shearer, Tyrone Power, John Barrymore, Gladys George, Robert Morley, Anita Louise, Joseph Schildkraut, Albert Dekker, Scotty Becket, Alma Kruger, George Meeker, Wade Crosby, Anthony Warde, John Burton.

George Watts. *The Remarkable Andrew* (US/1942/80m/BW) D: Stuart Heisler. B/on the novel by Dalton Trumbo. C: William Holden, Ellen Drew, Brian Donlevy, Rod Cameron, Richard Webb, Frances Gifford, Brandon Hurst, Gilbert Emery, Montagu Love.

Orson Welles. *Royal Affairs in Versailles* (aka *Versailles*) (aka *Affairs in Versailles*) (aka *If Versailles Were Told to Me*) (aka *Si Versailles M'Eétait Couté*) (France/1953/180–152m/C) D: Sacha Guitry. C: Sacha Guitry, Claudette Colbert, Gerard Phillippe, Micheline Presle, Jean Marais, Georges Marchal, Gilbert Boka, Lana Marconi, Gino Cervi, Fernand Gravet, Louis Arbessier, Jacques Berthier, Samson Fainsilber, Gilbert Gil, Emile Drain, Jacques de Feraudy, Gaston Rey, Philippe Richard.

Charles Coburn. *John Paul Jones* (US/1959/126m/C) D: John Farrow. B/on the story *Nor'wester* by Clements Ripley. C: Robert Stack, Bette Davis, Marisa Pavan, Jean-Pierre Aumont, Macdonald Carey, Susana Canales, John Crawford, Eric Pohlmann.

Orson Welles. *Lafayette* (France/1962/110m/C) D: Jean Dreville. C: Michel Le Royer, Howard St. John, Jack Hawkins, Wolfgang Priess, Vittorio De Sica, Edmund Purdom, Liselotte Pulver, Albert Remy, Renee Saint-Cyr.

Howard Da Silva. *1776* (US/1972/141m/C) D: Peter H. Hunt. B/on the musical by Sherman Edwards and Peter Stone. C: William Daniels, Ken Howard, Donald Madden, Ron Holgate, David Ford, Blythe Danner, Roy Poole, Virginia Vestoff, John Cullum.

Don Forney. *Bill and Ted's Bogus Journey* (US/1991/95m/C) D: Pete Hewitt. C: Keanu Reeves, Alex Winter, George Carlin, William Sadler, Amy Stock-Poynton, Joss Ackland, John Ehrin, Ed Cambridge, Tad Horino.

Jeff Nuttall. *Beaumarchais the Scoundrel* (France/1996/60m/C) D: Edouard Molinaro. Inspired by an unpublished manuscript of Sacha Guitry. C: Fabrice Luchini, Manuel Blanc, Sandrine Kiberlane, Michel Serrault, Jacques Weber, Dominique Besnehard, Murray Head, Judith Godreche.

John Adams (William Daniels, left) and Ben Franklin (Howard Da Silva) con-
fer over the musical affairs of state as they re-create their Broadway roles in *1776*
(1972). (Museum of Modern Art Film Stills Archive)

199 Franz Josef (1830–1916)

Emperor Franz Josef has probably been portrayed in more films than any other
Austrian short of **Adolf Hitler**. His life was marked by great personal tragedy
including the suicide of his only son, the assassination of his wife, and finally
the assassination of his nephew, Franz Ferdinand, an act that led to the outbreak
of World War I.

Anton Vaverka. *Melody Man* (US/1930/75m/C) D: R. William Neill. B/on
the play by Richard Rodgers & Lorenz Hart. C: William Collier, Jr., Alice Day,
John St. Polis.

Paul Otto. *Elisabeth of Austria* (Germany/1931/110–74m/BW) D: Adolf Trotz.
C: Lil Dagover, Maria Solveg, Ekkehard Arend, Gert Pilary, Ida Perry, Ludwig
Stoessel.

Walter Janssen. *Kaiserliebchen* (Germany/1931/82m/BW) D: Hans Tintner. C:
Liane Haid, Wilhelm Bendow, Colette Jell, Hans Jaray, August Jonker.

Eugen Klöepfer. *1914: The Last Days Before the War* (Germany/1931/110m/BW)
D: Richard Oswald. C: Albert Basserman, Wolfgang von Schwind, Heinrich
Schroth, Reinhold Schunzel, Lucie Hoeflich, Ferdinand Hart, Oskar Homolka,
Theodor Loos, Alfred Abel, Paul Mederow, Heinrich George, Varl Goetz, Paul Bildt.

Jean Dax. *Mayerling* (France/1935/96m/BW) D: Anatole Litvak. B/on the novel *Idyl's End* by Claude Anet. C: Charles Boyer, Danielle Darrieux, Suzy Prim, Gabrielle Dorziat, Jean Debucourt, Vladimir Sokoloff.

Curt Jurgens. *The Royal Waltz* (Germany/1935/80m/BW) D: Herbert Maisch. C: Paul Hoerbiger, Carola Hoehn, Anton Pointer, Willi Forst.

Paul Otto. *Ein Liebesroman Im Hause Habsburg* (aka *Das Geheimnis Um Johannes Orth*) (Germany/1936/81m/BW) D: Willi Wolff. C: Paul Richter, Karl Ludwig Diehl, Fritz Albertl, Paul Wegener.

Franchot Tone. *The King Steps Out* (US/1936/85m/BW) D: Josef von Sternberg. B/on the play *Cissy* by Gustav Hohn & Ernest Decsey and the operetta by Ernst & Hubert Marischka. C: Grace Moore, Walter Connolly, Raymond Walburn.

Earl Ehmann. *Love at Court* (aka *Mein Liebster Ist Ein Jaegersman*) (Germany/1936/84m/BW) D: Walter Kolm. C: Georg Alexander, Fred von Bohlen.

Henry Hull. *The Great Waltz* (US/1938/107m/BW) D: Julien Duvivier. C: Luise Rainer, Fernand Gravet, Miliza Korjus, Hugh Herbert, Lionel Atwill, Curt Bois, George Houston.

Reginald Owen. *Florian* (US/1940/91m/BW) D: Edwin L. Marin. B/on the novel by Felix Salten. C: Robert Young, Helen Gilbert, Lee Bowman, William B. Davidson.

Jean Worms. *From Mayerling to Serajevo* (aka *De Mayerling a Sarajevo*) (France/1940/95m/BW) D: Max Ophuls. C: John Lodge, Edwige Feuilliere, Gabrielle Dorziat.

Richard Haydn. *The Emperor Waltz* (US/1948/105m/C) D: Billy Wilder. C: Bing Crosby, Joan Fontaine, Roland Culver, Lucile Watson, Sig Rumann, Julia Dean.

Jean Debucourt. *The Secret of Mayerling* (aka *Le Secret de Mayerling*) (France/1949/90m/BW) D: Jean Delannoy. C: Jean Marais, Dominique Blanchar, Jacques Dacquime.

Karl Schoenboeck. *Die Försterchristl* (Germany/1952/95m/BW) D: Arthur M. Rabenalt. B/on the operetta by George Jarno & M. Buchbinder. C: Hannerl Matz.

Rudolf Forster. *The White Horse Inn* (Austria/1952/C) D: Willi Forst. B/on the operetta by Leo Benatzky. C: Johanna Matz, Johannes Heesters, Walter Muller, Paul Westermeier.

Eric Frey. *The Eternal Waltz* (aka *Ewiger Walzer*) (Germany/1954/97m/C) D: Paul Verhoeven. C: Bernhard Wicki, Hilde Krahl, Annemarie Dueringer, Friedl Loor, Arnulf Schroeder, Hans Putz, Eduard Strauss, Jr.

Karl Boehm. *Forever My Love* (Austria/1962/147m/C) D: Ernest Marischka. U.S. theatrical release edited from three Austrian films: *Sissi* (55), *Sissi Die Junge Kaiserin* (56), and *Sissi-Schicksalsjare Einer Kaiserin* (57). C: Romy Schneider, Magda Schneider, Vilma Degischer, Gustav Knuth, Uta Franz.

James Mason. *Mayerling* (GB/1968/140m/C) D: Terence Young. B/on the novel *Mayerling* by Claude Anet and on the novel *The Archduke* by Michael Arnold. C: Omar Sharif, Catherine Deneuve, Ava Gardner, Genevieve Page, James Robertson Justice.

Jack Hawkins. *Oh! What a Lovely War* (GB/1969/144m/C) D: Richard Attenborough. B/on the musical play by Joan Littlewood and the play *The Long, Long Trail* by Charles Chilton. Best English Language Foreign Film (GG), and the United Nations Award (BFA). C: Pamela Abbott, Laurence Olivier, Ralph Richardson, John Mills, John Gabriel, Paul Daneman, Dirk Bogarde, Vanessa Redgrave, Kenneth More, Michael Redgrave, Ian Holm, Wensley Pithey, Frank Forsyth, John Gielgud, Maggie Smith, Guy Middleton.

J. Schonburg-Hartenstein. *The Great Waltz* (US/1972/135m/C) D: Andrew L. Stone. C: Horst Bucholz, Mary Costa, Rossano Brazzi, Nigel Patrick, Yvonne Mitchell, Dominique Weber.

200 Fräulein Doktor (1887–1940)

(Elsbeth Schragmüller) A famous German spy of the first World War, Fräulein Doktor did no field work, but trained spies at a school in Antwerp where one of her students was **Mata Hari.**

Myrna Loy. *Stamboul Quest* (US/1934/88m/BW) D: Sam Wood. C: George Brent, Lionel Atwill, C. Henry Gordon, Douglas Dumbrille, Judith Vosselli, Mischa Auer, Joseph Sawyer.

Dito Parlo. *Mademoiselle Docteur* (France/1936/87m/BW) D: G.W. Pabst. C: Pierre Blanchar, Pierre Fresnay, Charles Dullin, Louis Jouvet, Viviane Romance.

Dito Parlo. *Under Secret Orders* (GB-France/1937/66m/BW) D: Edmond Greville. English language version of *Mademoiselle Docteur* (36). C: John Loder, Erich von Stroheim.

Suzy Kendall. *Fräulein Doctor* (Italy-Yugoslavia/1969/102m/C) D: Alberto Lattuada. C: Kenneth More, Capucine, James Booth, Alexander Knox, Walter Williams.

Gaye Brown. *Mata Hari* (GB-US/1985/108m/C) D: Curtis Harrington. C: Sylvia Kristel, Christopher Cazenove, Gottfried John, Oliver Tobias.

201 Freed, Alan (1922–1965)

A noted radio personality, Freed helped popularize the term (and the music) "Rock and Roll." He appeared as himself in several films including *Rock Around the Clock* (56), *Rock, Rock, Rock!* (56), and *Mr. Rock and Roll* (57) which supposedly told the story of how he "invented" Rock and Roll. Freed was portrayed by Judd Nelson in the TV film *Mr. Rock 'n' Roll: The Alan Freed Story* (99).

Tim McIntire. *American Hot Wax* (US/1978/91m/C) D: Floyd Mutrux. C: Fran Drescher, Jay Leno, Laraine Newman, Carl Earl Weaver, Jeff Altman, John Lehne.

Jeffrey Alan Chandler. *La Bamba* (US/1987/108m/C) D: Luis Valdez. C: Lou Diamond Phillips, Esai Morales, Rosana De Soto, Elizabeth Pena, Marshall Crenshaw.

Robert Lesser. *Great Balls of Fire* (US/1989/108m/C) D: Jim McBride. B/on the book by Myra Lewis & Murray Silver. C: Dennis Quaid, Winona Ryder, Alec Baldwin, John Doe, Stephen Toblowsky, Trey Wilson, Michael St. Gerard, Lisa Jane Persky, Steve Allen.

202 Frémont, John Charles (1813–1890)

An early explorer of the American West, Frémont was a pivotal figure in the annexation of California. He was portrayed by Richard Chamberlain in the television mini-series *Dream West* (86).

Charles Trowbridge. *Mutiny on the Blackhawk* (US/1939/67m/BW) D: Christy Cabanne. C: Richard Arlen, Andy Devine, Constance Moore, Noah Beery, Sr., Richard Lane.

Dana Andrews. *Kit Carson* (US/1940/97m/BW) D: George B. Seitz. C: Jon Hall, Lynn Bari, Raymond Hatton, Edwin Maxwell, Harold Huber.

LeRoy Mason. *Along the Oregon Trail* (US/1947/64m/BW) D: R.G. Springsteen. C: Monte Hale, Adrian Booth, Roy Barcroft, Will Wright, Forrest Taylor, Kermit Maynard.

George Eldridge. *California Conquest* (US/1952/78m/C) D: Lew Landers. C: Cornel Wilde, Teresa Wright, Alfonzo Bedoya, Lisa Ferraday, John Dehner, Eugene Iglesias.

203 Freud, Sigmund (1856–1939)

Renowned Austrian physician and neurologist, Freud was the founder of psychoanalysis (and thus, I suppose, father of the Oedipus Complex).

Montgomery Clift. *Freud* (aka *The Secret Passion*) (US/1962/140–120m/BW) D: John Huston. C: Susannah York, Larry Parks, Susan Kohner, Eric Portman.

Alan Arkin. *The Seven Percent Solution* (GB/1977/113m/C) D: Herbert Ross. B/on the novel by Nicholas Meyer. C: Vanessa Redgrave, Robert Duvall, Nicol Williamson.

Alec Guinness. *Lovesick* (US/1983/95m/C) D: Marshall Brickman. C: Dudley Moore, Elizabeth McGovern, Christine Baranski, Gene Saks, John Huston.

Bud Cort. *The Secret Diary of Sigmund Freud* (US/1984/99m/C) D: Danford B. Greene. C: Carol Kane, Klaus Kinski, Marisa Berenson, Carroll Baker, Dick Shawn, Ferdinand Mayne.

Frank Finlay (voice only). *1919* (GB/1985/99m/BW/C) D: Hugh Brody. C: Paul Scofield, Maria Schell, Dianna Quick, Clare Higgins, Colin Firth.

Tim McKew. *Young Einstein* (Australia/1988/91m/C) D: Yahoo Serious. C: Yahoo Serious, Odile Le Clezio, Pee Wee Wilson, Basil Clarke, Ian James Tait, Nick Conroy.

Rod Loomis. *Bill and Ted's Excellent Adventure* (US/1989/90m/C) D: Stephen Herek. C: Keanu Reeves, Alex Winter, George Carlin, Amy Stock-Poynton, Terry Camilleri, Dan Shor, Clifford David, Al Leong, Jane Wiedlin, Robert V. Barron, Tony Steedman, Fee Waybill.

Sieghardt Rupp. *Weininger's Last Night* (Austria /1991/100m/C) D: Paulus Manker. B/on the play *The Soul of a Jew* by Joshua Sobol. C: Paulus Manker, Hermann Schmid.

Peter Michael Goetz. *The Empty Mirror* (US/1997/129m/C) D: Barry J. Hershey. C: Norman Rodway, Camilla Søeberg, Doug McKeon, Glenn Shadix, Joel Grey, Hope Allen, Lori Scott, Raul Kobrinsky, Randy Zielinski, Shannon Yowell, Courtney Dale, Elizabeth Hershey, Christopher Levitus, Chip Marks.

204 Fulton, Robert (1765–1815)

American inventor and engineer, Fulton developed the first commercially successful steamboat and had also built a working submarine (named The Nautilas) as early as 1800.

Richard Greene. *Little Old New York* (US/1940/99m/BW) D: Henry King. B/on the play by Rida Johnson Young. C: Alice Faye, Fred MacMurray, Brenda Joyce, Roger Imhof, Theodore von Eltz, Robert Middlemass, Andy Devine.

Orson Welles. *Austerlitz* (aka *The Battle of Austerlitz*) (France-Italy-Yugoslavia/1959/166m/C) D: Abel Gance. C: Pierre Mondy, Jean Mercure, Martine Carol, Jack Palance, Claudia Cardinale, Georges Marchal, Roland Bartrop, Anthony Stuart, Jean Marais, Vittorio De Sica, Ettore Manni.

205 Gable, William Clark (1901–1960)

The "King of Hollywood," Gable appeared in more than 70 films including *Mutiny on The Bounty* (35), *It Happened One Night* (34), and his career peak as Rhett Butler in *Gone With the Wind* (39). His third wife, Carole Lombard (1908–1942), was played by Jill Clayburgh in *Gable and Lombard*. TV portrayals of Gable and Lombard include: Edward Winter and Sharon Gless in *Moviola: The Scarlett O'Hara War* (80), and Gary Wayne and Denise Crosby in *Malice in Wonderland* (85).

James Brolin. *Gable and Lombard* (US/1976/131m/C) D: Sidney J. Furie. C: Jill Clayburgh, Red Buttons, Allen Garfield, Joanne Linville, Alice Backes, Morgan Brittany.

Larry Pennell. *Marilyn: The Untold Story* (US/1980/156m/C) D: John Flynn, Jack Arnold & Lawrence Schiller. B/on the book *Marilyn* by Norman Mailer. C: Catherine Hicks, Richard Basehart, Frank Converse, John Ireland, Viveca Lindfors, Jason Miller, Sheree North.

Nick Conroy. *Young Einstein* (Australia/1988/91m/C) D: Yahoo Serious. C: Yahoo Serious, Odile Le Clezio, Pee Wee Wilson, Basil Clarke, Tim McKew, Ian James Tait.

Gene Daily. *The Rocketeer* (US/1991/108m/C) D: Joe Johnston. B/on the book by Dave Stevens. C: Bill Campbell, Jennifer Connelly, Alan Arkin, Timothy Dalton, Paul Sorvino, Terry O'Quinn, Bob Leeman, James Handy.

206 Galileo Galilei (1564–1642)

Italian physicist and developer of the first astronomical telescope, Galileo was condemned to life imprisonment by the Catholic Church for his belief that the Earth rotated around the Sun.

Cyril Cusack. *Galileo* (Italy-Bulgaria/1968/108m/C) D: Liliana Cavani. C: Lou Castel, Piero Vida, Gigi Ballista, Irene Kokonova, Paolo Graziosi.

Topol. *Galileo* (GB/1973/145m/C) D: Joseph Losey. B/on Charles Laughton's adaption of the play *Galileo* by Bertolt Brecht. C: Edward Fox, Colin Blakely, Georgia Brown, Michael Lonsdale, Margaret Leighton, John Gielgud, Michael Gough.

207 Gandhi, Mahatma (1869–1948)

(Mohandas Karamchand Gandhi) Religious, social, political leader, Gandhi's program of civil disobedience hastened the end of the British Raj in India.

J.S. Casshyap. *Nine Hours to Rama* (aka *Nine Hours to Live*) (US-GB/1963/ 125m/C) D: Mark Robson. B/on the book by Stanley Wolpert. C: Horst Bucholz, Jose Ferrer, Diane Baker.

Ben Kingsley * Best Actor (AA, BFA, NYC). *Gandhi* (GB-India/1982/188m/C) D: Richard Attenborough. Best Picture (AA, BFA, NYC), Best Director (AA, BFA, DGA). C: Candice Bergen, Edward Fox, John Gielgud, Trevor Howard, Peter Harlowe, Martin Sheen, Roshan Seth, Alyque Padamsee.

Sam Dastor. *Jinnah* (Pakistan/1998/110m/C) D: Jamil Dehlavi. C: Christopher Lee, James Fox, Maria Aitken, Shashi Kapoor, Richard Lintern, Shireen Shah, Robert Ashby, Indira Varma, Shakeel, Vaneeza Ahmed, Roger Brierley, Rowena Cooper, James Curran, Vernon Dobtcheff, Michael Elwyn, Ian Gelder, Christopher Godwin, John Grillo, Talat Hussain, John Nettleton, Alyque Padamsee.

A powerful character study of Ben Kingsley in his Academy Award winning performance as Mohandas K. Gandhi. From *Gandhi* (1982); which received 8 Oscars, including Best Picture, Director, Actor, and Screenplay. (Museum of Modern Art Film Stills Archive)

Garfield, James A. see 581

208 Garrett, Patrick Floyd "Pat" (1850–1908)

As with **Bob Ford**, Garrett is remembered for shooting a famous outlaw (who had once been his friend) in the back. In Garrett's case it was **Billy the Kid**, and, as with Ford, Garrett's life didn't improve much with the notoriety gained from the killing and he, himself, was shot to death years later. In *Outcasts of the Trail* (49) Monte Hale plays a hero named Pat Garrett, though the story has nothing to do with Billy the Kid.

Wallace Beery. *Billy the Kid* (aka *The Highwayman Rides*) (US/1930/95m/BW) D: King Vidor. B/on the novel *The Saga of Billy the Kid* by Walter Noble Burns.

C: Johnny Mack Brown, Karl Dane, Wyndham Standing, Russell Simpson, Blanche Frederici.

Wade Boteler. *Billy the Kid Returns* (US/1938/51m/BW) D: Joseph Kane. C: Roy Rogers, Smiley Burnette, Lynne Roberts, Morgan Wallace, Fred Kohler, Joseph Crehan.

Brian Donlevy (as Jim Sherwood). *Billy the Kid* (US/1941/94m/C) D: David Miller. B/on the novel *The Saga of Billy the Kid* by Walter Noble Burns. C: Robert Taylor, Ian Hunter.

Thomas Mitchell. *The Outlaw* (US/1943/126m/BW) D: Howard Hughes. C: Jack Buetel, Jane Russell, Walter Huston, Mimi Aguglia, Joe Sawyer, Dickie Jones.

Charles Bickford. *Four Faces West* (aka *They Passed This Way*) (US/1948/96m/BW) D: Alfred E. Green. B/on the novel *Paso Por Aqui* by Eugene Manlove Rhodes. C: Joel McCrea, Frances Dee, Joseph Calleia, William Conrad, Martin Garralaga.

Frank Wilcox. *The Kid from Texas* (aka *Texas Kid, Outlaw*) (US/1950/78m/C) D: Kurt Neumann. C: Audie Murphy, Gale Storm, Shepperd Strudwick, Will Geer, Robert Barrat.

Robert Lowrey. *I Shot Billy the Kid* (US/1950/57m/BW) D: William Berke. C: Donald Barry, Wally Vernon, Tom Neal, Wendy Lee, Claude Stroude, Richard Farmer.

James Griffith. *The Law vs. Billy the Kid* (US/1954/72m/C) D: William Castle. C: Scott Brady, Betta St. John, Alan Hale, Jr., Paul Cavanagh, Bill Phillips, Otis Garth, Robert Griffin.

James Craig. *Last of the Desperadoes* (US/1955/56m/BW) D: Sam Newfield. C: Jim Davis, Barton MacLane, Margia Dean, Donna Martel, Bob Steele, Stanley Clements.

John Dehner. *The Left-Handed Gun* (US/1958/102m/BW) D: Arthur Penn. B/on the teleplay *The Death of Billy the Kid* by Gore Vidal. C: Paul Newman, Lita Milan, Hurd Hatfield, James Congdon, Colin Keith-Johnston, John Dierkes, Denver Pyle.

George Montgomery. *Badman's Country* (US/1958/85m/BW) D: Fred F. Sears. C: Buster Crabbe, Neville Brand, Karin Booth, Gregory Wolcott, Malcolm Atterbury, Russell Johnson, Richard Devon, Morris Ankrum.

Rod Cameron. *Bullets Don't Argue* (aka *The Last Two from Rio Bravo*) (Germany-Italy-Spain/1965/93m/C) D: Manfred Rieger. C: Dick Palmer, Vivi Bach, Kai Fisher.

Fausto Tozzi. *The Man Who Killed Billy the Kid* (aka *For a Few Bullets More*) (Spain-Italy/1967/90m/C) D: Julio Buchs. C: Peter Lee Lawrence, Diane Zura, Gloria Milland.

Glenn Corbett. *Chisum* (US/1970/110m/C) D: Andrew McLaglen. C: John Wayne, Forrest Tucker, Christopher George, Ben Johnson, Geoffrey Deuel, Andrew Prine, Patric Knowles, Lynda Day, John Agar, Robert Donner, Ray Teal, Ron Soble.

James Coburn. *Pat Garrett and Billy the Kid* (US/1973/122–106m/C) D: Sam Peckinpah. C: Kris Kristofferson, Bob Dylan, Jason Robards, Richard Jaeckel, Katy Jurado, Barry Sullivan.

Patrick Wayne. *Young Guns* (US/1988/97m/C) D: Chris Cain. C: Emilio Estevez, Kiefer Sutherland, Lou Diamond Phillips, Charlie Sheen, Casey Siemaszko, Terence Stamp.

William Petersen. *Young Guns II* (US/1990/105m/C) D: Geoff Murphy. C: Emilio Estevez, Kiefer Sutherland, Lou Diamond Phillips, Christian Slater, James Coburn, Balthazar Getty, Scott Wilson, Chief Buddy Redbow, Alan Ruck, R.D. Call, Jack Kehoe.

209 Garrick, David (1717–1779)

The most renowned English actor of the 18th century, Garrick was noted for his performances of Macbeth and King Lear. He was also a partner and manager of London's Drury Lane from 1747 to 1776 when he sold his interest in the theatre to **Richard B. Sheridan**.

Cedric Hardwicke. *Peg of Old Drury* (GB/1935/74m/BW) D: Herbert Wilcox. B/on the play *Masks and Faces* by Charles Reade. C: Anna Neagle, Margaretta Scott, Robert Atkins, Jack Hawkins, Maire O'Neill, Leslie French, Sara Allgood, Tom Heslewood.

Brian Aherne. *The Great Garrick* (US/1937/82m/BW) D: James Whale. B/on the play *Ladies and Gentlemen* by Ernest Vadja. C: Olivia de Havilland, Edward Everett Horton, Melville Cooper, Lionel Atwill, Henry O'Neill, Lana Turner, Albert Dekker.

George Baxter. *The Lady and the Bandit* (aka *Dick Turpin's Ride*) (US/1951/79m/BW) D: Ralph Murphy. B/on the poem "The Highwayman" by Alfred Noyes. C: Louis Hayward, Patricia Medina, Suzanne Dalbert, John Williams, Alan Mowbray, Ivan Triesault.

210 Gauguin (1848–1903)

(Eugène Henri Paul Gaugin) French painter and contemporary of **Van Gogh**, Gaugin is remembered for his works made in Tahiti using bright, non-naturalistic colors. He was played by David Carradine in the TV movie *Gaugin the Savage* (80).

George Sanders (as Charles Strickland). *The Moon and Sixpence* (US/1943/89m/BW) D: Albert Lewin. B/on the novel by W. Somerset Maugham. C: Herbert Marshall, Steve Geray, Doris Dudley.

Anthony Quinn * Best Supporting Actor (AA). *Lust for Life* (US/1956/122m/C) D: Vincente Minnelli. B/on the novel by Irving Stone. C: Kirk Douglas, James Donald, Pamela Brown, Jerry Bergen.

Donald Sutherland. *The Wolf at the Door* (France-Denmark/1986/102m/C) D: Henning Carlsen. C: Valerie Morea, Max von Sydow, Sofie Graboel, Yves Barsack.

Wladimir Yordanoff. *Vincent and Theo* (France-GB/1990/138m/C) D: Robert Altman. C: Tim Roth, Paul Rhys, Adrian Brine, Johanna Ter Steege, Peter Tuinman.

211 Gehrig, Henry Louis "Lou" (1903–1941)

Baseball's "Iron Horse," Gehrig died at the age of 37 of amyotrophic lateral sclerosis which has come to be known as "Lou Gehrig's Disease." Lou was portrayed by Edward Herrmann in the TV film *A Love Affair: The Eleanor and Lou Gehrig Story* (78).

    Gary Cooper. *The Pride of the Yankees* (US/1942/127m/BW) D: Sam Wood. C: Teresa Wright, Dan Duryea, Walter Brennan, Babe Ruth, Ernie Adams, David Manley, Harry Harvey.

    Michael McGrady. *The Babe* (US/1992/115m/C) D: Arthur Hiller. C: John Goodman, Kelly McGillis, Trini Alvarado, Bruce Boxleitner, Joe Ragno, Bernie Gigliotti, Randy Steinmeyer, Michael Nicolasi, Bernard Kates, Harry Hutchinson, Guy Barile.

212 Genghis Khan (1167?–1227)

(Jenghiz Khan) Mongol conqueror, the Khan's empire included much of China, Korea, Siberia and the Middle East.

    Marvin Miller. *The Golden Horde* (aka *The Golden Horde of Genghis Khan*) (US/1951/77m/C) D: George Sherman. C: Ann Blyth, David Farrar, George Macready.

    Manuel Conde. *Genghis Khan* (Phillipines/1952/88m/BW) D: Lou Salvador & Manuel Conde. C: Elvira Reyes, Lou Salvador, Andres Centenera, Darmo Acosta.

    John Wayne. *The Conqueror* (US/1956/111m/C) D: Dick Powell. C: Susan Hayward, Pedro Armendariz, Agnes Moorehead, Thomas Gomez, William Conrad, Lee Van Cleef.

    Roldano Lupi. *The Mongols* (France-Italy/1961/115m/C) D: Andre De Toth, Leopoldo Savona & Riccardo Freda. C: Jack Palance, Anita Ekberg, Franco Silva.

    Omar Sharif. *Genghis Khan* (US/1965/124m/C) D: Henry Levin. C: Stephen Boyd, James Mason, Eli Wallach, Françoise Dorleac, Telly Savalas, Robert Morley.

    Mondo. *Shanks* (US/1974/93m/C) D: William Castle. C: Marcel Marceau, Tsilla Chelton, Philippe Clay, Cindy Eilbacher, Helena Kallianiotes, Don Calfa, Larry Bishop, Phil Adams, William Castle.

    Al Leong. *Bill and Ted's Excellent Adventure* (US/1989/90m/C) D: Stephen Herek. C: Keanu Reeves, Alex Winter, George Carlin, Amy Stock-Poynton, Terry Camilleri, Dan Shor, Clifford David, Rod Loomis, Jane Wiedlin, Robert V. Barron, Tony Steedman, Fee Waybill.

213 Genovese, Vito (1897–1969)

Powerful New York gangster, Genovese headed a national crime syndicate even after being arrested on drug charges in 1959.

    Lino Ventura. *The Valachi Papers* (Italy-France/1972/125m/C) D: Terence Young. B/on the book by Peter Maas. C: Charles Bronson, Jill Ireland, Fausto Tozzi, Angelo Infante, Giancomino De Michelis, Joseph Wiseman, Walter Chiari.

    Charles Cioffi. *Lucky Luciano* (aka *Re: Lucky Luciano*) (Italy-France/1973/113m/C) D: Francesco Rosi. C: Gian Maria Volonte, Rod Steiger, Charles Siragusa, Edmond O'Brien, Vincent Gardenia, Silverio Blasi.

Don Carrara. *Bugsy* (US/1991/135m/C) D: Barry Levinson. B/on the book *We Only Kill Each Other: The Life and Bad Times of Bugsy Siegel* by Dean Jennings. C: Warren Beatty, Annette Bening, Harvey Keitel, Ben Kingsley, Joe Mantegna, Elliott Gould, Wendy Phillips, Bill Graham, Carmine Caridi, Ksenia Prohaska.

George I *see* 608

George II *see* 609

214 George III (1738–1820)

English king who ruled over the loss of the American colonies, George's mental instability (caused by the disease porphyria) so incapacitated him that **George IV** succeeded as Regent in 1811. Television portrayals have been by John Tillinger in the mini-series *The Adams Chronicles* (76), and Alex Jennings in *Liberty, the American Revolution* (97).

Henry Mowbray. *The Pursuit of Happiness* (US/1934/72m/BW) D: Alexander Hall. B/on the play by Lawrence Langner & Armina Marshall. C: Francis Lederer, Joan Bennett, Boyd Irwin.

Raymond Lovell. *The Young Mr. Pitt* (GB/1942/118m/BW) D: Carol Reed. C: Robert Donat, Robert Morley, Phyllis Calvert, Max Adrian, Felix Aylmer, Albert Lieven, Stephen Haggard, Geoffrey Atkins, John Mills, Herbert Lom, Agnes Laughlan.

Frederick Valk. *Mrs. Fitzherbert* (GB/1947/99m/BW) D: Montgomery Tully. B/on the novel *Princess Fitz* by Winifred Carter. C: Peter Graves, Joyce Howard, Leslie Banks, Margaretta Scott, Wanda Rotha, Mary Clare, Ralph Truman, John Stuart, Barry Morse, Henry Oscar, Arthur Dulay, Moira Lister, Julian Dallas, Lily Kann.

Robert Morley. *Beau Brummell* (US-GB/1954/111m/C) D: Curtis Bernhardt. B/on the play by Clyde Fitch. C: Stewart Granger, Elizabeth Taylor, Peter Ustinov, James Donald, James Hayter, Rosemary Harris, Paul Rogers, Noel Willman, Peter Bull.

Eric Pohlmann. *John Paul Jones* (US/1959/126m/C) D: John Farrow. B/on the story *Nor'wester* by Clements Ripley. C: Robert Stack, Bette Davis, Marisa Pavan, Charles Coburn, Jean-Pierre Aumont, Macdonald Carey, Susana Canales, John Crawford.

Eric Pohlmann. *Dr. Syn, Alias the Scarecrow* (aka *The Scarecrow of Romney Marsh*) (US-GB/1962/129–84m/C) D: James Nielson. B/on a book by Russell Thorndyke & William Buchanan. C: Patrick McGoohan, George Cole, Tony Britton, Michael Hordern.

Ralph Richardson. *Lady Caroline Lamb* (GB/1972/122m/C) D: Robert Bolt. C: Sarah Miles, Jon Finch, Richard Chamberlain, John Mills, Margaret Leighton, Laurence Olivier.

Nigel Hawthorne. *The Madness of King George* (aka *The Madness of George III*) (GB/1994/107m/C) D: Nicholas Hytner. B/on the play by Alan Bennett. C: Helen Mirren, Rupert Everett, Amanda Donohoe, Julian Wadham, Caroline

Harker, Ian Holm, Rupert Graves, Geoffrey Palmer, Barry Stanton, Jim Carter, Peter Bride-Kirk, Cyril Shaps.

215 George IV (1762–1830)

The son of **George III,** George was never popular with the English people but has proved very popular with filmakers on both sides of the Atlantic. Though never featured in his own biopic, the Prince Regent has been depicted in more films than any other British King.

Wlliam F. Schoeller. *The Royal Box* (US/1930/76m/BW) D: Bryan Foy. B/on the play *Kean* by Alexandre Dumas. C: Alexander Moissi, Camilla Horn, Sig Rumann.

Lumsden Hare. *The House of Rothschild* (US/1934/94m/C) D: Alfred Werker. B/on the play by George Humbert Westley. C: George Arliss, Boris Karloff, Loretta Young, Robert Young, C. Aubrey Smith, Florence Arliss, Alan Mowbray, Georges Renavent, Holmes Herbert.

Olaf Hytten. *Becky Sharp* (US/1935/83m/C) D: Rouben Mamoulian. B/on the play by Langdon Mitchell and the novel *Vanity Fair* by William Makepeace Thackeray. C: Miriam Hopkins, Frances Dee, Cedric Hardwicke, Billie Burke, William Faversham.

Nigel Bruce. *The Scarlet Pimpernel* (GB/1935/85m/BW) D: Harold Young. B/on the novel by the Baroness Orczy. C: Leslie Howard, Merle Oberon, Raymond Massey, Bramwell Fletcher, Anthony Bushell, Walter Rilla, Ernest Milton, Bruce Belfrage.

Hugh Huntley. *Lloyds of London* (US/1936/115m/BW) D: Henry King. C: Freddie Bartholomew, Madeleine Carroll, Sir Guy Standing, Tyrone Power, George Sanders, C. Aubrey Smith, John Burton, Thomas Pogue, Yorke Sherwood, William Wagner.

Gilbert Davis. *Amateur Gentleman* (GB/1936/93m/BW) D: Thornton Freeland. B/on the novel by Jeffrey Farnol. C: Douglas Fairbanks, Jr., Elissa Landi, Gordon Harker.

Evelyn Roberts. *The Return of the Scarlet Pimpernel* (GB/1937/94–80m/BW) D: Hans Schwartz. C: Barry K. Barnes, Sophie Stewart, Margareta Scott, James Mason, Henry Oscar, Esme Percy.

Raymond Lovell. *The Man in Grey* (GB/1943/93m/BW) D: Leslie Arliss. B/on the novel by Lady Eleanor Smith. C: James Mason, Margaret Lockwood, Phyllis Calvert, Stewart Granger, Nora Swinburne, Martita Hunt, Helen Haye.

Michael Dyne. *Kitty* (US/1945/103m/BW) D: Mitchell Leisen. B/on the novel by Rosamund Marshall. C: Paulette Goddard, Ray Milland, Patric Knowles, Reginald Owen, Cecil Kellaway, Gordon Richards, Constance Collier, Dennis Hoey.

Peter Graves. *The Laughing Lady* (GB/1946/100m/C) D: Paul L. Stein. B/on the play by Ingram d'Abbes. C: Anne Ziegler, Webster Booth, Charles Goldner, Anthony Nicholls.

Peter Graves. *Mrs. Fitzherbert* (GB/1947/99m/BW) D: Montgomery Tully. B/ on the novel *Princess Fitz* by Winifred Carter. C: Joyce Howard, Leslie Banks, Margaretta Scott, Wanda Rotha, Mary Clare, Frederick Valk, Ralph Truman, John Stuart, Barry Morse, Henry Oscar, Arthur Dulay, Moira Lister, Julian Dallas, Lily Kann.

Cecil Parker. *The First Gentleman* (aka *The Affairs of a Rogue*) (GB/1948/111–95m/BW) D: Alberto Cavalcanti. B/on the play by Norman Ginsbury. C: Jean-Pierre Aumont, Joan Hopkins, Margaretta Scott, Hugh Griffith, Tom Gil, Frances Waring, Jack Livesy.

Jack Hawkins. *The Elusive Pimpernel* (aka *The Fighting Pimpernel*) (GB/1950/109m/C) D: Michael Powell & Emeric Pressburger. B/on the novel *The Scarlet Pimpernel* by Baroness Orczy. C: David Niven, Margaret Leighton, Cyril Cusack, Arthur Wontner.

Peter Ustinov. *Beau Brummell* (US-GB/1954/111m/C) D: Curtis Bernhardt. B/on the play by Clyde Fitch. C: Stewart Granger, Elizabeth Taylor, Robert Morley, James Donald, James Hayter, Rosemary Harris, Paul Rogers, Noel Willman, Peter Bull.

Roy Kinnear. *On a Clear Day You Can See Forever* (US/1970/129m/C) D: Vincente Minelli. B/on the musical play by Alan Jay Lerner & Burton Lane. C: Barbra Streisand, Yves Montand, Bob Newhart, Pamela Brown, Larry Blyden, Simon Oakland, Jack Nicholson.

Rupert Everett. *The Madness of King George* (aka *The Madness of George III*) (GB/1994/107m/C) D: Nicholas Hytner. B/on the play by Alan Bennett. C: Nigel Hawthorne, Helen Mirren, Amanda Donohoe, Julian Wadham, Caroline Harker, Ian Holm, Rupert Graves, Geoffrey Palmer, Barry Stanton, Jim Carter, Peter Bride-Kirk, Cyril Shaps.

John Sessions. *Princess Caraboo* (US/1994/94m/C) D: Michael Austin. C: Phoebe Cates, Jim Broadbent, Wendy Hughes, Kevin Kline, John Lithgow, Steven Rea, Peter Eyre.

216 Geronimo (1829–1909)

Leader of the Chiricahua Apaches after the death of **Cochise**, Geronimo led raids in Arizona and Mexico for years until his final capture in 1886.

Chief White Horse. *Stagecoach* (US/1939/97m/BW) D: John Ford. B/on the story *Stage to Lordsburg* by Ernest Haycox. Best Direction (NYC). C: Claire Trevor, John Wayne, John Carradine, Thomas Mitchell, Andy Devine, Donald Meek.

Chief Thundercloud. *Geronimo!* (US/1939/89m/BW) D: Paul H. Sloane. C: Preston Foster, Ellen Drew, Andy Devine, Joseph Crehan, William Henry, Ralph Morgan.

Tom Tyler. *Valley of the Sun* (US/1942/84m/BW) D: George Marshall. B/on the book by Clarence Budington Kelland. C: Lucille Ball, James Craig, Cedric Hardwicke, Dean Jagger, Billy Gilbert, Antonio Moreno, George Cleveland, Stanley Andrews.

Chief Thundercloud. *I Killed Geronimo* (US/1950/62m/BW) D: John Hoffman. C: James Ellison, Virginia Herrick, Smith Ballew, Ted Adams.

Jay Silverheels (as Goklia). *Broken Arrow* (US/1950/93m/C) D: Delmer Daves. B/on the novel *Blood Brother* by Elliott Arnold. C: James Stewart, Jeff Chandler, Debra Paget.

Miguel Inclan. *Indian Uprising* (US/1951/75m/C) D: Ray Nazarro. C: George Montgomery, Audrey Long, Carl Benton Reid, Eugene Iglesias, John Baer, Joe Sawyer, Fay Roope.

John War Eagle. *The Last Outpost* (US/1951/88m/C) D: Lewis R. Foster. C: Ronald Reagan, Rhonda Fleming, Bruce Bennett, Bill Williams, Noah Beery, Jr., Chief Yowlachie.

Jay Silverheels. *The Battle at Apache Pass* (US/1952/85m/C) D: George Sherman. C: Jeff Chandler, John Lund, Beverly Tyler, Bruce Cowling, Hugh O'Brian, Jack Elam.

Ian MacDonald. *Taza, Son of Cochise* (US/1954/79m/C) D: Douglas Sirk. C: Rock Hudson, Barbara Rush, Gregg Palmer, Morris Ankrum, Eugene Iglesias, Jeff Chandler.

Monte Blue. *Apache* (US/1954/91m/C) D: Robert Aldrich. B/on the novel *Bronco Apache* by Paul I. Wellman. C: Burt Lancaster, Jean Peters, Charles Bronson.

Jay Silverheels. *Walk the Proud Land* (US/1956/88m/C) D: Jesse Hibbs. B/on the book *Apache Agent* by Woodworth Clum. C: Audie Murphy, Anne Bancroft, Pat Crowley, Charles Drake, Eugene Iglesias, Robert Warwick, Anthony Caruso, Addison Richards.

Chuck Connors. *Geronimo* (US/1962/101m/C) D: Arnold Laven. C: Ross Martin, Kamala Devi, Pat Conway, Larry Dobkin, Adam West, Denver Pyle, Enid James.

Pat Hogan. *Geronimo's Revenge* (US/1965/61m/C) D: James Neilson. C: Tom Tryon, Darryl Hickman, Betty Lynn, Harry Carey, Jr., Allan Lane, Jay Silverheels.

Giso Weissbach. *Trini* (aka *Stirb für Zapata*) (East Germany/1976) D: Walter Beck. C: Gunnar Helm, Dmitrina Sawowa, Gunter Friedrich, Iwan Tomow, Michael Kann.

Wes Studi. *Geronimo: An American Legend* (US/1993/115m/C) D: Walter Hill. C: Jason Patric, Gene Hackman, Robert Duvall, Matt Damon, Rodney A. Grant, Kevin Tighe, Steve Reevis, Carlos Palomino, Victor Aaron, Stuart Proud Eagle Grant, Stephen McHattie.

217 Gershwin, George (1898–1937)

Popular American composer, Gershwin is remembered for his "Rhapsody in Blue," "Porgy and Bess" and dozens of popular tunes.

Robert Alda. *Rhapsody in Blue* (US/1945/139m/BW) D: Irving Rapper. C: Joan Leslie, Alexis Smith, Charles Coburn, Julie Bishop, Oscar Levant, Herbert Rudley, Eddie Marr.

William Boyett. *So This Is Love* (aka *The Grace Moore Story*) (US/1953/101m/C) D: Gordon Douglas. B/on the autobiography *You're Only Human Once* by Grace Moore. C: Kathryn Grayson, Merv Griffin, Joan Weldon, Walter Abel, Ray Kellogg.

218 Gershwin, Ira (1896–1983)

American librettist/lyricist, Ira collaborated with brother George on all his songs and shows and later with such artists as **Moss Hart**, Kurt Weill and Jerome Kern.

Herbert Rudley. *Rhapsody in Blue* (US/1945/139m/BW) D: Irving Rapper. C: Robert Alda, Joan Leslie, Alexis Smith, Charles Coburn, Julie Bishop, Oscar Levant, Eddie Marr.

Alex Gerry. *Three Sailors and a Girl* (US/1953/95m/C) D: Roy Del Ruth. B/on the play *The Butter and Egg Man* by George S. Kaufman. C: Jane Powell, Gordon MacRae, David Bond.

219 Gilbert, William Schwenk (1836–1911)

Gilbert was the lyricist half of Gilbert and **Sullivan**, famous for their comic operas which included "H.M.S. Pinafore" and "The Mikado."

Nigel Bruce. *Lillian Russell* (US/1940/127m/BW) D: Irving Cummings. C: Alice Faye, Edward Arnold, Don Ameche, Henry Fonda, Warren William, Claud Allister, Eddie Foy, Jr., William B. Davidson, Leo Carillo, Milburn Stone.

Robert Morley. *The Great Gilbert and Sullivan* (aka *The Story of Gilbert and Sullivan*) (GB/1953/105m/C) D: Sydney Gilliat. B/on The *Gilbert and Sullivan Book* by Leslie Bailey. C: Maurice Evans, Eileen Herlie, Peter Finch, Martyn Green, Muriel Aked.

Jim Broadbent. *Topsy-Turvy* (US-GB/1999/160m/C) D: Mike Leigh. NYC Directors Award. C: Allan Corduner, Lesley Manville, Eleanor David, Ron Cook, Timothy Spall, Kevin McKidd, Martin Savage, Shirley Henderson, Dorothy Atkinson, Wendy Nottingham, Jonathan Aris, Louise Gold.

220 Ginsberg, Allen (1926–1997)

American poet of the Beat Generation and guru of the 1960's counterculture. His best known work is *Howl*, written in 1956, a brutal indictment of American values. He became friends with **Jack Kerouac** and **William S. Burroughs** while attending Columbia University in New York.

John Turturro. *The Source* (US/1999/88m/BW/C) D: Chuck Workman. C: Johnny Depp, Dennis Hopper.

Ron Livingston. *Beat* (US/2000/89m/C) D: Gary Walkow. C: Courtney Love, Norman Reedus, Kiefer Sutherland, Daniel Martínez, Kyle Secor, Sam Trammell, Lisa Sheridan, Rene Rubio, Georgiana Sîrbu, Tommy Perna, Alec Von Bargen, Steve Hedden, Patricia De Llaca, Luis Felipe Tovar, Luisa Huertas, Darren Ross, Serafina De Lorca.

221 Gladstone, William Ewart (1809–1898)

A rival of **Disraeli**, strongly disliked by **Queen Victoria**, Gladstone was the British Prime Minister four times between 1868 and 1894.

Montagu Love. *Parnell* (US/1937/115m/BW) D: John M. Stahl. B/on the play by Elsie Tough Schauffler. C: Clark Gable, Myrna Loy, Edna May Oliver, Edmund Gwenn, Alan Marshall, Billie Burke, Donald Crisp, George Zucco, Donald Meek.

Arthur Young. *Victoria the Great* (GB/1937/110m/C) D: Herbert Wilcox. B/on the play *Victoria Regina* by Laurence Housman. C: Anna Neagle, Anton Walbrook, H.B. Warner, James Dale, Charles Carson, Hubert Harben, Felix Aylmer,

Derrick De Marney, Hugh Miller, Percy Parsons, Henry Hallatt, Gordon McLeod, Wyndham Goldie.

George Zucco. *Suez* (US/1938/104m/BW) D: Allan Dwan. C: Tyrone Power, Loretta Young, Miles Mander, Annabella, Leon Ames, Victor Varconi, Brandon Hurst.

Malcolm Keen. *Sixty Glorious Years* (aka *Queen of Destiny*) (GB/1938/90m/C) D: Herbert Wilcox. C: Anna Neagle, Anton Walbrook, C. Aubrey Smith, Charles Carson, Felix Aylmer, Pamela Standish, Gordon McLeod, Henry Hallatt, Wyndham Goldie, Derrick De Marney, Joyce Bland, Harvey Braban, Aubrey Dexter, Laidman Browne.

Stephen Murray. *The Prime Minister* (GB/1940/94m/BW) D: Thorold Dickinson. C: John Gielgud, Diana Wynyard, Will Fyfe, Owen Nares, Fay Compton, Lyn Harding, Leslie Perrins, Vera Bogetti, Frederick Leister, Nicolas Hannan, Kynaston Reeves, Gordon McLeod.

Gordon Richards. *The Imperfect Lady* (US/1947/97m/BW) D: Lewis Allen. C: Ray Milland, Teresa Wright, Anthony Quinn, Cedric Hardwicke, Reginald Owen, Rhys Williams.

Arthur Young. *The Lady With a Lamp* (aka *The Lady With the Lamp*) (GB/1951/112m/BW) D: Herbert Wilcox. B/on the play *The Lady With the Lamp* by Reginald Berkeley. C: Anna Neagle, Michael Wilding, Felix Aylmer, Helena Pickard, Peter Graves.

Ralph Richardson. *Khartoum* (GB/1966/134m/C) D: Basil Deardon. C: Charlton Heston, Laurence Olivier, Richard Johnson, Alexander Knox, Michael Hordern, Johnny Sekka, Peter Arne, Nigel Green, Ralph Michael.

222 Glinka, Mikhail Ivanovich (1804–1857)

The first prominent Russian composer, Glinka's works include the operas *A Life for the Czar* and *Russlan and Ludmilla*.

Boris Chirkov. *The Great Glinka* (aka *Glinka*) (USSR/1946/100m/BW) D: Leo Arnstam. C: Sasha Sobolyev, Valentina Serova, Boris Livanov, Peter Aleynikov.

Boris Smirnov. *Man of Music* (aka *Glinka*) (USSR/1952/100m/C) D: Grigori Alexandrov. C: Lubov Orlova, L. Durasov, Svyatoslav Richter, Mikhail Nazvanov, B. Vinogradova.

223 Goebbels, Paul Joseph (1897–1945)

The Nazi minister of propaganda, Goebbels remained with **Hitler** to the very end in the bunker where, after poisoning his six children, he committed suicide. In Hitler's will he had named Goebbels his successor, so, for one day Goebbels was the Fuhrer of the Third Reich.

Martin Kosleck. *Confessions of a Nazi Spy* (US/1939/110m/BW) D: Anatole Litvak. B/on Leon Turrou's articles *Storm Over America*. C: Edward G. Robinson, Francis Lederer, George Sanders, Paul Lukas, Lya Lys, Sig Rumann, Joe Sawyer, Henry O'Neill.

Charles Rogers. *That Nazty Nuisance* (aka *Nazty Nuisance*) (US/1943/50m/

BW) D: Glenn Tryon. C: Bobby Watson, Joe Devlin, Johnny Arthur, Rex Evans, Wedgewood Nowell.

Paul Andor. *Enemy of Women* (aka *The Private Life of Paul Joseph Goebbels*) (aka *Mad Lover*) (aka *Dr. Paul Joseph Goebbels*) (US/1944/86m/BW) D: Alfred Zeisler. C: Claudia Drake, Donald Woods, H.B. Warner, Sigrid Gurie, Ralph Morgan.

Martin Kosleck. *The Hitler Gang* (US/1944/101m/BW) D: John Farrow. C: Bobby Watson, Roman Bohnen, Victor Varconi, Luis Van Rooten, Alexander Pope, Ivan Triesault, Sig Rumann, Reinhold Schunzel, Alexander Granach, Fritz Kortner.

Philip Wade. *Dreaming* (GB/1944/78m/BW) D: John Baxter. C: Bud Flannagan, Chesney Allen, Hazel Court, Dick Francis, Kay Kendall, Gerry Wilmott.

M. Petrunkin. *The Fall of Berlin* (USSR/1949/124m/C) D: Mikhail Chiaureli. C: Mikhail Gelovani, Oleg Froelich, V. Savelyev, M. Novakova, Victor Stanitsin, Y. Verikh.

Willy Krause. *The Last Ten Days* (aka *Ten Days to Die*) (aka *Last Ten Days of Adolf Hitler*) (aka *Der Letzte Akt*) (aka *The Last Act*) (Germany/1955/115m/BW) D: G.W. Pabst. B/on the novel *Ten Days to Die* by M.A. Mussanno. C: Albin Skoda, Oskar Werner, Lotte Tobisch, Erich Stuckmann, Edmund Erlandsen, Kurt Eilers, Helga Dohrn, Leopold Hainisch, Otto Schmoele.

Martin Kosleck. *Hitler* (aka *Women of Nazi Germany*) (US/1962/107m/BW) D: Stuart Heisler. C: Richard Basehart, Cordula Trantow, Maria Emo, John Banner, Martin Brandt, William Sargent, Gregory Gay, Theodore Marcuse, Rick Traeger, John Mitchum, G. Stanley Jones, Walter Kohler, Carl Esmond, Berry Kroeger.

John Bennett. *Hitler: The Last Ten Days* (GB-Italy/1973/106m/C) D: Ennio De Concini. B/on the book *The Last Days of the Chancellery* by Gerhardt Boldt. C: Alec Guinness, Simon Ward, Gabriele Ferzetti, Doris Kunstmann, Philip Stone, Mark Kingston.

David Mauro. *The Hindenburg* (US/1975/125m/C) D: Robert Wise. B/on the book by Michael M. Mooney. C: George C. Scott, Anne Bancroft, William Atherton, Roy Thinnes, Gig Young, Burgess Meredith, Charles Durning, Richard Dysart.

Joel Grey. *The Empty Mirror* (US/1997/129m/C) D: Barry J. Hershey. C: Norman Rodway, Camilla Søeberg, Peter Michael Goetz, Doug McKeon, Glenn Shadix, Hope Allen, Lori Scott, Raul Kobrinsky, Randy Zielinski, Shannon Yowell, Courtney Dale, Elizabeth Hershey, Christopher Levitus, Chip Marks.

224 Gordon, (Gen.) Charles George (1833–1885)

Known as "Chinese" Gordon following his service in the Second Opium War in China, Gordon later lead British troops in the Sudan where he was sent to quell the revolution lead by The Mahdi. His forces were defeated and he was killed two days before relief arrived.

Laidman Browne. *Sixty Glorious Years* (aka *Queen of Destiny*) (GB/1938/90m/C) D: Herbert Wilcox. C: Anna Neagle, Anton Walbrook, C. Aubrey Smith, Charles Carson, Felix Aylmer, Pamela Standish, Gordon McLeod, Henry Hallatt, Wyndham Goldie, Malcolm Keen, Derrick De Marney, Joyce Bland, Harvey Braban, Aubrey Dexter.

Charlton Heston. *Khartoum* (GB/1966/134m/C) D: Basil Deardon. C: Laurence Olivier, Richard Johnson, Ralph Richardson, Alexander Knox, Michael Hordern, Johnny Sekka, Peter Arne, Nigel Green, Ralph Michael.

225 Göring, Hermann Wilhelm (1893–1946)

Founder of the Nazi's Gestapo and the commander of Germany's air force in WW II, Goering had led **Richtoven's** Flying Circus in the First World War. A morphine addict and reported transvestite he committed suicide in his prison cell two hours before he was to be hanged for his war crimes. Brian Cox portrayed Hermann Goering in the TV movie *Nuremberg* (2000).

Rex Evans. *That Nazty Nuisance* (aka *Nazty Nuisance*) (US/1943/50m/BW) D: Glenn Tryon. C: Bobby Watson, Joe Devlin, Johnny Arthur, Charles Rogers, Wedgewood Nowell.

Alexander Pope. *The Hitler Gang* (US/1944/101m/BW) D: John Farrow. C: Bobby Watson, Roman Bohnen, Martin Kosleck, Victor Varconi, Luis Van Rooten, Ivan Triesault, Sig Rumann, Reinhold Schunzel, Alexander Granach, Fritz Kortner.

Y. Verikh. *The Fall of Berlin* (USSR/1949/124m/C) D: Mikhail Chiaureli. C: Mikhail Gelovani, Oleg Froelich, V. Savelyev, M. Novakova, Victor Stanitsin, M. Petrunkin.

Herman Erhardt. *The Magic Face* (Austria/1951/88m/BW) D: Frank Tuttle. C: Luther Adler, Patricia Knight, William L. Shirer, Ilka Windish, Sukman, Hans Sheel.

John Mitchum. *Hitler* (aka *Women of Nazi Germany*) (US/1962/107m/BW) D: Stuart Heisler. C: Richard Basehart, Cordula Trantow, Maria Emo, Martin Kosleck, John Banner, Martin Brandt, William Sargent, Gregory Gay, Theodore Marcuse, Rick Traeger, G. Stanley Jones, Walter Kohler, Carl Esmond, Berry Kroeger.

Hein Reiss. *The Battle of Britain* (GB/1969/132m/C) D: Guy Hamilton. B/on the book *The Narrow Margin* by Derek Wood & Derek Dempster. C: Harry Andrews, Michael Caine, Kenneth More, Trevor Howard, Curt Jurgens, Ian McShane, Laurence Olivier, Nigel Patrick, Christopher Plummer, Michael Redgrave, Ralph Richardson, Robert Shaw, Patrick Wymark, Susannah York, Barry Foster, Rolf Stiefel, Peter Hager.

Barry Primus. *Von Richtofen and Brown* (aka *The Red Baron*) (US/1970/97m/C) D: Roger Corman. C: John Philip Law, Don Stroud, Peter Masterson, Hurd Hatfield, Karen Huston.

Volker Spengler. *Der Unhold* (aka *The Ogre*) (aka *Le Roi des aulnes*) (France-Germany-GB/1996/118m/C) D: Volker Schlöndorff. B on the novel *Le Roi des Aulnes* by Michel Tournier. C: John Malkovich, Gottfried John, Marianne Sägebrecht, Heino Ferch, Dieter Laser, Agnès Soral, Sasha Hanau, Vernon Dobtcheff, Simon McBurney, Ilja Smoljanski, Luc Florian, Laurent Spielvogel.

Glenn Shadix. *The Empty Mirror* (US/1997/129m/C) D: Barry J. Hershey. C: Norman Rodway, Camilla Søeberg, Peter Michael Goetz, Doug McKeon, Joel Grey, Hope Allen, Lori Scott, Raul Kobrinsky, Randy Zielinski, Shannon Yowell, Courtney Dale, Elizabeth Hershey, Christopher Levitus, Chip Marks.

226 Gorky, Maxim (1868–1936)

(Alexei Maximovich Peshkov) Russian/Soviet writer Gorky, was active in the revolutions of 1905 and 1917. He later served as head of the state publishing department and was a propagandist for **Stalin**.

Alexei Lyarsky. *Childhood of Maxim Gorky* (USSR/1938/101m/BW) D: Mark Donskoi. B/on the book *My Childhood* by Maxim Gorky. C: Y. Valbert, Valeria Massalitnova.

Nikolai Cherkasov. *Lenin in 1918* (USSR/1939/133m/BW) D: Mikhail Romm. C: Boris Shchukin, Mikhail Gelovani, Nikolai Okhlopkov, Vasily Vanin, V. Markov.

Alexei Lyarsky. *On His Own* (aka *Among People*) (aka *In the World*) (USSR/1939/96m/BW) D: Mark Donskoi. B/on the memoirs of Maxim Gorky. C: Varvara Massalitinova, Mikhail Troyanovsky, I. Kudriavtse.

Y. Valbert. *University of Life* (aka *My Universities*) (USSR/1940/90m/BW) D: Mark Donskoi. B/on the book *My Universities* by Maxim Gorky. C: S. Kayukov, N. Dorokhin.

Pavel Kadochnikov. *Yakov Sverdlov* (USSR/1940/128m/BW) D: Sergei Yutkevich. B/on the play by B. Levin & Pyotr Pavlenko. C: Maxim Strauch, Nikolai Okhlopkov.

Nikolai Cherkasov. *Ivan Pavlov* (USSR/1950/93m/BW) D: Gregory Roshal. C: Alexander Borisov, Natalia Alisova, F. Nikitin, M. Safonova.

Pavel Kadochnikov. *Prologue* (USSR/1956/100m/C) D: Yefim Dzigan. C: Nikolai Plotnikov, Marina Pastukhova.

Alexei Lotkev. *On the Roads of Russia* (USSR/1968/95m/BW) D: Fyodor Filippov. B/on the story by Maxim Gorky. C: Roman Filippov, Yelyena Sanayeva.

Alexander Kochetov. *I Am An Actress* (USSR/1981/93m/BW) D: Viktor Sokolov. C: Natalya Saiko, Oleg Vavilov, P. Merkuriev.

227 Goya (1746–1828)

(Francisco José de Goya y Lucientes) Spanish artist considered the greatest painter of his time. The Duchess of Alba, known for her beauty and intrigue, was painted by Goya several times. She was portrayed by Ava Gardner in the *Naked Maja* and by Maribel Verdu in *Goya in Bordeaux*.

Anthony Franciosa. *The Naked Maja* (US-Italy/1959/111m/C) D: Henry Koster & Mario Russo. C: Ava Gardner, Amedeo Nazzari, Gino Cervi, Massimo Serato.

Francisco Rabal. *Goya* (Spain/1971/118m/C) D: Nino Quevedo. C: Irina Demick.

Donatas Banionis. *Goya* (USSR-Yugoslavia-Bulgaria/1971/C) D: Konrad Wolf. C: Katarina Olivera, Ernst Busch.

Francisco Rabal. Jose Coronado (Young Goya). *Goya in Bordeaux* (Italy/2000/104m/C) D: Carlos Saura. AKA *Goya*. C: Serge Lopez, Mathilde Seigner, Sophie Guillemin, Maribel Verdu.

228 Grant, Ulysses Simpson (1822–1885)

Commander of the Union armies in the Civil War, Grant's successes on the battlefield led to his nomination and election as the 18th President of the U.S. However, he was ill suited for the office and his administration was plagued by corruption and scandal.

Fred Warren. *Abraham Lincoln* (US/1930/97m/BW) D: D.W. Griffith. C: Walter Huston, Una Merkel, Kay Hammond, E. Alyn Warren, Edgar Deering, Hobart Bosworth, Frank Campeau, Francis Ford, Ian Keith, Oscar Apfel, Cameron Prud'Homme.

Guy Oliver. *Only the Brave* (US/1930/66m/BW) D: Frank Tuttle. C: Gary Cooper, Mary Brian, Phillips Holmes, James Neill, John H. Elliott, Morgan Farley.

Fred Warren. *Secret Service* (US/1931/69m/BW) D: J. Walter Ruben. B/on the play by William Gillette. C: Richard Dix, Shirley Grey, William Post, Jr., Gavin Gordon.

Walter Rogers. *Silver Dollar* (US/1932/84m/BW) D: Alfred E. Green. B/on the book *Silver Dollar; The Story of the Tabors* by David Karsner. C: Edward G. Robinson, Bebe Daniels, Emmett Corrigan, Niles Welch, Aline MacMahon, DeWitt Jennings.

Fred Warren. *Operator 13* (aka *Spy 13*) (US/1934/86m/BW) D: Richard Boleslavsky. B/on the novel by Robert W. Chambers. C: Marion Davies, Gary Cooper, Jean Parker, Katharine Alexander, Ted Healy, Sidney Toler, Douglas Dumbrille, John Elliot, Franklin Parker.

Joseph Crehan. *Union Pacific* (US/1939/135m/BW) D: Cecil B. DeMille. B/on the novel *Trouble Shooter* by Ernest Haycox. C: Barbara Stanwyck, Joel McCrea, Ernie Adams.

Jack Smith. *Frontier Scout* (US/1939/60m/BW) D: Sam Newfield. C: George Houston, Al St. John, Beth Marion, Dave O'Brien, Budd Buster, Mantan Moreland.

Joseph Crehan. *Geronimo!* (US/1939/89m/BW) D: Paul H. Sloane. C: Preston Foster, Ellen Drew, Chief Thundercloud, Andy Devine, William Henry, Ralph Morgan.

Harrison Greene. *The Son of Davy Crockett* (aka *Blue Clay*) (US/1941/59m/BW) D: Lambert Hillyer. C: Bill Elliott, Iris Meredith, Dub Taylor, Kenneth MacDonald, Lloyd Bridges.

Joseph Crehan. *They Died With Their Boots On* (US/1941/140m/BW) D: Raoul Walsh. C: Errol Flynn, Olivia de Havilland, Arthur Kennedy, Charles Grapewin, Gene Lockhart, Anthony Quinn, John Litel, Stanley Ridges, Sydney Greenstreet, Regis Toomey, Hattie McDaniel.

Harrison Greene. *Tennessee Johnson* (aka *The Man on America's Conscience*) (US/1942/103m/BW) D: William Dieterle. C: Van Heflin, Ruth Hussey, Lionel Barrymore, Marjorie Main, Regis Toomey, Montagu Love, Porter Hall, Morris Ankrum, Harry Worth, Ed O'Neill, Charles Dingle, Grant Withers, Lynne Carver, Noah Beery, Sr.

Reginald Sheffield. *Centennial Summer* (US/1946/104m/C) D: Otto Preminger. B/on the novel by Albert E. Idell. C: Jeanne Crain, Cornel Wilde, Linda Darnell, William Eythe.

John Hamilton. *The Fabulous Texan* (US/1947/97m/BW) D: Edward Ludwig. C: William Elliott, John Carroll, Catherine McLeod, Albert Dekker, Andy Devine, Jim Davis.

Joseph Crehan. *Silver River* (US/1948/108m/BW) D: Raoul Walsh. C: Errol Flynn, Ann Sheridan, Thomas Mitchell, Bruce Bennett, Tom D'Andrea, Barton MacLane.

Joseph Crehan. *Red Desert* (US/1949/59m/BW) D: Ford Beebe. C: Don Barry, Tom Neal, Jack Holt, Margia Dean, Byron Foulger, John Cason.

Hayden Rorke. *Drum Beat* (US/1954/111m/C) D: Delmer Daves. C: Alan Ladd, Audrey Dalton, Marisa Pavan, Robert Keith, Charles Bronson, Warner Anderson.

John Hamilton. *Sitting Bull* (US/1954/105m/C) D: Sidney Salkow. C: J. Carrol Naish, Dale Robertson, Mary Murphy, Iron Eyes Cody, John Litel, Douglas Kennedy.

Emile Avery. *Run of the Arrow* (US/1957/86m/C) D: Samuel Fuller. C: Rod Steiger, Sarita Montiel, Brian Keith, Ralph Meeker, Charles Bronson, Frank De Kova, Frank Baker.

Morris Ankrum. *From the Earth to the Moon* (US/1958/100m/C) D: Byron Haskin. B/on the novel by Jules Verne. C: Joseph Cotten, George Sanders, Debra Paget, Carl Esmond.

Stan Jones. *The Horse Soldiers* (US/1959/119m/C) D: John Ford. B/on the novel by Harold Sinclair. C: John Wayne, William Holden, Constance Towers, Hoot Gibson.

Harry Morgan. *How the West Was Won* (US/1962/165m/C) D: John Ford, Henry Hathaway & George Marshall. C: John Wayne, James Stewart, Gregory Peck, Carroll Baker, George Peppard, Henry Fonda, Carolyn Jones, Robert Preston, Raymond Massey, Karl Malden, Debbie Reynolds, Richard Widmark, Eli Wallach, Walter Brennan.

Jason Robards. *The Legend of the Lone Ranger* (US/1981/98m/C) D: William A. Fraker. C: Klinton Spilsbury, Michael Horse, Ted Flicker, Richard Farnsworth, Lincoln Tate.

Kevin Kline (*Triple role: Amtemus Gordon, President Grant, plus Gordon impersonating President Grant). *Wild, Wild West* (US/1999/152m/C) D: Barry Sonnenfeld. B/on the TV Series. C: Will Smith, Kenneth Branagh, Salma Hayek, Ted Levine, M. Emmet Walsh, Bai Ling, Frederique van der Wal, Musetta Vander, E.J. Callhan.

229 Grey, Edward, 1st Viscount Grey of Fallodon (1862–1933)

British politician and statesman, Grey was instrumental in cementing Great Britain's alliances in the years prior to the first World War.

Paul Mederow. *1914: The Last Days Before the War* (Germany/1931/110m/BW) D: Richard Oswald. C: Albert Basserman, Wolfgang von Schwind, Heinrich Schroth, Reinhold Schunzel, Lucie Hoeflich, Ferdinand Hart, Oskar Homolka, Theodor Loos, Alfred Abel, Heinrich George, Varl Goetz, Paul Bildt, Eugen Klöepfer.

H. Saxon-Snell. *Regal Cavalcade* (aka *Royal Cavalcade*) (GB/1935/100m/BW) D: Thomas Bentley, Herbert Brenton, Norman Lee, Walter Summers, Will Kellino & Marcel Varnel. C: Marie Lohr, Esme Percy, Pearl Argyle, Frank Vosper, Austin Trevor, Harry Brunning, John Mills, C.M. Hallard, Patric Knowles, Matheson Lang, Athene Seyler.

Ralph Richardson. *Oh! What a Lovely War* (GB/1969/144m/C) D: Richard Attenborough. B/on the musical play by Joan Littlewood and the play *The Long, Long Trail* by Charles Chilton. Best English Language Foreign Film (GG), and the United Nations Award (BFA). C: Pamela Abbott, Jack Hawkins, Laurence Olivier, John Mills, John Gabriel, Paul Daneman, Dirk Bogarde, Vanessa Redgrave, Kenneth More, Michael Redgrave, Ian Holm, Wensley Pithey, Frank Forsyth, John Gielgud, Maggie Smith, Guy Middleton.

230 Grey, Lady Jane (1537–1554)

Queen of England for nine days after having been named successor by **Edward VI**, Lady Jane was imprisoned and executed when **Mary I** seized the throne.

Nova Pilbeam. *Tudor Rose* (aka *Lady Jane Grey*) (aka *Nine Days a Queen*) (GB/1936/78m/BW) D: Robert Stevenson. C: Cedric Hardwicke, John Mills, Felix Aylmer, Frank Cellier, Desmond Tester, Gwen Frangcon-Davies, Sybil Thorndike.

Ann Howard. *The Prince and the Pauper* (US/1937/120m/BW) D: William Keighley. B/on the novel by Mark Twain and the play by Catherine C. Cushing. C: Errol Flynn, Claude Rains, Henry Stephenson, Billy Mauch, Bobby Mauch, Montagu Love, Alan Hale, Robert Warwick, Helen Valkis, Halliwell Hobbes, Barton MacLane.

Jane Asher. *The Prince and the Pauper* (GB/1962/93m/C) D: Don Chaffey. B/on the novel by Mark Twain. C: Sean Scully, Paul Rogers, Guy Williams, Laurence Naismith.

Felicity Dean. *Crossed Swords* (aka *The Prince and the Pauper*) (US/1977/121m/C) D: Richard Fleischer. B/on the novel *The Prince and the Pauper* by Mark Twain. C: Oliver Reed, Raquel Welch, Mark Lester, Ernest Borgnine, Charlton Heston, Lalla Ward, George C. Scott, Rex Harrison, Harry Andrews, David Hemmings.

Helena Bonham Carter. *Lady Jane* (GB/1986/144m/C) D: Trevor Nunn. C: Cary Elwes, John Wood, Michael Hordern, Jane Laportaire, David Waller, Warren Saire.

231 Grissom, Virgil Ivan "Gus" (1926–1967)

The second American in space, Grissom became one of the space program's first casualties when he was killed during testing for the first Apollo mission.

Fred Ward. *The Right Stuff* (US/1983/192m/C) D: Philip Kaufman. B/on the book by Tom Wolfe. C: Sam Shepard, Scott Glenn, Ed Harris, Dennis Quaid, Barbara Hershey, Kim Stanley, Veronica Cartwright, Donald Moffat, Robert Beer.

Steve Bernie. *Apollo 13* (US/1995/140m/C) D: Ron Howard. C: Tom Hanks, Bill Paxton, Kevin Bacon, Gary Sinise, Ed Harris, Kathleen Quinlan, Emily Ann Lloyd.

232 Groves, Leslie Richard (1896–1970)

American general of the Army Corps of Engineers, Groves headed the Manhattan Project, which was the United States' effort to develop the Atomic Bomb during WWII. In TV films Gen. Groves has been played by George R. Robertson in *F.D.R—The Last Year* (80), Richard Herd in *Enola Gay* (83), Brian Dennehy in *Day One* (89), and Richard D. Masur in *Hiroshima* (95).

Brian Donlevy. *The Beginning Or the End* (US/1947/110m/BW) D: Norman Taurog. C: Beverly Tyler, Hume Cronyn, Godfrey Tearle, Barry Nelson, Art Baker, Ludwig Stossel.

George Bartenieff. *Dead End Kids* (aka *Dead End Kids: A Story of Nuclear Power*) (US/1986/90m/C) D: JoAnne Akalaitis. B/on the play by Mabou Mines. C: Ellen McElduff, Ruth Maleczech, David Brisbin, John Schofield, Terry O'Reilly.

Paul Newman. *Fat Man and Little Boy* (US/1989/126m/C) D: Roland Joffe. C: Dwight Schultz, Bonnie Bedelia, John Cusack, Laura Dern, Ron Frazier, Natasha Richardson.

233 Guevera, Che (1928–1967)

(Ernesto Guevera de la Sarne) An Argentinian physician, Guevera became a revolutionary and was **Castro's** chief lieutenant in the overthrow of the Cuban government.

Francisco Rabal. *El Che Guevera* (aka *Rebel With a Cause*) (Italy/1968/C) D: Paolo Heusch. B/on the novel by Adriano Bolzoni. C: John Ireland, Giacomo Rossi Stuart.

Omar Sharif. *Che!* (US/1969/96m/C) D: Richard Fleischer. C: Jack Palance, Cesare Danova, Robert Loggia, Woody Strode, Barbara Luna, Frank Silvera.

234 Guinan, Texas (1884–1933)

(Mary Louise Cecilia Guinan) Brash New York speakeasy hostess whose "Hello, Suckers" greeting became a catch phrase of the Roaring Twenties.

Betty Hutton. *Incendiary Blond* (US/1945/113m/BW) D: George Marshall. B/on the book *The Life of Texas Guinan* by Thomas and W.D. Guinan. C: Arturo De Cordova, Charles Ruggles, Albert Dekker, Barry Fitzgerald.

Barbara Nichols. *The George Raft Story* (aka *Spin of a Coin*) (US/1961/105m/BW) D: Joseph M. Newman. C: Ray Danton, Jayne Mansfield, Julie London, Barrie Chase, Frank Gorshin, Brad Dexter, Neville Brand, Robert Strauss, Herschel Bernardi.

Phyllis Diller. *Splendor in the Grass* (US/1961/124m/C) D: Elia Kazan. C: Natalie Wood, Warren Beatty, Pat Hingle, Audrey Christie, Barbara Loden, Zohra Lampert.

Guthrie, Arlo *see* Guthrie, Woody

235 Guthrie, Woodrow Wilson "Woody" (1912–1967)

One of the most influential American folksinger-songwriters, Guthrie was a champion of union workers, migrant laborers and other exploited people. His son Arlo (1947–   ), also a popular folksinger, played himself in *Alice's Restaraunt* and was played by Calvin Butler in *Chicago 70* (70).

Joseph Boley. *Alice's Restaraunt* (US/1969/111m/C) D: Arthur Penn. C: Arlo Guthrie.

David Carradine * Best Actor (NBR). *Bound for Glory* (US/1976/147m/C) D: Hal Ashby. B/on the book by Woody Guthrie. C: Ronny Cox, Melinda Dillon, Gail Strickland, Randy Quaid.

236 Gwyn, Nell (1650–1687)

(Eleannor Gwyn, Gwynn or Gwynne) Starting out as an orange peddler at the Drury Lane Theatre, "pretty, witty Nell" became a noted (if not overly talented) actor and finally, from 1669 until his death, the favorite and most famous mistress to **Charles II**.

Anna Neagle. *Nell Gwyn* (GB/1934/75m/BW) D: Herbert Wilcox. B/on diaries of Samuel Pepys, Charles II and Nell Gwyn. C: Cedric Hardwicke, Muriel George, Esme Percy.

Virginia Field. *Hudson's Bay* (US/1940/95m/BW) D: Irving Pichel. C: Paul Muni, Gene Tierney, Laird Cregar, John Sutton, Vincent Price, Nigel Bruce, Chief Thundercloud.

Margaret Lockwood. *The Cardboard Cavalier* (GB/1949/97m/BW) D: Walter Forde. C: Sid Field, Anthony Hulme, Edmund Willard, Mary Clare.

Anna Neagle. *Let's Make Up* (aka *Lilacs in the Spring*) (GB/1954/94m/C) D: Herbert Wilcox. B/on the play *The Glorious Days* by Harold Purcell. C: Errol Flynn, David Farrar, Kathleen Harrison, Peter Graves, Sean Connery.

Teresa Codling. *The Wicked Lady* (GB/1983/99m/C) D: Michael Winner. B/on the novel *The Life and Death of the Wicked Lady Skelton* by Magdalen King-Hall. C: Faye Dunaway, Alan Bates, John Gielgud, Denholm Elliott, Prunella Scales, Mark Burns.

237 Halsey, William Frederick "Bull" (1882–1959)

Admiral Halsey was the Commander of the Allied naval forces in the Pacific during World War II.

John Maxwell. *The Eternal Sea* (US/1955/103m/BW) D: John H. Auer. C: Sterling Hayden, Alexis Smith, Dean Jagger, Ben Cooper, Virginia Grey.

Jack Diamond. *Battle Stations* (US/1956/81m/BW) D: Bryan Foy. C: John Lund, William Bendix, Keefe Brasselle, Richard Boone, Claude Akins, Eddie Foy III.

James Cagney. *The Gallant Hours* (US/1960/115m/BW) D: Robert Montgomery. C: Dennis Weaver, Ward Costello, Richard Jaeckel, James T. Goto, Selmer Jackson.

James Whitmore. *Tora! Tora! Tora!* (US-Japan/1970/143m/C) D: Richard Fleischer, Toshio Masuda & Kinji Fukasaku. B/on the books *Tora! Tora! Tora!* by Gordon Prange and *The Broken Seal* by Ladislas Farago. C: Martin Balsam, Soh Yamamura, Jason Robards, Joseph Cotten, Tatsuya Mihashi, E.G. Marshall, Wesley Addy, Leon Ames, Keith Andes, Richard Anderson, George Macready, Neville Brand.

Robert Mitchum. *Midway* (aka *The Battle of Midway*) (US/1976/132m/C) D:

Jack Smight. C: Charlton Heston, Henry Fonda, James Coburn, Glenn Ford, Hal Holbrook, Toshiro Mifune, Robert Wagner, Cliff Robertson, James Shigeta. Kenneth Tobey. *MacArthur* (US/1977/128m/C) D: Joseph Sargent. C: Gregory Peck, Ed Flanders, Dan O'Herlihy, Ivan Bonar, Ward Costello, Nicholas Coster, Art Fleming, Addison Powell, Marj Dusay, John Fujioka, Fred Stuthman, Sandy Kenyon.

238 Hamilton, Alexander (1755–1804)

An important figure in the Revolutionary period of the U.S., Hamilton was the country's first Secretary of the Treasury. He was killed in a duel with Aaron Burr who was portrayed by David Niven in *Magnificent Doll*. Television portrayals have been by Jeremiah Sullivan in the mini-series *The Adams Chronicles* (76), Colm Feore in *Liberty, the American Revolution* (97), and by Michael York in *Founding Fathers* (2000).

George Arliss. *Alexander Hamilton* (US/1931/73m/BW) D: John G. Adolfi. B/on the play by George Arliss & Mary Hamlin. C: Doris Kenyon, Alan Mowbray, Montagu Love, Morgan Wallace, Gwendolyn Logan, John T. Murray, Charles Middleton, Lionel Belmore.

Arthur Space. *Magnificent Doll* (US/1946/93m/BW) D: Frank Borzage. C: Ginger Rogers, Burgess Meredith, David Niven, Robert Barrat, Grandon Rhodes, Larry Steers.

239 Hamilton, Lady Emma (1765–1815)

(Emma Lyon) The mistress of **Lord Horatio Nelson** whose daughter she bore, Emma's life after his death included bankruptcy and a year spent in debtor's prison.

Corinne Griffith. *The Divine Lady* (US/1929/110m/BW) D: Frank Lloyd. Best Director (AA). C: Victor Varconi, Ian Keith, H.B. Warner, Marie Dressler, William Conklin.

Vivian Leigh. *That Hamilton Woman* (aka *Lady Hamilton*) (US/1941/128m/BW) D: Alexander Korda. C: Laurence Olivier, Alan Mowbray, Sara Allgood, Gladys Cooper.

Michele Mercier. *Lady Hamilton* (aka *The Making of a Lady*) (Germany-Italy-France/1969/98m/C) D: Christian-Jaque. B/on the novel by Alexandre Dumas. C: Richard Johnson, John Mills, Harald Leipnitz, Robert Hundar, Mirko Ellis.

Glenda Jackson. *The Nelson Affair* (aka *A Bequest to the Nation*) (GB/1973/118m/C) D: James Cellan Jones. B/on the play *A Bequest to the Nation* by Terence Rattigan. C: Peter Finch, Michael Jayston, Anthony Quayle, Margaret Leighton, Dominic Guard, Nigel Stock, Barbara Leigh-Hunt, Roland Culver.

240 Hammerstein, Oscar (1846–1919)

German-American operatic impresario and the grandfather of **Oscar Hammerstein II,** Hammerstein built the Harlem (1888) and Manhattan (1906) Opera Houses in New York City.

Robert Middlemass. *The Dolly Sisters* (US/1945/114m/C) D: Irving Cummings. C: Betty Grable, John Payne, June Haver, Frank Latimore, Sig Rumann, S.Z. Sakall.

Robert Morley. *Melba* (GB/1953/113m/C) D: Lewis Milestone. C: Patrice Munsel, John McCallum, Sybil Thorndyke, John Justin, Alec Clunes, Theodore Bikel.

Peter Carlisle. *After the Ball* (GB/1957/89m/C) D: Compton Bennett. B/on *Recollections of Vesta Tilley* by Lady de Frece. C: Pat Kirkwood, Laurence Harvey, Mark Baker.

241 Hammerstein, Oscar, II (1895–1960)

The world's most famous lybrettist/lyricist, Hammerstein gave us such shows as *Show Boat, Oklahoma, South Pacific, The King and I,* and *The Sound of Music.*

Edwin Maxwell. *The Jolson Story* (US/1946/128m/C) D: Alfred E. Green. C: Larry Parks, Evelyn Keyes, William Demarest, Ludwig Donath, Bill Goodwin, Eddie Kane.

Paul Langton. *Till the Clouds Roll By* (US/1946/120m/C) D: Richard Whorf. C: Robert Walker, Judy Garland, Lucille Bremer, Joan Wells, Van Heflin, Dorothy Patrick, Paul Maxey.

Mitchell Kowell. *Deep in My Heart* (US/1954/130m/C) D: Stanley Donen. B/on the book by Elliott Arnold. C: Jose Ferrer, Merle Oberon, Walter Pidgeon, Paul Henreid.

242 Hammett, Samuel Dashiell (1894–1961)

Once a private investigator himself, Hammett was the author who created Sam Spade, who appeared in only one of Hammett's novels. Hammett was portrayed by Sam Shepard in the TV movie *Dash and Lilly* (99).

Jason Robards. *Julia* (US/1977/116m/C) D: Fred Zinnemann. B/on the book *Pentimento* by Lillian Hellman. C: Jane Fonda, Vanessa Redgrave, Rosemary Murphy.

Frederic Forrest. *Hammett* (US/1982/100m/C) D: Wim Wenders. B/on the novel by Joe Gores. C: Peter Boyle, Marilu Henner, Roy Kinnear, Elisha Cook, Jr.

243 Hannibal (247–183 BC)

Carthaginian general whose battles with Rome included his famed crossing of the Alps utilizing elephants to carry troops and supplies.

Camillo Pilotto. *The Defeat of Hannibal* (aka *Scipio the African*) (Italy/1937/109m/BW) D: Carmine Gallone. C: Annibale Ninchi, Isa Miranda, Memo Benassi, Franco Coop.

Howard Keel. *Jupiter's Darling* (US/1955/95m/C) D: George Sidney. B/on the play *Road to Rome* by Robert Sherwood. C: Esther Williams, Marge Champion, Gower Champion, George Sanders, Richard Haydn, Norma Varden.

Victor Mature. *Hannibal* (US-Italy/1960/103m/C) D: Edgar G. Ulmer. C: Rita Gam, Gabriele Ferzetti, Milly Vitale, Rik Battaglia, Mario Girotti.

244 Hardin, John Wesley (1853–1895)

Though **Billy the Kid** received more noteriety, Hardin was the West's most prolific killer, having shot more than 40 men. After spending 16 years in prison he was shot in the back while gambling in a Texas saloon.

　　John Dehner. *The Texas Rangers* (US/1951/68m/C) D: Phil Karlson. C: George Montgomery, Gale Storm, Noah Beery, Jr., William Bishop, Ian MacDonald, John Doucette.

　　Rock Hudson. *The Lawless Breed* (US/1952/83m/C) D: Raoul Walsh. C: Julia Adams, John McIntire, Mary Castle, Hugh O'Brian, Forrest Lewis, Robert Anderson.

　　Jack Elam. *Dirty Dingus Magee* (US/1970/90m/C) D: Burt Kennedy. B/on the novel *The Ballad of Dingus Magee* by David Markson. C: Frank Sinatra, George Kennedy, Anne Jackson, Lois Nettleton, Michele Carey, John Dehner, Paul Fix, Donald Barry.

245 Harlow, Jean (1911–1937)

(Harlean Carpenter) Hollywood's original "blonde bombshell," Harlow was the subject of two film biographies in 1965. She was also played by Susan Buckner in the TV production *The Amazing Howard Hughes* (77).

　　Carol Lynley. *Harlow* (US/1965/107m/C) D: Alex Segal. C: Efrem Zimalist, Jr., Ginger Rogers, Barry Sullivan, Hurd Hatfield, Lloyd Bochner, Buddy Lewis, Hermione Baddeley, Jack Kruschen, Celia Lovesky, Robert Strauss, John Fox, Jim Plunkett.

　　Caroll Baker. *Harlow* (US/1965/125m/C) D: Gordon Douglas. B/on the book *An Intimate Biography* by Irving Shulman & Arthur Landau. C: Martin Balsam, Peter Lawford, Red Buttons, Angela Lansbury, Raf Vallone, Leslie Nielsen, Mary Murphy.

　　Lindsay Bloom. *Hughes and Harlow: Angels in Hell* (US/1978/94m/C) D: Larry Buchanan. C: Victor Holchak, Royal Dano, Adam Roarke, David McLean, Linda Cristal.

Harrison, Benjamin *see* 584

Harrison, William H. *see* 575

246 Hart, Moss (1904–1961)

American playwright, Hart co-wrote (with **George S. Kaufman**) such stage successes as *The Man Who Came to Dinner* and *You Can't Take It With You.*

　　David Bond. *Three Sailors and a Girl* (US/1953/95m/C) D: Roy Del Ruth. B/on the play *The Butter and Egg Man* by George S. Kaufman. C: Jane Powell, Gordon MacRae, Alex Gerry.

　　George Hamilton. *Act One* (US/1964/110m/BW) D: Dore Schary. B/on the book by Moss Hart. C: Jason Robards, Jack Klugman, Ruth Ford, Eli Wallach, Earl Montgomery.

247 Hay, John Milton (1838–1905)

American diplomat, Hay served in many posts (Ambassador to Great Britain, Secretary of State, etc.) beginning in the administration of **Abraham Lincoln** and ending in that of **Theodore Roosevelt.**

Cameron Prud'Homme. *Abraham Lincoln* (US/1930/97m/BW) D: D.W. Griffith. C: Walter Huston, Una Merkel, Kay Hammond, E. Alyn Warren, Edgar Deering, Hobart Bosworth, Fred Warren, Frank Campeau, Francis Ford, Ian Keith, Oscar Apfel.

Franklin Parker. *Operator 13* (aka *Spy 13*) (US/1934/86m/BW) D: Richard Boleslavsky. B/on the novel by Robert W. Chambers. C: Marion Davies, Gary Cooper, Jean Parker, Katharine Alexander, Ted Healy, Sidney Toler, Douglas Dumbrille, John Elliott, Fred Warren.

John Huston. *The Wind and the Lion* (US/1975/119m/C) D: John Milius. C: Sean Connery, Candice Bergen, Brian Keith, Shirley Rothman, Steve Kanaly, Larry Cross, Alex Weldon.

248 Haydn, Franz Joseph (1732–1809)

Prolific Austrian composer, Haydn wrote 107 symphonies, 68 string quartets, 62 piano sonatas and 19 operas.

Edward Vedder. *The Mozart Story* (aka *Whom the Gods Love*) (aka *Mozart*) (aka *Wenn Die Gotter Lieben*) (Germany/1942/91m/C) D: Karl Hartl. C: Hans Holt, Rene Deltgen, Winnie Markus, Irene von Meyendorf, Wilton Graff, Curt Jurgens, Carol Forman, Walther Jansson, Paul Hoerbiger.

Arthur Dulay. *Mrs. Fitzherbert* (GB/1947/99m/BW) D: Montgomery Tully. B/on the novel *Princess Fitz* by Winifred Carter. C: Peter Graves, Joyce Howard, Leslie Banks, Margaretta Scott, Wanda Rotha, Mary Clare, Frederick Valk, Ralph Truman, John Stuart, Barry Morse, Henry Oscar, Moira Lister, Julian Dallas, Lily Kann.

Ernst Nadhering. *The Magnificent Rebel* (US/1961/94m/C) D: Georg Tressler. C: Karl Boehm, Giulia Rubini, Ivan Desny, Gabriele Porks, Peter Arens.

Ladislav Chudik. *Forget Mozart!* (Germany-Czechoslovakia/1985/90m/C) D: Miloslav Luther. C: Max Tidof, Armin Muller Stahl, Franz Glatzeder, Zdenek Hradilak.

Hayes, Rutherford B. *see* 580

249 Hearst, William Randolph (1863–1951)

Powerful controversial millionaire who published the largest chain of newspapers in the United States. Through his publications, films, and investments, he was able to strongly influence American public opinion. TV film portrayals of Hearst have been *The Hearst and Davies Affair* (85) with Robert Mitchum, *Rough Riders* (97) with George Hamilton, and *RKO 281* (99) with James Cromwell.

Orson Welles (Charles Foster Kane). *Citizen Kane* (US/1941/119m/BW) D: Orson Welles. AA Best Screenplay, Orson Welles and Herman Mankiewicz. NYF: Best Picture. C: Joseph Cotton, Everett Sloan, Agnes Moorehead, Dorothy

Comingore, Ray Collins, George Coulouris, Ruth Warrick, William Alland, Paul Stewart, Erskine Sanford.

John Carpenter. *Cradle Will Rock* (US/1999/109m/C) D: Tim Robbins. C: Hank Azaria, Rubén Blades, Joan Cusack, John Cusack, Cary Elwes, Philip Baker Hall, Cherry Jones, Angus MacFadyen, Bill Murray, Vanessa Redgrave, Susan Sarandon, John Turturro, Barnard Hughes, Gretchen Mol, Corina Katt.

Edward Herrmann. *The Cat's Meow* (Canada-Germany-GB/2001/110m/BW/ C) D: Peter Bogdanovich. C: Kirsten Dunst, Cary Elwes, Eddie Izzard, Joanna Lumley, Victor Slezak, Jennifer Tilly, James Laurenson, Ronan Vibert, Chiara Schoras, Ingrid Lacey, John C. Vennema, Claudia Harrison, Claudie Blakley.

250 Hemingway, Ernest Miller (1899–1961)

American journalist and author, Hemingway wrote many novels considered classics of modern literature including *The Sun Also Rises* and *The Old Man and the Sea*. Many of his semi-autobiographical works have been adapted for the screen including *Islands in the Stream* (77) starring George Scott, and the Nick Adams stories in *Adventures of a Young Man* (62) featuring Richard Beymer. He was portrayed by Stacy Keach in the TV mini-series *Hemingway* (88). *In Love and War* was based on the *Diaries of Agnes von Kurowsky*, she was portrayed by Sandra Bullock in the film.

Bruce McGill. *Waiting for the Moon* (US/1987/88m/C) D: Jill Godmillow. C: Linda Hunt, Linda Bassett, Bernadette LaFont, Jacques Boudet, Andrew McCarthy.

Kevin J. O'Connor. *The Moderns* (US/1988/126m/C) D: Alan Rudolph. C: Keith Carradine, Linda Fiorentino, Genevieve Bujold, Geraldine Chaplin, Elsa Raven, Ali Giron, John Lone, Wallace Shawn.

Chris O'Donnell. *In Love and War* (US-GB/1996/115m/C) D: Richard Attenborough. B/on the Agnes von Kurowsky diaries and the book *Hemingway in Love and War: The Lost Diary of Agnes von Kurowsky* by Henry S. Villard and James Nagel. C: MacKenzie Astin, Margot Steinberg, Sandra Bullock, Alan Bennett, Ingrid Lacey, Terence Sach, Carlo Croccolo, Tara Hugo, Gigi Vivan, Houston Kenyon, Kay Hawtrey, Roseline Garland, Evan Smirnow.

Albert Finney. *Hemingway, the Hunter of Death* (US-Kenya-Spain-Colombia/ 2001/C) D: Sergio Dow. B/on the novel by Manuel Zapata. C: Paul Guilfoyle, Fele Martínez.

Henri II *see* 621

Henri III *see* 624

Henri IV *see* 625

251 Henry II (1133–1189)

Henry's attempts to curb the Church's power in England brought him into conflict with **Thomas Becket**, ending in Becket's murder. His stormy marriage to **Eleanor of Acquitaine** was depicted in *The Lion in Winter*.

Henry II (Peter O'Toole) and his wife, Eleanor of Aquitaine (Katherine Hep-burn) have one of their calmer moments during the Christmas Holidays. *The Lion in Winter* (1968). Hepburn received her third Oscar for this performance. (Museum of Modern Art Film Stills Archive)

Alexander Gauge. *Murder in the Cathedral* (GB/1951/140m/BW) D: George Hoellering. B/on the play by T.S. Eliot. C: Father John Groser, David Ward, T.S. Eliot, Michael Aldridge.

Peter O'Toole * Best Actor/Drama (GG). *Becket* (GB/1964/148m/C) D: Peter Glenville. B/on the play by Jean Anouilh. Best Picture (GG). C: Richard Burton, Donald Wolfit, John Gielgud, Martita Hunt, Pamela Brown, Sian Phillips, Paolo Stoppa, Felix Aylmer.

Peter O'Toole * Best Actor/Drama (GG). *The Lion in Winter* (GB/1968/134m/C) D: Anthony Harvey. B/on the play by James Goldman. Best Picture (GG [Drama], NYC). Best Director (DGA). C: Katharine Hepburn, Jane Merrow, John Castle, Anthony Hopkins, Timothy Dalton, Nigel Terry, Nigel Stock, Kenneth Griffith.

Henry III *see* 593

Henry IV *see* 597

252 Henry V (1387–1422)

English king whose victory over the superior forces of the French at Agincourt in 1415 has been depicted in several films.

Matheson Lang. *Regal Cavalcade* (aka *Royal Cavalcade*) (GB/1935/100m/BW) D: Thomas Bentley, Herbert Brenton, Norman Lee, Walter Summers, Will Kellino & Marcel Varnel. C: Marie Lohr, Esme Percy, Pearl Argyle, Frank Vosper, Austin Trevor, Harry Brunning, John Mills, C.M. Hallard, H. Saxon-Snell, Patric Knowles, Athene Seyler.

Laurence Olivier * Best Actor (NYC, NBR), Special Academy Award. *Henry V* (GB/1945/127m/C) D: Laurence Olivier. B/on the play by Wm. Shakespeare. Best Picture (NBR), Special Academy Award to Laurence Olivier "for his outstanding achievement as actor, producer and director." C: Robert Newton, Leslie Banks, Renee Asherson, Esmond Knight, Harcourt Williams, Max Adrian.

Dan O'Herlihy. *The Black Shield of Falworth* (US/1954/98m/C) D: Rudolph Mate. B/on the novel *Men of Iron* by Howard Pyle. C: Tony Curtis, Janet Leigh, David Farrar, Ian Keith.

Keith Baxter. *Chimes at Midnight* (aka *Falstaff*) (aka *Campanadas A Medianoche*) (Spain-Switzerland/1967/115m/BW) D: Orson Welles. B/on plays by Wm. Shakespeare and the book *The Chronicles of England* by Raphael Holinshed. C: Orson Welles, Jeanne Moreau, Margaret Rutherford, John Gielgud, Marina Vlady, Norman Rodway, Michael Aldridge, Fernando Rey.

Kenneth Branagh. *Henry V* (GB/1989/138m/C) D: Kenneth Branagh. B/on the play by Wm. Shakespeare. Best Director (NBR), Best New Director (NYC). C: Derek Jacobi, Brian Blessed, Alec McCowen, Ian Holm, Michael Williams, Richard Briers, Robert Stephens, Robbie Coltrane, Judi Dench, Paul Scofield, Michael Maloney.

Henry VI *see* 598

Henry VII *see* 601

253 Henry VIII (1491–1547)

The English King who broke with the Catholic Church establishing the Church of England (See **Cranmer** and **Wolsey**), it was Henry's six wives that brought him far more attention in the cinema.

Charles Laughton. *The Private Life of Henry VIII* (GB/1933/97m/BW) D: Alexander Korda. C: Robert Donat, Binnie Barnes, Elsa Lanchester, Merle Oberon, Wendy Barrie, Everley Gregg, Franklyn Dyall, Miles Mander, Claude Allister, John Loder, Lawrence Hanray.

Frank Cellier. *Tudor Rose* (aka *Lady Jane Grey*) (aka *Nine Days a Queen*) (GB/1936/78m/BW) D: Robert Stevenson. C: Cedric Hardwicke, John Mills, Felix Aylmer, Desmond Tester, Nova Pilbeam, Gwen Frangcon-Davies, Sybil Thorndike.

Alexandre Rignault. *Francis The First* (aka *François Ier*) (France/1937/BW) D: Christian-Jaque. C: Fernandel, Mona Goya, Henri Bosc, Sinoel, Mihalesco, Aime-Simon Girard.

Lyn Harding. *The Pearls of the Crown* (France/1937/120–100m/BW) D: Sacha

Guitry & Christian-Jaque. C: Sacha Guitry, Jacqueline Delubac, Ermete Zacconi, Marguerite Moreno, Yvette Plenne, Catalano, Arletty, Percy Marmont, Derrick De Marney, Barbara Shaw, Simone Renant, Jean Louis Barrault, Emile Drain, Enrico Glori, Renee Saint-Cyr, Pizani, Claude Dauphin, Aime-Simon Gerard.

Montagu Love. *The Prince and the Pauper* (US/1937/120m/BW) D: William Keighley. B/on the novel by Mark Twain and the play by Catherine C. Cushing. C: Errol Flynn, Claude Rains, Henry Stephenson, Billy Mauch, Bobby Mauch, Alan Hale, Robert Warwick, Helen Valkis, Ann Howard, Halliwell Hobbes, Barton MacLane.

James Robertson Justice. *The Sword and the Rose* (aka *When Knighthood Was in Flower*) (GB/1953/91m/C) D: Ken Annakin. B/on the novel *When Knighthood Was in Flower* by Charles Major. C: Richard Todd, Glynis Johns, Michael Gough, Jane Barrett, Rosalie Crutchley, Peter Copley, D.A. Clarke-Smith, Bryan Coleman, Jean Mercure.

Charles Laughton. *Young Bess* (US/1953/112m/C) D: George Sidney. B/on the novel by Margaret Irwin. C: Jean Simmons, Stewart Granger, Deborah Kerr, Kay Walsh, Cecil Kellaway, Rex Thompson, Elaine Stewart, Dawn Addams, Lumsden Hare.

Paul Rogers. *The Prince and the Pauper* (GB/1962/93m/C) D: Don Chaffey. B/on the novel by Mark Twain. C: Sean Scully, Jane Asher, Guy Williams, Laurence Naismith.

Robert Shaw. *A Man for All Seasons* (GB/1966/120m/C) D: Fred Zinnemann. B/on the play by Robert Bolt. Best Picture Awards: (AA, NBR, GG, NYC, BFA Any Source and Best British Film), Best Director Awards: (AA, NBR, GG, NYC, DGA). C: Paul Scofield, Wendy Hiller, Leo McKern, Orson Welles, Susannah York, Nigel Davenport, Vanessa Redgrave, Cyril Luckham.

Richard Burton. *Anne of the Thousand Days* (GB/1969/145m/C) D: Charles Jarrott. B/on the play by Maxwell Anderson. C: Genevieve Bujold, Irene Papas, Anthony Quayle, John Colicos, Michael Hordern, Katharine Blake, William Squire, Lesley Patterson, Nicola Pagett.

Sidney James. *Carry on Henry VIII* (GB/1970/89m/C) D: Gerald Thomas. C: Kenneth Williams, Joan Sims, Charles Hawtrey, Terry Scott, Peter Gilmore, Monica Dietrich, Patsy Rowlands.

Keith Michell. *The Six Wives of Henry VIII* (aka *Henry VIII and His Six Wives*) (GB/1972/125m/C) D: Waris Hussein. C: Frances Cuka, Charlotte Rampling, Jane Asher, Jenny Bos, Lynne Frederick, Barbara Leigh-Hunt, Donald Pleasence, Simon Henderson, Annette Crosbie, John Bryans, Michael Goodliffe, Bernard Hepton, Dorothy Tutin.

Charlton Heston. *Crossed Swords* (aka *The Prince and the Pauper*) (US/1977/121m/C) D: Richard Fleischer. B/on the novel *The Prince and the Pauper* by Mark Twain. C: Oliver Reed, Raquel Welch, Mark Lester, Ernest Borgnine, Lalla Ward, Felicity Dean, George C. Scott, Rex Harrison, Harry Andrews, David Hemmings.

254 Henry, Partick (1736–1799)

American Revolutionary leader remembered for his pronouncement "Give me liberty, or give me death." In TV mini-series he has been portrayed by Harry

Groener in *George Washington* (84), Daniel Davis in *George Washington II: The Forging of a Nation* (86), William Shust in the mini-series *The Adams Chronicles* (76), James Naughton in *Liberty, the American Revolution* (97), and by Burt Reynolds in *Founding Fathers* (2000).

    Richard Gaines. *The Howards of Virginia* (aka *Tree of Liberty*) (US/1940/117m/ BW) D: Frank Lloyd. B/on the novel *The Tree of Liberty* by Elizabeth Page. C: Cary Grant, Martha Scott, Cedric Hardwicke, Alan Marshal, Richard Carlson, George Houston.

    Macdonald Carey. *John Paul Jones* (US/1959/126m/C) D: John Farrow. B/on the story *Nor'wester* by Clements Ripley. C: Robert Stack, Bette Davis, Marisa Pavan, Charles Coburn, Jean-Pierre Aumont, Susana Canales, John Crawford, Eric Pohlmann.

255 Herbert, Victor (1859–1924)

Irish-American composer, Herbert is best remembered for his operettas "Babes in Toyland," "The Red Mill" and "Naughty Marietta."

    Walter Connally. *The Great Victor Herbert* (US/1939/96m/BW) D: Andrew L. Stone. C: Allan Jones, Mary Martin, Lee Bowman, Susanna Foster, Jerome Cowan, Richard Tucker.

    Paul Maxey. *Till the Clouds Roll By* (US/1946/120m/C) D: Richard Whorf. C: Robert Walker, Judy Garland, Lucille Bremer, Joan Wells, Van Heflin, Paul Langton, Dorothy Patrick.

256 Herod Antipas (21 BC–AD 39)

Herod Antipas, son of **Herod the Great**, was the Herod who had **John the Baptist** executed (See **Salome**), and who was ruling at the time of the crucifiction of **Jesus Christ**. He was played by Christopher Plummer in the TV mini-series *Jesus of Nazareth* (77), by Jonathan Pryce in the TV film *The Day Christ Died* (80), and by Luca Barbareschi in *Jesus* (99). Note: In *Salome's Last Dance* Stratford Johns plays an actor portraying Herod Antipas in a staged performance of the Oscar Wilde play *Salome*.

    Harry Baur. *Golgotha* (France/1935/97m/BW) D: Julien Duvivier. C: Robert Le Vigan, Jean Gabin, Charles Granval, Andre Bacque, Hubert Prelier, Lucas Gridoux, Edwige Feuillere, Juliette Verneuil, Vana Yami, Van Daele.

    Charles Laughton. *Salome* (US/1953/103m/C) D: William Dieterle. C: Rita Hayworth, Stewart Granger, Judith Anderson, Cedric Hardwicke, Alan Badel, Basil Sydney, Rex Reason, Robert Warwick, Maurice Schwartz.

    Herbert Lom. *The Big Fisherman* (US/1959/180m/C) D: Frank Borzage. B/on the novel by Lloyd C. Douglas. C: Howard Keel, Susan Kohner, John Saxon, Martha Hyer, Alexander Scourby, Jay Barney, Rhodes Reason, Brian Hutton, Thomas Troupe, Herbert Rudley.

    Carlos Casaravilla. *The Redeemer* (Spain/1959/93m/C) D: Joseph Breen. C: Luis Alvarez, Maruchi Fresno, Manuel Monroy, Felix Acaso, Antonio Vilar, Virgilio Teixeira, Sebastian Cabot (Narrator).

    Frank Thring. *King of Kings* (US/1961/168m/C) D: Nicholas Ray. C: Jeffrey

Hunter, Siobahn McKenna, Hurd Hatfield, Viveca Lindfors, Rita Gam, Carmen
Sevilla, Rip Torn, Brigid Bazlen, Harry Guardino, Guy Rolfe, Maurice Marsac,
Gregoire Aslan, Royal Dano, Robert Ryan, Gerard Tichy, Michael Wager, Tino
Barrero, Jose Antonio, Orson Welles (Narrator).

Francesco Leonetti. *The Gospel According to St. Matthew* (France-Italy/1964/
142m/BW) D: Pier Paolo Pasolini. B/on the *New Testament book of Matthew*. C:
Enrique Irazoqui, Susanna Pasolini, Mario Socrate, Marcello Morante, Alfonso
Gatto, Rodolfo Wilcock, Amerigo Bevilacqua, Otello Sestilli, Settimio Di Porto,
Ferruccio Nuzzo, Alessandro Tosca, Paolo Tedesco, Franca Cupane, Giacomo
Morante, Rosario Migale.

Jose Ferrer. *The Greatest Story Ever Told* (US/1965/141m/C) D: George Stevens.
B/on the book by Fulton Oursler. C: Max von Sydow, Dorothy McGuire, Robert
Loggia, Claude Rains, Charlton Heston, Donald Pleasence, David McCallum,
Gary Raymond, Robert Blake, John Considine, David Hedison, Joanna Dun-
ham, Sal Mineo, Van Heflin, Ed Wynn, Martin Landau, Telly Savalas, Sidney
Poitier, Roddy McDowell, Angela Lansbury, Richard Conte, Carroll Baker, Janet
Margolin, Burt Brinckerhoff, Tom Reese.

Joshua Mostel. *Jesus Christ, Superstar* (US/1973/107m/C) D: Norman Jewison. B/on the rock opera by Tim Rice & Andrew Lloyd Webber. C: Ted Neeley, Carl Anderson, Yvonne Elliman, Barry Dennen, Bob Bingham, Larry T.
Marshall, Philip Toubus.

Richard Peterson. *Jesus* (US/1979/117m/C) D: Peter Sykes & John Kirsh. B/on
the *New Testament book of Luke*. C: Brian Deacon, Rivka Noiman, Yossef Shiloah,
Niko Nitai, Gadi Rol, Eli Cohen, Shmuel Tal, Kobi Assaf, Talia Shapira, Eli
Danker, Mosko Alkalai, Nisim Gerama, Leonid Weinstein, Peter Frye, David
Goldberg.

Nehemiah Persoff. *In Search of Historic Jesus* (US/1979/91m/C) D: Henning
Schellerup. B/on the book by Lee Roddy & Charles E. Seller. C: John Rubin-
stein, John Anderson, Andrew Bloch, Morgan Brittany, Walter Brooke, Annette
Charles, Royal Dano, Anthony DeLongis, Lawrence Dobkin, David Opatoshu,
John Hoyt, Jeffrey Druce.

Tomas Milian. *Salome* (France-Italy/1985/97m/C) D: Claude d'Anna. B/on
the play by Oscar Wilde. C: Pamela Salem, Tim Woodward, Jo Ciampa, Fabrizio Bentivoglio, Fabiana Torrente.

257 Herod the Great (72?–4 BC)

Backed by the Romans and given the title of "King" by **Augustus Caesar**, Herod
was responsible for the massacring of all male babies in Bethlehem in his attempt
to kill the new born **Jesus Christ**. He was played by Peter Ustinov in the TV
mini-series *Jesus of Nazareth* (77).

Joseph Schildkraut. *Cleopatra* (US/1934/102m/BW) D: Cecil B. DeMille. C:
Claudette Colbert, Warren William, Henry Wilcoxon, Gertrude Michael, Ian
Keith, Ian Maclaren, Arthur Hohl, Claudia Dell, Robert Warwick, Charles Mor-
ris.

Edmund Purdom. *Herod the Great* (Italy/1959/93m/C) D: Arnaldo Genoino.
C: Sylvia Lopez, Massimo Girotti, Sandra Milo, Alberto Lupo.

Gregoire Aslan. *King of Kings* (US/1961/168m/C) D: Nicholas Ray. C: Jeffrey Hunter, Siobahn McKenna, Hurd Hatfield, Viveca Lindfors, Rita Gam, Carmen Sevilla, Rip Torn, Brigid Bazlen, Harry Guardino, Frank Thring, Guy Rolfe, Maurice Marsac, Royal Dano, Robert Ryan, Gerard Tichy, Michael Wager, Tino Barrero, Jose Antonio, Orson Welles (Narrator).

Amerigo Bevilacqua. *The Gospel According to St. Matthew* (France-Italy/1964/142m/BW) D: Pier Paolo Pasolini. B/on the *New Testament book of Matthew*. C: Enrique Irazoqui, Susanna Pasolini, Mario Socrate, Marcello Morante, Alfonso Gatto, Rodolfo Wilcock, Francesco Leonetti, Otello Sestilli, Settimio Di Porto, Ferruccio Nuzzo, Alessandro Tosca, Paolo Tedesco, Franca Cupane, Giacomo Morante, Rosario Migale.

Claude Rains. *The Greatest Story Ever Told* (US/1965/141m/C) D: George Stevens. B/on the book by Fulton Oursler. C: Max von Sydow, Dorothy McGuire, Robert Loggia, Jose Ferrer, Charlton Heston, Donald Pleasence, David McCallum, Gary Raymond, Robert Blake, John Considine, David Hedison, Joanna Dunham, Sal Mineo, Van Heflin, Ed Wynn, Martin Landau, Telly Savalas, Sidney Poitier, Roddy McDowell, Angela Lansbury, Richard Conte, Carroll Baker, Janet Margolin, Burt Brinckerhoff, Tom Reese.

David Opatoshu. *In Search of Historic Jesus* (US/1979/91m/C) D: Henning Schellerup. B/on the book by Lee Roddy & Charles E. Seller. C: John Rubinstein, John Anderson, Nehemiah Persoff, Andrew Bloch, Morgan Brittany, Walter Brooke, Annette Charles, Royal Dano, Anthony DeLongis, Lawrence Dobkin, John Hoyt, Jeffrey Druce.

258 Heydrich, Reinhardt (1904–1942)

Hitler's notoriously brutal governor in Czechoslovakia, Heydrich was shot by members of the Resistance in May 1942. As reprisal for his death **Himmler** had the town of Lidice destroyed and all male villagers killed. In the TV mini-series *Holocaust* (78) Heydrich was played by David Warner, and in the TV film *Conspiracy* (2001) by Kenneth Branagh.

Hans von Twardowski. *Hangmen Also Die* (aka *Lest We Forget*) (US/1943/131m/BW) D: Fritz Lang. C: Brian Donlevy, Walter Brennan, Anna Lee, Gene Lockhart, Dennis O'Keefe.

John Carradine. *Hitler's Madman* (aka *Hitler's Hangman*) (US/1943/84m/BW) D: Douglas Sirk. B/on the story *Hangman's Village* by Bart Lytton. C: Patricia Morison, Ralph Morgan, Alan Curtis, Howard Freeman, Ludwig Stossel, Edgar Kennedy, Al Shean.

Martin Held. *Canaris* (Germany/1954/113m/BW) D: Alfred Weldenmann. C: O.E. Hasse, Adrian Hovan, Barbara Ruetting, Wolfgang Priess, Charles Regnier.

Anton Diffring. *Operation Daybreak* (aka *Price of Freedom.*) (GB-US/1976/118m/C) D: Lewis Gilbert. B/on the novel *Seven Men at Daybreak* by Alan Burgess. C: Timothy Bottoms, Martin Shaw, Joss Ackland, Nicola Pagett, Anthony Andrews.

Siegfried Loyda. *The Assault* (aka *Atentát*) (Czechoslovakia/1964/BW) D: Jiří Sequens. C: Radoslav Brzobohaty, Vladimír Hlavaty, Jiří Holy, Rudolph Jelínek, Jiří Kodet, Ludek Munzar, Harry Studt, Josef Vinklár, Pavel Bartl.

David Warner. *Hitler's SS: Portrait in Evil* (US/1985/150m/C) D: Jim Goddard. Made for U.S. TV, released theatrically elsewhere. C: John Shea, Bill Nighy, Lucy Gutteridge, Michael Elphick, John Normington, Colin Jeavons, Jose Ferrer, Carroll Baker.

Dietrich Mattausch. *The Wannsee Conference* (Germany-Austria/1987/87m/C) D: Heinz Schirk. C: Robert Artzorn, Friedrich Beckhaus, Gerd Bockmann, Jochen Busse.

259 Hickok, James Butler "Wild Bill" (1837–1876)

A famous frontier lawman and marksman, Hickock kept the peace in several Kansas towns following the Civil War. He also appeared on stage with **Buffalo Bill** and was rumored to have had an affair with **Calamity Jane**. He was shot in the back while playing cards by **Jack McCall**. Hickok was portrayed by Sam Shepard in the TV film *Purgatory* (99). (See Appendix F for the PRC "**Wild Bill Hickok**" series.)

Tim McCoy. *Aces and Eights* (US/1936/62m/BW) D: Sam Newfield. C: Jimmy Aubrey, Luana Walters, Wheeler Oakman, Earl Hodgins, Rex Lease, Frank Ellis.

Gary Cooper. *The Plainsman* (US/1936/115m/BW) D: Cecil B. DeMille. B/on the novel *Wild Bill Hickok* by Frank J. Wilstach. C: Jean Arthur, James Ellison, Porter Hall, John Miljan, Frank McGlynn, Edwin Maxwell, Leila McIntyre, Charles H. Herzinger.

George Houston. *Frontier Scout* (US/1939/60m/BW) D: Sam Newfield. C: Al St. John, Beth Marion, Dave O'Brien, Jack Smith, Budd Buster, Mantan Moreland.

Roy Rogers. *Young Bill Hickok* (US/1940/59m/BW) D: Joseph Kane. C: George "Gabby" Hayes, Jacqueline Wells (Julie Bishop), Sally Payne, John Miljan, Monte Blue.

Richard Dix. *Badlands of Dakota* (US/1941/74m/BW) D: Alfred E. Green. C: Robert Stack, Ann Rutherford, Frances Farmer, Andy Devine, Lon Chaney, Jr., Addison Richards.

Bruce Cabot. *Wild Bill Hickok Rides* (US/1942/81m/BW) D: Ray Enright. C: Trevor Bardette, Constance Bennett, Warren William, Betty Brewer, Walter Catlett, Ward Bond, Ray Teal.

Reed Hadley. *Dallas* (US/1950/94m/C) D: Stuart Heisler. C: Gary Cooper, Ruth Roman, Steve Cochran, Raymond Massey, Barbara Payton, Leif Erickson.

Robert Anderson. *The Lawless Breed* (US/1952/83m/C) D: Raoul Walsh. C: Rock Hudson, Julia Adams, John McIntire, Mary Castle, Hugh O'Brian, Forrest Lewis.

Howard Keel. *Calamity Jane* (US/1953/100m/C) D: David Butler. C: Doris Day, Allyn McLerie, Philip Carey, Dick Wesson, Paul Harvey, Chubby Johnson.

Douglas Kennedy. *Jack McCall, Desperado* (US/1953/76m/C) D: Sidney Salkow. C: George Montgomery, Angela Stevens, James Seay, Eugene Iglesias, Jay Silverheels.

Forrest Tucker. *Pony Express* (US/1953/101m/C) D: Jerry Hopper. C: Charlton Heston, Rhonda Fleming, Jan Sterling, Porter Hall, Michael Moore, Pat Hogan.

Ewing Brown. *Son of the Renegade* (US/1953/57m/BW) D: Reg Brown. C: John Carpenter, Lori Irving, John McKellen, Valley Keene, Jack Ingram.

Tom Brown. *I Killed Wild Bill Hickok* (US/1956/63m/C) D: Richard Talmadge. C: John (Carpenter) Forbes, Helen Westcott, Virginia Gibson, Denver Pyle.

Adrian Hoven. *Seven Hours of Gunfire* (Italy-Germany-Spain/1964/C) D: Joaquim Marchent. C: Gloria Milland, Rick van Nutter.

Robert Culp. *The Raiders* (US/1964/75m/C) D: Herschel Daugherty. C: Brian Keith, Judi Meredith, James McMullan, Alfred Ryder, Simon Oakland, Ben Cooper.

Robert Dix. *Deadwood '76* (US/1965/94m/C) D: James Landis. C: Arch Hall, Jr., Melissa Morgan, Jack Lester, Rex Marlow.

Paul Shannon. *The Outlaws Is Coming* (US/1965/88m/BW) D: Norman Maurer. C: Larry Fine, Moe Howard, Joe De Rita, Nancy Kovack, Murray Alper, Joe Bolton, Bill Camfield, Hal Fryar, Johnny Ginger, Wayne Mack, Ed McDonnell, Bruce Sedley, Sally Starr.

Don Murray. *The Plainsman* (US/1966/92m/C) D: David Lowell Rich. C: Guy Stockwell, Abby Dalton, Brad Dillman, Leslie Nielsen, Simon Oakland, Emily Banks.

Jeff Corey. *Little Big Man* (US/1970/147m/C) D: Arthur Penn. B/on the novel by Thomas Berger. C: Dustin Hoffman, Faye Dunaway, Martin Balsam, Richard Mulligan.

Charles Bronson. *The White Buffalo* (aka *Hunt to Kill*) (US/1977/97m/C) D: J. Lee Thompson. B/on the novel by Richard Sale. C: Jack Warden, Will Sampson, Kim Novak, Clint Walker, Stuart Whitman, Slim Pickens, John Carradine, Martin Kove.

Richard Farnsworth. *The Legend of the Lone Ranger* (US/1981/98m/C) D: William A. Fraker. C: Klinton Spilsbury, Michael Horse, Jason Robards, Ted Flicker, Lincoln Tate.

Jeff Bridges. *Wild Bill* (US/1995/98m/C) D: Walter Hill. B/on the novel *Deadwood* by Pete Dexter and the play *Fathers and Sons* by Thomas Babe. C: Ellen Barkin, John Hurt, Diane Lane, Susannah Moore, David Arquette, Keith Carradine.

260 Himmler, Heinrich (1900–1945)

Nazi leader of the Gestapo, Himmler was responsible for executing **Hitler's** "Final Solution," the extermination of six million Jews.

Howard Freeman. *Hitler's Madman* (aka *Hitler's Hangman*) (US/1943/84m/ BW) D: Douglas Sirk. B/on the story *Hangman's Village* by Bart Lytton. C: John Carradine, Patricia Morison, Ralph Morgan, Alan Curtis, Ludwig Stossel, Edgar Kennedy, Al Shean.

Wedgewood Nowell. *That Nazty Nuisance* (aka *Nazty Nuisance*) (US/1943/ 50m/BW) D: Glenn Tryon. C: Bobby Watson, Joe Devlin, Johnny Arthur, Rex Evans, Charles Rogers.

Fred Giermann. *The Strange Death of Adolf Hitler* (US/1943/72m/BW) D: James Hogan. C: Ludwig Donath, Gale Sondergaard, George Dolenz, Fritz Kortner, Ivan Triesault, Ludwig Stossel.

Luis Van Rooten. *The Hitler Gang* (US/1944/101m/BW) D: John Farrow. C: Bobby Watson, Roman Bohnen, Martin Kosleck, Victor Varconi, Alexander Pope, Ivan Triesault, Sig Rumann, Reinhold Schunzel, Alexander Granach, Fritz Kortner.

Sukman. *The Magic Face* (Austria/1951/88m/BW) D: Frank Tuttle. C: Luther Adler, Patricia Knight, William L. Shirer, Ilka Windish, Herman Ehrhardt, Hans Sheel.

Erich Stuckmann. *The Last Ten Days* (aka *Ten Days to Die*) (aka *Last Ten Days of Adolf Hitler*) (aka *Der Letzte Akt*) (aka *The Last Act*) (Germany/1955/115m/BW) D: G.W. Pabst. B/on the novel *Ten Days to Die* by M.A. Mussanno. C: Albin Skoda, Oskar Werner, Lotte Tobisch, Willy Krause, Edmund Erlandsen, Kurt Eilers, Helga Dohrn, Leopold Hainisch, Otto Schmoele.

Julian Somers. *Battle of The V.1* (aka *Missile from Hell*) (aka *Unseen Heroes*) (GB/1958/104–85m/BW) D: Vernon Sewell. B/on the book *They Saved London* by Bernard Newman. C: Michael Rennie, Patricia Medina, Christopher Lee, Milly Vitale.

Eric Zuckmann. *I Aim at the Stars* (US/1960/106m/BW) D: J. Lee Thompson. C: Curt Jurgens, Victoria Shaw, Herbert Lom, Gia Scala, Gunther Mruwka, Adrian Hoven.

Luis Van Rooten. *Operation Eichmann* (US/1961/92m/BW) D: R.G. Springsteen. C: Werner Klemperer, Ruta Lee, Donald Buka, Barbara Turner, John Banner, Hans Gudegast.

Rick Traeger. *Hitler* (aka *Women of Nazi Germany*) (US/1962/107m/BW) D: Stuart Heisler. C: Richard Basehart, Cordula Trantow, Maria Emo, Martin Kosleck, John Banner, Martin Brandt, William Sargent, Gregory Gay, Theodore Marcuse, John Mitchum, G. Stanley Jones, Walter Kohler, Carl Esmond, Berry Kroeger.

Donald Pleasence. *The Eagle Has Landed* (GB/1976/134m/C) D: John Sturges. B/on the novel by Jack Higgins. C: Michael Caine, Donald Sutherland, Robert Duvall, Jenny Agutter, Leigh Dilley, Anthony Quayle, Jean Marsh, Judy Geeson, Larry Hagman.

Hans Korte. *Death Is My Trade* (Germany/1977/145m/C) D: Theodor Kotulla. B/on the novel *La Mort est Mon Metier* by Robert Merle. C: Goetz George, Elisabeth Schwarz, Kurt Hubner, Walter Czaschke, Kai Taschner, Sigurd Fitzek.

Erich Thiede. *Death Sentence* (aka *Wyrok Smierci*) (Poland/1980/105m/C) D: Witold Orzechowski. C: Doris Kuntsmann, Wojciech Wysocki, Jerzy Bonczak, Stanislaw Igar.

John Normington. *Hitler's SS: Portrait in Evil* (US/1985/150m/C) D: Jim Goddard. Made for U.S. TV, released theatrically elsewhere. C: John Shea, Bill Nighy, Lucy Gutteridge, Michael Elphick, David Warner, Colin Jeavons, Jose Ferrer, Carroll Baker.

261 Hitler, Adolf (1889–1945)

The Nazi Fuhrer of Germany's Third Reich, Hitler was the man responsible for 40 million deaths in WWII. Anthony Hopkins won an Emmy Award for his portrayal of Hitler in the TV movie *The Bunker* (81).

Line-up of *The Hitler Gang* (1944): left to right, Bobby Watson as Hitler, Victor Varcone as Rudolph Hess, Alexander Pope as Göring, and Luis Van Rooten as Himmler. Bobby Watson was a character actor with a remarkable resemblance to Hitler, portraying him in 8 films.Watson's career suffered from this type-casting, and he made very few films after the end of World War II. (Museum of Modern Art Film Stills Archive)

Billy Russell. *For Freedom* (GB/1940/87m/BW) D: Maurice Elvey Knight. C: Will Fyffe, Anthony Hulme, E.V.H. Emmett, Guy Middleton, Albert Lieven, Hugh McDermott.

Carl Ekberg. *Man Hunt* (US/1941/105m/BW) D: Fritz Lang. B/on the novel *Rogue Male* by Geoffrey Household. C: Walter Pidgeon, Joan Bennett, George Sanders.

Carl Ekberg. *Once Upon a Honeymoon* (US/1942/117m/BW) D: Leo McCarey. C: Ginger Rogers, Cary Grant, Walter Slezak, Albert Dekker, Albert Basserman, John Banner.

Bobby Watson. *The Devil With Hitler* (aka *The Devil Checks Up*) (US/1942/44m/BW) D: Gordon Douglas. C: Alan Mowbray, Joe Devlin, George E. Stone, Marjorie Woodworth.

Billy Russell. *The Goose Steps Out* (GB/1942/79m/BW) D: Will Hay & Basil Dearden. C: Will Hay, Frank Pettingel, Charles Hawtrey, Barry Morse, Peter Ustinov.

Carl Ekberg. *The Wife Takes a Flyer* (aka *A Yank in Dutch*) (US/1942/86m/BW)

D: Richard Wallace. C: Joan Bennett, Franchot Tone, Allyn Joslyn, Cecil Cunningham, Chester Clute.

Bobby Watson. *Hitler — Dead Or Alive* (US/1942/72m/BW) D: Nick Grinde. C: Ward Bond, Dorothy Tree, Warren Hymer, Paul Fix, Russell Hicks.

Bobby Watson. *That Nazty Nuisance* (aka *Nazty Nuisance*) (US/1943/50m/BW) D: Glenn Tryon. C: Joe Devlin, Johnny Arthur, Rex Evans, Charles Rogers, Wedgewood Nowell.

Ludwig Donath. *The Strange Death of Adolf Hitler* (US/1943/72m/BW) D: James Hogan. C: Gale Sondergaard, George Dolenz, Fritz Kortner, Fred Giermann, Ivan Triesault, Ludwig Stossel.

Bobby Watson. *The Hitler Gang* (US/1944/101m/BW) D: John Farrow. C: Roman Bohnen, Martin Kosleck, Victor Varconi, Luis Van Rooten, Alexander Pope, Ivan Triesault, Sig Rumann, Reinhold Schunzel, Alexander Granach, Fritz Kortner.

Bobby Watson. *The Miracle of Morgan's Creek* (US/1944/99m/BW) D: Preston Sturges. C: Eddie Bracken, Betty Hutton, Diana Lynn, Brian Donlevy, Akim Tamiroff, Porter Hall, Joe Devlin.

Bobby Watson. *A Foreign Affair* (US/1948/116m/BW) D: Billy Wilder. C: Jean Arthur, Marlene Dietrich, John Lund, Millard Mitchell, Bill Murphy, Stanley Prager, Raymond Bond.

V. Savelyev. *The Fall of Berlin* (USSR/1949/124m/C) D: Mikhail Chiaureli. C: Mikhail Gelovani, Oleg Froelich, M. Novakova, Victor Stanitsin, Y. Verikh, M. Petrunkin.

M. Astangov. *The First Front* (USSR/1949/81m/BW) D: Vladimir Petrov. Part I of *Battle of Stalingrad* (50). C: Alexei Diki, Y. Shumsky, V. Merkuryev, B. Livanov, Nikolai Cherkasov, Victor Stanitsin, K. Mikhailov, N. Simonov.

M. Astangov. *The Battle of Stalingrad (Parts I and II)* (USSR/1950/BW) D: Vladimir Petrov. *Part I of The Battle of Stalingrad* was released as *The First Front* in 1949. C: Alexei Diki, Yuri Shumsky, Boris Livanov, Nikolai Simonov, Nikolai Plotnikov.

Luther Adler. *The Desert Fox* (aka *Rommel — Desert Fox*) (US/1951/88m/BW) D: Henry Hathaway. B/on the book *Rommel* by Desmond Young. C: James Mason, Cedric Hardwicke, Jessica Tandy, Leo G. Carroll, Eduard Franz, John Hoyt, Jack Baston.

Luther Adler. *The Magic Face* (Austria/1951/88m/BW) D: Frank Tuttle. C: Patricia Knight, William L. Shirer, Ilka Windish, Sukman, Herman Ehrhardt, Hans Sheel.

Albin Skoda. *The Last Ten Days* (aka *Ten Days to Die*) (aka *Last Ten Days of Adolf Hitler*) (aka *Der Letzte Akt*) (aka *The Last Act*) (Germany/1955/115m/BW) D: G.W. Pabst. B/on the novel *Ten Days to Die* by M.A. Mussanno. C: Oskar Werner, Lotte Tobisch, Willy Krause, Erich Stuckmann, Edmund Erlandsen, Kurt Eilers, Helga Dohrn, Leopold Hainisch, Otto Schmoele.

Bobby Watson. *The Story of Mankind* (US/1957/100m/C) D: Irwin Allen. B/on the book by Hendrik Van Loon. C: Ronald Colman, Hedy Lamarr, Virginia Mayo, Agnes Moorehead, Peter Lorre, Dennis Hopper, Marie Wilson, Helmut Dantine, Edward Everett Horton, Reginald Gardiner, Marie Windsor, Francis X. Bushman, Anthony Dexter, Austin Green, Jim Ameche, Harpo Marx, Reginald Sheffield, Cedric Hardwicke, Cesar Romero.

Kenneth Griffith. *The Two-Headed Spy* (GB/1959/93m/BW) D: Andre De Toth. C: Jack Hawkins, Gia Scala, Erik Schumann, Alexander Knox, Felix Aylmer, Laurence Naismith, Richard Grey, Walter Hudd, Donald Pleasence, Michael Caine, Bernard Fox.

Bobby Watson. *On the Double* (US/1961/92m/C) D: Melville Shavelson. C: Danny Kaye, Dana Wynter, Wilfrid Hyde-White, Margaret Rutherford, Diana Dors, Jesse White.

Richard Basehart. *Hitler* (aka *Women of Nazi Germany*) (US/1962/107m/BW) D: Stuart Heisler. C: Cordula Trantow, Maria Emo, Martin Kosleck, John Banner, Martin Brandt, William Sargent, Gregory Gay, Theodore Marcuse, Rick Traeger, John Mitchum, G. Stanley Jones, Walter Kohler, Carl Esmond, Berry Kroeger.

Billy Frick. *Is Paris Burning?* (US-France/1966/173m/C) D: Rene Clement. C: Jean-Paul Belmondo, Charles Boyer, Leslie Caron, Jean-Pierre Casal, George Chakiris, Claude Dauphin, Alain Delon, Kirk Douglas, Glenn Ford, Gert Frobe, Daniel Gelin, Orson Welles, E.G. Marshall, Simone Signoret, Hannes Messemer, Robert Stack.

Carl Ekberg. *What Did You Do in the War, Daddy?* (US/1966/116m/C) D: Blake Edwards. C: James Coburn, Dick Shawn, Sergio Fantoni, Aldo Ray, Harry Morgan, Carroll O'Connor, Leon Askin.

Pitt Herbert. *The Search for the Evil One* (US/1967/C) D: Joseph Kane. C: Lee Patterson, Lisa Pera, Henry Brandon, James Dobson, Anna Lisa, H.M. Wynant.

Rolf Stiefel. *The Battle of Britain* (GB/1969/132m/C) D: Guy Hamilton. B/on the book *The Narrow Margin* by Derek Wood & Derek Dempster. C: Harry Andrews, Michael Caine, Kenneth More, Trevor Howard, Curt Jurgens, Ian McShane, Laurence Olivier, Nigel Patrick, Christopher Plummer, Michael Redgrave, Ralph Richardson, Robert Shaw, Patrick Wymark, Susannah York, Barry Foster, Hein Reiss, Peter Hager.

Fritz Diez. *The Great Battle* (aka *Liberation*) (USSR-Poland-Yugoslavia-Italy/1969/118m/C) D: Yuri Ozerov. C: Buhuti Zakariadze, Stanislav Yaskevich, Ivo Garani, Yuri Durov.

Sidney Miller. *Which Way to the Front?* (US/1970/96m/C) D: Jerry Lewis. C: Jerry Lewis, Jan Murray, Willie Davis, John Wood, Dack Rambo, Kaya Ballard, George Takei.

Gunnar Mollar. *Days of Treason* (aka *Days of Betrayal*) (aka *Dny Zrady*) (Czechoslovakia/1973/198m/C) D: Otakar Vavra. C: Jiri Pleskot, Bohus Pastorek, Martin Gregor, Jaroslav Radimecky, Alexander Fred, Rudolf Jurda, Vladimir Stach, Stanislav Zindulka, Vladimir Paviar, Bonvoj Navartil, Otakar Brousek, Josef Langmiller.

Alec Guinness. *Hitler: The Last Ten Days* (GB-Italy/1973/106m/C) D: Ennio De Concini. B/on the book *The Last Days of the Chancellery* by Gerhardt Boldt. C: Simon Ward, Gabriele Ferzetti, Doris Kunstmann, John Bennett, Philip Stone, Mark Kingston.

Henri Tisot. *The Fuhrer Runs Amok* (France/1974/95m/C) D: Philippe Clair. C: Alice Sapritch, Luis Rego, Maurice Risch, Michel Galabru.

Peter Sellers. *Undercovers Hero* (aka *Soft Beds, Hard Battles*) (GB/1974/107–

95m/C) D: Roy Boulting. C: Lila Kedrova, Curt Jurgens, Beatrice Romand, Rex Stallings.

Helmut Quatlinger. *Ice-Age* (Germany-Norway/1975/115m/BW) D: Peter Zadek. B/on the play by Tankred Dorst. C: O.E. Hasse, Hannelore Hoger.

Kurt Raab. *Adolf and Marlene* (Germany/1976/92m/C) D: Ulli Lommel. C: Margit Carstensen, Ila von Hasperg, Harry Baer, Ulli Lommel, Andrea Schober.

Heinz Schubert. *Hitler, A Film from Germany* (aka *Our Hitler*) (Germany/ 1977/420m/C) D: Hans-Jurgen Syberberg. C: Harry Baer, Peter Kern, Hellmut Lange, Rainer von Artenfels, Martin Sperr.

Ted Lehmann. *Under the Rainbow* (US/1981/98m/C) D: Steve Rash. C: Chevy Chase, Carrie Fisher, Billy Barty, Eve Arden, Robert Donner, Mako, Pat McCormick.

Gunter Meisner. *Ace of Aces* (France-Germany/1982/100m/C) D: Gerard Oury. C: Jean-Paul Belmondo, Marie-France Pisier, Frank Hoffman.

Doug McGrath. *The Return of Captain Invincible* (aka *Legend in Leotards*) (Australia-US/1982/90m/C) D: Philippe Mora. C: Alan Arkin, Christopher Lee, Kate Fitzpatrick.

Roy Goldman. *To Be or Not to Be* (US/1983/108m/C) D: Alan Johnson. C: Mel Brooks, Anne Bancroft, Tim Matheson, Charles Durning, Jose Ferrer, Christopher Lloyd.

Colin Jeavons. *Hitler's SS: Portrait in Evil* (US/1985/150m/C) D: Jim Goddard. Made for U.S. TV, released theatrically elsewhere. C: John Shea, Bill Nighy, Lucy Gutteridge, Michael Elphick, David Warner, John Normington, Jose Ferrer, Carroll Baker.

Ira Lewis. *Loose Cannons* (US/1990/94m/C) D: Bob Clark. C: Gene Hackman, Dan Aykroyd, Dom Deluise, Ronny Cox, Nancy Travis, Margaret Klenck, Robert Prosky.

Gilbert Gottfried. *Highway to Hell* (US/1992/93m/C) D: Ate De Jong. C: Patrick Bergin, Chad Lowe, Kristy Swanson, Adam Storke, Richard Farnsworth, Lita Ford.

Ludwig Haas. *Shining Through* (US/1992/127m/C) D: David Seltzer. B/on the novel by Susan Isaacs. C: Melanie Griffith, Michael Douglas, Liam Neeson, John Gielgud.

Ernst Jacobi. *Hamsun* (Sweden-Denmark-Norway-Germany/1997/160m) D: Jan Troell. B/on the book *Processen mod Hamsun* by Thorkild Hansen. C: Max von Sydow, Ghita Norby, Anette Hoff, Asa Sodering, Gard B. Eidsvold, Eindride Eidsvold, Sverre Anker Ousdal, Erik Hivju.

Norman Rodway. *The Empty Mirror* (US/1997/129m/C) D: Barry J. Hershey. C: Camilla Søeberg, Peter Michael Goetz, Doug McKeon, Glenn Shadix, Joel Grey, Hope Allen, Lori Scott, Raul Kobrinsky, Randy Zielinski, Shannon Yowell, Courtney Dale, Elizabeth Hershey, Christopher Levitus, Chip Marks.

262 Hoffman, Abbott "Abbie" 1936–1989

Political activist and writer, Hoffman was a national spokesman for the counter culture of the late 1960s and early 1970s. Anita Hoffman was played by Janeane Garofalo in *Steal This Movie!*.

Peter Faulkner. *Chicago 70* (US/1970/93m/C) D: Kerry Feltham. B/on the transcripts of the "Chicago 7" trial. C: Mel Dixon, Jim Lawrence, Calvin Butler, Neil Walsh.

Richard D'Allesandro. *Forrest Gump* (US/1994/142m/C) D: Robert Zemeckis. B/on the novel by Winston Groom. Best Picture (AA), Best Director (AA). C: Tom Hanks, Gary Sinise, Robin Wright, Sally Field, Mykelti Williamson, Peter Dobson, and the voices of Jed Gillin, John William Galt, Joe Stefanelli, and Joe Alaskey.

Vincent D'Onofrio. *Steal This Movie!* (aka *Abbie!*) (US/2000/111m/C) D: Robert Greenwald. B/on the book by Anita Hoffman. C: Janeane Garofalo, Jeanne Tripplehorn, Kevin Pollak, Donal Logue, Kevin Corrigan, Alan Van Sprang, Troy Garity, Ingrid Veninger, Stephen Marshall, Keith Jones, Marc Aubin, Michael Capellupo, Michael Cera, Todd Kozan, Ken Kramer, Panou, Michael Segovia, Robert N. Smith, Timm Zemanek.

263 Hogan, Ben (1912–1997)

Professional golfer from Texas, Hogan was the leading money winner in American golf from 1941 through 1948. He was also winner of the PGA in 1946 and 1948, the U.S. Open in 1948, 1950, 1951, 1953, and the British Open in 1953.

Glenn Ford. Harold Blake (Young Ben). *Follow the Sun* (US/1951/93m/BW) D: Sidney Lanfield. B/on writings by Frederick Hazlitt Brennan. C: Anne Baxter, Dennis O'Keefe, June Havoc, Larry Keating, Roland Winters, Nana Bryant, Anne Burr, Warren Stevens.

Michael O'Neill. *The Legend of Bagger Vance* (US/2000/126m/C) D: Robert Redford. C: Will Smith, Matt Damon, Andrea Powell, Dermot Crowley, Peter Gerety, Joel Gretsch, Trip Hamilton, Dearing Paige Hockman, Jack Lemmon, Bruce McGill, L. Michael Moncrief, Danny Nelson, Harve Presnell, Carrie Preston, Thomas Jay Ryan, Lane Smith, Charlize Theron.

264 Holiday, Billie (1915–1959)

(Eleanora Fagen) Influential American singer, Holiday is considered by many to be the finest vocalist of the Big Band era of the 1930s and 40s.

Diana Ross. *Lady Sings the Blues* (US/1972/144m/C) D: Sidney J. Furie. B/on the book by Billie Holiday. C: Billie Dee Williams, Richard Pryor, James Callahan, Scatman Crothers.

Miki Howard. *Malcolm X* (US/1992/201m/C) D: Spike Lee. C: Denzel Washington, Steve Reed, Jodie Farber, Angela Bassett, Albert Hall, Al Freeman, Jr., Delroy Lindo, Spike Lee, Theresa Randle, Kate Vernon, Lonette McKee, Tommy Hollis, James McDaniel, Ernest Thomas, Jean LaMarre, Craig Wasson, Ricky Gordon.

265 Holliday, John Henry "Doc" (1852–1887)

A dentist by vocation and a gambler by avocation, Holliday was **Wyatt Earp's** friend and partner in the O.K. Corral gunfight. He eventually died of the tuberculosis which had plagued him throughout his life. Holliday was portrayed by Randy Quaid in the TV film *Purgatory* (99).

Harvey Clark. *Law for Tombstone* (US/1937/59m/BW) D: Buck Jones & B. Reeves Eason. C: Buck Jones, Muriel Evans, Carl Stockdale, Earle Hodgins.

Cesar Romero. *Frontier Marshal* (US/1939/71m/BW) D: Allan Dwan. B/on the novel *Wyatt Earp, Frontier Marshal* by Stuart N. Lake. C: Randolph Scott, Nancy Kelly, Binnie Barnes, John Carradine, Edward Norris, Eddie Foy, Jr., Joe Sawyer, Charles Stevens.

Kent Taylor. *Tombstone, The Town Too Tough to Die* (US/1942/79m/BW) D: William McGann. B/on the book *Tombstone, The Toughest Town in Arizona* by Walter Noble Burns. C: Richard Dix, Edgar Buchanan, Frances Clifford, Don Castle, Victor Jory, Rex Bell, Dick Curtis.

Walter Huston. *The Outlaw* (US/1943/126m/BW) D: Howard Hughes. C: Jack Buetel, Jane Russell, Thomas Mitchell, Mimi Aguglia, Joe Sawyer, Dickie Jones.

Victor Mature. *My Darling Clementine* (US/1946/97m/BW) D: John Ford. B/on the novel *Wyatt Earp, Frontier Marshal* by Stuart N. Lake. C: Henry Fonda, Linda Darnell, Walter Brennan, Tim Holt, Ward Bond, Don Garner, John Ireland, Grant Withers, Cathy Downs, Alan Mowbray, Roy Roberts, Jane Darwell, J. Farrell MacDonald.

James Griffith. *Masterson of Kansas* (US/1954/72m/C) D: William Castle. C: George Montgomery, Nancy Gates, Jean Willes, Benny Rubin, Bruce Cowling, Donald Murphy.

Kirk Douglas. *Gunfight at the O.K. Corral* (US/1957/122m/C) D: John Sturges. B/on the story *The Killer* by George Scullin. C: Burt Lancaster, Rhonda Fleming, Jo Van Fleet, John Ireland, Lyle Bettger, Frank Faylen, Earl Holliman, Whit Bissell, DeForrest Kelley, Martin Milner, Kenneth Tobey, Lee Van Cleef, Jack Elam, Bing Russell.

Arthur Kennedy. *Cheyenne Autumn* (US/1964/159m/C) D: John Ford. B/on the novel by Mari Sandoz. C: Richard Widmark, Carroll Baker, Karl Malden, James Stewart.

Jason Robards. *Hour of the Gun* (aka *The Law and Tombstone*) (US/1967/101m/ C) D: John Sturges. B/on the novel *Tombstone's Epitaph* by Douglas D. Martin. C: James Garner, Robert Ryan, Albert Salmi, Charles Aidman, Frank Converse, Larry Gates.

Stacy Keach. *Doc* (US/1971/95m/C) D: Frank Perry. C: Faye Dunaway, Harris Yulin, Mike Witney, Dan Greenburg, Bruce M. Fischer, Ferdinand Zogbaum, Fred Dennis.

William Berger. *Verflucht Dies Amerika* (aka *Yankee Dudler*) (Germany/1973/C) D: Volker Vogeler. C: Geraldine Chaplin, Arthur Brauss, Francisco Algora, Sigi Graue.

Val Kilmer. *Tombstone* (US/1993/128m/C) D: George Pan Kosmatos. C: Kurt Russell, Michael Biehn, Powers Booth, Robert Blake, Dana Delaney, Sam Elliott, Stephen Lang, Terry O'Quinn, Joanna Pacula, Bill Paxton, Jason Priestley, Michael Rooker.

Dennis Quaid. *Wyatt Earp* (US/1994/195m/C) D: Lawrence Kasdan. C: Kevin Costner, Gene Hackman, David Andrews, Linden Ashby, Jeff Fahey, Mark Harmon, Michael Madsen, Catherine O'Hara, Bill Pullman, Isabella Rossellini, Tom Sizemore, JoBeth Williams, Norman Howell, Mare Winningham, Rex Linn, Randle Mell.

266 Holly, Buddy (1938–1959)

(Charles Hardin Holley) Early Rock and Roll star, Holly wrote and recorded such hits as "Peggy Sue" and "That'll Be the Day" before dying in a plane crash.

Gary Busey. *The Buddy Holly Story* (US/1978/113m/C) D: Steve Rash. B/on the book by John Coldrosen. C: Don Stroud, Charles Martin Smith, Maria Richwine, Gilbert Melgar.

Marshall Crenshaw. *La Bamba* (US/1987/108m/C) D: Luis Valdez. C: Lou Diamond Phillips, Esai Morales, Rosana De Soto, Elizabeth Pena, Jeffrey Allen Chandler.

267 Hood, Samuel (1724–1816)

(1st Viscount Hood) British Lord of the Admiralty, Hood's naval career spanned more than 50 years.

David Torrence. *Mutiny on the Bounty* (US/1935/132m/BW) D: Frank Lloyd. B/on the novels *Mutiny on the Bounty, Men Against the Sea*, and *Pitcairn's Island* by Charles Nordhoff & James Norman Hall. Best Picture (AA). C: Charles Laughton, Clark Gable, Franchot Tone, Eddie Quillan, Dudley Digges, Donald Crisp, Francis Lister, Ian Wolfe.

Kynaston Reeves. *Captain Horatio Hornblower* (GB/1951/116m/C) D: Raoul Walsh. B/on the novel by C.S. Forester. C: Gregory Peck, Virginia Mayo, James Robertson Justice.

Laurence Olivier. *The Bounty* (US/1984/132m/C) D: Roger Donaldson. B/on the novel *Captain Bligh and Mr. Christian* by Richard Hough. C: Mel Gibson, Anthony Hopkins, Edward Fox, Daniel Day-Lewis, Liam Neeson, Bernard Hill.

268 Hoover, John Edgar (1895–1972)

Director of the Federal Bureau of Investigation for nearly fifty years, Hoover instituted many of the methods that made the FBI famous for its apprehension of criminals. Numerous TV portrayals include: Dolph Sweet in the mini-series *King* (78), Vincent Gardenia in the mini-series *Kennedy* (83), Ernest Borgnine in *Blood Feud* (83), and Treat Williams in the cable film *J. Edgar Hoover* (87).

Dorthi Fox. *Bananas* (US/1971/82m/C) D: Woody Allen. C: Woody Allen, Louise Lasser, Carlos Montalban, Natividad Abascal, Howard Cosell, Rene Enriquez.

Erwin Fuller. *Lepke* (US/1975/110–98m/C) D: Menahem Golan. C: Tony Curtis, Anjanette Comer, Michael Callan, Warren Berlinger, Gianni Russo, Vic Tayback, Milton Berle, Jack Ackerman, Vaughn Meader, Zitto Kazan, John Durren.

Sheldon Leonard. *The Brink's Job* (US/1978/118m/C) D: William Friedkin. B/on the book *Big Stick Up at Brinks* by Noel Behn. C: Peter Falk, Peter Boyle, Allen Goorwitz, Warren Oates, Gena Rowlands, Paul Sorvino, Kevin O'Connor.

Broderick Crawford. James Wainwright (as a young man). *The Private Files of J. Edgar Hoover* (US/1978/112m/C) D: Larry Cohen. C: Jose Ferrer, Michael Parks, Ronee Blakely, Michael Sacks, Raymond St. Jacques, Andrew Duggan, Howard Da Silva, Brad Dexter, William Jordan, Richard M. Dixon, Gordon Zimmerman, Lloyd Nolan, June Havoc, Dan Dailey, John Marley, Lloyd Gough.

Kevin Dunn. *Chaplin* (US/1992/144m/C) D: Richard Attenborough. B/on the books *Chaplin:His Life & Art* by David Robinson and *My Autobiography* by Charlie Chaplin. C: Robert Downey, Jr., Kevin Kline, Moira Kelly, Geraldine Chaplin, John Thaw.

Bob Hoskins. *Nixon* (US/1995/190m/C) D: Oliver Stone. C: Anthony Hopkins, Joan Allen, Powers Boothe, Ed Harris, E.G. Marshall, David Paymer, David Hyde Pierce, Paul Sorvino, Mary Steenburgen, J.T. Walsh, James Woods, Bryan Bedford.

Richard Dysart. *Panther* (US/1995/125m/C) D: Mario Van Peebles. C: Kadeem Hardison, Bokeem Woodbine, Joe Don Baker, Courtney B. Vance, Tyrin Turner, Huey Newton, Anthony Griffith, Bobby Brown, Nefertiti, James Russo, Chris Rock, Dick Gregory, Melvin Van Peebles, Jay Koch, Jerry Rubin, Mario Van Peebles.

269 Horn, Tom (1861–1903)
Once an Army scout who assisted in the capture of **Geronimo**, Horn wound up in Wyoming where he was (according to many sources) unjustly hanged for the murder of a 13 year old boy. He was portrayed by David Carradine in the 1980 TV movie *Mr. Horn.*

George Montgomery. *Dakota Lil* (US/1950/87m/C) D: Lesley Selander. C: Rod Cameron, Marie Windsor, John Emery, Wallace Ford, James Flavin.

John Ireland. *Fort Utah* (US/1967/84m/C) D: Lesley Selander. C: Virginia Mayo, Scott Brady, John Russell, Robert Strauss, James Craig, Jim Davis.

Steve McQueen. *Tom Horn* (US/1980/98m/C) D: William Wiard. B/on *Life of Tom Horn, Government Scout and Interpreter* by Tom Horn. C: Linda Evans, Richard Farnsworth, Billy Green Bush, Slim Pickens, Elisha Cook, Jr., Steve Oliver.

270 Houdini, Harry (1874–1926)
(Erich Weiss) The world's most famous escape artist and magician, Houdini has been portrayed by Paul Michael Glaser in the TV movie *The Great Houdini* (76); in *Young Harry Houdini* (87), young Houdini (Eric Weiss) was played by Wil Wheaton, the adult by Jeffrey DeMunn; and in *Houdini* (99) by Jonathan Saech.

Tony Curtis. *Houdini* (US/1953/105m/C) D: George Marshall. B/on the book by Harold Kellock. C: Janet Leigh, Torin Thatcher, Angela Clark, Stefan Schnabel.

Jeff DeMunn. *Ragtime* (US/1981/155m/C) D: Milos Forman. B/on the novel by E.L. Doctorow. C: James Cagney, Brad Dourif, Moses Gunn, Elizabeth McGovern, Pat O'Brien, Kenneth McMillan, Donald O'Connor, James Olson, Mandy Patinkin, Howard E. Rollins, Robert Boyd, Robert Joy, Norman Mailer, Mary Steenburgen.

Harvey Keitel. *Fairy Tale: A True Story* (US-GB/1997/99m) D: Charles Sturridge. C: Florence Hoath, Elizabeth Earl, Paul McGann, Phoebe Nicholls, Peter O'Toole, Jason Salkey, Lara Morgan, Adam Franks, Guy Wichter, Joseph May,

John Bradley, Anna Chancellor, Leonard Kavanagh, Anton Lesser, Bob Peck, Lynn Farleigh, Sarah Marsden, Tara Marie, Alannah McGahan, Bill Nighy, Tim McInnerny, Peter Mullan, John Wiggins, David Calder, Anthony Calf, Mel Gibson (cameo role).

Norman Mailer. *Cremaster 2* (US/1999/79m/C) D: Mathew Barney C: Mathew Barney, Anonymous, Lauren Pine, Scot Ewalt, Patty Griffin, Michael Thompson, David A. Lombardo, Bruce Steele, Steve Tucker, Cat Kubic, Sam Jalhej, Jacqueline Molasses.

271 Houston, Samuel "Sam" (1793–1863)

Once the governor of Tennessee, Houston moved to Texas in 1832 and successfully commanded the army when Texas revolted against Mexico.

Edward Piel. *Heroes of the Alamo* (aka *Remember the Alamo*) (US/1937/80m/BW) D: Harry Fraser. C: Earl Hodgins, Lane Chandler, Roger Williams, Rex Lease, Julian Rivero, Lee Valianos, Ruth Findlay, Jack Smith, Tex Cooper.

Richard Dix. *Man of Conquest* (US/1939/97m/BW) D: George Nichols, Jr. C: Edward Ellis, Victor Jory, Robert Barrat, Ralph Morgan, Robert Armstrong, C. Henry Gordon, George "Gabby" Hayes, Gail Patrick, Joan Fontaine, Max Terhune, Lane Chandler.

Paul Newlan. *Down Rio Grande Way* (US/1942/57m/BW) D: William Berke. C: Charles Starrett, Russell Hayden, Britt Wood, Rose Anne Stevens, Edmund Cobb.

William Farnum. *Men of Texas* (US/1942/82m/BW) D: Ray Enright. B/on the story *Frontier* by Harold Shumate. C: Robert Stack, Broderick Crawford, Anne Gwynn, Ralph Bellamy, Jane Darwell, Leo Carillo.

Moroni Olsen. *Lone Star* (US/1952/94m/BW) D: Vincent Sherman. C: Clark Gable, Ava Gardner, Lionel Barrymore, Broderick Crawford, Beulah Bondi, Ed Begley.

Ward Negley. *The Man from the Alamo* (US/1953/79m/C) D: Budd Boetticher. C: Glenn Ford, Julia Adams, Chill Wills, Victor Jory, Stuart Randall, Trevor Bardette, Arthur Space.

Hugh Sanders. *The Last Command* (US/1955/110m/C) D: Frank Lloyd. B/on the story *The Last Command* by Sy Bartlett. C: Sterling Hayden, Richard Carlson, Arthur Hunnicutt, J. Carroll Naish, Otto Kruger, Don Kennedy, Anna Maria Alberghetti, Ernest Borgnine, Ben Cooper, Virginia Grey, John Russell, Edward Colmans, Jim Davis.

Joel McCrea. *The First Texan* (US/1956/82m/C) D: Byron Haskin. C: Jeff Morrow, Dayton Lummis, William Hopper, David Silva, James Griffith, Carl Benton Reid, Felicia Farr, Wallace Ford, Chubby Johnson, Jody McCrea, Abraham Sofaer.

Richard Boone. *The Alamo* (US/1960/192m/C) D: John Wayne. C: John Wayne, Richard Widmark, Laurence Harvey, Patrick Wayne, Ruben Padilla, Joseph Calleia.

272 Howard, Catherine (1521–1542)

Henry VIII's fifth wife, she was beheaded for adultery less than two years after marrying him.

Binnie Barnes. *The Private Life of Henry VIII* (GB/1933/97m/BW) D: Alexander Korda. C: Charles Laughton, Robert Donat, Elsa Lanchester, Merle Oberon, Wendy Barrie, Everley Gregg, Franklyn Dyall, Miles Mander, Claude Allister, John Loder, Lawrence Hanray.

Dawn Addams. *Young Bess* (US/1953/112m/C) D: George Sidney. B/on the novel by Margaret Irwin. C: Jean Simmons, Stewart Granger, Deborah Kerr, Charles Laughton, Kay Walsh, Cecil Kellaway, Rex Thompson, Elaine Stewart, Lumsden Hare.

Monica Dietrich. *Carry on Henry VIII* (GB/1970/89m/C) D: Gerald Thomas. C: Sidney James, Kenneth Williams, Joan Sims, Charles Hawtrey, Terry Scott, Peter Gilmore, Patsy Rowlands.

Lynne Frederick. *The Six Wives of Henry VIII* (aka *Henry VIII and His Six Wives*) (GB/1972/125m/C) D: Waris Hussein. C: Keith Michell, Frances Cuka, Charlotte Rampling, Jane Asher, Jenny Bos, Barbara Leigh-Hunt, Donald Pleasence, Simon Henderson, Annette Crosbie, John Bryans, Michael Goodliffe, Bernard Hepton, Dorothy Tutin.

273 Huerta, Victoriano (1854–1916)

Mexican revolutionary and dictator, Huerta succeeded **Madero** as the President of Mexico.

Frank Silvera. *Viva Zapata!* (US/1952/113m/BW) D: Elia Kazan. B/on the book *Zapata the Unconquerable* by Edgcumb Pinchon. C: Marlon Brando, Anthony Quinn, Jean Peters, Alan Reed, Harold Gordon, Margo, Frank De Kova, Fay Roope, Joseph Wiseman, Lou Gilbert.

Herbert Lom. *Villa Rides* (US/1968/125m/C) D: Buzz Kulik. B/on the book *Pancho Villa* by William Douglas Lansford. C: Yul Brynner, Robert Mitchum, Charles Bronson, Alexander Knox, Fernando Rey, Jill Ireland, John Ireland.

274 Hughes, Howard (1905–1976)

American billionaire and Hollywood producer, Hughes was once the owner of RKO Studios. He was portrayed by Tommy Lee Jones in the TV mini-series *The Amazing Howard Hughes* (77).

Victor Holchak. *Hughes and Harlow: Angels in Hell* (US/1978/94m/C) D: Larry Buchanan. C: Lindsay Bloom, Royal Dano, Adam Roarke, David McLean, Linda Cristal.

Jason Robards. *Melvin and Howard* (US/1980/93m/C) D: Jonathan Demme. C: Paul LeMat, Elizabeth Cheshire, Mary Steenburgen, Melvin E. Dummar, Gloria Grahame.

Dean Stockwell. *Tucker: the Man and His Dream* (US/1988/111m/C) D: Francis Ford Coppola. C: Jeff Bridges, Joan Allen, Martin Landau, Frederic Forrest, Lloyd Bridges, Christian Slater.

Terry O'Quinn. *The Rocketeer* (US/1991/108m/C) D: Joe Johnston. B/on the book by Dave Stevens. C: Bill Campbell, Jennifer Connelly, Alan Arkin, Timothy Dalton, Paul Sorvino, Bob Leeman, Gene Daily, James Handy.

275 Hull, Cordell (1871–1955)

American politician, Hull served as Secretary of State (under **Franklin Roosevelt** from 1933–1944) longer than anyone in U.S. history.

    Charles Trowbridge. *Sergeant York* (US/1941/134m/BW) D: Howard Hawks. B/on the diary of Alvin York as edited by Tom Skeyhill, and on the books: *War Diary of Sergeant York and Seargeant York and His People* by Sam K. Cowan and *Sergeant York: Last of the Long Hunters* by Tom Skeyhill. C: Gary Cooper, Walter Brennan, Joan Leslie, George Tobias, Stanley Ridges, Margaret Wycherly, Ward Bond, Joseph Girard.

    Charles Trowbridge. *Mission to Moscow* (US/1943/123m/BW) D: Michael Curtiz. B/on the book by Joseph E. Davies. C: Walter Huston, Ann Harding, Oscar Homolka, George Tobias, Gene Lockhart, Frieda Inescourt, Eleanor Parker, Richard Travis, Henry Daniell, Dudley Field Malone, Manart Kippen, Georges Renavent, Clive Morgan, Captain Jack Young, Leigh Whipper, Doris Lloyd, Olaf Hytten, Moroni Olsen.

    George Macready. *Tora! Tora! Tora!* (US–Japan/1970/143m/C) D: Richard Fleischer, Toshio Masuda & Kinji Fukasaku. B/on the books *Tora! Tora! Tora!* by Gordon Prange and *The Broken Seal* by Ladislas Farago. C: Martin Balsam, Soh Yamamura, Jason Robards, Joseph Cotten, Tatsuya Mihashi, E.G. Marshall, James Whitmore, Wesley Addy, Leon Ames, Keith Andes, Richard Anderson, Neville Brand.

276 Innocent III, Pope (1160?–1216)

(Lotario di Segni) One of the most powerful of the medieval Popes (1198–1216), Innocent has been depicted in films for his relationship with **Saint Francis** whom he gave permission to begin the Franciscan Order.

    Finlay Currie. *Francis of Assisi* (US/1961/105m/C) D: Michael Curtiz. B/on the novel *The Joyful Beggar* by Louis De Wohl. C: Bradford Dillman, Dolores Hart, Stuart Whitman, Pedro Armendariz, Cecil Kellaway, Eduard Franz, Mervyn Johns, Feodor Chaliapin.

    Alec Guinness. *Brother Sun, Sister Moon* (GB–Italy/1972/121m/C) D: Franco Zeffirelli. C: Graham Faulkner, Judi Bowker, Leigh Lawson, Valentina Cortese, Lee Montague.

    Hans Zischler. *Francesco* (Italy–Germany/1989/155–115m/C) D: Liliana Cavani. B/on the novel *Francis of Assisi* by Herman Hesse. C: Mickey Rourke, Helena Bonham Carter, Paolo Bonacelli, Mario Adorf, Peter Berling.

277 Isabella, Queen (1451–1504)

The Queen of Castille, Isabella, and her husband, **Ferdinand V**, sponsored **Columbus**' trips to the New World. She was portrayed by Faye Dunaway in the TV mini-series *Christopher Columbus* (85).

    Florence Eldridge. *Christopher Columbus* (GB/1949/104m/C) D: David MacDonald. C: Fredric March, Francis L. Sullivan, Kathleen Ryan, Francis Lister, Derek Bond.

    Robin Burroughs. *Stuck on You* (US/1983/88m/C) D: Samuel Weil & Michael Herz. C: Irwin Corey, Daniel Harris, Carl Sturmer, Julie Newdow, Barbie Kielian.

Christopher Columbus (Frederic March) presenting his treasures from the New World to Queen Isabella (Florence Eldridge) and King Ferdinand (Francis Lister) in this elaborate court scene from *Christopher Columbus* (1949). (Museum of Modern Art Film Stills Archive)

Sigourney Weaver. *1492: Conquest of Paradise* (US-GB-France-Spain/1992/145m/C) D: Ridley Scott. C: Gérard Depardieu, Armand Assante, Frank Langella, Loren Dean, Angela Molina, Fernando Rimida, Fernando Rey, Michael Wincott, Tcheky Karyo.

June Whitfield. *Carry on Columbus* (GB/1992/91m/C) D: Gerald Thomas. C: Jim Dale, Bernard Cribbins, Maureen Lipman, Rik Mayall, Alexei Sayle, Larry Miller, Leslie Phillips.

Rachel Ward. *Christopher Columbus: The Discovery* (US-Spain/1992/122m/C) D: John Glen. C: George Corraface, Tom Selleck, Marlon Brando, Robert Davi, Catherine Zeta-Jones.

Anna Paquin. *Amistad* (US/1997/152m/C) D: Steven Spielberg. C: Morgan Freeman, Nigel Hawthorne, Anthony Hopkins, Djimon Hounsou, Matthew McConaughey, David Paymer, Pete Postlewaithe, Stellan Skarsgard, Razaaq Adoti, Abu Bakaar Fofanah, Tomas Milian, Chitwetel Ejiofor, Derrick N. Ashong, Geno Silva, John Ortiz, Ralph Brown, Darren Burroughs, Allan Rich, Paul Guilfoyle, Peter Firth, Xander Berkeley, Jeremy Northan, Arliss Howard, Austen Pendleton, Daniel von Bargen, Rusty Schwimmer, Pedro Armendariz.

Ivan IV (The Terrible) *see* 632

278 Jackson, Andrew (1767–1845)

The 7th President of the U.S. and the first of humble origins, Jackson gained national popularity for his military defeats of the Creek Indians and the British in the War of 1812. He retained his personal popularity through two scandalous and racist administrations though was censured by the Senate for his dictatorial and unconstitutional behavior.

Lionel Barrymore. *The Gorgeous Hussey* (US/1936/103m/BW) D: Clarence Brown. B/on the novel by Samuel Hopkins Adams. C: Joan Crawford, Robert Taylor, Melvyn Douglas, James Stewart, Franchot Tone, Frank Conroy, Charles Trowbridge, Sidney Toler.

Hugh Sothern. *The Buccaneer* (US/1938/124m/BW) D: Cecil B. DeMille. B/on the novel *Lafitte the Pirate* by Lyle Saxon. C: Fredric March, Franciska Gaal, Akim Tamiroff, Margot Grahame, Walter Brennan, Ian Keith, Spring Byington, Anthony Quinn.

Edward Ellis. *Man of Conquest* (US/1939/97m/BW) D: George Nichols, Jr. C: Richard Dix, Victor Jory, Robert Barrat, Ralph Morgan, Robert Armstrong, C. Henry Gordon, George "Gabby" Hayes, Gail Patrick, Joan Fontaine, Max Terhune, Lane Chandler.

Brian Donlevy. *The Remarkable Andrew* (US/1942/80m/BW) D: Stuart Heisler. B/on the novel by Dalton Trumbo. C: William Holden, Ellen Drew, Rod Cameron, Richard Webb, Frances Gifford, Brandon Hurst, Gilbert Emery, George Watts, Montagu Love.

Lionel Barrymore. *Lone Star* (US/1952/94m/BW) D: Vincent Sherman. C: Clark Gable, Ava Gardner, Broderick Crawford, Beulah Bondi, Moroni Olsen, Ed Begley.

Charlton Heston. *The President's Lady* (US/1953/96m/BW) D: Henry Levin. B/on the novel by Irving Stone. C: Susan Hayward, John McIntire, George Spaulding, Jim Davis.

Basil Ruysdael. *Davy Crockett, King of the Wild Frontier* (US/1955/90m/C) D: Norman Foster. C: Fess Parker, Buddy Ebsen, Hans Conried, Kenneth Tobey, Pat Hogan, Helene Stanley, Don Megowan.

Carl Benton Reid. *The First Texan* (US/1956/82m/C) D: Byron Haskin. C: Joel McCrea, Jeff Morrow, Dayton Lummis, William Hopper, David Silva, James Griffith, Felicia Farr, Wallace Ford, Chubby Johnson, Jody McCrea, Abraham Sofaer.

Charlton Heston. *The Buccaneer* (US/1958/121m/C) D: Anthony Quinn. C: Yul Brynner, Claire Bloom, Charles Boyer, Inger Stevens, Henry Hull, E.G. Marshall.

279 Jackson, "Shoeless" Joe (1889–1951)

Star American baseball player, Jackson was thrown out of the game permanently for his involvement in gambling during the 1919 World Series.

D.B. Sweeney. *Eight Men Out* (US/1988/120m/C) D: John Sayles. B/on the book by Eliot Asinof. C: John Cusack, Clifton James, David Strathairn, Michael Lerner, John Sayles.

Ray Liotta. *Field of Dreams* (US/1989/106m/C) D: Phil Alden Robinson. B/on the book *Shoeless Joe* by W. P. Kinsella. C: Kevin Costner, Amy Madigan, James Earl Jones, Burt Lancaster, Timothy Busfield, Gaby Hoffman, Steve Eastin, Michael Milhoan.

280 James, Alexander Franklin "Frank" (1843–1915)

The elder brother of **Jesse James**, Frank turned himself in six months after Jesse's death. Due to his own popularity and a surplus of sentiment generated over the nature of Jesse's killing, Frank was acquitted of all charges.

Michael Worth. *Days of Jesse James* (US/1939/63m/BW) D: Joseph Kane. C: Roy Rogers, George "Gabby" Hayes, Don Barry, Pauline Moore, Harry Woods, Glenn Strange.

Henry Fonda. *Jesse James* (US/1939/105m/C) D: Henry King. C: Tyrone Power, Nancy Kelly, Randolph Scott, Henry Hull, Jane Darwell, John Carradine, Charles Tannen.

Henry Fonda. *The Return of Frank James* (US/1940/92m/C) D: Fritz Lang. C: Gene Tierney, Jackie Cooper, Henry Hull, John Carradine, Donald Meek, Charles Tannen, Eddie Collins.

Tom Tyler. *Badman's Territory* (US/1946/98m/BW) D: Tim Whelan. C: Randolph Scott, Ann Richards, George "Gabby" Hayes, Chief Thundercloud, Lawrence Tierney, Steve Brodie, Phil Warren, William Moss, Nestor Paiva, Isabell Jewell, Emory Parnell.

Tom Tyler. *I Shot Jesse James* (US/1949/81m/BW) D: Samuel Fuller. C: Preston Foster, Barbara Britton, John Ireland, Reed Hadley, Barbara Woodell, Tom Noonan.

Don Barry. *Gunfire* (US/1950/59m/BW) D: William Berke. C: Robert Lowery, Wally Vernon, Pamela Blake, Claude Stroud, Roger Anderson, Gaylord Pendleton.

Richard Long. *Kansas Raiders* (US/1950/80m/C) D: Ray Enright. C: Audie Murphy, Brian Donlevy, Scott Brady, James Best, Dewey Martin, Richard Egan, Tony Curtis.

Reed Hadley. *The Return of Jesse James* (US/1950/75m/BW) D: Arthur Hilton. C: John Ireland, Ann Dvorak, Henry Hull, Clifton Young, Tom Noonan, Hugh O'Brian, Sid Melton.

Tom Tyler. *Best of the Badmen* (US/1951/84m/C) D: William D. Russell. C: Robert Ryan, Claire Trevor, Jack Buetel, Lawrence Tierney, Bruce Cabot, Bob Wilke, John Cliff.

Wendell Corey. *The Great Missouri Raid* (US/1950/84m/C) D: Gordon Douglas. C: MacDonald Carey, Ward Bond, Ellen Drew, Bruce Bennett, Bill Williams, Anne Revere, Edgar Buchanan, Louis Jean Heydt, Lois Chartrand, James Millican, Whit Bissell.

James Brown. *The Woman They Almost Lynched* (US/1953/90m/BW) D: Allan Dwan. B/on the story by Michael Fessier. C: Brian Donlevy, Ben Cooper, Jim Davis, Audrey Totter, John Lund.

Jack Buetel. *Jesse James' Women* (US/1954/83m/C) D: Don Barry. C: Donald Barry, Peggie Castle, Lita Baron, Joyce Rhed, Betty Brueck, Sam Keller, Laura Lee.

Jeffrey Hunter. *The True Story of Jesse James* (aka *The James Brothers*) (US/1957/92m/C) D: Nicholas Ray. C: Robert Wagner, Hope Lange, Agnes Moorehead, Alan Hale, Jr., Carl Thayler.

Douglas Kennedy. *Hell's Crossroads* (US/1957/73m/C) D: Franklin Andreon. C: Stephen McNally, Peggie Castle, Robert Vaughn, Harry Shannon, Henry Brandon, Myron Healy.

Jim Davis. *Alias Jesse James* (US/1959/92m/C) D: Norman McLeod. C: Bob Hope, Rhonda Fleming, Wendell Corey, Hugh O'Brian, James Arness, Fess Parker, Gail Davis.

Robert Dix. *Young Jesse James* (US/1960/73m/BW) D: William F. Claxton. C: Ray Stricklyn, Willard Parker, Merry Anders, Emile Meyer, Bob Palmer, Johnny O'Neil.

Antonio Vico. *Up the MacGregors* (Italy-Spain/1967/93m/C) D: Franco Giraldi. C: David Bailey, Agata Flori, Leo Anchoriz, Robert Carmardiel.

William Fosterwick. *Ride a Wild Stud* (aka *Ride the Wild Stud*) (US/1969) D: Revilo Ekard. C: Cliff Alexander, Tex Gates, Frenchy LeBoyd, Bill Ferrill.

John Pearce. *The Great Northfield Minnesota Raid* (US/1972/91m/C) D: Philip Kaufman. C: Cliff Robertson, Robert Duvall, Luke Askew, R.G. Armstrong, Dana Elcar, Donald Moffat, Matt Clark.

Stacy Keach. *The Long Riders* (US/1980/99m/C) D: Walter Hill. C: David Carradine, Keith Carradine, Robert Carradine, James Keach, Dennis Quaid, Randy Quaid, Kevin Brophy, Christopher Guest, Nicholas Guest, Pamela Reed, James Remar, Fran Ryan, Savannah Smith, Harry Carey, Jr., James Whitmore, Jr., Shelby Leverington.

Bill Paxton. *Frank and Jesse* (US/1994/105m/C) D: Robert Boris. C: Rob Lowe, Randy Travis, Dana Wheeler-Nicholson, Maria Pitillo, Luke Askew, Sean Patrick Flanery, Alexis Arquette, Todd Field, John Pyper-Ferguson, Nicholas Sadler, William Atherton, Tom Chick, Mary Neff, Richard Maynard.

Gabriel Macht. *American Outlaws* (US/2001/93m/C) D: Les Mayfield. B/on a story by Roderick Taylor. C: Colin Farrell, Scott Caan, Ali Larter, Gregory Smith, Harris Yulin, Will McCormack, Ronny Cox, Terry O'Quinn, Nathaniel Arcand, Kathy Bates, Timothy Dalton, Craig Erickson, Ty O'Neal, Joe Stevens.

281 James, Jesse Woodson (1847–1882)

The most notorious of the Western bank and train robbers, Jesse was extremely popular in his time (and since) as a frontier Robin Hood. Though an outlaw, he has usually been portrayed as a tragic hero, his criminal acts being blamed on the personal devastation brought by the Civil War.

Don Barry. *Days of Jesse James* (US/1939/63m/BW) D: Joseph Kane. C: Roy Rogers, George "Gabby" Hayes, Pauline Moore, Harry Woods, Michael Worth, Glenn Strange.

Tyrone Power. *Jesse James* (US/1939/105m/C) D: Henry King. C: Henry Fonda, Nancy Kelly, Randolph Scott, Henry Hull, Jane Darwell, John Carradine, Charles Tannen.

The James gang cautiously view the main street in Northfield, Minnesota, prior to their fateful bank robbery. Pictured (left to right), David Carradine, Randy Quaid, Stacey Keach, James Keach, and Keith Carradine. Novel casting in *The Long Riders* (1980) was having actual brothers portraying the outlaw brothers; Stacey and James Keach as Frank and Jesse James, David Carradine as Cole Younger, his brothers Keith and Robert as Jim and Bob Younger; Christopher and Nicholas Guest as Charlie and Bob Ford, and Dennis and Randy Quaid as Ed and Clell Miller. (Museum of Modern Art Film Stills Archive)

Alan Baxter. *Bad Men of Missouri* (US/1941/75m/BW) D: Ray Enright. C: Dennis Morgan, Jane Wyman, Wayne Morris, Arthur Kennedy, Victor Jory, Faye Emerson, Russell Simpson.

Roy Rogers. *Jesse James at Bay* (US/1941/56m/BW) D: Joseph Kane. C: George "Gabby" Hayes, Sally Payne, Hal Taliaferro, Gale Storm, Roy Barcroft.

Rod Cameron. *The Remarkable Andrew* (US/1942/80m/BW) D: Stuart Heisler. B/on the novel by Dalton Trumbo. C: William Holden, Ellen Drew, Brian Donlevy, Richard Webb, Frances Gifford, Brandon Hurst, Gilbert Emery, George Watts, Montagu Love.

Lawrence Tierney. *Badman's Territory* (US/1946/98m/BW) D: Tim Whelan. C: Randolph Scott, Ann Richards, George "Gabby" Hayes, Chief Thundercloud, Tom Tyler, Steve Brodie, Phil Warren, William Moss, Nestor Paiva, Isabell Jewell, Emory Parnell.

Dale Robertson. *Fighting Man of the Plains* (US/1949/94m/C) D: Edwin L. Marin. C: Randolph Scott, Bill Williams, Victor Jory, Jane Nigh, Douglas Kennedy, James Griffith, Rhys Williams.

Reed Hadley. *I Shot Jesse James* (US/1949/81m/BW) D: Samuel Fuller. C: Preston Foster, Barbara Britton, John Ireland, Barbara Woodell, Tom Tyler, Tom Noonan.

Audie Murphy. *Kansas Raiders* (US/1950/80m/C) D: Ray Enright. C: Brian Donlevy, Scott Brady, Richard Long, James Best, Dewey Martin, Richard Egan, Tony Curtis.

Lawrence Tierney. *Best of the Badmen* (US/1951/84m/C) D: William D. Russell. C: Robert Ryan, Claire Trevor, Jack Buetel, Bruce Cabot, Tom Tyler, Bob Wilke, John Cliff.

Macdonald Carey. *The Great Missouri Raid* (US/1950/84m/C) D: Gordon Douglas. C: Wendell Corey, Ward Bond, Ellen Drew, Bruce Bennett, Bill Williams, Anne Revere, Edgar Buchanan, Louis Jean Heydt, Lois Chartrand, James Millican, Whit Bissell.

Willard Parker. *The Great Jesse James Raid* (US/1953/73m/BW) D: Reginald Le Borg. C: Barbara Payton, Tom Neal, Wallace Ford, Barbara Woodell, Earl Hodgins, Jim Bannon, Tom Walker.

Ben Cooper. *The Woman They Almost Lynched* (US/1953/90m/BW) D: Allan Dwan. B/on the story by Michael Fessier. C: Brian Donlevy, James Brown, Jim Davis, Audrey Totter, John Lund.

Donald Barry. *Jesse James' Women* (US/1954/83m/C) D: Don Barry. C: Jack Beutel, Peggie Castle, Lita Baron, Joyce Rhed, Betty Brueck, Sam Keller, Laura Lee.

Robert Wagner. *The True Story of Jesse James* (aka *The James Brothers*) (US/1957/92m/C) D: Nicholas Ray. C: Jeffrey Hunter, Hope Lange, Agnes Moorehead, Alan Hale, Jr., Carl Thayler.

Henry Brandon. *Hell's Crossroads* (US/1957/73m/C) D: Franklin Andreon. C: Stephen McNally, Peggie Castle, Robert Vaughn, Harry Shannon, Myron Healy, Douglas Kennedy.

Wendell Corey. *Alias Jesse James* (US/1959/92m/C) D: Norman McLeod. C: Bob Hope, Rhonda Fleming, Jim Davis, Hugh O'Brian, James Arness, Fess Parker, Gail Davis.

Ray Stricklyn. *Young Jesse James* (US/1960/73m/BW) D: William F. Claxton. C: Willard Parker, Merry Anders, Robert Dix, Emile Meyer, Bob Palmer, Johnny O'Neil.

Wayne Mack. *The Outlaws Is Coming* (US/1965/88m/BW) D: Norman Maurer. C: Larry Fine, Moe Howard, Joe De Rita, Nancy Kovack, Murray Alper, Joe Bolton, Bill Camfield, Hal Fryar, Johnny Ginger, Ed McDonnell, Bruce Sedley, Paul Shannon, Sally Starr.

John Lupton. *Jesse James Meets Frankenstein's Daughter* (US/1966/82m/C) D: William Beaudine. C: Cal Bolder, Narda Onyx, Steven Geray, Felipe Turich, Nestor Paiva.

Robert Hundar. *Jesse James' Kid* (aka *Solo Contro Tutti*) (Spain-Italy/1965/91m/C) D: Antonio Del Amo. C: Mercedes Alonso, Adrian Hoven, Luis Induni, Roberto Camardiel.

Audie Murphy. *A Time for Dying* (US/1969/87m/C) D: Budd Boetticher. C: Richard Lapp, Anne Randall, Victor Jory, Beatrice Kay, Burt Mustin.

Robert Duvall. *The Great Northfield Minnesota Raid* (US/1972/91m/C) D:

Philip Kaufman. C: Cliff Robertson, Luke Askew, R.G. Armstrong, Dana Elcar, Donald Moffat, John Pearce, Matt Clark.

James Keach. *The Long Riders* (US/1980/99m/C) D: Walter Hill. C: David Carradine, Keith Carradine, Robert Carradine, Stacy Keach, Dennis Quaid, Randy Quaid, Kevin Brophy, Christopher Guest, Nicholas Guest, Pamela Reed, James Remar, Fran Ryan, Savannah Smith, Harry Carey, Jr., James Whitmore, Jr., Shelby Leverington.

Rob Lowe. *Frank and Jesse* (US/1994/105m/C) D: Robert Boris. C: Bill Paxton, Randy Travis, Dana Wheeler-Nicholson, Maria Pitillo, Luke Askew, Sean Patrick Flanery, Alexis Arquette, Todd Field, John Pyper-Ferguson, Nicholas Sadler, William Atherton, Tom Chick, Mary Neff, Richard Maynard.

Colin Farrell. *American Outlaws* (US/2001/93m/C) D: Les Mayfield. B/on a story by Roderick Taylor. C: Scott Caan, Ali Larter, Gabriel Macht, Gregory Smith, Harris Yulin, Will McCormack, Ronny Cox, Terry O'Quinn, Nathaniel Arcand, Kathy Bates, Timothy Dalton, Craig Erickson, Ty O'Neal, Joe Stevens.

James I *see* 603

James II *see* 604

282 Jefferson, Thomas (1743–1826)

The author of the Declaration of Independence and the 3rd President of the U.S., Jefferson is also remembered as the man responsible for the Louisiana Purchase (from France in 1803) which doubled the U.S. in area. Television portrayals have been by Albert Stratton in the mini-series *The Adams Chronicles* (76), Kevin Tighe in *The Rebels* (79), Sam Neill in *Sally Hemmings: An American Scandal* (2000), and by Peter Coyote in *Founding Fathers* (2000).

Montagu Love. *Alexander Hamilton* (US/1931/73m/BW) D: John G. Adolfi. B/on the play by George Arliss & Mary Hamlin. C: George Arliss, Doris Kenyon, Alan Mowbray, Morgan Wallace, Gwendolyn Logan, John T. Murray, Charles Middleton, Lionel Belmore.

George Irving. *Hearts Divided* (US/1936/70m/BW) D: Frank Borzage. B/on the play *Glorious Betsy* by Rida Johnson Young. C: Marion Davies, Dick Powell, Charles Ruggles, Claude Rains, Beulah Bondi, Edward Everett Horton, Hattie McDaniel.

Allan Cavan. *Old Louisiana* (aka *Treason*) (aka *Louisiana Gal*) (US/1938/63m/BW) D: Irvin Willat. C: Tom Keene, Rita Cansino (Hayworth), Robert Fiske, Ramsey Hill.

Richard Carlson. *The Howards of Virginia* (aka *Tree of Liberty*) (US/1940/117m/BW) D: Frank Lloyd. B/on the novel *The Tree of Liberty* by Elizabeth Page. C: Cary Grant, Martha Scott, Cedric Hardwicke, Alan Marshal, Richard Gaines, George Houston.

Gilbert Emery. *The Loves of Edgar Allan Poe* (US/1942/67m/BW) D: Harry Lachman. C: Linda Darnell, John Sheppard, Virginia Gilmore, Jane Darwell, Mary Howard, Morton Lowry.

Gilbert Emery. *The Remarkable Andrew* (US/1942/80m/BW) D: Stuart Heisler. B/on the novel by Dalton Trumbo. C: William Holden, Ellen Drew, Brian Donlevy, Rod Cameron, Richard Webb, Frances Gifford, Brandon Hurst, George Watts, Montagu Love.

Grandon Rhodes. *Magnificent Doll* (US/1946/93m/BW) D: Frank Borzage. C: Ginger Rogers, Burgess Meredith, David Niven, Robert Barrat, Larry Steers, Arthur Space.

Holmes Herbert. *Barbary Pirate* (US/1949/64m/BW) D: Lew Landers. C: Donald Woods, Trudy Marshall, Lenore Aubert, John Dehner, Matthew Boulton.

Herbert Hayes. *The Far Horizons* (aka *The Untamed West*) (US/1955/108m/C) D: Rudolph Mate. B/on the novel *Sacajawea of the Shosones* by Della Gould Emmons. C: Fred MacMurray, Charlton Heston, Donna Reed, Barbara Hale, William Demarest, Alan Reed.

Ken Howard. *1776* (US/1972/141m/C) D: Peter H. Hunt. B/on the musical by Sherman Edwards and Peter Stone. C: William Daniels, Howard Da Silva, Donald Madden, Ron Holgate, David Ford, Blythe Danner, Roy Poole, Virginia Vestoff, John Cullum.

Nick Nolte. *Jefferson in Paris* (US/1995/144m/C) D: James Ivory. C: Greta Scacchi, Jean-Pierre Aumont, Simon Callow, Seth Gilliam, James Earl Jones, Michael Lonsdale, Gwyneth Paltrow, Lambert Wilson, Charlotte de Turckheim, Damien Groelle.

283 Jesus Christ (6 BC?–AD 30)

In Christian belief Jesus is the Son of God. He has been portrayed in many TV productions, among them by Robert Powell, in the TV mini-series *Jesus of Nazareth* (77); by Chris Sarandon in the TV film *The Day Christ Died* (80); in the Italian/West German mini series *A Child Called Jesus* (87) by Matteo Bellina as the child, and Alessandro Gassman as the adult; by Jeremy Sisto in the TV film **Jesus** (99); and in *Jesus: The Complete Story* (2001) the child, by Amit Aton and the man, by Liron Levo.

Charles Requa. *Are We Civilized?* (US/1934/70m/BW) D: Edwin Carewe. C: Frank McGlynn, Alin Cavin, Harry Burkhart, Bert Lindley, Aaron Edwards, William Humphrey.

Robert Le Vigan. *Golgotha* (France/1935/97m/BW) D: Julien Duvivier. C: Harry Baur, Jean Gabin, Charles Granval, Andre Bacque, Hubert Prelier, Lucas Gridoux, Edwige Feuillere, Juliette Verneuil, Vana Yami, Van Daele.

Millard Coody. *The Lawton Story* (aka *The Prince of Peace*) (US/1949/120–101m/C) D: William Beaudine & Harold Dan. C: Darlene Bridges, A.S. Fisher, Hazel Lee Becker.

Luis Alcoriza. *The Sinner of Magdala* (aka *Mary Magdalene*) (Mexico/1950/95m/BW) D: Miguel Torres. C: Medea de Novara, Carlos Villatios, Louana Alcanir, Jose Bavera.

Robert Wilson. *Day of Triumph* (US/1954/110m/C) D: Irving Pichel & John T. Coyle. C: Lee J. Cobb, Ralph Freud, Tyler McVey, Michael Connors, Joanne

Dru, James Griffith, Lowell Gilmore, Anthony Warde, Peter Whitney, Everett Glass.

Claude Heater. *Ben Hur* (US/1959/212m/C) D: William Wyler. B/on the novel by Lew Wallace. Best Picture (AA, BFA, NYC, GG), Best Director (AA, GG, DGA). C: Charlton Heston, Stephen Boyd, Jack Hawkins, Haya Harareet, Hugh Griffith, Sam Jaffe, Jose Greci, Laurence Payne, Frank Thring, George Relph, Finlay Currie.

Luis Alvarez. *The Redeemer* (Spain/1959/93m/ C) D: Joseph Breen. C: Maruchi Fresno, Manuel Monroy, Felix Acaso, Antonio Vilar, Virgilio Teixeira, Carlos Casaravilla, Sebastian Cabot (Narrator).

Jeffrey Hunter. *King of Kings* (US/1961/168m/C) D: Nicholas Ray. C: Siobhan McKenna, Hurd Hatfield, Viveca Lindfors, Rita Gam, Carmen Sevilla,

Willem Dafoe's sensitive, yet intense portrayal of Jesus Christ in Martin Scorsese's (controversial at the time) *The Last Temptation of Christ* (1988). (Museum of Modern Art Film Stills Archive)

Rip Torn, Brigid Bazlen, Harry Guardino, Frank Thring, Guy Rolfe, Maurice Marsac, Gregoire Aslan, Royal Dano, Robert Ryan, Gerard Tichy, Michael Wager, Tino Barrero, Jose Antonio, Orson Welles (Narrator).

John Drew Barrymore. *Pontius Pilate* (Italy-France/1962/100m/C) D: Irving Rapper. C: Jean Marais, Jeanne Crain, Basil Rathbone, Leticia Roman, Livio Lorenzon.

Roy Mangano. *Barabbas* (Italy/1962/144m/C) D: Richard Fleischer. B/on the novel by Pär Lagerkvist. C: Anthony Quinn, Silvana Mangano, Arthur Kennedy, Katy Jurado, Harry Andrews, Ivan Triesault, Michael Gwynn, Arnold Foa.

Enrique Irazoqui. *The Gospel According to St. Matthew* (France-Italy/1964/ 142m/BW) D: Pier Paolo Pasolini. B/on the *New Testament book of Matthew*. C: Susanna Pasolini, Mario Socrate, Marcello Morante, Alfonso Gatto, Rodolfo Wilcock, Francesco Leonetti, Amerigo Bevilacqua, Otello Sestilli, Settimio Di Porto, Ferruccio Nuzzo, Alessandro Tosca, Paolo Tedesco, Franca Cupane, Giacomo Morante, Rosario Migale.

Max von Sydow. *The Greatest Story Ever Told* (US/1965/141m/C) D: George Stevens. B/on the book by Fulton Oursler. C: Dorothy McGuire, Robert Loggia, Claude Rains, Jose Ferrer, Charlton Heston, Donald Pleasence, David McCallum, Gary Raymond, Robert Blake, John Considine, David Hedison, Joanna Dunham, Sal Mineo, Van Heflin, Ed Wynn, Martin Landau, Telly Savalas, Sidney Poitier, Roddy McDowell, Angela Lansbury, Richard Conte, Carroll Baker, Janet Margolin, Burt Brinckerhoff, Tom Reese.

Bernard Verley. *The Milky Way* (France-Italy/1969/105m/C) D: Luis Bunuel. C: Paul Frankeur, Laurent Terzieff, Alain Cuny, Edith Scob, Michel Piccoli, Jean Clarieux, Christian van Cau, Pierre Clementi, Georges Marchal, Delphine Seyrig.

Radomir Reljic. *The Master and Margarita* (Yugoslavia-Italy/1972/101m/C) D: Aleksander Petrovic. C: Ugo Tognazzi, Alain Cuny, Ljuba Tadic, Mimsy Farmer, Bata Zivojinovic.

Ted Neeley. *Jesus Christ, Superstar* (US/1973/107m/C) D: Norman Jewison. B/on the rock opera by Tim Rice & Andrew Lloyd Webber. C: Carl Anderson, Yvonne Elliman, Barry Dennen, Bob Bingham, Larry T. Marshall, Joshua Mostel, Philip Toubus.

Robert Elfstrom, Jr. *The Gospel Road* (US/1973/93m/C) D: Robert Elfstrom. C: June Carter Cash, Larry Lee, Paul Smith, Alan Dater, John Paul Kay, Gelles LaBlanc, Terrance W. Mannock, Thomas Levanthal, Sean Armstrong, Lyle Nicholson, Steven Chernoff, Jonathan Sanders, Ulf Pollack.

Victor Garber. *Godspell* (US/1973/103m/C) D: David Greene. B/on the musical play by John-Michael Tebelak & Stephen Schwartz. C: David Haskell, Jerry Sroka, Lynne Thigpen, Katie Hanley, Robin Lamont, Gilmer McCormick.

Zalman King. *The Passover Plot* (Israel/1976/108m/C) D: Michael Campus. B/on the book by Hugh Schonfield. C: Harry Andrews, Hugh Griffith, Donald Pleasence, Scott Wilson, Dan Ades, Michael Baselon, Lewis van Bergen, William Burns, Dan Hedaya, Kevin O'Connor, Robert Walker.

Brian Deacon. *Jesus* (US/1979/117m/C) D: Peter Sykes & John Kirsh. B/on the *New Testament book of Luke.* C: Rivka Noiman, Yossef Shiloah, Niko Nitai, Gadi Rol, Richard Peterson, Eli Cohen, Shmuel Tal, Kobi Assaf, Talia Shapira, Eli Danker, Mosko Alkalai, Nisim Gerama, Leonid Weinstein, Peter Frye, David Goldberg.

Ken Colley. *Monty Python's Life of Brian* (aka *Life of Brian*) (GB/1979/93m/C) D: Terry Jones. C: Graham Chapman, Eric Idle, Michael Palin, John Cleese, Terry Gilliam, Terry Jones, John Case.

John Rubinstein. *In Search of Historic Jesus* (US/1979/91m/C) D: Henning Schellerup. B/on the book by Lee Roddy & Charles E. Seller. C: John Anderson, Nehemiah Persoff, Andrew Bloch, Morgan Brittany, Walter Brooke, Annette Charles, Royal Dano, Anthony DeLongis, Lawrence Dobkin, David Opatoshu, John Hoyt, Jeffrey Druce.

John Hurt. *History of the World, Part I* (US/1981/92m/C) D: Mel Brooks. C: Mel Brooks, Dom DeLuise, Madeline Kahn, Harvey Korman, Cloris Leachman, Gregory Hines, Art Metrano.

Willem Dafoe. *The Last Temptation of Christ* (US/1988/164m/C) D: Martin Scorsese. B/on the novel by Nikos Kazantzakis. C: Harvey Keitel, Paul Greco, Verna Bloom, Barbara Hershey, Gary Basaraba, Victor Argo, Michael Been, John

Lurie, Harry Dean Stanton, David Bowie, Nehemiah Persoff, Leo Burmester, Irvin Kershner, Andre Gregory, Tomas Arana, Juliette Caton, Roberts Blossom, Barry Miller, Alan Rosenberg.

Sebastien Roche. *Household Saints* (US/1993/124–109m/C) D: Nancy Savoca. B/on the novel by Francine Prose. C: Tracey Ullman, Lili Taylor, Vincent D'Onofrio, Judith Malina, Joe Grifasi.

Martin Donovan. *The Book of Life* (US-France/1999/63m/C) D: Hal Hartley. C: P.J. Harvey, Thomas Jay Ryan.

284 Jinnah, Muhammad Ali (1876–1948)

Leader of the Indian Muslim League, who worked for Hindu/Mulsim unity. In 1947 Jinnah became the Founding Father and first Governor General of Pakistan.

Alyque Padamsee. *Gandhi* (GB-India/1982/188m/C) D: Richard Attenborough. Best Picture (AA, BFA, NYC), Best Director (AA, BFA, DGA). C: Ben Kingsley, Candice Bergen, Edward Fox, John Gielgud, Trevor Howard, Peter Harlowe, Martin Sheen, Roshan Seth.

Christopher Lee. Richard Lintern (Young Jinnah). *Jinnah* (Pakistan/1998/110m/C) D: Jamil Dehlavi. C: James Fox, Maria Aitken, Shashi Kapoor, Shireen Shah, Robert Ashby, Indira Varma, Sam Dastor, Shakeel, Vaneeza Ahmed, Roger Brierley, Rowena Cooper, James Curran, Vernon Dobtcheff, Michael Elwyn, Ian Gelder, Christopher Godwin, John Grillo, Talat Hussain, John Nettleton.

285 Joan of Arc (1412?–1431)

Acting upon voices that only she heard, Joan became an inspirational leader of the French army at the Siege of Orleans during the Hundred Years War with England. She was captured, tried and convicted as a heretic and burned at the stake. In 1920 she was canonized by the Catholic Church. Joan was portrayed by Leelee Sobieski in the TV film *Joan of Arc* (99).

Simone Genevois. *Saint Joan—The Maid* (aka *La Merveilleuse Vie de Jeanne d'Arc*) (France/1929/BW) D: Marco De Gastyne.

Angela Salloker. *Das Mädchen Johanna* (Germany/1935/BW) D: Gustav Ucicky. C: Gustaf Gruendgens, Rene Deltgen, Heinrich George, Erich Pante.

Ingrid Bergman. *Joan of Arc* (US/1948/145–100m/C) D: Victor Fleming. B/on the play *Joan of Lorraine* by Maxwell Anderson. C: Jose Ferrer, Hurd Hatfield, Ward Bond.

Michèle Morgan. *Daughters of Destiny* (aka *Destinées*) (aka *Love and the Frenchwoman*) (aka *Love, Soldiers and Women*) (France/1953/105m/BW) D: Marcel Pagliero, Jean Delannoy & Christian-Jaque. C: Claudette Colbert, Eleanora Rossi-Drago, Martine Carol, Raf Vallone, Andre Clement, Paolo Stoppa.

Ingrid Bergman. *Joan at the Stake* (Italy-France/1954/80m/C) D: Roberto Rossellini. B/on the opera by Paul Claudel & Arthur Honegger. C: Carminati, Giacinto Prantelli.

Jean Seberg. *Saint Joan* (US/1957/110m/BW) D: Otto Preminger. B/on the play by George Bernard Shaw. C: Richard Widmark, Richard Todd, Anton Walbrook.

Hedy Lamarr. *The Story of Mankind* (US/1957/100m/C) D: Irwin Allen. B/on the book by Hendrik Van Loon. C: Ronald Colman, Virginia Mayo, Agnes Moorehead, Peter Lorre, Dennis Hopper, Marie Wilson, Helmut Dantine, Edward Everett Horton, Reginald Gardiner, Marie Windsor, Francis X. Bushman, Anthony Dexter, Austin Green, Jim Ameche, Harpo Marx, Bobby Watson, Reginald Sheffield, Cedric Hardwicke, Cesar Romero.

Florence Carrez. *The Trial of Joan of Arc* (France/1962/65m/BW) D: Robert Bresson. C: Jean-Claude Fourneau, Marc Jacquier, Roger Honorat, Jean Gillibert, Michael Williams.

Jane Wiedlin. *Bill and Ted's Excellent Adventure* (US/1989/90m/C) D: Stephen Herek. C: Keanu Reeves, Alex Winter, George Carlin, Amy Stock-Poynton, Terry Camilleri, Dan Shor, Clifford David, Rod Loomis, Al Leong, Robert V. Barron, Tony Steedman, Fee Waybill.

Sandrine Bonnaire. *Jeanne la Pucelle 1. Les batailles* (aka *Joan the Maid 1.: The Battles*) (France/1994/160m/C) D: Jacques Rivette. C: Tatiana Moukhine, Jean-Marie Richier, Baptiste Roussillon, Jean-Luc Petit, Bernadette Giraud, Jean-Claude Jay, Olivier Cruveiller, Benjamin Rataud, Cyril Haouzi, Réginald Huguenin, Patrick Adomian, Nicolas Vian, André Marcon, Jean-Louis Richard.

Sandrine Bonnaire. *Jeanne la Pucelle 2. Les prisons* (aka *Joan the Maid 2.: The Prisons*) (France/1994/176m/C) D: Jacques Rivette. C: André Marcon, Jean-Louis Richard, Marcel Bozonnet, Patrick Le Mauff, Didier Sauvegrain, Jean-Pierre Lorit, Bruno Wolkowitch, Florence Darel, Nathalie Richard, Yann Collette, Edith Scob, Hélène de Fougerolles, Monique Mélinand, Olivier Cruveiller.

Milla Jovovich. *The Messenger: The Story of Joan of Arc* (aka *Jeanne d'Arc*) (France/1999/180m/Color) D: Luc Besson. C: John Malkovich, Faye Dunaway, Dustin Hoffman, Pascal Greggory, Vincent Cassel, Tchéky Karyo, Richard Ridings, Desmond Harrington, Timothy West, Andrew Birkin, Philippe Du Janerand, Christian Erickson, Mathieu Kassovitz, Gina McKee, John Merrick, Olivier Rabourdin.

286 Jodl, Alfred (1890–1946)

Field Marshal Jodl was the strategic planner responsible for many of Germany's early victories in World War II. In TV productions he's been portrayed by Wolfgang Priess in *Ike* (79), Tony Steedman in *The Bunker* (81), and Joachim Hansen in *The Winds of War* (83).

Jack Baston. *The Desert Fox* (aka *Rommel—Desert Fox*) (US/1951/88m/BW) D: Henry Hathaway. B/on the book *Rommel* by Desmond Young. C: James Mason, Cedric Hardwicke, Jessica Tandy, Luther Adler, Leo G. Carroll, Eduard Franz, John Hoyt.

Otto Schmoele. *The Last Ten Days* (aka *Ten Days to Die*) (aka *Last Ten Days of Adolf Hitler*) (aka *Der Letzte Akt*) (aka *The Last Act*) (Germany/1955/115m/BW) D: G.W. Pabst. B/on the novel *Ten Days to Die* by M.A. Mussanno. C: Albin Skoda, Oskar Werner, Lotte Tobisch, Willy Krause, Erich Stuckmann, Edmund Erlandsen, Kurt Eilers, Helga Dohrn, Leopold Hainisch.

Walter Kohler. *Hitler* (aka *Women of Nazi Germany*) (US/1962/107m/BW) D: Stuart Heisler. C: Richard Basehart, Cordula Trantow, Maria Emo, Martin Kosleck,

John Banner, Martin Brandt, William Sargent, Gregory Gay, Thodore Marcuse, Rick Traeger, John Mitchum, G. Stanley Jones, Carl Esmond, Berry Kroeger.

Wolfgang Lukschy. *The Longest Day* (US/1962/180m/BW) D: Andrew Marton, Ken Annakin & Bernherd Wicki. B/on the novel by Cornelius Ryan. Best English Language Picture (NBR). C: John Wayne, Robert Mitchum, Henry Fonda, Robert Ryan, Rod Steiger, Robert Wagner, Sal Mineo, Roddy McDowall, Curt Jurgens, Paul Hartman, Nicholas Stuart, Henry Grace, Werner Hinz, Trevor Reid, Alexander Knox.

Hannes Messemer. *Is Paris Burning?* (US-France/1966/173m/C) D: Rene Clement. C: Jean-Paul Belmondo, Charles Boyer, Leslie Caron, Jean-Pierre Casal, George Chakiris, Claude Dauphin, Alain Delon, Kirk Douglas, Glenn Ford, Gert Frobe, Daniel Gelin, Orson Welles, E.G. Marshall, Simone Signoret, Billy Frick, Robert Stack.

Richard Muench. *Patton* (aka *Patton — Lust for Glory*) (US/1970/170m/C) D: Franklin J. Schaffner. B/on *Patton: Ordeal and Triumph* by Ladislas Farago and *A Soldier's Story* by Omar Bradley. Best Picture, Best Direction (AA). Best English-Language Picture (NBR). Best Director (DGA). C: George C. Scott, Karl Malden, Michael Bates, Edward Binns, Lawrence Dobkin, John Doucette, Stephen Young, Michael Strong, Frank Latimore, James Edwards, Karl Michael Vogler.

Philip Stone. *Hitler: The Last Ten Days* (GB-Italy/1973/106m/C) D: Ennio De Concini. B/on the book *The Last Days of the Chancellery* by Gerhardt Boldt. C: Alec Guinness, Simon Ward, Gabriele Ferzetti, Doris Kunstmann, John Bennett, Mark Kingston.

287 John, Prince/King (1167–1216)

The youngest son of **Henry II**, John was the evil Prince in all the films about Robin Hood. He ascended the throne upon **King Richard's** death and in 1215 was forced by the English barons to sign the Magna Carta.

Ramsay Hill. *The Crusades* (US/1935/123m/BW) D: Cecil B. DeMille, Waldemar Young & Dudley Nichols. B/on the book *The Crusades: Iron Men and Saints* by Harold Lamb. C: Loretta Young, Henry Wilcoxon, Ian Keith, Katherine De Mille, C. Aubrey Smith, Joseph Schildkraut, Alan Hale, C. Henry Gordon.

Claude Rains. *The Adventures of Robin Hood* (US/1938/102m/C) D: Michael Curtiz. C: Errol Flynn, Olivia de Havilland, Basil Rathbone, Ian Hunter, Patric Knowles, Montagu Love.

George Macready. *Rogues of Sherwood Forest* (US/1950/80m/C) D: Gordon Douglas. C: John Derek, Diana Lynn, Alan Hale, Paul Cavanaugh, Lowell Gilmore, John Dehner.

Guy Rolfe. *Ivanhoe* (GB/1952/106m/C) D: Richard Thorpe. B/on the novel by Sir Walter Scott C: Robert Taylor, Elizabeth Taylor, Joan Fontaine, George Sanders, Emlyn Williams, Robert Douglas, Norman Wooland, Felix Aylmer, Finlay Currie, Francis de Wolff, Basil Sydney, Sebastian Cabot.

Hubert Gregg. *The Story of Robin Hood* (aka *The Story of Robin Hood and His Merrie Men*) (GB/1952/84m/C) D: Ken Annakin. C: Richard Todd, Joan Rice, Peter Finch, James Hayter, James Robertson Justice, Martita Hunt, Patrick Barr, Antony Eustrel.

Nigel Terry. *The Lion in Winter* (GB/1968/134m/C) D: Anthony Harvey. B/on the play by James Goldman. Best Picture (GG (Drama), NYC). Best Director (DGA). C: Peter O'Toole, Katharine Hepburn, Jane Merrow, John Castle, Anthony Hopkins, Timothy Dalton, Nigel Stock, Kenneth Griffith.

Ian Holm. *Robin and Marian* (GB/1976/106m/C) D: Richard Lester. C: Sean Connery, Audrey Hepburn, Richard Harris, Robert Shaw, Nicol Williamson, Denholm Elliott.

Edward Fox. *Robin Hood* (US-GB/1991/150–116m/C) D: John Irvin. C: Patrick Bergen, Jurgen Prochnow, Uma Thurman, Jeroen Krabbe, Jeff Nuttal, David Morrisey.

Richard Lewis. *Robin Hood: Men in Tights* (US/1993/102m/C) D: Mel Brooks. C: Cary Elwes, Roger Rees, Amy Yasbeck, Mark Blankfield, Patrick Stewart, Tracey Ullman.

288 John, Saint (3?–100?)

Called the "Beloved Disciple" of **Jesus Christ's** Apostles, it was to John that Jesus entrusted the care of His mother, **Mary**, at the time of His crucifixtion. He has been played by John Duttine in the TV mini-series *Jesus of Nazareth* (77), by Oliver Cotton in the 1980 TV film *The Day That Christ Died*, and by Ian Duncan in *Jesus* (99).

Brian Hutton. *The Big Fisherman* (US/1959/180m/C) D: Frank Borzage. B/on the novel by Lloyd C. Douglas. C: Howard Keel, Susan Kohner, John Saxon, Martha Hyer, Herbert Lom, Alexander Scourby, Jay Barney, Rhodes Reason, Thomas Troupe, Herbert Rudley.

Jose Antonio. *King of Kings* (US/1961/168m/C) D: Nicholas Ray. C: Jeffrey Hunter, Siobhan McKenna, Hurd Hatfield, Viveca Lindfors, Rita Gam, Carmen Sevilla, Rip Torn, Brigid Bazlen, Harry Guardino, Frank Thring, Guy Rolfe, Maurice Marsac, Gregoire Aslan, Royal Dano, Robert Ryan, Gerard Tichy, Michael Wager, Tino Barrero, Orson Welles (Narrator).

Giacomo Morante. *The Gospel According to St. Matthew* (France-Italy/1964/142m/BW) D: Pier Paolo Pasolini. B/on the *New Testament book of Matthew*. C: Enrique Irazoqui, Susanna Pasolini, Mario Socrate, Marcello Morante, Alfonso Gatto, Rodolfo Wilcock, Francesco Leonetti, Amerigo Bevilacqua, Otello Sestilli, Settimio Di Porto, Ferruccio Nuzzo, Alessandro Tosca, Paolo Tedesco, Franca Cupane, Rosario Migale.

John Considine. *The Greatest Story Ever Told* (US/1965/141m/C) D: George Stevens. B/on the book by Fulton Oursler. C: Max von Sydow, Dorothy McGuire, Robert Loggia, Claude Rains, Jose Ferrer, Charlton Heston, Donald Pleasence, David McCallum, Gary Raymond, Robert Blake, David Hedison, Joanna Dunham, Sal Mineo, Van Heflin, Ed Wynn, Martin Landau, Telly Savalas, Sidney Poitier, Roddy McDowell, Angela Lansbury, Richard Conte, Carroll Baker, Janet Margolin, Burt Brinckerhoff, Tom Reese.

Gelles LeBlanc. *The Gospel Road* (US/1973/93m/C) D: Robert Elfstrom. C: Robert Elfstrom, June Carter Cash, Larry Lee, Paul Smith, Alan Dater, John Paul Kay, Robert Elfstrom, Jr., Terrance W. Mannock, Thomas Levanthal, Sean Armstrong, Lyle Nicholson, Steven Chernoff, Jonathan Sanders, Ulf Pollack.

Andrew Bloch. *In Search of Historic Jesus* (US/1979/91m/C) D: Henning Schellerup. B/on the book by Lee Roddy & Charles E. Seller. C: John Rubinstein, John Anderson, Nehemiah Persoff, Morgan Brittany, Walter Brooke, Annette Charles, Royal Dano, Anthony DeLongis, Lawrence Dobkin, David Opatoshu, John Hoyt, Jeffrey Druce.

Shmuel Tal. *Jesus* (US/1979/117m/C) D: Peter Sykes & John Kirsh. B/on the *New Testament book of Luke.* C: Brian Deacon, Rivka Noiman, Yossef Shiloah, Niko Nitai, Gadi Rol, Richard Peterson, Eli Cohen, Kobi Assaf, Talia Shapira, Eli Danker, Mosko Alkalai, Nisim Gerama, Leonid Weinstein, Peter Frye, David Goldberg.

Michael Been. *The Last Temptation of Christ* (US/1988/164m/C) D: Martin Scorsese. B/on the novel by Nikos Kazantzakis. C: Willem Dafoe, Harvey Keitel, Paul Greco, Verna Bloom, Barbara Hershey, Gary Basaraba, Victor Argo, John Lurie, Harry Dean Stanton, David Bowie, Nehemiah Persoff, Leo Burmester, Irvin Kershner, Andre Gregory, Tomas Arana, Juliette Caton, Roberts Blossom, Barry Miller, Alan Rosenberg.

289 John the Baptist (6 BC?–28 AD)

The New Testament prophet who paved the way for **Jesus Christ,** John was imprisoned and eventually beheaded by **Herod Antipas.** He was portrayed by Michael York in the TV mini-series *Jesus of Nazareth* (77), and by David O'Hara in the TV film *Jesus* (99).

Alan Badel. *Salome* (US/1953/103m/C) D: William Dieterle. C: Rita Hayworth, Stewart Granger, Charles Laughton, Judith Anderson, Cedric Hardwicke, Basil Sydney, Rex Reason, Robert Warwick, Maurice Schwartz.

Jay Barney. *The Big Fisherman* (US/1959/180m/C) D: Frank Borzage. B/on the novel by Lloyd C. Douglas. C: Howard Keel, Susan Kohner, John Saxon, Martha Hyer, Herbert Lom, Alexander Scourby, Rhodes Reason, Brian Hutton, Thomas Troupe, Herbert Rudley.

Robert Ryan. *King of Kings* (US/1961/168m/C) D: Nicholas Ray. C: Jeffrey Hunter, Siobhan McKenna, Hurd Hatfield, Viveca Lindfors, Rita Gam, Carmen Sevilla, Rip Torn, Brigid Bazlen, Harry Guardino, Frank Thring, Guy Rolfe, Maurice Marsac, Gregoire Aslan, Royal Dano, Gerard Tichy, Michael Wager, Tino Barrero, Jose Antonio, Orson Welles (Narrator).

Mario Socrate. *The Gospel According to St. Matthew* (France-Italy/1964/142m/ BW) D: Pier Paolo Pasolini. B/on the *New Testament book of Matthew.* C: Enrique Irazoqui, Susanna Pasolini, Marcello Morante, Alfonso Gatto, Rodolfo Wilcock, Francesco Leonetti, Amerigo Bevilacqua, Otello Sestilli, Settimio Di Porto, Ferruccio Nuzzo, Alessandro Tosca, Paolo Tedesco, Franca Cupane, Giacomo Morante, Rosario Migale.

Charlton Heston. *The Greatest Story Ever Told* (US/1965/141m/C) D: George Stevens. B/on the book by Fulton Oursler. C: Max von Sydow, Dorothy McGuire, Robert Loggia, Claude Rains, Jose Ferrer, Donald Pleasence, David McCallum, Gary Raymond, Robert Blake, John Considine, David Hedison, Joanna Dunham, Sal Mineo, Van Heflin, Ed Wynn, Martin Landau, Telly Savalas, Sidney Poitier, Roddy McDowell, Angela Lansbury, Richard Conte, Carroll Baker, Janet Margolin, Burt Brinckerhoff, Tom Reese.

Larry Lee. *The Gospel Road* (US/1973/93m/C) D: Robert Elfstrom. C: Robert Elfstrom, June Carter Cash, Paul Smith, Alan Dater, John Paul Kay, Gelles LaBlanc, Robert Elfstrom, Jr., Terrance W. Mannock, Thomas Levanthal, Sean Armstrong, Lyle Nicholson, Steven Chernoff, Jonathan Sanders, Ulf Pollack.

David Haskell. *Godspell* (US/1973/103m/C) D: David Greene. B/on the musical play by John-Michael Tebelak & Stephen Schwartz. C: Victor Garber, Jerry Sroka, Lynne Thigpen, Katie Hanley, Robin Lamont, Gilmer McCormick.

Harry Andrews. *The Passover Plot* (Israel/1976/108m/C) D: Michael Campus. B/on the book by Hugh Schonfield. C: Hugh Griffith, Zalman King, Donald Pleasence, Scott Wilson, Dan Ades, Michael Baselon, Lewis van Bergen, William Burns, Dan Hedaya, Kevin O'Connor, Robert Walker.

Eli Cohen. *Jesus* (US/1979/117m/C) D: Peter Sykes & John Kirsh. B/on the *New Testament book of Luke.* C: Brian Deacon, Rivka Noiman, Yossef Shiloah, Niko Nitai, Gadi Rol, Richard Peterson, Shmuel Tal, Kobi Assaf, Talia Shapira, Eli Danker, Mosko Alkalai, Nisim Gerama, Leonid Weinstein, Peter Frye, David Goldberg.

Fabrizio Bentivoglio. *Salome* (France-Italy/1985/97m/C) D: Claude d'Anna. B/on the play by Oscar Wilde. C: Tomas Milian, Pamela Salem, Tim Woodward, Jo Ciampa, Fabiana Torrente.

Andre Gregory. *The Last Temptation of Christ* (US/1988/164m/C) D: Martin Scorsese. B/on the novel by Nikos Kazantzakis. C: Willem Dafoe, Harvey Keitel, Paul Greco, Verna Bloom, Barbara Hershey, Gary Basaraba, Victor Argo, Michael Been, John Lurie, Harry Dean Stanton, David Bowie, Nehemiah Persoff, Leo Burmester, Irvin Kershner, Tomas Arana, Juliette Caton, Roberts Blossom, Barry Miller, Alan Rosenberg.

Raoul Bhaneja. *Extrodinary Visitor* (Canada/1999/90m/C) D: John W. Doyle. C: Mary Walsh, Andy Jones, Jordan Caney, Rick Boland, Greg Malone, Brian Hennessy, Ken Campbell, Maisie Rillie, Roger Maunder, James Mitchell, Bill Rowe.

Johnson, Andrew *see* 579

290 Johnson, Lyndon Baines (1908–1973)

The 36th President of the U.S., Johnson became the President upon the assassination of **John F. Kennedy** in 1963. TV portrayals of L.B.J. include: Warren Kemmerling in *King* (78), Forrest Tucker in *Blood Feud* (83), Nesbitt Blaisdell in *Kennedy* (83), G.D. Spradlin in *Robert Kennedy and His Times* (85), Randy Quaid in *LBJ: The Early Years* (87), and Rip Torn in *J. Edgar Hoover* (87).

Ivan Volkman. *How to Succeed in Business Without Really Trying* (US/1967/121m/C) D: David Swift. B/on the novel by Shepherd Mead and the musical play by Abe Burrows, Willie Gilbert & Jack Weinstock. C: Robert Morse, Michele Lee, Rudy Vallee, Anthony Teague, Maureen Arthur.

Bebert H. Marboutie. *Colpo di Stato* (Italy/1968) D: Luciano Salce. C: Attilio Zingarelli.

Andrew Duggan. *The Private Files of J. Edgar Hoover* (US/1978/112m/C) D: Larry Cohen. C: Broderick Crawford, Jose Ferrer, Michael Parks, Ronee Blakely,

Michael Sacks, Raymond St. Jacques, Howard Da Silva, James Wainwright, Brad Dexter, William Jordan, Richard M. Dixon, Gordon Zimmerman, Lloyd Nolan, June Havoc, Dan Dailey, John Marley, Lloyd Gough.

Donald Moffat. *The Right Stuff* (US/1983/192m/C) D: Philip Kaufman. B/on the book by Tom Wolfe. C: Sam Shepard, Scott Glenn, Ed Harris, Dennis Quaid, Fred Ward, Barbara Hershey, Kim Stanley, Veronica Cartwright, Robert Beer.

Kenneth Mars. *Prince Jack* (US/1984/100m/C) D: Bert Lovitt. C: Robert Hogan, James F. Kelly, Lloyd Nolan, Cameron Mitchell, Robert Guillame, Theodore Bikel.

Tom Howard. *JFK* (US/1991/189m/C) D: Oliver Stone. B/on *Crossfire* by Jim Marrs and *On the Trail of the Assassins* by Jim Garrison. C: Kevin Costner, Sissy Spacek, Kevin Bacon, Gary Oldman, Brian Doyle-Murray, Steve Reed, Jodi Farber.

John William Galt (voice only). *Forrest Gump* (US/1994/142m/C) D: Robert Zemeckis. B/on the novel by Winston Groom. Best Picture (AA), Best Director (AA). C: Tom Hanks, Gary Sinise, Robin Wright, Sally Field, Mykelti Williamson, Peter Dobson, Richard D'Allesandro, and the voices of Jed Gillin, Joe Stefanelli, and Joe Alaskey.

Walter Adrian. *Thirteen Days* (US/2000/145m/C/BW) D: Roger Donaldson. B/on the book *The Kennedy Tapes—Inside the White House During the Cuban Missile Crisis* by Ernest R. May and Philip D.Zelikow. C: Kevin Costner, Bruce Greenwood, Steven Culp, Dylan Baker, Henry Strozier, Frank Wood, Len Cariou, Janet Coleman, Stephanie Romanov, Bill Smitrovich, Ed Lauter, Dakin Matthews, Peter White, Tim Kelleher.

291 Johnson, Samuel (1709–1784)

English man of letters, Dr. Johnson's works include plays, poetry, essays, satires and his monumental *Dictionary of the English Language*.

Robert Atkins. *Peg of Old Drury* (GB/1935/74m/BW) D: Herbert Wilcox. B/on the play *Masks and Faces* by Charles Reade. C: Anna Neagle, Cedric Hardwicke, Margaretta Scott, Jack Hawkins, Maire O'Neill, Leslie French, Sara Allgood, Tom Heslewood.

Yorke Sherwood. *Lloyds of London* (US/1936/115m/BW) D: Henry King. C: Freddie Bartholomew, Madeleine Carroll, Sir Guy Standing, Tyrone Power, George Sanders, C. Aubrey Smith, John Burton, Hugh Huntley, Thomas Pogue, William Wagner.

Robert Atkins. *I'll Never Forget You* (aka *The House in the Square*) (US/1951/89m/C) D: Roy Baker. B/on the play *Berkeley Square* by John L. Balderston. C: Tyrone Power, Ann Blyth, Michael Rennie, Ronald Simpson, Alexander McCrindle.

292 Jolson, Al (1886–1950)

(Asa Yoelson) Popular American (born in Russia) singer and actor, Jolson starred in the first talking feature film *The Jazz Singer* in 1927. In the TV mini-series *Ellis Island* (84) he was played by Jonathan Burn.

Harry Brunning. *Regal Cavalcade* (aka *Royal Cavalcade*) (GB/1935/100m/BW)

D: Thomas Bentley, Herbert Brenton, Norman Lee, Walter Summers, Will Kellino & Marcel Varnel. C: Marie Lohr, Esme Percy, Pearl Argyle, Frank Vosper, Austin Trevor, John Mills, C.M. Hallard, H. Saxon-Snell, Patric Knowles, Matheson Lang, Athene Seyler.

Larry Parks. *The Jolson Story* (US/1946/128m/C) D: Alfred E. Green. C: Evelyn Keyes, William Demarest, Ludwig Donath, Bill Goodwin, Eddie Kane, Edwin Maxwell.

Larry Parks. *Jolson Sings Again* (US/1949/96m/C) D: Henry Levin. C: Barbara Hale, William Demarest, Ludwig Donath.

Norman Brooks. *The Best Things in Life Are Free* (US/1956/104m/C) D: Michael Curtiz. C: Gordon MacRae, Dan Dailey, Ernest Borgnine, Sheree North, Larry Keating, Tommy Noonan.

Buddy Lewis. *Harlow* (US/1965/107m/C) D: Alex Segal. C: Carol Lynley, Efrem Zimalist, Jr., Ginger Rogers, Barry Sullivan, Hurd Hatfield, Lloyd Bochner, Hermione Baddeley, Jack Kruschen, Celia Lovesky, Robert Strauss, John Fox, Jim Plunkett.

293 Joseph, Saint

The earthly father of **Jesus Christ**, Joseph is not mentioned in the gospels after Jesus begins his ministry and it is assumed that he had died by that time. Television portrayals of Saint Joseph have been by Yorgo Voyagis in the mini-series *Jesus of Nazareth* (77), Jeff East in *Mary and Joseph: A Story of Faith* (79), and Bekim Fehmiu in *A Child Called Jesus* mini series (87), and by Armin Mueller-Stahl in the TV film *Jesus* (99).

Laurence Payne. *Ben Hur* (US/1959/212m/C) D: William Wyler. B/on the novel by Lew Wallace. Best Picture (AA, BFA, NYC, GG), Best Director (AA, GG, DGA). C: Charlton Heston, Stephen Boyd, Jack Hawkins, Haya Harareet, Hugh Griffith, Sam Jaffe, Jose Greci, Frank Thring, Claude Heater, George Relph, Finlay Currie.

Gerard Tichy. *King of Kings* (US/1961/168m/C) D: Nicholas Ray. C: Jeffrey Hunter, Siobhan McKenna, Hurd Hatfield, Viveca Lindfors, Rita Gam, Carmen Sevilla, Rip Torn, Brigid Bazlen, Harry Guardino, Frank Thring, Guy Rolfe, Maurice Marsac, Gregoire Aslan, Royal Dano, Robert Ryan, Michael Wager, Tino Barrero, Jose Antonio, Orson Welles (Narrator).

Marcello Morante. *The Gospel According to St. Matthew* (France-Italy/1964/142m/BW) D: Pier Paolo Pasolini. B/on the *New Testament book of Matthew*. C: Enrique Irazoqui, Susanna Pasolini, Mario Socrate, Alfonso Gatto, Rodolfo Wilcock, Francesco Leonetti, Amerigo Bevilacqua, Otello Sestilli, Settimio Di Porto, Ferruccio Nuzzo, Alessandro Tosca, Paolo Tedesco, Franca Cupane, Giacomo Morante, Rosario Migale.

Robert Loggia. *The Greatest Story Ever Told* (US/1965/141m/C) D: George Stevens. B/on the book by Fulton Oursler. C: Max von Sydow, Dorothy McGuire, Claude Rains, Jose Ferrer, Charlton Heston, Donald Pleasence, David McCallum, Gary Raymond, Robert Blake, John Considine, David Hedison, Joanna Dunham, Sal Mineo, Van Heflin, Ed Wynn, Martin Landau, Telly Savalas, Sidney Poitier, Roddy McDowell, Angela Lansbury, Richard Conte, Carroll Baker, Janet Margolin, Burt Brinckerhoff, Tom Reese.

Walter Brooke. *In Search of Historic Jesus* (US/1979/91m/C) D: Henning Schellerup. B/on the book by Lee Roddy & Charles E. Seller. C: John Rubinstein, John Anderson, Nehemiah Persoff, Andrew Bloch, Morgan Brittany, Annette Charles, Royal Dano, Anthony DeLongis, Lawrence Dobkin, David Opatoshu, John Hoyt, Jeffrey Druce.

Yossef Shiloah. *Jesus* (US/1979/117m/C) D: Peter Sykes & John Kirsh. B/on the *New Testament book of Luke*. C: Brian Deacon, Rivka Noiman, Niko Nitai, Gadi Rol, Richard Peterson, Eli Cohen, Shmuel Tal, Kobi Assaf, Talia Shapira, Eli Danker, Mosko Alkalai, Nisim Gerama, Leonid Weinstein, Peter Frye, David Goldberg.

294 Joseph II (1741–1790)

Holy Roman Emperor (1765–90) and the brother of **Marie-Antionette**, Joseph was responsible for widespread changes during his reign but has been depicted in films due to his patronage of **Mozart**.

Paul Richter. *Die Försterchristl* (Germany/1931/90m/BW) D: Friedrich Zelnik. C: Irene Elsinger, Oskar Karlweis, Andre Pilot, Adele Sandrock.

Frederick Leister. *Mozart* (aka *Whom the Gods Love*) (GB/1936/78m/BW) D: Basil Dean. C: Stephen Haggard, Victoria Hopper, John Loder, Liane Haid, Jean Cadell.

Curt Jurgens. *The Mozart Story* (aka *Whom the Gods Love*) (aka *Mozart*) (aka *Wenn Die Gotter Lieben*) (Germany/1942/91m/C) D: Karl Hartl. C: Hans Holt, Rene Deltgen, Winnie Markus, Irene von Meyendorf, Edward Vedder, Wilton Graff, Carol Forman, Walther Jansson, Paul Hoerbiger.

Jeffrey Jones. *Amadeus* (US/1984/158m/C) D: Milos Forman. B/on the play by Peter Shaffer. Best Picture (AA, GG), Best Director (AA, DGA, GG). C: Tom Hulce, F. Murray Abraham, Elizabeth Berridge, Simon Callow, Roy Dotrice.

Zdenek Hradilak. *Forget Mozart!* (Germany-Czechoslovakia/1985/90m/C) D: Miloslav Luther. C: Max Tidof, Armin Muller Stahl, Franz Glatzeder, Ladislav Chudik.

295 Josephine (1763–1814)

(Marie Josèphe Rose Tascher de la Pagerie) The wife of **Napoleon** and the grandmother of **Napoleon III**, Josephine was Empress of France for less than six years before Bonaparte divorced her for not bearing him any sons.

Gina Manés. *Napoleon Bonaparte* (France/1934/140m/BW) D: Abel Gance. Three-dimensional sound version of Gance's 1927 epic *Napoléon*. C: Albert Dieudonné, Edmond von Daele, Alexandre Koubitsky, Antonin Artaud, Boudreau, Alberty, Jack Rye, Favière, Suzanne Blanchetti, Marguerite Gance, Simone Genevois, Genica Missirio.

Jacqueline Delubac. *The Pearls of the Crown* (France/1937/120–100m/BW) D: Sacha Guitry & Christian-Jaque. C: Sacha Guitry, Lyn Harding, Ermete Zacconi, Marguerite Moreno, Yvette Plenne, Catalano, Arletty, Percy Marmont, Derrick De Marney, Barbara Shaw, Simone Renant, Jean Louis Barrault, Emile Drain, Enrico Glori, Renee Saint-Cyr, Pizani, Claude Dauphin, Aime-Simon Gerard.

Ruth Chatterton. *A Royal Divorce* (GB/1938/85m/BW) D: Jack Raymond. B/on the novel *Josephine* by Jacques Thery. C: Pierre Blanchar, Frank Cellier, John Laurie, Jack Hawkins, David Farrar, Allan Jeayes, Lawrence Hanray, Auriol Lee.

Lise Delamare. *Mademoiselle Désirée* (aka *Le Destin Fabuleux de Désirée Clary*) (France/1942/95m/BW) D: Sacha Guitry. C: Sacha Guitry, Jean-Louis Barrault, Genevieve Guitry, Gaby Morlay, Aime Clariond, Jacques Varenne.

Hedy Lamarr. *The Loves of Three Queens* (aka *The Face That Launched a Thousand Ships*) (aka *Eternal Woman*) (aka *Helen of Troy*) (Italy-France/1953/90m/C) D: Marc Allegret. C: Gerard Oury, Massimo Serato, Robert Beatty, Cathy O'Donnell.

Merle Oberon. *Désirée* (US/1954/110m/C) D: Henry Koster. B/on the novel by Annemarie Selinko. C: Marlon Brando, Jean Simmons, Michael Rennie, John Hoyt, Elizabeth Sellars, Cameron Mitchell, Cathleen Nesbitt, Sam Gilman, Alan Napier.

Michèle Morgan. *Napoleon* (France/1954/190m/C) D: Sacha Guitry. C: Jean-Pierre Aumont, Gianna Maria Canale, Jeanne Boitel, Pierre Brasseur, Daniel Gelin, Sacha Guitry, O.W. Fisher, Raymond Pellegrin, Danielle Darrieux, Lana Marconi, Erich von Stroheim, Dany Roby, Henri Vidal, Clement Duhour, Serge Regianni, Maria Schell.

Marie Windsor. *The Story of Mankind* (US/1957/100m/C) D: Irwin Allen. B/on the book by Hendrik Van Loon. C: Ronald Colman, Hedy Lamarr, Virginia Mayo, Agnes Moorehead, Peter Lorre, Dennis Hopper, Marie Wilson, Helmut Dantine, Edward Everett Horton, Reginald Gardiner, Francis X. Bushman, Anthony Dexter, Austin Green, Jim Ameche, Harpo Marx, Bobby Watson, Reginald Sheffield, Cedric Hardwicke, Cesar Romero.

Martine Carol. *Austerlitz* (aka *The Battle of Austerlitz*) (France-Italy-Yugoslavia/1959/166m/C) D: Abel Gance. C: Pierre Mondy, Jean Mercure, Jack Palance, Orson Welles, Claudia Cardinale, Georges Marchal, Roland Bartrop, Anthony Stuart, Jean Marais, Vittorio De Sica, Ettore Manni.

Micheline Presle. *Imperial Venus* (Italy-France/1962/140m/C) D: Jean Delannoy. C: Gina Lollobrigida, Stephen Boyd, Gabrielle Ferzetti, Raymond Pellegrin.

Monica Randal. *The Sea Pirate* (France-Italy-Spain/1967/85m/C) D: Roy Rowland. C: Gerard Barray, Antonella Lualdi, Terence Morgan, Giani Esposito, Frank Oliveras.

Ursula Andress. *The Loves and Times of Scaramouche* (aka *Scaramouche*) (Italy/1976/91m/C) D: Enzo Castellari. C: Michael Sarrazin, Aldo Maccione, Michael Forest.

Barbie Kielan. *Stuck on You* (US/1983/88m/C) D: Samuel Weil & Michael Herz. C: Irwin Corey, Daniel Harris, Robin Burroughs, Carl Sturmer, Julie Newdow.

296 Joyce, James (1882–1941)

Irish novelist and poet, considered to be one of the greatest writers of the 20th century. His best known works are *Ulysses* and *Finnegans Wake*. These are autobiographical, with the hero, Stephen Dedalus, representing Joyce. In 1904 Joyce left Ireland to wander Europe with Nora Barnacle. They had two children but did not marry until 1931. Nora is portrayed by Susan Lynch in the film *Nora*.

Maurice Roeves (as Stephen Dedalus). *Ulysses* (Ireland-GB-US/1967/140m) D: Joseph Strick. B/on the novel by James Joyce. C: Barbara Jefford, Milo O'Shea, T. P. McKenna, Martin Dempsey, Sheila O'Sullivan, Tony Doyle, Fionnula Flanagan, Eddie Golden, Maire Hastings, David Kelly, Rosaleen Linehan, Graham Lines, Joe Lynch, Anna Manahan, Pauline Melville, Desmond Perry, Charles Roberts, Cecil Sheehan, Maureen Toal, O.Z. Whitehead.

Bosco Hogan (as Stephen Dedalus). Luke Johnson (Young Stephen). *A Portrait of the Artist as a Young Man* (Ireland/1979/98m/C) D: Joseph Strick. B/on the novel by James Joyce. C: T. P. McKenna, John Gielgud, Rosaleen Linehan, Maureen Potter, Niall Buggy, Brian Murray, Brendan Caudwell, Desmond Cave, Danny Figgis, Susan Fitzgerald, Adrian Grenell, Leslie Laller, Desmond Perry, Cecel Sheehan.

Ewan McGregor. *Nora* (aka *Nora — Die leidenschaftliche Liebe von James Joyce*) (Ireland-GB-Italy-Germany/2000/106m/C) D: Pat Murphy. B/on the book by Brenda Maddox. C: Susan Lynch, Andrew Scott, Vinnie McCabe, Veronica Duffy, Aedin Moloney, Pauline McLynn, Darragh Kelly, Alan Devine, Peter McDonald, Paul Hickey, Kate O'Toole, Martin Murphy, Karl Scully.

297 Juarez, Benito Pablo (1806–1872)

Mexican revolutionary and statesman, Juarez first became President after the overthrow of **Santa Anna** and again after the fall of **Maximillian's** government. He died during a further rebellion, started by **Porfirio Diaz**.

Paul Muni. *Juarez* (US/1939/132m/BW) D: William Dieterle. B/on the novel *The Phantom Crown* by Bertita Harding and the play *Juarez and Maximillian* by Franz Werfel. C: Bette Davis, Brian Aherne, Claude Rains, John Garfield, Donald Crisp, Walter Kingsford, Harry Davenport, Gale Sondergaard, Joseph Calleia.

Jason Robards, Sr. *The Mad Empress* (aka *Juarez and Maximillian*) (Mexico-US /1939/72m/BW) D: Miguel Contreras Torres. C: Medea Novara, Lionel Atwill, Conrad Nagel, Guy Bates Post, Evelyn Brent, Earl Gunn, Frank McGlynn, Duncan Renaldo.

Fausto Tozzi. *The Treasure of the Aztecs* (aka *Der Schatz Der Azteken*) (aka *Die Pyramide Des Sonnengottes*) (Germany-France-Italy-Yugoslavia/1965/102–90m/C) D: Robert Siodmark. C: Lex Barker, Gerard Barray, Jeff Corey, Michele Girardon.

298 Judas Iscariot

The man who sold **Jesus Christ** for thirty pieces of silver, Judas realized he had made a bum deal and committed suicide. He was portrayed by Ian McShane in the TV mini-series *Jesus of Nazareth* (77), by Barrie Houghton in the TV film *The Day Christ Died* (80), and by Thomas Lockyer in *Jesus* (99).

Lucas Gridoux. *Golgotha* (France/1935/97m/BW) D: Julien Duvivier. C: Harry Baur, Robert Le Vigan, Jean Gabin, Charles Granval, Andre Bacque, Hubert Prelier, Edwige Feuillere, Juliette Verneuil, Vana Yami, Van Daele.

Marc Lobell. *The Great Commandment* (US/1941/78m/BW) D: Irving Pichel. C: John Beal, Marjorie Cooley, Albert Dekker, Harold Minjir, Olaf Hytten, Maurice Moscovich.

Michael Ansara. *The Robe* (US/1953/135m/C) D: Henry Koster. B/on the novel by Lloyd C. Douglas. Best Picture — Drama (GG). C: Richard Burton, Jean Simmons, Victor Mature, Michael Rennie, Jay Robinson, Dean Jagger, Torin Thatcher, Richard Boone, Ernest Thesiger, Cameron Mitchell (the voice of Jesus Christ).

James Griffith. *Day of Triumph* (US/1954/110m/C) D: Irving Pichel & John T. Coyle. C: Lee J. Cobb, Robert Wilson, Ralph Freud, Tyler McVey, Michael Connors, Joanne Dru, Lowell Gilmore, Anthony Warde, Peter Whitney, Everett Glass.

Manuel Monroy. *The Redeemer* (Spain/1959/93m/C) D: Joseph Breen. C: Luis Alvarez, Maruchi Fresno, Felix Acaso, Antonio Vilar, Virgilio Teixeira, Carlos Casaravilla, Sebastian Cabot (Narrator).

Rip Torn. *King of Kings* (US/1961/168m/C) D: Nicholas Ray. C: Jeffrey Hunter, Siobhan McKenna, Hurd Hatfield, Viveca Lindfors, Rita Gam, Carmen Sevilla, Brigid Bazlen, Harry Guardino, Frank Thring, Guy Rolfe, Maurice Marsac, Gregoire Aslan, Royal Dano, Robert Ryan, Gerard Tichy, Michael Wager, Tino Barrero, Jose Antonio, Orson Welles (Narrator).

John Drew Barrymore. *Pontius Pilate* (Italy-France/1962/100m/C) D: Irving Rapper. C: Jean Marais, Jeanne Crain, Basil Rathbone, Leticia Roman, Livio Lorenzon.

Otello Sestilli. *The Gospel According to St. Matthew* (France-Italy/1964/142m/ BW) D: Pier Paolo Pasolini. B/on the *New Testament book of Matthew*. C: Enrique Irazoqui, Susanna Pasolini, Mario Socrate, Marcello Morante, Alfonso Gatto, Rodolfo Wilcock, Francesco Leonetti, Amerigo Bevilacqua, Settimio Di Porto, Ferruccio Nuzzo, Alessandro Tosca, Paolo Tedesco, Franca Cupane, Giacomo Morante, Rosario Migale.

David McCallum. *The Greatest Story Ever Told* (US/1965/141m/C) D: George Stevens. B/on the book by Fulton Oursler. C: Max von Sydow, Dorothy McGuire, Robert Loggia, Claude Rains, Jose Ferrer, Charlton Heston, Donald Pleasence, Gary Raymond, Robert Blake, John Considine, David Hedison, Joanna Dunham, Sal Mineo, Van Heflin, Ed Wynn, Martin Landau, Telly Savalas, Sidney Poitier, Roddy McDowell, Angela Lansbury, Richard Conte, Carroll Baker, Janet Margolin, Burt Brinckerhoff, Tom Reese.

Carl Anderson. *Jesus Christ, Superstar* (US/1973/107m/C) D: Norman Jewison. B/on the rock opera by Tim Rice & Andrew Lloyd Webber. C: Ted Neeley, Yvonne Elliman, Barry Dennen, Bob Bingham, Larry T. Marshall, Joshua Mostel, Philip Toubus.

Thomas Leventhal. *The Gospel Road* (US/1973/93m/C) D: Robert Elfstrom. C: Robert Elfstrom, June Carter Cash, Larry Lee, Paul Smith, Alan Dater, John Paul Kay, Gelles LaBlanc, Robert Elfstrom, Jr., Terrance W. Mannock, Sean Armstrong, Lyle Nicholson, Steven Chernoff, Jonathan Sanders, Ulf Pollack.

David Haskell. *Godspell* (US/1973/103m/C) D: David Greene. B/on the musical play by John-Michael Tebelak & Stephen Schwartz. C: Victor Garber, Jerry Sroka, Lynne Thigpen, Katie Hanley, Robin Lamont, Gilmer McCormick.

Scott Wilson. *The Passover Plot* (Israel/1976/108m/C) D: Michael Campus. B/on the book by Hugh Schonfield. C: Harry Andrews, Hugh Griffith, Zalman King, Donald Pleasence, Dan Ades, Michael Baselon, Lewis van Bergen, William Burns, Dan Hedaya, Kevin O'Connor, Robert Walker.

Eli Danker. *Jesus* (US/1979/117m/C) D: Peter Sykes & John Kirsh. B/on the *New Testament book of Luke*. C: Brian Deacon, Rivka Noiman, Yossef Shiloah, Niko Nitai, Gadi Rol, Richard Peterson, Eli Cohen, Shmuel Tal, Kobi Assaf, Talia Shapira, Mosko Alkalai, Nisim Gerama, Leonid Weinstein, Peter Frye, David Goldberg.

Harvey Keitel. *The Last Temptation of Christ* (US/1988/164m/C) D: Martin Scorsese. B/on the novel by Nikos Kazantzakis. C: Willem Dafoe, Paul Greco, Verna Bloom, Barbara Hershey, Gary Basaraba, Victor Argo, Michael Been, John Lurie, Harry Dean Stanton, David Bowie, Nehemiah Persoff, Leo Burmester, Irvin Kershner, Andre Gregory, Tomas Arana, Juliette Caton, Roberts Blossom, Barry Miller, Alan Rosenberg.

299 Julius II, Pope (1443–1513)

(Giuliano della Rovere) A powerful Pope during the Renaissance, Julius is remembered as a great patron of artists including such men as **Michealangelo** and **Bramante**.

F.B.J. Sharpe. *The Cardinal* (GB/1936/70m/BW) D: Sinclair Hill. B/on the play by Louis N. Parker. C: Matheson Lang, Eric Portman, Wilfred Fletcher, Robert Atkins.

Rex Harrison. *The Agony and the Ecstasy* (US/1965/136m/C) D: Carol Reed. B/on the novel by Irving Stone. C: Charlton Heston, Diane Cilento, Harry Andrews, Tomas Milian.

300 Kahlo, Frida (1907–1954)

One of the great painters of Mexico, whose work is extremely passionate, reflecting physical pain and the emotional anguish of her life with husband, **Diego Rivera**. They had a loving, but tempestuous relationship, divorcing, remarrying, but separating again. They opened their home to **Leon Trotsky** when he fled to Mexico.

Ofelia Medina. *Frida* (Mexico/1984/108m/C) D: Paul Leduc. C: Juan Jose Gurrola, Max Kerlow, Salvador Sanchez, Valentina Leduc, Claudio Brook.

Corina Katt. *Cradle Will Rock* (US/1999/109m/C) D: Tim Robbins. C: Hank Azaria, Rubén Blades, Joan Cusack, John Cusack, Cary Elwes, Philip Baker Hall, Cherry Jones, Angus MacFadyen, Bill Murray, Vanessa Redgrave, Susan Sarandon, John Turturro, Barnard Hughes, John Carpenter, Gretchen Mol.

301 Karpis, Alvin (1908–1979)

Once a member of **Ma Barker's** gang, Karpis was one of the last of the famous Depression era gangsters and the only one to be personally arrested by **J. Edgar Hoover**. In the TV movie *The FBI Story — Alvin Karpis* (74) he was played by Robert Foxworth.

Paul Dubov. *Guns Don't Argue* (US/1955/92m/BW) D: Bill Karn & Richard Kahn. Feature film edited from the TV series *Gangbusters*. C: Myron Healey, Lyle Talbot, Jean Harvey, Sam Edwards, Richard Crane, Tamar Cooper, Baynes Barron, Doug Wilson.

Paul Dubov. *Ma Barker's Killer Brood* (US/1960/82m/BW) D: Bill Karn. C: Lurene Tuttle, Tris Coffin, Robert Kendall, Vic Lundin, Don Grady, Eric Sinclair, Ronald Foster.

Brad Dexter. *The Private Files of J. Edgar Hoover* (US/1978/112m/C) D: Larry Cohen. C: Broderick Crawford, Jose Ferrer, Michael Parks, Ronee Blakely, Michael Sacks, Raymond St. Jacques, Andrew Duggan, Howard Da Silva, James Wainwright, William Jordan, Richard M. Dixon, Gordon Zimmerman, Lloyd Nolan, June Havoc, Dan Dailey, John Marley, Lloyd Gough.

302 Katherine of Aragon (1485–1536)

The first of **Henry VIII's** wives, Katharine was the mother of **Mary I,** but having borne him no sons Henry had the marriage annulled.

Rosalie Crutchley. *The Sword and the Rose* (aka *When Knighthood Was in Flower*) (GB/1953/91m/C) D: Ken Annakin. B/on the novel When *Knighthood Was in Flower* by Charles Major. C: Richard Todd, Glynis Johns, James Robertson Justice, Michael Gough, Jane Barrett, Peter Copley, D.A. Clarke-Smith, Bryan Coleman, Jean Mercure.

Irene Papas. *Anne of the Thousand Days* (GB/1969/145m/C) D: Charles Jarrott. B/on the play by Maxwell Anderson. C: Richard Burton, Genevieve Bujold, Anthony Quayle, John Colicos, Michael Hordern, Katharine Blake, William Squire, Lesley Patterson, Nicola Pagett.

Frances Cuka. *The Six Wives of Henry VIII* (aka *Henry VIII and His Six Wives*) (GB/1972/125m/C) D: Waris Hussein. C: Keith Michell, Charlotte Rampling, Jane Asher, Jenny Bos, Lynne Frederick, Barbara Leigh-Hunt, Donald Pleasence, Simon Henderson, Annette Crosbie, John Bryans, Michael Goodliffe, Bernard Hepton, Dorothy Tutin.

303 Kaufman, George Simon (1889–1961)

American playwright, Kaufman wrote (with **Moss Hart**) *The Man Who Came to Dinner* and *You Can't Take it With You*. He also worked on such screenplays as *Star Spangled Rhythm* (42) and *A Night at the Opera* (35).

Jason Robards, Jr. *Act One* (US/1964/110m/BW) D: Dore Schary. B/on the book by Moss Hart. C: George Hamilton, Jack Klugman, Ruth Ford, Eli Wallach, Earl Montgomery.

David Thornton. *Mrs. Parker and the Vicious Circle* (US/1994/125m/C) D: Alan Rudolph. C: Jennifer Jason Leigh, Campbell Scott, Matthew Broderick, Peter Gallagher, Tom McGowan, Lili Taylor, Keith Carradine, Nick Cassavetes, Malcolm Gets, Gwyneth Paltrow.

304 Keitel, Wilhelm (1882–1946)

Supreme Commander of **Hitler's** armies, Keitel was convicted and executed at the Nuremburg Trials for his crimes against humanity.

John Hoyt. *The Desert Fox* (aka *Rommel — Desert Fox*) (US/1951/88m/BW) D: Henry Hathaway. B/on the book *Rommel* by Desmond Young. C: James Mason, Cedric Hardwicke, Jessica Tandy, Luther Adler, Leo G. Carroll, Eduard Franz, Jack Baston.

Jochen Hauer. *The Jackboot Mutiny* (aka *Es Geschah Am 20 Juli*) (Germany/1955/85m/BW) D: G.W. Pabst. C: Bernhard Wicki, Karl Ludwig Diehl, Carl Wery, Kurt Meisel.

Leopold Hainisch. *The Last Ten Days* (aka *Ten Days to Die*) (aka *Last Ten Days of Adolf Hitler*) (aka *Der Letzte Akt*) (aka *The Last Act*) (Germany/1955/115m/BW) D: G.W. Pabst. B/on the novel *Ten Days to Die* by M.A. Mussanno. C: Albin Skoda, Oskar Werner, Lotte Tobisch, Willy Krause, Erich Stuckmann, Edmund Erlandsen, Kurt Eilers, Helga Dohrn, Otto Schmoele.

Richard Grey. *The Two-Headed Spy* (GB/1959/93m/BW) D: Andre De Toth. C: Jack Hawkins, Gia Scala, Erik Schumann, Alexander Knox, Felix Aylmer, Laurence Naismith, Kenneth Griffith, Walter Hudd, Donald Pleasence, Michael Caine, Bernard Fox.

Carl Esmond. *Hitler* (aka *Women of Nazi Germany*) (US/1962/107m/BW) D: Stuart Heisler. C: Richard Basehart, Cordula Trantow, Maria Emo, Martin Kosleck, John Banner, Martin Brandt, William Sargent, Gregory Gay, Thodore Marcuse, Rick Traeger, John Mitchum, G. Stanley Jones, Walter Kohler, Berry Kroeger.

Gabriele Ferzetti. *Hitler: The Last Ten Days* (GB-Italy/1973/106m/C) D: Ennio De Concini. B/on the book *The Last Days of the Chancellery* by Gerhardt Boldt. C: Alec Guinness, Simon Ward, Doris Kunstmann, John Bennett, Philip Stone, Mark Kingston.

305 Kelly, George "Machine Gun" (1897–1954)

A small-time bank robber and kidnapper, Kelly was captured and sent to Alcatraz Prison where he died in 1954.

Charles Bronson. *Machine Gun Kelly* (US/1958/84m/BW) D: Roger Corman. C: Susan Cabot, Barboura Morris, Morey Amsterdam, Wally Campo, Jack Lambert, Connie Gilchrist.

Vic Lundin. *Ma Barker's Killer Brood* (US/1960/82m/BW) D: Bill Karn. C: Lurene Tuttle, Tris Coffin, Paul Dubov, Robert Kendall, Don Grady, Eric Sinclair, Ronald Foster.

Harris Yulin. *Melvin Purvis: G-Man* (aka *The Legend of Machine Gun Kelly*) (US/1974/78m/C) D: Dan Curtis. C: Dale Robertson, Margaret Blye, Matt Clark, David Canary.

306 Kelly, Ned (1854–1880)

Australia's legendary outlaw, Kelly's criminal career lasted less than two years before he was caught and hanged.

Hay Simpson. *When the Kellys Rode* (Australia/1934/79m/BW) D: Harry Southwell. C: George Randall, Jack Appleton, Norman Waite.

Bob Chitty. *The Glenrowan Affair* (Australia/1951/70m/BW) D: Rupe Kathner. C: Ben Crowe, Larry Crowhurst, Bill Crowe, Rupe Kathner.

Mick Jagger. *Ned Kelly* (aka *Ned Kelly, Outlaw*) (GB/1970/103m/C) D: Tony Richardson. C: Allen Bickford, Geoff Gilmour, Mark McManus, Clarissa Kaye.

307 Kennedy, Jackie (1929–1995)

(Jacqueline Lee Bouvier Kennedy Onassis) The widow of **John F. Kennedy**, Jackie became the world's number one celebrity following her marriage to Aristotle Onassis. In TV movies she has been played by Jaclyn Smith in *Jacqueline Bouvier Kennedy* (81), Blair Brown in *Kennedy* (83), Juanin Clay in *Robert Kennedy and His Times* (85), Francesca Annis in *Onassis: The Richest Man in the World* (88), and Joanne Whalley in the TV mini-series *Jacqueline Bouvier Kennedy Onassis* (2000).

Jodi Farber. *JFK* (US/1991/189m/C) D: Oliver Stone. B/on *Crossfire* by Jim Marrs and *On the Trail of the Assassins* by Jim Garrison. C: Kevin Costner, Sissy Spacek, Kevin Bacon, Gary Oldman, Brian Doyle-Murray, Tom Howard, Steve Reed.

Rhoda Griffis. *Love Field* (US/1992/104m/C) D: Jonathan Kaplan. C: Michelle Pfeiffer, Dennis Haysbert, Stephanie McFadden, Louise Latham, Peggy Rea, Bob Gill.

Jodie Farber. *Malcolm X* (US/1992/201m/C) D: Spike Lee. C: Denzel Washington, Steve Reed, Miki Howard, Angela Bassett, Albert Hall, Al Freeman, Jr., Delroy Lindo, Spike Lee, Theresa Randle, Kate Vernon, Lonette McKee, Tommy Hollis, James McDaniel, Ernest Thomas, Jean LaMarre, Craig Wasson, Ricky Gordon.

Chris Wall. *Ruby* (US/1992/110m/C) D: John MacKenzie. B/on the play *Love Child* by Stephen Davis. C: Danny Aiello, Joe Viterelli, Gerard David, Kevin Wiggins, Willie Garson, Sherilyn Fenn, Jane Hamilton, Carmine Caridi.

Stephanie Romanov. *Thirteen Days* (US/2000/145m/C/BW) D: Roger Donaldson. B/on the book *The Kennedy Tapes — Inside the White House During the Cuban Missile Crisis* by Ernest R. May and Philip D. Zelikow. C: Kevin Costner, Bruce Greenwood, Steven Culp, Dylan Baker, Henry Strozier, Frank Wood, Len Cariou, Janet Coleman, Bill Smitrovich, Ed Lauter, Dakin Matthews, Walter Adrian, Peter White, Tim Kelleher.

308 Kennedy, John Fitzgerald (1917–1963)

The 35th President of the U.S., JFK was assassinated on November 22, 1963. He has been played in many TV movies and mini-series including *The Kennedys of Massachusetts* by Steven Weber (90), *Onassis: The Richest Man in the World* by David Gilliam (88), *LBJ: The Early Years* by Charles Frank (87), *J. Edgar Hoover* by Art Hindle (87), *Robert Kennedy and His Times* by Cliff DeYoung (85), *Blood Feud* by Sam Groom (83), *Kennedy* by Martin Sheen (83), *Jacqueline Bouvier Kennedy* by James Franciscus (81), *King* by Will Jordan (78), *Young Joe, The Forgotten Kennedy* by Sam Chew, Jr. (77), *Johnny, We Hardly Knew Ye* by Paul Rudd (77), *The Missiles of October* by William Devane (74), and the TV mini-series *Jacqueline Bouvier Kennedy Onassis* by Tim Matheson (2000).

Cliff Robertson. *PT 109* (US/1963/140m/BW) D: Leslie H. Martinson. C: Ty Hardin, James Gregory, Robert Culp, Grant Williams, Michael Pate, Robert Blake.

William Jordan. *The Private Files of J. Edgar Hoover* (US/1978/112m/C) D: Larry Cohen. C: Broderick Crawford, Jose Ferrer, Michael Parks, Ronee Blakely, Michael Sacks, Raymond St. Jacques, Andrew Duggan, Howard Da Silva, James Wainwright, Brad Dexter, Richard M. Dixon, Gordon Zimmerman, Lloyd Nolan, June Havoc, Dan Dailey, John Marley, Lloyd Gough.

Robert Hogan. *Prince Jack* (US/1984/100m/C) D: Bert Lovitt. C: James F. Kelly, Kenneth Mars, Lloyd Nolan, Cameron Mitchell, Robert Guillame, Theodore Bikel.

Steve Reed. *JFK* (US/1991/189m/C) D: Oliver Stone. B/on *Crossfire* by Jim Marrs and *On the Trail of the Assassins* by Jim Garrison. C: Kevin Costner, Sissy Spacek, Kevin Bacon, Gary Oldman, Brian Doyle-Murray, Tom Howard, Jodi Farber.

Steve Reed. *Malcolm X* (US/1992/201m/C) D: Spike Lee. C: Denzel Washington, Jodie Farber, Miki Howard, Angela Bassett, Albert Hall, Al Freeman, Jr., Delroy Lindo, Spike Lee, Theresa Randle, Kate Vernon, Lonette McKee, Tommy Hollis, James McDaniel, Ernest Thomas, Jean LaMarre, Craig Wasson, Ricky Gordon.

Bob Gill. *Love Field* (US/1992/104m/C) D: Jonathan Kaplan. C: Michelle Pfeiffer, Dennis Haysbert, Stephanie McFadden, Louise Latham, Peggy Rea, Rhoda Griffis.

Gerard David (in Las Vegas scene). Kevin Wiggins (in Dallas scene). *Ruby* (US/1992/110m/C) D: John MacKenzie. B/on the play *Love Child* by Stephen Davis. C: Danny Aiello, Joe Viterelli, Willie Garson, Chris Wall, Sherilyn Fenn, Jane Hamilton, Carmine Caridi.

Jed Gillin (voice only). *Forrest Gump* (US/1994/142m/C) D: Robert Zemeckis. B/on the novel by Winston Groom. Best Picture (AA), Best Director (AA). C: Tom Hanks, Gary Sinise, Robin Wright, Sally Field, Mykelti Williamson, Peter Dobson, Richard D'Allesandro, and the voices of John William Galt, Joe Stefanelli, and Joe Alaskey.

Bruce Greenwood. *Thirteen Days* (US/2000/145m/C/BW) D: Roger Donaldson. B/on the book *The Kennedy Tapes—Inside the White House During the Cuban Missile Crisis* by Ernest R. May and Philip D. Zelikow. C: Kevin Costner, Steven Culp, Dylan Baker, Henry Strozier, Frank Wood, Len Cariou, Janet Coleman, Stephanie Romanov, Bill Smitrovich, Ed Lauter, Dakin Matthews, Walter Adrian, Peter White, Tim Kelleher.

Tuck Milligan. *Company Man* (France-GB-US/2000/86m/C) D: Peter Askin, Douglas McGrath. C: Paul Guilfoyle, Jeffrey Jones, Reathel Bean, Harriet Koppel, Douglas McGrath, Sigourney Weaver, Terry Beaver, Sean Dugan, Grant Walden, Nathan Dean, Nathan Bean, John Randolph Jones, Ryan Phillippe, Kim Merrill, Merwin Goldsmith, Anthony LaPaglia, Meredith Patterson.

309 Kennedy, Robert Francis (1925–1968)

The brother of **John F. Kennedy**, RFK was assassinated while campaigning for the Presidency in June 1968. Portrayals in TV productions include: Randle Mell in *The Kennedys of Massachusetts* (90), Brad Davis in *Robert Kennedy and His Times* (85), John Shea in *Kennedy* (83), Cotter Smith in *Blood Feud* (83), Cliff DeYoung in *King* (78), Sam Chew, Jr. in *Tail Gunner Joe* (77), Shane Kerwin in *Young Joe, The Forgotten Kennedy* (77), Jim McMullen in *Francis Gary Powers: The True Story of the U2 Spy Incident* (76), Martin Sheen in *The Missiles of October* (74), Andrew McCarthy in the TV mini-series *Jacqueline Bouvier Kennedy Onassis* (2000). James F. Kelly has played Kennedy many times in TV films such as *Jacqueline Bouvier Kennedy* (81), *J. Edgar Hoover* (87), *LBJ: The Early Years* (87), *Onassis: The Richest Man in the World* (88), and *Marilyn and Bobby* (93).

Michael Parks. *The Private Files of J. Edgar Hoover* (US/1978/112m/C) D: Larry Cohen. C: Broderick Crawford, Jose Ferrer, Ronee Blakely, Michael Sacks, Raymond St. Jacques, Andrew Duggan, Howard Da Silva, James Wainwright, Brad Dexter, William Jordan, Richard M. Dixon, Gordon Zimmerman, Lloyd Nolan, June Havoc, Dan Dailey, John Marley, Lloyd Gough.

James F. Kelly. *Prince Jack* (US/1984/100m/C) D: Bert Lovitt. C: Robert Hogan, Kenneth Mars, Lloyd Nolan, Cameron Mitchell, Robert Guillame, Theodore Bikel.

Kevin Anderson. *Hoffa* (US/1992/140m/C) D: Danny De Vito. C: Jack Nicholson, Danny De Vito, Armand Assante, J.T. Walsh, John C. Reilly, Frank Whaley.

Steven Culp. *Thirteen Days* (US/2000/145m/C/BW) D: Roger Donaldson. B/on the book *The Kennedy Tapes — Inside the White House During the Cuban Missile Crisis* by Ernest R. May and Philip D. Zelikow. C: Kevin Costner, Bruce Greenwood, Dylan Baker, Henry Strozier, Frank Wood, Len Cariou, Janet Coleman, Stephanie Romanov, Bill Smitrovich, Ed Lauter, Dakin Matthews, Walter Adrian, Peter White, Tim Kelleher.

310 Kerouac, Jack (1922–1969)

American writer and chronicler of the "Beat Generation," Kerouac's best known work is *On the Road*. (See **Burroughs, William S.** and **Ginsberg, Allen**)

John Heard. *Heart Beat* (US/1979/109m/C) D: John Byrum. B/on the book by Carolyn Cassady. C: Nick Nolte, Sissy Spacek, Ray Sharkey, Anne Dusenberry.

Jack Coulter. Seth Gordon (Young Jack). *Kerouac* (aka *Jack Kerouac's America*) (US/1985/78m/C) D: John Antonelli. C: David Andrews, Jonah Pearson, John Rousseau, Patrick Turner.

Johnny Depp. *The Source* (US/1999/88m/BW/C) D: Chuck Workman C: Dennis Hopper, John Turturro.

Daniel Martínez. *Beat* (US/2000/89m/C) D: Gary Walkow. C: Courtney Love, Norman Reedus, Ron Livingston, Kiefer Sutherland, Kyle Secor, Sam Trammell, Lisa Sheridan, Rene Rubio, Georgiana Sîrbu, Tommy Perna, Alec Von Bargen, Steve Hedden, Patricia De Llaca, Luis Felipe Tovar, Luisa Huertas, Darren Ross, Serafina De Lorca.

311 Kidd, (Captain) William (1645?–1701)

A British pirate who operated off the African coast and in the West Indies, Kidd was captured and hanged leaving behind rumors of vast fortunes of buried treasure. Some of his treasure was found in the tropical paradise of Long Island, New York but the rest may still be out there.

Charles Laughton. *Captain Kidd* (US/1945/89m/BW) D: Rowland V. Lee. C: Randolph Scott, Barbara Britton, Reginald Owen, Miles Mander, John Carradine.

Alan Napier. *Double Crossbones* (US/1950/75m) D: Charles Barton. C: Donald O'Connor, Helena Carter, Will Geer, John Emery, Hope Emerson, Robert Barrat, Louis Bacigalupi.

Charles Laughton. *Abbott and Costello Meet Captain Kidd* (US/1952/70m/C) D: Charles Lamont. C: Bud Abbott, Lou Costello, Hillary Brooke, Fran Warren, Leif Erickson, Rex Lease.

Robert Warwick. *Against All Flags* (US/1952/83m/C) D: George Sherman. C: Errol Flynn, Maureen O'Hara, Anthony Quinn, Olaf Hytten, Mildred Natwick.

Anthony Dexter. *Captain Kidd and the Slave Girl* (aka *The Slave Girl*) (US/1954/82m/C) D: Lew Landers. C: Zsa Zsa Gabor, Alan Hale, Jr., James Seay, Lyle Talbot.

Gary Reinike. *George's Island* (Canada/1992/89m/C) D: Paul Donovan. C: Ian Bannen, Sheila McCarthy, Maury Chaykin, Nathaniel Moreau, Vicki Ridler.

312 King, Martin Luther, Jr. (1929–1968)

The primary figure in the American Civil Rights movement, King was assassinated in April 1968. Television portrayals of King have been by Charles Brown in the mini-series *Kennedy* (83), Paul Winfield in the mini-series *King* (78), and in *Boycott* (2001) by Jeffrey Wright.

Raymond St. Jacques. *The Private Files of J. Edgar Hoover* (US/1978/112m/C) D: Larry Cohen. C: Broderick Crawford, Jose Ferrer, Michael Parks, Ronee Blakely, Michael Sacks, Andrew Duggan, Howard Da Silva, James Wainwright, Brad Dexter, William Jordan, Richard M. Dixon, Gordon Zimmerman, Lloyd Nolan, June Havoc, Dan Dailey, John Marley, Lloyd Gough.

Robert Guillaume. *Prince Jack* (US/1984/100m/C) D: Bert Lovitt. C: Robert Hogan, James F. Kelly, Kenneth Mars, Lloyd Nolan, Cameron Mitchell, Theodore Bikel.

LeVar Burton. *Ali* (US/2001/158m/C) D: Michael Mann. C: Will Smith, Jamie Foxx, Jon Voight, Mario Van Peebles, Ron Silver, Jeffrey Wright, Mykelti Williamson, Vincent De Paul, Jon A. Barnes, Michael Bentt, Malick Bowens, Candy Ann Brown, David Cubitt, Lee Cummings, James Currie, Rufus Dorsey, Martha Edgerton, Giancarlo Esposito, Sheldon Fogel, Themba Gasa, Nona M. Gaye, Ross Haines, Maestro Harrell, Michael Michele, Joe Morton, Patrick New, Al Quinn, Paul Rodriguez, Gailard Sartain, Charles Shufford, Jada Pinkett Smith, James Toney, Jack Truman, William Utay, Wade Williams.

313 Kipling, Joseph Rudyard (1865–1936)

The first English winner of the Nobel Prize for Literature (in 1907), Kipling's works include *The Jungle Book, Captains Courageous* and *Kim.*

Reginald Sheffield. *Gunga Din* (US/1939/117m/BW) D: George Stevens. B/on the poem by Rudyard Kipling. C: Cary Grant, Victor McLaglen, Douglas Fairbanks, Jr., Sam Jaffe, Eduardo Cianelli, Joan Fontaine, Montagu Love, Robert Coote.

Paul Scardon. *The Adventures of Mark Twain* (US/1944/130m/BW) D: Irving Rapper. C: Fredric March, Alexis Smith, C. Aubrey Smith, John Carradine, Brandon Hurst, Douglas Wood.

Christopher Plummer. *The Man Who Would Be King* (GB/1975/129m/C) D: John Huston. B/on the story by Rudyard Kipling. C: Sean Connery, Michael Caine, Saeed Jaffrey.

314 Kissinger, Henry Alfred (1923–   )

Secretary of State to **Richard Nixon** and **Gerald Ford**, Kissinger negotiated the cease fire between the U.S. and North Viet Nam in 1973. TV portrayals have been by Theodore Bikel in *The Final Days* (89) and Ron Silver in *Kissinger and Nixon* (95).

Roger Bowen. *Tunnelvision* (US/1976/75m/C) D: Neal Israel & Brad Swirnoff. C: Phil Proctor, Rick Hurst, Laraine Newman, Howard Hesseman, Ernie Anderson.

Byron Kane. *The Pink Panther Strikes Again* (US/1976/103m/C) D: Blake Edwards. C: Peter Sellers, Herbert Lom, Colin Blakely, Leslie-Anne Down, Burt Kwouk, Dick Crockett.

Jules Kreitzer. *The Cayman Triangle* (US/1977/92m/C) D: Anderson Humphreys. C: Reid Dennis, Anderson Humphreys, Ed Beheler, John Morgan.

Peter Jurasik. *Born Again* (US/1978/110m/C) D: Irving Rapper. B/on the book by Charles Colson. C: Dean Jones, Anne Francis, Jay Robinson, Harry Spillman.

Paul Sorvino. *Nixon* (US/1995/190m/C) D: Oliver Stone. C: Anthony Hopkins, Joan Allen, Powers Boothe, Ed Harris, Bob Hoskins, E.G. Marshall, David Paymer, David Hyde Pierce, Mary Steenburgen, J.T. Walsh, James Woods, Bryan Bedford.

Saul Rubinek. *Dick* (US/1999/95m) D: Andrew Fleming. C: Kirsten Dunst, Michelle Williams, Dan Hedaya, Will Ferrell, Bruce McCulloch, Dave Foley, Jim Breuer, Terri Garr, Ana Gasteyer, Harry Shearer, Richard Fitzpatrick, Len Doncheff, Deborah Grover.

315 Kitchner, Horatio Herbert, 1st Earl of Kitchener (1850–1916)

British soldier who successfully reconquered the Sudan (See **Gordon, Gen. Charles**), Kitchener was killed while serving in WWI as the Secretary of War.

Jean Galland. *Entente Cordiale* (France/1938/95m/BW) D: Marcel L'Herbier. B/on *Edward VII and His Times* by Andre Maurois. C: Victor Francen, Gaby Morlay, Andre Lefaur, Marcelle Praince, Jeanine Darcey, Arlette Marchal, Andre Roanne, Jacques Catelain, Jean Toulot, Jacques Baumer, Jean d'Yd, Jean Perrier.

Peter Arne. *Khartoum* (GB/1966/134m/C) D: Basil Deardon. C: Charlton Heston, Laurence Olivier, Richard Johnson, Ralph Richardson, Alexander Knox, Michael Hordern, Johnny Sekka, Nigel Green, Ralph Michael.

John Mills. *Young Winston* (GB/1972/145m/C) D: Richard Attenborough. B/on the book *My Early Life: A Roving Commission* by Winston Churchill. Best English-Language Foreign Film (GG). C: Simon Ward, Peter Cellier, Ronald Hines, Anne Bancroft, Robert Shaw, Laurence Naismith, William Dexter, Basil Dignam, Reginald Marsh, Anthony Hopkins, Robert Hardy, Colin Blakely, Michael Audreson, Jack Hawkins.

Alan Cassell. *Breaker Morant* (Australia/1980/107m/C) D: Bruce Beresford. B/on a play by Kenneth Ross. C: Edward Woodward, Jack Thompson, Bryan Brown.

316 Kublai Khan (1215–1294)

Mongol ruler of China, it was to Kublai's court that **Marco Polo** journeyed.

George Barbier. *The Adventures of Marco Polo* (US/1938/100m/BW) D: Archie Mayo. C: Gary Cooper, Sigrid Gurie, Basil Rathbone, Ernest Truex, Binnie Barnes, Alan Hale, H.B. Warner.

Camillo Pilotto. *Marco Polo* (aka *Grand Khan*) (Italy-France/1962/95m/C) D: Hugo Fregonese & Piero Pierot. C: Rory Calhoun, Yoko Tani, Robert Hundar.

Anthony Quinn. *Marco the Magnificent* (aka *The Fabulous Adventures of Marco Polo*) (France-Italy-Afghanistan-Egypt-Yugoslavia/1965/115–100m/C) D: Denys De la Patèlliere, Noel Howard, Christian-Jaque & Cliff Lyons. C: Horst Bucholz, Orson Welles.

Zero Mostel. *Marco* (US/1973/109m/C) D: Seymour Robbie. C: Desi Arnaz, Jr., Jack Weston, Cie Cie Win, Aimee Eccles, Romeo Muller, Fred Sadoff.

317 Kutuzov, Mikhail Ilarianovich (1745–1813)

Russian field marshal, Kutuzov successfully commanded the Russian armies during **Napoleon's** invasion of 1812.

Alexei Diki. *1812* (aka *Kutuzov*) (USSR/1944/95m/BW) D: Vladimir Petrov. C: Sergei Mezhinsky, Y. Kaluzhsky, Sergo Zaqariadze, Nikolai Okhlopkov, Sergei Blinnikov, V. Gotovtsev, A. Polyakov, Nikolai Brilling, Boris Chirkov, Mikhail Pugovkin, Ivan Ryzhov, K. Shilovtsev, Aleksandr Stepanov, Ivan Skuratov, G. Terekhov, N. Timchenko, Vladimir Yershov.

Oscar Homolka. *War and Peace* (US-Italy/1956/208m/C) D: King Vidor. B/on the novel by Leo Tolstoy. C: Audrey Hepburn, Henry Fonda, Mel Ferrer, Vittorio Gassman, John Mills, Herbert Lom, Anita Ekberg, Helmut Dantine, Savo Raskovitch.

Igor Ilyinsky. *Ballad of a Hussar* (USSR/1963/94m/C) D: Eldar Ryazanov. C: Larissa Golubkina.

Boris Zakhava. *War and Peace* (USSR/1966/373m/C) D: Sergei Bondarchuk. B/on the novel by Leo Tolstoy. C: Lyudmila Savelyeva, Sergei Bondarchuk, Viktor Stanitsin, Vyacheslav Tihonov, Hira Ivanov-Gubanova, Vladislav Strzhelchik, V. Murganov.

318 Lafayette, Marquis de 1757–1834

(Marie Joseph Paul Yves Roch Gilbert du Motier) French soldier and statesman, Lafayette fought for the Americans during the Revolution, and was given the rank of Major General at the age of 20. He has been portrayed by Ike Eisenman in the TV mini-series *The Bastard* (78), and by Sebastian Roché in *Liberty, the American Revolution* (97).

Boudreau. *Napoleon Bonaparte* (France/1934/140m/BW) D: Abel Gance. Three-dimensional sound version of Gance's 1927 epic *Napoléon*. C: Albert Dieudonné, Edmond von Daele, Alexandre Koubitsky, Antonin Artaud, Alberty, Jack Rye, Favière, Gina Manès, Suzanne Blanchetti, Marguerite Gance, Simone Genevois, Genica Missirio.

John Burton. *Marie Antoinette* (US/1938/160m/BW) D: W.S. Van Dyke II. B/on the book by Stefan Zweig. C: Norma Shearer, Tyrone Power, John Barrymore, Gladys George, Robert Morley, Anita Louise, Joseph Schildkraut, Albert Dekker, Scotty Becket, Alma Kruger, George Meeker, Wade Crosby, Anthony Warde, Walter Walker.

Larry Steers. *Magnificent Doll* (US/1946/93m/BW) D: Frank Borzage. C: Ginger Rogers, Burgess Meredith, David Niven, Robert Barrat, Grandon Rhodes, Arthur Space.

Wilton Graff. *The Black Book* (aka *Reign of Terror*) (US/1949/89m/BW) D: Anthony Mann. C: Robert Cummings, Arlene Dahl, Richard Hart, Arnold Moss, Richard Basehart, Wade Crosby, Jess Barker, Norman Lloyd, John Doucette.

Michel Le Royer. *Lafayette* (France/1962/110m/C) D: Jean Dreville. C: Howard St. John, Jack Hawkins, Wolfgang Priess, Orson Welles, Vittorio De Sica, Edmund Purdom, Liselotte Pulver, Albert Remy, Renee Saint-Cyr.

Lambert Wilson. *Jefferson in Paris* (US/1995/144m/C) D: James Ivory. C: Nick Nolte, Greta Scacchi, Jean-Pierre Aumont, Simon Callow, Seth Gilliam, James Earl Jones, Michael Lonsdale, Gwyneth Paltrow, Charlotte de Turckheim, Damien Groelle.

Michael Neeley (uncredited role). *The Patriot* (US/2000/164m/C) D: Roland Emmerich. C: Mel Gibson, Heath Ledger, Joely Richardson, Jason Isaacs, Donal Logue, Rene Auberjonois, Adam Baldwin, Lisa Brenner, Beatrice Bush, Bryan Chafin, Chris Cooper, Mary Jo Deschanel, Shan Omar Huey, Jay Arlen Jones, Tchéky Karyo, Terry Layman, Logan Lerman, Skye McCole Bartusiak, Trevor Morgan, Jamieson Price, Hank Stone, Kristian Truelsen, Mark Twogood, Joey D. Vieira, Tom Wilkinson, Grahame Wood, Peter Woodward.

319 Laffite, Jean (1780?–1826?)

A French born Louisiana pirate, Laffite received a general pardon from the U.S. for his help at the Battle of New Orleans in 1814.

Fredric March. *The Buccaneer* (US/1938/124m/BW) D: Cecil B. DeMille. B/on the novel *Lafitte the Pirate* by Lyle Saxon. C: Franciska Gaal, Akim Tamiroff, Margot Grahame, Walter Brennan, Ian Keith, Spring Byington, Anthony Quinn, Hugh Sothern.

Paul Henreid. *Last of the Buccaneers* (US/1950/78m/C) D: Lew Landers. C: Jack Oakie, Karin Booth, Mary Anderson, Edgar Barrier, John Dehner.

197 Lansky / 323

Yul Brynner. *The Buccaneer* (US/1958/121m/C) D: Anthony Quinn. C: Charlton Heston, Claire Bloom, Charles Boyer, Inger Stevens, Henry Hull, E.G. Marshall.

320 La Guardia, Fiorello Henrico (1882–1947)

Fiery U.S. politician and Mayor of New York City (1933–45), the "Little Flower" was also the subject of the 1959 Broadway musical *Fiorello!* He was played by Sorrell Booke in the TV movie *The Amazing Howard Hughes* (77).

David Manley. *The Pride of the Yankees* (US/1942/127m/BW) D: Sam Wood. C: Gary Cooper, Teresa Wright, Dan Duryea, Walter Brennan, Babe Ruth, Ernie Adams, Harry Harvey.

Phil Arnold. *The Court-Martial of Billy Mitchell* (aka *One Man Mutiny*) (US/1955/100m/C) D: Otto Preminger. C: Gary Cooper, Charles Bickford, Ralph Bellamy, Rod Steiger, Elizabeth Montgomery, James Daly, Dayton Lumis, Herbert Heyes, Tom McKee, Ian Wolfe.

321 Lamb, Lady Caroline (1785–1828)

Eccentric English novelist married to **Lord Melbourne**, Lady Caroline went mad in 1825 following the death of her former lover, **Lord Byron**.

Joan Greenwood. *The Bad Lord Byron* (GB/1949/83m/BW) D: David MacDonald. C: Dennis Price, Mai Zetterling, Linden Travers, Sonia Holm, Nora Swinburne, Irene Browne.

Sarah Miles. *Lady Caroline Lamb* (GB/1972/122m/C) D: Robert Bolt. C: Jon Finch, Richard Chamberlain, John Mills, Margaret Leighton, Ralph Richardson, Laurence Olivier.

322 Langtry, Lillie (1853–1929)

(Emily Charlotte Le Breton) An English actress reknowned for her great beauty, Lillie was also famous as the mistress of **Edward VII**.

Lillian Bond. *The Westerner* (US/1940/100m/BW) D: William Wyler. Best Supporting Actor (AA). C: Gary Cooper, Walter Brennan, Doris Davenport, Fred Stone, Forrest Tucker, Dana Andrews.

Naomi Chance. *The Trials of Oscar Wilde* (aka *The Man With the Green Carnation*) (aka *The Green Carnation*) (GB/1960/123m/C) D: Ken Hughes. B/on the book by Montgomery Hyde and the play *The Stringed Lute* by John Furnell. Best English-Language Foreign Film (GG). C: Peter Finch, John Fraser, Yvonne Mitchell, Lionel Jeffries, Nigel Patrick, James Mason, Emrys Jones, Laurence Naismith, Sonia Dresdel.

Ava Gardner. *The Life and Times of Judge Roy Bean* (US/1972/120m/C) D: John Huston. C: Paul Newman, John Huston, Jacqueline Bisset, Tab Hunter, Victoria Principal, Stacy Keach.

323 Lansky, Meyer (1902–1983)

(Maier Suchowljansky) Russian born, New York gambler and racketeer, Lansky was considered the financial genius of U.S. organized crime. The role of Hyman

Roth (played by Lee Strasburg) in *The Godfather, Part II* (74) was based on Lansky.

Mark Rydell. *Havana* (US/1990/140m/C) D: Sydney Pollack. C: Robert Redford, Lena Olin, Alan Arkin, Tomas Milian, Raul Julia, Tony Plana, Richard Farnsworth.

Ben Kingsley. *Bugsy* (US/1991/135m/C) D: Barry Levinson. B/on the book *We Only Kill Each Other: The Life and Bad Times of Bugsy Siegel* by Dean Jennings. C: Warren Beatty, Annette Bening, Harvey Keitel, Joe Mantegna, Elliott Gould, Wendy Phillips, Bill Graham, Don Carrara, Carmine Caridi, Ksenia Prohaska.

Patrick Dempsey. *Mobsters* (US/1991/104m/C) D: Michael Karbelnikoff. C: Christian Slater, Richard Grieco, Costas Mandylor, F. Murray Abraham, Anthony Quinn, Michael Gambon, Lara Flynn Boyle, Nicholas Sadler, Titus Welliver.

324 Lee, Robert Edward (1807–1870)

Commander of the southern armies, Lee's military brilliance and leadership sustained the Confederate States of America for nearly four years during the American Civil War.

Hobart Bosworth. *Abraham Lincoln* (US/1930/97m/BW) D: D.W. Griffith. C: Walter Huston, Una Merkel, Kay Hammond, E. Alyn Warren, Edgar Deering, Fred Warren, Frank Campeau, Francis Ford, Ian Keith, Oscar Apfel, Cameron Prud'Homme.

John Elliott. *Only the Brave* (US/1930/66m/BW) D: Franck Tuttle. C: Gary Cooper, Mary Brian, Phillips Holmes, James Neill, Guy Oliver, Morgan Farley.

John Elliott. *Carolina* (aka *House of Connelly*) (US/1934/83m/BW) D: Henry King. B/on the play *House of Connelly* by Paul Green. C: Janet Gaynor, Lionel Barrymore, Robert Young, Richard Cromwell, Roy Watson, Stepin Fetchit.

John Elliott. *Operator 13* (aka *Spy 13*) (US/1934/86m/BW) D: Richard Boleslavsky. B/on the novel by Robert W. Chambers. C: Marion Davies, Gary Cooper, Jean Parker, Katharine Alexander, Ted Healy, Sidney Toler, Douglas Dumbrille, Fred Warren. Franklin Parker.

Moroni Olson. *Santa Fe Trail* (US/1940/110m/BW) D: Michael Curtiz. C: Errol Flynn, Ronald Reagan, Olivia de Havilland, Raymond Massey, Alan Hale, Guinn Williams, Van Heflin, Charles Middleton, Erville Alderson, David Bruce, Frank Wilcox.

John Litel. *Salome, Where She Danced* (US/1945/90m/C) D: Charles Lamont. C: Yvonne De Carlo, Rod Cameron, David Bruce, Walter Slezak, Albert Dekker, Kurt Katch, Nestor Paiva.

Richard Cutting. *Seminole Uprising* (US/1955/74m/C) D: Earl Bellamy. B/on the novel *Bugle's Wake* by Curt Brandon. C: George Montgomery, Karin Booth, Steve Ritch.

Robert Osterloh. *Seven Angry Men* (US/1955/90m/BW) D: Charles Marquis Warren. C: Raymond Massey, Debra Paget, Jeffrey Hunter, Larry Pennell, Leo Gordon, Dennis Weaver.

Frank Baker. *Run of the Arrow* (US/1957/86m/C) D: Samuel Fuller. C: Rod Steiger, Sarita Montiel, Brian Keith, Ralph Meeker, Charles Bronson, Frank De Kova, Emile Avery.

Martin Sheen. *Gettysburg* (US/1993/248m/C) D: Ronald F. Maxwell. B/on the novel *The Killer Angels* by Michael Shaara. C: Tom Berenger, Jeff Daniels, Kevin Conway, C. Thomas Howell, Richard Jordan, Stephen Lang, Joseph Fuqua, Sam Elliott.

325 Leicester, Robert Dudley, Earl of (1532?–1588)

English soldier and statesman. During the reign of **Elizabeth I**, Robert Dudley became a favorite and was made Earl of Leicester. Elizabeth appointed him lieutenant general of the army sent to fight the Spanish. He died shortly thereafter.

Gavin Muir. *Mary of Scotland* (US/1936/123m/BW) D: John Ford. B/on the play by Maxwell Anderson. C: Katharine Hepburn, Fredric March, Florence Eldridge, Douglas Walton, John Carradine, Robert Barrat, Ian Keith, Ralph Forbes, Alan Mowbray, Walter Byron.

Herbert Marshall. *The Virgin Queen* (US/1955/92m/C) D: Henry Koster. C: Bette Davis, Richard Todd, Joan Collins, Jay Robinson, Dan O'Herlihy, Robert Douglas.

Daniel Massey. *Mary, Queen of Scots* (GB/1971/128m/C) D: Charles Jarrot. C: Vanessa Redgrave, Glenda Jackson, Patrick McGoohan, Timothy Dalton, Nigel Davenport, Trevor Howard, Ian Holm, Andrew Keir, Katherine Kath, Robert James, Richard Denning, Rick Warner.

Joseph Fiennes. *Elizabeth* (US/1998/124m/C) D: Shekar Kapur. AA Best makeup. GG Best Actress. C: Cate Blanchett, Fanny Ardant, James Frain, Richard Attenborough, Christopher Eccleston, Vincent Cassel, George Yiasoumi, Geoffrey Rush, Kathy Burke.

326 Lenin, Vladimir Ilych (1870–1924)

(Vladimir Ilyich Ulyanov) Bolshevik leader in the Russian Revolution, Lenin was the major force in the formation of the Soviet Union. In the mini-series *Stalin* (92) he was played by Maximilian Schell.

Tenen Holtz. *British Agent* (US/1934/75m/BW) D: Michael Curtiz. B/on the book *Memoirs of a British Agent* by Robert Bruce Lockhart. C: Leslie Howard, Kay Francis, William Gargan, Philip Reed, J. Carrol Naish, George Pearce, Cesar Romero, Olaf Hytten.

Boris Shchukin. *Lenin in October* (USSR/1937/111m/BW) D: Mikhail Romm. C: I. Golshtab, Vasily Vanin, Nikolai Okhlopkov, N. Svobodin.

K. Miuffko. *Great Dawn* (aka *They Wanted Peace*) (USSR/1938/73m/BW) D: Mikhail Chiaureli. C: F. Bagaschvili, Mikhail Gelovani, Tamara Makarova.

Maxim Strauch. *The Man With the Gun* (aka *The Man With a Gun*) (USSR/1938/88m/BW) D: Sergei Yutkevich. C: Mikhail Gelovani, Boris Tenin, Zoya Federova, Nikolai Cherkasov.

Boris Shchukin. *Lenin in 1918* (USSR/1939/133m/BW) D: Mikhail Romm. C: Mikhail Gelovani, Nikolai Cherkassov, Nikolai Okhlopkov, Vasily Vanin, V. Markov.

Maxim Strauch. *The Vyborg Side* (aka *New Horizons*) (USSR/1939/117–92m/BW) D: Grigori Kozintsev & Leonid Trauberg. C: Boris Chirkov, Mikhail Gelovani, Mikhail Zharov.

Maxim Strauch. *Yakov Sverdlov* (USSR/1940/128m/BW) D: Sergei Yutkevich. B/on the play by B. Levin & Pyotr Pavlenko. C: Pavel Kadochnikov, Nikolai Okhlopkov.

Maxim Strauch. *His Name Is Sukhe-Bator* (USSR/1942/BW) D: Alexander Zarkhi & Josif Heif. C: Lev Sverdlin, Nikolai Cherkasov, S. Goldstab.

I. Molchanov. *The Unforgettable Year: 1919* (USSR/1952/C) D: Mikhail Chiaureli. B/on the play by Vsevold Vishnevsky. C: Mikhail Gelovani, Boris Andreyev, M. Kovaleva, Yevgeni Samoilov, Victor Stanitsine, V. Koltsov, Gnat Yura, L. Korsakov, Sergei Lukyanov.

Nikolai Plotnikov. *Prologue* (USSR/1956/100m/C) D: Yefim Dzigan. C: Marina Pastukhova, Pavel Kadochnikov.

G. Yuchenkov. *The First Day* (USSR/1958/C) D: Friedrich Ermler. C: Olga Petrenko, Eduard Bredun.

V. Chestnokov. *In the October Days* (USSR/1958/116m/C) D: Sergei Vasiliev. C: V. Brener, A. Kobaladze, A. Fyodorinov, Galina Vodyanitskaya.

Maxim Strauch. *Stories About Lenin* (USSR/1958/C) D: Sergei Yutkevich. C: Marina Pastukhova.

Maxim Strauch. *Lenin in Poland* (aka *Portrait of Lenin*) (USSR-Poland/1965/100m/BW) D: Sergei Yutkevich. C: Anna Lisyanskaya, Antonina Pavlychyova, Ilona Kusmierska.

Rodion Nakhapetov. *Heart of a Mother* (aka *Sons and Mothers*) (aka *A Mother's Heart*) (USSR/1966/100m/BW) D: Mark Donskoi. C: Elena Fadeyeva, Danili Sagal.

Rodion Nakhapetov. *A Mother's Devotion* (aka *Vernost Materi*) (USSR/1967/90m/BW) D: Mark Donskoi. C: Elena Fadeyeva, Guennady Tchertov, T. Loginova.

Yuri Kayurov. *The Sixth of July* (USSR/1968/BW) D: Yuli Karasik. C: Alla Demidova, Vladimir Tatosov, Vasili Lanovoi.

John Gabriel. *Oh! What a Lovely War* (GB/1969/144m/C) D: Richard Attenborough. B/on the musical play by Joan Littlewood and the play *The Long, Long Trail* by Charles Chilton. Best English Language Foreign Film (GG), and the United Nations Award (BFA). C: Pamela Abbott, Jack Hawkins, Laurence Olivier, Ralph Richardson, John Mills, Paul Daneman, Dirk Bogarde, Vanessa Redgrave, Kenneth More, Michael Redgrave, Ian Holm, Wensley Pithey, Frank Forsyth, John Gielgud, Maggie Smith, Guy Middleton.

Michael Bryant. *Nicholas and Alexandra* (GB/1971/183m/C) D: Franklin J. Schaffner. B/on the book by Robert K. Massie. C: Michael Jayston, Janet Suzman, Roderic Noble, Fiona Fullerton, Harry Andrews, Irene Worth, Tom Baker, Ralph Truman, Alexander Knox, John McEnery, James Hazeldine, Brian Cox, Ian Holm, Roy Dotrice, Martin Potter.

Peter Steen. *Lenin, You Rascal, You* (Denmark/1972/96m/C) D: Kirston Stenbaek. C: Dirch Paser, Joergen Ryg, Judy Gringer, Eva Dann.

Yuri Kayurov. *Lenin in Paris* USSR/1981/110m/C) D: Sergei Yutkevich. C: Valentina Svetlova, Vladimir Antonik.

Roger Sloman. *Reds* (US/1981/200m/C) D: Warren Beatty. Best Picture (NYC), Best Director (AA,DGA). C: Warren Beatty, Diane Keaton, Edward Herrmann, Jerzy Kosinski, Jack Nicholson, Paul Sorvino, Maureen Stapleton, Stuart Richman.

Anatoly Ustiuzhaninov. *Red Bells* (aka *Red Bells: I've Seen the Birth of the New World*) (aka *Ten Days That Shook the World*) (USSR-Mexico-Italy/1982/137m/C) D: Sergei Bondarchuk. C: Franco Nero, Sydne Rome.

327 Lennon, John Winston (Ono) (1940–1980)

As a co-founder of and a co-principal writer for The Beatles, Lennon was one of the most influential musicians of the rock era, as well as a driving force of the pop culture that was the 1960s. The man who asked us all to "Give Peace a Chance" was murdered by Mark Chapman on Dec. 8, 1980. Lennon's film appearences include: *A Hard Day's Night* (64), *Help!* (65), *How I Won the War* (67) and the documentaries *Let It Be* (70) and *Imagine: John Lennon* (88). In TV movies he has been played by Stephen Mackenna in *Birth of the Beatles* (79), Mark McGann in *John and Yoko* (85), Jared Harris in *The Two of Us* (2000), and by Phillip McQuillan in *In His Life: The John Lennon Story* (2000).

Mitch Weissman. *Beatlemania* (US/1981/95–86m/C) D: Joseph Manduke. C: Ralph Castelli, David Leon, Tom Teeley.

Ian Hart. *The Hours and Times* (US/1992/60m/BW) D: Christopher Munch. C: David Angus, Stephanie Pack, Robin McDonald, Sergio Moreno, Unity Grimwood.

Ian Hart. *Backbeat* (GB/1994/100m/C) D: Iain Softley. C: Stephen Dorff, Sheryl Lee, Chris O'Neill, Scot Williams, Gary Bakewell, Kai Wiesinger, Jennifer Ehle.

Joe Stefanelli. (voice only). *Forrest Gump* (US/1994/142m/C) D: Robert Zemeckis. B/on the novel by Winston Groom. Best Picture (AA), Best Director (AA). C: Tom Hanks, Gary Sinise, Robin Wright, Sally Field, Mykelti Williamson, Peter Dobson, Richard D'Allesandro, and the voices of Jed Gillin, John William Galt, and Joe Alaskey.

328 Leonardo da Vinci (1452–1519)

Italian artist and scientist, famous for painting "The Last Supper" and "Mona Lisa," Leonardo made a living as an architect and civil engineer.

Ben Webster. *Conquest of the Air* (GB/1936/71m/BW) D: Zoltan Korda, Alexander Esway, Donald Taylor, Alexander Shaw & John Saunders. C: Frederick Culley, Franklin Dyali, Laurence Olivier, John Trumbell, Charles Lefaux, Charles Hickman, Michael Rennie.

Art Metrano. *History of the World, Part I* (US/1981/92m/C) D: Mel Brooks. C: Mel Brooks, Dom DeLuise, Madeline Kahn, Harvey Korman, Cloris Leachman, Gregory Hines, John Hurt.

Stephano Molinari. *Hudson Hawk* (US/1991/95m/C) D: Michael Lehmann. C: Bruce Willis, Danny Aiello, Andie McDowell, Sandra Bernhard, James Coburn, David Caruso, Frank Stallone.

Lepke, Louis *see* Buchalter, Louis

329 Lincoln, Abraham (1809–1865)

As the 16th President of the U.S., Abraham Lincoln guided the Union through the Civil War. With the war's successful outcome Lincoln had ended slavery and preserved the Union but within a week of victory he was assassinated by **John Wilkes Booth**. Lincoln has been portrayed in countless television productions, among them are *The Blue and the Grey* mini-series by Gregory Peck (82), *Dream West* (86) with F. Murray Abraham, *North and South I* and *II* (86) with Hal Halbrook; *The Civil War* miniseries (90), and *Abraham Lincoln* (88) in both by Sam Waterson; *The Perfect Tribute* (91), and *Lincoln* (92) in both by Jason Robards; *Tad* by Kris Kristofferson (95), and *Abraham and Mary Lincoln: A House Divided* mini-series by David Morse (voice) (2001).

Walter Huston. *Abraham Lincoln* (US/1930/97m/BW) D: D.W. Griffith. C: Una Merkel, Kay Hammond, E. Alyn Warren, Edgar Deering, Hobart Bosworth, Fred Warren, Frank Campeau, Francis Ford, Ian Keith, Oscar Apfel, Cameron Prud'Homme.

Charles Middleton. *The Phantom President* (US/1932/80m/BW) D: Norman Taurog. B/on a novel by George F. Worts. C: George M. Cohan, Claudette Colbert, Alan Mowbray.

Frank McGlynn. *Are We Civilized?* (US/1934/70m/BW) D: Edwin Carewe. C: Alin Cavin, Harry Burkhart, Charles Requa, Bert Lindley, Aaron Edwards, William Humphrey.

Frank McGlynn. *The Littlest Rebel* (US/1935/73m/BW) D: David Butler. B/on the play by Edward Peple. C: Shirley Temple, John Boles, Jack Holt, Bill Robinson.

Budd Buster. *Cavalry* (US/1936/63m/BW) D: Robert N. Bradbury. C: Bob Steele, Frances Grant, Karl Hackett, William Welch, Earl Ross, Hal Price.

Frank McGlynn. *Hearts in Bondage* US/1936/72m/BW) D: Lew Ayres. C: James Dunn, Mae Clark, Charlotte Henry, David Manner, Erville Alderson, Douglas Wood.

Frank McGlynn. *The Plainsman* (US/1936/115m/BW) D: Cecil B. DeMille. B/on the novel *Wild Bill Hickok* by Frank J. Wilstach. C: Gary Cooper, Jean Arthur, James Ellison, Porter Hall, John Miljan, Edwin Maxwell, Leila McIntyre, Charles H. Herzinger.

Frank McGlynn. *The Prisoner of Shark Island* (US/1936/95m/BW) D: John Ford. C: Warner Baxter, Gloria Stuart, Joyce Kay, Claude Gillenwater, Francis McDonald, Leila McIntyre, Harry Carey, Paul Fix, John Carradine, Arthur Byron, Ernest Whitman.

Robert Barrat. *Trailin' West* (aka *On Secret Service*) (US/1936/56m/BW) D: Noel Smith. B/on the story *On Secret Service* by Anthony Coldeway. C: Dick Foran, Paula Stone, Gordon (Bill) Elliott, Joseph Crehan, Stuart Holmes, Jim Thorpe.

Albert Russell. *Courage of the West* (US/1937/56m/BW) D: Joseph H. Lewis. C: Bob Baker, Lois January, J. Farrell MacDonald, Thomas Monk, Charles French.

Percy Parsons. *Victoria the Great* (GB/1937/110m/C) D: Herbert Wilcox. B/on the play *Victoria Regina* by Laurence Housman. C: Anna Neagle, Anton Walbrook, H.B. Warner, James Dale, Charles Carson, Hubert Harben, Felix Aylmer, Arthur Young, Derrick De Marney, Hugh Miller, Henry Hallatt, Gordon McLeod, Wyndham Goldie.

Frank McGlynn. *Wells Fargo* (US/1937/115–94m/BW) D: Frank Lloyd. C: Joel McCrea, Bob Burns, Frances Dee, Lloyd Nolan, Porter Hall, Ralph Morgan, Rebecca Wassem.

Frank McGlynn. *Western Gold* (aka *The Mysterious Stranger*) (US/1937/57m/BW) D: Howard Bretherton. B/on the novel *Helen of the Old House* by Harold Bell Wright. C: Smith Ballew, Heather Angel, Leroy Mason, Ben Alexander, Otis Harlan.

John Carradine. *Of Human Hearts* (US/1938/100m/BW) D: Clarence Brown. B/on the novel *Benefits Forgot* by Honore Morrow. C: Walter Huston, James Stewart, Beulah Bondi, Guy Kibbee, Charles Coburn, Charley Grapewin, Ann Rutherford, Gene Lockhart.

Frank McGlynn. *The Mad Empress* (aka *Juarez and Maximillian*) (Mexico-US /1939/72m/BW) D: Miguel Contreras Torres. C: Medea Novara, Lionel Atwill, Conrad Nagel, Guy Bates Post, Evelyn Brent, Earl Gunn, Jason Robards, Sr., Duncan Renaldo.

Henry Fonda. *Young Mr. Lincoln* (US/1939/100m/BW) D: John Ford. C: Alice Brady, Marjorie Weaver, Arlene Whelan, Richard Cromwell, Milburn Stone, Pauline Moore.

Raymond Massey. *Abe Lincoln in Illinois* (aka *Spirit of The People*) (US/1940/110m/BW) D: John Cromwell. B/on the play by Robert E. Sherwood. C: Gene Lockhart, Ruth Gordon, Mary Howard, Dorothy Tree, Harvey Stephens, Howard Da Silva.

Charles Middleton. *Santa Fe Trail* (US/1940/110m/BW) D: Michael Curtiz. C: Errol Flynn, Ronald Reagan, Olivia de Havilland, Raymond Massey, Alan Hale, Guinn Williams, Van Heflin, Moroni Olsen, Erville Alderson, David Bruce, Frank Wilcox.

Victor Kilian. *Virginia City* (US/1940/121m/BW) D: Michael Curtiz. C: Errol Flynn, Miriam Hopkins, Randolph Scott, Humphrey Bogart, Thurston Hall, Charles Middleton.

Frank McGlynn. *Hi-Yo Silver* (US/1940/69m/BW) D: William Witney & John English. Feature film edited from the 15-chapter serial *The Lone Ranger* (38). C: Lee Powell, Chief Thundercloud, Herman (Bruce Bennett) Brix, Lynn Roberts, Stanley Andrews.

Ed O'Neill. *Tennessee Johnson* (aka *The Man on America's Conscience*) (US/1942/103m/BW) D: William Dieterle. C: Van Heflin, Ruth Hussey, Lionel Barrymore, Marjorie Main, Regis Toomey, Montagu Love, Porter Hall, Morris Ankrum, Harry Worth, Harrison Greene, Charles Dingle, Grant Withers, Lynne Carver, Noah Beery, Sr.

Joel Day. *Days of Buffalo Bill* (US/1946/56m/BW) D: Thomas Carr. C: Sunset Carson, Peggy Stewart, Tom London, James Craven, Rex Lease, Edmund Cobb.

Jeff Corey. *Rock Island Trail* (aka *Transcontinent Express*) (US/1950/90m/C) D: Joseph Kane. B/on the novel *A Yankee Dared* by Frank J. Nevins. C: Forrest

Tucker, Adele Mara, Adrian Booth, Bruce Cabot, Barbara Fuller, Grant Withers, Roy Barcroft.

Hans Conreid. *New Mexico* (US/1951/76m/C) D: Irving Reis. C: Lew Ayres, Marilyn Maxwell, Robert Hutton, Andy Devine, Raymond Burr, Jeff Corey, Lloyd Corrigan.

Leslie Kimmell. *The Tall Target* (US/1951/78m/BW) D: Anthony Mann. C: Dick Powell, Paula Raymond, Adolphe Menjou, Marshall Thompson, Ruby Dee, Will Geer, James Harrison.

Richard Hale. *San Antone* (US/1953/90m/BW) D: Joseph Kane. B/on the novel *The Golden Herd* by Curt Carroll. C: Rod Cameron, Arleen Whelan, Roy Roberts, Bob Steele.

James Griffith. *Apache Ambush* (US/1955/68m/BW) D: Fred F. Sears. C: Bill Williams, Richard Jaeckel, Alex Montoya, Tex Ritter, Movita, Adele August.

Stanley Hall. *Prince of Players* (US/1955/102m/BW) D: Philip Dunne. B/on the book by Eleanor Ruggles. C: Richard Burton, John Derek, Raymond Massey, Sarah Padden.

Austin Green. *The Story of Mankind* (US/1957/100m/C) D: Irwin Allen. B/on the book by Hendrik Van Loon. C: Ronald Colman, Hedy Lamarr, Virginia Mayo, Agnes Moorehead, Peter Lorre, Dennis Hopper, Marie Wilson, Helmut Dantine, Edward Everett Horton, Reginald Gardiner, Marie Windsor, Francis X. Bushman, Anthony Dexter, Jim Ameche, Harpo Marx, Bobby Watson, Reginald Sheffield, Cedric Hardwicke, Cesar Romero.

Raymond Massey. *How the West Was Won* (US/1962/165m/C) D: John Ford, Henry Hathaway & George Marshall. C: John Wayne, James Stewart, Gregory Peck, Carroll Baker, George Peppard, Henry Fonda, Carolyn Jones, Robert Preston, Harry Morgan, Karl Malden, Debbie Reynolds, Richard Widmark, Eli Wallach, Walter Brennan.

Jeff Corey. *The Treasure of the Aztecs,* (aka *Der Schatz Der Azteken*) (aka *Die Pyramide Des Sonnengottes*) (Germany-France-Italy-Yugoslavia/1965/102–90m/C) D: Robert Siodmark. C: Lex Barker, Gerard Barray, Fausto Tozzi, Michele Girardon.

Ford Rainey. *Guardian of the Wilderness* (aka *Mountain Man*) (US/1977/112m/C) D: David O'Malley. C: Denver Pyle, John Dehner, Ken Barry, Cheryl Miller, Don Shanks.

John Anderson. *The Lincoln Conspiracy.* (US/1977/90m/C) D: James L. Conway. B/on the book by David Balsiger & Charles E. Sellier, Jr. C: Bradford Dillman, Frances Fordham, Robert Middleton, E.J. Andre, Wallace K. Wilkinson, John Dehner, Whit Bissell.

Robert V. Barron. *Bill and Ted's Excellent Adventure* (US/1989/90m/C) D: Stephen Herek. C: Keanu Reeves, Alex Winter, George Carlin, Amy Stock-Poynton, Terry Camilleri, Dan Shor, Clifford David, Rod Loomis, Al Leong, Jane Wiedlin, Tony Steedman, Fee Waybill.

330 Lincoln, Mary Ann Todd (1818–1882)

The death of her husband, **Abraham Lincoln**, and of three of her sons proved too much for Mrs. Lincoln and she was committed to an asylum in 1875. Mrs.

Lincoln has been portrayed in many television productions, among them *The Blue and the Gray* mini-series by Janice Carroll (82), *The Last of Mrs. Lincoln* by Julie Harris (84), *Gore Vidal's Lincoln* by Mary Tyler Moore (88), *Tad* by Jane Curtin (92), and *Abraham and Mary Lincoln: A House Divided* mini-series by Holly Hunter (voice) (2001).

Kay Hammond. *Abraham Lincoln* (US/1930/97m/BW) D: D.W. Griffith. C: Walter Huston, Una Merkel, E. Alyn Warren, Edgar Deering, Hobart Bosworth, Fred Warren, Frank Campeau, Francis Ford, Ian Keith, Oscar Apfel, Cameron Prud'Homme.

Leila McIntyre. *The Plainsman* (US/1936/115m/BW) D: Cecil B. DeMille. B/on the novel *Wild Bill Hickok* by Frank J. Wilstach. C: Gary Cooper, Jean Arthur, James Ellison, Porter Hall, John Miljan, Frank McGlynn, Edwin Maxwell, Charles H. Herzinger.

Leila McIntyre. *The Prisoner of Shark Island* (US/1936/95m/BW) D: John Ford. C: Warner Baxter, Gloria Stuart, Joyce Kay, Claude Gillenwater, Francis McDonald, Frank McGlynn, Harry Carey, Paul Fix, John Carradine, Arthur Byron, Ernest Whitman.

Marjorie Weaver. *Young Mr. Lincoln* (US/1939/100m/BW) D: John Ford. C: Henry Fonda, Alice Brady, Arlene Whelan, Richard Cromwell, Milburn Stone, Pauline Moore.

Ruth Gordon. *Abe Lincoln in Illinois* (aka *Spirit of The People*) (US/1940/110m/BW) D: John Cromwell. B/on the play by Robert E. Sherwood. C: Raymond Massey, Gene Lockhart, Mary Howard, Dorothy Tree, Harvey Stephens, Howard Da Silva.

Sarah Padden. *Prince of Players* (US/1955/102m/BW) D: Philip Dunne. B/on the book by Eleanor Ruggles. C: Richard Burton, John Derek, Raymond Massey, Stanley Hall.

Frances Fordham. *The Lincoln Conspiracy.* (US/1977/90m/C) D: James L. Conway. B/on the book by David Balsiger & Charles E. Sellier, Jr. C: Bradford Dillman, John Anderson, Robert Middleton, E.J. Andre, Wallace K. Wilkinson, John Dehner, Whit Bissell.

331 Lind, Jenny (1820–1887)

(Johanna Maria Lind-Goldschmidt) Popular soprano known as "The Swedish Nightingale," Lind performed throughout Europe and the States in the mid–nineteenth century. On one U.S. tour she was managed by **P.T. Barnum**. Jenny was portrayed by Janet Heitmeyer in the TV mini-series *P.T. Barnum* (99).

Grace Moore. *A Lady's Morals* (aka *Jenny Lind*) (aka *The Soul Kiss*) (US/1930/86m/BW) D: Sidney Franklin. C: Wallace Beery, Reginald Denny, Gus Shy, Jobyna Howland.

Virginia Bruce. *The Mighty Barnum* (US/1934/87m/BW) D: Walter Lang. C: Wallace Beery, Adolphe Menjou, Janet Beecher, Herman Bing, Davison Clark, George MacQuarrie.

Helga Gorlin. *The Great John Ericsson* (Sweden/1938/94m/BW) D: Gustav Edgren. C: Victor Seastrom, Marta Ekstrom, Anders Henrikson, Hilda Borgstrom.

Ilse Werner. *Die Schwedische Nachtigall* (Germany/1940/BW) D: Peter Paul Brauer. C: Joachim Gottschalk, Karl Diehl, Bernhard Goetzke, Karl Tiedtke.
June Elvin. *Mr. H.C. Andersen* (GB/1950/62m/BW) D: Ronald Haines. B/on the book *The True Story of My Life* by Hans Christian Anderson. C: Asley Glynne, Constance Lewis, Terence Noble, Stuart Sanders, Edward Sullivan, Victor Rietty.

Liszt, Cosima *see* Wagner, Cosima

332 Liszt, Franz (1811–1886)

A dynamic figure in the Romantic school of music, Liszt was considered the greatest pianist of his day and as a composer is remembered for his Hungarian Rhapsodies and Paganini Etudes among his nearly 400 works.

Claudio Arrau. *Suenos de Amor* (Mexico/1935/BW) D: Jose Bohr. C: Consuelo Frank.

Ferenc Taray. *Szerelmi Almok* (Hungary/1935/103m/BW) D: Heinz Hille. C: Maria Sulyok, Giza Bathory, T.M. Laszlo, Geza Foldesy, Bela Fay.

Luis Rainer. *Liszt Rhapsody* (aka *Wenn Die Musik Nicht Waer*) (Germany/1935/90m/BW) D: Carmine Gallone. B/on the novel *Der Kraft-Mayer* by Ernest von Wolzogen. C: Paul Horbiger, Willi Schaeffers, Ida Wuest, Harry Hardt, Karin Hardt.

Zoltan Szakaca. *Szenzacio* (Hungary/1937/78m/BW) D: Stefen Szekely & Ladislau Vaj. C: Irene Agai, Ann Somogyi, Frank Kiss, Julius Kabos.

Brandon Hurst. *Suez* (US/1938/104m/BW) D: Allan Dwan. C: Tyrone Power, Loretta Young, Miles Mander, Annabella, George Zucco, Leon Ames, Victor Varconi.

Fritz Leiber. *The Phantom of the Opera* (US/1943/92m/C) D: Arthur Lubin. B/on the novel by Gaston Leroux. C: Nelson Eddy, Susanna Foster, Claude Rains, Edgar Barrier.

Stephen Bekassy. *A Song to Remember* (US/1945/113m/C) D: Charles Vidor. C: Cornel Wilde, Merle Oberon, Paul Muni, Nina Foch, George Coulouris, George Macready, Roxy Roth.

Pierre Richard Willm. *Dreams of Love* (aka *Reves d'Amour*) (France/1947/100m) D: Christian Stengel. B/on the play by Rene Fauchois. C: Annie Ducaux.

Henry Daniell. *Song of Love* (US/1947/119m/BW) D: Clarence Brown. B/on the play by Bernard Schubert & Mario Silva. C: Katharine Hepburn, Paul Henried, Robert Walker, Leo G. Carroll, Else Janssen, Gigi Perreau, Henry Stephenson.

Svyatoslav Richter. *Man of Music* (aka *Glinka*) (USSR/1952/100m/C) D: Grigori Alexandrov. C: Boris Smirnov, Lubov Orlova, L. Durasov, Mikhail Nazvanov, B. Vinogradova.

Jacques François. *At the Order of the Czar* (France/1954/100m/C) D: Andre Haguet. C: Michel Simon, Colette Marchand, Lucienne Lemarchand, Willy Fritsch.

Will Quadflieg. *Lola Montes* (aka *The Sins of Lola Montes*) (aka *The Fall of Lola Montes*) (France-Germany/1955/110m/C) D: Max Ophuls. C: Martine Carol, Peter Ustinov, Anton Walbrook, Ivan Desnu, Oskar Werner.

Carlos Thompson. *Magic Fire* (US/1956/94m/C) D: William Dieterle. B/on the novel by Bertita Harding. C: Yvonne De Carlo, Rita Gam, Valentina Cortesa,

Alan Badel, Peter Cushing, Gerhard Riedmann, Eric Schumann, Frederick Valk.

Dirk Bogarde. *Song Without End* (US/1960/145m/C) D: George Cukor & Charles Vidor. C: Capucine, Genevieve Page, Patricia Morison, Ivan Desny, Martita Hunt, Lou Jacobi, Lyndon Brook, E. Erlandsen, Alex Davion, Hans Unterkirchner, Katherine Squire.

Henry Gilbert. *Song of Norway* (US/1970/142m/C) D: Andrew L. Stone. B/on the musical play by Milton Lazarus, Robert Wright & George Forrest. C: Toralv Maurstad, Edward G. Robinson, Florence Henderson, Robert Morley, Richard Wordsworth.

Imre Sinkovits. *The Loves of Liszt* (Hungary-USSR/1970) D: Marton Keleti. C: Larissa Trembovelska.

Roger Daltrey. *Lisztomania* (GB/1975/105m/C) D:

Franz Liszt (Roger Daltry), according to Ken Russell. *Lisztomania* (1975), not your usual bio-pic, but an eccentric, electric, Rock Opera of the Romantic Era musicians' lives and loves. (Museum of Modern Art Film Stills Archive)

Ken Russell. C: Sara Kestelman, Paul Nicholas, Fiona Lewis, Veronica Qilligan, Ken Colley, Andrew Reilly, Murray Melvin, Otto Diamant, Anulka Dziubinska, Imogen Claire, Ken Parry.

Ekkerhard Schall. *Wagner* (GB-Austria-Hungary/1983/540–300m/C) D: Tony Palmer. C: Richard Burton, Vanessa Redgrave, Gemma Craven, Laszlo Galffi, John Gielgud, Ralph Richardson, Laurence Olivier, Ronald Pickup, Miguel Herz-Kestranek, Marthe Keller, Gwyneth Jones, Franco Nero.

Julian Sands. *Impromptu* (GB/1990/107m/C) D: James Lapine. C: Judy Davis, Hugh Grant, Mandy Patinkin, Bernadette Peters, Ralph Brown, Emma Thompson.

Little Britches *see* Stevens, Jenny

333 Livingstone, (Dr.) David (1813–1873)

Scottish missionary and African explorer, Livingstone was so well known, that when he disappeared, an expedition led by **H.M. Stanley** was sent to find him. He died while searching for the source of the Nile.

Percy Marmont. *David Livingstone* (GB/1936/71m/BW) D: James A. Fitz-patrick. C: Marian Spencer, Pamela Stanley, Hugh McDermott, James Carew.

Cedric Hardwicke. *Stanley and Livingstone* (US/1939/101m/BW) D: Henry King. C: Spencer Tracy, Nancy Kelly, Richard Greene, Walter Brennan, Charles Coburn, Henry Hull.

Neal Arden. *The Best House in London* (GB/1969/97m/C) D: Philip Savile. C: David Hemmings, Joanna Pettet, Arnold Diamond, John DeMarco, George Reynolds, Suzanne Hunt.

Bernard Hill. *Mountains of the Moon* (US/1990/135m/C) D: Bob Rafelson. B/on the book by William Harrison. C: Patrick Bergen, Iain Glen, Richard E. Grant, Fiona Shaw.

334 Lloyd George, David, 1st Earl of Dwyfor (1863–1945)

British Prime Minister (1916–22), Lloyd George led England through the latter part of WW I and later helped negotiate the Treaty of Versailles.

George Pearce. *British Agent* (US/1934/75m/BW) D: Michael Curtiz. B/on the book *Memoirs of a British Agent* by Robert Bruce Lockhart. C: Leslie Howard, Kay Francis, William Gargan, Philip Reed, J. Carrol Naish, Cesar Romero, Tenen Holz, Olaf Hytten.

Esme Percy. *Regal Cavalcade* (aka *Royal Cavalcade*) (GB/1935/100m/BW) D: Thomas Bentley, Herbert Brenton, Norman Lee, Walter Summers, Will Kellino & Marcel Varnel. C: Marie Lohr, Pearl Argyle, Frank Vosper, Austin Trevor, Harry Brunning, John Mills, C.M. Hallard, H. Saxon-Snell, Patric Knowles, Matheson Lang, Athene Seyler.

Clifford Brooke. *Wilson* (US/1944/154m/C) D: Henry King. C: Alexander Knox, Charles Coburn, Geraldine Fitzgerald, Cedric Hardwicke, Vincent Price, Sidney Blackmer, Eddie Foy, Jr., Marcel Dalio, Edwin Maxwell, Francis X. Bushman.

V. Koltsov. *The Unforgettable Year: 1919* (USSR/1952/C) D: Mikhail Chiaureli. B/on the play by Vsevold Vishnevsky. C: I. Molchanov, Mikhail Gelovani, Boris Andreyev, M. Kovaleva, Yevgeni Samoilov, Victor Stanitsine, Gnat Yura, L. Korsakov, Sergei Lukyanov.

Anthony Hopkins. *Young Winston* (GB/1972/145m/C) D: Richard Attenborough. B/on the book *My Early Life: A Roving Commission* by Winston Churchill. Best English-Language Foreign Film (GG). C: Simon Ward, Peter Cellier, Ronald Hines, John Mills, Anne Bancroft, Robert Shaw, Laurence Naismith, William Dexter, Basil Dignam, Reginald Marsh, Robert Hardy, Colin Blakely, Michael Audreson, Jack Hawkins.

335 Logan, Harvey (1865–1903)

"Kid Curry" to his outlaw partners **Butch Cassidy** and the **Sundance Kid**, Logan reportedly shot himself when about to be captured by a posse. Some evidence indicates that he escaped to Bolivia and rode with Cassidy and Sundance for a time and that he was spotted there as late as 1913.

Rod Cameron. *Dakota Lil* (US/1950/87m/C) D: Lesley Selander. C: George Montgomery, Marie Windsor, John Emery, Wallace Ford, James Flavin.

John Dehner. *Powder River* (US/1953/78m/C) D: Louis King. B/on the novel by Stuart N. Lake. C: Rory Calhoun, Corrine Calvet, Cameron Mitchell, Penny Edwards, Carl Betz.

Richard Devon. *Badman's Country* (US/1958/85m/BW) D: Fred F. Sears. C: George Montgomery, Buster Crabbe, Neville Brand, Karin Booth, Gregory Wolcott, Malcolm Atterbury, Russell Johnson, Morris Ankrum.

Ted Cassidy. *Butch Cassidy and the Sundance Kid* (US/1969/112m/C) D: George Roy Hill. Best Film, Best Director (BFA-1970). C: Paul Newman, Robert Redford, Katherine Ross, Strother Martin, Jeff Corey, Henry Jones, Charles Dierkop, Cloris Leachman, Sam Elliott.

John Schuck. *Butch and Sundance: the Early Days* (US/1979/110m/C) D: Richard Lester. C: William Katt, Tom Berenger, Jill Eikenberry, Brian Dennehy, Paul Plunkett, Jeff Corey, Peter Weller.

Lombard, Carole *see* Gable, William Clark

336 London, Jack (1876–1916)

(John Griffith London) An author, sailor and Alaskan gold miner, London is remembered for his tales of adventure such as *The Call of the Wild*, *The Sea Wolf* and *White Fang*, all of which have been made into feature films.

Michael O'Shea. *Jack London* (aka *The Adventures of Jack London*) (US/1943/94m/BW) D: Alfred Santell. B/on The Book of *Jack London* by Charmian London. C: Susan Hayward, Osa Massen, Virginia Mayo, Morgan Conway, Wallis Clark.

Jeff East. *Klondike Fever* (aka *Jack London's Klondike Fever*) (US/1980/106m/C) D: Peter Carter. C: Rod Steiger, Angie Dickinson, Lorne Greene, Barry Morse.

Louis III *see* 613

Louis VII *see* 614

Louis XI *see* 618

Louis XII *see* 619

337 Louis XIII (1601–1643)

King of France (in regency from 1610, then from 1617), Louis left most of the governing chores to others, including (from 1624 on) **Cardinal Richelieu**. In the 1976 TV movie *Panache* he was portrayed by Harvey Solin. (See **Anne of Austria**)

Rolfe Sedan. *The Iron Mask*, (US/1929/95m/BW) D: Allan Dwan. B/on *The Three Musketeers* and *The Viscount of Bragelonne* by Alexandre Dumas. C: Douglas Fairbanks, Belle Bennett, Dorothy Revier, William Bakewell, Nigel De Brulier.

Fernand Francell. *The Three Musketeers* (France/1932/128m/BW) D: Henri

Diamant-Berger. B/on the novel by Alexandre Dumas. C: Aime Simon-Girard, Edith Mera, Samson Fainsilber, Harry Baur, Andree Lafayette, Maurice Escande.

Fernand Francell. *Milady* (France/1933/120m/BW) D: Henri Diamant-Berger. C: Aime Simon-Girard, Samson Fainsilber, Harry Baur, Blanche Montel, Andree Lafayette, Edith Mera, Louis Allibert, Tommy Bourdelle, Henri Rollan, Maurice Escande.

Edward Arnold. *Cardinal Richelieu* (US/1935/83m/BW) D: Rowland V. Lee. B/on the play *Richelieu* by Edward Bulwer-Lytton. C: George Arliss, Katherine Alexander.

Miles Mander. *The Three Musketeers* (US/1935/97m/BW) D: Rowland V. Lee. B/on the novel by Alexandre Dumas. C: Walter Abel, Paul Lukas, Margot Grahame, Heather Angel, Ian Keith, Onslow Stevens, Rosamond Pinchot, Ralph Forbes, Nigel De Brulier.

Shayle Gardner. *Under the Red Robe* (GB/1937/80m/BW) D: Victor Seastrom. B/on the play by Edward Rose and the novel by Stanley J. Weyman. C: Conrad Veidt, Annabella, Raymond Massey, Romney Brent, Sophie Stewart, Edie Martin, Ralph Truman.

Raymond Galle. *Champs-Elysées* (aka *Remontons Les Champs-Elysées*) (France/1938/100m/BW) D: Sacha Guitry. C: Sacha Guitry, Lucien Baroux, Jacqueline Delubac, Germaine Dermoz, Jeanne Boitel, Raymonde Allain, Jean Davy, Emile Drain, Jacques Erwin, Rene Fauchois, Liane Pathe, Robert Pizani, Claude Martin, Andre Laurent.

Albert Dekker. *The Man in the Iron Mask* (US/1939/110m/BW) D: James Whale. B/on the novel by Alexandre Dumas. C: Louis Hayward, Joan Bennett, Warren William, Joseph Schildkraut, Alan Hale, Miles Mander, Walter Kingsford, Doris Kenyon, Nigel De Brulier.

Joseph Schildkraut. *The Three Musketeers* (aka *The Singing Musketeer*) (US/1939/73m/BW) D: Allan Dwan. B/on the novel by Alexandre Dumas. C: Don Ameche, The Ritz Brothers, Binnie Barnes, Lionel Atwill, Gloria Stuart, Pauline Moore, Miles Mander, John Carradine, Douglas Dumbrille, John King, Lester Matthews.

Julio Villarreal. *The Three Musketeers* (aka *Tres Mosqueteros*) (Mexico/1942/139m/BW) D: Miguel M. Delgado. B/on the novel by Alexandre Dumas. C: Cantinflas, Angel Garasa, Raquel Rojas, Consuelo Frank, Andres Soler, Jorge Reyes.

Frank Morgan. *The Three Musketeers* (US/1948/126m/C) D: George Sidney. B/on the novel by Alexandre Dumas. C: Lana Turner, Gene Kelly, June Allyson, Van Heflin, Angela Lansbury, Vincent Price, Kennan Wynn, John Sutton, Gig Young, Robert Coote.

Don Beddoe. *Blades of the Musketeers* (aka *The Sword of D'Artagnan*) (US/1953/54m/BW) D: Budd Boetticher. B/on the novel *The Three Musketeers* by Alexandre Dumas. C: Robert Clarke, John Hubbard, Mel Archer, Paul Cavanagh, Marjorie Lord, Charles Lang.

Louis Arbessier. *Royal Affairs in Versailles* (aka *Versailles*) (aka *Affairs in Versailles*) (aka *If Versailles Were Told to Me*) (aka *Si Versailles M'Eétait Couté*) (France/1953/180–152m/C) D: Sacha Guitry. C: Sacha Guitry, Claudette Colbert, Orson Welles, Gerard Phillippe, Micheline Presle, Jean Marais, Georges

Marchal, Gilbert Boka, Lana Marconi, Gino Cervi, Fernand Gravet, Jacques
Berthier, Samson Fainsilber, Gilbert Gil, Emile Drain, Jacques de Feraudy, Gaston Rey, Philippe Richard.

Christian Fourcade. *Le Capitan* (France/1960/111m/C) D: Andre Hunebelle.
B/on a novel by Michel Zavaco. C: Jean Marais, Bourvil, Elsa Martinelli.

Graham Armitage. *The Devils* (GB/1971/111m/C) D: Ken Russell. B/on the
play by John Whiting and the book *The Devils of Louden* by Aldous Huxley. C:
Oliver Reed, Vanessa Redgrave, Dudley Sutton, Christopher Logue, Kenneth
Colley.

Daniel Ceccaldi. *The Four Charlots Musketeers* (France/1974/110m/C) D: Andre
Hunnebelle. B/on the novel *The Three Musketeers* by Alexandre Dumas. C: The
Charlots, Gerard Rinaldi, Josephine Chaplin, Catherine Jourdan, Bernard Haller.

Jean-Pierre Cassel. *The Three Musketeers* (GB-US-Panama/1974/105m/C) D:
Richard Lester. B/on the novel by Alexandre Dumas. C: Oliver Reed, Richard
Chamberlain, Michael York, Frank Finlay, Geraldine Chaplin, Simon Ward,
Charlton Heston.

Jean-Pierre Cassel. *The Four Musketeers* (aka *The Revenge of Milady*) (GB-
US/1975/108m/C) D: Richard Lester. B/on the novel *The Three Musketeers* by
Alexandre Dumas. C: Michael York, Charlton Heston, Oliver Reed, Richard
Chamberlain, Christopher Lee, Frank Finlay, Geraldine Chaplin, Raquel Welch,
Simon Ward.

Hugh O'Connor. *The Three Musketeers* (US/1993/105m/C) D: Stephen Herek.
B/on the novel by Alexandre Dumas. C: Charlie Sheen, Kiefer Sutherland, Chris
O'Donnell, Oliver Platt, Tim Curry, Rebecca DeMornay, Gabrielle Anwar,
Michael Wincott.

Daniel Mesguich. *The Musketeer* (Germany-Luxemburg-US/2001/105m/C)
D: Peter Hyams. B/on the novel by Alexandre Dumas. C: Catherine Deneuve,
Mena Suvari, Stephen Rea, Tim Roth, Justin Chambers, Bill Treacher, David
Schofield, Nick Moran, Steven Spiers, Jan Gregor Kremp, Jeremy Clyde, Michael
Byrne, Jean-Pierre Castaldi, Tsilla Chelton, Bertrand Witt.

Louis XIV *see* 626

Louis XV *see* 627

338 Louis XVI (1754–1793)
The King of France (1774–93) during the French Revolution, Louis and his wife
Marie-Antoinette were guillotined in January of 1793.

Stuart Holmes. *Captain of the Guard* (US/1930/85m/BW) D: John S. Robertson. C: John Boles, Laura La Plante, Sam De Grasse, George Hackathorne,
Richard Cramer, Evelyn Hall.

Ernst Stahl-Nachbaur. *Danton* (Germany/1931/94m/BW) D: Hans Behrendt.
B/on the book by Hans Rehfisch. C: Fritz Kortner, Gustaf Gründgens, Lucie
Mannheim, Alexander Granach, Walter Werner, Gustav von Wangenheim.

Jack Rye. *Napoleon Bonaparte* (France/1934/140m/BW) D: Abel Gance. Three-
dimensional sound version of Gance's 1927 epic *Napoléon*. C: Albert Dieudonné,

Edmond von Daele, Alexandre Koubitsky, Antonin Artaud, Boudreau, Alberty, Favière, Gina Manès, Suzanne Blanchetti, Marguerite Gance, Simone Genevois, Genica Missirio.

Pierre Renoir. *La Marseillaise* (France/1938/130m/BW) D: Jean Renoir. C: Lise Delamare, Leon Larive, Louis Jouvet, William Haguet, Jaque Catelain.

Robert Morley. *Marie Antoinette* (US/1938/160m/BW) D: W.S. Van Dyke II. B/on the book by Stefan Zweig. C: Norma Shearer, Tyrone Power, John Barrymore, Gladys George, Anita Louise, Joseph Schildkraut, Albert Dekker, Scotty Becket, Alma Kruger, George Meeker, Wade Crosby, Anthony Warde, Walter Walker, John Burton.

Lloyd Corrigan. *The Fighting Guardsman* (US/1945/84m/BW) D: Henry Levin. B/on the novel *Companions of Jehu* by Alexandre Dumas. C: Willard Parker, Anita Louise, Janis Carter, John Loder, Edgar Buchanan, George Macready, Ian Wolfe, Ray Teal.

Lee Kresel. *Black Magic* (US/1949/105m/BW) D: Gregory Ratoff. B/on the novel *Joseph Balsamo* by Alexandre Dumas. C: Orson Welles, Nancy Guild, Akim Tamiroff, Raymond Burr, Margot Grahame, Berry Kroeger, Charles Goldner, Robert Atkins.

Gilbert Boka. *Royal Affairs in Versailles* (aka *Versailles*) (aka *Affairs in Versailles*) (aka *If Versailles Were Told to Me*) (aka *Si Versailles M'Eétait Couté*) (France/1953/180–152m/C) D: Sacha Guitry. C: Sacha Guitry, Claudette Colbert, Orson Welles, Gerard Phillippe, Micheline Presle, Jean Marais, Georges Marchal, Lana Marconi, Gino Cervi, Fernand Gravet, Louis Arbessier, Jacques Berthier, Samson Fainsilber, Gilbert Gil, Emile Drain, Jacques de Feraudy, Gaston Rey, Philippe Richard.

Gilbert Boka. *If Paris Were Told to Us* (France/1955/135m/C) D: Sacha Guitry. C: Danielle Darrieaux, Jean Marais, Robert Lamoureaux, Sacha Guitry, Michelle Morgan, Lana Marconi, Jeanne Boitel, Renee Saint-Cyr, Gerard Philipe.

Jacques Morel. *Marie-Antoinette* (aka *Shadow of the Guillotine*) (France/1956/120m/C) D: Jean Delannoy. C: Michele Morgan, Richard Todd, Aime Clariond, Jeanne Boitel.

Jean-Pierre Aumont. *John Paul Jones* (US/1959/126m/C) D: John Farrow. B/on the story *Nor'wester* by Clements Ripley. C: Robert Stack, Bette Davis, Marisa Pavan, Charles Coburn, Macdonald Carey, Susana Canales, John Crawford, Eric Pohlmann.

Albert Remy. *Lafayette* (France/1962/110m/C) D: Jean Dreville. C: Michel Le Royer, Howard St. John, Jack Hawkins, Wolfgang Priess, Orson Welles, Vittorio De Sica, Edmund Purdom, Liselotte Pulver, Renee Saint-Cyr.

Hugh Griffith. *Start the Revolution Without Me* (US/1970/90m/C) D: Bud Yorkin. B/on the story *Two Times Two* by Fred Freeman. C: Gene Wilder, Donald Sutherland, Jack MacGowan, Billie Whitelaw, Victor Spinetti, Helen Fraser, Ewa Aulin, Orson Welles (Narrator).

Mel Brooks. *History of the World, Part I* (US/1981/92m/C) D: Mel Brooks. C: Dom DeLuise, Madeline Kahn, Harvey Korman, Cloris Leachman, Gregory Hines, Art Metrano, John Hurt.

Michel Piccoli. *La Nuit de Varennes* (France-Italy/1983/150–133m/C) D: Ettore Scola. C: Marcello Mastroianni, Jean-Louis Barrault, Hanna Schygulla,

Harvey Keitel, Jean-Claude Brialy, Jean-Louis Trintignant, Eleonore Hirt, Daniel Gelin.

Michael Lonsdale. *Jefferson in Paris* (US/1995/144m/C) D: James Ivory. C: Nick Nolte, Greta Scacchi, Jean-Pierre Aumont, Simon Callow, Seth Gilliam, James Earl Jones, Gwyneth Paltrow, Lambert Wilson, Charlotte de Turckheim, Damien Groelle.

Dominique Besnehard. *Beaumarchais the Scoundrel* (France/1996/101m/C) D: Edouard Molinaro. Inspired by an unpublished manuscript of Sacha Guitry. C: Fabrice Luchini, Manuel Blanc, Sandrine Kiberlane, Michel Serrault, Jacques Weber, Murray Head, Judith Godreche, Jeff Nuttall.

Simon Shackleton. *The Affair of the Necklace* (US/2001/120m/C) D: Charles Shyer. C: Hilary Swank, Simon Baker, Adrien Brody, Jonathan Pryce, Joely Richardson, Christopher Walken, Eva Aichmajerová, John Comer, Brian Cox, Skye McCole Bartusiak, Hayden Panettiere, Victoria Shalet.

Louis XVII *see* 628

Louis XVIII *see* 629

Louis Philippe *see* 631

339 Luciano, Charles "Lucky" (1897–1962)

(Salvatore Lucania) Boss of the New York rackets and one of the early Mafia heads, Luciano was imprisoned for his crimes and later deported to his native Italy. He was portrayed by Billy Drago in the 1993 video release *The Outfit.*

Cesar Romero. *A House Is Not a Home* (US/1964/98m/BW) D: Russell Rouse. B/on the book by Polly Adler. C: Shelley Winters, Robert Taylor, Ralph Taeger, Kaye Ballard.

Gian Maria Volonte. *Lucky Luciano* (aka *Re: Lucky Luciano*) (Italy-France/1973/113m/C) D: Francesco Rosi. C: Rod Steiger, Charles Siragusa, Edmond O'Brien, Vincent Gardenia, Silverio Blasi, Charles Cioffi.

Angelo Infanti. *The Valachi Papers* (Italy-France/1972/125m/C) D: Terence Young. B/on the book by Peter Maas. C: Charles Bronson, Lino Ventura, Jill Ireland, Fausto Tozzi, Giancomino De Michelis, Joseph Wiseman, Walter Chiari.

Vic Tayback. *Lepke* (US/1975/110–98m/C) D: Menahem Golan. C: Tony Curtis, Anjanette Comer, Michael Callan, Warren Berlinger, Gianni Russo, Milton Berle, Erwin Fuller, Jack Ackerman, Vaughn Meader, Zitto Kazan, John Durren.

Lee Montague. *Brass Target* (US/1978/111m/C) D: John Hough. B/on the novel *The Algonquin Project* by Frederick Nolan. C: Sophia Loren, John Cassavetes, George Kennedy, Robert Vaughn, Patrick McGoohan, Bruce Davison, Edward Hermann.

Joe Dallesandro. *The Cotton Club* (US/1984/127m/C) D: Francis Coppola. C: Richard Gere, Gregory Hines, Diane Lane, Lonette McKee, Bob Hoskins, James Remar, Nicolas Cage, Rosalind Harris, Fred Gwynne, Gregory Rozakis, Larry

Marshall, Maurice Hines, Gwen Verdon, Lisa Jane Persky, Woody Strode, Zane Mark.

Stanley Tucci. *Billy Bathgate* (US/1991/106m/C) D: Robert Benton. B/on the novel by E.L. Doctorow. C: Dustin Hoffman, Nicole Kidman, Loren Dean, Bruce Willis.

Bill Graham. *Bugsy* (US/1991/135m/C) D: Barry Levinson. B/on the book *We Only Kill Each Other: The Life and Bad Times of Bugsy Siegel* by Dean Jennings. C: Warren Beatty, Annette Bening, Harvey Keitel, Ben Kingsley, Joe Mantegna, Elliott Gould, Wendy Phillips, Don Carrara, Carmine Caridi, Ksenia Prohaska.

Christian Slater. *Mobsters* (US/1991/104m/C) D: Michael Karbelnikoff. C: Patrick Dempsey, Richard Grieco, Costas Mandylor, F. Murray Abraham, Anthony Quinn, Michael Gambon, Lara Flynn Boyle, Nicholas Sadler, Titus Welliver.

Matt Servitto. *Mad Dog Coll* (aka *Killer Instinct*) (US-Russia/1993/101m/C) D: Greydon Clark & Ken Stein. C: Christopher Bradley, Bruce Nozick, Rachel York, Jeff Griggs, Thomas McHugh, Eddie Bowz, Jack Conley, Will Kempe, Dennis Predovic.

Andy Garcia. *Hoodlum* (US/1997/130m/C) D: Bill Duke. C: Laurence Fishburne, Tim Roth, Vanessa L. Williams, Cicely Tyson, Chi McBride, Clarence Williams III, Richard Bradford, William Athertin, Loretta Devine, Queen Latifah, Michael McCary, Dick Djonola.

340 Ludwig II (1845–1886)

Bavaria's "Mad King" was one of **Wagner's** early patrons and spent much of his country's wealth building castles. He was declared insane, removed from the throne and eventually drowned himself.

O.W. Fischer. *Ludwig II* (Germany/1955) D: Helmut Kautner. C: Friedrich Domin, Paul Bildt, Klaus Kinski, Marianne Koch, Ruth Leuwerik.

Gerhard Riedman. *Magic Fire* (US/1956/94m/C) D: William Dieterle. B/on the novel by Bertita Harding. C: Yvonne De Carlo, Carlos Thompson, Rita Gam, Valentina Cortesa, Alan Badel, Peter Cushing, Eric Schumann, Frederick Valk.

Harry Baer. *Ludwig—Requiem for a Virgin King* (Germany/1972/134m/C) D: Hans Jurgen Syberberg. C: Ingrid Caven, Gerhard Marz, Balthasar Thomas, Peter Kern.

Helmut Berger. *Ludwig* (Italy-Germany-France/1973/186m/C) D: Luchino Visconti. C: Romy Schneider, Trevor Howard, Silvana Mangano, Mark Burns.

Laszlo Galffi. *Wagner* (GB-Austria-Hungary/1983/540–300m/C) D: Tony Palmer. C: Richard Burton, Vanessa Redgrave, Gemma Craven, John Gielgud, Ralph Richardson, Laurence Olivier, Ekkerhard Schall, Ronald Pickup, Miguel Herz-Kestranek, Marthe Keller, Gwyneth Jones, Franco Nero.

341 Luther, Martin (1483–1546)

Once an Augustinian monk, Luther later broke with the Catholic Church and led the Protestant Reformation.

Niall MacGinnis. *Martin Luther* (US/1953/105m/BW) D: Irving Pichel. C:

John Ruddock, Pierre Lefevre, Guy Verney, Philip Leaver, Alastair Hunter, Hans Lefebre.

Stacy Keach. *Luther* (US/1974/112m/C) D: Guy Green. B/on the play by John Osborne. C: Patrick Magee, Hugh Griffith, Robert Stephens, Alan Badel, Judi Dench, Leonard Rossiter, Maurice Denham, Malcolm Stoddard.

342 MacArthur, Douglas (1880–1964)

American general and commander of Allied forces in Southeast Asia during WW II, MacArthur was relieved of his command during the Korean War following serious military policy disputes with President **Harry Truman.**

Robert Barrat. *They Were Expendable* (US/1945/135m/BW) D: John Ford. B/on the book by William L. White. C: Robert Montgomery, John Wayne, Donna Reed, Jack Holt.

Robert Barrat. *An American Guerrilla in the Philippines* (aka *I Shall Return*) (US/1950/105m/C) D: Fritz Lang. B/on the novel by Ira Wolfert. C: Tyrone Power, Micheline Presle, Tom Ewell.

Dayton Lummis. *The Court-Martial of Billy Mitchell* (aka *One Man Mutiny*) (US/1955/100m/C) D: Otto Preminger. C: Gary Cooper, Charles Bickford, Ralph Bellamy, Rod Steiger, Elizabeth Montgomery, James Daly, Herbert Heyes, Tom McKee, Phil Arnold, Ian Wolfe.

Gregory Peck. *MacArthur* (US/1977/128m/C) D: Joseph Sargent. C: Ed Flanders, Dan O'Herlihy, Ivan Bonar, Ward Costello, Nicholas Coster, Art Fleming, Addison Powell, Marj Dusay, Kenneth Tobey, John Fujioka, Fred Stuthman, Sandy Kenyon.

Laurence Olivier. *Inchon* (US/1981/140–105m/C) D: Terence Young. C: Jacqueline Bisset, Ben Gazzara, Toshiro Mifune, Richard Roundtree, David Janssen.

Jon Sidney. *Death of a Soldier* (Australia/1986/93m/C) D: Phillippe Mora. C: James Coburn, Reb Brown, Bill Hunter, Maurie Fields, Belinda Davey, Michael Pate.

John Bennett Perry. *Farewell to the King* (US/1989/117m/C) D: John Milius. B/on the novel by Pierre Schoendoerffer. C: Nick Nolte, Nigel Havers, Frank McRae, Michael Nissman.

343 Madden, Owen "Owney" (1892–1964)

English born, American raised gangster, Madden was one of the major New York crime figures during Prohibition.

Bob Hoskins. *The Cotton Club* (US/1984/127m/C) D: Francis Coppola. C: Richard Gere, Gregory Hines, Diane Lane, Lonette McKee, James Remar, Nicolas Cage, Rosalind Harris, Fred Gwynne, Gregory Rozakis, Larry Marshall, Joe Dallesandro, Maurice Hines, Gwen Verdon, Lisa Jane Persky, Woody Strode, Zane Mark.

Jack Conley. *Mad Dog Coll* (aka *Killer Instinct*) (US-Russia/1993/101m/C) D: Greydon Clark & Ken Stein. C: Christopher Bradley, Bruce Nozick, Rachel York, Jeff Griggs, Thomas McHugh, Eddie Bowz, Matt Servitto, Will Kempe, Dennis Predovic.

Dick Djonola. *Hoodlum* (US/1997/130m/C) D: Bill Duke. C: Laurence Fishburne, Tim Roth, Vanessa L. Williams, Andy Garcia, Cicely Tyson, Chi McBride, Clarence Williams III, Richard Bradford, William Athertin, Loretta Devine, Queen Latifah, Michael McCary.

344 Madero, Francisco Indalecio (1873–1913)

The President of Mexico following the **Diaz** dictatorship, Madero attempted reforms but was imprisoned and murdered when **Huerta** came to power.

Henry B. Walthall. *Viva Villa!* (US/1934/115m/BW) D: Jack Conway & Howard Hawks (uncredited). B/on the book by Edgcumb Pinchon & O.B. Strade. C: Wallace Beery, Fay Wray, Stuart Erwin, Leo Carillo, Donald Cook, Joseph Schildkraut.

Harold Gordon. *Viva Zapata!* (US/1952/113m/BW) D: Elia Kazan. B/on the book *Zapata the Unconquerable* by Edgcumb Pinchon. C: Marlon Brando, Anthony Quinn, Jean Peters, Alan Reed, Margo, Frank Silvera, Frank De Kova, Fay Roope, Joseph Wiseman, Lou Gilbert.

Ben Wright. *Villa!* (US/1958/72m/C) D: James B. Clark. C: Rodolfo Hoyos, Brian Keith, Cesar Romero, Margia Dean, Rosenda Monteros.

Alexander Knox. *Villa Rides* (US/1968/125m/C) D: Buzz Kulik. B/on the book *Pancho Villa* by William Douglas Lansford. C: Yul Brynner, Robert Mitchum, Charles Bronson, Herbert Lom, Fernando Rey, Jill Ireland, John Ireland.

Madison, James *see* 571

345 Mahler, Gustav (1860–1911)

Austrian composer and conductor, whose orchestrations greatly influenced the 20th century. Considered to be the heir of **Beethoven** and **Wagner**, Mahler wrote nine symphonies; songs, and song cycles. One of his greatest works is his 8th Symphony, *The Symphony of a Thousand.* In *Death in Venice* the character (von Aschenbach) is made up to resemble Mahler, and the film score uses Mahler's compositions. In films, his wife Alma is played by Georgina Hale in 74, Sarah Wynter in 2001, and in *Death in Venice* Frau von Aschenbach by Marisa Berenson. In the Yugoslavian TV film *Nedrovrsena simfonia* (98) Mahler was portrayed by Slobodan Ljubicic, and Alma by Vladislava Milosavljevic.

Dirk Bogarde (Gustav von Aschenbach). *Death in Venice* (Italy/1971/130m/C) D: Luchino Visconti. B/on the story by Thomas Mann. C: Mark Burns, Marisa Berenson, Bjorn Andresen, Silvana Mangano, Luigi Battaglia.

Robert Powell. *Mahler* (GB/1974/115m/C) D: Ken Russell. C: Georgina Hale, Richard Morant, Lee Montague, Antonia Ellis, Rosalie Crutchley, David Collings.

Jonathan Pryce. *Bride of the Wind* (Germany-GB/2001/99m/C) D: Bruce Beresford. C: Sarah Wynter, Vincent Perez, Simon Verhoeven, Gregor Seberg, Dagmar Schwarz, August Schmölzer, Wolfgang Hübsch, Marion Rottenhofer, Sophie Schweighofer, Johannes Silberschneider, Daniela Dadieu, Brigitte Antonius, Johanna Mertinz, Erwin Ebenbauer, Hans Steunzer, Robert Herzl, Werner Prinz, Patricia Hirschbichler.

346 Malcolm X (1925–1965)

(Malcolm Little) Militant black American leader and a primary spokesman for the Black Muslim religion, Malcolm was assassinated in February 1965. The film *Death of a Prophet* does not refer to the the Prophet by name, but there is no doubt that it is meant to be Malcolm X. Television portrayals have been by Dick Anthony in the mini-series *King* (78), Al Freeman, Jr. in *Roots* (79), and Joe Morton in *Ali: an American Hero* (2000).

James Earl Jones. *The Greatest* (US-GB/1977/101m/C) D: Tom Gries. B/on the book *The Greatest: My Own Story* by Muhammad Ali. C: Muhammad Ali, Ernest Borgnine, Lloyd Haynes, John Marley, Robert Duvall, Dina Merrill, Ben Johnson, Chip McAllister.

Morgan Freeman (the Prophet). *Death of a Prophet* (US/1981/60m/B&W/C) D: Woodie King, Jr. C: Yolanda King, Sam Singleton, Tommy Redmond Hicks, Yusef Iman, Sonny Jim Gaines, Kirk Kirksey, James DeJongh, Salaelo Maredi, Ossie Davis, Yuri Kochiyama, Amiri Baraka, Morgana Freeman, Terria Joseph, Daud Lateef, Mansoor Najeeullah, Alkiis Papoutsis, Shauneille Perry.

Denzel Washington. *Malcolm X* (US/1992/201m/C) D: Spike Lee. C: Steve Reed, Jodie Farber, Miki Howard, Angela Bassett, Albert Hall, Al Freeman, Jr.,

Malcolm X (Denzel Washington) giving a speech in front of the Apollo Theater in Harlem, this scene from *Malcolm X* (1992). Washington received the Chicago and New York Film Critics Awards as Best Actor and an Academy Award nomination for his convincing portrayal of Malcolm. (Museum of Modern Art Film Stills Archive)

Delroy Lindo, Spike Lee, Theresa Randle, Kate Vernon, Lonette McKee, Tommy Hollis, James McDaniel, Ernest Thomas, Jean LaMarre, Craig Wasson, Ricky Gordon.

Mario Van Peebles. *Ali* (US/2001/158m/C) D: Michael Mann. C: Will Smith, Jamie Foxx, Jon Voight, Ron Silver, Jeffrey Wright, Mykelti Williamson, Vincent De Paul, Jon A. Barnes, Michael Bentt, Malick Bowens, Candy Ann Brown, LeVar Burton, David Cubitt, Lee Cummings, James Currie, Rufus Dorsey, Martha Edgerton, Giancarlo Esposito, Sheldon Fogel, Themba Gasa, Nona M. Gaye, Ross Haines, Maestro Harrell, Michael Michele, Joe Morton, Patrick New, Al Quinn, Paul Rodriguez, Gailard Sartain, Charles Shufford, Jada Pinkett Smith, James Toney, Jack Truman, William Utay, Wade Williams.

347 Marat, Jean Paul (1743–1793)

French revolutionary Marat's radical views led to his own death when he was stabbed to death in his bath by **Charlotte Corday**.

Alexander Granach. *Danton* (Germany/1931/94m/BW) D: Hans Behrendt. B/on the book by Hans Rehfisch. C: Fritz Kortner, Gustaf Gründgens, Lucie Mannheim, Ernst Stahl-Nachbaur, Walter Werner, Gustav von Wangenheim.

Antonin Artaud. *Napoleon Bonaparte* (France/1934/140m/BW) D: Abel Gance. Three-dimensional sound version of Gance's 1927 epic *Napoléon*. C: Albert Dieudonné, Edmond von Daele, Alexandre Koubitsky, Boudreau, Alberty, Jack Rye, Favière, Gina Manès, Suzanne Blanchetti, Marguerite Gance, Simone Genevois, Genica Missirio.

Renee Fauchois. *Champs-Elysées* (aka *Remontons Les Champs-Elysées*) (France/1938/100m/BW) D: Sacha Guitry. C: Sacha Guitry, Lucien Baroux, Jacqueline Delubac, Germaine Dermoz, Jeanne Boitel, Raymonde Allain, Jean Davy, Emile Drain, Jacques Erwin, Liane Pathe, Robert Pizani, Claude Martin, Raymond Galle, Andre Laurent.

Anthony Ward. *Marie Antoinette* (US/1938/160m/BW) D: W.S. Van Dyke II. B/on the book by Stefan Zweig. C: Norma Shearer, Tyrone Power, John Barrymore, Gladys George, Robert Morley, Anita Louise, Joseph Schildkraut, Albert Dekker, Scotty Becket, Alma Kruger, George Meeker, Wade Crosby, Walter Walker, John Burton.

Ian Richardson. *Marat/Sade* (aka *The Persecution and Assassination of Jean-Paul Marat As Performed By the Inmates of Charenton Under the Direction of the Marquis de Sade*) (GB/1966/115m/C) D: Peter Brook. B/on the play by Peter Weiss. C: Patrick Magee, Clifford Rose, Glenda Jackson, John Harwood, Brenda Kempner, Ruth Baker, Michael Williams, Freddie Jones, Henry Woolf.

Marco Polo *see* Polo, Marco

348 Marie-Antoinette (1755–1793)

Though her callous solution to the bread famine ("Let them eat cake") is apochryphal, Marie-Antoinette was not popular with the French people and she followed her husband (**Louis XVI**) to the guillotine in October 1793.

Evelyn Hall. *Captain of the Guard* (US/1930/85m/BW) D: John S. Robertson. C: John Boles, Laura La Plante, Sam De Grasse, George Hackathorne, Richard Cramer, Stuart Holmes.

Suzanne Blanchetti. *Napoleon Bonaparte* (France/1934/140m/BW) D: Abel Gance. Three-dimensional sound version of Gance's 1927 epic *Napoléon*. C: Albert Dieudonné, Edmond von Daele, Alexandre Koubitsky, Antonin Artaud, Boudreau, Alberty, Jack Rye, Favière, Gina Manès, Marguerite Gance, Simone Genevois, Genica Missirio.

Anita Louise. *Madame du Barry* (US/1934/79m/BW) D: William Dieterle. C: Dolores Del Rio, Reginald Owen, Victor Jory, Osgood Perkins, Verree Teasdale, Maynard Holmes.

Tina Lattanzi. *The Count of Brechard* (aka *Il Conte di Brechard*) (Italy/1938/BW) D: Mario Bonnard. B/on the play by Giaocchino Forzano. C: Amedeo Nazzari, Louisa Ferida.

Lise Delamare. *La Marseillaise* (France/1938/130m/BW) D: Jean Renoir. C: Pierre Renoir, Leon Larive, Louis Jouvet, William Haguet, Jaque Catelain.

Norma Shearer. *Marie Antoinette* (US/1938/160m/BW) D: W.S. Van Dyke II. B/on the book by Stefan Zweig. C: Tyrone Power, John Barrymore, Gladys George, Robert Morley, Anita Louise, Joseph Schildkraut, Albert Dekker, Scotty Becket, Alma Kruger, George Meeker, Wade Crosby, Anthony Warde, Walter Walker, John Burton.

Marion Doran. *The Queen's Necklace* (aka *L'Affaire du Collier de la Reine*) (France/1946/BW) D: Marcel L'Herbier.

Nancy Guild. *Black Magic* (US/1949/105m/BW) D: Gregory Ratoff. B/on the novel *Joseph Balsamo* by Alexandre Dumas. C: Orson Welles, Akim Tamiroff, Raymond Burr, Margot Grahame, Berry Kroeger, Charles Goldner, Lee Kresel, Robert Atkins.

Nina Foch. *Scaramouche* (US/1952/118m/C) D: George Sidney. B/on the novel by Rafael Sabatini. C: Stewart Granger, Eleanor Parker, Janet Leigh, Mel Ferrer.

Lana Marconi. *Royal Affairs in Versailles* (aka *Versailles*) (aka *Affairs in Versailles*) (aka *If Versailles Were Told to Me*) (aka *Si Versailles M'Eétait Couté*) (France/1953/180–152m/C) D: Sacha Guitry. C: Sacha Guitry, Claudette Colbert, Orson Welles, Gerard Phillippe, Micheline Presle, Jean Marais, Georges Marchal, Gilbert Boka, Gino Cervi, Fernand Gravet, Louis Arbessier, Jacques Berthier, Samson Fainsilber, Gilbert Gil, Emile Drain, Jacques de Feraudy, Gaston Rey, Philippe Richard.

Isabelle Pia. *Madame du Barry* (aka *Mistress du Barry*) (France-Italy/1954/110m/C) D: Christian-Jaque. C: Martine Carol, Andre Luguet, Daniel Ivernel, Dennis Gianna Maria Canale, Massimo Serato, Denis d'Ines, Jean Paredes.

Lana Marconi. *If Paris Were Told to Us* (France/1955/135m/C) D: Sacha Guitry. C: Danielle Darrieaux, Jean Marais, Robert Lamoureaux, Sacha Guitry, Michelle Morgan, Jeanne Boitel, Gilbert Boka, Renee Saint-Cyr, Gerard Philipe.

Michèle Morgan. *Marie-Antoinette* (aka *Shadow of the Guillotine*) (France/1956/120m/C) D: Jean Delannoy. C: Richard Todd, Jacques Morel, Aime Clariond, Jeanne Boitel.

Marie Wilson. *The Story of Mankind* (US/1957/100m/C) D: Irwin Allen. B/on the book by Hendrik Van Loon. C: Ronald Colman, Hedy Lamarr, Virginia

Mayo, Agnes Moorehead, Peter Lorre, Dennis Hopper, Helmut Dantine, Edward Everett Horton, Reginald Gardiner, Marie Windsor, Francis X. Bushman, Anthony Dexter, Austin Green, Jim Ameche, Harpo Marx, Bobby Watson, Reginald Sheffield, Cedric Hardwicke, Cesar Romero.

Susana Canales. *John Paul Jones* (US/1959/126m/C) D: John Farrow. B/on the story *Nor'wester* by Clements Ripley. C: Robert Stack, Bette Davis, Marisa Pavan, Charles Coburn, Jean-Pierre Aumont, Macdonald Carey, John Crawford, Eric Pohlmann.

Liselotte Pulver. *Lafayette* (France/1962/110m/C) D: Jean Dreville. C: Michel Le Royer, Howard St. John, Jack Hawkins, Wolfgang Priess, Orson Welles, Vittorio De Sica, Edmund Purdom, Albert Remy, Renee Saint-Cyr.

Billie Whitelaw. *Start the Revolution Without Me* (US/1970/90m/C) D: Bud Yorkin. B/on the story *Two Times Two* by Fred Freeman. C: Gene Wilder, Donald Sutherland, Hugh Griffith, Jack MacGowan, Victor Spinetti, Helen Fraser, Ewa Aulin, Orson Welles (Narrator).

Christina Bohm. *Lady Oscar* (France-Japan/1979/125m/C) D: Jacques Demy. B/on the comic strip *Rose of Versailles* by Ryoko Ikeda. C: Catriona Maccoll, Barry Stokes.

Eleonore Hirt. *La Nuit de Varennes* (France-Italy/1983/150–133m/C) D: Ettore Scola. C: Marcello Mastroianni, Jean-Louis Barrault, Hanna Schygulla, Harvey Keitel, Jean-Claude Brialy, Jean-Louis Trintignant, Michel Piccoli, Daniel Gelin.

Ursula Andress. *Liberty, Equality and Sauerkraut* (aka *Liberte, Egalite, Choucroute*) (France/1985/C) D: Jean Yanne. C: Oliver de Kersauzon, Roland Giraud.

Charlotte de Turckheim. *Jefferson in Paris* (US/1995/144m/C) D: James Ivory. C: Nick Nolte, Greta Scacchi, Jean-Pierre Aumont, Simon Callow, Seth Gilliam, James Earl Jones, Michael Lonsdale, Gwyneth Paltrow, Lambert Wilson, Damien Groelle.

Judith Godreche. *Beaumarchais the Scoundrel* (France/1996/101m/C) D: Edouard Molinaro. Inspired by an unpublished manuscript of Sacha Guitry. C: Fabrice Luchini, Manuel Blanc, Sandrine Kiberlane, Michel Serrault, Jacques Weber, Dominique Besnehard, Murray Head, Jeff Nuttall.

Joely Richardson. *The Affair of the Necklace* (US/2001/120m/C) D: Charles Shyer. C: Hilary Swank, Simon Baker, Adrien Brody, Jonathan Pryce, Christopher Walken, Eva Aichmajerová, John Comer, Brian Cox, Skye McCole Bartusiak, Hayden Panettiere, Simon Shackleton, Victoria Shalet.

349 Marion, Francis, General (1732–1795)

South Carolina farmer who became a soldier in the American Revolution. The British gave him the nickname "The Swamp Fox" for his guerrilla warfare tactics and habit of disappearing into the swamps. Marion was portrayed by Leslie Nielsen in the television series *The Swamp Fox* (59).

Mel Gibson (as Colonel Benjamin "The Ghost" Martin). *The Patriot* (US/2000/164m/C) D: Roland Emmerich. C: Heath Ledger, Joely Richardson, Jason Isaacs, Donal Logue, Michael Neeley, Rene Auberjonois, Adam Baldwin, Lisa Brenner, Beatrice Bush, Bryan Chafin, Chris Cooper, Mary Jo Deschanel, Shan Omar Huey, Jay Arlen Jones, Tchéky Karyo, Terry Layman, Logan Lerman, Skye

McCole Bartusiak, Trevor Morgan, Jamieson Price, Hank Stone, Kristian Truelsen, Mark Twogood, Joey D. Vieira, Tom Wilkinson, Grahame Wood, Peter
Woodward.

350 Marshall, George Catlett (1880–1959)

American soldier and statesman, General Marshall was awarded the Nobel Peace
Prize for authoring the Marshall Plan for European recovery following WWII.
In TV films he has been played by John Anderson in *Tail Gunner Joe* (77), Dana
Andrews in *Ike* (79), Bill Morey in *Enola Gay* (83), and Harris Yulin in *Truman*
(95).

Keith Andes. *Tora! Tora! Tora!* (US-Japan/1970/143m/C) D: Richard Fleis-
cher, Toshio Masuda & Kinji Fukasaku. B/on the books *Tora! Tora! Tora!* by
Gordon Prange and *The Broken Seal* by Ladislas Farago. C: Martin Balsam, Soh
Yamamura, Jason Robards, Joseph Cotten, Tatsuya Mihashi, E.G. Marshall, James
Whitmore, Wesley Addy, Leon Ames, Richard Anderson, George Macready,
Neville Brand.

Ward Costello. *MacArthur* (US/1977/128m/C) D: Joseph Sargent. C: Gregory Peck, Ed Flanders, Dan O'Herlihy, Ivan Bonar, Nicholas Coster, Art Fleming, Addison Powell, Marj Dusay, Kenneth Tobey, John Fujioka, Fred Stuthman,
Sandy Kenyon.

Herve Presnell. *Saving Private Ryan* (US/1998/169m/C) D: Steven Spielberg.
Best Director, Cinematography, Best Sound, Best Sound Effects Editing, Best
Film Editing (AA). Best Director, Best Motion Picture — Drama (GG). C: Tom
Hanks, Matt Damon, Tom Sizemore, Vin Diesel, Barry Pepper, Amanda Bixer,
Jeremy Davis, Giovanne Ribisi, Edward Burns, Harrison Young, Ted Danson.

351 Marshall, John (1755–1835)

American jurist, Marshall served as Chief Justice of the Supreme Court from
1801–35 and established many judicial precedents that exist today. In the TV
movie *The Man Without a Country* (73) he was played by Addison Powell.

Brandon Hurst. *The Remarkable Andrew* (US/1942/80m/BW) D: Stuart
Heisler. B/on the novel by Dalton Trumbo. C: William Holden, Ellen Drew,
Brian Donlevy, Rod Cameron, Richard Webb, Frances Gifford, Gilbert Emery,
George Watts, Montagu Love.

George Spaulding. *The President's Lady* (US/1953/96m/BW) D: Henry Levin.
B/on the novel by Irving Stone. C: Charlton Heston, Susan Hayward, John McIntire, Jim Davis.

352 Mary

In Christian belief, Mary was the virgin mother of **Jesus Christ.** She has been
portrayed by Olivia Hussey in the TV mini-series *Jesus of Nazareth* (77), by
Blanche Baker in *Mary and Joseph, a Story of Faith* (79), Eleanor Bron in the TV
film *The Day Christ Died* (80), María del Carmen San Martín in *A Child Called
Jesus* mini-series (87), and by Jacqueline Bisset in the TV film *Jesus* (99).

Juliette Verneuil. *Golgotha* (France/1935/97m/BW) D: Julien Duvivier. C: Harry Baur, Robert Le Vigan, Jean Gabin, Charles Granval, Andre Bacque, Hubert Prelier, Lucas Gridoux, Edwige Feuillere, Vana Yami, Van Daele.

Darlene Bridges. *The Lawton Story* (aka *The Prince of Peace*) (US/1949/120–101m/C) D: William Beaudine & Harold Dan. C: Millard Coody, A.S. Fisher, Hazel Lee Becker.

Louana Alcanir. *The Sinner of Magdala* (aka *Mary Magdalene*) (Mexico/1950/95m/BW) D: Miguel Torres. C: Medea de Novara, Luis Alcoriza, Carlos Villatios, Jose Bavera.

Jose Greci. *Ben Hur* (US/1959/212m/C) D: William Wyler. B/on the novel by Lew Wallace. Best Picture (AA,BFA,NYC,GG). Best Director (AA,GG,DGA). C: Charlton Heston, Stephen Boyd, Jack Hawkins, Haya Harareet, Hugh Griffith, Sam Jaffe, Laurence Payne, Frank Thring, Claude Heater, George Relph, Finlay Currie.

Maruchi Fresno. *The Redeemer* (Spain/1959/93m/C) D: Joseph Breen. C: Luis Alvarez, Manuel Monroy, Felix Acaso, Antonio Vilar, Virgilio Teixeira, Carlos Casaravilla, Sebastian Cabot (Narrator).

Siobhan McKenna. *King of Kings* (US/1961/168m/C) D: Nicholas Ray. C: Jeffrey Hunter, Hurd Hatfield, Viveca Lindfors, Rita Gam, Carmen Sevilla, Rip Torn, Brigid Bazlen, Harry Guardino, Frank Thring, Guy Rolfe, Maurice Marsac, Gregoire Aslan, Royal Dano, Robert Ryan, Gerard Tichy, Michael Wager, Tino Barrero, Jose Antonio, Orson Welles (Narrator).

Dorothy McGuire. *The Greatest Story Ever Told* (US/1965/141m/C) D: George Stevens. B/on the book by Fulton Oursler. C: Max von Sydow, Robert Loggia, Claude Rains, Jose Ferrer, Charlton Heston, Donald Pleasence, David McCallum, Gary Raymond, Robert Blake, John Considine, David Hedison, Joanna Dunham, Sal Mineo, Van Heflin, Ed Wynn, Martin Landau, Telly Savalas, Sidney Poitier, Roddy McDowell, Angela Lansbury, Richard Conte, Carroll Baker, Janet Margolin, Burt Brinckerhoff, Tom Reese.

Susanna Pasolini. *The Gospel According to St. Matthew* (France-Italy/1964/142m/BW) D: Pier Paolo Pasolini. B/on the *New Testament book of Matthew*. C: Enrique Irazoqui, Mario Socrate, Marcello Morante, Alfonso Gatto, Rodolfo Wilcock, Francesco Leonetti, Amerigo Bevilacqua, Otello Sestilli, Settimio Di Porto, Ferruccio Nuzzo, Alessandro Tosca, Paolo Tedesco, Franca Cupane, Giacomo Morante, Rosario Migale.

Edith Scob. *The Milky Way* (France-Italy/1969/105m/C) D: Luis Bunuel. C: Paul Frankeur, Laurent Terzieff, Alain Cuny, Bernard Verley, Michel Piccoli, Jean Clarieux, Christian van Cau, Pierre Clementi, Georges Marchal, Delphine Seyrig.

Rivka Noiman. *Jesus* (US/1979/117m/C) D: Peter Sykes & John Kirsh. B/on the *New Testament book of Luke*. C: Brian Deacon, Yossef Shiloah, Niko Nitai, Gadi Rol, Richard Peterson, Eli Cohen, Shmuel Tal, Kobi Assaf, Talia Shapira, Eli Danker, Mosko Alkalai, Nisim Gerama, Leonid Weinstein, Peter Frye, David Goldberg.

Morgan Brittany. *In Search of Historic Jesus* (US/1979/91m/C) D: Henning Schellerup. B/on the book by Lee Roddy & Charles E. Seller. C: John Rubinstein, John Anderson, Nehemiah Persoff, Andrew Bloch, Walter Brooke, Annette Charles, Royal Dano, Anthony DeLongis, Lawrence Dobkin, David Opatoshu, John Hoyt, Jeffrey Druce.

Verna Bloom. *The Last Temptation of Christ* (US/1988/164m/C) D: Martin Scorsese. B/on the novel by Nikos Kazantzakis. C: Willem Dafoe, Harvey Keitel, Paul Greco, Barbara Hershey, Gary Basaraba, Victor Argo, Michael Been, John Lurie, Harry Dean Stanton, David Bowie, Nehemiah Persoff, Leo Burmester, Irvin Kershner, Andre Gregory, Tomas Arana, Juliette Caton, Roberts Blossom, Barry Miller, Alan Rosenberg.

Sinéad O'Connor (in a hallucination). *The Butcher Boy* (US-Ireland/1997/109m/C) D: Neil Jordan. B/on the novel by Patrick McCabe. C: Eamonn Owens, Sean McGinley, Peter Gowen, Alan Boyle, Andrew Fullerton, Fiona Shaw, Aisling O'Sullivan, Stephen Rea, John Kavanagh, Rosaleen Linehan, Anita Reeves, Gina Moxley, Niall Buggy, Ian Hart, Anne O'Neill, Milo O'Shea.

Mary I *see* 602

Mary II *see* 606

353 Mary Magdalene

In the Gospel stories, Mary Magdalene was the harlot whose virtue was restored through her faith in **Jesus Christ**. She has been portrayed by Anne Bancroft in the TV mini-series *Jesus of Nazareth* (77), by Delia Boccardo in TV the film *The Day Christ Died* (80), and by Debra Messing in *Jesus* (99).

Vana Yami. *Golgotha* (France/1935/97m/BW) D: Julien Duvivier. C: Harry Baur, Robert Le Vigan, Jean Gabin, Charles Granval, Andre Bacque, Hubert Prelier, Lucas Gridoux, Edwige Feuillere, Juliette Verneuil, Van Daele.

Hazel Lee Becker. *The Lawton Story* (aka *The Prince of Peace*) (US/1949/120–101m/C) D: William Beaudine & Harold Dan. C: Millard Coody, Darlene Bridges, A.S. Fisher.

Medea de Novara. *The Sinner of Magdala* (aka *Mary Magdalene*) (Mexico/1950/95m/BW) D: Miguel Torres. C: Luis Alcoriza, Carlos Villatios, Louana Alcanir, Jose Bavera.

Joanne Dru. *Day of Triumph* (US/1954/110m/C) D: Irving Pichel & John T. Coyle. C: Lee J. Cobb, Robert Wilson, Ralph Freud, Tyler McVey, Michael Connors, James Griffith, Lowell Gilmore, Anthony Warde, Peter Whitney, Everett Glass.

Yvonne De Carlo. *Mary Magdalene* (aka *La Spada E La Croce*) (Italy/1958/C) D: Carlo Ludovico Bragaglia. C: Jorge Mistral.

Carmen Sevilla. *King of Kings* (US/1961/168m/C) D: Nicholas Ray. C: Jeffrey Hunter, Siobhan McKenna, Hurd Hatfield, Viveca Lindfors, Rita Gam, Rip Torn, Brigid Bazlen, Harry Guardino, Frank Thring, Guy Rolfe, Maurice Marsac, Gregoire Aslan, Royal Dano, Robert Ryan, Gerard Tichy, Michael Wager, Tino Barrero, Jose Antonio, Orson Welles (Narrator).

Joanna Dunham. *The Greatest Story Ever Told* (US/1965/141m/C) D: George Stevens. B/on the book by Fulton Oursler. C: Max von Sydow, Dorothy McGuire, Robert Loggia, Claude Rains, Jose Ferrer, Charlton Heston, Donald Pleasence, David McCallum, Gary Raymond, Robert Blake, John Considine, David Hedison, Sal Mineo, Van Heflin, Ed Wynn, Martin Landau, Telly Savalas, Sidney

Poitier, Roddy McDowell, Angela Lansbury, Richard Conte, Carroll Baker, Janet Margolin, Burt Brinckerhoff, Tom Reese.

Yvonne Elliman. *Jesus Christ, Superstar* (US/1973/107m/C) D: Norman Jewison. B/on the rock opera by Tim Rice & Andrew Lloyd Webber. C: Ted Neeley, Carl Anderson, Barry Dennen, Bob Bingham, Larry T. Marshall, Joshua Mostel, Philip Toubus.

June Carter Cash. *The Gospel Road* (US/1973/93m/C) D: Robert Elfstrom. C: Robert Elfstrom, Larry Lee, Paul Smith, Alan Dater, John Paul Kay, Gelles LaBlanc, Robert Elfstrom, Jr., Terrance W. Mannock, Thomas Levanthal, Sean Armstrong, Lyle Nicholson, Steven Chernoff, Jonathan Sanders, Ulf Pollack.

Talia Shapira. *Jesus* (US/1979/117m/C) D: Peter Sykes & John Kirsh. B/on the *New Testament book of Luke*. C: Brian Deacon, Rivka Noiman, Yossef Shiloah, Niko Nitai, Gadi Rol, Richard Peterson, Eli Cohen, Shmuel Tal, Kobi Assaf, Eli Danker, Mosko Alkalai, Nisim Gerama, Leonid Weinstein, Peter Frye, David Goldberg.

Annette Charles. *In Search of Historic Jesus* (US/1979/91m/C) D: Henning Schellerup. B/on the book by Lee Roddy & Charles E. Seller. C: John Rubinstein, John Anderson, Nehemiah Persoff, Andrew Bloch, Morgan Brittany, Walter Brooke, Royal Dano, Anthony DeLongis, Lawrence Dobkin, David Opatoshu, John Hoyt, Jeffrey Druce.

Lina Sastri. *The Inquiry* (aka *L'Inchiesta*) (aka *The Investigation*) (aka *The Inquest*) (Italy/1986/107m/C) D: Damiano Damiani. C: Keith Carradine, Harvey Keitel, Phyllis Logan, Angelo Infanti, Sylvan.

Barbara Hershey. *The Last Temptation of Christ* (US/1988/164m/C) D: Martin Scorsese. B/on the novel by Nikos Kazantzakis. C: Willem Dafoe, Harvey Keitel, Paul Greco, Verna Bloom, Gary Basaraba, Victor Argo, Michael Been, John Lurie, Harry Dean Stanton, David Bowie, Nehemiah Persoff, Leo Burmester, Irvin Kershner, Andre Gregory, Tomas Arana, Juliette Caton, Roberts Blossom, Barry Miller, Alan Rosenberg.

Harvey Hartley (as Magadelena). *The Book of Life* (US-France/1999/63m/C) D: Hal Hartley. C: P.J. Harvey, Martin Donovan, Thomas Jay Ryan.

354 Mary, Queen of Scots (1542–1587)

An heir to the English throne, Mary's life of intrigue (in Scotland and in England) eventually brought her to the chopping block after she was convicted of a conspiracy to murder **Elizabeth I**.

Katharine Hepburn. *Mary of Scotland* (US/1936/123m/BW) D: John Ford. B/on the play by Maxwell Anderson. C: Fredric March, Florence Eldridge, Douglas Walton, John Carradine, Robert Barrat, Gavin Muir, Ian Keith, Ralph Forbes, Alan Mowbray, Walter Byron.

Jacqueline Delubac. *The Pearls of the Crown* (France/1937/120–100m/BW) D: Sacha Guitry & Christian-Jaque. C: Sacha Guitry, Lyn Harding, Ermete Zacconi, Marguerite Moreno, Yvette Plenne, Catalano, Arletty, Percy Marmont, Derrick De Marney, Barbara Shaw, Simone Renant, Jean Louis Barrault, Emile Drain, Enrico Glori, Renee Saint-Cyr, Pizani, Claude Dauphin, Aime-Simon Gerard.

Zarah Leander. *Heart of a Queen* (aka *Das Herz Einer Königin*) (Germany/

Their Royal Highnesses, Elizabeth I (Glenda Jackson) and Mary of Scotland (Vanessa Redgrave), enjoying a royal smoking break between takes of *Mary Queen of Scots* (1971). (Museum of Modern Art Film Stills Archive)

1940/BW) D: Carl Froelich. C: Maria Koppenhofer, Axel von Ambesser, Willy Bergel, Erich Ponto.

   Esmerelda Ruspoli. *Seven Seas to Calais* (Italy/1962/99m/C) D: Rudolph Mate & Primo Zeglio. C: Rod Taylor, Irene Worth, Keith Michell, Anthony Dawson, Umberto Raho, Basil Dignam.

   Vanessa Redgrave. *Mary, Queen of Scots* (GB/1971/128m/C) D: Charles Jarrot. C: Glenda Jackson, Patrick McGoohan, Timothy Dalton, Nigel Davenport, Trevor Howard, Daniel Massey, Ian Holm, Andrew Keir, Katherine Kath, Robert James, Richard Denning, Rick Warner.

355 Masterson, William Barclay "Bat" (1853–1921)

One of the most famous lawmen of the Old West, Masterson was once the Sheriff of Dodge City and also helped **Wyatt Earp** keep the peace in Tombstone. He later made a living as a gambler and wound up his life as a sportswriter in New York City. Trivia Note: In the heavyweight title fight between **Jim Corbett** and **John L. Sullivan** Bat was the timekeeper.

Albert Dekker. *The Woman of the Town* (US/1943/90m/BW) D: George Archainbaud. C: Claire Trevor, Barry Sullivan, Henry Hull, Marion Martin, Porter Hall, Charley Foy, Beryl Wallace.

Randolph Scott. *Trail Street* (US/1947/84m/BW) D: Ray Enright. B/on the novel *Golden Horizon* by William Corcoran. C: Robert Ryan, Anne Jeffreys, George "Gabby" Hayes, Steve Brodie, Jason Robards, Sr., Sarah Padden.

Monte Hale. *Prince of the Plains* (US/1949/60m/BW) D: Philip Ford. C: Paul Hurst, Shirley Davis.

Steve Darrell. *Winchester '73* (US/1950/92m/BW) D: Anthony Mann. B/on the story by Stuart N. Lake. C: James Stewart, Shelley Winters, Dan Duryea, Will Geer.

Frank Ferguson. *Santa Fe* (US/1951/89m/C) D: Irving Pichel. B/on the novel by James L. Marshall. C: Randolph Scott, Janis Carter, Jerome Courtland, Peter Thompson.

George Montgomery. *Masterson of Kansas* (US/1954/72m/C) D: William Castle. C: Nancy Gates, James Griffith, Jean Willes, Benny Rubin, Bruce Cowling, Donald Murphy.

Keith Larsen. *Wichita* (US/1955/81m/C) D: Jacques Tourneur. C: Joel McCrea, Vera Miles, Lloyd Bridges, Wallace Ford, Edgar Buchanan, Peter Graves, John Smith.

Kenneth Tobey. *Gunfight at the O.K. Corral* (US/1957/122m/C) D: John Sturges. B/on the story *The Killer* by George Scullin. C: Burt Lancaster, Kirk Douglas, Rhonda Fleming, Jo Van Fleet, John Ireland, Lyle Bettger, Frank Faylen, Earl Holliman, Whit Bissell, DeForrest Kelley, Martin Milner, Lee Van Cleef, Jack Elam, Bing Russell.

Gregory Wolcott. *Badman's Country* (US/1958/85m/BW) D: Fred F. Sears. C: George Montgomery, Buster Crabbe, Neville Brand, Karin Booth, Malcolm Atterbury, Russell Johnson, Richard Devon, Morris Ankrum.

Joel McCrea. *The Gunfight at Dodge City* (US/1959/81m/C) D: Joseph M. Newman. C: Julie Adams, John McIntire, Nancy Gates, Richard Anderson.

Ed McDonnell. *The Outlaws Is Coming* (US/1965/88m/BW) D: Norman Maurer. C: Larry Fine, Moe Howard, Joe De Rita, Nancy Kovack, Murray Alper, Joe Bolton, Bill Camfield, Hal Fryar, Johnny Ginger, Wayne Mack, Bruce Sedley, Paul Shannon, Sally Starr.

Tom Sizemore. *Wyatt Earp* (US/1994/195m/C) D: Lawrence Kasdan. C: Kevin Costner, Dennis Quaid, Gene Hackman, David Andrews, Linden Ashby, Jeff Fahey, Mark Harmon, Michael Madsen, Catherine O'Hara, Bill Pullman, Isabella Rossellini, JoBeth Williams, Norman Howell, Mare Winningham, Rex Linn, Randle Mell.

356 Mata Hari (1876–1917)

(Margaretha Geertruida Zelle) Dutch dancer who worked as a spy for Germany in Paris during WWI, she was caught, tried and executed.

Greta Garbo. *Mata Hari* (US/1931/91m/BW) D: George Fitzmaurice. C: Ramon Navarro, Lionel Barrymore, Lewis Stone, C. Henry Gordon, Karen Morley.

Judith Vosselli. *Stamboul Quest* (US/1934/88m/BW) D: Sam Wood. C: Myrna Loy, George Brent, Lionel Atwill, C. Henry Gordon, Douglas Dumbrille, Mischa Auer, Joseph Sawyer.

Delia Col. *Marthe Richard* (France/1937/83m/BW) D: Raymond Bernard. C: Edwige Feuilliere, Erich von Stroheim, Jean Galland, Marcel Andre.

Jeanne Moreau. *Mata Hari, Agent H-21* (aka *Mata Hari*) (France-Italy/1964/99m/BW) D: Jean-Louis Richard. C: Jean-Louis Trintignant, Claude Rich, Frank Villard, Albert Remy.

Carmen de Lirio. *Operation Mata Hari* (Spain/1968/94m/C) D: Mariano Ozores. C: Gracita Morales.

Zsa Zsa Gabor. *Up the Front* (GB/1972/89m/C) D: Bob Kellett. C: Frankie Howerd, Bill Fraser, Stanley Holloway, Hermione Baddeley, Robert Coote, Lance Percival.

Helena Kallianiotes. *Shanks* (US/1974/93m/C) D: William Castle. C: Marcel Marceau, Tsilla Chelton, Philippe Clay, Cindy Eilbacher, Don Calfa, Larry Bishop, Mondo, Phil Adams, William Castle.

Sylvia Kristel. *Mata Hari* (GB-US/1985/108m/C) D: Curtis Harrington. C: Christopher Cazenove, Gaye Brown, Gottfried John, Oliver Tobias.

357 Maximilian (1832–1867)

Younger brother of **Franz Josef**, Maximilian was given the throne of Mexico by **Napoleon III**. When the French forces withdrew Maximilian was captured by **Juarez's** troops and executed.

Brian Aherne. *Juarez* (US/1939/132m/BW) D: William Dieterle. B/on the novel *The Phantom Crown* by Bertita Harding and the play *Juarez and Maximillian* by Franz Werfel. C: Paul Muni, Bette Davis, Claude Rains, John Garfield, Donald Crisp, Walter Kingsford, Harry Davenport, Gale Sondergaard, Joseph Calleia.

Conrad Nagel. *The Mad Empress* (aka *Juarez and Maximillian*) (Mexico-US /1939/72m/BW) D: Miguel Contreras Torres. C: Medea Novara, Lionel Atwill, Guy Bates Post, Evelyn Brent, Earl Gunn, Jason Robards, Sr., Frank McGlynn, Duncan Renaldo.

George Macready. *Vera Cruz* (US/1954/94m/C) D: Robert Aldrich. B/on the story by Borden Chase. C: Gary Cooper, Burt Lancaster, Denise Darcel, Cesar Romero, Sarita Montiel, Ernest Borgnine, Morris Ankrum, Charles Buchinsky (Bronson).

358 Mayer, Louis Burt (1885–1957)

The second "M" in MGM, Mayer was the production chief for that studio from 1924 to 1951. TV portrayals include: Martin Balsam in *Rainbow* (78), Richard Dysart in *Malice in Wonderland* (85), Harold Gould in *Moviola: The Silent Lovers* (80) and *Moviola: The Scarlett O'Hara War* (80), and by David Suchet in the TV film *RKO 281* (99).

Jack Kruschen. *Harlow* (US/1965/107m/C) D: Alex Segal. C: Carol Lynley, Efrem Zimalist, Jr., Ginger Rogers, Barry Sullivan, Hurd Hatfield, Lloyd Bochner,

Buddy Lewis, Hermione Baddeley, Celia Lovesky, Robert Strauss, John Fox, Jim Plunkett.

    Allen Garfield. *Gable and Lombard* (US/1976/131m/C) D: Sidney J. Furie. C: James Brolin, Jill Clayburgh, Red Buttons, Joanne Linville, Alice Backes, Morgan Brittany.

    Howard Da Silva. *Mommie Dearest* (US/1981/129m/C) D: Frank Perry. B/on the book by Christina Crawford. C: Faye Dunaway, Diana Scarwid, Steve Forrest, Mara Hobel.

359 Mazarin, Cardinal (1602–1661)

(Giulio Mazarini) The successor to **Cardinal Richelieu**, Mazarin effectively governed France during much of the reign of **Louis XIV**.

    Samson Fainsilber. *Royal Affairs in Versailles* (aka *Versailles*) (aka *Affairs in Versailles*) (aka *If Versailles Were Told to Me*) (aka *Si Versailles M'Eétait Couté*) (France/1953/180–152m/C) D: Sacha Guitry. C: Sacha Guitry, Claudette Colbert, Orson Welles, Gerard Phillippe, Micheline Presle, Jean Marais, Georges Marchal, Gilbert Boka, Lana Marconi, Gino Cervi, Fernand Gravet, Louis Arbessier, Jacques Berthier, Gilbert Gil, Emile Drain, Jacques de Feraudy, Gaston Rey, Philippe Richard.

    Enrico-Maria Salerno. *Le Masque de Fer* (aka *The Iron Mask*) (France-Italy/1962/130m/C) D: Henri Decoin. B/on the novel *The Man in the Iron Mask* by Alexandre Dumas. C: Jean Marais, Jean-François Poron, Claudine Auger, Jean Rochefort.

    Silvagni. *The Rise of Louis XIV* (France/1966/100m/BW) D: Roberto Rossellini. C: Jean-Marie Patte, Raymond Jourdan, Katherina Renn, Dominique Vincent, Pierre Barrat.

    Philippe Noiret. *The Return of the Musketeers* (GB-France-Spain/1989/101m/C) D: Richard Lester. B/on the novel *Twenty Years Later* by Alexandre Dumas. Shown on US cable in 1991, released theatrically elsewhere. C: Michael York, Oliver Reed, Frank Finlay, Richard Chamberlain, C. Thomas Howell, Geraldine Chaplin, Roy Kinnear.

360 McCall, Jack (1851–1877)

Western gunman, McCall was the man who killed **Wild Bill Hickok**, shooting him in the back, for which he was hanged on March 1, 1877.

    Porter Hall. *The Plainsman* (US/1936/115m/BW) D: Cecil B. DeMille. B/on the novel *Wild Bill Hickok* by Frank J. Wilstach. C: Gary Cooper, Jean Arthur, James Ellison, John Miljan, Frank McGlynn, Edwin Maxwell, Leila McIntyre, Charles H. Herzinger.

    Lon Chaney, Jr. *Badlands of Dakota* (US/1941/74m/BW) D: Alfred E. Green. C: Robert Stack, Richard Dix, Ann Rutherford, Frances Farmer, Andy Devine, Addison Richards.

    George Montgomery. *Jack McCall, Desperado* (US/1953/76m/C) D: Sidney Salkow. C: Angela Stevens, Douglas Kennedy, James Seay, Eugene Iglesias, Jay Silverheels.

    Martin Kove. *The White Buffalo* (aka *Hunt to Kill*) (US/1977/97m/C) D: J.

Lee Thompson. B/on the novel by Richard Sale. C: Charles Bronson, Jack Warden, Will Sampson, Kim Novak, Clint Walker, Stuart Whitman, Slim Pickens, John Carradine.

David Arquette. *Wild Bill* (US/1995/98m/C) D: Walter Hill. B/on the novel *Deadwood* by Pete Dexter and the play *Fathers and Sons* by Thomas Babe. C: Jeff Bridges, Ellen Barkin, John Hurt, Diane Lane, Susannah Moore, Keith Carradine.

McKinley, William *see* 585

361 Melbourne, Lord (1779–1848)

(William Lamb) The Prime Minister of England when **Victoria** ascended the throne (1837), Melbourne became her political tutor and one of her earliest trusted advisors. He was the husband of **Lady Caroline Lamb**. He was portrayed by Nigel Hawthorne the TV mini-series *Victoria and Albert* (2001).

Otto Tressler. *Mädchenjahre Einer Königin* (Germany/1936/BW) D: Erich Engel. C: Jennie Jugo, Olga Limburg, Friedrich Benfer, Paul Henckels, Ernst Schiffner, Renee Stobrawa.

H.B. Warner. *Victoria the Great* (GB/1937/110m/C) D: Herbert Wilcox. B/on the play *Victoria Regina* by Laurence Housman. C: Anna Neagle, Anton Walbrook, James Dale, Charles Carson, Hubert Harben, Felix Aylmer, Arthur Young, Derrick De Marney, Hugh Miller, Percy Parsons, Henry Hallatt, Gordon McLeod, Wyndham Goldie.

Frederick Leister. *The Prime Minister* (GB/1940/94m/BW) D: Thorold Dickinson. C: John Gielgud, Diana Wynyard, Will Fyfe, Stephen Murray, Owen Nares, Fay Compton, Lyn Harding, Leslie Perrins, Vera Bogetti, Nicolas Hannan, Kynaston Reeves, Gordon McLeod.

Karl Ludwig Diehl. *The Story of Vickie* (aka *Young Victoria*) (aka *Dover Interlude*) (aka *Girl Days of a Queen*) (aka *Mädchenjahre Einer Königin*) (Austria/1955/108–90m/C) D: Ernst Marischka. B/on the diaries of Queen Victoria. C: Romy Schneider, Adrian Hoven, Magda Schneider, Christl Mardayn, Paul Horbiger, Alfred Neugebauer, Otto Tressler, Rudolf Lenz, Fred Liewehr, Eduard Strauss, Peter Weck.

Jon Finch. *Lady Caroline Lamb* (GB/1972/122m/C) D: Robert Bolt. C: Sarah Miles, Richard Chamberlain, John Mills, Margaret Leighton, Ralph Richardson, Laurence Olivier.

362 Metternich, Prince (1773–1859)

(Klemens Wenzel Nepomuk Lothar von Metternich) Austrian statesman, Metternich was responsible for guiding Austria to a leading position in the European balance of power in the nineteenth century.

Conrad Veidt. *Congress Dances* (aka *Der Kongress Tanzt*) (Germany/1931/92m/BW) D: Eric Charell. C: Lilian Harvey, Henri Graat, Humberstone Wright.

Alan Mowbray. *The House of Rothschild* (US/1934/94m/C) D: Alfred Werker. B/on the play by George Humbert Westley. C: George Arliss, Boris Karloff,

Loretta Young, Robert Young, C. Aubrey Smith, Florence Arliss, Georges Renavent, Lumsden Hare, Holmes Herbert.

Farren Souter. *The Iron Duke* (GB/1935/80m/BW) D: Victor Saville. C: George Arliss, Gladys Cooper, Emlyn Williams, Ellaline Terriss, Allan Aynesworth, Felix Aylmer, Gerald Lawrence, Gibb McLaughlin, Frederick Leister, Edmund Willard.

Lamberto Picasso. *Campo di Maggio* (aka *100 Days of Napoleon*) (Italy/1936/100m/BW) D: Giovacchino Forzano. C: Corrado Racca, Emilia Varini, Pino Locchi, Rosa Stradner, Enzo Biliotti, Augusto Marcacci, Ernseto Marini.

Ien Wul. *Conquest* (aka *Marie Walewska*) (US/1937/115m/BW) D: Clarence Brown. B/on the novel *Pani Walewska* by Waclaw Gasiorowski. C: Greta Garbo, Charles Boyer, Reginald Owen, Alan Marshal, Henry Stephenson, Leif Erikson.

Paul Hoffman. *Fanny Elssler* (aka *Fanny Eissler*) (Germany/1937/83m/BW) D: Paul Martin. C: Lillian Harvey, Liselotte Schaak, Rolf Moeblus, Willy Birgel, Walter Werner.

Luigi Cimara. *Loyalty of Love* (Italy/1937/90m/BW) D: Guido Brignone. C: Marta Abba, Elsa de Giorgi, Tina Lottanzi, Riccardo Tassani, Nerio Bernardi.

Lawrence Hanray. *A Royal Divorce* (GB/1938/85m/BW) D: Jack Raymond. B/on the novel *Josephine* by Jacques Thery. C: Ruth Chatterton, Pierre Blanchar, Frank Cellier, John Laurie, Jack Hawkins, David Farrar, Allan Jeayes, Auriol Lee.

Walter Kingsford. *Juarez* (US/1939/132m/BW) D: William Dieterle. B/on the novel *The Phantom Crown* by Bertita Harding and the play *Juarez and Maximillian* by Franz Werfel. C: Paul Muni, Bette Davis, Brian Aherne, Claude Rains, John Garfield, Donald Crisp, Harry Davenport, Gale Sondergaard, Joseph Calleia.

O. W. Fisher. *Napoleon* (France/1954/190m/C) D: Sacha Guitry. C: Jean-Pierre Aumont, Gianna Maria Canale, Jeanne Boitel, Pierre Brasseur, Daniel Gelin, Sacha Guitry, Raymond Pellegrin, Danielle Darrieux, Lana Marconi, Michele Morgan, Erich von Stroheim, Dany Roby, Henri Vidal, Clement Duhour, Serge Regianni, Maria Schell.

Karl Schonbock. *Congress Dances* (Germany/1955/79m/BW) D: Franz Antel. C: Johanna Matz, Rudolf Prack, Hannelore Bollmann, Jester Naefe, Marte Harell.

Hannes Messemer. *Der Kongress Amüsiert Sich* (Germany-Austria/1966/98m/C) D: Geza von Radvanvi. C: Lilli Palmer, Curt Jurgens, Paul Meurisse, Wolfgang Kieling, Brett Halsey.

Barry Humphries. *Immortal Beloved* (US/1994/123m/C) D: Bernard Rose. C: Gary Oldman, Isabella Rosselini, Valeria Golino, Jeroen Krabbe, Gerard Horan.

363 Michelangelo Buonarroti (1475–1564)

A poet, sculptor (the statue of "David") and painter, Michaelangelo's most famous work was the painting on the ceiling of the Sistine Chapel.

Wilfred Fletcher. *The Cardinal* (GB/1936/70m/BW) D: Sinclair Hill. B/on the play by Louis N. Parker. C: Matheson Lang, Eric Portman, F.B.J. Sharpe, Robert Atkins.

Andrea Bosic. *The Magnificent Adventurer* (aka *Il Magnifico Avventuriero*) (France-Italy-Spain-/1963/93m/C) D: Riccardo Freda. Cast: Carmelo Artale, Bernard Blier, Carla Caló, Rossella Como, Umberto D'Orsi, Félix Dafauce, Sandro Dori, Françoise Fabian, Félix Fernández, Brett Halsey, Rafael Ibáñez, Giampiero Littera, Diego Michelotti, Claudia Mori, José Nieto, Elio Pandolfo, Dany París, Nazzareno Piana, Jancito San Emeterio, Bruno Scipioni, Mirko Valentin.

Charlton Heston. *The Agony and the Ecstasy* (US/1965/136m/C) D: Carol Reed. B/on the novel by Irving Stone. C: Rex Harrison, Diane Cilento, Harry Andrews, Tomas Milian.

364 Miller, Glenn (1904–1944)

Extremely popular bandleader of the War years, Miller's plane disappeared over the English Channel when he was preparing a show to entertain troops.

James Stewart. *The Glenn Miller Story* (US/1953/115m/C) D: Anthony Mann. C: June Allyson, Charles Drake, Harry Morgan, Barton MacLane, George Tobias, Marion Ross.

Ray Daley. *The Five Pennies* (US/1959/117m/C) D: Melville Shavelson. C: Danny Kaye, Barbara Bel Geddes, Ray Anthony, Bobby Troup, Tuesday Weld.

365 Miller, Henry (1891–1980)

American writer whose unconventional, sexually explicit, biographical novels changed the writings of the mid 20th century. They were banned in the United States and Britain until the1960's. His best known works are *Tropic of Capricorn* and *Tropic of Cancer*. His last major work was the trilogy *The Rosy Crucifiction: Sexus, Plexus*, and *Nexus*. *Henry and June* is based on the diaries of Anais Nin, portrayed in the film by Maria de Medeiros.

Rip Torn. *Tropic of Cancer* (France/1970/87m/C) D: Joseph Strick. B/on the novel by Henry Miller. C: James Callahan, Ellen Burstyn, David Bauer, Laurence Lingeres, Phil Brown.

Fred Ward. *Henry and June* (US/1990/134m/C) D: Philip Kaufman. B/on the dairies of Anais Nin. C: Uma Thurman, Maria de Medeiros, Richard E. Grant, Kevin Spacey, Jean-Philippe Ecoffey, Bruce Myers, Jean-Louis Bunuel, Fedor Ateba, Gaetan Bloom, Karine Couvelard, Alexandra de Gall, Artesu de Peguerni, Maurice Escargot, Pierre Etan, Annie Fratellini, Liz Hasse, Frank Heiler, Slyvie Huguel, Brigitte Lahie, Maite Maille, Marc Maury, Annie Vincent.

366 Miller, Marilyn (1898–1936)

Broadway singer/actress, Marilyn also starred in several early sound musicals including *Sally* (29), *Sunny* (30) and *Her Majesty Love* (31), which were less than successful attempts at recreating her Broadway achievements.

Rosina Lawrence. *The Great Ziegfeld* (US/1936/170m/BW) D: Robert Z. Leonard. Best Picture (AA). C: William Powell, Luise Rainer, Myrna Loy, Frank Morgan, Reginald Owen, Fannie Brice, Ray Bolger, A.A. Trimble, Buddy Doyle, Ruth Gillette.

Judy Garland. *Till the Clouds Roll By* (US/1946/120m/C) D: Richard Whorf. C: Robert Walker, Lucille Bremer, Joan Wells, Van Heflin, Paul Langton, Dorothy Patrick, Paul Maxey.

June Haver. *Look for the Silver Lining* (US/1949/106m/C) D: David Butler. B/on *The Life of Marilyn Miller* by Bert Kalmar & Harry Ruby. C: Ray Bolger, Gordon MacRae, Charlie Ruggles, Will Rogers, Jr.

367 Molière (1622–1673)

(Jean Baptiste Poquelin) Influential French playwright, Molière's works include The *Misanthrope, Amphitryon,* and *Tartuffe.*

Otto Gebuhr. *Nanon* (Germany/1938/BW) D: Herbert Maisch. C: Johannes Heester.

Fernand Gravet. *Royal Affairs in Versailles* (aka *Versailles*) (aka *Affairs in Versailles*) (aka *If Versailles Were Told to Me*) (aka *Si Versailles M'Eétait Couté*) (France/1953/180–152m/C) D: Sacha Guitry. C: Sacha Guitry, Claudette Colbert, Orson Welles, Gerard Phillippe, Micheline Presle, Jean Marais, Georges Marchal, Gilbert Boka, Lana Marconi, Gino Cervi, Louis Arbessier, Jacques Berthier, Samson Fainsilber, Gilbert Gil, Emile Drain, Jacques de Feraudy, Gaston Rey, Philippe Richard.

Philippe Cauberte. *Moliére* (France/1975/255m/C) D: Ariane Mnouchkine. C: Marie-France Audollent, Jonathan Sutton, Jean-Claude Penchenat, Frederic Ladonne.

Daniel J. Coplan. *The Man in the Iron Mask* (US/1998/85m/C) D: William Richert. B/on the novel by Alexandre Dumas. C: Edward Albert, Dana Barron, Timothy Bottoms, Brigid Conley Walsh, Fannie Brett, Meg Foster, James Gammon, Dennis Hayden, William Richert, Nick Richert, Rex Ryon, Brenda James, R.G. Armstrong, Robert Tena.

Monroe, James *see* 572

368 Monroe, Marilyn (1926–1962)

(Norma Jean Mortenson) The quintessential cinema sex goddess, Marilyn received top billing in only seven of her pictures including *Bus Stop* (56) and *Some Like It Hot* (59). Yet since her premature death (of a drug overdose), her popularity has only increased and she has been the subject of hundreds of books, films, articles and even popular songs. In the TV movie *Moviola: This Year's Blonde* (80) she was portrayed by Constance Forsland, and by Melody Anderson in *Marilyn and Bobby* (93).

Misty Rowe. *Goodbye, Norma Jean* (US-Australia/1976/95m/C) D: Larry Buchanan. C: Terrence Locke, Patch Mackenzie, Preston Hanson, Marty Zagon.

Catherine Hicks. *Marilyn: The Untold Story* (US/1980/156m/C) D: John Flynn, Jack Arnold & Lawrence Schiller. B/on the book *Marilyn* by Norman Mailer. C: Richard Basehart, Frank Converse, John Ireland, Viveca Lindfors, Jason Miller, Sheree North, Larry Pennell.

Paula Lane. *Goodnight, Sweet Marilyn* (US-Australia/1984/100m/C) D: Larry Buchanan. C: Phyllis Coates, Stuart Lancaster, Jeremy Slate, Misty Rowe.

Stephanie Anderson. *Death Becomes Her* (US/1992/105m/C) D: Robert Zemeckis. C: Meryl Streep, Bruce Willis, Goldie Hawn, Isabella Rossellini, Sydney Pollack, Ian Ogilvy, Michael Caine, Bonnie Cahoon, Bob Swain, Ron Stein, Eric Clark, Dave Brock.

Stephanie Anderson. Cortney Page (voice only). *Calendar Girl* (US/1993/92m/C) D: John Whitesell. C: Jason Priestley, Gabriel Olds, Jerry O'Connell, Joe Pantoliano, Steve Railsback.

Meredith Patterson. *Company Man* (France-GB-US/2000/86m/C) D: Peter Askin, Douglas McGrath. C: Paul Guilfoyle, Jeffrey Jones, Reathel Bean, Harriet Koppel, Douglas McGrath, Sigourney Weaver, Terry Beaver, Sean Dugan, Grant Walden, Nathan Dean, Nathan Bean, John Randolph Jones, Ryan Phillippe, Kim Merrill, Merwin Goldsmith, Anthony LaPaglia, Tuck Milligan.

369 Montez, Lola (1818–1861)

(Marie Dolores Eliza Gilbert) An Irish born dancer and actress, Montez was a mistress of **Franz Liszt**, Alexandre Dumas and the Bavarian King Ludwig I. She also toured America (and eventually died there), hence her inclusion in several Westerns.

Rebecca Wassem. *Wells Fargo* (US/1937/115–94m/BW) D: Frank Lloyd. C: Joel McCrea, Bob Burns, Frances Dee, Lloyd Nolan, Porter Hall, Ralph Morgan, Frank McGlynn.

Yvonne DeCarlo. *Black Bart* (US/1948/80m/C) D: George Sherman. C: Dan Duryea, Jeffrey Lynn, Percy Kilbride.

Carmen D'Antonio. *Golden Girl* (US/1951/107m/C) D: Lloyd Bacon. C: Mitzi Gaynor, Dale Robertson, Dennis Day, James Barton, Emory Parnell, Kermit Maynard.

Martine Carol. *Lola Montes* (aka *The Sins of Lola Montes*) (aka *The Fall of Lola Montes*) (France-Germany/1955/110m/C) D: Max Ophuls. C: Peter Ustinov, Anton Walbrook, Ivan Desnu, Will Quadflieg, Oskar Werner.

Larissa Trembovelskaya. *The Loves of Liszt* (Hungary-USSR/1970) D: Marton Keleti. C: Imre Sinkovits.

Ingrid Caven. *Ludwig — Requiem for a Virgin King* (Germany/1972/134m/C) D: Hans Jurgen Syberberg. C: Harry Baer, Gerhard Marz, Balthasar Thomas, Peter Kern.

Anulka Dziubinska. *Lisztomania* (GB/1975/105m/C) D: Ken Russell. C: Roger Daltrey, Sara Kestelman, Paul Nicholas, Fiona Lewis, Veronica Qilligan, Ken Colley, Andrew Reilly, Murray Melvin, Otto Diamant, Imogen Claire.

Florinda Balkan. *Royal Flash* (GB/1975/98m/C) D: Richard Lester. B/on the novel by George MacDonald Fraser. C: Malcolm McDowell, Alan Bates, Oliver Reed.

370 Montgomery, Bernard Law (1887–1976)

(1st Viscount Montgomery of Alamein) The English general who defeated **Rommell** in the North African campaign, Monty was made field marshal and led all British and Canadian forces during the invasion of Normandy.

M.E. Clifton James. *I Was Monty's Double* (aka *Hell, Heaven Or Hoboken*) (GB/1958/100m/BW) D: John Guillerman. B/on the book by M. E. Clifton-

James. C: John Mills, Patrick Allen, Patrick Holt, Leslie Phillips, Michael Hordern.

Trevor Reid. *The Longest Day* (US/1962/180m/BW) D: Andrew Marton, Ken Annakin & Bernherd Wicki. B/on the novel by Cornelius Ryan. Best English Language Picture (NBR). C: John Wayne, Robert Mitchum, Henry Fonda, Robert Ryan, Rod Steiger, Robert Wagner, Sal Mineo, Roddy McDowall, Curt Jurgens, Paul Hartman, Nicholas Stuart, Henry Grace, Wolfgang Lukschy, Werner Hinz, Alexander Knox.

Michael Rennie. *Desert Tanks* (aka *The Battle of El Alamein*) (aka *El Alamein*) (Italy-France/1968/109m/C) D: Calvin Padget (Giorgio Ferro). C: Frederick Stafford, George Hilton, Robert Hossein, Ettore Manni.

Michael Bates. *Patton* (aka *Patton — Lust for Glory*) (US/1970/170m/C) D: Franklin J. Schaffner. B/on *Patton: Ordeal and Triumph* by Ladislas Farago and *A Soldier's Story* by Omar Bradley. Best Picture, Best Direction (AA). Best English-Language Picture (NBR). Best Director (DGA). C: George C. Scott, Karl Malden, Edward Binns, Lawrence Dobkin, John Doucette, Stephen Young, Michael Strong, Frank Latimore, James Edwards, Richard Meunch, Karl Michael Vogler.

371 Moran, George "Bugs" (1893–1957)

Chicago Prohibition gangster and rival of **Al Capone**, Moran's gang (along with his power) was wiped out in the St. Valentine's Day Massacre. He died in Leavenworth prison having been convicted on a bank robbery charge.

Ben Hendricks, Jr. *The Public Enemy* (aka *Enemies of the Public*) (US/1931/83m/ BW) D: William Wellman. B/on the story *Beer and Blood* by John Bright. C: James Cagney, Jean Harlow, Edward Woods, Joan Blondell, Donald Cook, Mae Clarke.

Murvyn Vye. *Al Capone* (US/1959/105m/BW) D: Richard Wilson. C: Rod Steiger, Fay Spain, Lewis Charles, Nehemiah Persoff, James Gregory, Martin Balsam, Robert Gist.

Ralph Meeker. *The St. Valentine's Day Massacre* (US/1967/100m/C) D: Roger Corman. C: Jason Robards, George Segal, Jean Hale, Clint Ritchie, Frank Silvera, Joseph Campanella, Harold J. Stone, Bruce Dern, John Agar, Reed Hadley, Rico Cattani, Jack Nicholson.

Robert Phillips. *Capone* (US/1975/101m/C) D: Steve Carver. C: Ben Gazzara, Susan Blakely, Harry Guardino, John Cassavetes, Sylvester Stallone, John D. Chandler, John Orchard.

Sean Moran. *Verne Miller* (US/1987/95m/C) D: Rod Hewitt. C: Scott Glenn, Barbara Stock, Thomas G. Waites, Lucinda Jenney, Diane Salinger, Andrew Robinson.

372 More, Sir Thomas (1478–1535)

Lord Chancellor to **Henry VIII**, More resigned when pressured by Henry to arrange his divorce from **Katharine of Aragon**. He refused to accept Henry as the head of the church, was imprisoned for treason and beheaded. In 1935 he was canonized by the Roman Catholic Church. He was portrayed by Charlton Heston in the 1989 TV version of *A Man For All Seasons*.

Paul Scofield. *A Man for All Seasons* (GB/1966/120m/C) D: Fred Zinnemann. B/on the play by Robert Bolt. Best Picture Awards: (AA, NBR, GG, NYC, BFA Any Source and Best British Film). Best Director Awards: (AA, NBR, GG, NYC, DGA). C: Wendy Hiller, Leo McKern, Robert Shaw, Orson Welles, Susannah York, Nigel Davenport, Vanessa Redgrave, Cyril Luckham.

William Squire. *Anne of the Thousand Days* (GB/1969/145m/C) D: Charles Jarrott. B/on the play by Maxwell Anderson. C: Richard Burton, Genevieve Bujold, Irene Papas, Anthony Quayle, John Colicos, Michael Hordern, Katharine Blake, Lesley Patterson, Nicola Pagett.

Michael Goodliffe. *The Six Wives of Henry VIII* (aka *Henry VIII and His Six Wives*) (GB/1972/125m/C) D: Waris Hussein. C: Keith Michell, Frances Cuka, Charlotte Rampling, Jane Asher, Jenny Bos, Lynne Frederick, Barbara Leigh-Hunt, Donald Pleasence, Simon Henderson, Annette Crosbie, John Bryans, Bernard Hepton, Dorothy Tutin.

373 Morgan, Sir Henry (1634?–1688)

A Welsh pirate who raided Spanish possessions throughout the Caribbean, he was knighted by **Charles II**, and made deputy governor of Jamaica.

Laird Cregar. *The Black Swan* (US/1942/85m/C) D: Henry King. B/on the novel by Rafael Sabatini. C: Tyrone Power, Maureen O'Hara, Thomas Mitchell, George Sanders.

Robert Barrat. *Double Crossbones* (US/1950/75m) D: Charles Barton. C: Donald O'Connor, Helena Carter, Will Geer, John Emery, Hope Emerson, Alan Napier, Louis Bacigalupi.

Torin Thatcher. *Blackbeard the Pirate* (US/1952/98m/C) D: Raoul Walsh. C: Robert Newton, Linda Darnell, William Bendix, Irene Ryan, Alan Mowbray, Richard Egan.

Timothy Carey. *The Boy and the Pirates* (US/1960/84m/C) D: Bert I. Gordon. C: Charles Herbert, Susan Gordon, Murvyn Vye, Paul Guilfoyle, Joseph Turkel, Archie Duncan.

Steve Reeves. *Morgan the Pirate* (Italy/1961/95m/C) D: Andre De Toth & Primo Zeglio. C: Valerie Lagrange, Chelo Alonso, Lidia Alfonsi, Armand Mestral, Ivo Garrani.

Robert Stephens. *Pirates of Tortuga* (US/1961/97m/C) D: Robert D. Webb. C: Ken Scott, Leticia Roman, David King, John Richardson, Rafer Johnson, Rachel Stephens, Stanley Adams.

374 Morrison, Jim (1943–1971)

Charismatic rock star, song writer, and lead singer of The Doors, epitomized the deep, dark, psychedelic side of rock and roll. The "Lizard King" was elevated to cult status after his death.

Val Kilmer. Sean Stone (Young Jim). *The Doors* (US/1991/135m/C) D: Oliver Stone. C: Frank Whaley, Kevin Dillon, Meg Ryan, Kyle MacLachlan, Billy Idol, Dennis Burkley, Josh Evans, Michael Masden, Michael Wincott, Kathleen Quinlan, John Densmore, Will Jordan, Mimi Rogers, Paul Williams, Crispin Glover, Bill Graham, Billy Vera, Bill Kunstler, Wes Studi, Costas Mandylor.

Daniel Cosgrove. *Isn't She Great* (US/2000/93m/C) D: Andrew Bergman. C: Bette Midler, Nathan Lane, Stockard Channing, David Hyde Pierce, Amanda Peet, John Cleese, Jason Fuchs, John Larroquette, Richard McConomy, Rebekah Mintzer, Sarah Jessica Parker, Sam Street, Frank Vincent.

375 Moses

Hebrew leader and lawgiver, Moses led the Jewish people out of bondage in Egypt to the Promised Land in Palestine. He was portrayed by Bill Campbell in the TV mini-series *In the Beginning* (2000).

Alin Cavin. *Are We Civilized?* (US/1934/70m/BW) D: Edwin Carewe. C: Frank McGlynn, Harry Burkhart, Charles Requa, Bert Lindley, Aaron Edwards, William Humphrey.

Frank Wilson. *Green Pastures* (US/1936/93m/BW) D: Marc Connelly & William Keigh. C: Rex Ingram, Oscar Polk, Eddie Anderson, George Reed, Reginald Federson.

Charlton Heston. *The Ten Commandments* (US/1956/245–219m/C) D: Cecil B. DeMille. B/on the the books of the *Old Testament* and other ancient texts, and on the novels *The Prince of Egypt* by Dorothy Wilson, *Pillar of Fire* by the Rev. J.H. Ingraham, and *On Eagles' Wings* by the Rev. G.E. Southon. C: Yul Brynner, Anne Baxter, Edward G. Robinson, Debra Paget, John Derek, Cedric Hardwicke, John Carradine, Ian Keith.

Francis X. Bushman. *The Story of Mankind* (US/1957/100m/C) D: Irwin Allen. B/on the book by Hendrik Van Loon. C: Ronald Colman, Hedy Lamarr, Virginia Mayo, Agnes Moorehead, Peter Lorre, Dennis Hopper, Marie Wilson, Helmut Dantine, Edward Everett Horton, Reginald Gardiner, Marie Windsor, Anthony Dexter, Austin Green, Jim Ameche, Harpo Marx, Bobby Watson, Reginald Sheffield, Cedric Hardwicke, Cesar Romero.

Burt Lancaster. *Moses* (GB-Italy/1975/140m/C) D: Gianfranco de Bosio. Feature film edited from the TV mini-series *Moses—The Lawgiver*. C: Anthony Quayle, Ingrid Thulin, Irene Papas, Mariangela Melato, William Lancaster, Mario Ferrari.

Gunter Reich. *Moses and Aaron* (Germany-France-Italy/1975/105m/C) D: Jean-Marie Straub. B/on the opera by Arnold Schoenberg. C: Louis Devos, Roger Lucas, Eva Csapo, Richard Salter, Werner Mann.

Mel Brooks. *History of the World, Part I* (US/1981/92m/C) D: Mel Brooks. C: Dom DeLuise, Madeline Kahn, Harvey Korman, Cloris Leachman, Gregory Hines, Art Metrano, John Hurt.

376 Mountbatten, Lord Louis (1900–1979)

(1st Earl Mountbatten of Burma) Allied commander of Burmese operations during World War II, Mountbatten later served as the last British viceroy in India. In 1979 he was assassinated by a bomb planted by the IRA.

Peter Williams. *The Man Who Never Was* (GB/1956/103m/C) D: Ronald Neame. B/on the novel by Ewen Montagu. C: Clifton Webb, Gloria Grahame, Robert Flemyng, Stephen Boyd, Wolf Frees, Michael Hordern, Cyril Cusack, Peter Sellers (voice of Churchill).

Patric Knowles. *The Devil's Brigade* (US/1968/131m/C) D: Andrew McLaglen. B/on the book by Robert H. Adleman & Col. George Walton. C: William Holden, Cliff Robertson, Vince Edwards, Michael Rennie, Dana Andrews, Andrew Prine.

Peter Harlowe. *Gandhi* (GB-India/1982/188m/C) D: Richard Attenborough. Best Picture (AA, BFA ,NYC), Best Director (AA, BFA, DGA). C: Ben Kingsley, Candice Bergen, Edward Fox, John Gielgud, Trevor Howard, Martin Sheen, Roshan Seth, Alyque Padamsee.

James Fox. *Jinnah* (Pakistan/1998/110m/C) D: Jamil Dehlavi. C: Christopher Lee, Maria Aitken, Shashi Kapoor, Richard Lintern, Shireen Shah, Robert Ashby, Indira Varma, Sam Dastor, Shakeel, Vaneeza Ahmed, Roger Brierley, Rowena Cooper, James Curran, Vernon Dobtcheff, Michael Elwyn, Ian Gelder, Christopher Godwin, John Grillo, Talat Hussain, John Nettleton, Alyque Padamsee.

377 Mozart, Wolfgang Amadeus (1756–1791)

A genius who died in poverty at the age of 35, Mozart, creator of more than 600 works in all musical genres, is today considered one of the greatest composers of all time.

Oskar Karlweis. *Die Försterchristl* (Germany/1931/90m/BW) D: Friedrich Zelnik. C: Irene Elsinger, Paul Richter, Andre Pilot, Adele Sandrock.

Stephen Haggard. *Mozart* (aka *Whom the Gods Love*) (GB/1936/78m/BW) D: Basil Dean. C: Victoria Hopper, John Loder, Liane Haid, Jean Cadell, Frederick Leister.

Hannes Stelzer. *Ein Kleine Nachtmusik* (Germany/1939/BW) D: Leopold Hainisch. C: Axel von Ambesser, Kurt Meisel.

Gino Cervi. *Eternal Melodies* (Italy/1939/93m/BW) D: Carmine Gallone. C: Conchita Montenegro, Luisella Beghi, Maria Jacobini, Paolo Stoppa, Luigi Pavese.

Hans Holt. *The Mozart Story* (aka *Whom the Gods Love*) (aka *Mozart*) (aka *Wenn Die Gotter Lieben*) (Germany/1942/91m/C) D: Karl Hartl. C: Rene Deltgen, Winnie Markus, Irene von Meyendorf, Edward Vedder, Wilton Graff, Curt Jurgens, Carol Forman, Walther Jansson, Paul Hoerbiger.

Oskar Werner. *The Life and Loves of Mozart* (aka *Mozart— Put Your Hand in Mine Dear*) (aka *Give Me Your Hand My Love. Mozart*) (aka *Mozart*) (Austria/1955/100–87m/C) D: Karl Hartl. C: Johanna Matz, Albin Skoda, Gertrud Kuekelmann.

Santiago Ziesmer. *Mozart: A Childhood Chronicle* (Germany/1976/224m/BW) D: Klaus Kirschner. C: Diego Crovetti, Marianne Lowitz, Ingeborg Schroder, Nina Palmers, Karl-Maria Schley.

Tom Hulce. *Amadeus* (US/1984/158m/C) D: Milos Forman. B/on the play by Peter Shaffer. Best Picture (AA, GG), Best Director (AA, DGA, GG). C: F. Murray Abraham, Elizabeth Berridge, Jeffrey Jones, Simon Callow, Roy Dotrice.

Max Tidof. *Forget Mozart!* (Germany-Czechoslovakia/1985/90m/C) D: Miloslav Luther. C: Armin Muller Stahl, Franz Glatzeder, Ladislav Chudik, Zdenek Hradilak.

Philip Zander. *The Mozart Brothers* (Sweden/1986/111m/C) D: Suzanne Osten. C: Henry Bronnett, Loa Falkman, Agneta Ekmanner.

378 Munch, Edvard (1863–1944)

Norwegian painter considered one of the great masters of modern European art, Munch's most famous work is "The Scream," or "The Shriek" (1893).

Geir Westby. *Edvard Munch* (Sweden-Norway/1976/215m/C) D: Peter Watkins. C: Gro Fraas, Johan Halsborg, Alf Kare Strindberg, Iselin Bast.

Nils Ole Oftebro. *Dagny* (Poland-Norway/1977/88m/C) D: Haakon Sandy. C: Lise Fjeldstad, Daniel Olbrychski, Per Oscarsson, Maciej Englert.

379 Murat, Joachim (1767–1815)

French marshal, Murat served **Napoleon** as a brilliant cavalry officer in many of his campaigns, married his sister Caroline in 1800 and succeeded his brother Joseph as the King of Naples in 1808.

Genica Missirio. *Napoleon Bonaparte* (France/1934/140m/BW) D: Abel Gance. Three-dimensional sound version of Gance's 1927 epic *Napoléon*. C: Albert Dieudonné, Edmond von Daele, Alexandre Koubitsky, Antonin Artaud, Boudreau, Alberty, Jack Rye, Favière, Gina Manès, Suzanne Blanchetti, Marguerite Gance, Simone Genevois.

Allan Jeayes. *A Royal Divorce* (GB/1938/85m/BW) D: Jack Raymond. B/on the novel *Josephine* by Jacques Thery. C: Ruth Chatterton, Pierre Blanchar, Frank Cellier, John Laurie, Jack Hawkins, David Farrar, Lawrence Hanray, Auriol Lee.

Nikolai Brilling. *1812* (aka *Kutuzov*) (USSR/1944/95m/B&W) D: Vladimir Petrov. C: Aleksei Diki, Sergei Mezhinsky, Y. Kaluzhsky, Sergo Zaqariadze, Nikolai Okhlopkov, Sergei Blinnikov, V. Gotovtsev, A. Polyakov, Boris Chirkov, Mikhail Pugovkin, Ivan Ryzhov, K. Shilovtsev, Aleksandr Stepanov, Ivan Skuratov, G. Terekhov, N. Timchenko, Vladimir Yershov.

Henri Vidal. *Napoleon* (France/1954/190m/C) D: Sacha Guitry. C: Jean-Pierre Aumont, Gianna Maria Canale, Jeanne Boitel, Pierre Brasseur, Daniel Gelin, Sacha Guitry, O.W. Fisher, Raymond Pellegrin, Danielle Darrieux, Lana Marconi, Michele Morgan, Erich von Stroheim, Dany Roby, Clement Duhour, Serge Regianni, Maria Schell.

Ettore Manni. *Austerlitz* (aka *The Battle of Austerlitz*) (France-Italy-Yugoslavia/1959/166m/C) D: Abel Gance. C: Pierre Mondy, Jean Mercure, Martine Carol, Jack Palance, Orson Welles, Claudia Cardinale, Georges Marchal, Roland Bartrop, Anthony Stuart, Jean Marais, Vittorio De Sica.

380 Mureita, Joaquin (1832?–1853)

A Mexican outlaw whose raids and robberies throughout the California gold fields literally put a bounty on his head which was cut off, preserved in alcohol and put on display as a warning to other would-be bandits. The Buck Jones flick *The Avenger* (31) is loosely based on Murieta's story.

Warner Baxter. *Robin Hood of El Dorado* (US/1936/86m/BW) D: William A. Wellman. B/on the novel by Walter Noble Burns. C: Ann Loring, Bruce Cabot, Margo, J. Carroll Naish.

Bill Elliott. *Vengeance of the West* (US/1942/60m/BW) D: Lambert Hillyer. C: Tex Ritter, Adele Mara, Frank Mitchell, Dick Curtis, Edmund Cobb.

Philip Reed. *Bandit Queen* (US/1950/69m/BW) D: William Berke. C: Barbara Britton, Willard Parker, Barton MacLane, Thurston Hall.

Robert Cabal. *The Man Behind the Gun* (US/1952/82m/C) D: Felix Feist. C: Randolph Scott, Patrice Wymore, Dick Wesson, Philip Carey, Lina Romay, Roy Roberts, Morris Ankrum.

Carlos Thompson. *The Last Rebel* (Mexico/1961/83m/C) D: Miguel Contreras Torres. C: Ariadne Welter, Rodolfo Acosta, Charles Fawcett.

Valentin De Vargas. *The Firebrand* (US/1962/63m/BW) D: Maury Dexter. C: Kent Taylor, Lisa Montell, Chubby Johnson, Barbara Mancell, Joe Racitti.

Jeffrey Hunter. *Murieta* (aka *Vendetta*) (aka *Joaquin Murieta*) (Spain/1965/107m/C) D: George Sherman. C: Arthur Kennedy, Diana Lorys, Sara Lezana.

Ricardo Montalban. *The Desperate Mission* (aka *Joaquin Murieta*) (aka *Murieta*) (US/1970/98m/C) D: Earl Bellamy. C: Slim Pickens, Rosey Grier, Ina Balin, Earl Holliman.

381 Musset, Alfred de (1810–1857)

French poet and playwright of the Romantic movement, author of autobiographical, historic, and comic works, still performed today. Some of his finest works were inspired by his love affiar with **George Sand**, including *La Confession d'un enfant du siècle (A Confession of a Child of the Century)*.

George Macready. *A Song to Remember* (US/1945/113m/C) D: Charles Vidor. C: Cornel Wilde, Merle Oberon, Paul Muni, Stephen Bekassy, Nina Foch, George Coulouris, Roxy Roth.

Mandy Patinkin. *Impromptu* (GB/1990/107m/C) D: James Lapine. C: Judy Davis, Hugh Grant, Bernadette Peters, Julian Sands, Ralph Brown, Emma Thompson.

Benoît Magimel. *Les Enfants du siècle* (aka *The Children of the Century*) (France/2000/135m/C) D: Diane Kurys. C: Juliette Binoche, Stefano Dionisi, Robin Renucci, Karin Viard, Isabelle Carré, Arnaud Giovaninetti, Denis Podalydès, Olivier Foubert, Marie-France Mignal, Patrick Chesnais.

382 Mussolini, Benito (1883–1945)

Italian Fascist dictator known as "Il Duce," Mussolini ruled Italy for twenty years until his defeat and execution in World War II. TV portrayals include: Enzo Castellari in *The Winds of War* (83), Bob Hoskins in *Mussolini and I* (85), and George C. Scott in *Mussolini: The Untold Story* (85).

Joe Devlin. *The Devil with Hitler* (aka *The Devil Checks Up*) (US/1942/44m/BW) D: Gordon Douglas. C: Alan Mowbray, Bobby Watson, George E. Stone, Marjorie Woodworth.

Joe Devlin. *That Nazty Nuisance* (aka *Nazty Nuisance*) (US/1943/50m/BW) D: Glenn Tryon. C: Bobby Watson, Johnny Arthur, Rex Evans, Charles Rogers, Wedgewood Nowell.

Joe Devlin. *They Got Me Covered* (US/1943/95m/BW) D: David Butler. C: Bob Hope, Dorothy Lamour, Otto Preminger, Eduardo Ciannelli, Lenore Aubert.

Joe Devlin. *The Miracle of Morgan's Creek* (US/1944/99m/BW) D: Preston

Sturges. C: Eddie Bracken, Betty Hutton, Diana Lynn, Brian Donlevy, Akim Tamiroff, Porter Hall, Bobby Watson.

Ivo Garrani. *The Great Battle* (aka *Liberation*) (USSR-Poland-Yugoslavia-Italy/1969/118m/C) D: Yuri Ozerov. C: Buhuti Zakariadze, Stanislav Yaskevich, Fritz Diez, Yuri Durov.

Vladimir Stach. *Days of Treason* (aka *Days of Betrayal*) (aka *Dny Zrady*) (Czechoslovakia/1973/198m/C) D: Otakar Vavra. C: Jiri Pleskot, Bohus Pastorek, Martin Gregor, Gunnar Mollar, Jaroslav Radimecky, Alexander Fred, Rudolf Jurda, Stanislav Zindulka, Vladimir Paviar, Bonvoj Navartil, Otakar Brousek, Josef Langmiller.

Mario Adorf. *The Assassination of Matteotti* (Italy/1973/117m/C) D: Florestano Vancini. C: Franco Nero, Damiano Damiani, Giulio Girola, Vittorio De Sica.

Rod Steiger. *The Last Days of Mussolini* (aka *The Last Four Days*) (Italy/1974/126–91m/C) D: Carlo Lizzani. C: Lisa Gastoni, Henry Fonda, Franco Nero, Lino Capolicchio.

Rod Steiger. *Lion of the Desert* (aka *Omar Mukhtar*) (Libya-GB/1981/162m/C) D: Moustapha Akkad. C: Anthony Quinn, Oliver Reed, John Gielgud, Irene Pappas, Raf Vallone, Gastone Moschin, Stefano Patrizi, Sky Dumont.

Fernando Briamo. *Claretta* (Italy/1984/127m/C) D: Pasquale Squitieri. C: Claudia Cardinale, Catherine Spaak, Giuliano Gemma, Caterina Boratto.

Claudio Spadaro. *Tea with Mussolini* (GB-Italy/1999/117m/C) D: Franco Zeffirelli. C: Cher, Judi Dench, Joan Plowright, Maggie Smith, Lily Tomlin, Baird Wallace, Charlie Lucas, Massimo Ghini, Paolo Seganti.

383 Napoleon Bonaparte (1769–1821)

The historical character most often portrayed on film, Napoleon was the Emperor of France and controlled much of Europe for nearly ten years (1804–14). His retreat in the Russian campaign precipitated his exile and upon his return from the Isle of Elba he met his final defeat at Waterloo.

Emile Drain. *L'Aiglon* (France-Germany/1931/BW) D: Victor Tourjansky. French language version of the German film *Der Herzog von Reichstadt.* C: Alfred Abel.

Paul Gunther. *Luise, Königin von Preussen* (Germany/1931/112m/BW) D: Carl Froelich. B/on the novel Luise by Walter von Molo. C: Henny Porten, Ekkehard Arendt, Vladimir Galderow, Gustaf Gründgens.

Gianfranco Giachetti. *Cento di Questi Giorni* (Italy/1933/BW) D: Mario & Augusto Camerini.

Albert Dieudonné. *Napoleon Bonaparte* (France/1934/140m/BW) D: Abel Gance. Three-dimensional sound version of Gance's 1927 epic *Napoléon.* C: Edmond von Daele, Alexandre Koubitsky, Antonin Artaud, Boudreau, Alberty, Jack Rye, Favière, Gina Manès, Suzanne Blanchetti, Marguerite Gance, Simone Genevois, Genica Missirio.

William Humphrey. *Are We Civilized?* (US/1934/70m/BW) D: Edwin Carewe. C: Frank McGlynn, Alin Cavin, Harry Burkhart, Charles Requa, Bert Lindley, Aaron Edwards.

Paul Irving. *The Count of Monte Cristo* (US/1934/113m/BW) D: Rowland V.

Napoleon (Herbert Lom) surveys the landscape after his victory over the Austrian and Russian Armies at the battle of Austerlitz. *War and Peace* (1956). Lom portrayed Napoleon previously in *The Young Mr. Pitt* (1942). (Museum of Modern Art Film Stills Archive)

Lee. B/on the novel by Alexandre Dumas. C: Robert Donat, Elissa Landi, Louis Calhern, Clarence Wilson, Ferdinand Munier, Sidney Blackmer, Luis Alberni.

Esme Percy. *Invitation to the Waltz* (GB/1935/80m/BW) D: Paul Merzbach. B/on the radio play by Holt Marvell, Eric Maschwitz & George Posford. C: Lilian Harvey, Wendy Toye, Carl Esmond, Harold Warrender, Richard Bird, Eric Stanley.

Rollo Lloyd. *Anthony Adverse* (US/1936/139m/BW) D: Mervyn LeRoy. B/on the novel by Hervey Allen. C: Fredric March, Olivia de Havilland, Edmund Gwenn.

Corrado Racca. *Campo di Maggio* (aka *100 Days of Napoleon*) (Italy/1936/100m/BW) D: Giovacchino Forzano. C: Emilia Varini, Pino Locchi, Rosa Stradner, Enzo Biliotti, Lamberto Picasso, Augusto Marcacci, Ernseto Marini.

Claude Rains. *Hearts Divided* (US/1936/70m/BW) D: Frank Borzage. B/on the play *Glorious Betsy* by Rida Johnson Young. C: Marion Davies, Dick Powell, Charles Ruggles, George Irving, Beulah Bondi, Edward Everett Horton, Hattie McDaniel.

Hans Zesch-Ballot. *Die Nacht Mit Dem Kaiser* (Germany/1936/BW) D: Erich Engel. C: Jenny Jugo, Richard Romanowski, Friedrich Benfer, Otto Woegerer, Paul Henckels.

Charles Boyer. *Conquest* (aka *Marie Walewska*) (US/1937/115m/BW) D: Clarence Brown. B/on the novel *Pani Walewska* by Waclaw Gasiorowski. C: Greta Garbo, Reginald Owen, Alan Marshal, Henry Stephenson, Ien Wul, Leif Erikson.

Stanley Price. *The Firefly* (US/1937/140m/BW) D: Robert Z. Leonard. B/on the musical play by Rudolf Friml and Otto Harbach. C: Jeanette MacDonald, Allan Jones, Warren William, Douglas Dumbrille, Tom Rutherford, Matthew Boulton.

Emile Drain (as Napoleon I). Jean-Louis Barrault (as General Bonaparte). *The Pearls of the Crown* (France/1937/120–100m/BW) D: Sacha Guitry & Christian-Jaque. C: Sacha Guitry, Jacqueline Delubac, Lyn Harding, Ermete Zacconi, Marguerite Moreno, Yvette Plenne, Catalano, Arletty, Percy Marmont, Derrick De Marney, Barbara Shaw, Simone Renant, Enrico Glori, Renee Saint-Cyr, Pizani, Claude Dauphin, Aime-Simon Gerard.

Pierre Blanchar. *A Royal Divorce* (GB/1938/85m/BW) D: Jack Raymond. B/on the novel *Josephine* by Jacques Thery. C: Ruth Chatterton, Frank Cellier, John Laurie, Jack Hawkins, David Farrar, Allan Jeayes, Lawrence Hanray, Auriol Lee.

Emile Drain (as Napoleon I). Claude Martin (as General Bonaparte). *Champs-Elysées* (aka *Remontons Les Champs-Elysées*) (France/1938/100m/BW) D: Sacha Guitry. C: Sacha Guitry, Lucien Baroux, Jacqueline Delubac, Germaine Dermoz, Jeanne Boitel, Raymonde Allain, Jean Davy, Jacques Erwin, Rene Fauchois, Liane Pathe, Robert Pizani, Raymond Galle, Andre Laurent.

Albert Dieudonné. *Madame Sans Gene* (France/1941) D: Roger Richebe.

Jean-Louis Barrault. Sacha Guitry. *Mademoiselle Désirée* (aka *Le Destin Fabuleux de Désirée Clary*) (France/1942/95m/BW) D: Sacha Guitry. C: Genevieve Guitry, Gaby Morlay, Lise Delamare, Aime Clariond, Jacques Varenne.

Herbert Lom. *The Young Mr. Pitt* (GB/1942/118m/BW) D: Carol Reed. C: Robert Donat, Robert Morley, Phyllis Calvert, Raymond Lovell, Max Adrian, Felix Aylmer, Albert Lieven, Stephen Haggard, Geoffrey Atkins, John Mills, Agnes Laughlan.

Sergei Mezhinsky. *1812* (aka *Kutuzov*) (USSR/1944/95m/B&W) D: Vladimir Petrov. C: Aleksei Diki, Y. Kaluzhsky, Sergo Zaqariadze, Nikolai Okhlopkov, Sergei Blinnikov, V. Gotovtsev, A. Polyakov, Nikolai Brilling, Boris Chirkov, Mikhail Pugovkin, Ivan Ryzhov, K. Shilovtsev, Aleksandr Stepanov, Ivan Skuratov, G. Terekhov, N. Timchenko, Vladimir Yershov.

Emile Drain. *Le Diable Boiteux* (France/1948) D: Sacha Guitry. C: Sacha Guitry, Maurice Schutz.

Paul Dahlke. *Begegnung Mit Werther* (Germany/1949) D: Karl Heinz Stroux. C: Heidemarie Hatheyer.

Gerard Oury. *Sea Devils* (GB/1953/91m/C) D: Raoul Walsh. B/on *The Toilers of the Sea* by Victor Hugo. C: Yvonne De Carlo, Rock Hudson, Jacques Brunius.

Gerard Oury. *The Loves of Three Queens* (aka *The Face That Launched a Thousand Ships*) (aka *Eternal Woman*) (aka *Helen of Troy*) (Italy-France/1953/90m/C) D: Marc Allegret. C: Hedy Lamarr, Massimo Serato, Robert Beatty, Cathy O'Donnell.

Emile Drain. *Royal Affairs in Versailles* (aka *Versailles*) (aka *Affairs in Versailles*) (aka *If Versailles Were Told to Me*) (aka *Si Versailles M'Eétait Couté*) (France/1953/180–152m/C) D: Sacha Guitry. C: Sacha Guitry, Claudette Colbert, Orson

Welles, Gerard Phillippe, Micheline Presle, Jean Marais, Georges Marchal, Gilbert Boka, Lana Marconi, Gino Cervi, Fernand Gravet, Louis Arbessier, Jacques Berthier, Samson Fainsilber, Gilbert Gil, Jacques de Feraudy, Gaston Rey, Philippe Richard.

Marlon Brando. *Désirée* (US/1954/110m/C) D: Henry Koster. B/on the novel by Annemarie Selinko. C: Jean Simmons, Merle Oberon, Michael Rennie, John Hoyt, Elizabeth Sellars, Cameron Mitchell, Cathleen Nesbitt, Sam Gilman, Alan Napier.

Raymond Pellegrin. Daniel Gelin. *Napoleon* (France/1954/190m/C) D: Sacha Guitry. C: Jean-Pierre Aumont, Gianna Maria Canale, Jeanne Boitel, Pierre Brasseur, Sacha Guitry, O.W. Fisher, Danielle Darrieux, Lana Marconi, Michele Morgan, Erich von Stroheim, Dany Roby, Henri Vidal, Clement Duhour, Serge Regianni, Maria Schell.

Robert Cornthwaite. *The Purple Mask* (US/1955/82m/C) D: H. Bruce Humberstone. B/on the play *Le Chevalier Au Masques* by Paul Armont & Jean Manouss. C: Tony Curtis, Colleen Miller, Dan O'Herlihy, Gene Barry, Angela Lansbury, George Dolenz.

Herbert Lom. *War and Peace* (US-Italy/1956/208m/C) D: King Vidor. B/on the novel by Leo Tolstoy. C: Audrey Hepburn, Henry Fonda, Mel Ferrer, Vittorio Gassman, John Mills, Oscar Homolka, Anita Ekberg, Helmut Dantine, Savo Raskovitch.

Rene Deltgen. *Queen Luise* (aka *Königin Luise*) (Germany/1957/102m/C) D: Wolfgang Liebeneiner. C: Ruth Leuwerik, Dieter Borsche, Bernhard Wicki, Charles Regnier.

Dennis Hopper. *The Story of Mankind* (US/1957/100m/C) D: Irwin Allen. B/on the book by Hendrik Van Loon. C: Ronald Colman, Hedy Lamarr, Virginia Mayo, Agnes Moorehead, Peter Lorre, Marie Wilson, Helmut Dantine, Edward Everett Horton, Reginald Gardiner, Marie Windsor, Francis X. Bushman, Anthony Dexter, Austin Green, Jim Ameche, Harpo Marx, Bobby Watson, Reginald Sheffield, Cedric Hardwicke, Cesar Romero.

Pierre Mondy. *Austerlitz* (aka *The Battle of Austerlitz*) (France-Italy-Yugoslavia/1959/166m/C) D: Abel Gance. C: Jean Mercure, Martine Carol, Jack Palance, Orson Welles, Claudia Cardinale, Georges Marchal, Roland Bartrop, Anthony Stuart, Jean Marais, Vittorio De Sica, Ettore Manni.

Julien Bertheau. *Madame* (aka *Madame Sans-Gene*) (France-Italy-Spain/1961/104m/C) D: Christian-Jaque. B/on the play *Madame Sans Gene* by Emile Moreau & Victorien Sardou. C: Sophia Loren, Robert Hossein, Renaud Mary, Marina Berti, Carlo Giuffere, Gabriella Pallotta, Annalis Gade, Laura Valenzuela.

Raymond Pellegrin. *Imperial Venus* (Italy-France/1962/140m/C) D: Jean Delannoy. C: Gina Lollobrigida, Stephen Boyd, Gabrielle Ferzetti, Micheline Presle.

Janusz Zakrzenski. *Ashes* (aka *The Lost Army*) (aka *Popioly*) (Poland/1965/233m/BW) D: Andrzej Wajda. C: Daniel Olbrychski, Pola Raksa.

Gyula Bodrogi. *Hary Janos* (Hungary/1965) D: Miklos Szinetar.

Vladislav Strzhelchik. *War and Peace* (USSR/1966/373m/C) D: Sergei Bondarchuk. B/on the novel by Leo Tolstoy. C: Lyudmila Savelyeva, Sergei Bondarchuk, Viktor Stanitsin, Vyacheslav Tihonov, Hira Ivanov-Gubanova, Boris Zakhava, V. Murganov.

Giani Esposito. *The Sea Pirate* (France-Italy-Spain/1967/85m/C) D: Roy Rowland. C: Gerard Barray, Antonella Lualdi, Terence Morgan, Monica Randal, Frank Oliveras.

Heinrich Schweiger. *Sexy Susan at the King's Court* (aka *Sexy Susan Sins Again*) (aka *Frau Wirtin Hat Auch Einen Grafen*) (Austria-Germany-Italy-Hungary/1968/96m/C) D: François Legrand (Franz Antel). C: Terry Torday, Jeffrey Hunter, Harald Leipnitz.

Heinrich Schweiger. *Frau Wirtin Hat Auch Eine Nichte* (Germany-Austria-Italy/1968/98m/C) D: Franz Antel. C: Terry Torday, Claudio Brook, Margaret Lee.

Eli Wallach. *The Adventures of Gerard* (GB-Italy-Switzerland/1970/91m/C) D: Jerzy Skolimowski. B/on *The Exploits of Brigadier Gerard* stories by A. Conan Doyle. C: Peter McEnery, Claudia Cardinale, John Neville, Jack Hawkins, Mark Burns, Paolo Stoppa.

Rod Steiger. *Waterloo* (Italy-USSR/1970/123m/C) D: Sergei Bondarchuk. C: Orson Welles, Virginia McKenna, Michael Wilding, Donal Donnelly, Christopher Plummer, Jack Hawkins, Dan O'Herlihy, Rupert Davies, Aldo Cecconi, Rodolfo Lodi.

Kenneth Haig. *Eagle in a Cage* (US-GB-Yugoslavia/1971/97m/C) D: Fielder Cook. B/on the teleplay by Millard Lampell. C: John Gielgud, Ralph Richardson, Billie Whitelaw, Moses Gunn, Lee Montague, Michael Williams.

Larry Bishop. *Shanks* (US/1974/93m/C) D: William Castle. C: Marcel Marceau, Tsilla Chelton, Philippe Clay, Cindy Eilbacher, Helena Kallianiotes, Don Calfa, Mondo, Phil Adams, William Castle.

James Tolkan. *Love and Death* (US/1975/85m/C) D: Woody Allen. C: Woody Allen, Diane Keaton, Georges Adet, Frank Adu, Harold Gould, Alfred Lutter.

Aldo Maccione. *The Loves and Times of Scaramouche* (aka *Scaramouche*) (Italy/1976/91m/C) D: Enzo Castellari. C: Michael Sarrazin, Ursula Andress, Michael Forest.

Ian Holm. *Time Bandits* (GB/1981/116m/C) D: Terry Gilliam. C: John Cleese, Sean Connery, Shelley Duvall, Katherine Helmond, Michael Palin, Ralph Richardson.

Daniel Harris. *Stuck on You* (US/1983/88m/C) D: Samuel Weil & Michael Herz. C: Irwin Corey, Robin Burroughs, Carl Sturmer, Julie Newdow, Barbie Kielian.

Patrice Chéreau. *Adieu, Bonaparte* (France-Egypt/1985/120m/C) D: Youssef Chahine. C: Michel Piccoli, Mohsen Mohiedine, Mohamed Atef, Christian Patey.

Terry Camilleri. *Bill and Ted's Excellent Adventure* (US/1989/90m/C) D: Stephen Herek. C: Keanu Reeves, Alex Winter, George Carlin, Amy Stock-Poynton, Dan Shor, Clifford David, Rod Loomis, Al Leong, Jane Wiedlin, Robert V. Barron, Tony Steedman, Fee Waybill.

Ron Cook. *Quills* (GB-US/2000/123m/C) D: Philip Kaufman. B/on the play by Doug Wright. C: Geoffrey Rush, Kate Winslet, Joaquin Phoenix, Michael Caine, Billie Whitelaw, Patrick Malahide, Amelia Warner, Jane Menelaus, Stephen Moyer, Tony Pritchard, Michael Jenn, Danny Babington, George Yiasoumi, Elizabeth Berrington, Edward Tudor-Pole, Harry Jones, Bridget McConnell, Rebecca R. Palmer, Toby Sawyer, Daniel Ainsleigh, Terry O'Neill, Diana Morrison, Carol MacReady, Tom Ward, Richard Mulholland, Julian Tait, Tessa Vale, Howard Lew Lewis, Lisa Hammond, Mathew Fraser, Jamie Beddard.

384 Napoleon III (1808–1873)

(Louis Napoleon Bonaparte) The nephew of **Napoleon Bonaparte** and the Emperor of France (1852–70), Napoleon was deposed following his defeat in the Franco-Prussian War.

Frank Vosper. *Spy of Napoleon* (GB/1936/98m/BW) D: Maurice Elvey. B/on the novel by the Baroness Orczy. C: Richard Barthelmess, Dolly Haas, Joyce Bland, Lyn Harding.

Walter Kingsford. *The Story of Louis Pasteur* (US/1936/85m/BW) D: William Dieterle. C: Paul Muni, Josephine Hutchinson, Anita Louise, Donald Woods, Iphigenie Castiglioni.

Guy Bates Post. *Maytime* (US/1937/132m/BW) D: Robert Z. Leonard. B/on the operetta by Rida Johnson Young & Sigmund Romberg. C: Jeanette Mac-Donald, Nelson Eddy, John Barrymore, Herman Bing, Tom Brown, Iphigenie Castiglioni.

Sacha Guitry. *The Pearls of the Crown* (France/1937/120–100m/BW) D: Sacha Guitry & Christian-Jaque. C: Jacqueline Delubac, Lyn Harding, Ermete Zacconi, Marguerite Moreno, Yvette Plenne, Catalano, Arletty, Percy Marmont, Derrick De Marney, Barbara Shaw, Simone Renant, Jean Louis Barrault, Emile Drain, Enrico Glori, Renee Saint-Cyr, Pizani, Claude Dauphin, Aime-Simon Gerard.

Sacha Guitry. *Champs-Elysées* (aka *Remontons Les Champs-Elysées*) (France/1938/100m/BW) D: Sacha Guitry. C: Lucien Baroux, Jacqueline Delubac, Germaine Dermoz, Jeanne Boitel, Raymonde Allain, Jean Davy, Emile Drain, Jacques Erwin, Rene Fauchois, Liane Pathe, Robert Pizani, Claude Martin, Raymond Galle, Andre Laurent.

Leon Ames. *Suez* (US/1938/104m/BW) D: Allan Dwan. C: Tyrone Power, Loretta Young, Miles Mander, Annabella, George Zucco, Victor Varconi, Brandon Hurst.

Claude Rains. *Juarez* (US/1939/132m/BW) D: William Dieterle. B/on the novel *The Phantom Crown* by Bertita Harding and the play *Juarez and Maximillian* by Franz Werfel. C: Paul Muni, Bette Davis, Brian Aherne, John Garfield, Donald Crisp, Walter Kingsford, Harry Davenport, Gale Sondergaard, Joseph Calleia.

Guy Bates Post. *The Mad Empress* (aka *Juarez and Maximillian*) (Mexico-US/1939/72m/BW) D: Miguel Contreras Torres. C: Medea Novara, Lionel Atwill, Conrad Nagel, Evelyn Brent, Earl Gunn, Jason Robards, Sr., Frank McGlynn, Duncan Renaldo.

Walter Kingsford. *A Dispatch from Reuters* (aka *This Man Reuter*) (US/1940/89m/BW) D: William Dieterle. B/on the story *Reuter's News Agency* by Valentine Williams & Wolfgang Wilhelm. C: Edward G. Robinson, Albert Basserman, Gilbert Emery.

Jerome Cowan. *The Song of Bernadette* (US/1943/156m/BW) D: Henry King. B/on the novel by Franz Werfel. Best Picture (GG). C: Jennifer Jones, William Eythe, Charles Bickford, Vincent Price, Lee J. Cobb, Anne Revere, Patricia Morison, Gladys Cooper.

A. Khokhlov. *Admiral Nakhimov* (USSR/1947/95m/BW) D: Vsevolod Pudovkin. C: Alexi Dikki, Vsevolod Pudovkin, Eugene Samoilov, Vladimir Vladislavsky.

Kenneth Kent. *Idol of Paris* (GB/1948/106m/BW) D: Leslie Arliss. B/on the novel *Paiva, Queen of Love* by Alfred Shirkauer. C: Michael Rennie, Beryl Baxter, Christine Norden, Miles Malleson, Margaretta Scott.

Jean Debucourt. *Man To Men* (aka *D'Homme a Hommes*) (France/1948/112m/BW) D: Christian-Jaque. C: Jean-Louis Barrault, Bernard Blier, Helene Perdriere.

David Bond. *The Sword of Monte Cristo* (US/1951/80m/C) D: Maurice Geraghty. B/on a novel by Alexandre Dumas. C: George Montgomery, Paula Corday, Berry Kroeger, Steve Brodie.

Pierre Bertin. *The Amazing Monsieur Fabre* (aka *Monsieur Fabre*) (France/1952/90–78m/BW) D: Henri Diamond-Berger. C: Pierre Fresnay, Andre Randall, Georges Tabet, Espanita Cortez.

Jean Debucourt. *Nana* (France-Italy/1954/100m/C) D: Christian-Jaque. B/on the novel by Emile Zola. C: Martine Carol, Charles Boyer, Jacques Castelot.

Michel Duchaussoy. *Bernadette* (France/1988/118m/C) D: Jean Delannoy. C: Sydney Penny, Jean-Marc Bory, Roland Lesaffre, Michele Simonnet, Bernard Dheran.

385 Nehru, Jawaharlal (1889–1964)

Political leader who became the first Prime Minister of the newly independent India. Although a supporter of **Gandhi**, he did not share Gandhi's views on passive resistance.

Roshan Seth. *Gandhi* (GB-India/1982/188m/C) D: Richard Attenborough. Best Picture (AA,BFA,NYC), Best Director (AA,BFA,DGA). C: Ben Kingsley, Candice Bergen, Edward Fox, John Gielgud, Trevor Howard, Peter Harlowe, Martin Sheen, Alyque Padamsee.

Robert Ashby. *Jinnah* (Pakistan/1998/110m/C) D: Jamil Dehlavi. C: Christopher Lee, James Fox, Maria Aitken, Shashi Kapoor, Richard Lintern, Shireen Shah, Indira Varma, Sam Dastor, Shakeel, Vaneeza Ahmed, Roger Brierley, Rowena Cooper, James Curran, Vernon Dobtcheff, Michael Elwyn, Ian Gelder, Christopher Godwin, John Grillo, Talat Hussain, John Nettleton, Alyque Padamsee.

386 Nelson, George "Baby Face" (1908–1934)

(Lester Gillis) A psychotic, murderous, little, bank robber and partner of **John Dillinger**, Nelson was Public Enemy Number One until shot to death by Federal Agents.

Mickey Rooney. *Baby Face Nelson* (US/1957/85m/BW) D: Don Siegel. C: Carolyn Jones, Cedric Hardwicke, Leo Gordon, Elisha Cook, Jr., Ted De Corsia, Dan Terranova, Jack Elam.

William Phipps. *The FBI Story* (US/1959/149m/C) D: Mervyn LeRoy. B/on the book by Don Whitehead. C: James Stewart, Vera Miles, Murray Hamilton, Larry Pennell, Nick Adams, Scott Peters, Jean Willes, Diane Jergens.

Robert Kendall. *Ma Barker's Killer Brood* (US/1960/82m/BW) D: Bill Karn. C: Lurene Tuttle, Tris Coffin, Paul Dubov, Vic Lundin, Don Grady, Eric Sinclair, Ronald Foster.

John Ashley. *Young Dillinger* (US/1965/102m/BW) D: Terry Morse. C: Nick Adams, Robert Conrad, Dan Terranova, Mary Ann Mobley, Victor Buono, John Hoyt, Reed Hadley.

Richard Dreyfuss. *Dillinger* (US/1973/107m/C) D: John Milius. C: Warren Oates, Michelle Phillips, Ben Johnson, Harry Dean Stanton, Geoffrey Lewis, Steve Kanaly.

387 Nelson, Lord Horatio (1758–1805)

Great Britain's most honored naval hero, Nelson died of wounds sustained during his greatest victory at Trafalgar where he defeated the combined forces of the French and Spanish. (See **Hamilton, Emma**)

Victor Varconi. *The Divine Lady* (US/1929/110m/BW) D: Frank Lloyd. Best Director (AA). C: Corinne Griffith, Ian Keith, H.B. Warner, Marie Dressler, William Conklin.

Francis Lister. *Mutiny on the Bounty* (US/1935/132m/BW) D: Frank Lloyd. B/on the novels *Mutiny on the Bounty, Men Against the Sea,* and *Pitcairn's Island* by Charles Nordhoff & James Norman Hall. Best Picture (AA). C: Charles Laughton, Clark Gable, Franchot Tone, David Torrence, Eddie Quillan, Dudley Digges, Donald Crisp, Ian Wolfe.

John Burton. *Lloyds of London* (US/1936/115m/BW) D: Henry King. C: Freddie Bartholomew, Madeleine Carroll, Sir Guy Standing, Tyrone Power, George Sanders, C. Aubrey Smith, Hugh Huntley, Thomas Pogue, Yorke Sherwood, William Wagner.

Laurence Olivier. *That Hamilton Woman* (aka *Lady Hamilton*) (US/1941/128m/BW) D: Alexander Korda. C: Vivien Leigh, Alan Mowbray, Sara Allgood, Gladys Cooper.

Stephen Haggard. *The Young Mr. Pitt* (GB/1942/118m/BW) D: Carol Reed. C: Robert Donat, Robert Morley, Phyllis Calvert, Raymond Lovell, Max Adrian, Felix Aylmer, Albert Lieven, Geoffrey Atkins, John Mills, Herbert Lom, Agnes Laughlan.

Lester Matthews. *Tyrant of the Sea* (US/1950/70m/BW) D: Lew Landers. C: Rhys Williams, Ron Randell, Valentine Perkins, Doris Lloyd, Harry Cording, Terry Kilburn.

I. Solovyov. *Admiral Ushakov* (USSR/1953/C) D: Mikhail Romm. C: Ivan Pereverzev, Olga Zhizneva, Boris Livanov, V. Vasyliev, N. Volkov.

Roland Bartrop. *Austerlitz* (aka *The Battle of Austerlitz*) (France-Italy-Yugoslavia/1959/166m/C) D: Abel Gance. C: Pierre Mondy, Jean Mercure, Martine Carol, Jack Palance, Orson Welles, Claudia Cardinale, Georges Marchal, Anthony Stuart, Jean Marais, Vittorio De Sica, Ettore Manni.

Jimmy Thompson. *Carry on Jack* (aka *Carry on Venus*) (GB/1963/91m/C) D: Gerald Thomas. C: Bernard Cribbins, Juliet Mills, Charles Hawtrey, Kenneth Williams.

Richard Johnson. *Lady Hamilton* (aka *The Making of a Lady*) (Germany-Italy-France/1969/98m/C) D: Christian-Jaque. B/on the novel by Alexandre Dumas. C: Michele Mercier, John Mills, Harald Leipnitz, Robert Hundar, Mirko Ellis.

Peter Finch. *The Nelson Affair* (aka *A Bequest to the Nation*) (GB/1973/118m/C)

D: James Cellan Jones. B/on the play *A Bequest to the Nation* by Terence Ratti-gan. C: Glenda Jackson, Michael Jayston, Anthony Quayle, Margaret Leighton, Dominic Guard, Nigel Stock, Barbara Leigh-Hunt, Roland Culver.

388 Nero (37–68)

(Nero Claudius Caesar) Roman emperor and musician, Nero's last words upon committing suicide were "What an artist the world is losing in me."

Charles Laughton. *The Sign of the Cross* (US/1932/124m/BW) D: Cecil B. DeMille. B/on the play by Wilson Barrett. C: Fredric March, Elissa Landi, Claudette Colbert, Ian Keith, Vivian Tobin, Harry Beresford, Nat Pendleton, Joe Bonomo.

Francis L. Sullivan. *Fiddlers Three* (GB/1944/88m/BW) D: Harry Watt. C: Tommy Trinder, Frances Day, Sonnie Hale, Diana Decker, James Robertson Jus-tice, Kay Kendall.

Gino Cervi. *O.K. Nero!* (Italy/1951/111m/BW) D: Mario Soldati. C: Silvana Pampanini, Walter Chiari, Carlo Campanini, Jackie Frost, Alba Arnova.

Peter Ustinov * Best Supporting Actor (GG). *Quo Vadis* (US/1951/171m/C) D: Mervyn LeRoy. B/on the novel by Henryk Sienkiewicz. C: Robert Taylor, Deborah Kerr, Leo Genn, Patricia Laffan, Finlay Currie, Abraham Sofaer, Buddy Baer, Marina Berti, Norman Woodland.

Jacques Aubuchon. *The Silver Chalice* (US/1954/143m/C) D: Victor Saville. B/on the novel by Thomas B. Costain. C: Virginia Mayo, Jack Palance, Paul Newman, Pier Angeli, Lorne Greene, E.G. Marshall, Alexander Scourby, Joseph Wiseman.

Alberto Sordi. *Nero's Mistress* (aka *Nero's Big Weekend*) (aka *Nero's Weekend*) (aka *My Son Nero*) (aka *Mio Figlio Nerone*) (Italy/1956/104–86m/C) D: Steno (Stefano Vanzina). C: Gloria Swanson, Vittorio De Sica, Brigitte Bardot.

Peter Lorre. *The Story of Mankind* (US/1957/100m/C) D: Irwin Allen. B/on the book by Hendrik Van Loon. C: Ronald Colman, Hedy Lamarr, Virginia Mayo, Agnes Moorehead, Dennis Hopper, Marie Wilson, Helmut Dantine, Edward Everett Horton, Reginald Gardiner, Marie Windsor, Francis X. Bush-man, Anthony Dexter, Austin Green, Jim Ameche, Harpo Marx, Bobby Wat-son, Reginald Sheffield, Cedric Hardwicke, Cesar Romero.

Vladimir Medar. *Revenge of the Gladiators* (Italy/1963/C) D: Guido Malat-esta. C: Lang Jeffries.

Gianni Rizzo. *Ten Desperate Men* (aka *I Dieci Gladiatori*) (Italy/1964/C) D: Gianfranco Parolini. C: Roger Browne, Susan Paget.

Giancarlo Cobelli. *White, Red, Yellow, Pink* (aka *The Love Factory*) (aka *Bianco, Rosso, Gallo, Rosa*) (Italy/1966/94m/C) D: Massimo Mida. C: Maria Grazia Bucella, Agnes Spaak.

Patrick Cargill. *Up Pompeii* (GB/1971/90m/C) D: Bob Kellett. C: Frankie Howerd.

Dom Deluise. *History of the World, Part I* (US/1981/92m/C) D: Mel Brooks. C: Mel Brooks, Madeline Kahn, Harvey Korman, Cloris Leachman, Gregory Hines, Art Metrano, John Hurt.

Michal Bajor. *Quo Vadis* (Poland/2001/167m/C) D: Jerzy Kawalerowicz. C:

Pawel Delag, Magdalena Mielcarz, Boguslaw Linda, Danuta Stenka, Franciszek Pieczka, Krzysztof Majchrzak, Agnieszka Wagner, Jerzy Trela, Malgorzata Pieczynska, Rafal Kubacki, Jerzy Nowak, Anna Majcher, Eugeniusz Priwieziencew.

Nesbit, Evelyn *see* Thaw, Harry K.

389 Ness, Eliot (1903–1957)

A Federal investigator sent to Chicago in the early 1930s, Ness was one of the men responsible for the arrest and conviction of **Al Capone** on charges of tax evasion. Robert Stack returned to the role for which he is best known in the 1991 TV movie *The Return of Eliot Ness.*

Robert Stack. *The Scarface Mob* (US/1962/105m/BW) D: Phil Karlson. B/on the book *The Untouchables* by Eliot Ness & Oscar Fraley. C: Neville Brand, Bruce Gordon, Keenan Wynn, Barbara Nichols, Bill Williams, Pat Crowley, Walter Winchell (Narrator).

Phillip R. Allen. *The Lady in Red* (aka *Guns, Sin and Bathtub Gin*) (US/1979/93m/C) D: Lewis Teague. C: Robert Conrad, Pamela Sue Martin, Louise Fletcher, Robert Hogan, Laurie Heineman, Robert Forster, Alan Vint.

Kevin Costner. *The Untouchables* (US/1987/119m/C) D: Brian De Palma. C: Sean Connery, Charles Martin Smith, Robert De Niro, Andy Garcia, Billy Drago, Richard Bradford.

390 Netanyahu, Yonatan (1946–1976)

Decorated Israeli soldier, Colonel Netanyahu was the lone casualty in the daring rescue of hostages at Entebbe on July 4, 1976.

Richard Dreyfuss. *Victory at Entebbe* (US/1976/150m/C) D: Marvin J. Chomsky. C: Kirk Douglas, Burt Lancaster, Theodore Bikel, Linda Blair, Julius Harris, Harris Yulin.

Stephen Macht. *Raid on Entebbe* (US/1977/115m/C) D: Irvin Kershner. Made for US television, released theatrically in Europe. C: Peter Finch, Charles Bronson, Martin Balsam, Horst Bucholz, John Saxon, Sylvia Sidney, Yaphet Kotto, Tige Andrews, David Opatoshu.

Yehoram Gaon. *Operation Thunderbolt* (aka *Entebbe: Operation Thunderbolt*) (Israel/1977/120m/C) D: Menahen Golan. C: Klaus Kinski, Arik Lavi, Sybil Danning.

391 Newton, Sir Isaac (1642–1727)

British mathematician and astronomer who discovered the law of gravity, developed calculus, and built the first reflecting telescope. The author of many scholarly volumes explaining his theories, among them, *Philosophiae Naturalis Principia Mathematica (*Mathematical Principles of Natural Philosophy). Television portrayals of Sir Isaac have been by Trevor Howard in *Peter the Great* (86) and by Karl Pruner in *Newton: A Tale of Two Isaacs* (97).

Harpo Marx. *The Story of Mankind* (US/1957/100m/C) D: Irwin Allen. B/on the book by Hendrik Van Loon. C: Ronald Colman, Hedy Lamarr, Virginia Mayo, Agnes Moorehead, Peter Lorre, Dennis Hopper, Marie Wilson, Helmut Dantine, Edward Everett Horton, Reginald Gardiner, Marie Windsor, Francis X. Bushman, Anthony Dexter, Austin Green, Jim Ameche, Bobby Watson, Reginald Sheffield, Cedric Hardwicke, Cesar Romero.

Ron Moody. *Revelaton* (GB/2001/C) D: Stuart Urban. C: Charlotte Weston, James D'Arcy, Natasha Wightman, Terence Stamp, Udo Kier, Derek Jacobi, Liam Cunningham, Heathcote Williams, Celia Imrie.

392 Ney, Michel (1769–1815)

French Marshal, commanded armies in the Revolutionary Wars and for **Napoleon** to whom he remained loyal through the battle of Waterloo. Following Napoleon's defeat Marshal Ney was shot as a traitor.

Edmund Willard. *The Iron Duke* (GB/1935/80m/BW) D: Victor Saville. C: George Arliss, Gladys Cooper, Emlyn Williams, Ellaline Terriss, Allan Aynesworth, Felix Aylmer, Gerald Lawrence, Gibb McLaughlin, Frederick Leister, Farren Soutar.

Aleksandr Stepanov. *1812* (aka *Kutuzov*) (USSR/1944/95m/B&W) D: Vladimir Petrov. C: Aleksei Diki, Sergei Mezhinsky, Y. Kaluzhsky, Sergo Zaqariadze, Nikolai Okhlopkov, Sergei Blinnikov, V. Gotovtsev, A. Polyakov, Nikolai Brilling, Boris Chirkov, Mikhail Pugovkin, Ivan Ryzhov, K. Shilovtsev, Ivan Skuratov, G. Terekhov, N. Timchenko, Vladimir Yershov.

Clement Duhour. *Napoleon* (France/1954/190m/C) D: Sacha Guitry. C: Jean-Pierre Aumont, Gianna Maria Canale, Jeanne Boitel, Pierre Brasseur, Daniel Gelin, Sacha Guitry, O.W. Fisher, Raymond Pellegrin, Danielle Darrieux, Lana Marconi, Michele Morgan, Erich von Stroheim, Dany Roby, Henri Vidal, Serge Regianni, Maria Schell.

Dan O'Herlihy. *Waterloo* (Italy-USSR/1970/123m/C) D: Sergei Bondarchuk. C: Rod Steiger, Orson Welles, Virginia McKenna, Michael Wilding, Donal Donnelly, Christopher Plummer, Jack Hawkins, Rupert Davies, Aldo Cecconi, Rodolfo Lodi.

Nicholas I *see* 638

393 Nicholas II (1868–1918)

Russia's last Czar, Nicholas was deposed in 1917 with the Russian Revolution, and he and his family were executed by the Bolsheviks the following year. He was played by Omar Sharif in the TV movie *Anastasia: The Mystery of Anna* (86).

Reinhold Schunzel. *1914: The Last Days Before the War* (Germany/1931/110m/BW) D: Richard Oswald. C: Albert Basserman, Wolfgang von Schwind, Heinrich Schroth, Lucie Hoeflich, Ferdinand Hart, Oskar Homolka, Theodor Loos, Alfred Abel, Paul Mederow, Heinrich George, Varl Goetz, Paul Bildt, Eugen Klöepfer.

Paul Otto. *Rasputin* (Germany/1932/82m/BW) D: Adolf Trotz. C: Conrad Veidt, Hermine Sterler, Kenny Rieve, Alexandra Sorina, Brigitte Horney, Bernhard Goetzke.

Ralph Morgan. *Rasputin and the Empress* (aka *Rasputin the Mad Monk*) (US/1932/132m/BW) D: Richard Boleslawsky. Original story by Charles MacArthur. C: John Barrymore, Ethel Barrymore, Lionel Barrymore, Diana Wynyard, Tad Alexander, C. Henry Gordon, Edward Arnold.

Jean Worms. *Rasputin* (France/1939/93m/BW) D: Marcel L'Herbler. B/on the novel *Tragedie Imperiale* by Alfred Neumann. C: Harry Baur, Marcelle Chantal, Denis d'Ines.

Ugo Sasso. *The Night They Killed Rasputin* (aka *The Nights of Rasputin*) (France-Italy/1960/95m/BW) D: Pierre Chenal. C: Edmund Purdom, Gianna Maria Canale, Jany Clair.

William Hutt. *The Fixer* (US/1968/130m/C) D: John Frankenheimer. B/on the novel by Bernard Malamud. C: Alan Bates, Dirk Bogarde, Georgia Brown, Ian Holm.

Paul Daneman. *Oh! What a Lovely War* (GB/1969/144m/C) D: Richard Attenborough. B/on the musical play by Joan Littlewood and the play *The Long, Long Trail* by Charles Chilton. Best English Language Foreign Film (GG), and the United Nations Award (BFA). C: Pamela Abbott, Jack Hawkins, Laurence Olivier, Ralph Richardson, John Mills, John Gabriel, Dirk Bogarde, Vanessa Redgrave, Kenneth More, Michael Redgrave, Ian Holm, Wensley Pithey, Frank Forsyth, John Gielgud, Maggie Smith, Guy Middleton.

Michael Jayston. *Nicholas and Alexandra* (GB/1971/183m/C) D: Franklin J. Schaffner. B/on the book by Robert K. Massie. C: Janet Suzman, Roderic Noble, Fiona Fullerton, Harry Andrews, Irene Worth, Tom Baker, Ralph Truman, Alexander Knox, John McEnery, Michael Bryant, James Hazeldine, Brian Cox, Ian Holm, Roy Dotrice, Martin Potter.

Anatoly Romashin. *Agony* (aka *Rasputin*) (USSR/1975/148–107m/C) D: Elem Klimov. C: Alexei Petrenko, Velta Linei, Alisa Freindtlich.

394 Nightingale, Florence (1820–1910)

The first woman to receive the British Order of Merit, Florence Nightingale is considered the founder of modern nursing. In the TV movie *Florence Nightingale* (85) she was played by Jaclyn Smith.

Kay Francis. *The White Angel* (aka *The White Sister*) (US/1936/75m/BW) D: William Dieterle. B/on the *Florence Nightingale* chapter of *Eminent Victorians* by Lytton Strachey. C: Ian Hunter, Donald Woods, Nigel Bruce, Gaby Fay, Halliwell Hobbes.

Fay Compton. *Wrath of Jealousy* (aka *Wedding Group*) (GB/1936/70m/BW) D: Alex Bryce & Campbell Gullan. C: Patric Knowles, Barbara Greene, Alastair Sim, Bruce Seton.

Joyce Bland. *Sixty Glorious Years* (aka *Queen of Destiny*) (GB/1938/90m/C) D: Herbert Wilcox. C: Anna Neagle, Anton Walbrook, C. Aubrey Smith, Charles Carson, Felix Aylmer, Pamela Standish, Gordon McLeod, Henry Hallatt, Wyndham Goldie, Malcolm Keen, Derrick De Marney, Harvey Braban, Aubrey Dexter, Laidman Browne.

Anna Neagle. *The Lady with a Lamp* (aka *The Lady with the Lamp*) (GB/1951/112m/BW) D: Herbert Wilcox. B/on the play *The Lady with the Lamp* by Reginald Berkeley. C: Michael Wilding, Felix Aylmer, Arthur Young, Helena Pickard, Peter Graves.

395 Nijinsky, Vaslav (1890–1950)

Ranked among the greatest ballet dancers of all time, Nijinsky's career ended in 1918 when he went insane, the victim of schizophrenia.

Anthony Dowell. *Valentino* (GB/1977/132m/C) D: Ken Russell. B/on the story *Valentino, An Intimate Exposé of the Sheik* by Brad Steiger & Chaw Mank. C: Rudolf Nureyev, Leslie Caron, Michelle Phillips, Carol Kane, Felicity Kendal, Peter Vaughan, Huntz Hall, David De Keyser, William Hootkins, Anton Diffring.

George De La Pena. *Nijinsky* (GB/1980/129m/C) D: Herbert Ross. B/on The Diary of Vaslav Nijinsky and *Nijinsky* by Romola Nijinsky. C: Alan Bates, Leslie Browne, Alan Badel, Colin Blakely, Ronald Pickup, Jeremy Irons, Janet Suzman.

Max von Sydow (voice only). *She Dances Alone* (Austria-US/1981/87m/C) D: Robert Dornhelm. C: Kyra Nijinsky, Bud Cort, Patrick Dupond, Sauncey Le Sueur.

Michael Kradunin. *Pavlova* (aka *Pavlova—A Woman for All Time*) (GB-USSR/1984/133m/C) D: Emil Lotianou. C: Galina Beliaeva, James Fox, Serge Shakourov, Vsevolod Larinov, Martin Scorsese, Bruce Forsyth, Roy Kinnear, Lina Boultakova.

396 Nimitz, Chester William (1885–1966)

U.S. naval officer, Admiral Nimitz was Commander of the Pacific Fleet during World War II.

Selmer Jackson. *Hellcats of the Navy* (US/1957/81m/BW) D: Nathan Juran. B/on the book by Charles A. Lockwood & Hans Christian Adamson. C: Ronald Reagan, Nancy Davis, Arthur Franz, Robert Arthur, Harry Lauter, Joseph Turkel, William Phillips.

Selmer Jackson. *The Gallant Hours* (US/1960/115m/BW) D: Robert Montgomery. C: James Cagney, Dennis Weaver, Ward Costello, Richard Jaeckel, James T. Goto.

Henry Fonda. *Midway* (aka *The Battle of Midway*) (US/1976/132m/C) D: Jack Smight. C: Charlton Heston, James Coburn, Glenn Ford, Hal Holbrook, Toshiro Mifune, Robert Mitchum, Robert Wagner, Cliff Robertson, James Shigeta.

Addison Powell. *MacArthur* (US/1977/128m/C) D: Joseph Sargent. C: Gregory Peck, Ed Flanders, Dan O'Herlihy, Ivan Bonar, Ward Costello, Nicholas Coster, Art Fleming, Marj Dusay, Kenneth Tobey, John Fujioka, Fred Stuthman, Sandy Kenyon.

397 Nitti, Frank (1887–1943)

(Francesco Nittoni) **Al Capone's** "Enforcer" and his successor when Capone was imprisoned, Nitti committed suicide when facing federal charges of tax evasion. He was played by Anthony LaPaglia in the TV movie *Nitti: The Enforcer* (88).

Bruce Gordon. *The Scarface Mob* (US/1962/105m/BW) D: Phil Karlson. B/on the book *The Untouchables* by Eliot Ness & Oscar Fraley. C: Robert Stack, Neville

Brand, Keenan Wynn, Barbara Nichols, Bill Williams, Pat Crowley, Walter Winchell (Narrator).

Harold J. Stone. *The St. Valentine's Day Massacre* (US/1967/100m/C) D: Roger Corman. C: Jason Robards, George Segal, Ralph Meeker, Jean Hale, Clint Ritchie, Frank Silvera, Joseph Campanella, Bruce Dern, John Agar, Reed Hadley, Rico Cattani, Jack Nicholson.

Sylvester Stallone. *Capone* (US/1975/101m/C) D: Steve Carver. C: Ben Gazzara, Susan Blakely, Harry Guardino, John Cassavetes, Robert Phillips, John D. Chandler, John Orchard.

Billy Drago. *The Untouchables* (US/1987/119m/C) D: Brian De Palma. C: Kevin Costner, Sean Connery, Charles Martin Smith, Robert De Niro, Andy Garcia, Richard Bradford.

398 Nixon, Richard Milhouse (1913–1994)

37th president of the United States (1969–1974), who achieved a cease-fire in the Viet Nam War, initiated strategic arms limitation talks with the Soviet Union, and in 1972, visited the People's Republic of China. In 1974 his gains in domestic and foreign affairs were overshadowed by investigations of corrup-

High drama in the Oval Office as President Nixon (Anthony Hopkins, center pointing) squares off with Secretary of State Henry Kissinger (Paul Sorvino, left) blaming him for the Watergate Scandal. Seated around the table are (left to right) Chuck Colson (Kevin Dunn), John Mitchell (E.G. Marshall), Alexander Haig (Powers Boothe), Ron Ziegler (David Paymer), and H.R. Haldeman (James Woods). This scene from Oliver Stone's powerful and interpretive film, *Nixon* (1995). (Museum of Modern Art Film Stills Archive)

tion in his administration. Threatened with impeachment over the Watergate Scandal, Nixon became the first United States president to resign from office. (See **Kissinger, Henry; Woodward, Bob.**) Television portrayals of Nixon have been by Richard M. Dixon in *Tail Gunner Joe* (77), Rip Torn in *Blind Ambition, a* mini series (79), John Byner in *Will: the Autobiography of G. Gordon Liddy* (82), Peter Riegert in *Concealed Enemies* (84), Anthony Palmer in *J. Edgar Hoover* (87), Lane Smith in *The Final Days* (89), Beau Bridges in *Kissinger and Nixon* (95), John Wells in Pt. 1 of the series *Chalk* (97), and by Bob Gunton in *Elvis Meets Nixon* (97).

Jean-Pierre Biesse. *Made in USA* (aka *The Juggler*) (France/1966) D: Jean-Luc Godard. B/on *The Juggler* by Donald E. Westlake. C: Yves Alfonso, Claude Bakka, Jean-Claude Bouillon, Marc Dudicort, Marianne Faithful, Remo Forlani, Jean-Luc Godard, Anna Karena, Kyoko Koska, Philippe Labro, Jean-Pierre Léaud, Ernest Menzer, Laszlo Szabo.

Richard Nixon (Anthony Hopkins) pictured with his strong and always supportive wife, Pat (Joan Allen). *Nixon* (1995). (Museum of Modern Art Film Stills Archive)

Jim Dixon. *Is There Sex After Death?* (US/1971/97m/C) D: Jeanne & Alan Abel. C: Buck Henry, Alan Abel, Marshall Efron, Holly Woodlawn, Earl Doud.

Anderson Humphreys. *The Cayman Triangle* (US/1977/92m/C) D: Anderson Humphreys. C: Reid Dennis, Ed Beheler, Jules Kreitzer, John Morgan.

Harry Spillman. *Born Again* (US/1978/110m/C) D: Irving Rapper. B/on the book by Charles Colson. C: Dean Jones, Anne Francis, Jay Robinson, Peter Jurasik.

Richard M. Dixon. *The Private Files of J. Edgar Hoover* (US/1978/112m/C) D: Larry Cohen. C: Broderick Crawford, Jose Ferrer, Michael Parks, Ronee Blakely, Michael Sacks, Raymond St. Jacques, Andrew Duggan, Howard Da Silva, James Wainwright, Brad Dexter, William Jordan, Gordon Zimmerman, Lloyd Nolan, June Havoc, Dan Dailey, John Marley, Lloyd Gough.

Richard M. Dixon. *Hopscotch* (US/1980/104m/C) D: Ronald Neame. B/on the novel by Brian Garfield. C: Walter Matthau, Glenda Jackson, Sam Waterson, Ned Beaty, Herbert Lom.

Nixon (Anthony Hopkins) showing the strain of the Watergate scandal and an infamous tape recorder. *Nixon* (1995). (Museum of Modern Art Film Stills Archive)

Richard M. Dixon. *Where the Buffalo Roam* (US/1980/96m/C) D: Art Linson. C: Peter Boyle, Bill Murray, Bruno Kirby, Rene Aberjonois, R.G. Armstrong, Rafael Campos, Leonard Frey, Mark Metcalf, Craig T. Nelson.

Philip Baker Hall. *Secret Honor* (aka *Lords of Treason*) (US/1984/90m/C) D: Robert Altman. B/on the one-character play *The Last Will and Testament of Richard M. Nixon* by Donald Freed & Arnold Stone.

Buck McDancer. *Hot Shots! Part Deux* (US/1993/89m/C) D: Jim Abrahams. C: Charlie Sheen, Lloyd Bridges, Valeria Golino, Richard Crenna, Miguel Ferrer, Jay Koch, Jerry Haleva, Mitchell Ryan, Larry Lindsey, Ed Beheler, Daniel T. Healy.

Joe Alaskey (voice only). *Forrest Gump* (US/1994/142m/C) D: Robert Zemeckis. B/on the novel by Winston Groom. Best Picture (AA), Best Director (AA). C: Tom Hanks, Gary Sinise, Robin Wright, Sally Field, Mykelti Williamson, Peter Dobson, Richard D'Allesandro, and the voices of Jed Gillin, John William Galt, and Joe Stefanelli.

Anthony Hopkins. *Nixon* (US/1995/190m/C) D: Oliver Stone. C: Joan Allen, Powers Boothe, Ed Harris, Bob Hoskins, E.G. Marshall, David Paymer, David Hyde Pierce, Paul Sorvino, Mary Steenburgen, J.T. Walsh, James Woods, Bryan Bedford.

Dan Hedaya. *Dick* (US/1999/95m) D: Andrew Fleming. C: Kirsten Dunst, Michelle Williams, Will Ferrell, Bruce McCulloch, Dave Foley, Jim Breuer, Terri Garr, Ana Gasteyer, Harry Shearer, Saul Rubinek, Richard Fitzpatrick, Len Doncheff, Deborah Grover.

399 Oakley, Annie (1860–1926)

(Phoebe Anne Oakley Mosee) A star attraction with **Buffalo Bill's** Wild West Show, Annie made her mark as the greatest sharpshooter of her day. She was portrayed by Jamie Lee Curtis in the 1985 TV film *Annie Oakley*.

Barbara Stanwyck. *Annie Oakley* (US/1935/79m/BW) D: George Stevens. C: Preston Foster, Melvyn Douglas, Moroni Olsen, Chief Thundercloud, Dick Elliott.

Betty Hutton. *Annie Get Your Gun* (US/1950/107m/C) D: George Sidney. B/on the musical play, book by Herbert and Dorothy Fields. C: Howard Keel, Louis Calhern, J. Carrol Naish, Chief Yowlachie, Evelyn Beresford, John Mylong, Nino Pipitone.

Gail Davis. *Alias Jesse James* (US/1959/92m/C) D: Norman McLeod. C: Bob Hope, Rhonda Fleming, Wendell Corey, Jim Davis, Hugh O'Brian, James Arness, Fess Parker.

Angela Douglas. *Carry on Cowboy* (GB/1965/94m/C) D: Gerald Thomas. C: Sidney James, Kenneth Williams, Jim Dale, Charles Hawtrey, Joan Sims, Jon Pertwee.

Nancy Kovack. *The Outlaws Is Coming* (US/1965/88m/BW) D: Norman Maurer. C: Larry Fine, Moe Howard, Joe De Rita, Murray Alper, Joe Bolton, Bill Camfield, Hal Fryar, Johnny Ginger, Wayne Mack, Ed McDonnell, Bruce Sedley, Paul Shannon, Sally Starr.

Geraldine Chaplin. *Buffalo Bill and the Indians, Or Sitting Bull's History Lesson* (aka *Buffalo Bill and the Indians*) (US/1976/120m/C) D: Robert Altman. B/on the play *Indians* by Arthur Kopit. C: Paul Newman, Burt Lancaster, Joel Grey, Harvey Keitel, Frank Kaquitts, Will Sampsen, Pat McCormick.

400 O'Bannion, Charles Dion (1892–1924)

Chicago bootlegger-gangster of the Prohibition era, O'Bannion was one of the many victims of **Al Capone's** rise to the top; shot to death while working in his flower shop.

Robert Gist. *Al Capone* (US/1959/105m/BW) D: Richard Wilson. C: Rod Steiger, Fay Spain, Murvyn Vye, Lewis Charles, Nehemiah Persoff, James Gregory, Martin Balsam.

John Agar. *The St. Valentine's Day Massacre* (US/1967/100m/C) D: Roger Corman. C: Jason Robards, George Segal, Ralph Meeker, Jean Hale, Clint Ritchie, Frank Silvera, Joseph Campanella, Harold J. Stone, Bruce Dern, Reed Hadley, Rico Cattani, Jack Nicholson.

John Orchard. *Capone* (US/1975/101m/C) D: Steve Carver. C: Ben Gazzara, Susan Blakely, Harry Guardino, John Cassavetes, Sylvester Stallone, Robert Phillips, John D. Chandler.

401 Odets, Clifford (1906–1963)

American dramatist, Odets wrote many plays of social protest including *Awake and Sing* and *Golden Boy*. In the TV film *Will There Really Be a Morning?* (83) he was played by John Heard.

Jeffrey DeMunn. *Frances* (US/1982/140m/C) D: Graeme Clifford. C: Jessica Lange, Sam Shepard, Kim Stanley, Jordan Charney, Donald Craig, Bart Burns.

Lee Breuer. *Committed* (US/1984/77m/BW) D: Sheila McLaughlin & Lynne Tillman. C: Sheila McLaughlin, Victoria Boothby, John Erdman, Heinz Emigholz.

402 Offenbach, Jacques (1819–1880)

(Jacob Levy Eberst) German-French composer, Offenbach became famous for his operettas, but his greatest success (and the work for which he is most remembered) came in grand opera with *The Tales of Hoffman*.

Julius Falkenstein. *Ich Und Die Kaiserin* (Germany/1933/84m/BW) D: Friedrich Hollander. C: Mady Christians, Conrad Veidt, Lilian Harvey, Friedel Schuster, Heinz Ruchmann.

Julius Falkenstein. *The Only Girl* (aka *Heart Song*) (GB-Germany/1933/84m/BW) D: Friedrich Hollaender. English language version of the German film *Ich Und Die Kaiserin* (33). C: Lilian Harvey, Charles Boyer, Mady Christians, Ernest Thesiger.

Julius Falkenstein. *Moi Et L'Imperatrice* (France-Germany/1933/84m/BW) D: Friedrich Holländer. French version of *Ich Und de Kaiserin* (33). C: Lillian Harvey, Charles Boyer, Pierre Brasseur, Daniele Bregis, Pierre Stephen, Nilda Duplessy.

Miles Malleson. *Idol of Paris* (GB/1948/106m/BW) D: Leslie Arliss. B/on the novel *Paiva, Queen of Love* by Alfred Shirkauer. C: Michael Rennie, Beryl Baxter, Christine Norden, Kenneth Kent, Margaretta Scott.

Pierre Fresnay. *The Paris Waltz* (aka *La Valse de Paris*) (France/1949/101m/BW) D: Marcel Achard. C: Yvonne Printemps, Jacques Castelot, Pierre Dux, Andre Roussin.

Arnulf Schroeder. *The Eternal Waltz* (aka *Ewiger Walzer*) (Germany/1954/97m/C) D: Paul Verhoeven. C: Bernhard Wicki, Hilde Krahl, Annemarie Dueringer, Friedl Loor, Eric Frey, Hans Putz, Eduard Strauss, Jr.

Dominique Weber. *The Great Waltz* (US/1972/135m/C) D: Andrew L. Stone. C: Horst Bucholz, Mary Costa, Rossano Brazzi, Nigel Patrick, Yvonne Mitchell, J. Schonburg-Hartenstein.

403 Oppenheimer, James Robert (1904–1967)

A physicist and nuclear scientist, Oppenheimer was the scientific director of the Manhattan Project, the program that developed the first nuclear weapons. In the British mini-series *Oppenheimer* (81) he was portrayed by Sam Waterson. Other TV depictions include Robert Walden in *Enola Gay* (83), David Strathaird in *Day One* (89) and Jeff DeMunn in *Hiroshima* (95).

Hume Cronyn. *The Beginning Or the End* (US/1947/110m/BW) D: Norman Taurog. C: Brian Donlevy, Beverly Tyler, Godfrey Tearle, Barry Nelson, Art Baker, Ludwig Stossel.

Dwight Schultz. *Fat Man and Little Boy* (US/1989/126m/C) D: Roland Joffe. C: Paul Newman, Bonnie Bedelia, John Cusack, Laura Dern, Ron Frazier, Natasha Richardson.

404 Orgen, Jacob "Little Augie" (??–1927)

Legs Diamond's boss in the New York rackets of the Prohibition era, Little Augie was gunned down by Lepke Buchalter in October of 1927.

Sid Melton. *The Rise and Fall of Legs Diamond* (US/1960/101m/BW) D: Budd Boetticher. C: Ray Danton, Karen Steele, Elaine Stewart, Jesse White, Robert Lowery, Richard Gardner.

Giancomino De Micheli. *The Valachi Papers* (Italy-France/1972/125m/C) D: Terence Young. B/on the book by Peter Maas. C: Charles Bronson, Lino Ventura, Jill Ireland, Fausto Tozzi, Angelo Infante, Joseph Wiseman, Walter Chiari.

Jack Ackerman. *Lepke* (US/1975/110–98m/C) D: Menahem Golan. C: Tony Curtis, Anjanette Comer, Michael Callan, Warren Berlinger, Gianni Russo, Vic Tayback, Milton Berle, Erwin Fuller, Vaughn Meader, Zitto Kazan, John Durren.

405 Oswald, Lee Harvey (1939–1963)

John F. Kennedy's assassin, Oswald was shot and killed by Jack Ruby on November 24, 1963. In the TV movie *Ruby and Oswald* (77) he was played by Frederic Forrest.

George Mazyrack. *The Trial of Lee Harvey Oswald* (US/1964/100m/BW) D: Larry Buchanan. C: Arthur Nations, George Russell, George Edgley, Charles W. Tessmer.

Gary Oldman. *JFK* (US/1991/189m/C) D: Oliver Stone. B/on *Crossfire* by Jim Marrs and *On the Trail of the Assassins* by Jim Garrison. C: Kevin Costner, Sissy

Spacek, Kevin Bacon, Brian Doyle-Murray, Tom Howard, Steve Reed, Jodi Farber.

Willie Garson. *Ruby* (US/1992/110m/C) D: John MacKenzie. B/on the play *Love Child* by Stephen Davis. C: Danny Aiello, Joe Viterelli, Gerard David, Kevin Wiggins, Chris Wall, Sherilyn Fenn, Jane Hamilton, Carmine Caridi.

406 Paganini, Niccolo (1782–1840)

Italian composer and violin virtuoso; Paganini's playing so astounded audiences of his day that many accused him of demonic possession.

Hugh Miller. *The Divine Spark* (aka *Casta Diva*) (Italy-GB/1935/100–81m/BW) D: Carmine Gallone. C: Martha Eggerth, Phillips Holmes, Benita Hume, Edmund Breon.

Roxy Roth. *A Song to Remember* (US/1945/113m/C) D: Charles Vidor. C: Cornel Wilde, Merle Oberon, Paul Muni, Stephen Bekassy, Nina Foch, George Coulouris, George Macready.

Stewart Granger. *The Magic Bow* (GB/1947/105m/BW) D: Bernard Knowles. B/on the novel by Manuel Komroff. C: Phyllis Calvert, Jean Kent, Dennis Price, Cecil Parker.

Karel Dostal. *Bohemian Rapture* (Czechoslovakia/1948/88m/BW) D: Vaclav Krska. C: Jaromir Spol, Vaclav Voska, Vlasia Fabianova, Libuse Zemkova.

Gideon Kremer. *Spring Symphony* (aka *Frühlingssinfonie*) (West Germany-East Germany/1983/103m/C) D: Peter Schamoni. C: Nastassja Kinski, Herbert Gronemeyer, Rolf Hoppe, Bernhard Wicki, Andre Heller, Anja-Christine Preussler.

Klaus Kinski. *Paganini* (Italy/1989/C) D: Klaus Kinski.

407 Palmerston, Lord (1784–1865)

(Henry John Temple, 3rd Viscount Palmerston) Powerful British politician, Palmerston served twice as Prime Minister (1855–58, 1859–65).

Wallace Bosco. *Balaclava* (aka *Jaws of Hell*) (GB/1930/94m/BW) D: Maurice Elvey & Milton Rosmer. B/on *The Charge of the Light Brigade* by Alfred Lord Tennyson. Made as a silent in 1928, with sound added in 1930. C: Benita Hume, Cyril McLaglen, J. Fisher White, Bos Ranevsky, Marian Drada, Eugene Leahy.

Felix Aylmer. *Victoria the Great* (GB/1937/110m/C) D: Herbert Wilcox. B/on the play *Victoria Regina* by Laurence Housman. C: Anna Neagle, Anton Walbrook, H.B. Warner, James Dale, Charles Carson, Hubert Harben, Arthur Young, Derrick De Marney, Hugh Miller, Percy Parsons, Henry Hallatt, Gordon McLeod, Wyndham Goldie.

Felix Aylmer. *Sixty Glorious Years* (aka *Queen of Destiny*) (GB/1938/90m/C) D: Herbert Wilcox. C: Anna Neagle, Anton Walbrook, C. Aubrey Smith, Charles Carson, Pamela Standish, Gordon McLeod, Henry Hallatt, Wyndham Goldie, Malcolm Keen, Derrick De Marney, Joyce Bland, Harvey Braban, Aubrey Dexter, Laidman Browne.

Gilbert Emery. *A Dispatch from Reuters* (aka *This Man Reuter*) (US/1940/89m/BW) D: William Dieterle. B/on the story *Reuter's News Agency* by Valentine Williams & Wolfgang Wilhelm. C: Edward G. Robinson, Albert Basserman, Walter Kingsford.

Felix Aylmer. *The Lady with a Lamp* (aka *The Lady with the Lamp*) (GB/1951/112m/BW) D: Herbert Wilcox. B/on the play *The Lady with the Lamp* by Reginald Berkeley. C: Anna Neagle, Michael Wilding, Arthur Young, Helena Pickard, Peter Graves.

408 Parker, Bonnie (1911–1934)

Clyde **Barrow**'s bank-robbing partner, Bonnie was a self-styled poet who once wrote: "Some day they will go down together, And they will bury them side by side. To a few it means grief, To the law it's relief, But it's death to Bonnie and Clyde."

Tamar Cooper. *Guns Don't Argue* (US/1955/92m/BW) D: Bill Karn & Richard Kahn. Feature film edited from the TV series *Gangbusters*. C: Myron Healey, Lyle Talbot, Jean Harvey, Paul Dubov, Sam Edwards, Richard Crane, Baynes Barron, Doug Wilson.

Dorothy Provine. *The Bonnie Parker Story* (US/1958/79m/BW) D: William Witney. C: Jack Hogan, Richard Bakalyan, Joseph Turkel, William Stevens, Ken Lynch.

Faye Dunaway. *Bonnie and Clyde* (US/1967/111m/C) D: Arthur Penn. C: Warren Beatty, Gene Hackman, Michael J. Pollard, Estelle Parsons, Denver Pyle, Gene Wilder.

Joe Enterentree. *The Other Side of Bonnie and Clyde* (US/1968/75m/BW) D: Larry Buchanan. C: Lucky Mosley, Frank Hamer, Jr., Burl Ives (Narrator).

409 Parker, Dorothy (1893–1967)

(Dorothy Rothschild) American writer known for her acerbic wit, Parker was portrayed by Dolores Sutton in the TV movie *F. Scott Fitzgerald in Hollywood* (76), and by Bebe Neuwirth in *Dash and Lilly* (99).

Rosemary Murphy. *Julia* (US/1977/116m/C) D: Fred Zinnemann. B/on the book *Pentimento* by Lillian Hellman. C: Jane Fonda, Vanessa Redgrave, Jason Robards.

Jennifer Jason Leigh. *Mrs. Parker and the Vicious Circle* (US/1994/125m/C) D: Alan Rudolph. C: Campbell Scott, Matthew Broderick, Peter Gallagher, Tom McGowan, Lili Taylor, Keith Carradine, Nick Cassavetes, David Thornton, Malcolm Gets, Gwyneth Paltrow.

410 Parnell, Charles Stewart (1846–1891)

Irish nationalist politician, Parnell's career in Parliament was effectively ended when he was named as co-respondent in a divorce case.

Clark Gable. *Parnell* (US/1937/115m/BW) D: John M. Stahl. B/on the play by Elsie Tough Schauffler. C: Myrna Loy, Edna May Oliver, Edmund Gwenn, Alan Marshall, Billie Burke, Donald Crisp, Montagu Love, George Zucco, Donald Meek.

Robert Donat. *Captain Boycott* (GB/1947/93m/BW) D: Frank Launder. B/on the novel by Philip Rooney. C: Stewart Granger, Kathleen Ryan, Cecil Parker, Mervyn Johns.

411 Parr, Catherine (1512–1548)

The sixth wife of **Henry VIII**, Catherine had been married twice before (widowed twice) and after Henry's death she was married again, this time to Henry's former brother-in-law, Thomas Seymour. She died in childbirth.

Everley Gregg. *The Private Life of Henry VIII* (GB/1933/97m/BW) D: Alexander Korda. C: Charles Laughton, Robert Donat, Binnie Barnes, Elsa Lanchester, Merle Oberon, Wendy Barrie, Franklyn Dyall, Miles Mander, Claude Allister, John Loder, Lawrence Hanray.

Deborah Kerr. *Young Bess* (US/1953/112m/C) D: George Sidney. B/on the novel by Margaret Irwin. C: Jean Simmons, Stewart Granger, Charles Laughton, Kay Walsh, Cecil Kellaway, Rex Thompson, Elaine Stewart, Dawn Addams, Lumsden Hare.

Barbara Leigh-Hunt. *The Six Wives of Henry VIII* (aka *Henry VIII and His Six Wives*) (GB/1972/125m/C) D: Waris Hussein. C: Keith Michell, Frances Cuka, Charlotte Rampling, Jane Asher, Jenny Bos, Lynne Frederick, Donald Pleasence, Simon Henderson, Annette Crosbie, John Bryans, Michael Goodliffe, Bernard Hepton, Dorothy Tutin.

412 Parsons, Louella (1893–1972)

Gossip columnist who wielded a mighty pen for the Hearst newspapers in the heyday of the Hollywood studio system. Along with writing two volumes of memoirs, *The Gay Illiterate* (44) and *Tell it to Louella* (61), she appeared as herself in several films, including *Hollywood Hotel* (37), *Without Reservations* (46), and *Starlift* (51). The many TV portrayals have been by Anne Bellamy in *Bogie* (80), Priscilla Morrill in *Marilyn: The Untold Story* (80), Jane Kean in *The Scarlett O'Hara War* (80), Doris Belack in *The Hearst and Davies Affair* (85), Elizabeth Taylor in *Malice in Wonderland* (85), and in *RKO 281* (99) she was portrayed by Brenda Blethyn.

Beryl Wallace. *The Woman of the Town* (US/1943/90m/BW) D: George Archainbaud. C: Claire Trevor, Albert Dekker, Barry Sullivan, Henry Hull, Marion Martin, Porter Hall, Charley Foy.

Catherine Craig. (uncredited). *Incendiary Blond* (US/1945/113m/BW) D: George Marshall. B/on the book *The Life of Texas Guinan* by Thomas and W.D. Guinan. C: Betty Hutton, Arturo De Cordova, Charles Ruggles, Albert Dekker, Barry Fitzgerald.

Sandy Martin. *Marlene* (Germany-Italy/2000/125m/C) D: Joseph Vilsmaier. C: Katja Flint, Herbert Knaup, Heino Ferch, Hans Werner Meyer, Christiane Paul, Suzanne von Borsody, Armin Rohde, Josefina Vilsmaier, Theresa Vilsmaier, Janina Vilsmaier, Monika Bleibtreu, Cosma Shiva Hagen, Katharina Müller-Elmau, Oliver Elias.

Jennifer Tilly. *The Cat's Meow* (Canada-Germany-GB/2001/110m/BW/C) D: Peter Bogdanovich. C: Kirsten Dunst, Cary Elwes, Edward Herrmann, Eddie Izzard, Joanna Lumley, Victor Slezak, James Laurenson, Ronan Vibert, Chiara Schoras, Ingrid Lacey, John C. Vennema, Claudia Harrison, Claudie Blakley.

413 Pasteur, Louis (1822–1895)

French chemist noted for his studies in bacteriology, Pasteur discovered vaccines for Anthrax and Rabies and he developed the process to retard spoilage in liquids now known as Pasteurization.

Sacha Guitry. *Pasteur* (France/1935/85m/BW) D: Sacha Guitry. C: Jean Perier, Jose Squinquel, Bonvallet, Beuve, Louis Maurel.

Paul Muni. *The Story of Louis Pasteur* (US/1936/85m/BW) D: William Dieterle. C: Josephine Hutchinson, Anita Louise, Donald Woods, Walter Kingsford, Iphigenie Castiglioni.

Theodor Vogler. *Dr. Semmelweis* (aka *Semmelweis, Der Hetter Der Mutter*) (East Germany/1950/BW) D: Georg Klaren. C: Eduard von Winterstein, Camilla Spira.

414 Patton, George Smith (1885–1945)

Colorful American general of the Second World War, Patton commanded the 3rd army during the liberation of France.

John Larch. *Miracle of the White Stallions* (aka *The Flight of the White Stallions*) (US/1963/117m/C) D: Arthur Hiller. B/on the book *The Dancing White Stallions of Vienna* by Alois Podhajsky. C: Robert Taylor, Lilli Palmer, Curt Jurgens, James Franciscus.

Kirk Douglas. *Is Paris Burning?* (US-France/1966/173m/C) D: Rene Clement. C: Jean-Paul Belmondo, Charles Boyer, Leslie Caron, Jean-Pierre Casal, George Chakiris, Claude Dauphin, Alain Delon, Glenn Ford, Gert Frobe, Daniel Gelin, Orson Welles, E.G. Marshall, Simone Signoret, Billy Frick, Hannes Messemer, Robert Stack.

George C. Scott. *Patton* (aka *Patton — Lust for Glory*) (US/1970/170m/C) D: Franklin J. Schaffner. B/on *Patton: Ordeal and Triumph* by Ladislas Farago and *A Soldier's Story* by Omar Bradley. Best Picture, Best Direction (AA). Best English-Language Picture (NBR). Best Director (DGA). C: Karl Malden, Michael Bates, Edward Binns, Lawrence Dobkin, John Doucette, Stephen Young, Michael Strong, Frank Latimore, James Edwards, Richard Meunch, Karl Michael Vogler.

George Kennedy. *Brass Target* (US/1978/111m/C) D: John Hough. B/on the novel *The Algonquin Project* by Frederick Nolan. C: Sophia Loren, John Cassavetes, Robert Vaughn, Patrick McGoohan, Lee Montague, Bruce Davison, Edward Hermann.

Paul I *see* 636

415 Pavlova, Anna Pavlovna (1881–1931)

Russian ballerina, Pavlova was the most famous classical dancer of her era.

Pearl Argyle. *Regal Cavalcade* (aka *Royal Cavalcade*) (GB/1935/100m/BW) D: Thomas Bentley, Herbert Brenton, Norman Lee, Walter Summers, Will Kellino & Marcel Varnel. C: Marie Lohr, Esme Percy, Frank Vosper, Austin Trevor, Harry Brunning, John Mills, C.M. Hallard, H. Saxon-Snell, Patric Knowles, Matheson Lang, Athene Seyler.

Maria Tallchief. *Million Dollar Mermaid* (aka *The One-Piece Bathing Suit*) (US/1952/115m/C) D: Mervyn LeRoy. C: Esther Williams, Victor Mature, Walter Pidgeon.

Tamara Toumanova. *Tonight We Sing* (US/1953/109m/C) D: Mitchell Leisen. B/on the book *Impressario* by Sol Hurok & Ruth Goode. C: David Wayne, Ezio Pinza.

Galina Beliaeva. *Pavlova* (aka *Pavlova—A Woman for All Time*) (GB-USSR/ 1984/133m/C) D: Emil Lotianou. C: James Fox, Serge Shakourov, Vsevolod Larinov, Michael Kradunin, Martin Scorsese, Bruce Forsyth, Roy Kinnear, Lina Boultakova.

416 Peel, Sir Robert (1788–1850)

British politician and Prime Minister (1834–35, 1841–46), Peel's organization of the London police force immortalized him when the cops came to be known as "Bobbies." He was portrayed by Alec McCowen in the TV mini-series *Victoria and Albert* (2001).

Charles Carson. *Victoria the Great* (GB/1937/110m/C) D: Herbert Wilcox. B/on the play *Victoria Regina* by Laurence Housman. C: Anna Neagle, Anton Walbrook, H.B. Warner, James Dale, Hubert Harben, Felix Aylmer, Arthur Young, Derrick De Marney, Hugh Miller, Percy Parsons, Henry Hallatt, Gordon McLeod, Wyndham Goldie.

Charles Carson. *Sixty Glorious Years* (aka *Queen of Destiny*) (GB/1938/90m/C) D: Herbert Wilcox. C: Anna Neagle, Anton Walbrook, C. Aubrey Smith, Felix Aylmer, Pamela Standish, Gordon McLeod, Henry Hallatt, Wyndham Goldie, Malcolm Keen, Derrick De Marney, Joyce Bland, Harvey Braban, Aubrey Dexter, Laidman Browne.

Nicolas Hannan. *The Prime Minister* (GB/1940/94m/BW) D: Thorold Dickinson. C: John Gielgud, Diana Wynyard, Will Fyfe, Stephen Murray, Owen Nares, Fay Compton, Lyn Harding, Leslie Perrins, Vera Bogetti, Frederick Leister, Kynaston Reeves, Gordon McLeod.

417 Pepys, Samuel (1633–1703)

English government official, Pepys is remembered for his diary which included his accounts of the Plague and the Great Fire of London.

Arthur Chesney. *Colonel Blood* (GB/1934/98m/BW) D: W.P. Lipscomb. C: Frank Cellier, Anne Gray, Allan Jeayes, Mary Lawson, Stella Arbenina, Hilda Trevelyan.

Esme Percy. *Nell Gwyn* (GB/1934/75m/BW) D: Herbert Wilcox. B/on diaries of Samuel Pepys, Charles II and Nell Gwyn. C: Anna Neagle, Cedric Hardwicke, Muriel George.

Henry Oscar. *The Courageous Mr. Penn* (aka *Penn of Pennsylvania*) (GB/1941/ 78m/BW) D: Lance Comfort. B/on the book *William Penn* by C.E. Vulliamy. C: Clifford Evans, Deborah Kerr, Dennis Arundell, Aubrey Mallalieu, O.B. Clarence.

418 Perón, Eva Duarte "Evita" (1919–1952)

Powerful political figure and second wife of Argentinian president **Juan Perón**. Eva became politically active as a champion of women and the poor; her followers loved and worshiped her almost to the point of sainthood. Eva was portrayed by Fay Dunaway in the 1981 TV film *Evita Peron* (Allison Smith as the Young Eva).

Madonna. María Luján Hidalgo (Young Eva). *Evita* (US/1996/134m/C) D: Alan Parker. B/on the musical by Andrew Lloyd Weber & Tim Rice. C: Antonio Banderas, Jonathan Pryce, Jimmy Nail, Victoria Sus, Julian Littman, Olga Merediz, Laura Pallas, Julia Worsley, Servando Villamil, Andrea Corr, Peter Polycarpou, Gary Brooker, Maite Yerro.

Esther Goris. *Eva Perón* (Argentina/1996/119m/C) D: Juan Carlos Desanzo. C: Víctor Laplace, Christina Banegas, Pepe Nuvoa, Irma Córdoba, Lorenzo Quinteros.

419 Perón, Juan (1895–1974)

President of Argentina (1946–55 and 1973–74), one of the most influential political figures in Latin America. His policies were pro labor, nationalistic, and he was an admirer of **Musolinni**. Although an elected president, he ruled as a dictator. Perón was portrayed by James Farentino in the 1981 TV film *Evita Peron*.

Jonathan Pryce. *Evita* (US/1996/134m/C) D: Alan Parker. B/on the musical by Andrew Lloyd Weber & Tim Rice. C: Madonna, Antonio Banderas, Jimmy Nail, Victoria Sus, Julian Littman, Olga Merediz, Laura Pallas, Julia Worsley, María Luján Hidalgo, Servando Villamil, Andrea Corr, Peter Polycarpou, Gary Brooker, Maite Yerro.

Víctor Laplace. *Eva Perón* (Argentina/1996/119m/C) D: Juan Carlos Desanzo. C: Esther Goris, Christina Banegas, Pepe Nuvoa, Irma Córdoba, Lorenzo Quinteros.

420 Pershing, John Joseph (1860–1948)

U.S. general and commander of the American Expeditionary Force in WWI, Pershing had previously headed an unsuccessful punitive campaign in Mexico against **Pancho Villa**. Pershing was portrayed by Marshall R. Teague in the TV movie *Rough Riders* (97).

Joseph Girard. *Sergeant York* (US/1941/134m/BW) D: Howard Hawks. B/on the diary of Alvin York as edited by Tom Skeyhill, and on the books: *War Diary of Sergeant York* and *Sergeant York and His People* by Sam K. Cowan and *Sergeant York: Last of the Long Hunters* by Tom Skeyhill. C: Gary Cooper, Walter Brennan, Joan Leslie, George Tobias, Stanley Ridges, Margaret Wycherly, Ward Bond, Charles Trowbridge.

Herbert Heyes. *The Court-Martial of Billy Mitchell* (aka *One Man Mutiny*) (US/1955/100m/C) D: Otto Preminger. C: Gary Cooper, Charles Bickford, Ralph Bellamy, Rod Steiger, Elizabeth Montgomery, James Daly, Dayton Lumis, Tom McKee, Phil Arnold, Ian Wolfe.

Milburn Stone. *The Long Gray Line* (US/1955/138m/C) D: John Ford. B/on the novel *Bringing Up the Brass* by Marty Maher & Nardi Reeder. C: Tyrone Power, Maureen O'Hara, Robert Francis, Donald Crisp, Elbert Steele, Harry Carey, Jr., James Sears.

John Russell. *Cannon for Cordoba* (aka *Dragon Master*) (US/1970/104m/C) D: Paul Wendkos. C: George Peppard, Giovanna Ralli, Raf Vallone, Peter Duel, Don Gordon.

Walter Coy. *Pancho Villa* (aka *Challenge of Pancho Villa*) (Spain/1972/90m/C) D: Eugene Martin. C: Telly Savalas, Clint Walker, Anne Francis, Chuck Connors.

421 Peter (?–AD 64)

The most prominent apostle of **Jesus Christ**, Peter is believed to have been martyred in Rome at the time of **Nero's** Christian persecutions. He was portrayed by James Farentino in the TV mini-series *Jesus of Nazareth* (77), by Jay O. Sanders in the TV film *The Day Christ Died* (80), and by Luca Zingaretti in *Jesus* (99).

Hubert Prelier. *Golgotha* (France/1935/97m/BW) D: Julien Duvivier. C: Harry Baur, Robert Le Vigan, Jean Gabin, Charles Granval, Andre Bacque, Lucas Gridoux, Edwige Feuillere, Juliette Verneuil, Vana Yami, Van Daele.

A.S. Fisher. *The Lawton Story* (aka *The Prince of Peace*) (US/1949/120–101m/C) D: William Beaudine & Harold Dan. C: Millard Coody, Darlene Bridges, Hazel Lee Becker.

Carlos Villatios. *The Sinner of Magdala* (aka *Mary Magdalene*) (Mexico/1950/95m/BW) D: Miguel Torres. C: Medea de Novara, Luis Alcoriza, Louana Alcanir, Jose Bavera.

Finlay Currie. *Quo Vadis* (US/1951/171m/C) D: Mervyn LeRoy. B/on the novel by Henryk Sienkiewicz. C: Robert Taylor, Deborah Kerr, Leo Genn, Peter Ustinov, Patricia Laffan, Abraham Sofaer, Buddy Baer, Marina Berti, Norman Woodland.

Michael Rennie. *The Robe* (US/1953/135m/C) D: Henry Koster. B/on the novel by Lloyd C. Douglas. Best Picture — Drama (GG). C: Richard Burton, Jean Simmons, Victor Mature, Jay Robinson, Dean Jagger, Torin Thatcher, Richard Boone, Ernest Thesiger, Michael Ansara, Cameron Mitchell (the voice of Jesus Christ).

Tyler McVey. *Day of Triumph* (US/1954/110m/C) D: Irving Pichel & John T. Coyle. C: Lee J. Cobb, Robert Wilson, Ralph Freud, Michael Connors, Joanne Dru, James Griffith, Lowell Gilmore, Anthony Warde, Peter Whitney, Everett Glass.

Michael Rennie. *Demetrius and the Gladiators* (US/1954/101m/C) D: Delmer Daves. C: Victor Mature, Susan Hayward, Debra Paget, Anne Bancroft, Jay Robinson, Barry Jones.

Lorne Greene. *The Silver Chalice* (US/1954/143m/C) D: Victor Saville. B/on the novel by Thomas B. Costain. C: Virginia Mayo, Jack Palance, Paul Newman, Pier Angeli, E.G. Marshall, Alexander Scourby, Joseph Wiseman, Jacques Aubuchon.

Howard Keel. *The Big Fisherman* (US/1959/180m/C) D: Frank Borzage. B/on the novel by Lloyd C. Douglas. C: Susan Kohner, John Saxon, Martha Hyer, Herbert Lom, Alexander Scourby, Jay Barney, Rhodes Reason, Brian Hutton, Thomas Troupe, Herbert Rudley.

Antonio Vilar. *The Redeemer* (Spain/1959/93m/C) D: Joseph Breen. C: Luis Alvarez, Maruchi Fresno, Manuel Monroy, Felix Acaso, Virgilio Teixeira, Carlos Casaravilla, Sebastian Cabot (Narrator).

Royal Dano. *King of Kings* (US/1961/168m/C) D: Nicholas Ray. C: Jeffrey Hunter, Siobhan McKenna, Hurd Hatfield, Viveca Lindfors, Rita Gam, Carmen Sevilla, Rip Torn, Brigid Bazlen, Harry Guardino, Frank Thring, Guy Rolfe, Maurice Marsac, Gregoire Aslan, Robert Ryan, Gerard Tichy, Michael Wager, Tino Barrero, Jose Antonio, Orson Welles (Narrator).

Harry Andrews. *Barabbas* (Italy/1962/144m/C) D: Richard Fleischer. B/on the novel by Pär Lagerkvist. C: Anthony Quinn, Silvana Mangano, Arthur Kennedy, Katy Jurado, Roy Mangano, Ivan Triesault, Michael Gwynn, Arnold Foa.

Settimio Di Porto. *The Gospel According to St. Matthew* (France-Italy/1964/ 142m/BW) D: Pier Paolo Pasolini. B/on the *New Testament* book of *Matthew*. C: Enrique Irazoqui, Susanna Pasolini, Mario Socrate, Marcello Morante, Alfonso Gatto, Rodolfo Wilcock, Francesco Leonetti, Amerigo Bevilacqua, Otello Ses- tilli, Ferruccio Nuzzo, Alessandro Tosca, Paolo Tedesco, Franca Cupane, Gia- como Morante, Rosario Migale.

Gary Raymond. *The Greatest Story Ever Told* (US/1965/141m/C) D: George Stevens. B/on the book by Fulton Oursler. C: Max von Sydow, Dorothy McGuire, Robert Loggia, Claude Rains, Jose Ferrer, Charlton Heston, Donald Pleasence, David McCallum, Robert Blake, John Considine, David Hedison, Joanna Dun- ham, Sal Mineo, Van Heflin, Ed Wynn, Martin Landau, Telly Savalas, Sidney Poitier, Roddy McDowell, Angela Lansbury, Richard Conte, Carroll Baker, Janet Margolin, Burt Brinckerhoff, Tom Reese.

Jean Clarieux. *The Milky Way* (France-Italy/1969/105m/C) D: Luis Bunuel. C: Paul Frankeur, Laurent Terzieff, Alain Cuny, Bernard Verley, Edith Scob, Michel Piccoli, Christian van Cau, Pierre Clementi, Georges Marchal, Delphine Seyrig.

Philip Toubus. *Jesus Christ, Superstar* (US/1973/107m/C) D: Norman Jewi- son. B/on the rock opera by Tim Rice & Andrew Lloyd Webber. C: Ted Nee- ley, Carl Anderson, Yvonne Elliman, Barry Dennen, Bob Bingham, Larry T. Marshall, Joshua Mostel.

Paul Smith. *The Gospel Road* (US/1973/93m/C) D: Robert Elfstrom. C: Robert Elfstrom, June Carter Cash, Larry Lee, Alan Dater, John Paul Kay, Gelles LaBlanc, Robert Elfstrom, Jr., Terrance W. Mannock, Thomas Levanthal, Sean Armstrong, Lyle Nicholson, Steven Chernoff, Jonathan Sanders, Ulf Pollack.

Niko Nital. *Jesus* (US/1979/117m/C) D: Peter Sykes & John Kirsh. B/on the *New Testament* book of *Luke*. C: Brian Deacon, Rivka Noiman, Yossef Shiloah, Gadi Rol, Richard Peterson, Eli Cohen, Shmuel Tal, Kobi Assaf, Talia Shapira, Eli Danker, Mosko Alkalai, Nisim Gerama, Leonid Weinstein, Peter Frye, David Goldberg.

Anthony DeLongis. *In Search of Historic Jesus* (US/1979/91m/C) D: Henning

Schellerup. B/on the book by Lee Roddy & Charles E. Seller. C: John Rubinstein, John Anderson, Nehemiah Persoff, Andrew Bloch, Morgan Brittany, Walter Brooke, Annette Charles, Royal Dano, Lawrence Dobkin, David Opatoshu, John Hoyt, Jeffrey Druce.

Victor Argo. *The Last Temptation of Christ* (US/1988/164m/C) D: Martin Scorsese. B/on the novel by Nikos Kazantzakis. C: Willem Dafoe, Harvey Keitel, Paul Greco, Verna Bloom, Barbara Hershey, Gary Basaraba, Michael Been, John Lurie, Harry Dean Stanton, David Bowie, Nehemiah Persoff, Leo Burmester, Irvin Kershner, Andre Gregory, Tomas Arana, Juliette Caton, Roberts Blossom, Barry Miller, Alan Rosenberg.

Franciszek Pieczka. *Quo Vadis* (Poland/2001/167m/C) D: Jerzy Kawalerowicz. C: Pawel Delag, Magdalena Mielcarz, Boguslaw Linda, Danuta Stenka, Krzysztof Majchrzak, Agnieszka Wagner, Michal Bajor, Jerzy Trela, Malgorzata Pieczynska, Rafal Kubacki, Jerzy Nowak, Anna Majcher, Eugeniusz Priwieziencew.

Peter III *see* 635

422 Philip II, King (1527–1598)

Philip II ruled Spain at the height of its power and influence. During his reign Spanish colonies were established in what is now the southern U.S., and the Philippine Islands were named for him. His second of four wives was **Mary I** of England. His religious zeal led to the Inquisition and the 80 years war which resulted in the northern provinces winning their independence, eventually becoming the Netherlands. During the reign of **Elizabeth I**, Philip planned an invasion of England and built the Spanish Armada for this purpose.

Raymond Massey. *Fire Over England* (GB/1937/92m/BW) D: William K. Howard. B/on the novel by A.E.W. Mason. C: Laurence Olivier, Flora Robson, Leslie Banks, Vivien Leigh, Tamara Desni, Robert Newton, Lyn Harding, James Mason.

Montague Love. *The Sea Hawk* (US/1940/126m/BW) D: Michael Curtiz. C: Errol Flynn, Brenda Marshall, Claude Rains, Flora Robson, Donald Crisp, Henry Daniell, Alan Hale, Henry David.

Umberto Raho. *Seven Seas to Calais* (Italy/1962/99m/C) D: Rudolph Mate & Primo Zeglio. C: Rod Taylor, Irene Worth, Keith Michell, Anthony Dawson, Esmerelda Ruspoli, Basil Dignam.

George Yiasoumi. *Elizabeth* (US/1998/124m/C) D: Shekar Kapur. AA Best makeup. GG Best Actress. C: Cate Blanchett, Joseph Fiennes, Fanny Ardant, James Frain, Richard Attenborough, Christopher Eccleston, Vincent Cassel, Geoffrey Rush, Kathy Burke.

Philippe II *see* 615

423 Phillips, Sam (1923–)

Influential American record producer, Phillips owned Sun Records in Memphis and produced the earliest successes for such rock/country stars as **Elvis Presley**,

Jerry Lee Lewis, Johnny Cash, Carl Perkins and Roy Orbison. In the ABC series *Elvis* (90) he was played by Jordan Williams.

Charles Cyphers. *Elvis* (aka *Elvis—The Movie*) (US/1979/150–119m/C) D: John Carpenter. Made for U.S. TV, released theatrically elsewhere. C: Kurt Russell, Shelley Winters, Pat Hingle, Season Hubley, Bing Russell, Will Jordan.

Knox Phillips. *This Is Elvis* (US/1981/144–101m/C) D: Malcolm Leo & Andrew Solti. C: Paul Boensch III, David Scott, Dana MacKay, Johnny Harra, Lawrence Koller, Rhonda Lyn, Debbie Edge, Larry Raspberry, Furry Lewis, Ral Donner (Elvis' Narration).

Trey Wilson. *Great Balls of Fire* (US/1989/108m/C) D: Jim McBride. B/on the book by Myra Lewis & Murray Silver. C: Dennis Quaid, Winona Ryder, Alec Baldwin, John Doe, Stephen Toblowsky, Michael St. Gerard, Lisa Jane Persky, Steve Allen, Robert Lesser.

424 Piaf, Edith (1915–1963)

(Edith Giovanna Gassion) Popular French singer and cabaret entertainer.

Brigitte Ariel. Betty Mars (Singing voice of Edith Piaf). *Piaf—The Early Years* (aka *The Sparrow of Pigalle*) (US-France/1974/104m/C) D: Guy Casaril. B/on the book *Piaf* by Simone Berteaut. C: Pascale Christophe, Guy Trejan, Pierre Vernier, Jacques Duby.

Evelyne Bouix. *Edith and Marcel* (France/1983/162–104m/C) D: Claude Lelouch. C: Marcel Cerdan, Jr., Charles Aznavour, Jacques Villeret, Jean-Claude Brialy.

425 Picasso, Pablo Ruiz y (1881–1973)

Spanish painter and sculptor, considered to be the greatest artist of the 20th century. Innovator and explorer of form, styles, and techniques, he was the foremost developer of abstract painting, cubism, collage, and experimental construction. A extremely prolific artist, he created more than 20,000 works in his lifetime. He was the first living artist to have his work shown at the Louvre, a 1971 exhibition honoring him on his 90th birthday.

Gosta Ekman. *The Adventures of Picasso* (Sweden/1978/92m/C) D: Tage Daniellson. C: Hans Alfredson, Margaretha Krook, Bernard Cribbins, Wilfrid Brambell, Per Oscarsson.

Anthony Hopkins. *Surviving Picasso* (GB/1999/125m/C) D: James Ivory. C: Natascha McElhone, Julianne Moore, Joss Ackland, Peter Eyre, Jane Lapotaire, Joseph Maher, Bob Peck, Diane Venora, Joan Plowright.

Pierce, Franklin *see* 578

426 Pilate, Pontius

Roman Procurator of Judea from 26–36, Pilate was the governor at the time of the crucifixion of **Jesus Christ**. After his recall to Rome nothing is known of his life though one theory has it that he later became a Christian and was martyred. He is a saint in the Coptic and Abyssinian churches. He was portrayed by Rod Steiger in the TV mini-series *Jesus of Nazareth* (77), by Keith Michell in the TV film *The Day Christ Died* (80), and by Gary Oldman in *Jesus* (99).

Basil Gill. *The Wandering Jew* (GB/1933/111–85m/BW) D: Maurice Elvey. B/on the play by E. Temple Thurston. C: Conrad Veidt, Marie Ney, Anne Grey, Dennis Hoey.

Jean Gabin. *Golgotha* (France/1935/97m/BW) D: Julien Duvivier. C: Harry Baur, Robert Le Vigan, Charles Granval, Andre Bacque, Hubert Prelier, Lucas Gridoux, Edwige Feuillere, Juliette Verneuil, Vana Yami, Van Daele.

Basil Rathbone. *The Last Days of Pompeii* (US/1935/96m/BW) D: Ernest B. Schoedsack. C: Preston Foster, John Wood, Louis Calhern, Alan Hale, Ward Bond, Gloria Shea.

Jose Bavera. *The Sinner of Magdala* (aka *Mary Magdalene*) (Mexico/1950/95m/BW) D: Miguel Torres. C: Medea de Novara, Luis Alcoriza, Carlos Villatios, Louana Alcanir.

Basil Sydney. *Salome* (US/1953/103m/C) D: William Dieterle. C: Rita Hayworth, Stewart Granger, Charles Laughton, Judith Anderson, Cedric Hardwicke, Alan Badel, Rex Reason, Robert Warwick, Maurice Schwartz.

Richard Boone. *The Robe* (US/1953/135m/C) D: Henry Koster. B/on the novel by Lloyd C. Douglas. Best Picture — Drama (GG). C: Richard Burton, Jean Simmons, Victor Mature, Michael Rennie, Jay Robinson, Dean Jagger, Torin Thatcher, Ernest Thesiger, Michael Ansara, Cameron Mitchell (the voice of Jesus Christ).

Lowell Gilmore. *Day of Triumph* (US/1954/110m/C) D: Irving Pichel & John T. Coyle. C: Lee J. Cobb, Robert Wilson, Ralph Freud, Tyler McVey, Michael Connors, Joanne Dru, James Griffith, Anthony Warde, Peter Whitney, Everett Glass.

Frank Thring. *Ben Hur* (US/1959/212m/C) D: William Wyler. B/on the novel by Lew Wallace. Best Picture (AA,BFA,NYC,GG), Best Director (AA,GG,DGA). C: Charlton Heston, Stephen Boyd, Jack Hawkins, Haya Harareet, Hugh Griffith, Sam Jaffe, Jose Greci, Laurence Payne, Claude Heater, George Relph, Finlay Currie.

Antonio Vilar. *The Redeemer* (Spain/1959/93m/C) D: Joseph Breen. C: Luis Alvarez, Maruchi Fresno, Manuel Monroy, Felix Acaso, Virgilio Teixeira, Carlos Casaravilla, Sebastian Cabot (Narrator).

Hurd Hatfield. *King of Kings* (US/1961/168m/C) D: Nicholas Ray. C: Jeffrey Hunter, Siobhan McKenna, Viveca Lindfors, Rita Gam, Carmen Sevilla, Rip Torn, Brigid Bazlen, Harry Guardino, Frank Thring, Guy Rolfe, Maurice Marsac, Gregoire Aslan, Royal Dano, Robert Ryan, Gerard Tichy, Michael Wager, Tino Barrero, Jose Antonio, Orson Welles (Narrator).

Arthur Kennedy. *Barabbas* (Italy/1962/144m/C) D: Richard Fleischer. B/on the novel by Pär Lagerkvist. C: Anthony Quinn, Silvana Mangano, Katy Jurado, Harry Andrews, Roy Mangano, Ivan Triesault, Michael Gwynn, Arnold Foa.

Jean Marais. *Pontius Pilate* (Italy-France/1962/100m/C) D: Irving Rapper. C: Jeanne Crain, Basil Rathbone, Leticia Roman, John Drew Barrymore, Livio Lorenzon.

Alessandro Tosca. *The Gospel According to St. Matthew* (France-Italy/1964/142m/BW) D: Pier Paolo Pasolini. B/on the *New Testament* book of *Matthew*. C: Enrique Irazoqui, Susanna Pasolini, Mario Socrate, Marcello Morante, Alfonso Gatto, Rodolfo Wilcock, Francesco Leonetti, Amerigo Bevilacqua, Otello Sestilli, Settimio Di Porto, Ferruccio Nuzzo, Paolo Tedesco, Franca Cupane, Giacomo Morante, Rosario Migale.

Telly Savalas. *The Greatest Story Ever Told* (US/1965/141m/C) D: George Stevens. B/on the book by Fulton Oursler. C: Max von Sydow, Dorothy McGuire, Robert Loggia, Claude Rains, Jose Ferrer, Charlton Heston, Donald Pleasence, David McCallum, Gary Raymond, Robert Blake, John Considine, David Hedison, Joanna Dunham, Sal Mineo, Van Heflin, Ed Wynn, Martin Landau, Sidney Poitier, Roddy McDowell, Angela Lansbury, Richard Conte, Carroll Baker, Janet Margolin, Burt Brinckerhoff, Tom Reese.

Ljuba Tadic. *The Master and Margarita* (Yugoslavia-Italy/1972/101m/C) D: Aleksander Petrovic. C: Ugo Tognazzi, Alain Cuny, Radomir Reljic, Mimsy Farmer, Bata Zivojinovic.

Barry Dennen. *Jesus Christ, Superstar* (US/1973/107m/C) D: Norman Jewison. B/on the rock opera by Tim Rice & Andrew Lloyd Webber. C: Ted Neeley, Carl Anderson, Yvonne Elliman, Bob Bingham, Larry T. Marshall, Joshua Mostel, Philip Toubus.

Donald Pleasence. *The Passover Plot* (Israel/1976/108m/C) D: Michael Campus. B/on the book by Hugh Schonfield. C: Harry Andrews, Hugh Griffith, Zalman King, Scott Wilson, Dan Ades, Michael Baselon, Lewis van Bergen, William Burns, Dan Hedaya, Kevin O'Connor, Robert Walker.

Peter Frye. *Jesus* (US/1979/117m/C) D: Peter Sykes & John Kirsh. B/on the *New Testament* book of *Luke*. C: Brian Deacon, Rivka Noiman, Yossef Shiloah, Niko Nital, Gadi Rol, Richard Peterson, Eli Cohen, Shmuel Tal, Kobi Assaf, Talia Shapira, Eli Danker, Mosko Alkalai, Nisim Gerama, Leonid Weinstein, David Goldberg.

Michael Palin. *Monty Python's Life of Brian* (aka *Life of Brian*) (GB/1979/93m/C) D: Terry Jones. C: Graham Chapman, Eric Idle, John Cleese, Terry Gilliam, Terry Jones, Ken Colley, John Case.

Lawrence Dobkin. *In Search of Historic Jesus* (US/1979/91m/C) D: Henning Schellerup. B/on the book by Lee Roddy & Charles E. Seller. C: John Rubinstein, John Anderson, Nehemiah Persoff, Andrew Bloch, Morgan Brittany, Walter Brooke, Annette Charles, Royal Dano, Anthony DeLongis, David Opatoshu, John Hoyt, Jeffrey Druce.

Harvey Keitel. *The Inquiry* (aka *L'Inchiesta*) (aka *The Investigation*) (aka *The Inquest*) (Italy/1986/107m/C) D: Damiano Damiani. C: Keith Carradine, Lina Sastri, Phyllis Logan, Angelo Infanti, Sylvan.

David Bowie. *The Last Temptation of Christ* (US/1988/164m/C) D: Martin Scorsese. B/on the novel by Nikos Kazantzakis. C: Willem Dafoe, Harvey Keitel, Paul Greco, Verna Bloom, Barbara Hershey, Gary Basaraba, Victor Argo, Michael Been, John Lurie, Harry Dean Stanton, Nehemiah Persoff, Leo Burmester, Irvin Kershner, Andre Gregory, Tomas Arana, Juliette Caton, Roberts Blossom, Barry Miller, Alan Rosenberg.

427 Pinkerton, Allan (1819–1884)

American detective (Scottish born), founder of the Pinkerton National Detective Agency. He directed espionage operations behind Confederate lines during the Civil War, uncovering a plot to assassinate President **Lincoln**. Although Pinkerton was a secondary character in the films listed, Pinkerton himself, or a "Pinkerton Man" would arrive on the scene to foil bank and train robbers of the old west. In the TV movie *The Rose and the Jackal* (90) Pinkerton was played by Christopher Reeve.

Sidney Toler. *Operator 13* (aka *Spy 13*) (US/1934/86m/BW) D: Richard Boleslavsky. B/on the novel by Robert W. Chambers. C: Marion Davies, Gary Cooper, Jean Parker, Katharine Alexander, Ted Healy, Douglas Dumbrille, John Elliott, Fred Warren. Franklin Parker.

James Harrison. *The Tall Target* (US/1951/78m/BW) D: Anthony Mann. C: Dick Powell, Paula Raymond, Adolphe Menjou, Marshall Thompson, Ruby Dee, Will Geer, Leslie Kimmell.

Vít Olmer. *Fantom Morrisvillu* (Czechoslovakia/1966/C/BW) C: Rudolf Deyl, Kveta Fialová, Lubomír Kostelka, Jaroslav Marvan, Waldemar Matuska, Oldrich Novy.

William Atherton. *Frank and Jesse* (US/1994/105m/C) D: Robert Boris. C: Rob Lowe, Bill Paxton, Randy Travis, Dana Wheeler-Nicholson, Maria Pitillo, Luke Askew, Sean Patrick Flanery, Alexis Arquette, Todd Field, John Pyper-Ferguson, Nicholas Sadler, Tom Chick, Mary Neff, Richard Maynard.

E.J. Callahan. *Wild, Wild West* (US/1999/152m/C) D: Barry Sonnenfeld. B/on the TV Series. C: Will Smith, Kevin Kline, Kenneth Branagh, Salma Hayek, Ted Levine, M. Emmet Walsh, Bai Ling, Frederique van der Wal, Musetta Vander.

Timothy Dalton. *American Outlaws* (US/2001/93m/C) D: Les Mayfield. B/on a story by Roderick Taylor. C: Colin Farrell, Scott Caan, Ali Larter, Gabriel Macht, Gregory Smith, Harris Yulin, Will McCormack, Ronny Cox, Terry O'Quinn, Nathaniel Arcand, Kathy Bates, Craig Erickson, Ty O'Neal, Joe Stevens.

428 Pitt, William (1759–1806)

The youngest man to serve as Great Britain's Prime Minister, Pitt was appointed by **George III** at the age of 24 and he held the position for 18 years. He served as PM again from 1804 until his death.

Bruce Belfrage. *The Scarlet Pimpernel* (GB/1935/85m/BW) D: Harold Young. B/on the novel by the Baroness Orczy. C: Leslie Howard, Merle Oberon, Raymond Massey, Nigel Bruce, Bramwell Fletcher, Anthony Bushell, Walter Rilla, Ernest Milton.

Ian MacLaren. *The Last of the Mohicans* (US/1936/91m/BW) D: George B. Seitz. B/on the novel by James Fennimore Cooper. C: Randolph Scott, Binnie Barnes, Heather Angel, Hugh Buckler, Henry Wilcoxon, Bruce Cabot, Olaf Hytten.

Robert Donat. *The Young Mr. Pitt* (GB/1942/118m/BW) D: Carol Reed. C: Robert Morley, Phyllis Calvert, Raymond Lovell, Max Adrian, Felix Aylmer, Albert Lieven, Stephen Haggard, Geoffrey Atkins, John Mills, Herbert Lom, Agnes Laughlan.

Anthony Nicholls. *The Laughing Lady* (GB/1946/100m/C) D: Paul L. Stein. B/on the play by Ingram d'Abbes. C: Anne Ziegler, Webster Booth, Peter Graves, Charles Goldner.

Henry Oscar. *Mrs. Fitzherbert* (GB/1947/99m/BW) D: Montgomery Tully. B/on the novel *Princess Fitz* by Winifred Carter. C: Peter Graves, Joyce Howard, Leslie Banks, Margaretta Scott, Wanda Rotha, Mary Clare, Frederick Valk, Ralph Truman, John Stuart, Barry Morse, Arthur Dulay, Moira Lister, Julian Dallas, Lily Kann.

N. Volkov. *Admiral Ushakov* (USSR/1953/C) D: Mikhail Romm. C: Ivan Pereverzev, Olga Zhizneva, Boris Livanov, V. Vasyliev, I. Solovyov.

Paul Rogers. *Beau Brummell* (US-GB/1954/111m/C) D: Curtis Bernhardt. B/on the play by Clyde Fitch. C: Stewart Granger, Elizabeth Taylor, Peter Ustinov, Robert Morley, James Donald, James Hayter, Rosemary Harris, Noel Willman, Peter Bull.

Anthony Stuart. *Austerlitz* (aka *The Battle of Austerlitz*) (France-Italy-Yugoslavia/1959/166m/C) D: Abel Gance. C: Pierre Mondy, Jean Mercure, Martine Carol, Jack Palance, Orson Welles, Claudia Cardinale, Georges Marchal, Roland Bartrop, Jean Marais, Vittorio De Sica, Ettore Manni.

Julian Wadham. *The Madness of King George* (aka *The Madness of George III*) (GB/1994/107m/C) D: Nicholas Hytner. B/on the play by Alan Bennett. C: Nigel Hawthorne, Helen Mirren, Rupert Everett, Amanda Donohoe, Caroline Harker, Ian Holm, Rupert Graves, Geoffrey Palmer, Barry Stanton, Jim Carter, Peter Bride-Kirk, Cyril Shaps.

429 Poe, Edgar Allan (1809–1849)

American poet and short story writer, Poe is remembered for such stories as "The Tell-Tale Heart," "The Gold Bug" and "The Murders in the Rue Morgue" among many others.

John Shepperd. *The Loves of Edgar Allan Poe* (US/1942/67m/BW) D: Harry Lachman. C: Linda Darnell, Virginia Gilmore, Jane Darwell, Mary Howard, Morton Lowry, Gilbert Emery.

Joseph Cotten. *The Man with a Cloak* (US/1951/81m/BW) D: Fletcher Markle. B/on the story *Gentleman from Paris* by John Dickson Carr. C: Barbara Stanwyck, Louis Calhern, Leslie Caron, Joe De Santis, Jim Backus, Margaret Wycherly, Hank Worden.

Hedger Wallace. *The Torture Garden* (GB/1968/92m/C) D: Freddie Francis. B/on the stories: *Enoch, Terror Over Hollywood, Mr. Steinway, & The Man Who Collected Poe* by Robert Bloch. C: Jack Palance, Burgess Meredith, Beverly Adams, Peter Cushing.

Klaus Kinski. *Web of the Spider* (Italy-France-Germany/1970/93m/C) D: Anthony Dawson (Antonio Margheriti). B/on the story *Danse Macabre* by Edgar Allan Poe. C: Anthony Franciosa, Michele Mercier, Karin Field, Peter Carsten.

Robert Walker, Jr. *The Spectre of Edgar Allan Poe* (US/1974/87m/C) D: Mohy Quandour. C: Cesar Romero, Tom Drake, Mary Grover, Carol Ohmart, Paul Bryar.

430 Polidori, John William (1795–1821)

Lord Byron's physician, Polidori was in attendance the night in 1816 when he, Byron, **Percy** and **Mary Shelley** gathered to create their most frightening stories.

Mary Shelley's inspiration became *Frankenstein, or the Modern Prometheus.* Polidori later wrote the influential novel *The Vampyre.* James Mason played a character named "Dr. Polidori" in the made for TV movie *Frankenstein: The True Story* (73).

Timothy Spall. *Gothic* (GB/1987/90m/C) D: Ken Russell. C: Gabriel Byrne, Julian Sands, Natasha Richardson, Myriam Cyr, Andreas Wisniewski.

Alex Winter. *Haunted Summer* (US/1988/115m/C) D: Ivan Passer. B/on the novel by Anne Edwards. C: Philip Anglim, Laura Dern, Alice Krige, Eric Stolz.

Jose Luis Gomez. *Rowing with the Wind* (Spain/1988/96m/C) D: Gonzalo Suarez. C: Hugh Grant, Lizzy McInnerny, Valentine Pelka, Elizabeth Hurley, Bibi Andersson.

Polk, James J. *see* 576

431 Polo, Marco (1254–1324)

Venetian traveler and writer, Polo's accounts of his trips to **Kublai Khan's** China provided the Western world its first view of the Eastern world.

Gary Cooper. *The Adventures of Marco Polo* (US/1938/100m/BW) D: Archie Mayo. C: Sigrid Gurie, Basil Rathbone, Ernest Truex, George Barbier, Binnie Barnes, Alan Hale, H.B. Warner.

Rory Calhoun. *Marco Polo* (aka *Grand Khan*) (Italy-France/1962/95m/C) D: Hugo Fregonese & Piero Pierot. C: Camillo Pilotto, Yoko Tani, Robert Hundar.

Horst Bucholz. *Marco the Magnificent* (aka *The Fabulous Adventures of Marco Polo*) (France-Italy-Afghanistan-Egypt-Yugoslavia/1965/115–100m/C) D: Denys De la Patèlliere, Noel Howard, Christian-Jaque & Cliff Lyons. C: Anthony Quinn, Orson Welles.

Desi Arnaz, Jr. *Marco* (US/1973/109m/C) D: Seymour Robbie. C: Zero Mostel, Jack Weston, Cie Cie Win, Aimee Eccles, Romeo Muller, Fred Sadoff.

Richard Harrison. *Marco Polo* (Hong Kong/1975/106m/C) D: Chang Cheh. C: Alexander Fu Sheng, Chi Kuan-chun, Shih Szu.

432 Pompadour, Marquise de (1721–1764)

(Jeanne Antoinette Poisson) **Louis XV's** official mistress from 1745 to 1750; Madame de Pompadour's influence extended beyond the boudoir to all cultural, social and political areas of the French court.

Anny Ahlers. *Die Marquise von Pompadour* (Germany/1930/92m/BW) D: Willi Wolff. C: Kurt Gerron.

Doris Kenyon. *Voltaire* (US/1933/72m/BW) D: John G. Adolfi. B/on the novel by George Gibbs & E. Lawrence. C: George Arliss, Margaret Lindsay, Reginald Owen.

Lil Dagover. *Fridericus* (Germany/1936/98m/BW) D: Johannes Meyer. B/on the novel by Walter von Molo. C: Otto Gebuhr, Hilde Korber, Agnes Straub, Kathe Haack.

Thekla Ahrens. *The King Smiles — Paris Laughs* (aka *Der Postillon von Lon-*

jumeau) (aka *Der König Lächelt— Paris Lacht*) (Germany/1936/91m/BW) D: Carl Lamac. B/on an operetta by Adolf Adam. C: Alfred Neugebauer, Leo Slezak, Willy Eichberger, Rudolf Carl.

Jeanne Boitel. *Champs-Elysées* (aka *Remontons Les Champs-Elysées*) (France/1938/100m/BW) D: Sacha Guitry. C: Sacha Guitry, Lucien Baroux, Jacqueline Delubac, Germaine Dermoz, Raymonde Allain, Jean Davy, Emile Drain, Jacques Erwin, Rene Fauchois, Liane Pathe, Robert Pizani, Claude Martin, Raymond Galle, Andre Laurent.

Hillary Brooke. *Monsieur Beaucaire* (US/1946/93m/BW) D: George Marshall. B/on the novel by Booth Tarkington. C: Bob Hope, Joan Caulfield, Patric Knowles, Marjorie Reynolds, Reginald Owen, Douglas Dumbrille, Howard Freeman.

Genevieve Page. *Fanfan the Tulip* (France/1952/104m/BW) D: Christian-Jaque. C: Gerard Philipe, Gina Lollobrigida, Marcel Herrand, Noel Roquevert, Henri Rollan.

Micheline Presle. *Royal Affairs in Versailles* (aka *Versailles*) (aka *Affairs in Versailles*) (aka *If Versailles Were Told to Me*) (aka *Si Versailles M'Eétait Couté*) (France/1953/180–152m/C) D: Sacha Guitry. C: Sacha Guitry, Claudette Colbert, Orson Welles, Gerard Phillippe, Jean Marais, Georges Marchal, Gilbert Boka, Lana Marconi, Gino Cervi, Fernand Gravet, Louis Arbessier, Jacques Berthier, Samson Fainsilber, Gilbert Gil, Emile Drain, Jacques de Feraudy, Gaston Rey, Philippe Richard.

433 Poppaea, Sabina (?–65 AD)

Married to **Nero** (his second, her third) in 62 AD, the Roman Emperor kicked her to death three years later in a fit of rage.

Claudette Colbert. *The Sign of the Cross* (US/1932/124m/BW) D: Cecil B. DeMille. B/on the play by Wilson Barrett. C: Fredric March, Elissa Landi, Charles Laughton, Ian Keith, Vivian Tobin, Harry Beresford, Nat Pendleton, Joe Bonomo.

Frances Day. *Fiddlers Three* (GB/1944/88m/BW) D: Harry Watt. C: Francis L. Sullivan, Tommy Trinder, Sonnie Hale, Diana Decker, James Robertson Justice, Kay Kendall.

Silvana Pampanini. *O.K. Nero!* (Italy/1951/111m/BW) D: Mario Soldati. C: Gino Cervi, Walter Chiari, Carlo Campanini, Jackie Frost, Alba Arnova.

Patricia Laffan. *Quo Vadis* (US/1951/171m/C) D: Mervyn LeRoy. B/on the novel by Henryk Sienkiewicz. C: Robert Taylor, Deborah Kerr, Leo Genn, Peter Ustinov, Finlay Currie, Abraham Sofaer, Buddy Baer, Marina Berti, Norman Woodland.

Brigitte Bardot. *Nero's Mistress* (aka *Nero's Big Weekend*) (aka *Nero's Weekend*) (aka *My Son Nero*) (aka *Mio Figlio Nerone*) (Italy/1956/104–86m/C) D: Steno (Stefano Vanzina). C: Gloria Swanson, Alberto Sordi, Vittorio De Sica.

Maria Grazia Bucella. *White, Red, Yellow, Pink* (aka *The Love Factory*) (aka *Bianco, Rosso, Gallo, Rosa*) (Italy/1966/94m/C) D: Massimo Mida. C: Giancarlo Cobelli, Agnes Spaak.

Agnieszka Wagner. *Quo Vadis* (Poland/2001/167m/C) D: Jerzy Kawalerowicz. C: Pawel Delag, Magdalena Mielcarz, Boguslaw Linda, Danuta Stenka, Franciszek Pieczka, Krzysztof Majchrzak, Michal Bajor, Jerzy Trela, Malgorzata Pieczynska, Rafal Kubacki, Jerzy Nowak, Anna Majcher, Eugeniusz Priwieziencew.

434 Porter, Cole (1893–1964)

Sophisticated American songwriter, Porter's works include the songs "Begin the Beguine" and "Night and Day" as well as the scores for such films as *Anything Goes* (36 & 56), *Kiss Me Kate* (53) and *Silk Stockings* (57).

Cary Grant. *Night and Day* (US/1946/128m/C) D: Michael Curtiz. C: Alexis Smith, Monty Woolley, Ginny Simms, Jane Wyman, Eve Arden, Victor Francen, Alan Hale.

Ron Randell. *Kiss Me Kate* (US/1953/109m/C) D: George Sidney. B/on the musical play by Cole Porter, Samuel Spewack & Bella Spewack and *The Taming of the Shrew* by Wm. Shakespeare. C: Kathryn Grayson, Howard Keel, Ann Miller.

435 Prefontaine, Steve "Pre" (1951–1975)

Charismatic, outspoken athlete, who held 14 American Track and Field Records. He was coached at Oregon State by Bill Bowerman (R. Lee Emery in *Prefontaine*, Donald Sutherland in *Without Limits*), and Bill Dellinger (Ed O'Neill in *Prefontaine*, Dean Norris in *Without Limits*). (Note: Bob Bowerman made the running shoes for his team and later became a co-founder of Nike) Pre's criticism of the treatment of amateur athletes led to the passage of the Amateur Sports Act in 1978. He was a competitor in the 1972 Munich Olympics, finishing fourth, but was expected to win the Gold Medal at the 1976 Olympics. This was not to happen, he was killed in an automobile accident in May of 1975.

Jared Leto. Robert Karl Burke (Young Prefontaine). *Prefontaine* (US/1997/106m/C) D: Steve James. C: R. Lee Emery, Ed O'Neill, Brekin Meyer, Lindsay Crouse, Amy Locane, Laurel Holloman, Brain McGovern, Kurtwood Smith, Tracy Hollister.

Billy Crudup. *Without Limits* (US/1998/117m/C) D: Robert Towne. C: Donald Sutherland, Dean Norris, Monica Potter, Jeremy Sisto, Matthew Lillard, Billy Burke, Judith Ivey, Fred Long, Pat Porter, Ashley Johnson, Tom Ansberry.

436 Presley, Elvis Aron (1935–1977)

The undisputed King of Rock and Roll, Elvis' battle with prescription drugs and deep-fried peanut butter and banana sandwiches led to a sadly premature death. Elvis starred in more than 30 films himself including such classics as: *Girls! Girls! Girls!* (62), *Girl Happy* (65) and *The Trouble with Girls* (70). Dale Midkiff played the King in Priscilla Presley's TV film *Elvis and Me* (88), Rick Peters in *Elvis Meets Nixon* (97), and in the strangest bit of casting in the history of television, Don Johnson portrayed Elvis in the TV movie *Elvis and the Beauty Queen* (81).

Kurt Russell. *Elvis* (aka *Elvis—The Movie*) (US/1979/150–119m/C) D: John Carpenter. Made for U.S. TV, released theatrically elsewhere. C: Shelley Winters, Pat Hingle, Season Hubley, Bing Russell, Will Jordan, Charles Cyphers.

David Scott (playing Elvis at 18). Dana MacKay (playing Elvis at 35). Johnny Hara (playing Elvis at 42). Ral Donner (Elvis' Narration). *This Is Elvis* (US/1981/ 144–101m/C) D: Malcolm Leo & Andrew Solti. C: Paul Boensch III, Lawrence Koller, Rhonda Lyn, Debbie Edge, Larry Raspberry, Furry Lewis, Knox Phillips.

David Keith. *Heartbreak Hotel* (US/1988/90m/C) D: Chris Columbus. C: Tuesday Weld, Charlie Schlatter, Angela Goethals, Jacque Lynn Colton, T. Graham Brown.

Michael St. Gerard. *Great Balls of Fire* (US/1989/108m/C) D: Jim McBride. B/on the book by Myra Lewis & Murray Silver. C: Dennis Quaid, Winona Ryder, Alec Baldwin, John Doe, Stephen Toblowsky, Trey Wilson, Lisa Jane Persky, Steve Allen, Robert Lesser.

Ron Stein. *Death Becomes Her* (US/1992/105m/C) D: Robert Zemeckis. C: Meryl Streep, Bruce Willis, Goldie Hawn, Isabella Rossellini, Sydney Pollack, Ian Ogilvy, Michael Caine, Stephanie Anderson, Bonnie Cahoon, Bob Swain, Eric Clark, Dave Brock.

Val Kilmer. *True Romance* (US/1993/119m/C) D: Tony Scott. C: Christian Slater, Patricia Arquette, Dennis Hopper, Gary Oldman, Brad Pitt, Christopher Walken.

Peter Dobson. *Forrest Gump* (US/1994/142m/C) D: Robert Zemeckis. B/on the novel by Winston Groom. Best Picture (AA), Best Director (AA). C: Tom Hanks, Gary Sinise, Robin Wright, Sally Field, Mykelti Williamson, Richard D'Allesandro, and the voices of Jed Gillin, John William Galt, Joe Stefanelli, and Joe Alaskey.

437 Proust, Marcel (1871–1922)

French novelist whose autobiographical works chronicled the decay of the French aristocracy. The 17 volume *À la recherche du temps perdu (Remembrance of Things Past)*, written in the last decade of his life, is considered his greatest work.

Marcel Mazzarella. Georges Du Fresne (child Marcel). Pierre Mignard (adolescent Marcel). André Engel (Marcel in old age). Patrice Chéreau (voice [Marcel, narrator]). *Time Regained* (aka *Le Temps retrouvé*) (aka *O Tempo Reencontrado*) (aka *I Tempo ritrovato*) (France-Italy-Portugal/1999/169m/C) D: Raoul Ruiz. B/on the novel by Marcel Proust. C: Catherine Deneuve, Emmanuelle Béart, Vincent Pérez, John Malkovich, Pascal Greggory, Marie-France Pisier, Chiara Mastroianni, Arielle Dombasle, Edith Scob, Elsa Zylberstein, Christian Vadim, Dominique Labourier, Philippe Morier-Genoud, Melvil Poupaud, Mathilde Seigner, Jacques Pieiller, Hélène Surgère.

Stanislas Merhar (as Simon [Proust]). *La Captive* (aka *The Captive*) (France-Belgium/2000/118m/C) D: Chantal Akerman. B/on writings of Marcel Proust. C: Sylvie Testud, Olivia Bonamy, Liliane Rovère, Françoise Bertin, Aurore Clément.

438 Purvis, Melvin (??)

One of **J. Edgar Hoover's** top FBI agents, Purvis was involved in the capture (and deaths) of **John Dillinger** and **Pretty Boy Floyd**.

Myron Healy. *Guns Don't Argue* (US/1955/92m/BW) D: Bill Karn & Richard Kahn. Feature film edited from the TV series *Gangbusters*. C: Lyle Talbot, Jean Harvey, Paul Dubov, Sam Edwards, Richard Crane, Tamar Cooper, Baynes Barron, Doug Wilson.

Ben Johnson. *Dillinger* (US/1973/107m/C) D: John Milius. C: Warren Oates, Michelle Phillips, Harry Dean Stanton, Geoffrey Lewis, Richard Dreyfuss, Steve Kanaly.

Dale Robertson. *Melvin Purvis: G-Man* (aka *The Legend of Machine Gun Kelly*) (US/1974/78m/C) D: Dan Curtis. C: Harris Yulin, Margaret Blye, Matt Clark, David Canary.

Michael Sacks. *The Private Files of J. Edgar Hoover* (US/1978/112m/C) D: Larry Cohen. C: Broderick Crawford, Jose Ferrer, Michael Parks, Ronee Blakely, Raymond St. Jacques, Andrew Duggan, Howard Da Silva, James Wainwright, Brad Dexter, William Jordan, Richard M. Dixon, Gordon Zimmerman, Lloyd Nolan, June Havoc, Dan Dailey, John Marley, Lloyd Gough.

Alan Vint. *The Lady in Red* (aka *Guns, Sin and Bathtub Gin*) (US/1979/93m/C) D: Lewis Teague. C: Robert Conrad, Pamela Sue Martin, Louise Fletcher, Robert Hogan, Laurie Heineman, Phillip R. Allen, Robert Forster.

Christopher Kriesa. *Dillinger and Capone* (US/1995/95m/C) D: Jon Purdy. C: Martin Sheen, F. Murray Abraham, Stephen Davies, Catherine Hicks, Don Stroud, Debi A. Monahan.

439 Pushkin, Alexander Sergeyevich (1799–1837)

Russia's greatest poet, Pushkin created such works as *Eugene Onegin* and *Boris Gudenov*. He was killed in a duel defending his wife's honor.

V. Litovsky. *Young Pushkin* (USSR/1937/81m/BW) D: Arcady Naroditsky. C: L. Mazin, I. Paramonov, A. Mazurin, K. Smirnov.

Peter Aleynikov. *The Great Glinka* (aka *Glinka*) (USSR/1946/100m/BW) D: Leo Arnstam. C: Boris Chorkov, Sasha Sobolyev, Valentina Serova, Boris Livanov.

L. Durasov. *Man of Music* (aka *Glinka*) (USSR/1952/100m/C) D: Grigori Alexandrov. C: Boris Smirnov, Lubov Orlova, Svyatoslav Richter, Mikhail Nazvanov, B. Vinogradova.

Alexander Paleyes. *Wake Up Mukhin!* (USSR/1968/84m/C) D: Yakov Seghel. C: Sergei Shaqkurov, Lilia Alyoshnikova, Nikolai Ribnikov, Vladimir Kozinets, Nikolai Sergeyev.

440 Quanah Parker (1852?–1911)

Comanche leader, Quanah was the son of a Comanche chief and a white captive woman. He was the founder of the Peyote Religion.

John War Eagle. *They Rode West* (US/1954/84m/C) D: Phil Karlson. C: Robert Francis, Donna Reed, May Wynn, Phil Carey, Onslow Stevens, Roy Roberts, Jack Kelly, James Best.

Kent Smith. *Comanche* (US/1956/87m/C) D: George Sherman. C: Dana Andrews, Linda Cristal, Lowell Gilmore, Nestor Paiva, John Litel, Stacy Harris, Mike Mazurki.

Henry Brandon. *Two Rode Together* (US/1961/108m/C) D: John Ford. B/on the novel *Comanche Captives* by Will Cook. C: James Stewart, Richard Widmark, Shirley Jones, Linda Cristal, Andy Devine, John McIntire, Mae Marsh, Harry Carey, Jr.

441 Quantrill, William Clark (1837–1865)

Confederate guerrilla leader of the Civil War, Quantrill was responsible for the massacre and burning of the town of Lawrence, Kansas. He was killed by Union forces a month after the war ended. Among those who fought in Quantrill's Raiders were **Jesse** and **Frank James** and **Cole Younger**.

Walter Pidgeon (as William Cantrell). *Dark Command* (US/1940/91m/BW) D: Raoul Walsh. B/on the novel by W.R. Burnett. C: John Wayne, Roy Rogers, Claire Trevor, Marjorie Main.

Ray Corrigan. *Renegade Girl* (US/1946/65m/BW) D: William Berke. C: Alan Curtis, Ann Savage, Edward Brophy, Jack Holt, Russell Wade, Chief Thunder Cloud.

James Griffith. *Fighting Man of the Plains* (US/1949/94m/C) D: Edwin L. Marin. C: Randolph Scott, Bill Williams, Victor Jory, Jane Nigh, Douglas Kennedy, Dale Robertson, Rhys Williams.

Brian Donlevy. *Kansas Raiders* (US/1950/80m/C) D: Ray Enright. C: Audie Murphy, Scott Brady, Richard Long, James Best, Dewey Martin, Richard Egan, Tony Curtis.

John Ireland. *Red Mountain* (US/1951/84m/C) D: William Dieterle. C: Alan Ladd, Lizabeth Scott, Arthur Kennedy, Jeff Corey, James Bell, Bert Freed, Neville Brand.

Reed Hadley. *Kansas Pacific* (US/1953/73m/C) D: Ray Nazarro. C: Sterling Hayden, Eve Miller, Barton MacLane, Harry Shannon, Tom Fadden.

Brian Donlevy. *The Woman They Almost Lynched* (US/1953/90m/BW) D: Allan Dwan. B/on the story by Michael Fessier. C: Ben Cooper, James Brown, Jim Davis, Audrey Totter, John Lund.

Leo Gordon. *Quantrill's Raiders* (US/1958/68m/C) D: Edward Bernds. C: Steve Cochran, Diane Brewster, Myron Healey, Guy Prescott, Gale Robbins, Glenn Strange, Lane Chandler.

Emile Meyer. *Young Jesse James* (US/1960/73m/BW) D: William F. Claxton. C: Ray Stricklyn, Willard Parker, Merry Anders, Robert Dix, Bob Palmer, Johnny O'Neill.

Fred Graham. *Arizona Raiders* (US/1965/88m/C) D: William Witney. C: Audie Murphy.

Bill Ferrill. *Ride a Wild Stud* (aka *Ride the Wild Stud*) (US/1969) D: Revilo Ekard. C: Cliff Alexander, Tex Gates, Frenchy LeBoyd, William Fosterwick.

John Ales. *Ride with the Devil* (aka *Civil War, To Live On*) (US/1999/138m/C) D: Ang Lee. B/on the novel *Woe to Live On* by Daniel Woodrell. C: Skeet Ulrich, Tobey Maguire, Jewel Kilcher, Simon Baker-Denny, Jonathan Rhys-Meyers, James Caviezel, Tom Guiry, Tom Wilkinson, Jonathan Brandis, Matthew Faber, Stephen Mailer, Zach Grenier, Margo Martindale.

442 Raft, George (1895–1980)

(George Ranft) Hollywood star of the 1930s, Raft had grown up (in New York's Hell's Kitchen) with the kinds of tough guys he would play in such films as *Scarface* (32), *The Bowery* (33) and *Johnny Angel* (45).

Ray Danton. *The George Raft Story* (aka *Spin of a Coin*) (US/1961/105m/BW) D: Joseph M. Newman. C: Jayne Mansfield, Julie London, Barrie Chase, Frank Gorshin, Barbara Nichols, Brad Dexter, Neville Brand, Robert Strauss, Herschel Bernardi.

Joe Mantegna. *Bugsy* (US/1991/135m/C) D: Barry Levinson. B/on the book *We Only Kill Each Other: The Life and Bad Times of Bugsy Siegel* by Dean Jennings. C: Warren Beatty, Annette Bening, Harvey Keitel, Ben Kingsley, Elliott Gould, Wendy Phillips, Bill Graham, Don Carrara, Carmine Caridi, Ksenia Prohaska.

443 Raglan, Lord (1788–1855)

(Fitzroy James Henry Somerset, 1st Baron of Raglan) British soldier, Raglan is the general credited with the order that caused the slaughter of the English brigade during the Crimean War known as the Charge of the Light Brigade.

J. Fisher White. *Balaclava* (aka *Jaws of Hell*) (GB/1930/94m/BW) D: Maurice Elvey & Milton Rosmer. B/on *The Charge of the Light Brigade* by Alfred Lord Tennyson. Made as a silent in 1928, with sound added in 1930. C: Benita Hume, Cyril McLaglen, Bos Ranevsky, Wallace Bosco, Marian Drada, Eugene Leahy.

Brandon Hurst. *Charge of the Light Brigade* (US/1936/115m/BW) D: Michael Curtiz. C: Errol Flynn, Patric Knowles, Olivia de Havilland, David Niven, Charles Croker King, Nigel Bruce.

Halliwell Hobbes. *The White Angel* (aka *The White Sister*) (US/1936/75m/BW) D: William Dieterle. B/on the *Florence Nightingale* chapter of *Eminent Victorians* by Lytton Strachey. C: Kay Francis, Ian Hunter, Donald Woods, Nigel Bruce, Gaby Fay.

P. Galdeburov. *Admiral Nakhimov* (USSR/1947/95m/BW) D: Vsevolod Pudovkin. C: Alexi Dikki, Vsevolod Pudovkin, Eugene Samoilov, Vladimir Vladislavsky, A. Khokhlov.

John Gielgud. *Charge of the Light Brigade* (GB/1968/145–130m/C) D: Tony Richardson. C: Trevor Howard, Vanessa Redgrave, Harry Andrews, David Hemmings, Peter Bowles.

444 Raleigh, Sir Walter (1554?–1618)

British adventurer and favorite of **Elizabeth I**, Raleigh established the first English colony in America on Roanoke Island. He was later imprisoned for treason by James I and ultimately executed on that charge.

Vincent Price. *The Private Lives of Elizabeth and Essex* (aka *Elizabeth the Queen*) (US/1939/106m/C) D: Michael Curtiz. B/on the play *Elizabeth the Queen* by Maxwell Anderson. C: Bette Davis, Errol Flynn, Olivia de Havilland, Donald Crisp, Alan Hale, Robert Warwick.

Leslie Bradley. *Time Flies* (GB/1944/88m/BW) D: Walter Forde. C: Tommy

Handley, Evelyn Dall, George Moon, John Salew, Olga Lindo, Roy Emerson, Iris Lang.

Richard Todd. *The Virgin Queen* (US/1955/92m/C) D: Henry Koster. C: Bette Davis, Joan Collins, Jay Robinson, Herbert Marshall, Dan O'Herlihy, Robert Douglas.

Edward Everett Horton. *The Story of Mankind* (US/1957/100m/C) D: Irwin Allen. B/on the book by Hendrik Van Loon. C: Ronald Colman, Hedy Lamarr, Virginia Mayo, Agnes Moorehead, Peter Lorre, Dennis Hopper, Marie Wilson, Helmut Dantine, Reginald Gardiner, Marie Windsor, Francis X. Bushman, Anthony Dexter, Austin Green, Jim Ameche, Harpo Marx, Bobby Watson, Reginald Sheffield, Cedric Hardwicke, Cesar Romero.

445 Rasputin, Grigori Yefimovich (1872–1916)

The Russian "Mad Monk" who exerted tremendous influence over **Czarina Alexandra** (due to his ability to relieve the suffering of her hemophiliac son), Rasputin was murdered by a group of patriotic Russian noblemen.

Conrad Veidt. *Rasputin* (Germany/1932/82m/BW) D: Adolf Trotz. C: Paul Otto, Hermine Sterler, Kenny Rieve, Alexandra Sorina, Brigitte Horney, Bernhard Goetzke.

Lionel Barrymore. *Rasputin and the Empress* (aka *Rasputin the Mad Monk*) (US/1932/132m/BW) D: Richard Boleslawsky & Charles Brabin. C: John Barrymore, Ethel Barrymore, Ralph Morgan, Diana Wynyard, Tad Alexander, C. Henry Gordon, Edward Arnold.

Harry Baur. *Rasputin* (France/1939/93m/BW) D: Marcel L'Herbier. B/on the novel *Tragedie Imperiale* by Alfred Neumann. C: Marcelle Chantal, Jean Worms, Denis d'Ines.

Pierre Brasseur. *Raspoutine* (France/1954/105m/C) D: Georges Combret. C: Isa Miranda, Rene Faure, Jacques Berthier, Micheline Francey.

Edmund Purdom. *The Night They Killed Rasputin* (aka *The Nights of Rasputin*) (France-Italy/1960/95m/BW) D: Pierre Chenal. C: Gianna Maria Canale, Jany Clair, Ugo Sasso.

Christopher Lee. *Rasputin—The Mad Monk* (GB/1966/92m/C) D: Don Sharp. C: Barbara Shelley, Richard Pasco, Francis Matthews, Renee Asherson, Suzan Farmer, Joss Ackland.

Gert Frobe. *I Killed Rasputin* (France-Italy/1967/102m/C) D: Robert Hossein. C: Peter McEnery, Robert Hossein, Geraldine Chaplain, Ira Furstenburg, Patrick Balkany.

Wes Carter. *Why Russians Are Revolting* (US/1970/91m/BW) D: Neil Sullivan. C: Neil Sullivan, D.F. Barry, Saul Katz, Ed Maywood, Seneca Ames, George Badera.

Tom Baker. *Nicholas and Alexandra* (GB/1971/183m/C) D: Franklin J. Schaffner. B/on the book by Robert K. Massie. C: Michael Jayston, Janet Suzman, Roderic Noble, Fiona Fullerton, Harry Andrews, Irene Worth, Ralph Truman, Alexander Knox, John McEnery, Michael Bryant, James Hazeldine, Brian Cox, Ian Holm, Roy Dotrice, Martin Potter.

Alexei Petrenko. *Agony* (aka *Rasputin*) (USSR/1975/148–107m/C) D: Elem Klimov. C: Anatoly Romashin, Velta Linei, Alisa Freindtlich.

Rasputin (Tom Baker) comforts Czarina Alexandra (Janet Suzman), who worries about her seriously ill young son in *Nicholas and Alexandra* (1971). Sci-Fi fans will recognize Tom Baker from his role as Doctor Who in the British television series of the same name. (Museum of Modern Art Film Stills Archive)

Reagan, Ronald *see* 589

446 Red Cloud (1822–1909)

A leader of the Oglala Sioux, Red Cloud fought the U.S. Army in what became known as Red Cloud's War (1866–1868). "They made us many promises, but they never kept but one. They promised to take our land and they took it."

Chief White Eagle. *End of the Trail* (US/1932/60m/BW) D: Ross Lederman. C: Tim McCoy, Luana Walters, Wheeler Oakman, Wally Albright, Wade Boteler.

John War Eagle. *Tomahawk* (aka *Battle of Powder River*) (US/1951/82m/C) D: George Sherman. C: Van Heflin, Yvonne De Carlo, Preston Foster, Rock Hudson, Ann Doran.

Jay Silverheels. *Jack McCall, Desperado* (US/1953/76m/C) D: Sidney Salkow. C: George Montgomery, Angela Stevens, Douglas Kennedy, James Seay, Eugene Iglesias.

John War Eagle. *The Great Sioux Uprising* (US/1953/79m/C) D: Lloyd Bacon. C: Jeff Chandler, Faith Domergue, Lyle Bettger, Stacy Harris, Glenn Strange.

Robert Bice. *The Gun That Won the West* (US/1955/69m/C) D: William Castle. C: Dennis Morgan, Paula Raymond, Richard Cutting, Richard Denning, Howard Wright, Roy Gordon.

Morris Ankrum. *Chief Crazy Horse* (aka *Valley of Fury*) (US/1954/86m/C) D: George Sherman. C: Victor Mature, Suzan Ball, John Lund, Ray Danton, Keith Larsen.

Eduard Franz. *The Indian Fighter* (US/1955/88m/C) D: Andre de Toth. C: Kirk Douglas, Elsa Martinelli, Walter Matthau, Diana Douglas, Lon Chaney, Jr., Ray Teal.

Manuel Donde. *The Last Frontier* (aka *Savage Wilderness*) (US/1955/98m/C) D: Anthony Mann. B/on the novel *The Gilded Rooster* by Richard Emery Roberts. C: Victor Mature, Guy Madison, Robert Preston, James Whitmore, Pat Hogan.

Frank De Kova. *Run of the Arrow* (US/1957/86m/C) D: Samuel Fuller. C: Rod Steiger, Sarita Montiel, Brian Keith, Ralph Meeker, Charles Bronson, Frank Baker, Emile Avery.

Eddie Little Sky. *Revolt at Fort Laramie* (US/1957/73m/C) D: Lesley Selander. C: John Dehner, Gregg Palmer, Frances Helm, Don Gordon, Robert Keys, (Harry) Dean Stanton.

Alberto Mariscal. *The Return of a Man Called Horse* (US/1976/125m/C) D: Irvin Kershner. B/on characters created by Dorothy M. Johnson. C: Richard Harris, Gale Sondergaard, Geoffrey Lewis.

447 Reed, John (1887–1920)

A journalist, revolutionary and author (*Ten Days That Shook the World*), Reed is the only American buried at the Kremlin in Moscow.

A. Fyodorinov. *In the October Days* (USSR/1958/116m/C) D: Sergei Vasiliev. C: V. Chestnokov, V. Brener, A. Kobaladze, Galina Vodyanitskaya.

Claudio Obregon. *Reed: Insurgent Mexico* (Mexico/1971/110m) D: Paul Leduc. B/on the book *Insurgent Mexico* by John Reed. C: Eduardo Lopez Rojas, Eraclio Zepeda, Ernesto Gomez.

Warren Beatty. *Reds* (US/1981/200m/C) D: Warren Beatty. Best Picture (NYC). Best Director (AA,DGA). C: Diane Keaton, Edward Herrmann, Jerzy Kosinski, Jack Nicholson, Paul Sorvino, Maureen Stapleton, Roger Sloman, Stuart Richman.

Franco Nero. *Mexico in Flames* (aka *Red Bells*) (USSR-Mexico-Italy/1982/131m/C) D: Sergei Bondarchuk. C: Ursula Andress, Jorge Luke, Blanca Guerra, Heraclio Zepeda, Jorge Reynoso, Robery Ruy, Erika Carlson, Trinidad Escalva, Vitautas Tomkus, Sydney Rome.

Franco Nero. *Red Bells* (aka *Red Bells: I've Seen the Birth of the New World*) (aka *Ten Days That Shook the World*) (USSR-Mexico-Italy/1982/137m/C) D: Sergei Bondarchuk. C: Sydne Rome, Anatoly Ustiuzhaninov, Bogdan Stupka, Aleksandr Sajko, Vareri Barinov, Pytor Vorobyov.

448 Rembrandt Harmenzoon van Rijn (1606–1669)

The greatest master of the Dutch school of painting, Rembrandt was famous for his depiction of light. Among his numerous paintings are "The Night Watch," "Saul and David" and many self portraits.

Charles Laughton. *Rembrandt* (GB/1936/84m/BW) D: Alexander Korda. C: Gertrude Lawrence, Elsa Lanchester, Edward Chapman, Roger Livesey, Raymond Huntley.

Ewald Balser. *Rembrandt* (Germany/1942/BW) D: Hans Steinhoff. C: Hertha Feiler, Elisabeth Flickenschildt, Otto Hasse, Paul Henckels, Eduard von Winterstein.

Frans Stelling. *Rembrandt-Feigt 1669* (Netherlands/1978/114m/C) D: Jos Stelling. C: Tom de Koff, Aya Fil, Lucie Singeling

449 Reynolds, Sir Joshua (1723–1792)

Considered one of the most important English painters, Reynolds is famous for his portraits of leading British figures of the eighteenth century.

Olaf Hytten. *Berkeley Square* (US/1933/87m/BW) D: Frank Lloyd. B/on the play by John L. Balderston. C: Leslie Howard, Heather Angel, Valerie Taylor, Beryl Mercer, Colin Keith-Johnston, Alan Mowbray, Lionel Barrymore, David Torrence.

Henry O'Neill. *The Great Garrick* (US/1937/82m/BW) D: James Whale. B/on the play *Ladies and Gentlemen* by Ernest Vadja. C: Brian Aherne, Olivia de Havilland, Edward Everett Horton, Melville Cooper, Lionel Atwill, Lana Turner, Albert Dekker.

Gordon Richards. *Kitty* (US/1945/103m/BW) D: Mitchell Leisen. B/on the novel by Rosamund Marshall. C: Paulette Goddard, Ray Milland, Patric Knowles, Reginald Owen, Cecil Kellaway, Michael Dyne, Constance Collier, Dennis Hoey.

Ronald Simpson. *I'll Never Forget You* (aka *The House in the Square*) (US/1951/89m/C) D: Roy Baker. B/on the play *Berkeley Square* by John L. Balderston. C: Tyrone Power, Ann Blyth, Michael Rennie, Robert Atkins, Alexander McCrindle.

450 Rhodes, Cecil John (1853–1902)

Rhodes was a driving force in the expansion of British imperialism in South Africa during the latter part of the 19th century.

Walter Huston. *Rhodes* (aka *Rhodes of Africa*) (GB/1936/94m/BW) D: Berthold Viertel. B/on the book by Sarah Millin. C: Oscar Homolka, Peggy Ashcroft.

Wyndham Goldie. *Victoria the Great* (GB/1937/110m/C) D: Herbert Wilcox. B/on the play *Victoria Regina* by Laurence Housman. C: Anna Neagle, Anton Walbrook, H.B. Warner, James Dale, Charles Carson, Hubert Harben, Felix Aylmer, Arthur Young, Derrick De Marney, Hugh Miller, Percy Parsons, Henry Hallatt, Gordon McLeod.

Ferdinand Marian. *Ohm Krüger* (Germany/1941/135m/BW) D: Hans Steinhoff. C: Emil Jannings, Hedwig Wangel, Franz Schafheitlin, Gustav Gründgens.

451 Ribbentrop, Joachim von (1893–1946)

Hitler's Foreign Minister, Von Ribbentrop was hanged for war crimes following the trials at Nuremberg. Benoît Girard portrayed Ribbentrop in the TV movie *Nuremberg* (2000).

Henry Daniel. *Mission to Moscow* (US/1943/123m/BW) D: Michael Curtiz. B/on the book by Joseph E. Davies. C: Walter Huston, Ann Harding, Oscar Homolka, George Tobias, Gene Lockhart, Frieda Inescourt, Eleanor Parker, Richard Travis, Dudley Field Malone, Manart Kippen, Charles Trowbridge, Georges Renavent, Clive Morgan, Captain Jack Young, Leigh Whipper, Doris Lloyd, Olaf Hytten, Moroni Olsen.

Stanislav Zindulka. *Days of Treason* (aka *Days of Betrayal*) (aka *Dny Zrady*) (Czechoslovakia/1973/198m/C) D: Otakar Vavra. C: Jiri Pleskot, Bohus Pastorek, Martin Gregor, Gunnar Mollar, Jaroslav Radimecky, Alexander Fred, Rudolf Jurda, Vladimir Stach, Vladimir Paviar, Bonvoj Navartil, Otakar Brousek, Josef Langmiller.

452 Richard I (1157–1199)

The son of **Henry II** and **Eleanor of Aquitaine**, Richard the Lionheart spent most of his ten year reign as King of England on Crusades in the Middle East, imprisoned in Austria, or at war in France where he was killed in battle. He was succeeded by his brother **John**. In TV films he's been played by Julian Glover in *Ivanhoe* (82) and by Robert Hardy in *The Zany Adventures of Robin Hood* (84).

Henry Wilcoxon. *The Crusades* (US/1935/123m/BW) D: Cecil B. DeMille. Waldemar Young & Dudley Nichols. B/on the book *The Crusades: Iron Men and Saints* by Harold Lamb. C: Loretta Young, Ian Keith, Katherine De Mille, C. Aubrey Smith, Joseph Schildkraut, Alan Hale, C. Henry Gordon, Ramsay Hill.

Ian Hunter. *The Adventures of Robin Hood* (US/1938/102m/C) D: Michael Curtiz. C: Errol Flynn, Olivia de Havilland, Claude Rains, Basil Rathbone, Patric Knowles, Montagu Love.

Norman Wooland. *Ivanhoe* (GB/1952/106m/C) D: Richard Thorpe. B/on the novel by Sir Walter Scott C: Robert Taylor, Elizabeth Taylor, Joan Fontaine, George Sanders, Emlyn Williams, Robert Douglas, Guy Rolfe, Felix Aylmer, Finlay Currie, Francis de Wolff, Basil Sydney, Sebastian Cabot.

Patrick Barr. *The Story of Robin Hood* (aka *The Story of Robin Hood and His Merrie Men*) (GB/1952/84m/C) D: Ken Annakin. C: Richard Todd, Joan Rice, Peter Finch, James Hayter, James Robertson Justice, Martita Hunt, Hubert Gregg, Antony Eustrel.

George Sanders. *King Richard and the Crusaders* (US/1954/113m/C) D: David Butler. B/on the novel *The Talisman* by Sir Walter Scott. C: Rex Harrison, Virginia Mayo, Laurence Harvey, Robert Douglas, Michael Pate, Paula Raymond, Henry Corden.

Patrick Holt. *Men of Sherwood Forest* (GB/1954/77m/C) D: Val Guest. C: Don Taylor, Reginald Beckwith, Eileen Moore, David King-Wood, Douglas Wilmer, Leonard Sachs.

Salah Zulficar. *Saladin* (Egypt/1963/180m/C) D: Youssef Chanine. C: Ahmed Mazhar, Nadia Loufti.

Anthony Hopkins. *The Lion in Winter* (GB/1968/134m/C) D: Anthony Harvey. B/on the play by James Goldman. Best Picture (GG (Drama), NYC). Best

Director (DGA). C: Peter O'Toole, Katharine Hepburn, Jane Merrow, John Castle, Timothy Dalton, Nigel Terry, Nigel Stock, Kenneth Griffith.

Frankie Howerd. *Up the Chastity Belt* (GB/1971/94m/C) D: Bob Kellett. C: Graham Crowden, Bill Fraser, Roy Hudd, Hugh Paddick, Anna Quayle, Eartha Kitt.

Richard Harris. *Robin and Marian* (GB/1976/106m/C) D: Richard Lester. C: Sean Connery, Audrey Hepburn, Ian Holm, Robert Shaw, Nicol Williamson, Denholm Elliott.

Neil Dickson. *Lionheart* (US/1987/105m/C) D: Franklin J. Schaffner. C: Eric Stoltz, Gabriel Byrne, Nicola Cowper, Dexter Fletcher, Deborah Barrymore, Nicholas Clay.

Sean Connery. *Robin Hood: Prince of Thieves* (US/1991/143m/C) D: Kevin Reynolds. C: Kevin Costner, Morgan Freeman, Mary Elizabeth Mastrantonio, Christian Slater, Alan Rickman.

Patrick Stewart. *Robin Hood: Men in Tights* (US/1993/102m/C) D: Mel Brooks. C: Cary Elwes, Richard Lewis, Roger Rees, Amy Yasbeck, Mark Blankfield, Tracey Ullman.

453 Richard III (1452–1485)

After usurping the throne of England from his young nephew, **Edward V** (whom he had murdered), Richard's reign lasted little more than two years before he was killed in battle with the forces of the future King **Henry VII**.

Basil Rathbone. *Tower of London* (US/1939/92m/BW) D: Rowland Lee. C: Boris Karloff, Barbara O'Neill, Ian Hunter, Nan Grey, Miles Mander, Ronald Sinclair, Ralph Forbes.

Laurence Olivier. *Richard III* (GB/1955/158m/C) D: Laurence Olivier. B/on the play by Wm. Shakespeare. Best Film (Any Source/British) (BFA), Best English-Language Foreign Film (GG). C: Ralph Richardson, Claire Bloom, John Gielgud, Cedric Hardwicke, Mary Kerridge, Pamela Brown, Paul Huson, Stanley Baker.

Vincent Price. *Tower of London* (US/1962/79m/BW) D: Roger Corman. C: Michael Pate, Joan Freeman, Robert Brown, Justice Watson, Sarah Selby, Eugene Martin, Donald Losby.

Ian McKellen. *Richard III* (GB-US/1995/104m/C) D: Richard Loncraine. B/on the play by Wm. Shakespeare. C: Annette Bening, Maggie Smith, Nigel Hawthorne, John Wood, Robert Downey, Jr., Edward Jewesbury, Marco Williamson.

454 Richelieu, Cardinal (1585–1642)

(Armand Jean du Plessis, Duc de Richelieu) Appointed chief minister to **Louis XIII** in 1624, Richelieu was effectively France's ruler from then until his own death in 1642. Note: In *Madame du Barry* (34) characters named Richelieu were played by Osgood Perkins and Dennis d'Ines, respectively. Some sources list these characters as the Cardinal which seems questionable since the good Madame was born a century after the Cardinal died.

Anne of Austria (Belle Bennett, left) receives a stern admonition from Cardinal Richelieu (Nigel De Brulier, center) in this scene from *The Iron Mask* (1929). One of the earliest films listed in this book, a silent film with "talkie" sequences, this was Douglas Fairbanks' last swashbuckler. Most prints in release today are the 1944 version with narration by Douglas Fairbanks, Jr. (Museum of Modern Art Film Stills Archive)

Nigel De Brulier. *The Iron Mask* (US/1929/95m/BW) D: Allan Dwan. B/on *The Three Musketeers* and *The Viscount of Bragelonne* by Alexandre Dumas. C: Douglas Fairbanks, Belle Bennett, Dorothy Revier, William Bakewell, Rolfe Sedan.

Samson Fainsilber. *The Three Musketeers* (France/1932/128m/BW) D: Henri Diamant-Berger. B/on the novel by Alexandre Dumas. C: Aime Simon-Girard, Edith Mera, Harry Baur, Andree Lafayette, Maurice Escande, Fernand Francell.

George Arliss. *Cardinal Richelieu* (US/1935/83m/BW) D: Rowland V. Lee. B/on the play *Richelieu* by Edward Bulwer-Lytton. C: Edward Arnold, Katherine Alexander.

Nigel De Brulier. *The Three Musketeers* (US/1935/97m/BW) D: Rowland V. Lee. B/on the novel by Alexandre Dumas. C: Walter Abel, Paul Lukas, Margot Grahame, Heather Angel, Ian Keith, Onslow Stevens, Rosamond Pinchot, Ralph Forbes, Miles Mander.

Raymond Massey. *Under the Red Robe* (GB/1937/80m/BW) D: Victor Seastrom. B/on the play by Edward Rose and the novel by Stanley J. Weyman. C: Conrad Veidt, Annabella, Romney Brent, Shayle Gardner, Sophie Stewart, Edie Martin, Ralph Truman.

Nigel De Brulier. *The Man in the Iron Mask* (US/1939/110m/BW) D: James Whale. B/on the novel by Alexandre Dumas. C: Louis Hayward, Joan Bennett, Warren William, Joseph Schildkraut, Alan Hale, Miles Mander, Walter Kingsford, Albert Dekker, Doris Kenyon.

Miles Mander. *The Three Musketeers* (aka *The Singing Musketeer*) (US/1939/73m/BW) D: Allan Dwan. B/on the novel by Alexandre Dumas. C: Don Ameche, The Ritz Brothers, Binnie Barnes, Lionel Atwill, Gloria Stuart, Pauline Moore, Joseph Schildkraut, John Carradine, Douglas Dumbrille, John King, Lester Matthews.

Angel Garasa. *The Three Musketeers* (aka *Tres Mosqueteros*) (Mexico/1942/139m/BW) D: Miguel M. Delgado. B/on the novel by Alexandre Dumas. C: Cantinflas, Raquel Rojas, Consuelo Frank, Andres Soler, Julio Villarreal, Jorge Reyes.

Aime Clariond. *Monsieur Vincent* (France/1947/73m/BW) D: Maurice Cloche. Special Academy Award as the most outstanding foreign film of 1948. C: Pierre Fresnay, Lisa Delamare, Jean Debucourt, Germaine Dermoz, Gabrielle Dorziat, Yvonne Godeau.

Vincent Price. *The Three Musketeers* (US/1948/126m/C) D: George Sidney. B/on the novel by Alexandre Dumas. C: Lana Turner, Gene Kelly, June Allyson, Van Heflin, Angela Lansbury, Frank Morgan, Kennan Wynn, John Sutton, Gig Young, Robert Coote.

Paul Cavanagh. *Blades of the Musketeers* (aka *The Sword of D'Artagnan*) (US/1953/54m/BW) D: Budd Boetticher. B/on the novel *The Three Musketeers* by Alexandre Dumas. C: Robert Clarke, John Hubbard, Mel Archer, Don Beddoe, Marjorie Lord, Charles Lang.

Renaud-Mary. *The Three Musketeers* (France/1953/120m/C) D: Andre Hunnebelle. B/on the novel by Alexandre Dumas. C: Georges Marchal, Gino Cervi, Yvonne Sanson, Bourvil.

Daniel Sorano. *The Three Musketeers* (France/1961/100m/C) D: Bernard Borderie. B/on the novel by Alexandre Dumas. C: Gerard Barry, Georges Descrieres, Bernard Woringer, Jacques Toja, Francoise Christophe, Mylene Demongeot, Henri Nassiet.

Rafael Rivelles. *Cyrano and D'Artagnan* (France/1962/145m/C) D: Abel Gance. C: Jose Ferrer, Jean-Pierre Cassel, Sylva Koscina, Daliah Lavi, Philippe Noiret, Michel Simon.

Massimo Serato. *The Secret Mark of D'Artagnan* (France-Italy/1962/95m/C) D: Siro Marcellini. C: George Nader, Magali Noel, Georges Marchal, Mario Petri.

Christopher Logue. *The Devils* (GB/1971/111m/C) D: Ken Russell. B/on the play by John Whiting and the book *The Devils of Louden* by Aldous Huxley. C: Oliver Reed, Vanessa Redgrave, Dudley Sutton, Graham Armitage, Kenneth Colley.

Charlton Heston. *The Three Musketeers* (GB-US-Panama/1974/105m/C) D:

Richard Lester. B/on the novel by Alexandre Dumas. C: Oliver Reed, Richard Chamberlain, Michael York, Frank Finlay, Jean-Pierre Cassel, Geraldine Chaplin, Simon Ward.

Charlton Heston. *The Four Musketeers* (aka *The Revenge of Milady*) (GB-US/1975/108m/C) D: Richard Lester. B/on the novel *The Three Musketeers* by Alexandre Dumas. C: Michael York, Oliver Reed, Richard Chamberlain, Christopher Lee, Frank Finlay, Geraldine Chaplin, Raquel Welch, Jean-Pierre Cassel, Simon Ward.

Tim Curry. *The Three Musketeers* (US/1993/105m/C) D: Stephen Herek. B/on the novel by Alexandre Dumas. C: Charlie Sheen, Kiefer Sutherland, Chris O'Donnell, Oliver Platt, Rebecca DeMornay, Gabrielle Anwar, Michael Wincott, Hugh O'Connor.

Stephen Rea. *The Musketeer* (Germany-Luxemburg-US/2001/105m/C) D: Peter Hyams. B/on the novel by Alexandre Dumas. C: Catherine Deneuve, Mena Suvari, Tim Roth, Justin Chambers, Bill Treacher, Daniel Mesguich, David Schofield, Nick Moran, Steven Spiers, Jan Gregor Kremp, Jeremy Clyde, Michael Byrne, Jean-Pierre Castaldi, Tsilla Chelton, Bertrand Witt.

455 Richthofen, Manfred, Baron von (1892–1918)

Germany's leading ace in World War I, the "Bloody Red Baron" was credited with shooting down 80 Allied planes before being shot down himself. Trivia Note: The Baron's sister, Frieda, was married to D.H. Lawrence.

William von Brincken. *Hell's Angels* (US/1930/135m/C) D: Howard Hughes. C: Ben Lyon, James Hall, Jean Harlow, John Darrow, Lucien Prival, Wyndham Standing.

Carl Schell. *The Blue Max* (US/1966/155m/C) D: John Guillermin. B/on the novel by Jack D. Hunter. C: George Peppard, James Mason, Ursula Andress, Jeremy Kemp.

Ingo Mogendorf. *Darling Lili* (US/1970/136m/C) D: Blake Edwards. C: Julie Andrews, Rock Hudson, Jeremy Kemp, Lance Percival, Jacques Marin, Nial MacGinnis.

John Phillip Law. *Von Richthofen and Brown* (aka *The Red Baron*) (US/1970/97m/C) D: Roger Corman. C: Don Stroud, Barry Primus, Peter Masterson, Hurd Hatfield, Karen Huston.

456 Rickenbacker, Edward Vernon "Eddie" (1890–1973)

The U.S.'s leading air ace in WWI with 26 kills (22 planes & 4 balloons), Rickenbacker later became the first president of Eastern Airlines.

Fred MacMurray. *Captain Eddie* (US/1945/107m/BW) D: Lloyd Bacon. C: Lynn Bari, Charles Bickford, Thomas Mitchell, Lloyd Nolan, James Gleason, Darryl Hickman.

Tom McKee. *The Court-Martial of Billy Mitchell* (aka *One Man Mutiny*) (US/1955/100m/C) D: Otto Preminger. C: Gary Cooper, Charles Bickford, Ralph Bellamy, Rod Steiger, Elizabeth Montgomery, James Daly, Dayton Lumis, Herbert Heyes, Phil Arnold, Ian Wolfe.

457 Rimsky-Korsakov (1844–1908)

(Nikolai Andreyevitch Rimsky-Korsakov) Russian composer, Rimsky-Korsakov is remembered for his symphonic suite "Scheherazade" and his opera "The Snow Maiden" among other works.

Jean-Pierre Aumont. *Song of Scheherazade* (US/1947/105m/C) D: Walter Reisch. C: Yvonne De Carlo, Brian Donlevy, Eve Arden, Philip Reed, John Qualen, George Dolenz.

David Leonard. *Song of My Heart* (US/1947/85m/BW) D: Benjamin Glazer. C: Frank Sundstrom, Audrey Lang, Cedric Hardwicke, John Hamilton, Lewis Howard, Robert Barron.

Andrei Popov. *Mussorgsky* (aka *Musorgskij*) (USSR/1950/116m/C) D: Grigori Roshal. C: Alexander Borisov, Nikolai Cherkassov, Lubov Orlova.

Grigori Belov. *Rimsky-Korsakov* (USSR/1952/88m/C) D: Grigori Roshal. C: Nikolai Cherkasov, L. Griasenko, A. Ognivtsev, L. Sukharevskaya.

458 Ringo, Johnny (1844–1882)

(John Ringgold) Little was known about this Western outlaw except that he was educated (he spoke Latin and Greek) and that he was a killer with a fast gun. Found shot to death, an apparent suicide, **Wyatt Earp** later claimed responsibility for Ringo's death.

Richard Boone. *City of Bad Men* (US/1953/81m/C) D: Harmon Jones. C: Jeanne Crain, Dale Robertson, Lloyd Bridges, Carole Mathews, Carl Betz, John Day, Gil Perkins.

John Ireland. *Gunfight at the O.K. Corral* (US/1957/122m/C) D: John Sturges. B/on the story *The Killer* by George Scullin. C: Burt Lancaster, Kirk Douglas, Rhonda Fleming, Jo Van Fleet, Lyle Bettger, Frank Faylen, Earl Holliman, Whit Bissell, DeForrest Kelley, Martin Milner, Kenneth Tobey, Lee Van Cleef, Jack Elam, Bing Russell.

Lee Morgan. *The Last of the Fast Guns* (US/1958/82m/C) D: George Sherman. C: Jock Mahoney, Gilbert Roland, Linda Cristal, Eduard Franz, Milton Bernstein.

Jim Davis. *Toughest Gun in Tombstone* (US/1958/72m/BW) D: Earl Bellamy. C: George Montgomery, Beverly Tyler, Don Beddoe, Gerald Milton, Hank Worden, Lane Bradford.

Hal Fryar. *The Outlaws Is Coming* (US/1965/88m/BW) D: Norman Maurer. C: Larry Fine, Moe Howard, Joe De Rita, Nancy Kovack, Murray Alper, Joe Bolton, Bill Camfield, Johnny Ginger, Wayne Mack, Ed McDonnell, Bruce Sedley, Paul Shannon, Sally Starr.

Fred Dennis. *Doc* (US/1971/95m/C) D: Frank Perry. C: Stacy Keach, Faye Dunaway, Harris Yulin, Mike Witney, Dan Greenburg, Bruce M. Fischer, Ferdinand Zogbaum.

Michael Biehn. *Tombstone* (US/1993/128m/C) D: George Pan Kosmatos. C: Kurt Russell, Val Kilmer, Powers Booth, Robert Blake, Dana Delaney, Sam Elliott, Stephen Lang, Terry O'Quinn, Joanna Pacula, Bill Paxton, Jason Priestley, Michael Rooker.

Norman Howell. *Wyatt Earp* (US/1994/195m/C) D: Lawrence Kasdan. C: Kevin Costner, Dennis Quaid, Gene Hackman, David Andrews, Linden Ashby, Jeff Fahey, Mark Harmon, Michael Madsen, Catherine O'Hara, Bill Pullman, Isabella Rossellini, Tom Sizemore, JoBeth Williams, Mare Winningham, Rex Linn, Randle Mell.

459 Rivera, Diego (1886–1957)

One of Mexico's greatest painters and creator of outdoor murals depicting Mexican history and social problems. Due to his active membership in the Communist party, much of his artwork was considered controversial. He was the husband of painter **Frida Kahlo**, who shared his social views.

Juan José Gurrola. *Frida* (Mexico/1984/108m/C) D: Paul Leduc. C: Ofelia Medina, Max Kerlow, Salvador Sanchez, Valentina Leduc, Claudio Brook.

Rubén Blades. *Cradle Will Rock* (US/1999/109m/C) D: Tim Robbins. C: Hank Azaria, Joan Cusack, John Cusack, Cary Elwes, Philip Baker Hall, Cherry Jones, Angus MacFadyen, Bill Murray, Vanessa Redgrave, Susan Sarandon, John Turturro, Barnard Hughes, John Carpenter, Gretchen Mol, Corina Katt.

460 Rob Roy (1671–1734)

(Robert Roy MacGregor) A Highland outlaw known as the "Scottish Robin Hood," Rob's exploits were greatly embellished by Sir Walter Scott in his novel *Rob Roy* which was the basis for the 1954 Disney film.

Richard Todd. *Rob Roy, The Highland Rogue* (aka *Rob Roy*) (GB/1954/81m/C) D: Harold French. C: Glynis Johns, James Robertson Justice, Michael Gough, Eric Pohlmann.

Liam Neeson. *Rob Roy* (US/1995/134m/C) D: Michael Caton-Jones. C: Jessica Lange, Tim Roth, John Hurt, Eric Stoltz, Brian Cox, Andrew Keir.

461 Robespierre (1758–1794)

(Maximilien François Marie Isidore de Robespierre) French Revolutionary leader and the man most responsible for the Reign of Terror, Robespierre was overthrown and met the same fate that he had condemned so many others to: the guillotine. *L'Anglaise et le duc* is based in Grace Elliott's memoirs; she is portrayed by Lucy Russell in the 2001 film.

George Hackathorne. *Captain of the Guard* (US/1930/85m/BW) D: John S. Robertson. C: John Boles, Laura La Plante, Sam De Grasse, Richard Cramer, Evelyn Hall, Stuart Holmes.

Gustaf Gründgens. *Danton* (Germany/1931/94m/BW) D: Hans Behrendt. B/on the book by Hans Rehfisch. C: Fritz Kortner, Lucie Mannheim, Alexander Granach, Ernst Stahl-Nachbaur, Walter Werner, Gustav von Wangenheim.

Edmond van Daele. *Napoleon Bonaparte* (France/1934/140m/BW) D: Abel Gance. Three-dimensional sound version of Gance's 1927 epic *Napoléon*. C: Albert Dieudonné, Alexandre Koubitsky, Antonin Artaud, Boudreau, Alberty, Jack Rye, Favière, Gina Manès, Suzanne Blanchetti, Marguerite Gance, Simone Genevois, Genica Missirio.

Ernest Milton. *The Scarlet Pimpernel* (GB/1935/85m/BW) D: Harold Young. B/on the novel by the Baroness Orczy. C: Leslie Howard, Merle Oberon, Raymond Massey, Nigel Bruce, Bramwell Fletcher, Anthony Bushell, Walter Rilla, Bruce Belfrage.

Henry Oscar. *The Return of the Scarlet Pimpernel* (GB/1937/94–80m/BW) D: Hans Schwartz. C: Barry K. Barnes, Sophie Stewart, Margareta Scott, James Mason, Evelyn Roberts, Esme Percy.

George Meeker. *Marie Antoinette* (US/1938/160m/BW) D: W.S. Van Dyke II. B/on the book by Stefan Zweig. C: Norma Shearer, Tyrone Power, John Barrymore, Gladys George, Robert Morley, Anita Louise, Joseph Schildkraut, Albert Dekker, Scotty Becket, Alma Kruger, Wade Crosby, Anthony Warde, Walter Walker, John Burton.

Charles Goldner. *The Laughing Lady* (GB/1946/100m/C) D: Paul L. Stein. B/on the play by Ingram d'Abbes. C: Anne Ziegler, Webster Booth, Peter Graves, Anthony Nicholls.

Richard Basehart. *The Black Book* (aka *Reign of Terror*) (US/1949/89m/BW) D: Anthony Mann. C: Robert Cummings, Arlene Dahl, Richard Hart, Arnold Moss, Wade Crosby, Jess Barker, Wilton Graff, Norman Lloyd, John Doucette.

Jacques Berthier. *Royal Affairs in Versailles* (aka *Versailles*) (aka *Affairs in Versailles*) (aka *If Versailles Were Told to Me*) (aka *Si Versailles M'Était Couté*) (France/1953/180–152m/C) D: Sacha Guitry. C: Sacha Guitry, Claudette Colbert, Orson Welles, Gerard Phillippe, Micheline Presle, Jean Marais, Georges Marchal, Gilbert Boka, Lana Marconi, Gino Cervi, Fernand Gravet, Louis Arbessier, Samson Fainsilber, Gilbert Gil, Emile Drain, Jacques de Feraudy, Gaston Rey, Philippe Richard.

Peter Gilmore. *Don't Lose Your Head* (GB/1967/90m/C) D: Gerald Thomas. C: Sidney James, Kenneth Williams, Jim Dale, Charles Hawtrey, Joan Sims, Dany Robin.

Bernard Dhéran. *Valmy* (France/1967/C) D: Abel Gance. C: Jacques Castelot, Marc Eyraud, William Sabatier, Serge Gainsbourg.

Wojciech Pszoniak. *Danton* (France-Poland/1982/136m/C) D: Andrzej Wajda. B/on the play *The Danton Affair* by Stanislawa Przybyszewska. C: Gerard Depardieu, Patrice Chereau, Angela Winkler, Boguslaw Linda, Roland Blanche.

Roland Giraud. *Liberty, Equality and Sauerkraut* (aka *Liberte, Egalite, Choucroute*) (France/1985/C) D: Jean Yanne. C: Ursula Andress, Oliver de Kersauzon.

François-Marie Bernier. *L'Anglaise et le duc* (aka *The Lady and the Duke*) (France/2001/125m/C) D: Eric Rohmer. B/on Grace Elliott's memoir *Journal of My Life During the French Revolution*. C: Lucy Russell, Jean-Claude Dreyfus, François Marthouret, Léonard Cobiant, Caroline Morin, Alain Libolt, Héléna Dubiel, Laurent Le Doyen, Serge Wolfsperger, Daniel Tarrare, Charlotte Véry, Marie Rivière, Michel Demierre, Serge Renko.

462 Rockne, Knute Kenneth (1888–1931)

American football coach (born in Norway), Rockne was the head coach at the University of Notre Dame from 1918–1931.

Pat O'Brien. *Knute Rockne—All American* (aka *A Modern Hero*) (US/1940/

98m/BW) D: Lloyd Bacon. C: Gale Page, Ronald Reagan, Donald Crisp, John Qualen, George Reeves.

James Sears. *The Long Gray Line* (US/1955/138m/C) D: John Ford. B/on the novel *Bringing Up the Brass* by Marty Maher & Nardi Reeder. C: Tyrone Power, Maureen O'Hara, Robert Francis, Donald Crisp, Milburn Stone, Elbert Steele, Harry Carey, Jr.

463 Roehm (or Röhm), Ernst (1887–1934)

An early leader of the Nazi party, Roehm was murdered on orders from **Adolf Hitler** for suspected disloyalty.

Roman Bohnen. *The Hitler Gang* (US/1944/101m/BW) D: John Farrow. C: Bobby Watson, Martin Kosleck, Victor Varconi, Luis Van Rooten, Alexander Pope, Ivan Triesault, Sig Rumann, Reinhold Schunzel, Alexander Granach, Fritz Kortner.

Berry Kroeger. *Hitler* (aka *Women of Nazi Germany*) (US/1962/107m/BW) D: Stuart Heisler. C: Richard Basehart, Cordula Trantow, Maria Emo, Martin Kosleck, John Banner, Martin Brandt, William Sargent, Gregory Gay, Thodore Marcuse, Rick Traeger, John Mitchum, G. Stanley Jones, Walter Kohler, Carl Esmond.

Michael Elphick. *Hitler's SS: Portrait in Evil* (US/1985/150m/C) D: Jim Goddard. Made for U.S. TV, released theatrically elsewhere. C: John Shea, Bill Nighy, Lucy Gutteridge, David Warner, John Normington, Colin Jeavons, Jose Ferrer, Carroll Baker.

464 Rogers, Major Robert (1731–1795)

American colonial soldier, Rogers led several successful expeditions during the French and Indian War.

Spencer Tracy. *Northwest Passage* (US/1940/125m/C) D: King Vidor. B/on the novel by Kenneth Roberts. C: Robert Young, Walter Brennan, Ruth Hussey, Lumsden Hare.

Howard Petrie. *Fort Ti* (US/1953/73m/C) D: William Castle. C: George Montgomery, Joan Vohs, Irving Bacon, James Seay, Lester Matthews.

Keith Larsen. *Fury River* (US/1959/74m/BW) D: Jacques Tourneur. Feature film edited from the TV series *Northwest Passage*. C: Buddy Ebsen, Don Burnett, Pat Hogan.

465 Rogers, Will (1879–1935)

(William Penn Adair Rogers) American humorist and entertainer, Rogers was a star of **Ziegfeld's** Follies with his act of rope tricks and humorous comments and he became even more popular with his entry into the fields of journalism, radio and films.

Andrew A. Trimble. *The Great Ziegfeld* (US/1936/170m/BW) D: Robert Z. Leonard. Best Picture (AA). C: William Powell, Luise Rainer, Myrna Loy, Frank Morgan, Reginald Owen, Fannie Brice, Ray Bolger, Buddy Doyle, Rosina Lawrence, Ruth Gillette.

Andrew A. Trimble. *You're a Sweetheart* (US/1937/96m/BW) D: David Butler. C: Alice Faye, George Murphy, Ken Murray, William Gargan.

Will Rogers, Jr. *Look for the Silver Lining* (US/1949/106m/C) D: David Butler. B/on *The Life of Marilyn Miller* by Bert Kalmar & Harry Ruby. C: June Haver, Ray Bolger, Gordon MacRae, Charlie Ruggles.

Will Rogers, Jr. *The Story of Will Rogers* (US/1952/109m/C) D: Michael Curtiz. B/on the story *Uncle Clem's Boy* by Betty Blake Rogers. C: Jane Wyman, Carl Benton Reid, Eve Miller, James Gleason, Slim Pickens, Noah Beery, Jr., Steve Brodie, William Forrest, Earl Lee.

Will Rogers, Jr. *The Eddie Cantor Story* (US/1953/115m/C) D: Alfred E. Green. C: Keefe Brasselle, Marilyn Erskine, Aline MacMahon, Arthur Franz, William Forrest, Jackie Barnett.

Keith Carradine. *Mrs. Parker and the Vicious Circle* (US/1994/125m/C) D: Alan Rudolph. C: Jennifer Jason Leigh, Campbell Scott, Matthew Broderick, Peter Gallagher, Tom McGowan, Lili Taylor, Nick Cassavetes, David Thornton, Malcolm Gets, Gwyneth Paltrow.

466 Rommel, Erwin (1891–1944)

German field marshal of WW II known as "The Desert Fox" and famous for his victories in the African campaign, Rommel was later implicated in a plot to kill **Adolf Hitler** and he committed suicide rather than stand trial.

Erich von Stroheim. *Five Graves to Cairo* (US/1943/96m/BW) D: Billy Wilder. B/on the play *Hotel Imperial* by Lajos Biro. C: Franchot Tone, Anne Baxter, Akim Tamiroff.

James Mason. *The Desert Fox* (aka *Rommel — Desert Fox*) (US/1951/88m/BW) D: Henry Hathaway. B/on the book *Rommel* by Desmond Young. C: Cedric Hardwicke, Jessica Tandy, Luther Adler, Leo G. Carroll, Eduard Franz, John Hoyt, Jack Baston.

James Mason. *The Desert Rats* (US/1953/88m/BW) D: Robert Wise. C: Richard Burton, Robert Newton, Robert Douglas, Torin Thatcher, Chips Rafferty, Michael Pate.

Albert Lieven. *Foxhole in Cairo* (GB/1960/80m/BW) D: John Moxey. B/on the novel *The Cat and the Mice* by Leonard Mosley. C: Adrian Hoven, James Robertson Justice, Niall MacGinnes, Peter Van Eyck, Michael Caine, Lee Montague.

Gregory Gay. *Hitler* (aka *Women of Nazi Germany*) (US/1962/107m/BW) D: Stuart Heisler. C: Richard Basehart, Cordula Trantow, Maria Emo, Martin Kosleck, John Banner, Martin Brandt, William Sargent, Thodore Marcuse, Rick Traeger, John Mitchum, G. Stanley Jones, Walter Kohler, Carl Esmond, Berry Kroeger.

Werner Hinz. *The Longest Day* (US/1962/180m/BW) D: Andrew Marton, Ken Annakin & Bernherd Wicki. B/on the novel by Cornelius Ryan. Best English Language Picture (NBR). C: John Wayne, Robert Mitchum, Henry Fonda, Robert Ryan, Rod Steiger, Robert Wagner, Sal Mineo, Roddy McDowall, Curt Jurgens, Paul Hartman, Nicholas Stuart, Henry Grace, Wolfgang Lukschy, Trevor Reid, Alexander Knox.

Christopher Plummer. *The Night of the Generals* (GB-France/1967/148m/C) D: Anatole Litvak. B/on the novel by Hans Helmut Kirst and the story *The Wary Transgressor* by James Hadley Chase. C: Peter O'Toole, Omar Sharif, Tom Courtenay, Donald Pleasence, Joanna Pettet, Phillippe Noiret, Gerard Bahr, John Gregson, Coral Browne.

Robert Hossein. *Desert Tanks* (aka *The Battle of El Alamein*) (aka *El Alamein*) (Italy-France/1968/109m/C) D: Calvin Padget (Giorgio Ferro). C: Frederick Stafford, George Hilton, Michael Rennie, Ettore Manni.

Karl Michael Vogler. *Patton* (aka *Patton — Lust for Glory*) (US/1970/170m/C) D: Franklin J. Schaffner. B/on *Patton: Ordeal and Triumph* by Ladislas Farago and *A Soldier's Story* by Omar Bradley. Best Picture, Best Direction (AA). Best English-Language Picture (NBR). Best Director (DGA). C: George C. Scott, Karl Malden, Michael Bates, Edward Binns, Lawrence Dobkin, John Doucette, Stephen Young, Michael Strong, Frank Latimore, James Edwards, Richard Meunch.

Wolfgang Preiss. *Raid on Rommel* (US/1971/99m/C) D: Henry Hathaway. C: Richard Burton, John Colicos, Clinton Greyn, Danielle De Metz, Greg Mullavey.

467 Roosevelt, Anna Eleanor (1884–1962)

The wife of **Franklin Roosevelt**, Mrs. Roosevelt worked tirelessly, during and after her stay in the White House, for the improvement of social conditions in the U.S. and throughout the world. She has been depicted far more frequently on TV including: Jane Alexander's excellent portrayals in *Eleanor and Franklin* (76) and *Eleanor and Franklin: The White House Years* (77), Eileen Heckart in *Backstairs at the White House* (77) and *F.D.R.—The Last Year* (80), Jean Stapleton in *Eleanor, First Lady of the World* (82), Elizabeth Hoffman in *The Winds of War* (83) and Marian Seldes in *Truman* (95).

Greer Garson. *Sunrise at Campobello* (US/1960/144m/C) D: Vincent J. Donehue. B/on the play by Dore Schary. C: Ralph Bellamy, Hume Cronyn, Jean Hagen, Alan Bunce.

Lois DeBanzie. *Annie* (US/1982/130m/C) D: John Huston. B/on the musical play by Thomas Meehan, Charles Strouse & Martin Charnin and the comic strip Little Orphan Annie created by Harold Gray. C: Albert Finney, Carol Burnett, Aileen Quinn, Bernadette Peters, Tim Curry, Edward Hermann, Geoffrey Holder.

468 Roosevelt, Franklin Delano (1882–1945)

The 32nd President of the U.S., Roosevelt was the only man ever elected to that office four times (1932, 1936, 1940 and 1944). Numerous television portrayals include: Edward Hermann in *Eleanor and Franklin* (76) and in *Eleanor and Franklin: The White House Years* (77), Stephen Roberts in *Ring of Passion* (78), *Ike* (79), and *Enola Gay* (83), Ralph Bellamy in *Winds of War* (83) and *War and Remembrance* (87), Jason Robards in *F.D.R—The Last Year* (80), Robert Vaughn in *Murrow* (86), and David Ogden Stiers in *J. Edgar Hoover* (87).

Captain Jack Young. *Yankee Doodle Dandy* (US/1942/126m/BW) D: Michael

Curtiz. C: James Cagney, Joan Leslie, Walter Huston, George Tobias, Eddie Foy, Jr., Wallis Clark.

Captain Jack Young. *This Is the Army* (US/1943/120m/C) D: Michael Curtiz. B/on the play by Irving Berlin. C: George Murphy, Ronald Reagan, Joe Louis, Joan Leslie.

Captain Jack Young. *Mission to Moscow* (US/1943/123m/BW) D: Michael Curtiz. B/on the book by Joseph E. Davies. C: Walter Huston, Ann Harding, Oscar Homolka, George Tobias, Gene Lockhart, Frieda Inescourt, Eleanor Parker, Richard Travis, Henry Daniell, Dudley Field Malone, Manart Kippen, Charles Trowbridge, Georges Renavent, Clive Morgan, Leigh Whipper, Doris Lloyd, Olaf Hytten, Moroni Olsen.

Godfrey Tearle. *The Beginning Or the End* (US/1947/110m/BW) D: Norman Taurog. C: Brian Donlevy, Beverly Tyler, Hume Cronyn, Barry Nelson, Art Baker, Ludwig Stossel.

Oleg Fröelich. *The Fall of Berlin* (USSR/1949/124m/C) D: Mikhail Chiaureli. C: Mikhail Gelovani, V. Savelyev, M. Novakova, Victor Stanitsin, Y. Verikh, M. Petrunkin.

Nikolai Cherkasov. *The First Front* (USSR/1949/81m/BW) D: Vladimir Petrov. Part I of *Battle of Stalingrad* (50). C: Alexei Diki, Y. Shumsky, V. Merkuryev, B. Livanov, Victor Stanitsin, M. Astangov, K. Mikhailov, N. Simonov.

Ralph Bellamy. *Sunrise at Campobello* (US/1960/144m/C) D: Vincent J. Donehue. B/on the play by Dore Schary. C: Greer Garson, Hume Cronyn, Jean Hagen, Alan Bunce.

Richard Nelson. *The Pigeon That Took Rome* (US/1962/101m/BW) D: Melville Shavelson. B/on the novel *The Easter Dinner* by Donald Downes. C: Charlton Heston, Elsa Martinelli, Harry Guardino, Brian Donlevy, Baccaloni, Marietto, Gabriella Pallotta, Debbie Price.

Stephen Roberts. *First to Fight* (US/1967/97m/C) D: Christian Nyby. C: Chad Everett, Marilyn Devin, Dean Jagger, Bobby Troup, Claude Akins, Gene Hackman, James Best.

Stanislav Yaskevich. *The Great Battle* (aka *Liberation*) (USSR-Poland-Yugoslavia-Italy/1969/118m/C) D: Yuri Ozerov. C: Buhuti Zakariadze, Ivo Garani, Fritz Diez, Yuri Durov.

Dan O'Herlihy. *MacArthur* (US/1977/128m/C) D: Joseph Sargent. C: Gregory Peck, Ed Flanders, Ivan Bonar, Ward Costello, Nicholas Coster, Art Fleming, Addison Powell, Marj Dusay, Kenneth Tobey, John Fujioka, Fred Stuthman, Sandy Kenyon.

Howard Da Silva. *The Private Files of J. Edgar Hoover* (US/1978/112m/C) D: Larry Cohen. C: Broderick Crawford, Jose Ferrer, Michael Parks, Ronee Blakely, Michael Sacks, Raymond St. Jacques, Andrew Duggan, James Wainwright, Brad Dexter, William Jordan, Richard M. Dixon, Gordon Zimmerman, Lloyd Nolan, June Havoc, Dan Dailey, John Marley, Lloyd Gough.

Edward Hermann. *Annie* (US/1982/130m/C) D: John Huston. B/on the musical play by Thomas Meehan, Charles Strouse & Martin Charnin and the comic strip Little Orphan Annie created by Harold Gray. C: Albert Finney, Carol Burnett, Aileen Quinn, Bernadette Peters, Tim Curry, Lois DeBanzie, Geoffrey Holder.

Algimantas Masiulis. *Victory* (aka *Pobeda*) (USSR/1984/160m/C) D: Yevgeni Matveyev. B/on the novel by Aleksandr Chakovsky. C: Aleksandr Mikhajlov, Andrei Mironov, Klaus-Peter Thiele, Ramaz Chkhikvadze, Georgi Menglet, Mikhail Ulyanov, Viktor Ilyichyov, Nikolai Zasukhim.

Jon Voight. *Pearl Harbor* (US/2001/183m/C) D: Michael Bay. C: Ben Affleck, Josh Hartnett, Kate Beckinsale, William Lee Scott, Greg Zola, Ewen Bremner, Alec Baldwin, James King, Catherine Kellner, Jennifer Garner, Cuba Gooding, Jr., Michael Shannon, Matthew Davis, Mako.

469 Roosevelt, Theodore (1858–1919)

A hero in the Spanish-American War, Roosevelt was elected Vice-President in 1900 and with McKinley's assassination he became the 26th President of the U.S. At the age of 42 he was the youngest man ever to hold that office. He was portrayed by Tom Berenger in the TV movie *Rough Riders* (97).

E.J. Radcliffe. *I Loved a Woman* (US/1933/90m/BW) D: Alfred Green. B/on the novel by David Karsner. C: Kay Francis, Edward G. Robinson, Genevieve Tobin, Robert Barrat.

Erle C. Kenton. *End of the Trail* (US/1936/72m/BW) D: Erle C. Kenton. B/on the novel *Outlaws of Palouse* by Zane Grey. C: Jack Holt, Louise Henry, Douglas Dumbrille.

Sidney Blackmer. *This Is My Affair* (aka *His Affair*) (US/1937/99m/BW) D: William S. Seiter. B/on the novel *The McKinley Case* by Melville Crossman. C: Robert Taylor, Barbara Stanwyck, Victor McLaglen, John Carradine, Robert McWade, Frank Conroy.

Wallis Clark. *Yankee Doodle Dandy* (US/1942/126m/BW) D: Michael Curtiz. C: James Cagney, Joan Leslie, Walter Huston, George Tobias, Eddie Foy, Jr., Captain Jack Young.

Sidney Blackmer. *In Old Oklahoma* (aka *War of the Wildcats*) (US/1943/100m/BW) D: Albert S. Rogell. B/on the story *War of the Wildcats* by T. Burtis. C: John Wayne, Martha Scott, Albert Dekker, George "Gabby" Hayes, Dale Evans, Marjorie Rambeau.

Wallis Clark. *Jack London* (aka *The Adventures of Jack London*) (US/1943/94m/BW) D: Alfred Santell. B/on The Book of *Jack London* by Charmian London. C: Michael O'Shea, Susan Hayward, Osa Massen, Virginia Mayo, Morgan Conway.

Sidney Blackmer. *Buffalo Bill* (US/1944/90m/C) D: William Wellman. C: Joel McCrea, Maureen O'Hara, Linda Darnell, Thomas Mitchell, Edgar Buchanan, Anthony Quinn, Moroni Olsen, Chief Thundercloud, John Dilson, Evelyn Beresford.

John Merton. *I Wonder Who's Kissing Her Now* (US/1947/105m/C) D: Lloyd Bacon. C: June Haver, Mark Stevens, Martha Stewart, Reginald Gardiner, Lenore Aubert.

Sidney Blackmer. *My Girl Tisa* (US/1948/95m/BW) D: Elliott Nugent. B/on the play *Ever the Beginning* by Lucille S. Prumbs & Sara B. Smith. C: Lilli Palmer, Sam Wanamaker.

John Alexander. *Fancy Pants* (US/1950/92m/C) D: George Marshall. B/on the story *Ruggles of Red Gap* by Harry Leon Wilson. C: Bob Hope, Lucille Ball, Bruce Cabot.

Edward Cassidy. *The First Traveling Saleslady* (US/1956/92m/C) D: Arthur Lubin. C: Ginger Rogers, Barry Nelson, Carol Channing, David Brian, James Arness, Clint Eastwood, Ian Murray.

Karl Swenson. *Brighty of the Grand Canyon* (US/1967/92m/C) D: Norman Foster. B/on the book by Marguerite Henry. C: Joseph Cotten, Pat Conway, Dick Foran, Dandy Curran.

Brian Keith. *The Wind and the Lion* (US/1975/119m/C) D: John Milius. C: Sean Connery, Candice Bergen, John Huston, Shirley Rothman, Steve Kanaly, Larry Cross, Alex Weldon.

James Whitmore. *Bully* (US/1978/120m/C) D: Peter H. Hunt.

Robert Boyd. *Ragtime* (US/1981/155m/C) D: Milos Forman. B/on the novel by E.L. Doctorow. C: James Cagney, Brad Dourif, Moses Gunn, Elizabeth McGovern, Pat O'Brien, Kenneth McMillan, Donald O'Connor, James Olson, Mandy Patinkin, Howard E. Rollins, Jeff DeMunn, Robert Joy, Norman Mailer, Mary Steenburgen.

Robert Boyd. *The Indomitable Teddy Roosevelt* (US/1983/94m/C) D: Harrison Engle.

David James Alexander. *Newsies* (US/1992/125m/C) D: Kenny Ortega. C: Robert Duvall, Christian Bale, David Moscow, Luke Edwards, Max Casella, Ann-Margret.

470 Root, Elihu (1845–1937)

American statesman, Root was awarded the Nobel Peace Prize in 1912 for his work with the International Court at The Hague.

Alexander Knox. *Nicholas and Alexandra* (GB/1971/183m/C) D: Franklin J. Schaffner. B/on the book by Robert K. Massie. C: Michael Jayston, Janet Suzman, Roderic Noble, Fiona Fullerton, Harry Andrews, Irene Worth, Tom Baker, Ralph Truman, John McEnery, Michael Bryant, James Hazeldine, Brian Cox, Ian Holm, Roy Dotrice, Martin Potter.

Alex Weldon. *The Wind and the Lion* (US/1975/119m/C) D: John Milius. C: Sean Connery, Candice Bergen, Brian Keith, John Huston, Shirley Rothman, Steve Kanaly, Larry Cross.

471 Rossini, Gioacchino Antonio (1792–1868)

Italian composer, Rossini is remembered for his popular operas including "The Barber of Seville" and "William Tell."

Edmund Breon. *The Divine Spark* (aka *Casta Diva*) (Italy-GB/1935/100–81m/BW) D: Carmine Gallone. C: Martha Eggerth, Phillips Holmes, Benita Hume, Hugh Miller.

Nino Besozzi. *Rossini* (Italy/1946/90m/BW) D: Mario Bonnard. C: Paolo Barbara, Camillo Pilotto, Armando Falconi, Memo Benassi, Greta Gonda.

Roland Alexandre. *Casa Ricordi* (aka *House of Ricordi*) (France-Italy/1954/130–112m/C) D: Carmine Gallone. C: Fosco Giachetti, Maurice Ronet, Miriam Bru.

Ken Parry. *Lisztomania* (GB/1975/105m/C) D: Ken Russell. C: Roger Daltrey, Sara Kestelman, Paul Nicholas, Fiona Lewis, Veronica Qilligan, Ken Colley, Andrew Reilly, Murray Melvin, Otto Diamant, Anulka Dziubinska, Imogen Claire.

472 Rothstein, Arnold (1882–1928)

Known as the man who fixed the 1919 World Series, Rothstein was the underworld King of New York during the Roaring Twenties.

Spencer Tracy (as Murray Golden). *Now I'll Tell* (aka *While New York Sleeps*) (US/1934/72m/BW) D: Edwin Burke. B/on the book by Mrs. Arnold Rothstein. C: Helen Twelvetrees, Alice Faye.

Robert Lowery. *The Rise and Fall of Legs Diamond* (US/1960/101m/BW) D: Budd Boetticher. C: Ray Danton, Karen Steele, Elaine Stewart, Jesse White, Richard Gardner, Sid Melton.

David Janssen. *King of the Roaring Twenties* (aka *King of the Roaring Twenties — The Story of Arnold Rothstein*) (aka *The Big Bankroll*) (US/1961/106m/BW) D: Joseph M. Newman. B/on the book *The Big Bankroll* by Leo Katcher. C: Dianne Foster, Mickey Rooney, Jack Carson, Diana Dors, Dan O'Herlihy, Keenan Wynn, Joseph Schildkraut.

Michael Lerner. *Eight Men Out* (US/1988/120m/C) D: John Sayles. B/on the book by Eliot Asinof. C: John Cusack, Clifton James, David Strathairn, D.B. Sweeney, John Sayles.

F. Murray Abraham. *Mobsters* (US/1991/104m/C) D: Michael Karbelnikoff. C: Christian Slater, Patrick Dempsey, Richard Grieco, Costas Mandylor, Anthony Quinn, Michael Gambon, Lara Flynn Boyle, Nicholas Sadler, Titus Welliver.

473 Rousseau, Jean-Jacques (1712–1778)

French writer/philosopher whose works greatly influenced **Robespierre** and the French Revolutionists.

Alberty. *Napoleon Bonaparte* (France/1934/140m/BW) D: Abel Gance. Three-dimensional sound version of Gance's 1927 epic *Napoléon*. C: Albert Dieudonné, Edmond von Daele, Alexandre Koubitsky, Antonin Artaud, Boudreau, Jack Rye, Favière, Gina Manès, Suzanne Blanchetti, Marguerite Gance, Simone Genevois, Genica Missirio.

Andre Laurent. *Champs-Elysées* (aka *Remontons Les Champs-Elysées*) (France/1938/100m/BW) D: Sacha Guitry. C: Sacha Guitry, Lucien Baroux, Jacqueline Delubac, Germaine Dermoz, Jeanne Boitel, Raymonde Allain, Jean Davy, Emile Drain, Jacques Erwin, Rene Fauchois, Liane Pathe, Robert Pizani, Claude Martin, Raymond Galle.

Gilbert Gil. *Royal Affairs in Versailles* (aka *Versailles*) (aka *Affairs in Versailles*) (aka *If Versailles Were Told to Me*) (aka *Si Versailles M'Eétait Couté*) (France/1953/180–152m/C) D: Sacha Guitry. C: Sacha Guitry, Claudette Colbert, Orson Welles, Gerard Phillippe, Micheline Presle, Jean Marais, Georges Marchal, Gilbert Boka, Lana Marconi, Gino Cervi, Fernand Gravet, Louis Arbessier, Jacques Berthier, Samson Fainsilber, Emile Drain, Jacques de Feraudy, Gaston Rey, Philippe Richard.

Marc Eyraud. *Valmy* (France/1967/C) D: Abel Gance. C: Jacques Castelot, Bernard Dhéran, William Sabatier, Serge Gainsbourg.

François Simon. *The Roads of Exile* (France/1978/200–169m/C) D: Claude Goretta. C: Dominique Labourier, Roland Bertin, David Markham, John Sharp, William Fox.

Roger Jendley. *Alzire Oder Der Neue Kontinent* (Switzerland/1978/108m/C) D: Thomas Koerfer. C: François Simon.

474 Ruby, Jack (1911–1967)

(Jacob Leon Rubenstein) A Dallas strip-club owner, Ruby shot and killed **Lee Harvey Oswald** following the assassination of **John F. Kennedy**. He was played by Michael Lerner in the TV film *Ruby and Oswald* (78).

Oscar Orcini. *Executive Action* (US/1973/91m/C) D: David Miller. C: Burt Lancaster, Robert Ryan, Will Geer, Gilbert Green, John Anderson, Paul Carr, Dick Miller.

Brian Doyle-Murray. *JFK* (US/1991/189m/C) D: Oliver Stone. B/on *Crossfire* by Jim Marrs and *On the Trail of the Assassins* by Jim Garrison. C: Kevin Costner, Sissy Spacek, Kevin Bacon, Gary Oldman, Tom Howard, Steve Reed, Jodi Farber.

Danny Aiello. *Ruby* (US/1992/110m/C) D: John MacKenzie. B/on the play *Love Child* by Stephen Davis. C: Joe Viterelli, Gerard David, Kevin Wiggins, Willie Garson, Chris Wall, Sherilyn Fenn, Jane Hamilton, Carmine Caridi.

475 Russell, Lillian (1861–1922)

(Helen Louise Leonard) American singer/actress, Russell performed comic opera and was very successful in the works of **Gilbert** and **Sullivan**.

Binnie Barnes. *Diamond Jim* (US/1935/93m/BW) D: Edward Sutherland. B/on the book *Diamond Jim Brady* by Parker Morell. C: Edward Arnold, Jean Arthur, Bill Hoolahan.

Ruth Gillette. *The Gentleman from Louisiana* (US/1936/67m/BW) D: Irving Pichel. C: Edward Quillan, Chic Sale, Charlotte Henry, Charles Wilson, John Kelly, Matt McHugh, Holmes Herbert.

Ruth Gillette. *The Great Ziegfeld* (US/1936/170m/BW) D: Robert Z. Leonard. Best Picture (AA). C: William Powell, Luise Rainer, Myrna Loy, Frank Morgan, Reginald Owen, Fannie Brice, Ray Bolger, A.A. Trimble, Buddy Doyle, Rosina Lawrence.

Alice Faye. *Lillian Russell* (US/1940/127m/BW) D: Irving Cummings. C: Edward Arnold, Don Ameche, Henry Fonda, Warren William, Claud Allister, Nigel Bruce, Eddie Foy, Jr., William B. Davidson, Leo Carillo, Milburn Stone.

Louise Allbritton. *Bowery to Broadway* (US/1944/94m/BW) D: Charles Lamont. C: Maria Montez, Jack Oakie, Susanna Foster, Turhan Bey, Ann Blyth, Donald Cook, Frank McHugh.

Andrea King. *My Wild Irish Rose* (US/1947/101m/C) D: David Butler. B/on the book *Song in His Heart* by Rita Olcott. C: Dennis Morgan, Alan Hale, George Tobias.

476 Ruth, George Herman "Babe" (1895–1948)

Baseball's greatest slugger, and probably America's most famous sports figure, Ruth has been given the full Hollywood treatment twice, and has been depicted in several TV movies including Stephen Lang's portrayal in *Babe Ruth* (91). The Babe appearred as himself in several films including *Speedy* (28) and *The Pride of the Yankees* (42).

William Bendix. *The Babe Ruth Story* (US/1948/106m/BW) D: Roy Del Ruth. B/on the book by Bob Considine. C: Claire Trevor, Charles Bickford, Sam Levene.

John Goodman. *The Babe* (US/1992/115m/C) D: Arthur Hiller. C: Kelly McGillis, Trini Alvarado, Bruce Boxleitner, Joe Ragno, Michael McGrady, Bernie Gigliotti, Randy Steinmeyer, Michael Nicolasi, Bernard Kates, Harry Hutchinson, Guy Barile.

Art LeFleur. *The Sandlot* (US/1993/109m/C) D: David Mickey Evans. C: Tom Guiry, Mike Vitar, Patrick Renna, Chauncey Leopardi, James Earl Jones, Marty York.

477 Rutledge, Ann (1813?–1835)

Portrayed in the movies as **Abraham Lincoln's** first and possibly greatest love, there is little historical evidence of a full-blown romance between the future president and the innkeeper's daughter.

Una Merkel. *Abraham Lincoln* (US/1930/97m/BW) D: D.W. Griffith. C: Walter Huston, Kay Hammond, E. Alyn Warren, Edgar Deering, Hobart Bosworth, Fred Warren, Frank Campeau, Francis Ford, Ian Keith, Oscar Apfel, Cameron Prud'Homme.

Pauline Moore. *Young Mr. Lincoln* (US/1939/100m/BW) D: John Ford. C: Henry Fonda, Alice Brady, Marjorie Weaver, Arlene Whelan, Richard Cromwell, Milburn Stone, Pauline Moore.

Mary Howard. *Abe Lincoln in Illinois* (aka *Spirit of The People*) (US/1940/110m/BW) D: John Cromwell. B/on the play by Robert E. Sherwood. C: Raymond Massey, Gene Lockhart, Ruth Gordon, Dorothy Tree, Harvey Stephens, Howard Da Silva.

478 Sade, Marquis de (1740–1814)

(Donatien Alphonse François) French author noted for his erotic works extolling sexual deviance, de Sade spent nearly 30 years in prisons or asylums for various sexual offences.

Patrick Magee. *Marat/Sade* (aka *The Persecution and Assassination of Jean-Paul Marat As Performed By the Inmates of Charenton Under the Direction of the Marquis de Sade*) (GB/1966/115m/C) D: Peter Brook. B/on the play by Peter Weiss. C: Clifford Rose, Glenda Jackson, Ian Richardson, John Harwood, Brenda Kempner, Ruth Baker, Michael Williams, Freddie Jones, Henry Woolf.

Klaus Kinski. *Justine* (aka *Marquis de Sade: Justine*) (aka *Justine and Juliet*) (Italy-Spain/1968/89m/C) D: Jesse Franco. B/on the novel by the Marquis de Sade. C: Jack Palance, Mercedes McCambridge, Sylva Koscina, Maria Rohm.

Keir Dullea. *De Sade* (US-Germany/1969/113m/C) D: Cy Endfield. C: Senta Berger, Lilli Palmer, Anna Massey, John Huston, Sonja Ziemann, Maz Kiebach.

Michel Piccoli. *The Milky Way* (France-Italy/1969/105m/C) D: Luis Bunuel.

C: Paul Frankeur, Laurent Terzieff, Alain Cuny, Bernard Verley, Edith Scob, Jean Clarieux, Christian van Cau, Pierre Clementi, Georges Marchal, Delphine Seyrig.

Serge Gainsbourg. *Valmy* (France/1967/C) D: Abel Gance. C: Jacques Castelot, Bernard Dhéran, Marc Eyraud, William Sabatier.

Geoffry Rush. *Quills* (GB-US/2000/123m/C) D: Philip Kaufman. B/on the play by Doug Wright. C: Kate Winslet, Joaquin Phoenix, Michael Caine, Billie Whitelaw, Patrick Malahide, Amelia Warner, Jane Menelaus, Stephen Moyer, Tony Pritchard, Michael Jenn, Danny Babington, George Yiasoumi, Elizabeth Berrington, Edward Tudor-Pole, Harry Jones, Bridget McConnell, Rebecca R. Palmer, Toby Sawyer, Daniel Ainsleigh, Terry O'Neill, Diana Morrison, Carol MacReady, Tom Ward, Richard Mulholland, Ron Cook, Julian Tait, Tessa Vale, Howard Lew Lewis, Lisa Hammond, Mathew Fraser, Jamie Beddard.

479 Saladin (1137–1193)

(Salah ed-din Yusuf ibn Ayyub) Sultan of Egypt and Syria, Saladin lead the Moslems in the holy wars with the Crusaders.

Ian Keith. *The Crusades* (US/1935/123m/BW) D: Cecil B. DeMille. Waldemar Young & Dudley Nichols. B/on the book *The Crusades: Iron Men and Saints* by Harold Lamb. C: Loretta Young, Henry Wilcoxon, Katherine De Mille, C. Aubrey Smith, Joseph Schildkraut, Alan Hale, C. Henry Gordon, Ramsay Hill.

Rex Harrison. *King Richard and the Crusaders* (US/1954/113m/C) D: David Butler. B/on the novel *The Talisman* by Sir Walter Scott. C: George Sanders, Virginia Mayo, Laurence Harvey, Robert Douglas, Michael Pate, Paula Raymond, Henry Corden.

Ahmed Mazhar. *Saladin* (Egypt/1963/180m/C) D: Youssef Chanine. C: Salah Zulficar, Nadia Loufti.

480 Salieri, Antonio (1750–1825)

Italian composer and teacher; Salieri's students included **Schubert**, **Beethoven** and **Liszt**. He was also a great rival of **Mozart**, though he did not poison the young genius as has been suggested.

Cecil Humphreys. *The Unfinished Symphony* (GB-Austria/1934/90m/BW) D: Willi Forst & Anthony Asquith. C: Hans Yaray, Martha Eggerth, Helen Chandler, Esme Percy.

Wilton Graff. *The Mozart Story* (aka *Whom the Gods Love*) (aka *Mozart*) (aka *Wenn Die Gotter Lieben*) (Germany/1942/91m/C) D: Karl Hartl. C: Hans Holt, Rene Deltgen, Winnie Markus, Irene von Meyendorf, Edward Vedder, Curt Jurgens, Carol Forman, Walther Jansson, Paul Hoerbiger.

Albin Skoda. *The Life and Loves of Mozart* (aka *Mozart— Put Your Hand in Mine Dear*) (aka *Give Me Your Hand My Love, Mozart*) (aka *Mozart*) (Austria/1955/100–87m/C) D: Karl Hartl. C: Oskar Werner, Johanna Matz, Gertrud Kuekelmann.

F. Murray Abraham * Best Actor (AA, GG). *Amadeus* (US/1984/158m/C) D: Milos Forman. B/on the play by Peter Shaffer. Best Picture (AA, GG). Best Director (AA, DGA, GG). C: Tom Hulce, Elizabeth Berridge, Jeffrey Jones, Simon Callow, Roy Dotrice.

Mozart (Tom Hulce) places a fervent kiss of thanks on the hand of Salieri (F. Murray Abraham), thinking that Salieri is helping him win favor with Emperor Joseph II. Not so, the jealous Salieri is scheming to ruin the young composer. *Amadeus* (1984). (Museum of Modern Art Film Stills Archive)

Franz Glatzeder. *Forget Mozart!* (Germany-Czechoslovakia/1985/90m/C) D: Miloslav Luther. C: Max Tidof, Armin Muller Stahl, Ladislav Chudik, Zdenek Hradilak.

481 Salisbury, Lord (1830–1903)

(Robert Arthur Talbot Gascoyne-Cecil, 3rd Marquess of Salisbury) British politician and statesman, Salisbury served as Prime Minister three times: 1885–86, 1886–92, and 1895–1902.

Harvey Braban. *Sixty Glorious Years* (aka *Queen of Destiny*) (GB/1938/90m/C) D: Herbert Wilcox. C: Anna Neagle, Anton Walbrook, C. Aubrey Smith, Charles Carson, Felix Aylmer, Pamela Standish, Gordon McLeod, Henry Hallatt, Wyndham Goldie, Malcolm Keen, Derrick De Marney, Joyce Bland, Aubrey Dexter, Laidman Browne.

Jean Toulout. *Entente Cordiale* (France/1938/95m/BW) D: Marcel L'Herbier. B/on *Edward VII and His Times* by Andre Maurois. C: Victor Francen, Gaby Morlay, Andre Lefaur, Marcelle Praince, Jeanine Darcey, Arlette Marchal, Jean Galland, Andre Roanne, Jacques Catelain, Jacques Baumer, Jean d'Yd, Jean Perrier.

Leslie Perrins. *The Prime Minister* (GB/1940/94m/BW) D: Thorold Dickinson. C: John Gielgud, Diana Wynyard, Will Fyfe, Stephen Murray, Owen Nares, Fay Compton, Lyn Harding, Vera Bogetti, Frederick Leister, Nicolas Hannan, Kynaston Reeves, Gordon McLeod.

Cecil Parker. *A Study in Terror* (aka *Fog*) (GB/1965/95m/C) D: James Hill. B/on characters created by A. Conan Doyle. C: John Neville, Donald Houston, John Fraser, Anthony Quayle, Robert Morley, Barbara Windsor, Frank Finlay, Judi Dench.

Laurence Naismith. *Young Winston* (GB/1972/145m/C) D: Richard Attenborough. B/on the book *My Early Life: A Roving Commission* by Winston Churchill. Best English-Language Foreign Film (GG). C: Simon Ward, Peter Cellier, Ronald Hines, John Mills, Anne Bancroft, Robert Shaw, William Dexter, Basil Dignam, Reginald Marsh, Anthony Hopkins, Robert Hardy, Colin Blakely, Michael Audreson, Jack Hawkins.

John Gielgud. *Murder By Decree* (GB-Canada/1979/121m/C) D: Bob Clark. B/on characters created by A. Conan Doyle and the book *The Ripper File* by John Lloyd & Elwyn Jones. C: Christopher Plummer, James Mason, Victor Langley, Frank Finlay.

482 Salome

Salome, the niece of **Herod Antipas**, was the Biblical hoofer whose terpsichorean talents were responsible for the beheading of **John the Baptist**. She was portrayed by Isabel Mestres (uncredited) in the TV mini-series *Jesus of Nazareth* (77), and by Gabriella Pession in the TV film *Jesus* (99).

Andre Johnsen. *Dante's Inferno* (US/1935/88m/BW) D: Harry Lachman. C: Spencer Tracy, Claire Trevor, Henry B. Walthall, Scotty Becket, Lorna Lowe, Leone Lane.

Rita Hayworth. *Salome* (US/1953/103m/C) D: William Dieterle. C: Stewart Granger, Charles Laughton, Judith Anderson, Cedric Hardwicke, Alan Badel, Basil Sydney, Rex Reason, Robert Warwick, Maurice Schwartz.

Brigid Bazlen. *King of Kings* (US/1961/168m/C) D: Nicholas Ray. C: Jeffrey Hunter, Siobhan McKenna, Hurd Hatfield, Viveca Lindfors, Rita Gam, Carmen Sevilla, Rip Torn, Harry Guardino, Frank Thring, Guy Rolfe, Maurice Marsac, Gregoire Aslan, Royal Dano, Robert Ryan, Gerard Tichy, Michael Wager, Tino Barrero, Jose Antonio, Orson Welles (Narrator).

Paola Tedesco. *The Gospel According to St. Matthew* (France-Italy/1964/142m/BW) D: Pier Paolo Pasolini. B/on the *New Testament* book of *Matthew*. C: Enrique Irazoqui, Susanna Pasolini, Mario Socrate, Marcello Morante, Alfonso Gatto, Rodolfo Wilcock, Francesco Leonetti, Amerigo Bevilacqua, Otello Sestilli, Settimio Di Porto, Ferruccio Nuzzo, Alessandro Tosca, Franca Cupane, Giacomo Morante, Rosario Migale.

Donayle Luna. *Salome* (Italy/1972/77m/C) D: Carmelo Bene. C: Veruschka, Lydia Mancinelli, Piero Vida, Alfiero Vincenti, Giovanni Davoli.

Jo Ciampa. *Salome* (France-Italy/1985/97m/C) D: Claude d'Anna. B/on the play by Oscar Wilde. C: Tomas Milian, Pamela Salem, Tim Woodward, Fabrizio Bentivoglio, Fabiana Torrente.

Imogen Millais-Scott. *Salome's Last Dance* (GB/1988/89m/C) D: Ken Russell. B/on the play *Salome* by Oscar Wilde. C: Nickolas Grace, Douglas Hodge, Glenda Jackson, Stratford Johns, Denis Ull, Ken Russell, Imogen Claire.

483 Sand, George (1804–1876)

(Amandine Aurore Lucie Dupin, baronne Dudevant) French author, Sand was noted for her unconventional lifestyle and her progressive novels of open relationships and social reform. In *A Winter in Majorca* she wrote about her life with **Frédéric Chopin**, an affair that lasted nine years, and in *She and He* she wrote about her life with Musset.

Merle Oberon. *A Song to Remember* (US/1945/113m/C) D: Charles Vidor. C: Cornel Wilde, Paul Muni, Stephen Bekassy, Nina Foch, George Coulouris, George Macready, Roxy Roth.

Patricia Morison. *Song Without End* (US/1960/145m/C) D: George Cukor & Charles Vidor. C: Dirk Bogarde, Capucine, Genevieve Page, Ivan Desny, Martita Hunt, Lou Jacobi, Lyndon Brook, E. Erlandsen, Alex Davion, Hans Unterkirchner, Katherine Squire.

Lucia Bose. *Jutrzenka: A Winter in Majorca* (Spain/1971/105m/C) D: Jaime Camino. C: Christopher Sandford, Henri Serre, Maurice Dudevant, Solange Dudevant.

Anne Wiazemsky. *Georges Qui?* (France/1973/110m/C) D: Michele Rosier. C: Roger Pianchon.

Imogen Claire. *Lisztomania* (GB/1975/105m/C) D: Ken Russell. C: Roger Daltrey, Sara Kestelman, Paul Nicholas, Fiona Lewis, Veronica Qilligan, Ken Colley, Andrew Reilly, Murray Melvin, Otto Diamant, Anulka Dziubinska, Ken Parry.

Judy Davis. *Impromptu* (GB/1990/107m/C) D: James Lapine. C: Hugh Grant, Mandy Patinkin, Bernadette Peters, Julian Sands, Ralph Brown, Emma Thompson.

Juliette Binoche. *Les Enfants du siècle* (aka *The Children of the Century*) (France/2000/135m/C) D: Diane Kurys. C: Benoît Magimel, Stefano Dionisi, Robin Renucci, Karin Viard, Isabelle Carré, Arnaud Giovaninetti, Denis Podalydès, Olivier Foubert, Marie-France Mignal, Patrick Chesnais.

484 Santa Anna (1794–1876)

(Antonio López de Santa Anna) The Mexican general known for his victory at the Alamo, Santa Anna was also Mexico's dictator several times before his final overthrow in 1855.

Julien Rivero. *Heroes of the Alamo* (aka *Remember the Alamo*) (US/1937/80m/BW) D: Harry Fraser. C: Earl Hodgins, Lane Chandler, Roger Williams, Rex Lease, Edward Piel, Lee Valianos, Ruth Findlay, Jack Smith, Tex Cooper.

C. Henry Gordon. *Man of Conquest* (US/1939/97m/BW) D: George Nichols, Jr. C: Richard Dix, Edward Ellis, Victor Jory, Robert Barrat, Ralph Morgan, Robert Armstrong, George "Gabby" Hayes, Gail Patrick, Joan Fontaine, Max Terhune, Lane Chandler.

J. Carrol Naish. *The Last Command* (US/1955/110m/C) D: Frank Lloyd. B/on the story *The Last Command* by Sy Bartlett. C: Sterling Hayden, Richard Carlson, Arthur Hunnicutt, Otto Kruger, Hugh Sanders, Don Kennedy, Anna Maria Alberghetti, Ernest Borgnine, Ben Cooper, Virginia Grey, John Russell, Edward Colmans, Jim Davis.

David Silva. *The First Texan* (US/1956/82m/C) D: Byron Haskin. C: Joel McCrea, Jeff Morrow, Dayton Lummis, William Hopper, James Griffith, Carl Benton Reid, Felicia Farr, Wallace Ford, Chubby Johnson, Jody McCrea, Abraham Sofaer.

Ruben Padilla. *The Alamo* (US/1960/192m/C) D: John Wayne. C: John Wayne, Richard Widmark, Laurence Harvey, Patrick Wayne, Joseph Calleia, Richard Boone.

Schragmüller, Elsbeth *see* Fraülein Doktor

485 Schubert, Franz Peter (1797–1828)

Austrian composer famous for his lieder ("art songs") and as one of the early figures of the Romantic movement. Schubert gave only one public concert in his life before dying of typhoid fever at the age of 31.

Carl Joeken. *Schubert's Dream of Spring* (aka *Schubert's Frühlingstraum*) (Germany/1932/85m/BW) D: Richard Oswald. C: Lucie Englisch, Alfred Lauetner, Gretl Theimer.

Richard Tauber. *Blossom Time* (aka *April Blossoms*) (aka *April Romance*) (GB/1934/80m/BW) D: Paul Stein. C: Jane Baxter, Carl Esmond, Athene Seyler, Charles Carson.

Nils Asther. *Love Time* (US/1934/72m/BW) D: James Tinling. C: Pat Paterson, Herbert Mundlin, Henry Kolker, Harry Green, Henry B. Walthall.

Hans Yaray. *The Unfinished Symphony* (GB-Austria/1934/90m/BW) D: Willi Forst & Anthony Asquith. C: Martha Eggerth, Helen Chandler, Esme Percy, Cecil Humphreys.

Paul Hörbiger. *Drei Mäderl Um Schubert* (Germany/1936/60m/BW) D: E.W. Emo. C: Gustav Waldau, Julia Serda, Gretl Theimer, Maria Andergast, Else Eister.

Bernard Lancret. *Schubert's Serenade* (aka *Serenade*) (France/1940/90m/BW) D: Jean Boyer. C: Lilian Harvey, Auguste Boverio, Louis Jouvet, Marcel Vallee, Jelix Oudart.

Alan Curtis. *New Wine* (aka *The Great Awakening*) (aka *The Melody Master*) (US/1941/84m/BW) D: Reinhold Schunzel. C: Ilona Massey, Binnie Barnes, Albert Basserman, Billy Gilbert, Sterling Holloway, John Qualen, Forrest Tucker.

Tino Rossi. *La Belle Meunière* (France/1949/120m/C) D: Marcel Pagnol. C: Jacqueline Pagnol.

Karl Boehm. *The House of the Three Girls* (Austria/1958/102m/C) D: Ernst Marischka. B/on the novel *Schwammer* by Rudolf Bascht. C: Gustav Knuth, Magda Schneider, Ewald Balser.

Axel Shanda. *Fremd bin ich eingezogen* (Austria-Germany/1979/70m/C) D: Titus Leber. C: August Schnigg, Angelika Berlage, Ernst Dungl, Alicia Meyer-Stauffen.

486 Schultz, Dutch (1902–1935)

(Arthur Flegenheimer) Feared New York gangster of the early 30s, Schultz was responsible for the death of **Mad Dog Coll** and probably that of **Legs Diamond**.

Vincent Gardenia. *Mad Dog Coll* (US/1961/88m/BW) D: Burt Balaban. C: John Chandler, Neil Nephew, Brooke Hayward, Joy Harmon, Jerry Orbach, Telly Savalas, Gene Hackman.

Vic Morrow. *Portrait of a Mobster* (US/1961/108m/BW) D: Joseph Pevney. B/on the book by Harry Grey. C: Leslie Parrish, Peter Breck, Ray Danton, Evan McCord.

John Durren. *Lepke* (US/1975/110–98m/C) D: Menahem Golan. C: Tony Curtis, Anjanette Comer, Michael Callan, Warren Berlinger, Gianni Russo, Vic Tayback, Milton Berle, Erwin Fuller, Jack Ackerman, Vaughn Meader, Zitto Kazan.

James Remar. *The Cotton Club* (US/1984/127m/C) D: Francis Coppola. C: Richard Gere, Gregory Hines, Diane Lane, Lonette McKee, Bob Hoskins, Nicolas Cage, Rosalind Harris, Fred Gwynne, Gregory Rozakis, Joe Dallesandro, Maurice Hines, Gwen Verdon, Lisa Jane Persky, Woody Strode, Zane Mark, Larry Marshall.

Dustin Hoffman. *Billy Bathgate* (US/1991/106m/C) D: Robert Benton. B/on the novel by E.L. Doctorow. C: Nicole Kidman, Loren Dean, Bruce Willis, Stanley Tucci.

Bruce Nozick. *Hit the Dutchman* (US-Russia/1993/116m/C) D: Menahem Golan. C: Christopher Bradley, Eddie Bowz, Will Kempe, Sally Kirkland, Jeff Griggs, Jennifer Miller, Jack Conley, Matt Servitto, Menahem Golan.

Bruce Nozick. *Mad Dog Coll* (aka *Killer Instinct*) (US-Russia/1993/101m/C) D: Greydon Clark & Ken Stein. C: Christopher Bradley, Rachel York, Jeff Griggs, Thomas McHugh, Eddie Bowz, Jack Conley, Matt Servitto, Will Kempe, Dennis Predovic.

Tim Roth. *Hoodlum* (US/1997/130m/C) D: Bill Duke. C: Laurence Fishburne, Vanessa L. Williams, Andy Garcia, Cicely Tyson, Chi McBride, Clarence Williams III, Richard Bradford, William Athertin, Loretta Devine, Queen Latifah, Michael McCary, Dick Djonola.

487 Schumann, Clara Wiek (1819–1896)

Virtuoso pianist and the wife of **Robert Schumann**, Clara was, in her time, more famous for her playing than her husband was for his composing.

Katharine Hepburn. *Song of Love* (US/1947/119m/BW) D: Clarence Brown. B/on the play by Bernard Schubert & Mario Silva. C: Paul Henried, Robert Walker, Henry Daniell, Leo G. Carroll, Else Janssen, Gigi Perreau, Henry Stephenson.

Nastassja Kinski. *Spring Symphony* (aka *Frühlingssinfonie*) (West Germany-East Germany/1983/103m/C) D: Peter Schamoni. C: Herbert Gronemeyer, Rolf Hoppe, Bernhard Wicki, Andre Heller, Gideon Kremer, Anja-Christine Preussler.

488 Schumann, Robert Alexander (1810–1856)

A brilliant Romantic composer, Schumann was plagued throughout his life with mental problems and spent the last two years of his life in an asylum.

Paul Henreid. *Song of Love* (US/1947/119m/BW) D: Clarence Brown. B/on the play by Bernard Schubert & Mario Silva. C: Katharine Hepburn, Robert Walker, Henry Daniell, Leo G. Carroll, Else Janssen, Gigi Perreau, Henry Stephenson.

Herbert Gronemeyer. *Spring Symphony* (aka *Frühlingssinfonie*) (West Germany-East Germany/1983/103m/C) D: Peter Schamoni. C: Nastassja Kinski, Rolf Hoppe, Bernhard Wicki, Andre Heller, Gideon Kremer, Anja-Christine Preussler.

489 Schweitzer, Albert (1875–1965)

A distinguished musician, author, theologian and medical missionary, Scweitzer's work in Africa brought him the Nobel Peace Prize (1953).

Pierre Fresnay. *The Story of Albert Schweitzer* (France/1952) D: André Haguet.

Malcolm McDowell. *The Light in the Jungle* (US/1990/100m/C) D: Gray Hofmyer. C: Susan Strasburg, Andrew Davis, Helen Jessop, John Carson.

490 Scott, Robert Falcon (1868–1912)

English Antarctic explorer, Scott died in his attempt to be the first man to reach the South Pole. (See **Amundsen, Roald**)

Frank Vosper. *Regal Cavalcade* (aka *Royal Cavalcade*) (GB/1935/100m/BW) D: Thomas Bentley, Herbert Brenton, Norman Lee, Walter Summers, Will Kellino & Marcel Varnel. C: Marie Lohr, Esme Percy, Pearl Argyle, Austin Trevor, Harry Brunning, John Mills, C.M. Hallard, H. Saxon-Snell, Patric Knowles, Matheson Lang, Athene Seyler.

John Mills. *Scott of the Antarctic* (GB/1948/111m/C) D: Charles Friend. C: Derek Bond, Harold Warrender, James Robertson Justice, Reginald Beckwith, Kenneth More.

491 Seymour, Jane (1509?–1537)

The third wife of **Henry VIII**, Seymour died shortly after giving birth to their son **Edward VI**.

Wendy Barrie. *The Private Life of Henry VIII* (GB/1933/97m/BW) D: Alexander Korda. C: Charles Laughton, Robert Donat, Binnie Barnes, Elsa Lanchester, Merle Oberon, Everley Gregg, Franklyn Dyall, Miles Mander, Claude Allister, John Loder, Lawrence Hanray.

Helen Valkis. *The Prince and the Pauper* (US/1937/120m/BW) D: William Keighley. B/on the novel by Mark Twain and the play by Catherine C. Cushing. C: Errol Flynn, Claude Rains, Henry Stephenson, Billy Mauch, Bobby Mauch, Montagu Love, Alan Hale, Robert Warwick, Ann Howard, Halliwell Hobbes, Barton MacLane.

Lesley Patterson. *Anne of the Thousand Days* (GB/1969/145m/C) D: Charles Jarrott. B/on the play by Maxwell Anderson. C: Richard Burton, Genevieve Bujold, Irene Papas, Anthony Quayle, John Colicos, Michael Hordern, Katharine Blake, William Squire, Nicola Pagett.

Patsy Rowlands. *Carry on Henry VIII* (GB/1970/89m/C) D: Gerald Thomas.

C: Sidney James, Kenneth Williams, Joan Sims, Charles Hawtrey, Terry Scott, Peter Gilmore, Monica Dietrich.

Jane Asher. *The Six Wives of Henry VIII* (aka *Henry VIII and His Six Wives*) (GB/1972/125m/C) D: Waris Hussein. C: Keith Michell, Frances Cuka, Charlotte Rampling, Jenny Bos, Lynne Frederick, Barbara Leigh-Hunt, Donald Pleasence, Simon Henderson, Annette Crosbie, John Bryans, Michael Goodliffe, Bernard Hepton, Dorothy Tutin.

492 Shakespeare, William (1564–1616)

Though there is some controversy as to whether he wrote all of the plays with which he is credited, Shakespeare is still considered to be the greatest dramatist ever.

Basil Gill. *Immortal Gentleman* (GB/1935/61m/BW) D: Widgey R. Newman. C: Rosalinde Fuller, Dennis Hoey, Anne Bolt, Edgar Owen, J. Hubert Leslie, Leo Genn.

John Salew. *Time Flies* (GB/1944/88m/BW) D: Walter Forde. C: Tommy Handley, Evelyn Dall, George Moon, Leslie Bradley, Olga Lindo, Roy Emerson, Iris Lang.

Reginald Gardiner. *The Story of Mankind* (US/1957/100m/C) D: Irwin Allen. B/on the book by Hendrik Van Loon. C: Ronald Colman, Hedy Lamarr, Virginia Mayo, Agnes Moorehead, Peter Lorre, Dennis Hopper, Marie Wilson, Helmut Dantine, Edward Everett Horton, Marie Windsor, Francis X. Bushman, Anthony Dexter, Austin Green, Jim Ameche, Harpo Marx, Bobby Watson, Reginald Sheffield, Cedric Hardwicke, Cesar Romero.

Joseph Fiennes. *Shakespeare in Love* (GB/1998/153m/C) D: John Madden. Best Picture, Best Actress, Best Supporting Actress, Best Original Screenplay, Original Musical Score, Art Direction, Costume Design (AA). Best Picture (Comedy), Best Actress, Best Screenplay (GG). C: Gwyneth Paltrow, Judi Dench, Ben Affleck, Colin Firth, Geoffrey Rush, Antony Sher, Tom Wilkinson, Simon Callow, Steven O'Donnell, Tim McMullen, Rupert Everett (as Christopher Marlowe) uncredited.

493 Shelley, Mary Wollstonecraft (1797–1851)

English writer and the wife of poet **Percy Shelley**, Mary was the author of *Frankenstein, Or the Modern Prometheus*.

Elsa Lanchester. *The Bride of Frankenstein* (US/1935/80m/BW) D: James Whale. B/on the novel *Frankenstein, or the Modern Prometheus* by Mary Shelley. C: Boris Karloff, Colin Clive, Valerie Hobson, Una O'Connor, Gavin Gordon, Douglas Walton.

Natasha Richardson. *Gothic* (GB/1987/90m/C) D: Ken Russell. C: Gabriel Byrne, Julian Sands, Myriam Cyr, Timothy Spall, Andreas Wisniewski.

Alice Krige. *Haunted Summer* (US/1988/115m/C) D: Ivan Passer. B/on the novel by Anne Edwards. C: Philip Anglim, Laura Dern, Eric Stolz, Alex Winter.

Lizzy McInnerny. *Rowing with the Wind* (Spain/1988/96m/C) D: Gonzalo Suarez. C: Hugh Grant, Valentine Pelka, Elizabeth Hurley, Jose Luis Gomez, Bibi Andersson.

Bridget Fonda. *Frankenstein Unbound* (aka *Roger Corman's Frankenstein Unbound*) (US/1990/85m/C) D: Roger Corman. B/on the novel by Brian Aldiss. C: John Hurt, Raul Julia, Jason Patric, Michael Hutchence, Nick Brimble, Catherine Rabett.

Esther Mulligan. *Conceiving Ada* (aka *Leidenschaftliche Berechnung*) (Germany-US/1997/85m/C) D: Lynn Hershman-Leeson. B/on *Ada: The Enchantress of Numbers: A Selection from the Letters of Lord Byron's Daughter and Her Description of the First Computer* by Betty A. Toole. C: Tilda Swinton, Francesca Faridany, Timothy Leary, Karen Black, John O'Keefe, John Perry Barlow, J.D. Wolfe, Owen Murphy, David Brooks, Ellen Sebastian, Mark Capri, Joe Wemple, Chris von Sneidern, David Eppel, R.U. Sirius, Kashka Peck, Rose Lockwood, Jesse Talman Boss, Lillian L. Malmberg, Cyrus Mare, Michael Oosterom, Pollyanna Jacobs, CD-ROM characters/voices: Charles Pinion, Bruce Sterling, Dave Nelson, Henry S. Rosenthal, Melissa Howden, Josh Rosen, Roger Shaw, Lynn Hershman-Leeson.

494 Shelley, Percy Bysse (1792–1822)

English lyric poet, Shelley wrote such works as Prometheus Unbound and "Queen Mab" among others. (See **Shelley, Mary** and **Byron, Lord**)

Douglas Walton. *The Bride of Frankenstein* (US/1935/80m/BW) D: James Whale. B/on the novel *Frankenstein, or the Modern Prometheus* by Mary Shelley. C: Boris Karloff, Colin Clive, Valerie Hobson, Elsa Lanchester, Una O'Connor, Gavin Gordon.

Julian Sands. *Gothic* (GB/1987/90m/C) D: Ken Russell. C: Gabriel Byrne, Natasha Richardson, Myriam Cyr, Timothy Spall, Andreas Wisniewski.

Eric Stoltz. *Haunted Summer* (US/1988/115m/C) D: Ivan Passer. B/on the novel by Anne Edwards. C: Philip Anglim, Laura Dern, Alice Krige, Alex Winter.

Valentine Pelka. *Rowing with the Wind* (Spain/1988/96m/C) D: Gonzalo Suarez. C: Hugh Grant, Lizzy McInnerny, Elizabeth Hurley, Jose Luis Gomez, Bibi Andersson.

Michael Hutchence. *Frankenstein Unbound* (aka *Roger Corman's Frankenstein Unbound*) (US/1990/85m/C) D: Roger Corman. B/on the novel by Brian Aldiss. C: John Hurt, Raul Julia, Bridget Fonda, Jason Patric, Nick Brimble, Catherine Rabett.

495 Sheridan, (Gen.) Philip Henry (1831–1888)

After distinguished service in the Civil War, Gen. Sheridan was made military governor of Texas. He was removed from the post and made commander of the armies fighting the Sioux, Apache and other tribes — a logical military appointment for the man who once said "the only good Indians I ever saw were dead."

Frank Campeau. *Abraham Lincoln* (US/1930/97m/BW) D: D.W. Griffith. C: Walter Huston, Una Merkel, Kay Hammond, E. Alyn Warren, Edgar Deering, Hobart Bosworth, Fred Warren, Francis Ford, Ian Keith, Oscar Apfel, Cameron Prud'Homme.

Sidney Blackmer. *In Old Chicago* (US/1938/115m/BW) D: Henry King. AA for Best Assistant Director (1937) to Robert Webb. C: Tyrone Power, Alice Faye, Don Ameche, Alice Brady, Andy Devine, Brian Donlevy, Rondo Hatton.

Ernie Adams. *Union Pacific* (US/1939/135m/BW) D: Cecil B. DeMille. B/on the novel *Trouble Shooter* by Ernest Haycox. C: Barbara Stanwyck, Joel McCrea, Joseph Crehan.

David Bruce. *Santa Fe Trail* (US/1940/110m/BW) D: Michael Curtiz. C: Errol Flynn, Ronald Reagan, Olivia de Havilland, Raymond Massey, Alan Hale, Guinn Williams, Van Heflin, Moroni Olsen, Charles Middleton, Erville Alderson, Frank Wilcox.

John Litel. *They Died with Their Boots On* (US/1941/140m/BW) D: Raoul Walsh. C: Errol Flynn, Olivia de Havilland, Arthur Kennedy, Charles Grapewin, Gene Lockhart, Anthony Quinn, Stanley Ridges, Sydney Greenstreet, Regis Toomey, Hattie McDaniel, Joseph Crehan.

J. Carrol Naish. *Rio Grande* (US/1950/105m/BW) D: John Ford. B/on the story *Mission with No Record* by James Warner Bellah. C: John Wayne, Maureen O'Hara, Ben Johnson, Claude Jarman, Jr., Harry Carey, Jr., Chill Wills, Victor McLaglen.

Lawrence Tierney. *Custer of the West* (US-Spain/1967/143m/C) D: Robert Siodmark & Irving Lerner. C: Robert Shaw, Mary Ure, Jeffrey Hunter, Ty Hardin, Charles Stalnaker, Robert Hall, Kieron Moore, Robert Ryan, Marc Lawrence.

496 Sheridan, Richard Brinsley (1751–1816)

Irish born dramatist, Sheridan wrote *School for Scandal* and *The Rivals* among other works.

Esme Percy. *The Return of the Scarlet Pimpernel* (GB/1937/94–80m/BW) D: Hans Schwartz. C: Barry K. Barnes, Sophie Stewart, Margareta Scott, James Mason, Henry Oscar, Evelyn Roberts.

Max Adrian. *The Young Mr. Pitt* (GB/1942/118m/BW) D: Carol Reed. C: Robert Donat, Robert Morley, Phyllis Calvert, Raymond Lovell, Felix Aylmer, Albert Lieven, Stephen Haggard, Geoffrey Atkins, John Mills, Herbert Lom, Agnes Laughlan.

Ralph Truman. *Mrs. Fitzherbert* (GB/1947/99m/BW) D: Montgomery Tully. B/on the novel *Princess Fitz* by Winifred Carter. C: Peter Graves, Joyce Howard, Leslie Banks, Margaretta Scott, Wanda Rotha, Mary Clare, Frederick Valk, John Stuart, Barry Morse, Henry Oscar, Arthur Dulay, Moira Lister, Julian Dallas, Lily Kann.

Barry Stanton. *The Madness of King George* (aka *The Madness of George III*) (GB/1994/107m/C) D: Nicholas Hytner. B/on the play by Alan Bennett. C: Nigel Hawthorne, Helen Mirren, Rupert Everett, Amanda Donohoe, Julian Wadham, Caroline Harker, Ian Holm, Rupert Graves, Geoffrey Palmer, Jim Carter, Peter Bride-Kirk, Cyril Shaps.

497 Siegel, Benjamin "Bugsy" (1906–1947)

American gangster, Siegel built the first gambling palace (the Flamingo) in Las Vegas before being "removed" by the mob for not paying his bills. In the TV film *The Virginia Hill Story* (74) he was played by Harvey Kietel.

Brad Dexter. *The George Raft Story* (aka *Spin of a Coin*) (US/1961/105m/BW)

D: Joseph M. Newman. C: Ray Danton, Jayne Mansfield, Julie London, Barrie Chase, Frank Gorshin, Barbara Nichols, Neville Brand, Robert Strauss, Herschel Bernardi.

Warren Beatty. *Bugsy* (US/1991/135m/C) D: Barry Levinson. B/on the book *We Only Kill Each Other: The Life and Bad Times of Bugsy Siegel* by Dean Jennings. C: Annette Bening, Harvey Keitel, Ben Kingsley, Joe Mantegna, Elliott Gould, Wendy Phillips, Bill Graham, Don Carrara, Carmine Caridi, Ksenia Prohaska.

Armand Assante. *The Marrying Man* (US/1991/115m/C) D: Jerry Rees. C: Alec Baldwin, Kim Basinger, Robert Loggia, Elisabeth Shue, Paul Reiser, Fisher Stevens, Peter Dobson.

Richard Grieco. *Mobsters* (US/1991/104m/C) D: Michael Karbelnikoff. C: Christian Slater, Patrick Dempsey, Costas Mandylor, F. Murray Abraham, Anthony Quinn, Michael Gambon, Lara Flynn Boyle, Nicholas Sadler, Titus Welliver.

498 Sitting Bull (1832?–1890)

(Tanaka Yotanka) The most famous American Indian leader, Sitting Bull lead the combined Sioux, Cheyenne and Arapaho tribes in the defeat of **Custer** at the Little Big Horn. He was later shot and killed by Reservation police when fears arose that he would lead a rebellion over the Ghost Dance religion.

Chief Thundercloud. *Annie Oakley* (US/1935/79m/BW) D: George Stevens. C: Barbara Stanwyck, Preston Foster, Melvyn Douglas, Moroni Olsen, Dick Elliott.

J. Carrol Naish. *Annie Get Your Gun* (US/1950/107m/C) D: George Sidney. B/on the musical play, book by Herbert and Dorothy Fields. C: Betty Hutton, Howard Keel, Louis Calhern, Chief Yowlachie, Evelyn Beresford, John Mylong, Nino Pipitone.

Michael Granger. *Fort Vengeance* (US/1953/75m/C) D: Lesley Selander. C: James Craig, Rita Moreno, Keith Larsen, Reginald Denny, Morris Ankrum.

J. Carrol Naish. *Sitting Bull* (US/1954/105m/C) D: Sidney Salkow. C: Dale Robertson, Mary Murphy, Iron Eyes Cody, John Litel, Douglas Kennedy, John Hamilton.

John War Eagle. *Tonka* (aka *A Horse Named Comanche*) (US/1958/97m/C) D: Lewis R. Foster. B/on the novel *Comanche* by David Appel. C: Sal Mineo, Philip Carey, Jerome Courtland, Rafael Campos, Britt Lomond, Herbert Rudley.

Michael Pate. *The Great Sioux Massacre* (aka *Custer Massacre*) (aka *The Massacre at the Rosebud*) (US/1965/92m/C) D: Sidney Salkow. C: Joseph Cotten, Darren McGavin, Philip Carey, Julie Sommars, Nancy Kovack, Don Haggerty, Iron Eyes Cody.

Alain Cuny. *Do Not Touch the White Woman* (aka *Touche Pas La Femme Blanche*) (aka *Don't Touch White Women!*) (France/1974/108m/C) D: Marco Ferreri. C: Marcello Mastroianni, Catherine Deneuve, Michel Piccoli, Philippe Noiret, Ugo Tognazzi.

Frank Kaquitts. *Buffalo Bill and the Indians, Or Sitting Bull's History Lesson* (aka *Buffalo Bill and the Indians*) (US/1976/120m/C) D: Robert Altman. B/on the play *Indians* by Arthur Kopit. C: Paul Newman, Burt Lancaster, Joel Grey, Harvey Keitel, Geraldine Chaplin, Will Sampsen, Pat McCormick.

499 Smith, (Captain) Edward John (1850–1912)

Captain of the Titanic, Smith once told a reporter "I never saw a wreck and have never been wrecked, nor was I ever in any predicament that threatened to end in disaster. You see, I am not very good material for a story."

Brian Aherne. *Titanic* (US/1953/98m/BW) D: Jean Negulesco. C: Clifton Webb, Barbara Stanwyck, Robert Wagner, Audrey Dalton, Thelma Ritter, William Johnstone.

Laurence Naismith. *A Night to Remember* (GB/1958/91m/BW) D: Roy Baker. B/on the book by Walter Lord. C: Kenneth More, David McCallum, Jill Dixon, Tucker McGuire.

Harry Andrews. *S.O.S. Titanic* (GB-US/1980/105m/C) D: Billy Hale. C: David Janssen, Cloris Leachman, Susan Saint James, Helen Mirren, David Warner, Ian Holm.

Bernard Hill. *Titanic* (US/1997/193m/C) D: James Cameron. 11 Oscars, including: Best Picture, Director, Visual Effects, Music, Song, Cinematography, Sound, and Costumes. GG Best Film (drama), Best Director, Best Original Score, Best Original Song. C: Leonardo DeCaprio, Kate Winslet, Bily Zane, Kathy Bates, Frances Fisher, Gloria Stuart, Bill Paxton, David Warner, Victor Garber, Jonathan Hyde, Suzy Amis, Lewis Abernathy, Nicholas Cascone, Dr. Anatoly Sagalevitch, Danny Nucci, Jason Barry, Ewan Stewart, Ioan Gruffudd, Johnny Phillips, Mark Lindsay Chapman, Richard Graham, Paul Brightwell, Ron Danachie, Eric Braeden, Charlotte Chatton, Bernard Fox.

500 Spartacus (?–71 BC)

Roman gladiator who led a slave revolt against Rome (73 BC–71 BC), Spartacus was killed in battle and thousands of his followers were crucified.

Massimo Girotti. *Spartacus, the Gladiator* (aka *Sins of Rome*) (Italy/1953/72m/BW) D: Riccardo Freda. C: Gianna Maria Canale, Ludmilla Tcherina, Carlo Ninchi, Yves Vincent.

Kirk Douglas. *Spartacus* (US/1960/196m/C) D: Stanley Kubrick. B/on the novel by Howard Fast. Best Motion Picture, Drama (GG). C: Laurence Olivier, Tony Curtis, Jean Simmons, Charles Laughton, Peter Ustinov, John Gavin, Nina Foch.

Dan Vardis. *Spartacus and the Ten Gladiators* (aka *Day of Vengeance*) (Italy-Spain-France/1965/99m/C) D: Nick Nostro. C: Helga Line.

Vladimir Kozinets. *Wake Up Mukhin!* (USSR/1968/84m/C) D: Yakov Seghel. C: Sergei Shaqkurov, Lilia Alyoshnikova, Alexander Paleyes, Nikolai Ribnikov, Nikolai Sergeyev.

501 Stalin, Joseph Vissarionovich (1879–1953)

Successor to **V.I. Lenin**, Stalin ruled the Soviet Union for 30 years and is considered by many to have been as evil a dictator as **Adolf Hitler**. In films made for television he has been portrayed by Jose Ferrer in *Meeting at Pottsdam* (76),

Nehmiah Persoff in *F.D.R.—The Last Year* (80), David Burke in the mini series
Reilly: Ace of Spies (83), Colin Blakely in *Red Monarch* (83), Anatoly Chaguin-
ian in *The Winds of War* (83), Al Ruscio in *War and Remembrance* (89), Bernard
Kay in *The Kremlin Farewell* (90), Robert Duvall in *Stalin* (92), and by Michael
Caine in *World War II, When Lions Roared* (94). Stalin was also portrayed by
(who else but) Mikhail Gelovani in the unreleased Soviet film *Light Over Russia* (47).

I. Golshtab. *Lenin in October* (USSR/1937/111m/BW) D: Mikhail Romm. C:
Boris Shchukin, Vasily Vanin, Nikolai Okhlopkov, N. Svobodin.

Mikhail Gelovani. *Great Dawn* (aka *They Wanted Peace*) (USSR/1938/73m/
BW) D: Mikhail Chiaureli. C: F. Bagaschvili, K. Miuffko, Tamara Makarova.

Mikhail Gelovani. *The Man with the Gun* (aka *The Man with a Gun*) (USSR/
1938/88m/BW) D: Sergei Yutkevich. C: Maxim Shtrauch, Boris Tenin, Zoya
Federova, Nikolai Cherkasov.

Mikhail Gelovani. *Lenin in 1918* (USSR/1939/133m/BW) D: Mikhail Romm.
C: Boris Shchukin, Nikolai Cherkassov, Nikolai Okhlopkov, Vasily Vanin, V.
Markov.

Mikhail Gelovani, *Manhood* (aka *Courage*) (aka *Mut*) (aka *Muzhestvo*) (USSR/
1939/BW) D: Mikhail Kalatozov.

Mikhail Gelovani. *The Vyborg Side* (aka *New Horizons*) (USSR/1939/117–92m/
BW) D: Grigori Kozintsev & Leonid Trauberg. C: Boris Chirkov, Maxim Strauch,
Mikhail Zharov.

Mikhail Gelovani. *Wings of Victory* (aka *Valeri Chkalov*) (USSR/1941/97m/BW)
D: Mikhail Kalatozov. C: Vladimir Belokurov, Semyon Nedhinsky, Zenia
Tarasova.

Mikhail Gelovani. *Fortress on the Volga* (aka *Defence of Tsaritsin*) (USSR/1942/
77m/BW) D: Sergei & Georgi Vassiliev. C: Nikolai Bogoliubov, Mikhail Zharov,
Barbara Miasnikova.

Manart Kippen. *Mission to Moscow* (US/1943/123m/BW) D: Michael Curtiz.
B/on the book by Joseph E. Davies. C: Walter Huston, Ann Harding, Oscar
Homolka, George Tobias, Gene Lockhart, Frieda Inescourt, Eleanor Parker,
Richard Travis, Henry Daniell, Dudley Field Malone, Charles Trowbridge,
Georges Renavent, Clive Morgan, Captain Jack Young, Leigh Whipper, Doris
Lloyd, Olaf Hytten, Moroni Olsen.

Mikhail Gelovani. *The Vow* (USSR/1946/BW) D: Mikhail Chiaureli. C:
Sophia Giatsintova, Nikolai Bogolubov, Alexei Gribov.

Mikhail Gelovani. *The Fall of Berlin* (USSR/1949/124m/C) D: Mikhail Chiaureli. C: Oleg Froelich, V. Savelyev, M. Novakova, Victor Stanitsin, Y. Verikh,
M. Petrunkin.

Alexei Diki. *The First Front* (USSR/1949/81m/BW) D: Vladimir Petrov. Part
I of *Battle of Stalingrad* (50). C: Y. Shumsky, V. Merkuryev, B. Livanov, Nikolai
Cherkasov, Victor Stanitsin, M. Astangov, K. Mikhailov, N. Simonov.

Alexei Diki. *The Battle of Stalingrad, (Parts I and II)* (USSR/1950/BW) D:
Vladimir Petrov. Part I of *The Battle of Stalingrad* was released as *The First Front*
in 1949. C: Yuri Shumsky, Boris Livanov, Nikolai Simonov, M. Astangov, Nikolai Plotnikov.

Mikhail Gelovani. *Miners of the Don* (USSR/1951/93m/C) D: L. Lukov. C: V. Khokhriakov, S. Lukianov, Boris Chirkov, Katia Luchko, V. Merkuriev.

Mikhail Gelovani. *The Unforgettable Year: 1919* (USSR/1952/C) D: Mikhail Chiaureli. B/on the play by Vsevold Vishnevsky. C: I. Molchanov, Boris Andreyev, M. Kovaleva, Yevgeni Samoilov, Victor Stanitsine, V. Koltsov, Gnat Yura, L. Korsakov, Sergei Lukyanov.

Maurice Manson. *The Girl in the Kremlin* (US/1957/81m/BW) D: Russell Birdwell. C: Lex Barker, Zsa Zsa Gabor, Jeffrey Stone, William Schallert, Natalie Daryll, Michael Fox.

A. Kobaladze. *In the October Days* (USSR/1958/116m/C) D: Sergei Vasiliev. C: V. Chestnokov, V. Brener, A. Fyodorinov, Galina Vodyanitskaya.

Buhuti Zakariadze. *The Great Battle* (aka *Liberation*) (USSR-Poland-Yugoslavia-Italy/1969/118m/C) D: Yuri Ozerov. C: Stanislav Yaskevich, Ivo Garani, Fritz Diez, Yuri Durov.

Saul Katz. *Why Russians Are Revolting* (US/1970/91m/BW) D: Neil Sullivan. C: Neil Sullivan, D.F. Barry, Wes Carter, Ed Maywood, Seneca Ames, George Badera.

James Hazeldine. *Nicholas and Alexandra* (GB/1971/183m/C) D: Franklin J. Schaffner. B/on the book by Robert K. Massie. C: Michael Jayston, Janet Suzman, Roderic Noble, Fiona Fullerton, Harry Andrews, Irene Worth, Tom Baker, Ralph Truman, Alexander Knox, John McEnery, Michael Bryant, Brian Cox, Ian Holm, Roy Dotrice, Martin Potter.

Colin Blakely. *Red Monarch* (GB/1983/101m/C) D: Jack Gold. B/on short stories by Yuri Krotkov. C: David Suchet, Carroll Baker, Ian Hogg, Nigel Stock, Lee Montague.

Ramaz Chkhikvadze. *Victory* (aka *Pobeda*) (USSR/1984/160m/C) D: Yevgeni Matveyev. B/on the novel by Aleksandr Chakovsky. C: Aleksandr Mikhajlov, Andrei Mironov, Klaus-Peter Thiele, Georgi Menglet, Algimantas Masiulis, Mikhail Ulyanov, Viktor Ilyichyov, Nikolai Zasukhin.

Alexandre Zbruev. *The Inner Circle* (US/1991/137–122m/C) D: Andrei Konchalovsky. C: Tom Hulce, Lolita Davidovich, Bob Hoskins, Feodor Chaliapin, Jr., Viktor Balabanov.

F. Murray Abraham. *Children of the Revolution* (Australia/1996/1101m) D: Peter Duncan. C: Judy Davis, Sam Neill, Richard Roxborgh, Geoffrey Rush, Rachel Griffiths, Russell Kiefel, John Gaden.

502 Stanley, Sir Henry Morton (1841–1904)

Anglo-American journalist and explorer, Stanley is primarily remembered for his successful African expedition in search of **David Livingstone**.

Hugh McDermott. *David Livingstone* (GB/1936/71m/BW) D: James A. Fitzpatrick. C: Percy Marmont, Marian Spencer, Pamela Stanley, James Carew.

Spencer Tracy. *Stanley and Livingstone* (US/1939/101m/BW) D: Henry King. C: Nancy Kelly, Richard Greene, Walter Brennan, Charles Coburn, Cedric Hardwicke, Henry Hull.

503 Stanton, Edwin McMasters (1814–1869)

Secretary of War to **Abraham Lincoln**, Stanton was later appointed to the Supreme Court but died before he was able to serve.

Oscar Apfel. *Abraham Lincoln* (US/1930/97m/BW) D: D.W. Griffith. C: Walter Huston, Una Merkel, Kay Hammond, E. Alyn Warren, Edgar Deering, Hobart Bosworth, Fred Warren, Frank Campeau, Francis Ford, Ian Keith, Cameron Prud'Homme.

Edwin Maxwell. *The Plainsman* (US/1936/115m/BW) D: Cecil B. DeMille. B/on the novel *Wild Bill Hickok* by Frank J. Wilstach. C: Gary Cooper, Jean Arthur, James Ellison, Porter Hall, John Miljan, Frank McGlynn, Leila McIntyre, Charles H. Herzinger.

Stuart Holmes. *Trailin' West* (aka *On Secret Service*) (US/1936/56m/BW) D: Noel Smith. B/on the story *On Secret Service* by Anthony Coldeway. C: Dick Foran, Paula Stone, Gordon (Bill) Elliott, Robert Barrat, Joseph Crehan, Jim Thorpe.

Charles French. *Courage of the West* (US/1937/56m/BW) D: Joseph H. Lewis. C: Bob Baker, Lois January, J. Farrell MacDonald, Albert Russell, Thomas Monk.

Richard Cutting. *The Gun That Won the West* (US/1955/69m/C) D: William Castle. C: Dennis Morgan, Paula Raymond, Richard Denning, Robert Bice, Howard Wright, Roy Gordon.

Robert Middleton. *The Lincoln Conspiracy.* (US/1977/90m/C) D: James L. Conway. B/on the book by David Balsiger & Charles E. Sellier, Jr. C: Bradford Dillman, John Anderson, Frances Fordham, E.J. Andre, Wallace K. Wilkinson, John Dehner, Whit Bissell.

504 Starr, Belle (1848–1889)

(Myra Belle Shirley) The West's "Bandit Queen," Starr was actually a small-time horse thief who spent time with several outlaw lovers including **Cole Younger.** Her exploits and beauty have been much exaggerated in several Hollywood movies.

Natalie Moorhead. *Heart of Arizona* (US/1938/68m/BW) D: Lesley Selander. C: William Boyd, George "Gabby" Hayes, Russell Hayden, John Elliott, Dorothy Short.

Gene Tierney. *Belle Starr* (US/1941/87m/C) D: Irving Cummings. C: Randolph Scott, Dana Andrews, Shepperd Strudwick, Chill Wills, Charles Trowbridge, Kermit Maynard.

Sally Payne. *Robin Hood of the Pecos* (US/1941/59m/BW) D: Joseph Kane. C: Roy Rogers, George "Gabby" Hayes, Marjorie Reynolds, Eddie Acuff, Jay Novello, Roscoe Ates.

Isabel Jewell. *Badman's Territory* (US/1946/98m/BW) D: Tim Whelan. C: Randolph Scott, Ann Richards, George "Gabby" Hayes, Chief Thundercloud, Lawrence Tierney, Tom Tyler, Steve Brodie, Phil Warren, William Moss, Nestor Paiva, Emory Parnell.

Isabel Jewell. *Belle Starr's Daughter* (US/1947/86m/BW) D: Lesley Selander. C: George Montgemery, Rod Cameron, Ruth Roman, Wallace Ford, Charles Kemper.

Jane Russell. *Montana Belle* (US/1952/81m/BW) D: Allan Dwan. C: George Brent, Scott Brady, Forrest Tucker, Andy Devine, Ray Teal, Rory Mallinson, Holly Bane.

Merry Anders. *Young Jesse James* (US/1960/73m/BW) D: William F. Claxton. C: Ray Stricklyn, Willard Parker, Robert Dix, Emile Meyer, Bob Palmer, Johnny O'Neill.

Sally Starr. *The Outlaws Is Coming* (US/1965/88m/BW) D: Norman Maurer. C: Larry Fine, Moe Howard, Joe De Rita, Nancy Kovack, Murray Alper, Joe Bolton, Bill Camfield, Hal Fryar, Johnny Ginger, Wayne Mack, Ed McDonnell, Bruce Sedley, Paul Shannon.

Elsa Martinelli. *The Belle Starr Story* (aka *Il Mio Corpo Per Un Poker*) (aka *Belle Starr*) (Italy/1967/90m/C) D: Nathan Wich (Lina Wertmuller). C: Robert Wood.

Pat Quinn. *Zachariah* (US/1971/92m/C) D: George Englund. C: John Rubinstein, Don Johnson, Country Joe and the Fish, Elvin Jones, Doug Kershaw, Dick Van Patten, The James Gang, The New York Rock Ensemble.

Pamela Reed. *The Long Riders* (US/1980/99m/C) D: Walter Hill. C: David Carradine, Keith Carradine, Robert Carradine, James Keach, Stacy Keach, Dennis Quaid, Randy Quaid, Kevin Brophy, Christopher Guest, Nicholas Guest, James Remar, Fran Ryan, Savannah Smith, Harry Carey, Jr., James Whitmore, Jr., Shelby Leverington.

505 Stauffenburg, Claus, Graf von (1907–1944)

German general who attempted to assassinate **Adolf Hitler** with a bomb in 1944, Stauffenburg was caught and executed.

Eduard Franz. *The Desert Fox* (aka *Rommel—Desert Fox*) (US/1951/88m/BW) D: Henry Hathaway. B/on the book *Rommel* by Desmond Young. C: James Mason, Cedric Hardwicke, Jessica Tandy, Luther Adler, Leo G. Carroll, John Hoyt, Jack Baston.

Wolfgang Preiss. *Der 20 Juli* (aka *The 20th July*) (Germany/1955) D: Falk Harnack. C: Werner Hinz.

Bernhard Wicki. *The Jackboot Mutiny* (aka *Es Geschah Am 20 Juli*) (Germany/1955/85m/BW) D: G.W. Pabst. C: Karl Ludwig Diehl, Carl Wery, Jochen Hauer, Kurt Meisel.

William Sargent. *Hitler* (aka *Women of Nazi Germany*) (US/1962/107m/BW) D: Stuart Heisler. C: Richard Basehart, Cordula Trantow, Maria Emo, Martin Kosleck, John Banner, Martin Brandt, Gregory Gay, Thodore Marcuse, Rick Traeger, John Mitchum, G. Stanley Jones, Walter Kohler, Carl Esmond, Berry Kroeger.

Gerard Buhr. *The Night of the Generals* (GB-France/1967/148m/C) D: Anatole Litvak. B/on the novel by Hans Helmut Kirst and the story *The Wary Transgressor* by James Hadley Chase. C: Peter O'Toole, Omar Sharif, Tom Courtenay, Donald Pleasence, Joanna Pettet, Phillippe Noiret, Christopher Plummer, John Gregson, Coral Browne.

506 Stein, Gertrude (1874–1946)

American author who lived in Paris from 1905, Stein's works include *Three Lives* and *The Autobiography of Alice B. Toklas*. (See **Toklas, Alice B.**)

Bernard Cribbins. *The Adventures of Picasso* (Sweden/1978/92m/C) D: Tage Daniellson. C: Gosta Ekman, Hans Alfredson, Margaretha Krook, Wilfrid Brambell, Per Oscarsson.

Linda Bassett. *Waiting for the Moon* (US/1987/88m/C) D: Jill Godmillow. C: Linda Hunt, Bernadette LaFont, Bruce McGill, Jacques Boudet, Andrew McCarthy.

Elsa Raven. *The Moderns* (US/1988/126m/C) D: Alan Rudolph. C: Keith Carradine, Linda Fiorentino, Genevieve Bujold, Geraldine Chaplin, Kevin J. O'Connor, Ali Giron, John Lone, Wallace Shawn.

507 Stevens, Jenny (1878–?)

Known as "Little Britches" when she rode with the **Doolin-Dalton** gang, Jennie and her partner **Cattle Annie** were captured and sent to prison.

Diane Lane. *Cattle Annie and Little Britches* (US/1980/97m/C) D: Lamont Johnson. B/on the novel by Robert Ward. C: Burt Lancaster, Rod Steiger, John Savage, Scott Glenn, Amanda Plummer.

508 Stevens, Thaddeus (1792–1868)

A Northern Congressman and strict Reconstructionist following the Civil War, Stevens was the driving force in the impeachment of **Andrew Johnson**.

Lionel Barrymore. *Tennessee Johnson* (aka *The Man on America's Conscience*) (US/1942/103m/BW) D: William Dieterle. C: Van Heflin, Ruth Hussey, Marjorie Main, Regis Toomey, Montagu Love, Porter Hall, Morris Ankrum, Harry Worth, Ed O'Neill, Harrison Greene, Charles Dingle, Grant Withers, Lynne Carver, Noah Beery, Sr.

E.J. Andre. *The Lincoln Conspiracy.* (US/1977/90m/C) D: James L. Conway. B/on the book by David Balsiger & Charles E. Sellier, Jr. C: Bradford Dillman, John Anderson, Frances Fordham, Robert Middleton, Wallace K. Wilkinson, John Dehner, Whit Bissell.

509 Strauss, Johann, Sr. (1804–1849)

Creator of the Viennese Waltz, Strauss also composed in other musical forms including his most famous composition: "The Radetzky March."

Hans Junkermann. *So Lang Noch Ein Walzer von Strauss Erklingt* (Germany/1931) D: Conrad Wiene. C: Gustav Fröhlich.

Anton Walbrook (Adolf Wohlbruck). *Waltz Time in Vienna* (aka *Walzerkrieg*) (Germany/1933/80m/BW) D: Ludwig Berger. C: Hanna Waag, Heinz von Cleve, Willy Fritsch.

Edmund Gwenn. *Strauss' Great Waltz* (aka *Waltzes from Vienna*) (GB/1934/80m/BW) D: Alfred Hitchcock. B/on the musical play *Great Waltz* by Heinz Reichert, A.M. Willner & Ernst Marischka. C: Esmond Knight, Jessie Matthews, Fay Compton, Robert Hale.

Paul Hörbiger. *Unsterblicher Walzer* (Germany/1939/BW) D: E.W. Emo. C: Fred Liewehr.

Anton Walbrook. *Vienna Waltzes* (aka *Wien Tanzt*) (Austria/1951/93m/BW) D: Emile Edwin Reinert. C: Marthe Harell, Lilly Stepanek, Fritz Imhoff, Eva Leiter.

Eduard Strauss. *The Story of Vickie* (aka *Young Victoria*) (aka *Dover Interlude*) (aka *Girl Days of a Queen*) (aka *Mädchenjahre Einer Königin*) (Austria/1955/108–

90m/C) D: Ernst Marischka. B/on the diaries of Queen Victoria. C: Romy Schneider, Adrian Hoven, Magda Schneider, Karl Ludwig Diehl, Christl Mardayn, Paul Horbiger, Alfred Neugebauer, Otto Tressler, Rudolf Lenz, Fred Liewehr, Peter Weck.

Brian Aherne. *The Waltz King* (US/1963/95m/C) D: Steve Previn. C: Kerwin Matthews, Senta Berger, Peter Kraus, Fritz Eckhardt.

Nigel Patrick. *The Great Waltz* (US/1972/135m/C) D: Andrew L. Stone. C: Horst Bucholz, Mary Costa, Rossano Brazzi, Yvonne Mitchell, Dominique Weber, J. Schonburg-Hartenstein.

510 Strauss, Johann, Jr. (1825–1899)

Austrian composer known as "The Waltz King," Strauss' famous works include "The Blue Danube" and "Tales from the Vienna Woods."

Gustav Fröhlich. *So Lang Noch Ein Walzer von Strauss Erklingt* (Germany/1931) D: Conrad Wiene. C: Hans Junkermann.

Esmond Knight. *Strauss' Great Waltz* (aka *Waltzes from Vienna*) (GB/1934/80m/BW) D: Alfred Hitchcock. B/on the musical play *Great Waltz* by Heinz Reichert, A.M. Willner & Ernst Marischka. C: Jessie Matthews, Edmund Gwenn, Fay Compton, Robert Hale.

Alfred Jerger. *Immortal Melodies* (aka *Unsterbliche Melodien*) (Austria/1937/73m/BW) D: Heinz Paul. B/on the biography of *Johann Strauss* by Hella Moja. C: Maria Paudler, Leo Slezak, Lizzi Holzscruh, Hanns Homma.

Fernand Gravet. *The Great Waltz* (US/1938/107m/BW) D: Julien Duvivier. C: Luise Rainer, Miliza Korjus, Hugh Herbert, Lionel Atwill, Henry Hull, Curt Bois, George Houston.

Fred Liewehr. *Unsterblicher Walzer* (Germany/1939/BW) D: E.W. Emo. C: Paul Hörbiger.

Edmund Schellhammer. *Operetta* (Germany/1949/106m/BW) D: Willi Forst. C: Willi Forst, Maria Holst, Dora Komar, Paul Hoerbiger, Leo Slezak, Curd (Curt) Jurgens.

Bernhard Wicki. *The Eternal Waltz* (aka *Ewiger Walzer*) (Germany/1954/97m/C) D: Paul Verhoeven. C: Hilde Krahl, Annemarie Dueringer, Friedl Loor, Eric Frey, Arnulf Schroeder, Hans Putz, Eduard Strauss, Jr.

Kerwin Mathews. *The Waltz King* (US/1963/95m/C) D: Steve Previn. C: Brian Aherne, Senta Berger, Peter Kraus, Fritz Eckhardt.

Horst Bucholz. *The Great Waltz* (US/1972/135m/C) D: Andrew L. Stone. C: Mary Costa, Rossano Brazzi, Nigel Patrick, Yvonne Mitchell, Dominique Weber, J. Schonburg-Hartenstein.

Oliver Tobias. *Johann Strauss, The King Without a Crown* (Austria-Hungary/1988/95m/C) D: Franz Antel. C: Mary Crosby.

511 Strindberg, Johan August (1849–1912)

Swedish dramatist, Strindberg is best remembered for his plays *The Dance of Death* and *Miss Julie.*

Alf Kare Strindberg. *Edvard Munch* (Sweden-Norway/1976/215m/C) D: Peter Watkins. C: Geir Westby, Gro Fraas, Johan Halsborg, Iselin Bast.

Max von Sydow. *The Wolf at the Door* (France-Denmark/1986/102m/C) D: Henning Carlsen. C: Donald Sutherland, Valerie Morea, Sofie Graboel, Yves Barsack.

Hermann Schmid. *Weininger's Last Night* (Austria /1991/100m/C) D: Paulus Manker. B/on the play *The Soul of a Jew* by Joshua Sobol. C: Paulus Manker, Sieghardt Rupp.

512 Sullivan, Sir Arthur Seymour (1842–1900)

English composer, Sullivan wrote the music for the team of **Gilbert** and Sullivan.

Claud Allister. *Lillian Russell* (US/1940/127m/BW) D: Irving Cummings. C: Alice Faye, Edward Arnold, Don Ameche, Henry Fonda, Warren William, Nigel Bruce, Eddie Foy, Jr., William B. Davidson, Leo Carillo, Milburn Stone.

Muir Mathieson. *The Magic Box* (GB/1952/118m/C) D: John Boulting. B/on the book *Friese-Greene, Closeup of an Inventor* by Ray Allister. C: Robert Donat, Maria Schell, Robert Beatty, Margaret Johnston, Renee Asherson, Richard Attenborough, Leo Genn, Marius Goring, William Hartnell, Joan Hickson.

Maurice Evans. *The Great Gilbert and Sullivan* (aka *The Story of Gilbert and Sullivan*) (GB/1953/105m/C) D: Sydney Gilliat. B/on The *Gilbert and Sullivan Book* by Leslie Bailey. C: Robert Morley, Eileen Herlie, Peter Finch, Martyn Green, Muriel Aked.

Allan Corduner. *Topsy-Turvy* (US-GB/1999/160m/C) D: Mike Leigh. NYC Directors Award. C: Jim Broadbent, Lesley Manville, Eleanor David, Ron Cook, Timothy Spall, Kevin McKidd, Martin Savage, Shirley Henderson, Dorothy Atkinson, Wendy Nottingham, Jonathan Aris, Louise Gold.

513 Sullivan, John L. (Lawrence) (1858–1918)

The last bare-knuckles Heavyweight Champion of the World, when boxing gloves were introduced Sullivan lost the title to **James Corbett**.

George Walsh. *The Bowery* (US/1933/92m/BW) D: Raoul Walsh. B/on the novel *Chuck Connors* by Michael L. Simmons & Bessi Roth Solomon. C: Wallace Beery, George Raft, Jackie Cooper, Fay Wray, Pert Kelton, Lillian Harmer, Herman Bing.

Bill Hoolahan. *Diamond Jim* (US/1935/93m/BW) D: Edward Sutherland. B/on the book *Diamond Jim Brady* by Parker Morell. C: Edward Arnold, Jean Arthur, Binnie Barnes.

John Kelly. *The Gentleman from Louisiana* (US/1936/67m/BW) D: Irving Pichel. C: Edward Quillan, Chic Sale, Charlotte Henry, Charles Wilson, Matt McHugh, Ruth Gillette, Holmes Herbert.

Ward Bond. *Gentleman Jim* (US/1942/104m/BW) D: Raoul Walsh. B/on the book *The Roar of the Crowd* by James J. Corbett. C: Erroll Flynn, Alexis Smith, Jack Carson, Alan Hale, John Loder, William Frawley, Minor Watson, Rhys Williams.

John Kelly. *My Gal Sal* (US/1942/103m/C) D: Irving Cummings. B/on the book *My Brother Paul* by Theodore Dreiser. C: Rita Hayworth, Victor Mature, John Sutton, Carole Landis, James Gleason, Phil Silvers, Walter Catlett, Barry Downing, Mona Maris.

Greg McClure. *The Great John L.* (aka *A Man Called Sullivan*) (US/1945/ 96m/BW) D: Frank Tuttle. C: Linda Darnell, Barbara Britton, Lee Sullivan, Otto Kruger, Rory Calhoun.

514 Sundance Kid, The (1861–1908?)

(Harry Longbaugh) Considered one of the fastest gunmen of the West, Sundance had been robbing banks for several years before teaming up with **Butch Cassidy**. The pair moved to South America where they were reportedly killed in 1908.

Arthur Kennedy. *Cheyenne* (aka *The Wyoming Kid*) (US/1947/100m/BW) D: Raoul Walsh. C: Dennis Morgan, Jane Wyman, Janis Paige, Bruce Bennett, Alan Hale.

Robert Ryan. *Return of the Bad Men* (US/1948/90m/BW) D: Ray Enright. C: Randolh Scott, George "Gabby" Hayes, Anne Jeffreys, Steve Brodie, Richard Powers, Robert Bray, Lex Barker, Walter Reed, Michael Harvey, Dean White, Robert Armstrong.

Ian MacDonald. *The Texas Rangers* (US/1951/68m/C) D: Phil Karlson. C: George Montgomery, Gale Storm, Noah Beery, Jr., William Bishop, John Dehner, John Doucette.

William Bishop. *Wyoming Renegades* (US/1955/73m/C) D: Fred Sears. C: Phil Carey, Gene Evans, Martha Hyer, Douglas Kennedy, Roy Roberts, George Keymas, A. Guy Teague, Aaron Spelling, John (Bob) Cason, Don Beddoe.

Scott Brady. *The Maverick Queen* (US/1955/92m/C) D: Joseph Kane. B/on the novel by Zane Grey. C: Barbara Stanwyck, Barry Sullivan, Mary Murphy, Howard Petrie.

Alan Hale, Jr. *The Three Outlaws* (US/1956/74m/BW) D: Sam Newfield. C: Neville Brand, Bruce Bennett, Jose Gonzalez, Jeanne Carmen, Stanley Andrews.

Russell Johnson. *Badman's Country* (US/1958/85m/BW) D: Fred F. Sears. C: George Montgomery, Buster Crabbe, Neville Brand, Karin Booth, Gregory Wolcott, Malcolm Atterbury, Richard Devon, Morris Ankrum.

John David Chandler. *Return of the Gunfighter* (US/1967/100m/C) D: James Neilson. Made for U.S. TV, released theatrically in Europe. C: Robert Taylor, Ana Martin, Chad Everett, John Crawford, Lyle Bettger, Mort Mills, Michael Pate.

Robert Redford * Best Actor (BFA-1970). *Butch Cassidy and the Sundance Kid* (US/1969/112m/C) D: George Roy Hill. Best Film, Best Director (BFA-1970). C: Paul Newman, Katherine Ross, Strother Martin, Jeff Corey, Henry Jones, Ted Cassidy, Charles Dierkop, Cloris Leachman, Sam Elliott.

William Kaat. *Butch and Sundance: the Early Days* (US/1979/110m/C) D: Richard Lester. C: Tom Berenger, Jill Eikenberry, John Schuck, Brian Dennehy, Paul Plunkett, Jeff Corey, Peter Weller.

515 Sutherland, (Gen.) Richard Kerns (1893–1966)

Dynamic, efficient American general, Sutherland served as **MacArthur's** Chief of Staff throughout World War II.

Ivan Bonar. *MacArthur* (US/1977/128m/C) D: Joseph Sargent. C: Gregory

Peck, Ed Flanders, Dan O'Herlihy, Ward Costello, Nicholas Coster, Art Fleming, Addison Powell, Marj Dusay, Kenneth Tobey, John Fujioka, Fred Stuthman, Sandy Kenyon.

Michael Pate. *Death of a Soldier* (Australia/1986/93m/C) D: Phillippe Mora. C: James Coburn, Reb Brown, Bill Hunter, Jon Sidney, Maurie Fields, Belinda Davey.

Michael Nissman. *Farewell to the King* (US/1989/117m/C) D: John Milius. B/on the novel by Pierre Schoendoerffer. C: Nick Nolte, Nigel Havers, Frank McRae, John Bennett Perry.

516 Sutter, John Augustus (1803–1880)

A German immigrant, Sutter had established a successful ranch in California until gold was discovered in 1848. His lands were overrun with prospectors, he lost his holdings and eventually went bankrupt.

Edward Arnold. *Sutter's Gold* (US/1936/69m/BW) D: James Cruze. B/on the novel *L'Or* by Blaise Cendrars. C: Lee Tracy, Binnie Barnes, Katherine Alexander, Addison Richards, Harry Carey, Montagu Love, Harry Stubbs, John Miljan, Robert Warwick.

Luis Trenker. *The Emperor of California* (aka *Der Kaiser von Kalifornien*) (Germany/1936/100–80m/BW) D: Luis Trenker. B/on the novel *L'Or* by Blaise Cendrars. C: Victoria von Bellasko, Werner Konig, Karl Zwingmann, Elsie Aulinger.

Edwin Maxwell. *Kit Carson* (US/1940/97m/BW) D: George B. Seitz. C: Jon Hall, Lynn Bari, Dana Andrews, Raymond Hatton, Harold Huber.

517 Talleyrand (1754–1838)

(Charles Maurice de Talleyrand-Pèrigord) French statesman, Talleyrand served in various posts from 1789 until 1834, influencing the governments of **Robespierre, Napoleon, Louis XVIII and Louis Philippe**.

John T. Murray. *Alexander Hamilton* (US/1931/73m/BW) D: John G. Adolfi. B/on the play by George Arliss & Mary Hamlin. C: George Arliss, Doris Kenyon, Alan Mowbray, Montagu Love, Morgan Wallace, Gwendolyn Logan, Charles Middleton, Lionel Belmore.

Georges Renavent. *The House of Rothschild* (US/1934/94m/C) D: Alfred Werker. B/on the play by George Humbert Westley. C: George Arliss, Boris Karloff, Loretta Young, Robert Young, C. Aubrey Smith, Florence Arliss, Alan Mowbray, Lumsden Hare, Holmes Herbert.

Gibb McLaughlin. *The Iron Duke* (GB/1935/80m/BW) D: Victor Saville. C: George Arliss, Gladys Cooper, Emlyn Williams, Ellaline Terriss, Allan Aynesworth, Felix Aylmer, Gerald Lawrence, Frederick Leister, Edmund Willard, Farren Soutar.

Augusto Marcacci. *Campo di Maggio* (aka *100 Days of Napoleon*) (Italy/1936/100m/BW) D: Giovacchino Forzano. C: Corrado Racca, Emilia Varini, Pino Locchi, Rosa Stradner, Enzo Biliotti, Lamberto Picasso, Ernseto Marini.

Reginald Owen. *Conquest* (aka *Marie Walewska*) (US/1937/115m/BW) D:

Clarence Brown. B/on the novel *Pani Walewska* by Waclaw Gasiorowski. C: Greta Garbo, Charles Boyer, Alan Marshal, Henry Stephenson, Ien Wul, Leif Erikson.

Pizani. *The Pearls of the Crown* (France/1937/120–100m/BW) D: Sacha Guitry & Christian-Jaque. C: Sacha Guitry, Jacqueline Delubac, Lyn Harding, Ermete Zacconi, Marguerite Moreno, Yvette Plenne, Catalano, Arletty, Percy Marmont, Derrick De Marney, Barbara Shaw, Simone Renant, Jean Louis Barrault, Emile Drain, Enrico Glori, Renee Saint-Cyr, Claude Dauphin, Aime-Simon Gerard.

Frank Cellier. *A Royal Divorce* (GB/1938/85m/BW) D: Jack Raymond. B/on the novel *Josephine* by Jacques Thery. C: Ruth Chatterton, Pierre Blanchar, John Laurie, Jack Hawkins, David Farrar, Allan Jeayes, Lawrence Hanray, Auriol Lee.

Albert Lieven. *The Young Mr. Pitt* (GB/1942/118m/BW) D: Carol Reed. C: Robert Donat, Robert Morley, Phyllis Calvert, Raymond Lovell, Max Adrian, Felix Aylmer, Stephen Haggard, Geoffrey Atkins, John Mills, Herbert Lom, Agnes Laughlan.

Sacha Guitry. *Le Diable Boiteux* (France/1948) D: Sacha Guitry. C: Maurice Schutz, Emile Drain.

John Hoyt. *Désirée* (US/1954/110m/C) D: Henry Koster. B/on the novel by Annemarie Selinko. C: Marlon Brando, Jean Simmons, Merle Oberon, Michael Rennie, Elizabeth Sellars, Cameron Mitchell, Cathleen Nesbitt, Sam Gilman, Alan Napier.

Sacha Guitry. *Napoleon* (France/1954/190m/C) D: Sacha Guitry. C: Jean-Pierre Aumont, Gianna Maria Canale, Jeanne Boitel, Pierre Brasseur, Daniel Gelin, O.W. Fisher, Raymond Pellegrin, Danielle Darrieux, Lana Marconi, Michele Morgan, Erich von Stroheim, Dany Roby, Henri Vidal, Clement Duhour, Serge Regianni, Maria Schell.

Charles Regnier. *Queen Luise* (aka *Königin Luise*) (Germany/1957/102m/C) D: Wolfgang Liebeneiner. C: Ruth Leuwerik, Rene Deltgen, Dieter Borsche, Bernhard Wicki.

Jean Mercure. *Austerlitz* (aka *The Battle of Austerlitz*) (France-Italy-Yugoslavia/1959/166m/C) D: Abel Gance. C: Pierre Mondy, Martine Carol, Jack Palance, Orson Welles, Claudia Cardinale, Georges Marchal, Roland Bartrop, Anthony Stuart, Jean Marais, Vittorio De Sica, Ettore Manni.

Paul Meurisse. *Der Kongress Amüsiert Sich* (Germany-Austria/1966/98m/C) D: Geza von Radvanvi. C: Lilli Palmer, Curt Jurgens, Hannes Messemer, Wolfgang Kieling, Brett Halsey.

Taylor, Zachary *see* 577

518 Tchiakovsky, Peter Ilyich (1840–1893)

Influential Russian composer, Tchaikovsky's famous works include the ballets *Swan Lake, The Nutcracker* and *The Sleeping Beauty*.

Hans Stuwe. *Es War Eine Rauschende Ballnacht* (aka *It Was a Gay Ball Night*) (Germany/1939/BW) D: Carl Froelich. C: Paul Dahlke, Zarah Leander, Fritz Rasp, Marika Rokk, Leo Slezak.

Alfonso D'Artega. *Carnegie Hall* (US/1947/136m/BW) D: Edgar G. Ulmer. C: Marsha Hunt.

Frank Sundstrom. *Song of My Heart* (US/1947/85m/BW) D: Benjamin Glazer. C: Audrey Lang, Cedric Hardwicke, David Leonard, John Hamilton, Lewis Howard, Robert Barron.

Innokenti Smoktunovsky. *Tchaikovsky* (USSR/1970/150m/C) D: Igor Talankin. C: B. Strjeltchik, E. Larionov, Antonia Chouranova.

Richard Chamberlain. *The Music Lovers* (GB/1971/122m/C) D: Ken Russell. B/on the novel *Beloved Friend* by Catherine Drinker Bowen & Barbara von Meck. C: Glenda Jackson, Max Adrian, Christopher Gable, Ken Colley, Izabella Telezynska.

519 Tecumseh (1768?–1813)

Native American leader (Shawnee), Tecumseh tried to forge an alliance among Indian tribes to withstand the onslaught of the white invaders.

Noble Johnson. *Ten Gentlemen from West Point* (US/1942/102m/BW) D: Henry Hathaway. C: George Montgomery, Maureen O'Hara, John Sutton, Laird Cregar, Douglas Dumbrille, Ralph Byrd.

Jay Silverheels. *Brave Warrior* (US/1952/73m/C) D: Spencer G. Bennett. C: Jon Hall, Christine Larson, Michael Ansara, James Seay, Rory Mallinson.

520 Thaw, Harry Kendall (1872–1947)

A deranged millionaire, Thaw murdered **Stanford White** for believed prior indiscretions with Thaw's wife, showgirl Evelyn Nesbit. Thaw was found not guilty by reason of insanity and committed to the New York Asylum for the Criminally Insane. Nesbit was played by Joan Collins in *The Girl in the Red Velvet Swing* and by Elizabeth McGovern in *Ragtime*.

Farley Granger. *The Girl in the Red Velvet Swing* (US/1955/109m/C) D: Richard Fleischer. C: Ray Milland, Joan Collins, Luther Adler, Cornelia Otis Skinner, Glenda Farrell, Richard Travis.

Robert Joy. *Ragtime* (US/1981/155m/C) D: Milos Forman. B/on the novel by E.L. Doctorow. C: James Cagney, Brad Dourif, Moses Gunn, Elizabeth McGovern, Pat O'Brien, Kenneth McMillan, Donald O'Connor, James Olson, Mandy Patinkin, Howard E. Rollins, Robert Boyd, Jeff DeMunn, Norman Mailer, Mary Steenburgen.

521 Thomas, Saint

One of **Jesus Christ's** Apostles and the patron saint of Portugal, Thomas did not believe in the Resurrection until he had touched Jesus' wounds, which coined the phrase "Doubting Thomas." He was portrayed by Bruce Lidington in the TV mini-series *Jesus of Nazareth* (77), and by Leonardo Treviglio in the TV film *The Day Christ Died* (80).

Michael Wager. *King of Kings* (US/1961/168m/C) D: Nicholas Ray. C: Jeffrey Hunter, Siobhan McKenna, Hurd Hatfield, Viveca Lindfors, Rita Gam, Carmen Sevilla, Rip Torn, Brigid Bazlen, Harry Guardino, Frank Thring, Guy Rolfe, Maurice Marsac, Gregoire Aslan, Royal Dano, Robert Ryan, Gerard Tichy, Tino Barrero, Jose Antonio, Orson Welles (Narrator).

Rosario Migale. *The Gospel According to St. Matthew* (France-Italy/1964/ 142m/BW) D: Pier Paolo Pasolini. B/on the *New Testament* book of *Matthew*. C: Enrique Irazoqui, Susanna Pasolini, Mario Socrate, Marcello Morante, Alfonso Gatto, Rodolfo Wilcock, Francesco Leonetti, Amerigo Bevilacqua, Otello Sestilli, Settimio Di Porto, Ferruccio Nuzzo, Alessandro Tosca, Paolo Tedesco, Franca Cupane, Giacomo Morante.

Tom Reese. *The Greatest Story Ever Told* (US/1965/141m/C) D: George Stevens. B/on the book by Fulton Oursler. C: Max von Sydow, Dorothy McGuire, Robert Loggia, Claude Rains, Jose Ferrer, Charlton Heston, Donald Pleasence, David McCallum, Gary Raymond, Robert Blake, John Considine, David Hedison, Joanna Dunham, Sal Mineo, Van Heflin, Ed Wynn, Martin Landau, Telly Savalas, Sidney Poitier, Roddy McDowell, Angela Lansbury, Richard Conte, Carroll Baker, Janet Margolin, Burt Brinckerhoff.

Sean Armstrong. *The Gospel Road* (US/1973/93m/C) D: Robert Elfstrom. C: Robert Elfstrom, June Carter Cash, Larry Lee, Paul Smith, Alan Dater, John Paul Kay, Gelles LaBlanc, Robert Elfstrom, Jr., Terrance W. Mannock, Thomas Levanthal, Lyle Nicholson, Steven Chernoff, Jonathan Sanders, Ulf Pollack.

Jeffrey Druce. *In Search of Historic Jesus* (US/1979/91m/C) D: Henning Schellerup. B/on the book by Lee Roddy & Charles E. Seller. C: John Rubinstein, John Anderson, Nehemiah Persoff, Andrew Bloch, Morgan Brittany, Walter Brooke, Annette Charles, Royal Dano, Anthony DeLongis, Lawrence Dobkin, David Opatoshu, John Hoyt.

Nisin Gerama. *Jesus* (US/1979/117m/C) D: Peter Sykes & John Kirsh. B/on the *New Testament* book of *Luke*. C: Brian Deacon, Rivka Noiman, Yossef Shiloah, Niko Nitai, Gadi Rol, Richard Peterson, Eli Cohen, Shmuel Tal, Kobi Assaf, Talia Shapira, Eli Danker, Mosko Alkalai, Leonid Weinstein, Peter Frye, David Goldberg.

Alan Rosenberg. *The Last Temptation of Christ* (US/1988/164m/C) D: Martin Scorsese. B/on the novel by Nikos Kazantzakis. C: Willem Dafoe, Harvey Keitel, Paul Greco, Verna Bloom, Barbara Hershey, Gary Basaraba, Victor Argo, Michael Been, John Lurie, Harry Dean Stanton, David Bowie, Nehemiah Persoff, Leo Burmester, Irvin Kershner, Andre Gregory, Tomas Arana, Juliette Caton, Roberts Blossom, Barry Miller.

522 Thompson, Hunter S. (1939–)

American author whose collected essays and books define "Gonzo Journalism." Noted for his quirky, druggy accounts of trips to cover newsworthy events, he travels with Oscar Zeta Acosta, his friend and attorney. Acosta was portrayed by Peter Boyle (as Carl Laszlo, Esq.) in *Where the Buffalo Roam* and Benico Del Toro (as Dr. Gonzo) in *Fear and Loathing in Las Vegas*. Acosta wrote *Autobiography of a Brown Buffalo*, which may have been the inspiration for the movie title. Among Thompson's works are: *Hell's Angels: "A Strange and Terrible Saga of the Outlaw Motorcycle Gang,"* *Fear and Loathing in Las Vegas,* and *Curse of the Lono.*

Bill Murray. *Where the Buffalo Roam* (US/1980/96m/C) D: Art Linson. C:

Peter Boyle, Bruno Kirby, Rene Aberjonois, R.G. Armstrong, Rafael Campos, Leonard Frey, Mark Metcalf, Craig T. Nelson, Richard M. Dixon.

Johnny Depp (as Raoul Duke). *Fear and Loathing in Las Vegas* (US/1998/119m/C) D: Terry Gilliam. B/on the book by Hunter Thompson. C: Benico Del Toro, Tobey Maguire, Craig Bierko, Katherine Helman, Mark Harmon, Tim Thomerson, Penn Jillette, Cameron Diaz, Lyle Lovett, Flea, Gary Busey, Christina Ricci, Michael Jeter, Harry Dean Stanton, Ellen Barkin.

Lee Cummings *Ali* (US/2001/158m/C) D: Michael Mann. C: Will Smith, Jamie Foxx, Jon Voight, Mario Van Peebles, Ron Silver, Jeffrey Wright, Mykelti Williamson, Vincent De Paul, Jon A. Barnes, Michael Bentt, Malick Bowens, Candy Ann Brown, LeVar Burton, David Cubitt, James Currie, Rufus Dorsey, Martha Edgerton, Giancarlo Esposito, Sheldon Fogel, Themba Gasa, Nona M. Gaye, Ross Haines, Maestro Harrell, Michael Michele, Joe Morton, Patrick New, Al Quinn, Paul Rodriguez, Gailard Sartain, Charles Shufford, Jada Pinkett Smith, James Toney, Jack Truman, William Utay, Wade Williams.

523 Tibbets, (Col.) Paul (1915–)

Tibbets was the pilot of the plane that dropped the first Atomic Bomb on Hiroshima, August 6, 1945. He was played by Patrick Duffy in the TV film *Enola Gay* (83).

Barry Nelson. *The Beginning Or the End* (US/1947/110m/BW) D: Norman Taurog. C: Brian Donlevy, Beverly Tyler, Hume Cronyn, Godfrey Tearle, Art Baker, Ludwig Stossel.

Robert Taylor. *Above and Beyond* (US/1953/122m/BW) D: Melvin Frank & Frank Panama. C: Eleanor Parker, James Whitmore, Larry Keating, Jim Backus.

524 Tiberius Caesar (42 BC–AD 37)

The stepson, son-in-law, adopted son and successor (in that chronological order) of **Augustus Caesar**, Tiberius was Roman Emperor from 14–37 AD. He was portrayed by James Mason in the mini-series *A.D.* (85).

Cedric Hardwicke. *Salome* (US/1953/103m/C) D: William Dieterle. C: Rita Hayworth, Stewart Granger, Charles Laughton, Judith Anderson, Alan Badel, Basil Sydney, Rex Reason, Robert Warwick, Maurice Schwartz.

Ernest Thesiger. *The Robe* (US/1953/135m/C) D: Henry Koster. B/on the novel by Lloyd C. Douglas. Best Picture, Drama (GG). C: Richard Burton, Jean Simmons, Victor Mature, Michael Rennie, Jay Robinson, Dean Jagger, Torin Thatcher, Richard Boone, Michael Ansara, Cameron Mitchell (the voice of Jesus Christ).

George Relph. *Ben Hur* (US/1959/212m/C) D: William Wyler. B/on the novel by Lew Wallace. Best Picture (AA, BFA, NYC, GG). Best Director (AA, GG, DGA). C: Charlton Heston, Stephen Boyd, Jack Hawkins, Haya Harareet, Hugh Griffith, Sam Jaffe, Jose Greci, Laurence Payne, Frank Thring, Claude Heater, Finlay Currie.

Herbert Rudley. *The Big Fisherman* (US/1959/180m/C) D: Frank Borzage. B/on the novel by Lloyd C. Douglas. C: Howard Keel, Susan Kohner, John

Saxon, Martha Hyer, Herbert Lom, Alexander Scourby, Jay Barney, Rhodes Reason, Brian Hutton, Thomas Troupe.

    Ivan Triesault. *Barabbas* (Italy/1962/144m/C) D: Richard Fleischer. B/on the novel by Pär Lagerkvist. C: Anthony Quinn, Silvana Mangano, Arthur Kennedy, Katy Jurado, Harry Andrews, Roy Mangano, Michael Gwynn, Arnold Foa.

    Peter O'Toole. *Caligula* (US-Italy/1980/156m/C) D: Tinto Brass. C: Malcolm McDowell, Teresa Ann Savoy, Helen Mirren, John Gielgud, Anneka DiLorenzo.

525 Toklas, Alice Babette (1877–1967)

American writer and companion of **Gertrude Stein**, Toklas wrote *The Alice B. Toklas Cookbook* and *Staying on Alone*.

    Wilfrid Brambell. *The Adventures of Picasso* (Sweden/1978/92m/C) D: Tage Daniellson. C: Gosta Ekman, Hans Alfredson, Margaretha Krook, Bernard Cribbins, Per Oscarsson.

    Linda Hunt. *Waiting for the Moon* (US/1987/88m/C) D: Jill Godmillow. C: Linda Bassett, Bernadette LaFont, Bruce McGill, Jacques Boudet, Andrew McCarthy.

    Ali Giron. *The Moderns* (US/1988/126m/C) D: Alan Rudolph. C: Keith Carradine, Linda Fiorentino, Genevieve Bujold, Geraldine Chaplin, Kevin J. O'Connor, Elsa Raven, John Lone, Wallace Shawn.

526 Toulouse-Lautrec, Count Henri de (1864–1901)

French painter and lithographer; Toulouse-Lautrec's most famous works were posters of the cabarets and music halls on the Moulin Rouge.

    Jose Ferrer. *Moulin Rouge* (US/1952/123m/C) D: John Huston. B/on the novel by Pierre La Mure. C: Collette Marchand, Suzanne Flon, Zsa Zsa Gabor, Katherine Kath, Claude Nollier, Eric Pohlmann, Michael Balfour, Christopher Lee, Peter Cushing.

    Jerry Bergen. *Lust for Life* (US/1956/122m/C) D: Vincente Minnelli. B/on the novel by Irving Stone. C: Kirk Douglas, Anthony Quinn, James Donald, Pamela Brown.

    John Leguizamo. *Moulin Rouge!* (US-Australia/2001/127m/C) D: Baz Luhrmann. Best Musical, Best Actress, Musical; Best Original Score (GG). C: Nicole Kidman, Ewan McGregor, Jim Broadbent, Richard Roxburgh, Garry McDonald, Jacek Koman, Matthew Whittet, Kerry Walker, Caroline O'Connor, David Wenham, Christine Anu, Natalie Jackson Mendoza, Lara Mulcahy, Kylie Minogue.

527 Travis, William Barrett (1809–1836)

Travis commanded the Texas forces who defended the Alamo when sieged by **Santa Anna's** Mexican army in the fight for Texas' independence.

    Rex Lease. *Heroes of the Alamo* (aka *Remember the Alamo*) (US/1937/80m/BW) D: Harry Fraser. C: Earl Hodgins, Lane Chandler, Roger Williams, Edward Piel, Julian Rivero, Lee Valianos, Ruth Findlay, Jack Smith, Tex Cooper.

Victor Jory. *Man of Conquest* (US/1939/97m/BW) D: George Nichols, Jr. C: Richard Dix, Edward Ellis, Robert Barrat, Ralph Morgan, Robert Armstrong, C. Henry Gordon, George "Gabby" Hayes, Gail Patrick, Joan Fontaine, Max Terhune, Lane Chandler.

Arthur Space. *The Man from the Alamo* (US/1953/79m/C) D: Budd Boetticher. C: Glenn Ford, Julia Adams, Chill Wills, Victor Jory, Stuart Randall, Trevor Bardette, Ward Negley.

Don Megowan. *Davy Crockett, King of the Wild Frontier* (US/1955/90m/C) D: Norman Foster. C: Fess Parker, Buddy Ebsen, Basil Ruysdael, Hans Conried, Kenneth Tobey, Pat Hogan, Helene Stanley.

Richard Carlson. *The Last Command* (US/1955/110m/C) D: Frank Lloyd. B/on the story *The Last Command* by Sy Bartlett. C: Sterling Hayden, Arthur Hunnicutt, J. Carroll Naish, Otto Kruger, Hugh Sanders, Don Kennedy, Anna Maria Alberghetti, Ernest Borgnine, Ben Cooper, Virginia Grey, John Russell, Edward Colmans, Jim Davis.

William Hopper. *The First Texan* (US/1956/82m/C) D: Byron Haskin. C: Joel McCrea, Jeff Morrow, Dayton Lummis, David Silva, James Griffith, Carl Benton Reid, Felicia Farr, Wallace Ford, Chubby Johnson, Jody McCrea, Abraham Sofaer.

Laurence Harvey. *The Alamo* (US/1960/192m/C) D: John Wayne. C: John Wayne, Richard Widmark, Patrick Wayne, Ruben Padilla, Joseph Calleia, Richard Boone.

528 Trotsky, Leon (1879–1940)

(Lev Davidovich Bronstein) An early leader in the Russian Revolution, Trotsky was exiled from the Soviet Union when **Stalin** came to power. Finally settling in Mexico, he was assassinated by a Stalinist agent.

J. Carrol Naish. *British Agent* (US/1934/75m/BW) D: Michael Curtiz. B/on the book *Memoirs of a British Agent* by Robert Bruce Lockhart. C: Leslie Howard, Kay Francis, William Gargan, Philip Reed, George Pearce, Cesar Romero, Tenen Holz, Olaf Hytten.

D.F. Barry. *Why Russians Are Revolting* (US/1970/91m/BW) D: Neil Sullivan. C: Neil Sullivan, Wes Carter, Saul Katz, Ed Maywood, Seneca Ames, George Badera.

Brian Cox. *Nicholas and Alexandra* (GB/1971/183m/C) D: Franklin J. Schaffner. B/on the book by Robert K. Massie. C: Michael Jayston, Janet Suzman, Roderic Noble, Fiona Fullerton, Harry Andrews, Irene Worth, Tom Baker, Ralph Truman, Alexander Knox, John McEnery, Michael Bryant, James Hazeldine, Ian Holm, Roy Dotrice, Martin Potter.

Richard Burton. *The Assassination of Trotsky* (France-Italy-GB/1972/105m/C) D: Joseph Losey. C: Alain Delon, Romy Schneider, Valentina Cortese.

Yves Penereau. *Stavisky* (France/1974/115m/C) D: Alain Resnais. C: Jean-Paul Belmondo, Charles Boyer, François Perier, Anny Duperey, Michel Lonsdale.

Stuart Richman. *Reds* (US/1981/200m/C) D: Warren Beatty. Best Picture (NYC), Best Director (AA,DGA). C: Warren Beatty, Diane Keaton, Edward Herrmann, Jerzy Kosinski, Jack Nicholson, Paul Sorvino, Maureen Stapleton, Roger Sloman.

Pinkas Braun. *The Sailors of Kronstadt* (aka *Die Matrosen von Kronstadt*) (Germany/1983/120m/C) D: Jurgen Klauss. C: Siemen Ruehaak, Gottfried John, Gert Haucke.

Max Kerlow. *Frida* (Mexico/1984/108m/C) D: Paul Leduc. C: Ofelia Medina, Juan Jose Gurrola, Salvador Sanchez, Valentina Leduc, Claudio Brook.

529 Truman, Harry S (1884–1972)

As the 33rd President of the U.S. (1945–53), Truman authorized the use of nuclear weapons against Japan bringing an end to the Second World War.

Art Baker. *The Beginning Or the End* (US/1947/110m/BW) D: Norman Taurog. C: Brian Donlevy, Beverly Tyler, Hume Cronyn, Godfrey Tearle, Barry Nelson, Ludwig Stossel.

James Whitmore. *Give 'Em Hell, Harry* (US/1975/102m/C) D: Steve Binder.

Ed Flanders. *MacArthur* (US/1977/128m/C) D: Joseph Sargent. C: Gregory Peck, Dan O'Herlihy, Ivan Bonar, Ward Costello, Nicholas Coster, Art Fleming, Addison Powell, Marj Dusay, Kenneth Tobey, John Fujioka, Fred Stuthman, Sandy Kenyon.

Ed Nelson. *Brenda Starr* (US/1992/87m/C) D: Robert Ellis Miller. B/on the comic strip by Dale Messick. C: Brooke Shields, Timothy Dalton, Tony Peck.

530 Tunstall, John Henry (1853–1878)

An English-born rancher who in 1877 hired and befriended **Billy the Kid**. Tunstall's murder set off a range war (The Lincoln County War) and sent Billy further along his infamous path as The Kid reputedly tracked down and shot each of his boss' murderers.

Wyndham Standing (as Tunston). *Billy the Kid* (aka *The Highwayman Rides*) (US/1930/95m/BW) D: King Vidor. B/on the novel *The Saga of Billy the Kid* by Walter Noble Burns. C: Johnny Mack Brown, Wallace Beery, Karl Dane, Russell Simpson, Blanche Frederici.

Ian Hunter (as Eric Keating). *Billy the Kid* (US/1941/94m/C) D: David Miller. B/on the novel *The Saga of Billy the Kid* by Walter Noble Burns. C: Robert Taylor, Brian Donlevy.

Shepperd Strudwick (as Roger Jameson). *The Kid from Texas* (aka *Texas Kid, Outlaw*) (US/1950/78m/C) D: Kurt Neumann. C: Audie Murphy, Gale Storm, Will Geer, Robert Barrat, Frank Wilcox.

Paul Cavanagh. *The Law vs. Billy the Kid* (US/1954/72m/C) D: William Castle. C: Scott Brady, Betta St. John, James Griffith, Alan Hale, Jr., Bill Phillips, Otis Garth, Robert Griffin.

Colin Keith-Johnston. *The Left-Handed Gun* (US/1958/102m/BW) D: Arthur Penn. B/on the teleplay *The Death of Billy the Kid* by Gore Vidal. C: Paul Newman, Lita Milan, John Dehner, Hurd Hatfield, James Congdon, John Dierkes, Denver Pyle.

Patric Knowles. *Chisum* (US/1970/110m/C) D: Andrew McLaglen. C: John Wayne, Forrest Tucker, Christopher George, Ben Johnson, Glenn Corbett, Geoffrey Deuel, Andrew Prine, Lynda Day, John Agar, Robert Donner, Ray Teal, Ron Soble.

Terence Stamp. *Young Guns* (US/1988/97m/C) D: Chris Cain. C: Emilio Estevez, Kiefer Sutherland, Lou Diamond Phillips, Charlie Sheen, Casey Siemaszko, Patrick Wayne.

531 Turpin, Dick (1705?–1739)

Legendary English highwayman, Turpin was eventually hanged for stealing horses. He was portrayed by Tom Mix in the 1925 silent feature *Dick Turpin*.

Victor McLaglen. *Dick Turpin* (GB/1933/79m/BW) D: John Stafford & Victor Hanbur. B/on the novel *Rookwood* by W. Harrison Ainsworth. C: Jane Carr, Frank Vosper.

Louis Hayward. *The Lady and the Bandit* (aka *Dick Turpin's Ride*) (US/1951/79m/BW) D: Ralph Murphy. B/on the poem "The Highwayman" by Alfred Noyes. C: Patricia Medina, Suzanne Dalbert, John Williams, Alan Mowbray, George Baxter, Ivan Triesault.

David Weston. *The Legend of Young Dick Turpin* (GB/1965/83m/C) D: James Neilson. C: Bernard Lee, George Cole, Maurice Denham, William Franklyn, Leonard Whiting.

Sidney James. *Carry on Dick* (GB/1974/91m/C) D: Gerald Thomas. C: Barbara Windsor, Kenneth Williams, Joan Sims, Kenneth Connor.

532 Twain, Mark (1835–1910)

(Samuel Langhorne Clemens) American author; Twain's classics of life along the Mississippi River include *Tom Sawyer* and *Huck Finn*. TV movie portrayals include Christopher Connelley in *The Incredible Rocky Mountain Race* (77) and Jack Warden in *Helen Keller: The Miracle Continues* (84).

James Bush. *Battle of Greed* (US/1937/65m/BW) D: Howard Higgin. C: Tom Keene, Gwynne Shipman, Jimmy Butler, Robert Fiske, Carl Stockdale, Budd Buster.

Fredric March. *The Adventures of Mark Twain* (US/1944/130m/BW) D: Irving Rapper. C: Alexis Smith, C. Aubrey Smith, John Carradine, Paul Scardon, Brandon Hurst, Douglas Wood.

533 Valachi, Joseph Michael (1904–1971)

New York gangster, Valachi, when arrested on drug charges, turned informer and was the first to reveal inside information about the Cosa Nostra (Mafia).

Charles Bronson. *The Valachi Papers* (Italy-France/1972/125m/C) D: Terence Young. B/on the book by Peter Maas. C: Lino Ventura, Jill Ireland, Fausto Tozzi, Angelo Infante, Giancomino De Michelis, Joseph Wiseman, Walter Chiari.

Joe Viterelli. *Ruby* (US/1992/110m/C) D: John MacKenzie. B/on the play *Love Child* by Stephen Davis. C: Danny Aiello, Gerard David, Kevin Wiggins, Willie Garson, Chris Wall, Sherilyn Fenn, Jane Hamilton, Carmine Caridi.

534 Valens, Ritchie (1941–1959)

(Richard Valenzuela) Teenage pop star of the late 1950s, Valens was killed in the plane crash that also took the life of **Buddy Holly**.

Gilbert Melgar. *The Buddy Holly Story* (US/1978/113m/C) D: Steve Rash. B/on the book by John Coldrosen. C: Gary Busey, Don Stroud, Charles Martin Smith, Maria Richwine.

Lou Diamond Phillips. *La Bamba* (US/1987/108m/C) D: Luis Valdez. C: Esai Morales, Rosana De Soto, Elizabeth Pena, Jeffrey Allen Chandler, Marshall Crenshaw.

535 Valentino, Rudolph (1895–1926)

(Rudolpho Guglielmi) Italian born silent screen matinee idol, Valentino starred in *The Sheik* (21) and *Blood and Sand* (22) among other films.

Anthony Dexter. *Valentino* (US/1951/102m/C) D: Lewis Allen. C: Eleanor Parker, Richard Carlson, Patricia Medina, Joseph Calleia, Dona Drake, Lloyd Gough, Otto Kruger.

Matt Collins. *The World's Greatest Lover* (US/1977/89m/C) D: Gene Wilder. C: Gene Wilder, Carol Kane, Dom DeLuise, Fritz Feld, Carl Ballantine, Danny De Vito, Ronny Graham.

Rudolf Nureyev. *Valentino* (GB/1977/132m/C) D: Ken Russell. B/on the story *Valentino, An Intimate Exposé of the Sheik* by Brad Steiger & Chaw Mank. C: Leslie Caron, Michelle Phillips, Carol Kane, Felicity Kendal, Peter Vaughan, Huntz Hall, David De Keyser, Anthony Dowell, William Hootkins, Anton Diffring.

Van Buren, Martin *see* 574

536 Van Gogh, Vincent Willem (1853–1890)

Postimpressionist painter who suffered from manic-depression, Van Gogh was ignored during his own lifetime but became one of the most influential painters of all time. John Hurt provided his voice in the documentary *Vincent—The Life and Death of Vincent Van Gogh* (87).

Kirk Douglas * Best Actor (NYC, GG). *Lust for Life* (US/1956/122m/C) D: Vincente Minnelli. B/on the novel by Irving Stone. C: Anthony Quinn, James Donald, Pamela Brown, Jerry Bergen.

Tim Roth. *Vincent and Theo* (France-GB/1990/138m/C) D: Robert Altman. C: Paul Rhys, Andrian Brine, Johanna Ter Steege, Wladimir Yordanoff, Peter Tuinman.

Martin Scorsese. *Akira Kurosawa's Dreams* (Japan/1990/119m/C) D: Akira Kurosawa. C: Akira Terao, Mitsuko Baisho, Toshihiko Nakano, Mie Suzuki, Mieko Harada.

Jacques Dutronc. *Van Gogh* (France/1992/175m/C) D: Maurice Pialat. C: Alexandra London, Gerard Sety, Bernard LeCoq, Corinne Bourdon.

537 Van Meter, Homer (?–1934)

Van Meter was the bank robbing partner of **John Dillinger** and **Baby Face Nelson**.

Richard Crane. *Guns Don't Argue* (US/1955/92m/BW) D: Bill Karn & Richard

A cynical Gauguin (Anthony Quinn) and an overly enthusiastic Van Gogh (Kirk Douglas) out to enjoy the delights of Arles in *Lust for Life* (1956). Quinn received the Academy Award as Best Supporting Actor for his portrayal of Gauguin. (Museum of Modern Art Film Stills Archive)

Kahn. Feature film edited from the TV series *Gangbusters*. C: Myron Healey, Lyle Talbot, Jean Harvey, Paul Dubov, Sam Edwards, Tamar Cooper, Baynes Barron, Doug Wilson.

Elisha Cook, Jr. *Baby Face Nelson* (US/1957/85m/BW) D: Don Siegel. C: Mickey Rooney, Carolyn Jones, Cedric Hardwicke, Leo Gordon, Ted De Corsia, Dan Terranova, Jack Elam.

Dan Terranova. *Young Dillinger* (US/1965/102m/BW) D: Terry Morse. C: Nick Adams, Robert Conrad, John Ashley, Mary Ann Mobley, Victor Buono, John Hoyt, Reed Hadley.

Harry Dean Stanton. *Dillinger* (US/1973/107m/C) D: John Milius. C: Warren Oates, Michelle Phillips, Ben Johnson, Geoffrey Lewis, Richard Dreyfuss, Steve Kanaly.

538 Vanderbilt, Cornelius (1794–1877)

American billionaire, Vanderbilt made his money in shipping and railroads.

Clarence Kolb. *The Toast of New York* (US/1937/109m/BW) D: Rowland V. Lee. B/on the book *Robber Barons, The Great American Capitalists* by Matthew

Josephson. C: Edward Arnold, Cary Grant, Frances Farmer, Jack Oakie, Donald Meek, Billy Gilbert.

Peter Boyle. *Walker* (US/1987/95m/C) D: Alex Cox. C: Ed Harris, Richard Masur.

539 Verdi, Giuseppe (1813–1901)

Foremost composer of Italian opera; Verdi's works include "Rigoletto," "La Traviata," "Il Trovatore" and "Aida."

Fosco Gaichetti. *The Life and Music of Giuseppe Verdi* (aka *Giuseppe Verdi*) (Italy/1938/123m/BW) D: Carmine Gallone. C: Germana Paolieri, Gaby Morlay, Maria Cebotari, Pierre Brasseur.

Nerio Bernardi. *The Lost One* (aka *La Traviata*) (Italy/1947/84m/BW) D: Carmine Gallone. B/on the opera "La Traviata" by Giuseppe Verdi & F.M. Piave, and the novel *The Lady of the Camelias* by Alexandre Dumas. C: Massimo Serato, Nelly Corradi.

Pierre Cressoy. *The Life and Music of Verdi* (aka *Giuseppe Verdi*) (aka *The Life and Music of Giuseppe Verdi*) (Italy/1953) D: Raffaello Matarazzo.

Fosco Gaichetti. *Casa Ricordi* (aka *House of Ricordi*) (France-Italy/1954/130–112m/C) D: Carmine Gallone. C: Roland Alexandre, Maurice Ronet, Miriam Bru.

540 Victoria, Queen (1819–1901)

England's longest reigning monarch, Victoria has been given more screen portrayals than any other Queen. In the TV mini-series *Victoria and Albert* (2001) she was portrayed as a young woman by Victoria Hamilton; and in old age, by Joyce Redman.

Margaret Mann. *Disraeli* (US/1929/90m/BW) D: Alfred E. Green. B/on the play by Louis N. Parker. C: George Arliss, Joan Bennett, Florence Arliss, Anthony Bushell.

Marian Drada. *Balaclava* (aka *Jaws of Hell*) (GB/1930/94m/BW) D: Maurice Elvey & Milton Rosmer. B/on *The Charge of the Light Brigade* by Alfred Lord Tennyson. Made as a silent in 1928, with sound added in 1930. C: Benita Hume, Cyril McLaglen, J. Fisher White, Bos Ranevsky, Wallace Bosco, Eugene Leahy.

Madeleine Ozeray. *War of the Waltzes* (aka *Walzerkrieg*) (Germany-France/1933/BW) D: Ludwig Berger. French language version of *Waltz Time in Vienna* (33).

Hanna Waag. *Waltz Time in Vienna* (aka *Walzerkrieg*) (Germany/1933/80m/BW) D: Ludwig Berger. C: Adolf Wohlbruck (Anton Walbrook), Heinz von Cleve, Willy Fritsch.

Pamela Stanley. *David Livingstone* (GB/1936/71m/BW) D: James A. Fitzpatrick. C: Percy Marmont, Marian Spencer, Hugh McDermott, James Carew.

Jennie Jugo. *Mädchenjahre Einer Königin* (Germany/1936/BW) D: Erich Engel. C: Otto Tressler, Olga Limburg, Friedrich Benfer, Paul Henckels, Ernst Schiffner, Renee Stobrawa.

Gaby Fay. *The White Angel* (aka *The White Sister*) (US/1936/75m/BW) D: William Dieterle. B/on the *Florence Nightingale* chapter of *Eminent Victorians* by

After the death of her beloved Albert, Queen Victoria (Judi Dench) went into seclusion for almost five years. John Brown (Billy Connolly), Albert's horseman at Balmoral, was brought to Windsor Castle hoping to encourage the queen to be in touch with her people again. *Mrs. Brown* (1997). Dame Judi Dench received the Golden Globe Award as Best Actress for her portrayal of Queen Victoria. (Museum of Modern Art Film Stills Archive)

Lytton Strachey. C: Kay Francis, Ian Hunter, Donald Woods, Nigel Bruce, Halliwell Hobbes.

Yvette Plenne. *The Pearls of the Crown* (France/1937/120–100m/BW) D: Sacha Guitry & Christian-Jaque. C: Sacha Guitry, Jacqueline Delubac, Lyn Harding, Ermete Zacconi, Marguerite Moreno, Catalano, Arletty, Percy Marmont, Derrick De Marney, Barbara Shaw, Simone Renant, Jean Louis Barrault, Emile Drain, Enrico Glori, Renee Saint-Cyr, Pizani, Claude Dauphin, Aime-Simon Gerard.

Anna Neagle. *Victoria the Great* (GB/1937/110m/C) D: Herbert Wilcox. B/on the play *Victoria Regina* by Laurence Housman. C: Anton Walbrook, H.B. Warner, James Dale, Charles Carson, Hubert Harben, Felix Aylmer, Arthur Young, Derrick De Marney, Hugh Miller, Percy Parsons, Henry Hallatt, Gordon McLeod, Wyndham Goldie.

Gaby Morlay. *Entente Cordiale* (France/1938/95m/BW) D: Marcel L'Herbier. B/on *Edward VII and His Times* by Andre Maurois. C: Victor Francen, Andre Lefaur, Marcelle Praince, Jeanine Darcey, Arlette Marchal, Jean Galland, Andre Roanne, Jacques Catelain, Jean Toulot, Jacques Baumer, Jean d'Yd, Jean Perrier.

Pamela Stanley. *Marigold* (GB/1938/74m/BW) D: Thomas Bentley. B/on the play by Charles Garvice, Allen Harker & F. Prior. C: Sophie Stewart, Patrick Barr.

Anna Neagle. *Sixty Glorious Years* (aka *Queen of Destiny*) (GB/1938/90m/C)

D: Herbert Wilcox. C: Anton Walbrook, C. Aubrey Smith, Charles Carson, Felix Aylmer, Pamela Standish, Gordon McLeod, Henry Hallatt, Wyndham Goldie, Malcolm Keen, Derrick De Marney, Joyce Bland, Harvey Braban, Aubrey Dexter, Laidman Browne.

Beryl Mercer. *The Little Princess* (US/1939/91m/C) D: Walter Lang. B/on the novel *The Fantasy* by Frances Hodgson Burnett. C: Shirley Temple, Richard Greene, Anita Louise, Ian Hunter, Cesar Romero, Arthur Treacher.

Beryl Mercer. *The Story of Alexander Graham Bell* (aka *The Modern Miracle*) (US/1939/97m/BW) D: Irving Cummings. C: Don Ameche, Loretta Young, Henry Fonda, Charles Coburn, Sally Blaine.

Hedwig Wangel. *Ohm Krüger* (Germany/1941/135m/BW) D: Hans Steinhoff. C: Emil Jannings, Ferdinand Marian, Franz Schafheitlin, Gustav Gründgens.

Fay Compton. *The Prime Minister* (GB/1940/94m/BW) D: Thorold Dickinson. C: John Gielgud, Diana Wynyard, Will Fyfe, Stephen Murray, Owen Nares, Lyn Harding, Leslie Perrins, Vera Bogetti, Frederick Leister, Nicolas Hannan, Kynaston Reeves, Gordon McLeod.

Evelyn Beresford. *Buffalo Bill* (US/1944/90m/C) D: William Wellman. C: Joel McCrea, Maureen O'Hara, Linda Darnell, Thomas Mitchell, Edgar Buchanan, Anthony Quinn, Moroni Olsen, Chief Thundercloud, John Dilson, Sidney Blackmer.

Evelyn Beresford. *Annie Get Your Gun* (US/1950/107m/C) D: George Sidney. B/on the musical play, book by Herbert and Dorothy Fields. C: Betty Hutton, Howard Keel, Louis Calhern, J. Carrol Naish, Chief Yowlachie, John Mylong, Nino Pipitone.

Irene Dunne. *The Mudlark* (GB/1950/98m/BW) D: Jean Negulesco. B/on the novel by Theodore Bonnet. C: Alec Guinness, Andrew Ray, Beatrice Campbell, Finlay Currie, Anthony Steel, Wilfrid Hyde-White, Robin Stevens, Kynaston Reeves, Vi Stevens.

Pamela Brown. *Alice in Wonderland* (GB-France/1951/83m/C) D: Dallas Bower. B/on stories by Lewis Carroll. C: Stephen Murray, Carol Marsh, David Read.

Helena Pickard. *The Lady with a Lamp* (aka *The Lady with the Lamp*) (GB/1951/112m/BW) D: Herbert Wilcox. B/on the play *The Lady with the Lamp* by Reginald Berkeley. C: Anna Neagle, Michael Wilding, Felix Aylmer, Arthur Young, Peter Graves.

Sybil Thorndike. *Melba* (GB/1953/113m/C) D: Lewis Milestone. C: Patrice Munsel, Robert Morley, John McCallum, John Justin, Alec Clunes, Theodore Bikel.

Muriel Aked. *The Great Gilbert and Sullivan* (aka *The Story of Gilbert and Sullivan*) (GB/1953/105m/C) D: Sydney Gilliat. B/on The *Gilbert and Sullivan Book* by Leslie Bailey. C: Robert Morley, Maurice Evans, Eileen Herlie, Peter Finch, Martyn Green.

Anna Neagle. *Let's Make Up* (aka *Lilacs in the Spring*) (GB/1954/94m/C) D: Herbert Wilcox. B/on the play *The Glorious Days* by Harold Purcell. C: Errol Flynn, David Farrar, Kathleen Harrison, Peter Graves, Sean Connery.

Romy Schneider. *The Story of Vickie* (aka *Young Victoria*) (aka *Dover Interlude*) (aka *Girl Days of a Queen*) (aka *Mädchenjahre Einer Königin*) (Austria/1955/108–90m/C) D: Ernst Marischka. B/on the diaries of Queen Victoria. C: Adrian Hoven, Magda Schneider, Karl Ludwig Diehl, Christl Mardayn, Paul Horbiger,

Alfred Neugebauer, Otto Tressler, Rudolf Lenz, Fred Liewehr, Eduard Strauss, Peter Weck.

Avis Bunnage. *The Wrong Box* (GB/1966/107m/C) D: Bryan Forbes. B/on the novel by Robert Louis Stevenson & Lloyd Osbourne. C: John Mills, Ralph Richardson, Michael Caine, Peter Cook, Dudley Moore, Nanette Newman, Peter Sellers.

Joan Sterndale Bennett. *Those Fantastic Flying Fools* (aka *Jules Verne's Rocket to the Moon*) (aka *Blast-Off*) (GB/1967/95m/C) D: Don Sharp. B/on the novel *Rocket to the Moon* by Jules Verne. C: Burl Ives, Troy Donahue, Gert Frobe.

Mollie Maureen. *The Private Life of Sherlock Holmes* (GB/1970/125m/C) D: Billy Wilder. C: Robert Stephens, Colin Blakely, Irene Handl, Christopher Lee, Genevieve Page, Stanley Holloway.

Susan Field. *The Adventure of Sherlock Holmes' Smarter Brother* (US/1975/91m/C) D: Gene Wilder. C: Gene Wilder, Madeline Kahn, Marty Feldman, Dom DeLuise, Leo McKern, Douglas Wilmer.

Peter Sellers. *The Great McGonagall* (GB/1975/95m/C) D: Joseph McGrath. C: Spike Milligan, Julia Foster, Julian Chagrin, Victor Spinetti, John Bluthal, Valentine Dyall.

Judy Dench *GG, BAFTA, Best Actress. *Mrs. Brown* (GB-Ireland-US/1997/103m/C) D: John Madden. C: Billy Connolly, Geoffry Palmer, Antony Sher, Gerald Butler, Richard Pasco, David Westhead.

Fay Masterson. *Amistad* (US/1997/152m/C) D: Steven Spielberg. C: Morgan Freeman, Nigel Hawthorne, Anthony Hopkins, Djimon Hounsou, Matthew McConaughey, David Paymer, Pete Postlewaithe, Stellan Skarsgard, Razaaq Adoti, Abu Bakaar Fofanah, Anna Paquin, Tomas Milian, Chitwetel Ejiofor, Derrick N. Ashong, Geno Silva, John Ortiz, Ralph Brown, Darren Burroughs, Allan Rich, Paul Guilfoyle, Peter Firth, Xander Berkeley, Jeremy Northan, Arliss Howard, Austen Pendleton, Daniel von Bargen, Rusty Schwimmer, Pedro Armendariz.

Liz Moscrop. *From Hell* (Czech Republic-US/2001/121m/C) D: Albert and Allen Hughes. C: Johnny Depp, Heather Graham, Ian Holm, Jason Flemyng, Robbie Coltran, Lesley Sharp, Susan Lynch, Terence Harvey, Katrin Cartlidge, Estelle Skornik, Paul Rhys, Nicholas McGaughey, Ian Richardson, Annabelle Apsion, Joanna Page, Mark Dexter.

541 Villa, Pancho (1877–1923)

(Doroteo Arango) A Mexican revolutionary who fought for **Madero** and against **Diaz** and **Huerta**, Villa has become something of a folk hero representing the peasants' struggle for freedom, equality and opportunity.

Wallace Beery. *Viva Villa!* (US/1934/115m/BW) D: Jack Conway & Howard Hawks (uncredited). B/on the book by Edgcumb Pinchon & O.B. Strade. C: Fay Wray, Stuart Erwin, Leo Carillo, Donald Cook, Joseph Schildkraut, Henry B. Walthall.

Domingo Soler. *Let's Go with Pancho Villa* (aka *Vamonos Con Pancho Villa*) (Mexico/1936/BW) D: Fernando de Fuentes. C: Ramon Vallarino, Antonio R. Frausto, Manuel Tames.

Maurice Black. *Under Strange Flags* (US/1937/61m/BW) D: I.V. Willat. C: Tom Keene, Luana Walters. Budd Buster, Roy D'Arcy.

Leo Carillo. *Pancho Villa Returns* (Mexico/1949/95m/BW) D: Miguel Contreras Torres. C: Esther Fernandez, Jaenette Comber, Rodolfo Acosta, Rafael Alcayde, Jorge Trevino.

Alan Reed. *Viva Zapata!* (US/1952/113m/BW) D: Elia Kazan. B/on the book *Zapata the Unconquerable* by Edgcumb Pinchon. C: Marlon Brando, Anthony Quinn, Jean Peters, Harold Gordon, Margo, Frank Silvera, Frank De Kova, Fay Roope, Joseph Wiseman, Lou Gilbert.

Pedro Armendariz. *Pancho Villa and Valentina* (Mexico/1958/90m/C) D: Ismael Rodriguez. C: Elsa Aguirre, Carlos Moctezuma, Humberto Almazon.

Pedro Armendariz. *This Was Pancho Villa* (aka *Cuando 1Viva Villa! Es La Muerte*) (Mexico/1958/90m/C) D: Ismael Rodriguez. C: Carlos Moctezuma, Maria Elena Marques.

Rodolfo Hoyos. *Villa!* (US/1958/72m/C) D: James B. Clark. C: Brian Keith, Cesar Romero, Margia Dean, Ben Wright, Rosenda Monteros.

Ricardo Palacios. *Seven for Pancho Villa* (Spain/1966/C) D: José M. Elorrieta (Joe Levy). C: John Ericson, Nuria Torray, Gustavo Rojo, Mara Cruz, James Philbrook, Pastor Serrador.

Yul Brynner. *Villa Rides* (US/1968/125m/C) D: Buzz Kulik. B/on the book *Pancho Villa* by William Douglas Lansford. C: Robert Mitchum, Charles Bronson, Herbert Lom, Alexander Knox, Fernando Rey, Jill Ireland, John Ireland.

Eraclio Zepeda. *Reed: Insurgent Mexico* (Mexico/1971/110m) D: Paul Leduc. B/on the book *Insurgent Mexico* by John Reed. C: Claudio Obregon, Eduardo Lopez Rojas, Ernesto Gomez.

Telly Savalas. *Pancho Villa* (aka *Challenge of Pancho Villa*) (Spain/1972/90m/C) D: Eugene Martin. C: Clint Walker, Anne Francis, Chuck Connors, Walter Coy.

Freddy Fender. *She Came to the Valley* (aka *Texas in Flames*) (US/1979/90m/C) D: Albert Band. B/on the novel by Cleo Dawson. C: Ronee Blakely, Dean Stockwell.

Pedro Armendariz, Jr. *Old Gringo* (US/1989/119m/C) D: Luis Puenzo. B/on the novel *Gringo Viejo* by Carlos Fuentes. C: Gregory Peck, Jane Fonda, Jimmy Smits.

Carlos Roberto Majul. *Ah! Silenciosa* (Mexico-US/1999/C) D: Marcos Cline-Márquez. C: Jim Beaver, Ana Sobero, Alberto Tejada, Ricardo Cárdenas, Lourdes Castillo, Chico Hernandez.

542 Villon, François (1431–1471?)

French poet considered the greatest poet of the Middle Ages; Villon's major works include *Grand Testament* and *Petite Testament*.

Dennis King. *The Vagabond King* (US/1930/104m/C) D: Ludwig Berger. B/on the operetta by William H. Post, Brian Hooker & Rudolph Friml, and the play *If I Were King* by Justin Huntly McCarthy. C: Jeanette MacDonald, O.P. Heggie, Lillian Roth.

Ronald Colman. *If I Were King* (US/1938/100m/BW) D: Frank Lloyd. B/on the play by Justin Huntly McCarthy. C: Basil Rathbone, Frances Dee, Ellen Drew.

Serge Reggiani. *François Villon* (France/1949/81m/BW) D: Andre Zwobada.

C: Renee Faure, Jacques-Henri Duval, Garcherry, Salabert, Helene Sauvaneix, Albert Remy.

Oreste. *The Vagabond King* (US/1956/88m/C) D: Michael Curtiz. B/on the operetta by William H. Post, Brian Hooker & Rudolph Friml, and the play *If I Were King* by Justin Huntly McCarthy. C: Kathryn Grayson, Rita Moreno, Walter Hampden, Leslie Nielsen.

543 Voltaire, François Marie Arouet de (1694–1778)

French writer/philosopher and leading figure of the 18th century Enlightenment; Voltaire's works include *The Philosophical Dictionary* and *Candide*.

Karl Meinhardt. *Trenck* (Germany/1932/84m/BW) D: Ernst Neubach & Heinz Paul. B/on the story *Trenck, The Story of a Favorite* by Bruno Franck. C: Hans Stuewe, Paul Horbiger, Theodor Loos, Olga Tschechowa, Dorothea Wieck.

George Arliss. *Voltaire* (US/1933/72m/BW) D: John G. Adolfi. B/on the novel by George Gibbs & E. Lawrence. C: Doris Kenyon, Margaret Lindsay, Reginald Owen.

Fernand Bercher. *Adrienne Lecouvreur* (France/1938/110m/BW) D: Marcel L'Herbier. C: Pierre Fresnay, Yvonne Printemps, Junie Astor, Andre Lefaur.

Maurice Schutz. *Le Diable Boiteux* (France/1948) D: Sacha Guitry. C: Sacha Guitry, Emile Drain.

Jacques de Feraudy. *Royal Affairs in Versailles* (aka *Versailles*) (aka *Affairs in Versailles*) (aka *If Versailles Were Told to Me*) (aka *Si Versailles M'Était Couté*) (France/1953/180–152m/C) D: Sacha Guitry. C: Sacha Guitry, Claudette Colbert, Orson Welles, Gerard Phillippe, Micheline Presle, Jean Marais, Georges Marchal, Gilbert Boka, Lana Marconi, Gino Cervi, Fernand Gravet, Louis Arbessier, Jacques Berthier, Samson Fainsilber, Gilbert Gil, Emile Drain, Gaston Rey, Philippe Richard.

François Simon. *Alzire Oder Der Neue Kontinent* (Switzerland/1978/108m/C) D: Thomas Koerfer. C: Roger Jendly.

544 Wagner, Cosima Liszt (1837–1930)

The illegitimate daughter of **Franz Liszt**, Cosima was the second wife of **Richard Wagner**. After his death she continued to produce the Wagner festivals at Bayreuth until her retirement in 1906.

Rita Gam. *Magic Fire* (US/1956/94m/C) D: William Dieterle. B/on the novel by Bertita Harding. C: Yvonne De Carlo, Carlos Thompson, Valentina Cortesa, Alan Badel, Peter Cushing, Gerhard Riedmann, Eric Schumann, Frederick Valk.

Silvana Mangano. *Ludwig* (Italy-Germany-France/1973/186m/C) D: Luchino Visconti. C: Helmut Berger, Romy Schneider, Trevor Howard, Mark Burns.

Antonia Ellis. *Mahler* (GB/1974/115m/C) D: Ken Russell. C: Robert Powell, Georgina Hale, Richard Morant, Lee Montague, Rosalie Crutchley, David Collings.

Veronica Quilligan. *Lisztomania* (GB/1975/105m/C) D: Ken Russell. C: Roger Daltrey, Sara Kestelman, Paul Nicholas, Fiona Lewis, Ken Colley, Andrew Reilly, Murray Melvin, Otto Diamant, Anulka Dziubinska, Imogen Claire, Ken Parry.

Vanessa Redgrave. *Wagner* (GB-Austria-Hungary/1983/540–300m/C) D:

Tony Palmer. C: Richard Burton, Gemma Craven, Laszlo Galffi, John Gielgud, Ralph Richardson, Laurence Olivier, Ekkerhard Schall, Ronald Pickup, Miguel Herz-Kestranek, Marthe Keller, Gwyneth Jones, Franco Nero.

545 Wagner, Wilhelm Richard (1813–1883)

Influential German operatic composer; Wagner's works include "The Flying Dutchman" and the four operas of "Der Ring des Nibelungen" (The Ring cycle).

Robert Pizani. *Champs-Elysées* (aka *Remontons Les Champs-Elysées*) (France/1938/100m/BW) D: Sacha Guitry. C: Sacha Guitry, Lucien Baroux, Jacqueline Delubac, Germaine Dermoz, Jeanne Boitel, Raymonde Allain, Jean Davy, Emile Drain, Jacques Erwin, Rene Fauchois, Liane Pathe, Claude Martin, Raymond Galle, Andre Laurent.

Paul Bildt. *Ludwig II* (Germany/1955) D: Helmut Kautner. C: Friedrich Domin, O.W. Fischer, Klaus Kinski, Marianne Koch, Ruth Leuwerik.

Alan Badel. *Magic Fire* (US/1956/94m/C) D: William Dieterle. B/on the novel by Bertita Harding. C: Yvonne De Carlo, Carlos Thompson, Rita Gam, Vale tina Cortesa, Peter Cushing, Gerhard Riedmann, Eric Schumann, Frederick Valk.

Lyndon Brook. *Song Without End* (US/1960/145m/C) D: George Cukor & Charles Vidor. C: Dirk Bogarde, Capucine, Genevieve Page, Patricia Morison, Ivan Desny, Martita Hunt, Lou Jacobi, E. Erlandsen, Alex Davion, Hans Unterkirchner, Katherine Squire.

Gerhard Marz. *Ludwig—Requiem for a Virgin King* (Germany/1972/134m/C) D: Hans Jurgen Syberberg. C: Harry Baer, Ingrid Caven, Balthasar Thomas, Peter Kern.

Trevor Howard. *Ludwig* (Italy-Germany-France/1973/186m/C) D: Luchino Visconti. C: Helmut Berger, Romy Schneider, Silvana Mangano, Mark Burns.

Paul Nicholas. *Lisztomania* (GB/1975/105m/C) D: Ken Russell. C: Roger Daltrey, Sara Kestelman, Fiona Lewis, Veronica Qilligan, Ken Colley, Andrew Reilly, Murray Melvin, Otto Diamant, Anulka Dziubinska, Imogen Claire, Ken Parry.

Richard Burton. *Wagner* (GB-Austria-Hungary/1983/540–300m/C) D: Tony Palmer. C: Vanessa Redgrave, Gemma Craven, Laszlo Galffi, John Gielgud, Ralph Richardson, Laurence Olivier, Ekkerhard Schall, Ronald Pickup, Miguel Herz-Kestranek, Marthe Keller, Gwyneth Jones, Franco Nero.

546 Walker, James John "Jimmy" (1881–1946)

Popular, flamboyant mayor of New York City (1926–32); Walker's administration was rife with corruption and he was forced to resign.

Ralph Gamble. *The Eddy Duchin Story* (US/1956/123m/C) D: George Sydney. C: Tyrone Power, Kim Novak, Victoria Shaw, James Whitmore, Rex Thompson, Mickey Maga.

Bob Hope. *Beau James* (US/1957/105m/C) D: Melville Shavelson. B/on the book by Gene Fowler. C: Vera Miles, Paul Douglas, Alexis Smith, Walter Catlett.

547 Wallace, Lewis "Lew" (1827–1905)

In 1878 Lew Wallace (who later wrote the novel *Ben-Hur*) was appointed governor of New Mexico to clean up the mess left by the Lincoln County War that involved **Billy the Kid**, **John Chisum** and **John Tunstall**.

Berton Churchill. *The Big Stampede* (US/1932/63m/BW) D: Tenny Wright. C: John Wayne, Noah Beery, Mae Madison, Luis Alberni, Paul Hurst.

Joseph King. *Land Beyond the Law* (US/1937/54m/BW) D: B. Reeves Easton. C: Dick Foran, Linda Perry, Wayne Morris, Irene Franklin, Glenn Strange, Edmund Cobb.

Claude Stroud. *I Shot Billy the Kid* (US/1950/57m/BW) D: William Berke. C: Donald Barry, Robert Lowery, Wally Vernon, Tom Neal, Wendy Lee, Richard Farmer.

Robert Barrat. *The Kid from Texas* (aka *Texas Kid, Outlaw*) (US/1950/78m/C) D: Kurt Neumann. C: Audie Murphy, Gale Storm, Shepperd Strudwick, Will Geer, Frank Wilcox.

Otis Garth. *The Law vs. Billy the Kid* (US/1954/72m/C) D: William Castle. C: Scott Brady, Betta St. John, James Griffith, Alan Hale, Jr., Paul Cavanagh, Bill Phillips, Robert Griffin.

Ralph Moody. *Strange Lady in Town* (US/1955/112m/C) D: Mervyn LeRoy. C: Greer Garson, Dana Andrews, Lois Smith, Cameron Mitchell, Walter Hampden, Nick Adams.

Jason Robards. *Pat Garrett and Billy the Kid* (US/1973/122–106m/C) D: Sam Peckinpah. C: Kris Kristofferson, James Coburn, Bob Dylan, Richard Jaeckel, Katy Jurado, Barry Sullivan.

Scott Wilson. *Young Guns II* (US/1990/105m/C) D: Geoff Murphy. C: Emilio Estevez, Kiefer Sutherland, Lou Diamond Phillips, Christian Slater, William Petersen, James Coburn, Balthazar Getty, Chief Buddy Redbow, Alan Ruck, R.D. Call, Jack Kehoe.

548 Walsingham, Sir Francis (1530?–1590)

English statesman and member of the parliament of **Elizabeth I**. Walsingham created an intelligence system which discovered a plot to assassinate Elizabeth. The evidence led to the execution of **Mary Queen of Scots**.

Walter Byron. *Mary of Scotland* (US/1936/123m/BW) D: John Ford. B/on the play by Maxwell Anderson. C: Katharine Hepburn, Fredric March, Florence Eldridge, Douglas Walton, John Carradine, Robert Barrat, Gavin Muir, Ian Keith, Ralph Forbes, Alan Mowbray.

Henry David. *The Sea Hawk* (US/1940/126m/BW) D: Michael Curtiz. C: Errol Flynn, Brenda Marshall, Claude Rains, Flora Robson, Donald Crisp, Henry Daniell, Alan Hale, Montagu Love.

Basil Dignam. *Seven Seas to Calais* (Italy/1962/99m/C) D: Rudolph Mate & Primo Zeglio. C: Rod Taylor, Irene Worth, Keith Michell, Anthony Dawson, Esmerelda Ruspoli, Umberto Raho.

Rick Warner. *Mary, Queen of Scots* (GB/1971/128m/C) D: Charles Jarrot. C: Vanessa Redgrave, Glenda Jackson, Patrick McGoohan, Timothy Dalton, Nigel

Davenport, Trevor Howard, Daniel Massey, Ian Holm, Andrew Keir, Katherine Kath, Robert James, Richard Denning.

Geoffrey Rush. *Elizabeth* (US/1998/124m/C) D: Shekar Kapur. AA Best makeup. GG Best Actress. C: Cate Blanchett, Joseph Fiennes, Fanny Ardant, James Frain, Richard Attenborough, Christopher Eccleston, Vincent Cassel, George Yiasoumi, Kathy Burke.

549 Warhol, Andy (1928–1987)

American painter, one of the leaders of the Pop Art movement, and under-ground film maker, coined the phrase "Everyone gets their 15 minutes of fame."

Crispin Glover. *The Doors* (US/1991/135m/C) D: Oliver Stone. C: Val Kilmer, Frank Whaley, Kevin Dillon, Meg Ryan, Kyle MacLachlan, Billy Idol, Dennis Burkley, Josh Evans, Michael Masden, Michael Wincott, Kathleen Quinlan, John Densmore, Will Jordan, Mimi Rogers, Paul Williams, Bill Graham, Billy Vera, Bill Kunstler, Wes Studi, Costas Mandylor, Sean Stone.

Jared Harris. *I Shot Andy Warhol* (GB-US/1996/103m/C) D: Mary Harron. C: Lili Taylor, Martha Plimpton, Lothaire Bluteau, Anna Levine, Peter Friedman, Tahnee Welch, Jamie Harrold, Donovan Leitch, Michael Imperioli, Reg Rogers, William Sage, Jill Hennessy, Coco McPherson, Myriam Cyr.

Sean Sullivan. *Studio 54* (aka *54*) (US/1998/89m/C) D: Mark Christopher. C: Ryan Phillippe, Salma Hayek, Neve Campbell, Mike Myers, Sela Ward, Breckin Meyer, Sherry Stringfield, Ellen Albertini Dow, Cameron Mathison, Michelle Risi, Noam Jenkins, Jay Goede, Patrick Taylor, Heather Matarazzo, Skipp Sudduth, Aemilia Robinson, Louis Negin, Lauren Hutton, Thelma Houston.

550 Washington, George (1732–1799)

American Revolutionary War hero and the 1st President of the United States (1789–97), Washington, surprisingly, has never been featured in a Hollywood biopic. In television mini-series he's been played by Barry Bostwick, in *George Washington* (84) and *George Washington II: The Forging of a Nation* (86); Peter Graves in *The Rebels* (79), Stephen Lang (voice only) in *Liberty, the American Revolution* (97), and by Brian Denehy in *Founding Fathers* (2000).

Alan Mowbray. *Alexander Hamilton* (US/1931/73m/BW) D: John G. Adolfi. B/on the play by George Arliss & Mary Hamlin. C: George Arliss, Doris Kenyon, Montagu Love, Morgan Wallace, Gwendolyn Logan, John T. Murray, Charles Middleton, Lionel Belmore.

Alan Mowbray. *The Phantom President* (US/1932/80m/BW) D: Norman Taurog. B/on a novel by George F. Worts. C: George M. Cohan, Claudette Colbert, Charles Middleton.

Aaron Edwards. *Are We Civilized?* (US/1934/70m/BW) D: Edwin Carewe. C: Frank McGlynn, Alin Cavin, Harry Burkhart, Charles Requa, Bert Lindley, William Humphrey.

George Houston. *The Howards of Virginia* (aka *Tree of Liberty*) (US/1940/117m/BW) D: Frank Lloyd. B/on the novel *The Tree of Liberty* by Elizabeth Page.

C: Cary Grant, Martha Scott, Cedric Hardwicke, Alan Marshal, Richard Carlson, Richard Gaines.

Montagu Love. *The Remarkable Andrew* (US/1942/80m/BW) D: Stuart Heisler. B/on the novel by Dalton Trumbo. C: William Holden, Ellen Drew, Brian Donlevy, Rod Cameron, Richard Webb, Frances Gifford, Brandon Hurst, Gilbert Emery, George Watts.

Alan Mowbray. *Where Do We Go from Here?* (US/1945/77m/C) D: Gregory Ratoff. C: Fred MacMurray, Joan Leslie, June Haver, Anthony Quinn, Fortunio Bonanova, John Davidson.

Douglas Dumbrille. *Monsieur Beaucaire* (US/1946/93m/BW) D: George Marshall. B/on the novel by Booth Tarkington. C: Bob Hope, Joan Caulfield, Patric Knowles, Marjorie Reynolds, Reginald Owen, Hillary Brooke, Howard Freeman.

Richard Gaines. *Unconquered* (US/1947/146m/BW) D: Cecil B. DeMille. B/on the novel *Unconquered, A Novel of the Pontiac Conspiracy* by Neil H. Swanson. C: Gary Cooper, Paulette Goddard, Howard Da Silva, Boris Karloff, Ward Bond, Frank Wilcox.

James Seay. *When the Redskins Rode* (US/1951/78m/C) D: Lew Landers. C: Jon Hall, Mary Castle, John Ridgley, Pedro De Cordoba, Lewis L. Russell.

John Crawford. *John Paul Jones* (US/1959/126m/C) D: John Farrow. B/on the story *Nor'wester* by Clements Ripley. C: Robert Stack, Bette Davis, Marisa Pavan, Charles Coburn, Jean-Pierre Aumont, Macdonald Carey, Susana Canales, Eric Pohlmann.

Howard St. John. *Lafayette* (France/1962/110m/C) D: Jean Dreville. C: Michel Le Royer, Jack Hawkins, Wolfgang Priess, Orson Welles, Vittorio De Sica, Edmund Purdom, Liselotte Pulver, Albert Remy, Renee Saint-Cyr.

Frank Windsor. *Revolution* (US/1985/125m/C) D: Hugh Hudson. C: Al Pacino, Donald Sutherland, Nastassja Kinski, Joan Plowright, Dave King, Annie Lennox.

Terry Layman. *The Patriot* (US/2000/164m/C) D: Roland Emmerich. C: Mel Gibson, Heath Ledger, Joely Richardson, Jason Isaacs, Donal Logue, Michael Neeley, Rene Auberjonois, Adam Baldwin, Lisa Brenner, Beatrice Bush, Bryan Chafin, Chris Cooper, Mary Jo Deschanel, Shan Omar Huey, Jay Arlen Jones, Tchéky Karyo, Logan Lerman, Skye McCole Bartusiak, Trevor Morgan, Jamieson Price, Hank Stone, Kristian Truelsen, Mark Twogood, Joey D. Vieira, Tom Wilkinson, Grahame Wood, Peter Woodward.

551 Webster, Daniel (1782–1852)

American lawyer and politician, Webster was famed for his oratorical skills.

George MacQuarrie. *The Mighty Barnum* (US/1934/87m/BW) D: Walter Lang. C: Wallace Beery, Adolphe Menjou, Virginia Bruce, Janet Beecher, Herman Bing, Davison Clark.

Sidney Toler. *The Gorgeous Hussey* (US/1936/103m/BW) D: Clarence Brown. B/on the novel by Samuel Hopkins Adams. C: Joan Crawford, Robert Taylor, Lionel Barrymore, Melvyn Douglas, James Stewart, Franchot Tone, Frank Conroy, Charles Trowbridge.

Edward Arnold. *The Devil and Daniel Webster* (aka *All That Money Can Buy*) (aka *Here Is a Man*) (aka *A Certain Mr. Scratch*) (US/1941/107m/BW) D: William Dieterle. B/on the story by Stephen Vincent Benet. C: Walter Huston, Jane Darwell, Simone Simon, Gene Lockhart, John Qualen, Jeff Corey, Frank Conlan.

552 Weiss, Hymie (1898–1926)

(Earl Wajcieckowski) Chicago bootlegger and gangster, Weiss was shot and killed by gunmen working for his rival, **Al Capone**.

Lewis Charles. *Al Capone* (US/1959/105m/BW) D: Richard Wilson. C: Rod Steiger, Fay Spain, Murvyn Vye, Nehemiah Persoff, James Gregory, Martin Balsam, Robert Gist.

Reed Hadley. *The St. Valentine's Day Massacre* (US/1967/100m/C) D: Roger Corman. C: Jason Robards, George Segal, Ralph Meeker, Jean Hale, Clint Ritchie, Frank Silvera, Joseph Campanella, Harold J. Stone, Bruce Dern, John Agar, Rico Cattani, Jack Nicholson.

John D. Chandler. *Capone* (US/1975/101m/C) D: Steve Carver. C: Ben Gazzara, Susan Blakely, Harry Guardino, John Cassavetes, Sylvester Stallone, Robert Phillips, John Orchard.

553 Welles, George Orson (1915–1985)

Actor-director-writer-producer, Welles' career, by his own admission, started at the top, *Citizen Kane* (41), and went down. His other films include *The Magnificent Ambersons* (42), *The Third Man* (49), and *Touch of Evil* (58). In TV movies he's been portrayed by Paul Shenar in *The Night That Panicked America* (75), Edward Edwards in *Rita Hayworth: The Love Goddess* (83), Eric Purcell in *Malice in Wonderland* (85), by Liev Schreiber in *RKO 281* (99) and the young Welles was portrayed by Aaron Keeling (non speaking role). *RKO 281* was awarded the Golden Globe as Best Motion Picture made for Television.

Arrigo Barnabe. *Nem Tudo E Verdade* (aka *Not Everything Is True*) (Brazil/1986/C) D: Rogerio Sganzerla.

Vincent D'Onofrio. *Ed Wood* (US/1994/127m/BW) D: Tim Burton. C: Johnny Depp, Martin Landau, Sarah Jessica Parker, Patricia Arquette, Jeffrey Jones.

Jean Guerin. *Heavenly Creatures* (New Zealand/1994/98m/C) D: Peter Jackson. C: Melanie Lynskey, Kate Winslet, Sarah Pierse, Diana Kent.

Angus MacFadyen. *Cradle Will Rock* (US/1999/109m/C) D: Tim Robbins. C: Hank Azaria, Rubén Blades, Joan Cusack, John Cusack, Cary Elwes, Philip Baker Hall, Cherry Jones, Bill Murray, Vanessa Redgrave, Susan Sarandon, John Turturro, Barnard Hughes, John Carpenter, Gretchen Mol, Corina Katt.

554 Wellington, Duke of (1769–1852)

(Arthur Wellesley) British general most remembered for his victory over **Napoleon** at Waterloo, Wellington also served as England's Prime Minister (1828–30, 1834). He was portrayed by John Wood in the TV mini-series *Victoria and Albert* (2001).

Humberstone Wright. *Congress Dances* (aka *Der Kongress Tanzt*) (Germany/1931/92m/BW) D: Eric Charell. C: Lilian Harvey, Conrad Veidt, Henri Graat.

C. Aubrey Smith. *The House of Rothschild* (US/1934/94m/C) D: Alfred Werker. B/on the play by George Humbert Westley. C: George Arliss, Boris Karloff, Loretta Young, Robert Young, Florence Arliss, Alan Mowbray, Georges Renavent, Lumsden Hare, Holmes Herbert.

William Faversham. *Becky Sharp* (US/1935/83m/C) D: Rouben Mamoulian. B/on the play by Langdon Mitchell and the novel *Vanity Fair* by William Makepeace Thackeray. C: Miriam Hopkins, Frances Dee, Cedric Hardwicke, Billie Burke, Olaf Hytten.

George Arliss. *The Iron Duke* (GB/1935/80m/BW) D: Victor Saville. C: Gladys Cooper, Emlyn Williams, Ellaline Terriss, Allan Aynesworth, Felix Aylmer, Gerald Lawrence, Gibb McLaughlin, Frederick Leister, Edmund Willard, Farren Soutar.

Matthew Boulton. *The Firefly* (US/1937/140m/BW) D: Robert Z. Leonard. B/on the musical play by Rudolf Friml and Otto Harbach. C: Jeanette MacDonald, Allan Jones, Warren William, Douglas Dumbrille, Tom Rutherford, Stanley Price.

James Dale. *Victoria the Great* (GB/1937/110m/C) D: Herbert Wilcox. B/on the play *Victoria Regina* by Laurence Housman. C: Anna Neagle, Anton Walbrook, H.B. Warner, Charles Carson, Hubert Harben, Felix Aylmer, Arthur Young, Derrick De Marney, Hugh Miller, Percy Parsons, Henry Hallatt, Gordon McLeod, Wyndham Goldie.

C. Aubrey Smith. *Sixty Glorious Years* (aka *Queen of Destiny*) (GB/1938/90m/C) D: Herbert Wilcox. C: Anna Neagle, Anton Walbrook, Charles Carson, Felix Aylmer, Pamela Standish, Gordon McLeod, Henry Hallatt, Wyndham Goldie, Malcolm Keen, Derrick De Marney, Joyce Bland, Harvey Braban, Aubrey Dexter, Laidman Browne.

Brandon Hurst. *Devotion* (US/1946/108m/BW) D: Curtis Bernhardt. C: Ida Lupino, Olivia de Havilland, Nancy Coleman, Paul Henried, Sydney Greenstreet, Arthur Kennedy, Dame May Whitty, Montagu Love, Reginald Sheffield, Victor Francen.

Torin Thatcher. *The Miracle* (US/1959/121m/C) D: Irving Rapper. B/on the play by Karl Vollmoeller. C: Carroll Baker, Roger Moore, Walter Slezak, Vittorio Gassman.

John Neville. *The Adventures of Gerard* (GB-Italy-Switzerland/1970/91m/C) D: Jerzy Skolimowski. B/on *The Exploits of Brigadier Gerard* stories by A. Conan Doyle. C: Peter McEnery, Claudia Cardinale, Eli Wallach, Jack Hawkins, Mark Burns, Paolo Stoppa.

Christopher Plummer. *Waterloo* (Italy-USSR/1970/123m/C) D: Sergei Bondarchuk. C: Rod Steiger, Orson Welles, Virginia McKenna, Michael Wilding, Donal Donnelly, Jack Hawkins, Dan O'Herlihy, Rupert Davies, Aldo Cecconi, Rodolfo Lodi.

Laurence Olivier. *Lady Caroline Lamb* (GB/1972/122m/C) D: Robert Bolt. C: Sarah Miles, Jon Finch, Richard Chamberlain, John Mills, Margaret Leighton, Ralph Richardson.

555 White, Stanford (1853–1906)

Noted American architect (Boston Public Library, the Washington Arch), White has been portrayed in films solely as **Harry K. Thaw's** murder victim over a previous affair White had had with Thaw's wife, Evelyn Nesbit.

Ray Milland. *The Girl in the Red Velvet Swing* (US/1955/109m/C) D: Richard Fleischer. C: Farley Granger, Joan Collins, Luther Adler, Cornelia Otis Skinner, Glenda Farrell, Richard Travis.

Norman Mailer. *Ragtime* (US/1981/155m/C) D: Milos Forman. B/on the novel by E.L. Doctorow. C: James Cagney, Brad Dourif, Moses Gunn, Elizabeth McGovern, Pat O'Brien, Kenneth McMillan, Donald O'Connor, James Olson, Mandy Patinkin, Howard E. Rollins, Robert Boyd, Jeff DeMunn, Robert Joy, Mary Steenburgen.

556 Wilde, Oscar (1854–1900)

(Oscar Fingall O'Flahertie Wills Wilde) Irish writer whose works include *The Picture of Dorian Gray* and *The Importance of Being Earnest*, Wilde's career and life were destroyed when he was sent to prison following a conviction on charges of homosexuality. (See **Douglas, Alfred**)

Robert Morley. *Oscar Wilde* (GB/1960/96m/BW) D: Gregory Ratoff. B/on the play by Leslie and Sewell Stokes. C: Phyllis Calvert, John Neville, Ralph Richardson, Dennis Price, Alexander Knox, Edward Chapman, Leonard Sachs.

Peter Finch. *The Trials of Oscar Wilde* (aka *The Man with the Green Carnation*) (aka *The Green Carnation*) (GB/1960/123m/C) D: Ken Hughes. B/on the book by Montgomery Hyde and the play *The Stringed Lute* by John Furnell. Best English-Language Foreign Film (GG). C: John Fraser, Yvonne Mitchell, Lionel Jeffries, Nigel Patrick, James Mason, Emrys Jones, Laurence Naismith, Naomi Chance, Sonia Dresdel.

John De Marco. *The Best House in London* (GB/1969/97m/C) D: Philip Savile. C: David Hemmings, Joanna Pettet, Arnold Diamond, Neal Arden, George Reynolds, Suzanne Hunt.

Nickolas Grace. *Salome's Last Dance* (GB/1988/89m/C) D: Ken Russell. B/on the play *Salome* by Oscar Wilde. C: Douglas Hodge, Glenda Jackson, Stratford Johns, Imogen Millais-Scott, Denis Ull, Ken Russell, Imogen Claire.

Stephen Fry. *Wilde* (GB/1998/115m/C) D: Brian Gilbert C: Jude Law, Tom Wilkinson, Vanessa Redgrave, Jennifer Ehle, Gemma Jones, Judy Parfitt, Zoe Wannamaker, Michael Sheen.

Michael Culkin. *An Ideal Husband* (GB-US/1999/97m/C) D: Oliver Parker. B/on the play by Oscar Wilde. C: Cate Blanchett, Minnie Driver, Rupert Everet, Julianne Moore, Jeremy Northam, John Wood, Peter Vaughan, Ben Pullen, Marsha Fitzalan, Lindsay Duncan, Neville Phillips, Nickolas Grace, Simon Russell Beale, Anna Patrick.

Wilhelm II *see* 640

William III *see* 605

William IV *see* 610

557 Williams, Hiram King "Hank" (1923–1953)

Pre-eminent figure in American Country music, Williams died at the age of 29 following extended bouts with alcohol and drug use.

George Hamilton. *Your Cheatin' Heart* (aka *The Hank Williams Story*) (US/ 1964/100m/BW) D: Gene Nelson. C: Susan Oliver, Red Buttons, Arthur O'Connell, Rex Ingram.

Sneezy Waters. *Hank Williams: The Show He Never Gave* (Canada/1982/ 86m/C) D: David Acomba. B/on the play by Maynard Collins. C: Sean McCann, Dixie Seatle, Sean Hewitt.

Wilson, Edith *see* Wilson, Thomas Woodrow

558 Wilson, Thomas Woodrow (1856–1924)

The 29th President of the U.S. (1913–21), Wilson was awarded the Nobel Peace prize for his work in establishing the League of Nations following the first World War. He suffered a stroke in 1919, and his wife Edith reportedly assumed many of his presidential responsibilities. Edith Bolling Galt Wilson (1872–1961) was played by Geraldine Fitzgerald in *Wilson* and by Adrienne Marden in *Birdman of Alcatraz* (62).

Alexander Knox * Best Actor (GG). *Wilson* (US/1944/154m/C) D: Henry King. C: Charles Coburn, Geraldine Fitzgerald, Cedric Hardwicke, Vincent Price, Sidney Blackmer, Eddie Foy, Jr., Marcel Dalio, Edwin Maxwell, Francis X. Bushman, Clifford Brooke.

L. Korsakov. *The Unforgettable Year: 1919* (USSR/1952/C) D: Mikhail Chiaureli. B/on the play by Vsevold Vishnevsky. C: I. Molchanov, Mikhail Gelovani, Boris Andreyev, M. Kovaleva, Yevgeni Samoilov, Victor Stanitsine, V. Koltsov, Gnat Yura, Sergei Lukyanov.

Earl Lee. *The Story of Will Rogers* (US/1952/109m/C) D: Michael Curtiz. B/on the story *Uncle Clem's Boy* by Betty Blake Rogers. C: Will Rogers, Jr., Jane Wyman, Carl Benton Reid, Eve Miller, James Gleason, Slim Pickens, Noah Beery, Jr., Steve Brodie, William Forrest.

Frank Forsyth. *Oh! What a Lovely War* (GB/1969/144m/C) D: Richard Attenborough. B/on the musical play by Joan Littlewood and the play *The Long, Long Trail* by Charles Chilton. Best English Language Foreign Film (GG), and the United Nations Award (BFA). C: Pamela Abbott, Jack Hawkins, Laurence Olivier, Ralph Richardson, John Mills, John Gabriel, Paul Daneman, Dirk Bogarde, Vanessa Redgrave, Kenneth More, Michael Redgrave, Ian Holm, Wensley Pithey, John Gielgud, Maggie Smith, Guy Middleton.

Jerzy Kaliszewski. *Polonia Restituta* (Poland-USSR-Hungary-Czechoslovakia/1981/C) D: Bohdan Poreba.

559 Winchell, Walter (1897–1972)

A dominating New York gossip columnist, Winchell has been the basis of many film characters including J.J. Hunsecker (played by Burt Lancaster) in *Sweet Smell of Success* (57). Winchell was portrayed by Mark Zimmerman in the TV movie *Dash and Lilly* (99).

   Vaughan Meader. *Lepke* (US/1975/110–98m/C) D: Menahem Golan. C: Tony Curtis, Anjanette Comer, Michael Callan, Warren Berlinger, Gianni Russo, Vic Tayback, Milton Berle, Erwin Fuller, Jack Ackerman, Zitto Kazan, John Durren.

   Lloyd Gough. *The Private Files of J. Edgar Hoover* (US/1978/112m/C) D: Larry Cohen. C: Broderick Crawford, Jose Ferrer, Michael Parks, Ronee Blakely, Michael Sacks, Raymond St. Jacques, Andrew Duggan, Howard Da Silva, James Wainwright, Brad Dexter, William Jordan, Richard M. Dixon, Gordon Zimmerman, Lloyd Nolan, June Havoc, Dan Dailey, John Marley.

560 Wolsey, Cardinal Thomas (1473?–1530)

Once a favorite of **Henry VIII**, Wolsey lost the King's backing when he failed to provide Henry with a quickie divorce from **Katharine of Aragon**.

   Percy Marmont. *The Pearls of the Crown* (France/1937/120–100m/BW) D: Sacha Guitry & Christian-Jaque. C: Sacha Guitry, Jacqueline Delubac, Lyn Harding, Ermete Zacconi, Marguerite Moreno, Yvette Plenne, Catalano, Arletty, Derrick De Marney, Barbara Shaw, Simone Renant, Jean Louis Barrault, Emile Drain, Enrico Glori, Renee Saint-Cyr, Pizani, Claude Dauphin, Aime-Simon Gerard.

   D.A. Clarke-Smith. *The Sword and the Rose* (aka *When Knighthood Was in Flower*) (GB/1953/91m/C) D: Ken Annakin. B/on the novel *When Knighthood Was in Flower* by Charles Major. C: Richard Todd, Glynis Johns, James Robertson Justice, Michael Gough, Jane Barrett, Rosalie Crutchley, Peter Copley, Bryan Coleman, Jean Mercure.

   Orson Welles. *A Man for All Seasons* (GB/1966/120m/C) D: Fred Zinnemann. B/on the play by Robert Bolt. Best Picture Awards: (AA, NBR, GG, NYC, BFA Any Source and Best British Film), Best Director Awards: (AA, NBR, GG, NYC, DGA). C: Paul Scofield, Wendy Hiller, Leo McKern, Robert Shaw, Susannah York, Nigel Davenport, Vanessa Redgrave, Cyril Luckham.

   Anthony Quayle. *Anne of the Thousand Days* (GB/1969/145m/C) D: Charles Jarrott. B/on the play by Maxwell Anderson. C: Richard Burton, Genevieve Bujold, Irene Papas, John Colicos, Michael Hordern, Katharine Blake, William Squire, Lesley Patterson, Nicola Pagett.

   Terry Scott. *Carry on Henry VIII* (GB/1970/89m/C) D: Gerald Thomas. C: Sidney James, Kenneth Williams, Joan Sims, Charles Hawtrey, Peter Gilmore, Monica Dietrich, Patsy Rowlands.

   John Bryans. *The Six Wives of Henry VIII* (aka *Henry VIII and His Six Wives*) (GB/1972/125m/C) D: Waris Hussein. C: Keith Michell, Frances Cuka, Charlotte Rampling, Jane Asher, Jenny Bos, Lynne Frederick, Barbara Leigh-Hunt, Donald Pleasence, Simon Henderson, Annette Crosbie, Michael Goodliffe, Bernard Hepton, Dorothy Tutin.

561 Woodward, Robert Upchurch "Bob" (1943–)

American journalist who, with his partner Carl Bernstein, broke the "Water-gate Scandal" that forced President **Richard M. Nixon** from office. Bernstein was portrayed by Dustin Hoffman in *All the President's Men* and was the basis for Jack Nicholson's role in *Heartburn*. (86).

Robert Redford. *All the President's Men* (US/1976/138m/C) D: Alan J. Pakula. B/on the book by Bob Woodward & Carl Bernstein. C: Dustin Hoffman, Jack Warden, Martin Balsam, Hal Holbrook, Jason Robards, Jane Alexander, Meredith Baxter, Ned Beatty.

J.T. Walsh. *Wired* (US/1989/110m/C) D: Larry Peerce. B/on the book by Bob Woodward. C: Michael Chiklis, Ray Sharkey, Patti D'Arbanville, Lucinda Jenney.

Will Ferill. *Dick* (US/1999/95m) D: Andrew Fleming. C: Kirsten Dunst, Michelle Williams, Dan Hedaya, Bruce McCulloch, Dave Foley, Jim Breuer, Terri Garr, Ana Gasteyer, Harry Shearer, Saul Rubinek, Richard Fitzpatrick, Len Doncheff, Deborah Grover.

562 Woolf, Virginia (1882–1941)

(Virginia Stephen) Influential English novelist and critic, whose London home was the center of the Bloomsbury Group. Like **James Joyce**, Woolf wrote in the stream-of-consciousness style, which greatly influenced the modern novel. Among her works adapted to film are *Mrs. Dalloway* and *Orlando*. Woolf was troubled by mental illness, and in a deep depression, committed suicide by drowning.

Joanna McCallum. *Tom & Viv* (GB/US/1994/115m/C) D: Brian Gilbert. B/on a play by Michael Hastings. C: Willem Dafoe, Miranda Richardson, Rosemary Harris, Tim Dutton, Nickolas Grace, Geoffrey Bayldon, Clare Holman, Philip Locke, Joseph O'Connor, John Savident, Michael Attwell, Sharon Bower, Linda Spurrier, Roberta Taylor.

Nicole Kidman. *The Hours* (US/2001/C) D: Stephen Daldry. B/on the novel by Michael Cunningham. C: Julianne Moore, Meryl Streep, Allison Janney, Ed Harris, Claire Danes, Toni Collette, Eileen Atkins, Stephen Dillane, Charley Ramm, John C. Reilly, Miranda Richardson.

563 Woollcott, Alexander Humphreys (1887–1943)

Theatre/literary critic and one of the acerbic wits of the famed Algonquin Round-table group (see **Parker, Dorothy**), Woollcott appeared in a few films, himself, *Babes on Broadway* (41), *Gift of Gab* (34), *The Scoundrel* (35), and was the basis for the character Sheridan Whiteside in *The Man Who Came to Dinner* (42).

Earl Montgomery. *Act One* (US/1964/110m/BW) D: Dore Schary. B/on the book by Moss Hart. C: George Hamilton, Jason Robards, Jr., Jack Klugman, Ruth Ford, Eli Wallach.

Jock Livingston. *Star!* (aka *Those Were the Happy Times*) (US/1968/175–120m/C) D: Robert Wise. C: Julie Andrews, Richard Crenna, Michael Craig, Daniel Massey, Bruce Forsyth, Jenny Agutter, Anna Lee, Lester Matthews, Bernard Fox.

Tom McGowan. *Mrs. Parker and the Vicious Circle* (US/1994/125m/C) D: Alan Rudolph. C: Jennifer Jason Leigh, Campbell Scott, Matthew Broderick, Peter Gallagher, Lili Taylor, Keith Carradine, Nick Cassavetes, David Thornton, Malcolm Gets, Gwyneth Paltrow.

564 Yamamoto, Isoruku (1884–1943)

Japanese Admiral and planner of the Pearl Harbor attack, Yamamoto was killed when his plane was shot down in the south Pacific.

Toshiro Mifune. *I Bombed Pearl Harbor* (aka *The Storm Over the Pacific*) (Japan/1960/100m/C) D: Shue Matsubayashi. C: Yosuke Natsuki, Koji Tsurata, Misa Uehara.

James T. Goto. *The Gallant Hours* (US/1960/115m/BW) D: Robert Montgomery. C: James Cagney, Dennis Weaver, Ward Costello, Richard Jaeckel, Selmer Jackson.

Toshiro Mifune. *Admiral Yamamoto* (Japan/1968/131m/C) D: Seiji Murayama. C: Yuzo Kayama.

Shogo Shimada. *Gateway to Glory* (Japan/1969/122m/C) D: Mitsuo Murayama. C: Kichiemon, Nakamura, Ryunosuke Minegishi.

Toshiro Mifune. *The Militarists* (Japan/1970) D: Hiromichi Horikawa.

Soh Yamamura. *Tora! Tora! Tora!* (US-Japan/1970/143m/C) D: Richard Fleischer, Toshio Masuda & Kinji Fukasaku. B/on the books *Tora! Tora! Tora!* by Gordon Prange and *The Broken Seal* by Ladislas Farago. C: Martin Balsam, Jason Robards, Joseph Cotten, Tatsuya Mihashi, E.G. Marshall, James Whitmore, Wesley Addy, Leon Ames, Keith Andes, Richard Anderson, George Macready, Neville Brand.

Toshiro Mifune. *Midway* (aka *The Battle of Midway*) (US/1976/132m/C) D: Jack Smight. C: Charlton Heston, Henry Fonda, James Coburn, Glenn Ford, Hal Holbrook, Robert Mitchum, Robert Wagner, Cliff Robertson, James Shigeta.

Mako. *Pearl Harbor* (US/2001/183m/C) D: Michael Bay. C: Ben Affleck, Josh Hartnett, Kate Beckinsale, William Lee Scott, Greg Zola, Ewen Bremner, Alec Baldwin, James King, Catherine Kellner, Jennifer Garner, Jon Voight, Cuba Gooding, Jr., Michael Shannon, Matthew Davis.

565 Young, Brigham (1801–1877)

Though not its founder, Young was the main leader of the Church of Jesus Christ of Latter Day Saints (The Mormons) in the religion's early years.

Dean Jagger. *Brigham Young—Frontiersman* (aka *Brigham Young*) (US/1940/114m/BW) D: Henry Hathaway. C: Tyrone Power, Linda Darnell, Brian Donlevy, Jane Darwell, John Carradine, Mary Astor, Vincent Price, Arthur Aylesworth, Jean Rogers.

Maurice Grandmaison. *Brigham* (US/1977/C) D: Philip Yordan & David Yeaman.

566 Younger, Thomas Coleman "Cole" (1844–1916)

A cousin of the **Daltons** and partners with **Frank** and **Jesse James**, Cole and his brothers robbed banks and trains throughout the midwest in the years following the Civil War. In 1876 his outlaw career ended when the townsfolk of Northfield, Minnesota, shot him up and sent him to prison from which he was paroled in 1901. Younger wrote an autobiography, *The Story of Cole Younger by Himself*, which was published in 1903.

Glenn Strange. *Days of Jesse James* (US/1939/63m/BW) D: Joseph Kane. C: Roy Rogers, George "Gabby" Hayes, Don Barry, Pauline Moore, Harry Woods, Michael Worth.

Dennis Morgan. *Bad Men of Missouri* (US/1941/75m/BW) D: Ray Enright. C: Jane Wyman, Wayne Morris, Arthur Kennedy, Victor Jory, Alan Baxter, Faye Emerson, Russell Simpson.

Steve Brodie. *Return of the Bad Men* (US/1948/90m/BW) D: Ray Enright. C: Randolh Scott, George "Gabby" Hayes, Robert Ryan, Anne Jeffreys, Richard Powers, Robert Bray, Lex Barker, Walter Reed, Michael Harvey, Dean White, Robert Armstrong.

Wayne Morris. *The Younger Brothers* (US/1949/77m/C) D: Edwin L. Marin. B/on the story *Three Bad Men* by Morton Grant. C: Janis Paige, Bruce Bennett, Geraldine Brooks, Robert Hutton, James Brown, Alan Hale, Fred Clark, Monte Blue, Tom Tyler, William Forrest, Ian Wolfe.

James Best. *Kansas Raiders* (US/1950/80m/C) D: Ray Enright. C: Audie Murphy, Brian Donlevy, Scott Brady, Richard Long, Dewey Martin, Richard Egan, Tony Curtis.

Bruce Bennett. *The Great Missouri Raid* (US/1950/84m/C) D: Gordon Douglas. C: Wendell Corey, MacDonald Carey, Ward Bond, Ellen Drew, Bill Williams, Anne Revere, Edgar Buchanan, Louis Jean Heydt, Lois Chartrand, James Millican, Whit Bissell.

Bruce Cabot. *Best of the Badmen* (US/1951/84m/C) D: William D. Russell. C: Robert Ryan, Claire Trevor, Jack Buetel, Lawrence Tierney, Tom Tyler, Bob Wilke, John Cliff.

Jim Davis. *The Woman They Almost Lynched* (US/1953/90m/BW) D: Allan Dwan. B/on the story by Michael Fessier. C: Brian Donlevy, Ben Cooper, James Brown, Audrey Totter, John Lund.

Sam Keller. *Jesse James' Women* (US/1954/83m/C) D: Don Barry. C: Donald Barry, Jack Beutel, Peggie Castle, Lita Baron, Joyce Rhed, Betty Brueck, Laura Lee.

Alan Hale, Jr. *The True Story of Jesse James* (aka *The James Brothers*) (US/1957/92m/C) D: Nicholas Ray. C: Robert Wagner, Jeffrey Hunter, Hope Lange, Agnes Moorehead, Carl Thayler.

Myron Healey. *Hell's Crossroads* (US/1957/73m/C) D: Franklin Andreon. C: Stephen McNally, Peggie Castle, Robert Vaughn, Harry Shannon, Henry Brandon, Douglas Kennedy.

Frank Lovejoy. *Cole Younger, Gunfighter* (US/1958/78m/C) D: R.G. Springsteen. B/on the novel *The Desperado* by Clifton Adams. C: James Best, Abby Dalton, Myron Healey.

Willard Parker. *Young Jesse James* (US/1960/73m/BW) D: William F. Claxton. C: Ray Stricklyn, Merry Anders, Robert Dix, Emile Meyer, Bob Palmer, Johnny O'Neill.

Bruce Sedley. *The Outlaws Is Coming* (US/1965/88m/BW) D: Norman Maurer. C: Larry Fine, Moe Howard, Joe De Rita, Nancy Kovack, Murray Alper, Joe Bolton, Bill Camfield, Hal Fryar, Johnny Ginger, Wayne Mack, Ed McDonnell, Paul Shannon, Sally Starr.

Cliff Robertson. *The Great Northfield Minnesota Raid* (US/1972/91m/C) D: Philip Kaufman. C: Robert Duvall, Luke Askew, R.G. Armstrong, Dana Elcar, Donald Moffat, John Pearce, Matt Clark.

David Carradine. *The Long Riders* (US/1980/99m/C) D: Walter Hill. C: Keith Carradine, Robert Carradine, James Keach, Stacy Keach, Dennis Quaid, Randy Quaid, Kevin Brophy, Christopher Guest, Nicholas Guest, Pamela Reed, James Remar, Fran Ryan, Savannah Smith, Harry Carey, Jr., James Whitmore, Jr., Shelby Leverington.

Randy Travis. *Frank and Jesse* (US/1994/105m/C) D: Robert Boris. C: Rob Lowe, Bill Paxton, Dana Wheeler-Nicholson, Maria Pitillo, Luke Askew, Sean Patrick Flanery, Alexis Arquette, Todd Field, John Pyper-Ferguson, Nicholas Sadler, William Atherton, Tom Chick, Mary Neff, Richard Maynard.

Ed Adams. *Lightning Jack* (Australia/1994/93m/C) D: Simon Wincer. C: Paul Hogan, Cuba Gooding, Jr., Beverly D'Angelo, Kamala Dawson, Pat Hingle.

Scott Caan. *American Outlaws* (US/2001/93m/C) D: Les Mayfield. B/on a story by Roderick Taylor. C: Colin Farrell, Ali Larter, Gabriel Macht, Gregory Smith, Harris Yulin, Will McCormack, Ronny Cox, Terry O'Quinn, Nathaniel Arcand, Kathy Bates, Timothy Dalton, Craig Erickson, Ty O'Neal, Joe Stevens.

567 Zapata, Emiliano (1879–1919)

Mexican revolutionary and fighter for the rights of Mexican Indians. Zapata joined with **Madero** in the struggle against **Diaz**, and when becoming disillusioned with Maderos' regime, he renewed his resistance against the government. When **Huerta** came to power Zapata joined with **Villa** in the marches on Mexico City. Upon returning to his homeland in Morales, Zapata was murdered by a government agent.

Marlon Brando. *Viva Zapata!* (US/1952/113m/BW) D: Elia Kazan. B/on the book *Zapata the Unconquerable* by Edgcumb Pinchon. C: Anthony Quinn, Jean Peters, Alan Reed, Harold Gordon, Margo, Frank Silvera, Frank De Kova, Fay Roope, Joseph Wiseman, Lou Gilbert.

Antonio Aguilar. *Emiliano Zapata* (aka *Zapata*) (Mexico/1970/C) D: Felipe Cazals. C: Mário Almada, Patricia Aspíllaga, Jaime Fernández.

Iwan Tomow. *Trini* (aka *Stirb für Zapata*) (East Germany/1976) D: Walter Beck. C: Gunnar Helm, Giso Weissbach, Dmitrina Sawowa, Gunter Friedrich, Michael Kann.

568 Ziegfeld, Florenz (1867–1932)

Famed theatrical producer, Ziegfeld is best known for his revue "The Ziegfeld Follies" which ran from 1907 until his death. He also produced the musical play *Showboat* and for a time managed **Fanny Brice** and **W.C. Fields**. In TV films

In their mountain hideout Zapata (Marlon Brando, right) and friend Pancho (Lou Gilbert) study the leaflet left by an emissary of Madero. Zapata is being urged to join Madero in the struggle against the dictatorial Diaz. *Viva Zapata!* (1952). (Corbis)

he has been portrayed by Paul Shenar in *Ziegfeld: The Man and His Women* (78) and by Julian Holloway in *Ellis Island* (84).

William Powell. *The Great Ziegfeld* (US/1936/170m/BW) D: Robert Z. Leonard. Best Picture (AA). C: Luise Rainer, Myrna Loy, Frank Morgan, Reginald Owen, Fannie Brice, Ray Bolger, A.A. Trimble, Buddy Doyle, Rosina Lawrence, Ruth Gillette.

William Powell. *Ziegfeld Follies* (US/1945/110m/C) D: Vincente Minelli. C: Judy Garland, Lucille Ball, Fred Astaire, Fanny Brice, Lena Horne, Red Skelton, Victor Moore, Lucille Bremer, Virginia O'Brien, Cyd Charisse, Gene Kelly, Edward Arnold, Esther Williams, Hume Cronyn, William Frawley, Ray Teal, Joseph Crehan, Kennan Wynn.

Eddie Kane. *The Jolson Story* (US/1946/128m/C) D: Alfred E. Green. C: Larry Parks, Evelyn Keyes, William Demarest, Ludwig Donath, Bill Goodwin, Edwin Maxwell.

William Forrest. *I'll See You in My Dreams* (US/1952/109m/BW) D: Michael Curtiz. C: Doris Day, Danny Thomas, Frank Lovejoy, Patrice Wymore, Ray Kellogg, James Gleason.

William Forrest. *The Story of Will Rogers* (US/1952/109m/C) D: Michael Curtiz. B/on the story *Uncle Clem's Boy* by Betty Blake Rogers. C: Will Rogers, Jr., Jane Wyman, Carl Benton Reid, Eve Miller, James Gleason, Slim Pickens, Noah Beery, Jr., Steve Brodie, Earl Lee.

William Forrest. *The Eddie Cantor Story* (US/1953/115m/C) D: Alfred E. Green. C: Keefe Brasselle, Marilyn Erskine, Aline MacMahon, Arthur Franz, Will Rogers, Jr., Jackie Barnett.

Wilton Graff. *The I Don't Care Girl* (US/1953/78m/C) D: Lloyd Bacon. C: Mitzi Gaynor, David Wayne, Oscar Levant, Bob Graham, Warren Stevens, Gwen Verdon.

Paul Henreid. *Deep in My Heart* (US/1954/130m/C) D: Stanley Donen. B/on the book by Elliott Arnold. C: Jose Ferrer, Merle Oberon, Walter Pidgeon, Mitchell Kowall.

Walter Woolf King. *The Helen Morgan Story* (aka *Both Ends of the Candle*) (US/1957/118m/BW) D: Michael Curtiz. C: Ann Blyth, Paul Newman, Richard Carlson, Gene Evans, Alan King, Cara Williams.

Walter Pidgeon. *Funny Girl* (US/1968/151m/C) D: William Wyler. B/on the musical play by Jule Styne, Bob Merrill & Isobel Lennart. C: Barbra Streisand, Omar Sharif, Kay Medford, Anne Francis, Lee Allen, Gerald Mohr, Frank Faylen.

Paul Stewart. *W.C. Fields and Me* (US/1976/111m/C) D: Arthur Hiller. B/on the book by Carlotta Monti & Cy Rice. C: Rod Steiger, Valerie Perrine, Jack Cassidy, Dana Elcar.

569 Zola, Emile Edouard Charles Antoine (1840–1902)

A famous French author of socially conscious novels, Zola has been portrayed in films most often for his involvement in the defense of Captain **Alfred Dreyfus**. In the TV movie *Prisoner of Honor* (91) he was played by Martin Friend.

Heinrich George. *The Dreyfus Case* (aka *Dreyfus*) (Germany/1930/BW) D:

Richard Oswald. C: Fritz Kortner, Grete Moshelm, Albert Basserman, Oscar Homolka, Paul Bildt, Ferdinand Hart

George Merritt. *Dreyfus* (aka *The Dreyfus Case*) (GB/1931/90m/BW) D: F.W. Kraemer. B/on the play *The Dreyfus Case* by Herzog and Rehfisch. C: Cedric Hardwicke, Charles Carson, Sam Livesey, Beatrix Thomson, Garry Marsh, Leonard Shepherd.

Paul Muni. *The Life of Emile Zola* (US/1937/123m/BW) D: William Dieterle. Best Picture (AA,NYC). C: Gale Sondergaard, Joseph Schildkraut, Gloria Holden, Donald Crisp, Morris Carnovsky, Louis Calhern, Ralph Morgan, Grant Mitchell, Vladimir Sokoloff.

Emlyn Williams. *I Accuse!* (GB/1958/99m/BW) D: Jose Ferrer. B/on the book *Captain Dreyfus — A Story of Mass Hysteria* by Nicholas Halasz. C: Jose Ferrer, Viveca Lindfors, Anton Walbrook, Leo Genn, David Farrar, Donald Wolfit, Peter Illing.

Appendix A: Presidents of the United States

Listed below in chronological order are film portrayals of the men who have served as President of the United States. See the Portrayals section for major entries on **George Washington**, **Andrew Jackson**, **Abraham Lincoln**, **Theodore Roosevelt**, **Franklin Roosevelt**, **Harry Truman**, **Dwight Eisenhower**, **John F. Kennedy**, **Lyndon Johnson**, and **Richard Nixon**.

570 Adams, John (1735–1826, served 1797–1801)
William Daniels. *1776* (US/1972/141m/C) D: Peter H. Hunt. B/on the musical by Sherman Edwards and Peter Stone. C: Howard Da Silva, Ken Howard, Donald Madden, Ron Holgate, David Ford, Blythe Danner, Roy Poole, Virginia Vestoff, John Cullum.

571 Madison, James (1751–1836, served 1809–1817)
Ramsey Hill. *Old Louisiana* (aka *Treason*) (aka *Louisiana Gal*) (US/1938/63m/BW) D: Irvin Willat. C: Tom Keene, Rita Cansino (Hayworth), Robert Fiske, Allan Cavan.
Burgess Meredith. *Magnificent Doll* (US/1946/93m/BW) D: Frank Borzage. C: Ginger Rogers, David Niven, Robert Barrat, Grandon Rhodes, Larry Steers, Arthur Space.

572 Monroe, James (1758–1831, served 1817–1825)
Morgan Wallace. *Alexander Hamilton* (US/1931/73m/BW) D: John G. Adolfi. B/on the play by George Arliss & Mary Hamlin. C: George Arliss, Doris Kenyon, Alan Mowbray, Montagu Love, Gwendolyn Logan, John T. Murray, Charles Middleton, Lionel Belmore.

573 Adams, John Quincy (1767–1848, served 1825–1829)
Anthony Hopkins. *Amistad* (US/1997/152m/C) D: Steven Spielberg. C: Morgan Freeman, Nigel Hawthorne, Djimon Hounsou, Matthew McConaughey, David

Paymer, Pete Postlewaithe, Stellan Skarsgard, Razaaq Adoti, Abu Bakaar Fofanah, Anna Paquin, Tomas Milian, Chitwetel Ejiofor, Derrick N. Ashong, Geno Silva, John Ortiz, Ralph Brown, Darren Burroughs, Allan Rich, Paul Guilfoyle, Peter Firth, Xander Berkeley, Jeremy Northan, Arliss Howard, Austen Pendleton, Daniel Von Bargen, Rusty Schwimmer, Pedro Armendariz, Fay Masterson.

574 Van Buren, Martin (1782–1862, served 1837–1841)

Charles Trowbridge. *The Gorgeous Hussey* (US/1936/103m/BW) D: Clarence Brown. B/on the novel by Samuel Hopkins Adams. C: Joan Crawford, Robert Taylor, Lionel Barrymore, Melvyn Douglas, James Stewart, Franchot Tone, Frank Conroy, Sidney Toler.

Nigel Hawthorne. *Amistad* (US/1997/152m/C) D: Steven Spielberg. C: Morgan Freeman, Anthony Hopkins, Djimon Hounsou, Matthew McConaughey, David Paymer, Pete Postlewaithe, Stellan Skarsgard, Razaaq Adoti, Abu Bakaar Fofanah, Anna Paquin, Tomas Milian, Chitwetel Ejiofor, Derrick N. Ashong, Geno Silva, John Ortiz, Ralph Brown, Darren Burroughs, Allan Rich, Paul Guilfoyle, Peter Firth, Xander Berkeley, Jeremy Northan, Arliss Howard, Austen Pendleton, Daniel Von Bargen, Rusty Schwimmer, Pedro Armendariz, Fay Masterson.

575 Harrison, William H. (1773–1841, served 1841)

Douglas Dumbrille. *Ten Gentlemen from West Point* (US/1942/102m/BW) D: Henry Hathaway. C: George Montgomery, Maureen O'Hara, John Sutton, Laird Cregar, Ralph Byrd, Noble Johnson.

James Seay. *Brave Warrior* (US/1952/73m/C) D: Spencer G. Bennett. C: Jon Hall, Christine Larson, Jay Silverheels, Michael Ansara, Rory Mallinson.

576 Polk, James J. (1795–1849, served 1845–1849)

Addison Richards. *Oregon Trail* (US/1959/86m/C) D: Gene Fowler, Jr. C: Fred MacMurray, William Bishop, Nina Shipman, Gloria Talbot, Henry Hull, John Caradine.

577 Taylor, Zachary (1784–1850, served 1849–1850)

Allan Cavan. *Rebellion* (US/1938/60m/BW) D: Lynn Shores. C: Gino Corrado, Roger Gray, Rita Hayworth, Jack Ingram, Tom Keene, Theodore Lorch, Merrill McCormack, Duncan Renaldo, William Royle.

Robert Barrat. *Distant Drums* (US/1951/101m/C) D: Raoul Walsh. C: Gary Cooper, Mari Aldon, Richard Webb, Ray Teal.

Fay Roope. *Seminole* (US/1953/87m/C) D: Budd Boetticher. C: Rock Hudson, Barbara Hale, Anthony Quinn, Richard Carlson, Hugh O'Brien, Russell Johnson, Lee Marvin, James Best.

James Gammon. *One Man's Hero* (aka *Héroes sin patria*) (US-Spain/1999/121m/C) D: Lance Hool. C: Tom Berenger, Joaquim de Almeida, Daniela Romo, Mark Moses, Stuart Graham, Stephen Tobolowsky, Carlos Carrasco, Patrick Bergin, Don Wycherley, Jorge Bosso.

578 Pierce, Franklin (1804–1869, served 1853–1857)

Porter Hall. *The Great Moment* (US/1944/83m/BW) D: Preston Sturges. C: Joel McCrea, Betty Field, Harry Carey, William Demarest, Franklin Pangborn, Grady Sutton, Louis Jean Heydt, Jimmy Conlin.

579 Johnson, Andrew (1808–1875, served 1865–1869)

Van Heflin. *Tennessee Johnson* (aka *The Man on America's Conscience*) (US/1942/103m/BW) D: William Dieterle. C: Ruth Hussey, Lionel Barrymore, Marjorie Main, Regis Toomey, Montagu Love, Porter Hall, Morris Ankrum, Harry Worth, Ed O'Neill, Harrison Greene, Charles Dingle, Grant Withers, Lynne Carver, Noah Beery, Sr.

580 Hayes, Rutherford B. (1822–1893, served 1877–1881)

John Dilson. *Buffalo Bill* (US/1944/90m/C) D: William Wellman. C: Joel McCrea, Maureen O'Hara, Linda Darnell, Thomas Mitchell, Edgar Buchanan, Anthony Quinn, Moroni Olsen, Chief Thundercloud, Sidney Blackmer, Evelyn Beresford.

581 Garfield, James A. (1831–1881, served 1881)

Lawrence Wolf. *No More Excuses* (US/1968/62m/BW) D: Robert Downey, Sr. C: Don Calfa, Aimee Eccles.

Van Johnson. *The Price of Power* (Italy-Spain/1969/96m/BW) D: Tonio Valeri. C: Guiliano Gemma, Fernando Rey, Warren Vanders.

582 Arthur, Chester A. (1831–1886, served 1881–1885)

Emmett Corrigan. *Silver Dollar* (US/1932/84m/BW) D: Alfred E. Green. B/on the book *Silver Dollar; The Story of the Tabors* by David Karsner. C: Edward G. Robinson, Bebe Daniels, Walter Rogers, Niles Welch, Aline MacMahon, DeWitt Jennings.

Larry Gates. *Cattle King* (US/1963/88m/C) D: Tay Garnett. C: Robert Taylor, Joan Caulfield, Robert Loggia, Robert Middleton, Malcolm Atterbury.

583 Cleveland, Grover (1837–1908, served 1885–1889 and 1893–1897)

William B. Davidson. *Lillian Russell* (US/1940/127m/BW) D: Irving Cummings. C: Alice Faye, Edward Arnold, Don Ameche, Henry Fonda, Warren William, Claud Allister, Nigel Bruce, Eddie Foy, Jr., Leo Carillo, Milburn Stone.

Pat McCormick. *Buffalo Bill and the Indians, Or Sitting Bull's History Lesson* (aka *Buffalo Bill and the Indians*) (US/1976/120m/C) D: Robert Altman. B/on the play *Indians* by Arthur Kopit. C: Paul Newman, Burt Lancaster, Joel Grey, Harvey Keitel, Geraldine Chaplin, Frank Kaquitts, Will Sampsen.

584 Harrison, Benjamin (1833–1901, served 1889–1893)

Roy Gordon. *Stars and Stripes Forever* (US/1952/89m/C) D: Henry Koster. C: Clifton Webb, Robert Wagner, Ruth Hussey, Debra Paget, Finlay Currie.

585 McKinley, William (1843–1901, served 1897–1901)

Dell Henderson. John Carradine (voice only). *Message to Garcia* (US/1936/77m/BW) D: George Marshall. C: Wallace Beery, Barbara Stanwyck, John Boles, Alan Hale, Mona Barrie, Herbert Mundin.

Frank Conroy. *This Is My Affair* (aka *His Affair*) (US/1937/99m/BW) D: William S. Seiter. B/on the novel *The McKinley Case* by Melville Crossman. C: Robert Taylor, Barbara Stanwyck, Victor McLaglen, John Carradine, Sidney Blackmer, Robert McWade.

586 Coolidge, Calvin (1872–1933, served 1923–1927)

Ian Wolfe. *The Court-Martial of Billy Mitchell* (aka *One Man Mutiny*) (US/1955/100m/C) D: Otto Preminger. C: Gary Cooper, Charles Bickford, Ralph Bellamy, Rod Steiger, Elizabeth Montgomery, James Daly, Dayton Lumis, Herbert Heyes, Tom McKee, Phil Arnold.

587 Ford, Gerald (b.1913, served 1974–1977)

Dick Crockett. *The Pink Panther Strikes Again* (US/1976/103m/C) D: Blake Edwards. C: Peter Sellers, Herbert Lom, Colin Blakely, Leslie-Anne Down, Burt Kwouk, Byron Kane.

Larry Lindsey. *Hot Shots! Part Deux* (US/1993/89m/C) D: Jim Abrahams. C: Charlie Sheen, Lloyd Bridges, Valeria Golino, Richard Crenna, Miguel Ferrer, Jay Koch, Jerry Haleva, Mitchell Ryan, Buck McDancer, Ed Beheler, Daniel T. Healy.

588 Carter, Jimmy (b.1924, served 1977–1981)

Ed Beheler. *The Cayman Triangle* (US/1977/92m/C) D: Anderson Humphreys. C: Reid Dennis, Anderson Humphreys, Jules Kreitzer, John Morgan.

Ed Beheler. *Hot Shots! Part Deux* (US/1993/89m/C) D: Jim Abrahams. C: Charlie Sheen, Lloyd Bridges, Valeria Golino, Richard Crenna, Miguel Ferrer, Jay Koch, Jerry Haleva, Mitchell Ryan, Buck McDancer, Larry Lindsey, Daniel T. Healy.

589 Reagan, Ronald (b.1911, served 1981–1989)

Jay Koch. *Back to the Future Part II* (US/1989/107m/C) D: Robert Zemeckis. C: Michael J. Fox, Christopher Lloyd, Lea Thompson, Thomas F. Wilson, Harry Waters, Jr., Charles Fleischer, Joe Flaherty, Elisabeth Shue, James Tolkan.

Bryan Clarke. *Pizza Man* (US/1991/90m/C) D: J.D. Athens & J.F. Lawton. C: Ron Darian, Bob Delegall, Annabelle Gurwich, Bill Maher, David McKnight, Cathy Shambley.

Jay Koch. *Hot Shots! Part Deux* (US/1993/89m/C) D: Jim Abrahams. C: Charlie Sheen, Lloyd Bridges, Valeria Golino, Richard Crenna, Miguel Ferrer, Jerry Haleva, Mitchell Ryan, Buck McDancer, Larry Lindsey, Ed Beheler, Daniel T. Healy.

Jay Koch. *Panther* (US/1995/125m/C) D: Mario Van Peebles. C: Kadeem Hardison, Bokeem Woodbine, Joe Don Baker, Courtney B. Vance, Tyrin Turner, Huey Newton, Anthony Griffith, Bobby Brown, Nefertiti, James Russo, Chris Rock, Richard Dysart, Dick Gregory, Melvin Van Peebles, Jerry Rubin, Mario Van Peebles.

590 Bush, George (b.1924, served 1989–1993)

John Roarke. *Naked Gun 2½: The Smell of Fear* (US/1991/85m/C) D: David Zucker. C: Leslie Nielsen, George Kennedy, Priscilla Presley, O.J. Simpson, Robert Goulet, Richard Griffiths, Jacqueline Brooks, Lloyd Bochner, Tim O'Connor, Peter Mark Richman.

Daniel T. Healy. *Hot Shots! Part Deux* (US/1993/89m/C) D: Jim Abrahams. C: Charlie Sheen, Lloyd Bridges, Valeria Golino, Richard Crenna, Miguel Ferrer, Jay Koch, Jerry Haleva, Mitchell Ryan, Buck McDancer, Larry Lindsey, Ed Beheler.

Appendix B:
British Monarchs

Listed below in chronological order are film portrayals of the men and women who have ruled England since 871. See the Portrayals section for major entries on **Henry II, Richard I, John, Henry V, Richard III, Henry VIII, Edward VI, Elizabeth I, Charles I, Charles II, George III, George IV, Victoria** and **Edward VII.**

591 Alfred the Great (849–900, r. 871–900)
David Hemmings. *Alfred the Great* (GB/1969/122m/C) D: Clive Donner. C: Michael York, Prunella Ransome, Colin Blakely, Julian Glover, Ian McKellan.

592 Edward the Confessor (1004–1066, r. 1043–1066)
Eduard Franz. *Lady Godiva* (US/1955/89m/C) D: Arthur Lubin. C: Maureen O'Hara, George Nader, Victor McLaglin, Torin Thatcher, Robert Warwick.

593 Henry III (1207–1272, r. 1216–1272)
Maurice R. Tauzin. *The Bandit of Sherwood Forest* (US/1946/86m/C) D: George Sherman and Henry Levin. C: Cornel Wilde, Anita Louise, Jill Esmond, Edgar Buchanan.

594 Edward I (1239–1307, r. 1272–1307)
Michael Rennie. *The Black Rose* (US/1950/120m/C) D: Henry Hathaway. C: Tyrone Power, Cecile Aubry, Orson Welles, Jack Hawkins, Herbert Lom, James Robertson Justice.

Patrick McGoohan. *Braveheart* (US/1995/177m/C) D: Mel Gibson. Best Director, Best Picture, Best Makeup, Best Cineamphotography, Best Sound (AA). C: Mel Gibson, Sophie Marceau, Catherine McCormack, Brendan Gleeson, James Cosmo, David O'Hara, Angus MacFadyen, Peter Henly, James Robinson, Alun Armstrong, Ian Bannen.

595 Edward II (1284–1327, r. 1307–1327)

Steven Waddington. *Edward II* (GB/1991/91m/C) D: Derek Jarman. B/on the play by Christopher Marlowe. C: Kevin Collins, Andrew Tiernan, John Lynch, Dudley Sutton, Tilda Swinton, Jerome Flynn, Jodie Graber, Nigel Terry, Annie Lennox.

Peter Henly. *Braveheart* (US/1995/177m/C) D: Mel Gibson. Best Director, Best Picture, Best Makeup, Best Cineamphotography, Best Sound (AA). C: Mel Gibson, Sophie Marceau, Patrick McGoohan, Catherine McCormack, Brendan Gleeson, James Cosmo, David O'Hara, Angus MacFadyen, James Robinson, Alun Armstrong, Ian Bannen.

596 Edward III (1312–1377, r. 1327–1377)

Michael Hordern. *The Warriors* (GB/1955/85m/C) D: Henry Levin. C: Errol Flynn, Joanne Dru, Peter Finch, Patrick Holt, Yvonne Furneaux, Christopher Lee.

Jody Graber. *Edward II* (GB/1991/91m/C) D: Derek Jarman. B/on the play by Christopher Marlowe. C: Steve Waddington, Kevin Collins, Andrew Tiernan, John Lynch, Dudley Sutton, Tilda Swinton, Jerome Flynn, Nigel Terry, Annie Lennox.

597 Henry IV (1367–1413, r. 1399–1413)

Ian Keith. *The Black Shield of Falworth* (US/1954/98m/C) D: Rudolph Mate. B/on the novel *Men of Iron* by Howard Pyle. C: Tony Curtis, Janet Leigh, David Farrar, Dan O'Herlihy.

John Gielgud. *Chimes at Midnight* (aka *Falstaff*) (aka *Campanadas A Medianoche*) (Spain-Switzerland/1967/115m/BW) D: Orson Welles. B/on plays by Wm. Shakespeare and the book *The Chronicles of England* by Raphael Holinshed. C: Orson Welles, Jeanne Moreau, Margaret Rutherford, Keith Baxter, Marina Vlady, Norman Rodway, Michael Aldridge, Fernando Rey.

598 Henry VI (1421–1471, r. 1422–1461, 1470–71)

Miles Mander. *Tower of London* (US/1939/92m/BW) D: Rowland Lee. C: Basil Rathbone, Boris Karloff, Barbara O'Neill, Ian Hunter, Nan Grey, Ronald Sinclair, Ralph Forbes.

599 Edward IV (1442–1483, r. 1461–1483)

Ian Hunter. *Tower of London* (US/1939/92m/BW) D: Rowland Lee. C: Basil Rathbone, Boris Karloff, Barbara O'Neill, Nan Grey, Miles Mander, Ronald Sinclair, Ralph Forbes.

Cedric Hardwicke. *Richard III* (GB/1955/158m/C) D: Laurence Olivier. B/on the play by Wm. Shakespeare. Best Film (Any Source/British) (BFA). Best English-Language Foreign Film (GG). C: Laurence Olivier, Ralph Richardson, Claire Bloom, John Gielgud, Mary Kerridge, Pamela Brown, Paul Huson, Stanley Baker.

Justice Watson. *Tower of London* (US/1962/79m/BW) D: Roger Corman. C: Vincent Price, Michael Pate, Joan Freeman, Robert Brown, Sarah Selby, Eugene Martin, Donald Losby.

John Wood. *Richard III* (GB-US/1995/104m/C) D: Richard Loncraine. B/on the play by Wm. Shakespeare. C: Ian McKellen, Annette Bening, Maggie Smith, Nigel Hawthorne, Robert Downey, Jr., Edward Jewesbury, Marco Williamson.

600 Edward V (1470–1483, r. 1483)

Ronald Sinclair. *Tower of London* (US/1939/92m/BW) D: Rowland Lee. C: Basil Rathbone, Boris Karloff, Barbara O'Neill, Ian Hunter, Nan Grey, Miles Mander, Ralph Forbes.

Paul Huson. *Richard III* (GB/1955/158m/C) D: Laurence Olivier. B/on the play by Wm. Shakespeare. Best Film (Any Source/British) (BFA). Best English-Language Foreign Film (GG). C: Laurence Olivier, Ralph Richardson, Claire Bloom, John Gielgud, Cedric Hardwicke, Mary Kerridge, Pamela Brown, Stanley Baker.

Eugene Martin. *Tower of London* (US/1962/79m/BW) D: Roger Corman. C: Vincent Price, Michael Pate, Joan Freeman, Robert Brown, Justice Watson, Sarah Selby, Donald Losby.

Marco Williamson. *Richard III* (GB-US/1995/104m/C) D: Richard Loncraine. B/on the play by Wm. Shakespeare. C: Ian McKellen, Annette Bening, Maggie Smith, Nigel Hawthorne, John Wood, Robert Downey, Jr., Edward Jewesbury.

601 Henry VII (1457–1509, r. 1485–1509)

Ralph Forbes. *Tower of London* (US/1939/92m/BW) D: Rowland Lee. C: Basil Rathbone, Boris Karloff, Barbara O'Neill, Ian Hunter, Nan Grey, Miles Mander, Ronald Sinclair.

Stanley Baker. *Richard III* (GB/1955/158m/C) D: Laurence Olivier. B/on the play by Wm. Shakespeare. Best Film (Any Source/British) (BFA). Best English-Language Foreign Film (GG). C: Laurence Olivier, Ralph Richardson, Claire Bloom, John Gielgud, Cedric Hardwicke, Mary Kerridge, Pamela Brown, Paul Huson.

Edward Jewesbury. *Richard III* (GB-US/1995/104m/C) D: Richard Loncraine. B/on the play by Wm. Shakespeare. C: Ian McKellen, Annette Bening, Maggie Smith, Nigel Hawthorne, John Wood, Robert Downey, Jr., Marco Williamson.

602 Mary I (1516–1558, r. 1553–1558)

Yvette Plenne. *The Pearls of the Crown* (France/1937/120–100m/BW) D: Sacha Guitry & Christian-Jaque. C: Sacha Guitry, Jacqueline Delubac, Lyn Harding, Ermete Zacconi, Marguerite Moreno, Catalano, Arletty, Percy Marmont, Derrick De Marney, Barbara Shaw, Simone Renant, Jean Louis Barrault, Emile Drain, Enrico Glori, Renee Saint-Cyr, Pizani, Claude Dauphin, Aime-Simon Gerard.

Nicola Pagett. *Anne of the Thousand Days* (GB/1969/145m/C) D: Charles Jarrott. B/on the play by Maxwell Anderson. C: Richard Burton, Genevieve Bujold, Irene Papas, Anthony Quayle, John Colicos, Michael Hordern, Katharine Blake, William Squire, Lesley Patterson.

Jane Lapotaire. *Lady Jane* (GB/1986/144m/C) D: Trevor Nunn. C: Helena Bonham Carter, Cary Elwes, John Wood, Michael Hordern, David Waller, Warren Saire.

Kathy Burke. *Elizabeth* (US/1998/124m/C) D: Shekar Kapur. Best makeup (AA). Best Actress (GG). C: Cate Blanchett, Joseph Fiennes, Fanny Ardant, James Frain, Richard Attenborough, Christopher Eccleston, Vincent Cassel, George Yiasoumi, Geoffrey Rush.

603 James I (1566–1625, r. 1603–1625)

Anthony Eustrel. *Captain John Smith and Pocahontas* (US/1953/75m/C) D: Lew Landers. C: Anthony Dexter, Jody Lawrence, Alan Hale, Jr., Douglass Dumbrille.

Dudley Sutton. *Orlando* (GB/1993/92m/C) D: Sally Potter. B/on the novel by Virginia Woolf. C: Tilda Swinton, Billy Zane, Lothaire Bluteau, Charlotte Valandrey, Quentin Crisp, Peter Eyre, Thom Hoffman, Sarah Crowden, Roger Hammond.

604 James II (1633–1701, r. 1685–1688)

Vernon Steele. *Captain Blood* (US/1935/119m/C) D: Michael Curtiz. C: Errol Flynn, Olivia de Havilland, Lionel Atwill, Basil Rathbone, Ross Alexander, Guy Kibbee, Henry Stevenson, Robert Barrat, Donald Meek, J. Carroll Naish, Ivan Simpson.

George Curzon. *Lorna Doone* (US/1951/88m/C) D: Phil Karlson. B/on the novel by Richard D. Blackmore. C: Barbara Hale, Richard Greene, William Bishop, Ron Randell, Lester Matthews.

Henry Oscar. *Bonnie Prince Charlie* (GB/1948/118m/C) D: Anthony Kimmins. C: David Niven, Margaret Leighton, Jack Hawkins, Judy Campbell, Morland Graham, Finlay Currie.

605 William III (1650–1702, r. 1689–1702)

Miles Mander. *Captain Kidd* (US/1945/89m/BW) D: Rowland V. Lee. C: Charles Laughton, Randolph Scott, Barbara Britton, Reginald Owen, John Carradine.

Olaf Hytten. *Against All Flags* (US/1952/83m/C) D: George Sherman. C: Errol Flynn, Maureen O'Hara, Anthony Quinn, Robert Warwick, Mildred Natwick.

Thom Hoffman. *Orlando* (GB/1993/92m/C) D: Sally Potter. B/on the novel by Virginia Woolf. C: Tilda Swinton, Billy Zane, Lothaire Bluteau, Charlotte Valandrey, Quentin Crisp, Peter Eyre, Dudley Sutton, Sarah Crowden, Roger Hammond.

606 Mary II (1662–1694, r. 1689–1694)

Sarah Crowden. *Orlando* (GB/1993/92m/C) D: Sally Potter. B/on the novel by Virginia Woolf. C: Tilda Swinton, Billy Zane, Lothaire Bluteau, Charlotte Valandrey, Quentin Crisp, Peter Eyre, Thom Hoffman, Dudley Sutton, Roger Hammond.

607 Anne (1665–1714, r. 1702–1714)

Liselotte (Lilo) Pulver. *A Glass of Water* (Germany/1962/85m/BW) D: Helmut Käuther. B/on the play *Le Verre d'Eau* by Eugene Scribe. C: Rudolf Forster, Gustaf Grüdens, Horst Jansen, Hilde Krahl, Sabine Sinjen, Herbert Weissbach.

608 George I (1660–1727, r. 1714–1727)

Peter Bull. *Saraband* (aka *Saraband for Dead Lovers*) (GB/1948/95m/C) D: Basil Dearden. C: Stewart Granger, Joan Greenwood, Flora Robson, Françios Rosay, Anthony Quayle, Michael Gough, Christopher Lee.

Otto Waldis. *The Iron Glove* (US/1954/77m/C) D: William Castle. C: Robert Stack, Ursula Thiess, Richard Stapley, Charles Irwin, Alan Hale, Jr.

Eric Pohlmann. *Rob Roy, The Highland Rogue* (aka *Rob Roy*) (GB/1954/81m/C) D: Harold French. C: Richard Todd, Glynis Johns, James Robertson Justice, Michael Gough.

Harold Kasket. *Where's Jack?* (GB/1969/119m/C) D: James Clavell. C: Tommy Steele, Stanley Baker, Fiona Lewis, Alan Badel, Dudley Foster, Sue Lloyd, Noel Pucell.

609 George II (1683–1760, r. 1727–1760)

Olaf Hytten. *The Last of the Mohicans* (US/1936/91m/BW) D: George B. Seitz. B/on the novel by James Fennimore Cooper. C: Randolph Scott, Binnie Barnes, Heather Angel, Hugh Buckler, Henry Wilcoxon, Bruce Cabot, Ian MacLaren.

Martin Miller. *Bonnie Prince Charlie* (GB/1948/118m/C) D: Anthony Kimmins. C: David Niven, Margaret Leighton, Jack Hawkins, Judy Campbell, Morland Graham, Finlay Currie.

Ivan Triesault. *The Lady and the Bandit* (aka *Dick Turpin's Ride*) (US/1951/79m/BW) D: Ralph Murphy. B/on the poem "The Highwayman" by Alfred Noyes. C: Louis Hayward, Patricia Medina, Suzanne Dalbert, John Williams, Alan Mowbray, George Baxter.

Arthur Young. *John Wesley* (GB/1954/80m/BW) D: Norman Walker. C: Neal Arden, Derek Aylward, George Bishop, Erik Chitty, Henry Hewitt, Vincent Holman, Partick Holt, Edward Jewesbury, Roger Maxwell, Julien Mitchell, Keith Pyott, Leonard Sachs.

610 William IV (1765–1837, r. 1830–1837)

Julian Dallas. *Mrs. Fitzherbert* (GB/1947/99m/BW) D: Montgomery Tully. B/on the novel *Princess Fitz* by Winifred Carter. C: Peter Graves, Joyce Howard, Leslie Banks, Margaretta Scott, Wanda Rotha, Mary Clare, Frederick Valk, Ralph Truman, John Stuart, Barry Morse, Henry Oscar, Arthur Dulay, Moira Lister, Lily Kann.

Tom Gil. *The First Gentleman* (aka *The Affairs of a Rogue*) (GB/1948/111–95m/BW) D: Alberto Cavalcanti. B/on the play by Norman Ginsbury. C: Jean-Pierre Aumont, Joan Hopkins, Cecil Parker, Margaretta Scott, Hugh Griffith, Frances Waring, Jack Livesy.

611 Edward VIII (1894–1972, r. 1936)

David Yelland. *Chariots of Fire* (GB/1981/123m/C) D: Hugh Hudson. C: Ben Cross, Ian Charleson, Nigel Havers, Nick Farrell, Alice Krige, Cheryl Campbell, Ian Holm, John Gielgud, Lindsay Anderson, Patrick Magee, Nigel Davenport, Lawrence Christopher, Brad Davis.

612 Elizabeth II (b.1926, r. 1952–)

Jeanette Charles. *National Lampoon's European Vacation* (US/1985/94m/C) D: Amy Heckerling. C: Chevy Chase, Beverly D'Angelo, Jason Lively, Dana Hill, Eric Idle, Victor Lanoux, John Astin.

Jeanette Charles. *Naked Gun* (US/1988/85m/C) D: David Zucker. C: Leslie Nielsen, George Kennedy, Priscilla Presley, Ricardo Montalban, O.J. Simpson, Nancy Marchand.

Mary Reynolds. *Bullseye!* (GB/1990/95m/C) D: Michael Willner. C: Michael Caine, Roger Moore, Sally Kirkland, Patsy Kinset, Jenny Seagrove, John Cleese, Lee Paterson, Deborah Barrymore.

Appendix C:
French Monarchs

Listed below in chronological order are film portrayals of the men who have ruled France as King since 879. See the Portrayals section for major entries on **Louis XIII** and **Louis XVI**.

613 Louis III (r. 879–882)

Franco Nero. *Pope Joan* (GB/1972/132m/C) D: Michael Anderson. C: Liv Ullmann, Keir Dullea, Robert Beatty, Jeremy Kemp, Olivia de Havilland, Patrick Magee, Maximiliam Schell, Trevor Howard, Nigel Havers, Lesley-Ann Down, Andre Morell.

614 Louis VII (1121–1180, r. 1137–1180)

John Gielgud. *Becket* (GB/1964/148m/C) D: Peter Glenville. B/on the play by Jean Anouilh. Best Picture (GG). C: Richard Burton, Peter O'Toole, Donald Wolfit, Martita Hunt, Pamela Brown, Sian Phillips, Paolo Stoppa, Felix Aylmer.

615 Philippe II (1165–1223, r. 1180–1223)

C. Henry Gordon. *The Crusades* (US/1935/123m/BW) D: Cecil B. De Mille. Waldemar Young & Dudley Nichols. B/on the book *The Crusades: Iron Men and Saints* by Harold Lamb. C: Loretta Young, Henry Wilcoxon, Ian Keith, Katherine De Mille, C. Aubrey Smith, Joseph Schildkraut, Alan Hale, Ramsay Hill.

Henry Corden. *King Richard and the Crusaders* (US/1954/113m/C) D: David Butler. B/on the novel *The Talisman* by Sir Walter Scott. C: George Sanders, Rex Harrison, Virginia Mayo, Laurence Harvey, Robert Douglas, Michael Pate, Paula Raymond.

Timothy Dalton. *The Lion in Winter* (GB/1968/134m/C) D: Anthony Harvey. B/on the play by James Goldman. Best Picture (GG [Drama] NYC). Best Director (DGA). C: Peter O'Toole, Katharine Hepburn, Jane Merrow, John Castle, Anthony Hopkins, Nigel Terry, Nigel Stock, Kenneth Griffith.

616 Charles VI (1368–1422, r. 1380–1422)

Harcourt Williams. *Henry V* (GB/1945/127m/C) D: Laurence Olivier. B/on the play by Wm. Shakespeare. Best Picture (NBR). Special Academy Award to Laurence Olivier "for his outstanding achievement as actor, producer and director." C: Laurence Olivier, Robert Newton, Leslie Banks, Renee Asherson, Esmond Knight, Max Adrian.

Paul Scofield. *Henry V* (GB/1989/138m/C) D: Kenneth Branagh. B/on the play by Wm. Shakespeare. Best Director (NBR). Best New Director (NYC). C: Kenneth Branagh, Derek Jacobi, Brian Blessed, Alec McCowen, Ian Holm, Michael Williams, Richard Briers, Robert Stephens, Robbie Coltrane, Judi Dench, Michael Maloney.

617 Charles VII (1403–1461, r. 1422–1461)

Gustaf Gründgens. *Das Mädchen Johanna* (Germany/1935/BW) D: Gustav Ucicky. C: Angela Salloker, Rene Deltgen, Heinrich George, Erich Pante.

Max Adrian. *Henry V* (GB/1945/127m/C) D: Laurence Olivier. B/on the play by Wm. Shakespeare. Best Picture (NBR). Special Academy Award to Laurence Olivier "for his outstanding achievement as actor, producer and director." C: Laurence Olivier, Robert Newton, Leslie Banks, Renee Asherson, Esmond Knight, Harcourt Williams.

Jose Ferrer. *Joan of Arc* (US/1948/145–100m/C) D: Victor Fleming. B/on the play *Joan of Lorraine* by Maxwell Anderson. C: Ingrid Bergman, Hurd Hatfield, Ward Bond.

Richard Widmark. *Saint Joan* (US/1957/110m/BW) D: Otto Preminger. B/on the play by George Bernard Shaw. C: Jean Seberg, Richard Todd, Anton Walbrook.

Michael Maloney. *Henry V* (GB/1989/138m/C) D: Kenneth Branagh. B/on the play by Wm. Shakespeare. Best Director (NBR). Best New Director (NYC). C: Kenneth Branagh, Derek Jacobi, Brian Blessed, Alec McCowen, Ian Holm, Michael Williams, Richard Briers, Robert Stephens, Robbie Coltrane, Judi Dench, Paul Scofield.

André Marcon. *Jeanne la Pucelle 1. Les batailles* (aka *Joan the Maid 1.: The Battles*) (France/1994/160m/C) D: Jacques Rivette. C: Tatiana Moukhine, Sandrine Bonnaire, Jean-Marie Richier, Baptiste Roussillon, Jean-Luc Petit, Bernadette Giraud, Jean-Claude Jay, Olivier Cruveiller, Benjamin Rataud, Cyril Haouzi, Réginald Huguenin, Patrick Adomian, Nicolas Vian, Jean-Louis Richard.

André Marcon. *Jeanne la Pucelle 2. Les prisons* (aka *Joan the Maid 2.: The Prisons*) (France/1994/176m/C) D: Jacques Rivette. C: Sandrine Bonnaire, Jean-Louis Richard, Marcel Bozonnet, Patrick Le Mauff, Didier Sauvegrain, Jean-Pierre Lorit, Bruno Wolkowitch, Florence Darel, Nathalie Richard, Yann Collette, Edith Scob, Hélène de Fougerolles, Monique Mélinand, Olivier Cruveiller.

John Malkovich. *The Messenger: The Story of Joan of Arc* (aka *Jeanne d'Arc*) (France/1999/180m/Color) D: Luc Besson. C: Milla Jovovich, Faye Dunaway, Dustin Hoffman, Pascal Greggory, Vincent Cassel, Tchéky Karyo, Richard Ridings, Desmond Harrington, Timothy West, Andrew Birkin, Philippe du Janerand, Christian Erickson, Mathieu Kassovitz, Gina McKee, John Merrick, Olivier Rabourdin.

618 Louis XI (1423–1483, r. 1461–1483)

O.P. Heggie. *The Vagabond King* (US/1930/104m/C) D: Ludwig Berger. B/on the operetta by William H. Post, Brian Hooker & Rudolph Friml, and the play *If I Were King* by Justin Huntly McCarthy. C: Dennis King, Jeanette MacDonald, Lillian Roth.

Basil Rathbone. *If I Were King* (US/1938/100m/BW) D: Frank Lloyd. B/on the play by Justin Huntly McCarthy. C: Ronald Colman, Frances Dee, Ellen Drew.

Harry Davenport. *The Hunchback of Notre Dame* (US/1939/115m/BW) D: William Dieterle. C: Charles Laughton, Cedric Hardwicke, Thomas Mitchell, Maureen O'Hara, Edmund O'Brien, Alan Marshal, Walter Hampden, George Zucco, Curt Bois, George Tobias, Rod LaRoque.

Sacha Guitry. *If Paris Were Told to Us* (France/1955/135m/C) D: Sacha Guitry. C: Danielle Darrieaux, Jean Marais, Robert Lamoureaux, Michelle Morgan, Lana Marconi, Jeanne Boitel, Gilbert Boka, Renee Saint-Cyr, Gerard Philipe.

Robert Morley. *Quentin Durward* (US/1955/101m/C) D: Richard Thorpe. B/on the character created by Sir Walter Scott. C: Robert Taylor, Kay Kendall, George Cole, Alec Clunes, Duncan Lamont, Marius Goring.

Walter Hampden. *The Vagabond King* (US/1956/88m/C) D: Michael Curtiz. B/on the operetta by William H. Post, Brian Hooker & Rudolph Friml, and the play *If I Were King* by Justin Huntly McCarthy. C: Kathryn Grayson, Oreste, Rita Moreno, Leslie Nielsen.

Jean Tissier. *The Hunchback of Notre Dame* (US/1957/104m/C) D: Jean Delannoy. C: Gina Lollobrigida, Anthony Quinn, Jean Danet, Alain Cuny.

619 Louis XII (1462–1515, r. 1498–1515)

Jean Mercure. *The Sword and the Rose* (aka *When Knighthood Was in Flower*) (GB/1953/91m/C) D: Ken Annakin. B/on the novel *When Knighthood Was in Flower* by Charles Major. C: Richard Todd, Glynis Johns, James Robertson Justice, Michael Gough, Jane Barrett, Rosalie Crutchley, Peter Copley, D.A. Clarke-Smith, Bryan Coleman.

620 François I (1494–1547, r. 1515–1547)

Aime-Simon Girard. *Francis The First* (aka *François 1st*) (France/1937/BW) D: Christian-Jaque. C: Fernandel, Mona Goya, Alexandre Rignault, Henri Bosc, Sinoel, Mihalesco.

Sacha Guitry. *The Pearls of the Crown* (France/1937/120–100m/BW) D: Sacha Guitry & Christian-Jaque. C: Jacqueline Delubac, Lyn Harding, Ermete Zacconi, Marguerite Moreno, Yvette Plenne, Catalano, Arletty, Percy Marmont, Derrick De Marney, Barbara Shaw, Simone Renant, Jean Louis Barrault, Emile Drain, Enrico Glori, Renee Saint-Cyr, Pizani, Claude Dauphin, Aime-Simon Gerard.

Pedro Armendariz. *Diane* (US/1955/110m/C) D: David Miller. B/on the novel *Diane de Poitier* by John Erskine. C: Lana Turner, Roger Moore, Marisa Pavan, Cedric Hardwicke, Ronald Green, Torin Thatcher, Henry Daniell, Basil Ruysdael.

Jean Marais. *If Paris Were Told to Us* (France/1955/135m/C) D: Sacha Guitry.

C: Danielle Darrieaux, Robert Lamoureaux, Sacha Guitry, Michelle Morgan, Lana Marconi, Jeanne Boitel, Gilbert Boka, Renee Saint-Cyr, Gerard Philipe.

Peter Gilmore. *Carry on Henry VIII* (GB/1970/89m/C) D: Gerald Thomas. C: Sidney James, Kenneth Williams, Joan Sims, Charles Hawtrey, Terry Scott, Monica Dietrich, Patsy Rowlands.

621 Henri II (1519–1559, r. 1547–1559)

Roger Moore. *Diane* (US/1955/110m/C) D: David Miller. B/on the novel *Diane de Poitier* by John Erskine. C: Lana Turner, Pedro Armendariz, Marisa Pavan, Cedric Hardwicke, Ronald Green, Torin Thatcher, Henry Daniell, Basil Ruysdael.

Raymond Gerome. *La Princesse de Cléves* (France/1961/115m/C) D: Jean Delannoy. B/on the novel by Madame De La Fayette. C: Jean Marais, Annie Ducaux, Lea Padovani.

Anthony Higgins. *Nostradamus* (GB-Germany/1994/118m/C) D: Roger Christian. C: Tcheky Karyo, Amanda Plummer, F. Murray Abraham, Rutger Hauer, Diana Quick.

622 François II (1544–1560, r. 1559–1560)

Ronald Green. *Diane* (US/1955/110m/C) D: David Miller. B/on the novel *Diane de Poitier* by John Erskine. C: Lana Turner, Pedro Armendariz, Roger Moore, Marisa Pavan, Cedric Hardwicke, Torin Thatcher, Henry Daniell, Basil Ruysdael.

Richard Denning. *Mary, Queen of Scots* (GB/1971/128m/C) D: Charles Jarrot. C: Vanessa Redgrave, Glenda Jackson, Patrick McGoohan, Timothy Dalton, Nigel Davenport, Trevor Howard, Daniel Massey, Ian Holm, Andrew Keir, Katherine Kath, Robert James, Rick Warner.

623 Charles IX (1550–1574, r. 1560–1574)

Robert Porte. *La Reine Margot* (France-Italy/1954/125m/C) D: Jean Dreville. B/on a novel by Alexandre Dumas. C: Jeanne Moreau, Armando Francioli, Francoise Rosay, Henri Genes, Andre Versini, Danile Ceccaldi, Nicole Riche.

Jean-Hugues Anglade. *Queen Margot* (aka *La Reine Margot*) (France-Germany-Italy/1994/159–143m/C) D: Patrice Chareau. B/on the novel by Alexandre Dumas. C: Isabelle Adjani, Vincent Perez, Virna Lisi, Daniel Auteuil, Pascal Greggory.

624 Henri III (1551–1589, r. 1574–1589)

Danile Ceccaldi. *La Reine Margot* (France-Italy/1954/125m/C) D: Jean Dreville. B/on a novel by Alexandre Dumas. C: Jeanne Moreau, Armando Francioli, Francoise Rosay, Henri Genes, Robert Porte, Andre Versini, Nicole Riche.

Pascal Greggory. *Queen Margot* (aka *La Reine Margot*) (France-Germany-Italy/1994/159–143m/C) D: Patrice Chareau. B/on the novel by Alexandre Dumas. C: Isabelle Adjani, Vincent Perez, Virna Lisi, Jean-Hugues Anglade, Daniel Auteuil.

625 Henri IV (1553–1610, r. 1589–1610)

Aime-Simon Girard. *The Pearls of the Crown* (France/1937/120–100m/BW) D: Sacha Guitry & Christian-Jaque. C: Sacha Guitry, Jacqueline Delubac, Lyn Harding, Ermete Zacconi, Marguerite Moreno, Yvette Plenne, Catalano, Arletty, Percy Marmont, Derrick De Marney, Barbara Shaw, Simone Renant, Jean Louis Barrault, Emile Drain, Enrico Glori, Renee Saint-Cyr, Pizani, Claude Dauphin.

Gaston Rey. *Royal Affairs in Versailles* (aka *Versailles*) (aka *Affairs in Versailles*) (aka *If Versailles Were Told to Me*) (aka *Si Versailles M'Était Couté*) (France/1953/180–152m/C) D: Sacha Guitry. C: Sacha Guitry, Claudette Colbert, Orson Welles, Gerard Phillippe, Micheline Presle, Jean Marais, Georges Marchal, Gilbert Boka, Lana Marconi, Gino Cervi, Fernand Gravet, Louis Arbessier, Jacques Berthier, Samson Fainsilber, Gilbert Gil, Emile Drain, Jacques de Feraudy, Philippe Richard.

Andre Versini. *La Reine Margot* (France-Italy/1954/125m/C) D: Jean Dreville. B/on a novel by Alexandre Dumas. C: Jeanne Moreau, Armando Francioli, Francoise Rosay, Henri Genes, Robert Porte, Danile Ceccaldi, Nicole Riche.

Daniel Auteuil. *Queen Margot* (aka *La Reine Margot*) (France-Germany-Italy/1994/159–143m/C) D: Patrice Chareau. B/on the novel by Alexandre Dumas. C: Isabelle Adjani, Vincent Perez, Virna Lisi, Jean-Hugues Anglade, Pascal Greggory.

626 Louis XIV (1638–1715, r. 1643–1715)

William Bakewell. *The Iron Mask* (US/1929/95m/BW) D: Allan Dwan. B/on *The Three Musketeers* and *The Viscount of Bragelonne* by Alexandre Dumas. C: Douglas Fairbanks, Belle Bennett, Dorothy Revier, Rolfe Sedan, Nigel De Brulier.

Randle Ayrton. *Me and Marlborough* (GB/1935/80m/BW) D: Victor Saville. C: Cicely Courtneidge, Tom Walls, Iris Ashley, Ivor McLaren, Gibb McLaughlin, Cecil Parker.

Michael Bohnen. *The Private Life of Louis XIV* (Germant/1936/95mBW) D: Carl Froelich. C: Hilde Hildebrand, Eugene Klopfer, Hans Stuewe, Dorothea Wieck, Ida Wuest.

Louis Hayward. *The Man in the Iron Mask* (US/1939/110m/BW) D: James Whale. B/on the novel by Alexandre Dumas. C: Joan Bennett, Warren William, Joseph Schildkraut, Alan Hale, Miles Mander, Walter Kingsford, Albert Dekker, Doris Kenyon, Nigel De Brulier.

Peter Miles. *At Sword's Point* (aka *Sons of the Musketeers*) (US/1951/81m/C) D: Lewis Allen. C: Cornel Wilde, Maureen O'Hara, Robert Douglas, Gladys Cooper.

Sacha Guitry. Georges Marchal. *Royal Affairs in Versailles* (aka *Versailles*) (aka *Affairs in Versailles*) (aka *If Versailles Were Told to Me*) (aka *Si Versailles M'Était Couté*) (France/1953/180–152m/C) D: Sacha Guitry. C: Claudette Colbert, Orson Welles, Gerard Phillippe, Micheline Presle, Jean Marais, Gilbert Boka, Lana Marconi, Gino Cervi, Fernand Gravet, Louis Arbessier, Jacques Berthier, Samson Fainsilber, Gilbert Gil, Emile Drain, Jacques de Feraudy, Gaston Rey, Philippe Richard.

Basil Sydney. *Star of India* (GB/1953/92m/C) D: Arthut Lubin. C: Cornell Wilde, Jean Wallace, Herbert Lom, Yvonne Sanson.

Jean-François Poron. *Le Masque de Fer* (aka *The Iron Mask*) (France-Italy/1962/130m/C) D: Henri Decoin. B/on the novel *The Man in the Iron Mask* by Alexandre Dumas. C: Jean Marais, Claudine Auger, Enrico-Maria Salerno, Jean Rochefort.

Jean-Marie Patte. *The Rise of Louis XIV* (France/1966/100m/BW) D: Roberto Rossellini. C: Raymond Jourdan, Silvagni, Katherina Renn, Dominique Vincent, Pierre Barrat.

Jean-Claude Penchena. *Moliére* (France/1975/255m/C) D: Ariane Mnouchkine. C: Philippe Caubere, Marie-France Audollent, Jonathan Sutton, Frederic Ladonne.

Beau Bridges. *The Fifth Musketeer* (aka *Behind the Iron Mask*) (Austria/1979/103–90m/C) D: Ken Annakin. B/on the novel *The Man in the Iron Mask* by Alexandre Dumas. C: Sylvia Kristel, Ursula Andress, Cornel Wilde, Olivia de Havilland, Ian McShane, Alan Hale Jr, Helmut Dantine, Jose Ferrer, Rex Harrison.

Leonardo DiCaprio. *Man in the Iron Mask* (US-GB/1998/132m/C) D: Randall Wallace. B/on the novel by Alexandre Dumas. C: Jeremy Irons, John Malkovich, Gérard Depardieu, Gabriel Byrne, Anne Parillaud, Judith Godrèche, Edward Atterton, Peter Sarsgaard, Hugh Laurie, David Lowe, Brigitte Boucher, Karine Belly, Emmanuel Guttierez.

Nick Richert. *The Man in the Iron Mask* (US/1998/85m/C) D: William Richert. B/on the novel by Alexandre Dumas. C: Edward Albert, Dana Barron, Timothy Bottoms, Brigid Conley Walsh, Fannie Brett, Meg Foster, James Gammon, Dennis Hayden, William Richert, Rex Ryon, Brenda James, R.G. Armstrong, Robert Tena, Daniel J. Coplan.

Julian Sands. *Vatel* (France-GB/2000/117m/C) D: Roland Joffee. B/on a 17th century story, English adaptation by Tom Stoppard. C: Gerard Depardieu, Uma Thurman, Tim Roth, Timothy Spall, Nathalie Cerda.

627 Louis XV (1710–1774, r. 1715–1774)

William Farnum. *Du Barry, Woman of Passion* (US/1930/88m/BW) D: Sam Taylor. B/on the play by David Belasco. C: Norma Talmadge, Hobart Bosworth, Conrad Nagel.

Kurt Gerron. *Die Marquise von Pompadour* (Germany/1930/92m/BW) D: Willi Wolff. C: Anny Ahlers.

Reginald Owen. *Voltaire* (US/1933/72m/BW) D: John G. Adolfi. B/on the novel by George Gibbs & E. Lawrence. C: George Arliss, Doris Kenyon, Margaret Lindsay.

Reginald Owen. *Madame du Barry* (US/1934/79m/BW) D: William Dieterle. C: Dolores Del Rio, Victor Jory, Osgood Perkins, Verree Teasdale, Anita Louise, Maynard Holmes.

Owen Nares. *I Give My Heart* (aka *The Loves of Madame du Barry*) (aka *Give Me Your Heart*) (GB/1935/90m/BW) D: Marcel Varnel. B/on the opera "The Dubarry" by Paul Knepler & J.M. Welleminsky. C: Gitta Alper, Patrick Waddington, Arthur Margeston, Hugh Miller, Hay Petrie.

Alfred Neugebauer. *The King Smiles—Paris Laughs* (aka *Der Postillon von Lonjumeau*) (aka *Der König Lächelt—Paris Lacht*) (Germany/1936/91m/BW) D: Carl

Lamac. B/on an operetta by Adolf Adam. C: Thekla Ahrens, Leo Slezak, Willy Eichberger, Rudolf Carl.

Sacha Guitry. *Champs-Elysées* (aka *Remontons Les Champs-Elysées*) (France/1938/100m/BW) D: Sacha Guitry. C: Lucien Baroux, Jacqueline Delubac, Germaine Dermoz, Jeanne Boitel, Raymonde Allain, Jean Davy, Emile Drain, Jacques Erwin, Rene Fauchois, Liane Pathe, Robert Pizani, Claude Martin, Raymond Galle, Andre Laurent.

John Barrymore. *Marie Antoinette* (US/1938/160m/BW) D: W.S. Van Dyke II. B/on the book by Stefan Zweig. C: Norma Shearer, Tyrone Power, Gladys George, Robert Morley, Anita Louise, Joseph Schildkraut, Albert Dekker, Scotty Becket, Alma Kruger, George Meeker, Wade Crosby, Anthony Warde, Walter Walker, John Burton.

Red Skelton. *Du Barry Was a Lady* (US/1943/96m/C) D: Roy Del Ruth. B/on the play by B.G. De Sylva & Herbert Fields. C: Lucille Ball, Gene Kelly, Zero Mostel, Rags Ragland.

Reginald Owen. *Monsieur Beaucaire* (US/1946/93m/BW) D: George Marshall. B/on the novel by Booth Tarkington. C: Bob Hope, Joan Caulfield, Patric Knowles, Marjorie Reynolds, Hillary Brooke, Douglas Dumbrille, Howard Freeman.

Robert Atkins. *Black Magic* (US/1949/105m/BW) D: Gregory Ratoff. B/on the novel *Joseph Balsamo* by Alexandre Dumas. C: Orson Welles, Nancy Guild, Akim Tamiroff, Raymond Burr, Margot Grahame, Berry Kroeger, Charles Goldner, Lee Kresel.

Marcel Herrand. *Fanfan the Tulip* (France/1952/104m/BW) D: Christian-Jaque. C: Gerard Philipe, Gina Lollobrigida, Genevieve Page, Noel Roquevert, Henri Rollan.

Jean Marais. *Royal Affairs in Versailles* (aka *Versailles*) (aka *Affairs in Versailles*) (aka *If Versailles Were Told to Me*) (aka *Si Versailles M'Était Couté*) (France/1953/180–152m/C) D: Sacha Guitry. C: Sacha Guitry, Claudette Colbert, Orson Welles, Gerard Phillippe, Micheline Presle, Georges Marchal, Gilbert Boka, Lana Marconi, Gino Cervi, Fernand Gravet, Louis Arbessier, Jacques Berthier, Samson Fainsilber, Gilbert Gil, Emile Drain, Jacques de Feraudy, Gaston Rey, Philippe Richard.

Andre Luguet. *Madame du Barry* (aka *Mistress du Barry*) (France-Italy/1954/110m/C) D: Christian-Jaque. C: Martine Carol, Daniel Ivernel, Isabelle Pia, Dennis Gianna Maria Canale, Massimo Serato, Denis d'Ines, Jean Paredes.

Michel Serrault. *Beaumarchais the Scoundrel* (France/1996/101m/C) D: Edouard Molinaro. Inspired by an unpublished manuscript of Sacha Guitry. C: Fabrice Luchini, Manuel Blanc, Sandrine Kiberlane, Jacques Weber, Dominique Besnehard, Murray Head, Judith Godreche, Jeff Nuttall.

628 Louis XVII (1785–1795?)

Scotty Beckett. *Marie Antoinette* (US/1938/160m/BW) D: W.S. Van Dyke II. B/on the book by Stefan Zweig. C: Norma Shearer, Tyrone Power, John Barrymore, Gladys George, Robert Morley, Anita Louise, Joseph Schildkraut, Albert Dekker, Alma Kruger, George Meeker, Wade Crosby, Anthony Warde, Walter Walker, John Burton.

Richard O'Sullivan. *Dangerous Exile* (GB/1958/90m/C) D: Brian Desmond Hurst. C: Louis Jourdan, Belinda Lee, Keith Mitchell.

Damien Groelle. *Jefferson in Paris* (US/1995/144m/C) D: James Ivory. C: Nick Nolte, Greta Scacchi, Jean-Pierre Aumont, Simon Callow, Seth Gilliam, James Earl Jones, Michael Lonsdale, Gwyneth Paltrow, Lambert Wilson, Charlotte de Turckheim.

629 Louis XVIII (1755–1824, r. 1814–1824)

Ferdinand Munier. *The Count of Monte Cristo* (US/1934/113m/BW) D: Rowland V. Lee. B/on the novel by Alexandre Dumas. C: Robert Donat, Elissa Landi, Louis Calhern, Clarence Wilson, Paul Irving, Sidney Blackmer, Luis Alberni.

Allan Aynesworth. *The Iron Duke* (GB/1935/80m/BW) D: Victor Saville. C: George Arliss, Gladys Cooper, Emlyn Williams, Ellaline Terriss, Felix Aylmer, Gerald Lawrence, Gibb McLaughlin, Frederick Leister, Edmund Willard, Farren Soutar.

Ernesto Marini. *Campo di Maggio* (aka *100 Days of Napoleon*) (Italy/1936/100m/BW) D: Giovacchino Forzano. C: Corrado Racca, Emilia Varini, Pino Locchi, Rosa Stradner, Enzo Biliotti, Lamberto Picasso, Augusto Marcacci.

Orson Welles. *Waterloo* (Italy-USSR/1970/123m/C) D: Sergei Bondarchuk. C: Rod Steiger, Virginia McKenna, Michael Wilding, Donal Donnelly, Christopher Plummer, Jack Hawkins, Dan O'Herlihy, Rupert Davies, Aldo Cecconi, Rodolfo Lodi.

630 Charles X (1757–1836, r. 1824–1830)

Aldo Cecconi. *Waterloo* (Italy-USSR/1970/123m/C) D: Sergei Bondarchuk. C: Rod Steiger, Orson Welles, Virginia McKenna, Michael Wilding, Donal Donnelly, Christopher Plummer, Jack Hawkins, Dan O'Herlihy, Rupert Davies, Rodolfo Lodi.

631 Louis Philippe (1773–1850, r. 1830–1848)

Philippe Richard. *Royal Affairs in Versailles* (aka *Versailles*) (aka *Affairs in Versailles*) (aka *If Versailles Were Told to Me*) (aka *Si Versailles M'Était Couté*) (France/1953/180–152m/C) D: Sacha Guitry. C: Sacha Guitry, Claudette Colbert, Orson Welles, Gerard Phillippe, Micheline Presle, Jean Marais, Georges Marchal, Gilbert Boka, Lana Marconi, Gino Cervi, Fernand Gravet, Louis Arbessier, Jacques Berthier, Samson Fainsilber, Gilbert Gil, Emile Drain, Jacques de Feraudy, Gaston Rey.

Appendix D: Russian Czars and Czarinas

Listed below in chronological order are film portrayals of some of the people who have ruled Russia as Czar or Czarina since 1533. See the Portrayals section for major entries on **Alexandra**, **Catherine the Great**, and **Nicholas II**.

632 Ivan IV (The Terrible) (1530–1584, r. 1533–1584)
Nikolai Cherkasov. *Ivan the Terrible Part I* (USSR/1943/96m/BW) D: Sergei Eisenstein. C: Ludmilla Tselikovskaya, Serafina Berman.

Nikolai Cherkasov. *Ivan the Terrible Part II* (USSR/1946/88m/BW) D: Sergei Eisenstein. C: Serafina Berman, Mikhail Nazvanov, Pavel Kadochnikov, Andrei Abrikosov.

Pyotr Glebov. *The Czar's Bride* (USSR/1966/95m/BW) D: Vladimir Gorikker. B/on an opera by Rimsky-Korsakov. C: Otar Koberidza, Raisa Nedashkovskaya, Natalya Rudnaya.

633 Boris Godunov (1551?–1605, r. 1598–1605)
A. Pirogov. *Boris Godunov* (USSR/1959/105m/BW) D: V. Stroyeva. B/on the opera by Moussorgksy. C: L. Audeyeva, I. Kozlovsky, A Krivchenva, G. Nellep.

634 Elizabeth (1709–1762, r. 1741–1762)
Flora Robson. *Catherine the Great* (aka *The Rise of Catherine the Great*) (GB/1934/94m/BW) D: Paul Czinner. B/on the play *The Czarina* by Melchior Lengyel & Lajos Biro. C: Elisabeth Bergner, Douglas Fairbanks, Jr., Gerald du Maurier.

Louise Dresser. *The Scarlet Empress* (US/1934/110m/BW) D: Josef von Sternberg. C: Marlene Dietrich, John Lodge, Sam Jaffe, Maria Sieber, Ruthelma Stevens, Gavin Gordon.

Agnes Straub. *Fridericus* (Germany/1936/98m/BW) D: Johannes Meyer. B/on the novel by Walter von Molo. C: Otto Gebuhr, Hilde Korber, Lil Dagover, Kathe Haack.

635 Peter III (1728–1762, r. 1762)

Douglas Fairbanks, Jr. *Catherine the Great* (aka *The Rise of Catherine the Great*) (GB/1934/94m/BW) D: Paul Czinner. B/on the play *The Czarina* by Melchior Lengyel & Lajos Biro. C: Elisabeth Bergner, Flora Robson, Gerald du Maurier.

Sam Jaffe. *The Scarlet Empress* (US/1934/110m/BW) D: Josef von Sternberg. C: Marlene Dietrich, John Lodge, Louise Dresser, Maria Sieber, Ruthelma Stevens, Gavin Gordon.

636 Paul I (1754–1801, r. 1796–1801)

Mikhail Yanshin. *The Czar Wants to Sleep* (USSR/1934/80m/BW) D: Alexander Feinzimmer.

Harry Baur. *The Patriot* (US-USSR/1928/113m/BW) D: Ernst Lubitsch. C: Harry Cording, Neil Hamilton, Emil Jannings, Lewis Stone, Florence Vidor, Vera Voronina.

637 Alexander I (1777–1825, r. 1801–1825)

Neil Hamilton. *The Patriot* (US-USSR/1928/113m/BW) D: Ernst Lubitsch. C: Harry Cording, Harry Bauer, Emil Jannings, Lewis Stone, Florence Vidor, Vera Voronina.

Henri Garat. *Congress Dances* (aka *Der Kongress Tanzt*) (Germany/1931/92m/BW) D: Eric Charell. C: Lilian Harvey, Conrad Veidt, Humberstone Wright.

Vladimir Galderow. *Luise, Königin von Preussen* (Germany/1931/112m/BW) D: Carl Froelich. B/on the novel Luise by Walter von Molo. C: Henny Porten, Paul Gunther, Ekkehard Arendt, Gustaf Gründgens.

Gerald Lawrence. *The Iron Duke* (GB/1935/80m/BW) D: Victor Saville. C: George Arliss, Gladys Cooper, Emlyn Williams, Ellaline Terriss, Allan Aynesworth, Felix Aylmer, Gibb McLaughlin, Frederick Leister, Edmund Willard, Farren Soutar.

Otto Woegerer. *Die Nacht Mit Dem Kaiser* (Germany/1936/BW) D: Erich Engel. C: Jenny Jugo, Richard Romanowski, Friedrich Benfer, Hans Zesch-Ballot, Paul Henckels.

N. Timchenko. *1812* (aka *Kutuzov*) (USSR/1944/95m/B&W) D: Vladimir Petrov. C: Aleksei Diki, Sergei Mezhinsky, Y. Kaluzhsky, Sergo Zaqariadze, Nikolai Okhlopkov, Sergei Blinnikov, V. Gotovtsev, A. Polyakov, Nikolai Brilling, Boris Chirkov, Mikhail Pugovkin, Ivan Ryzhov, K. Shilovtsev, Aleksandr Stepanov, Ivan Skuratov, G. Terekhov, Vladimir Yershov.

Rudolf Prack. *Congress Dances* (Germany/1955/79m/BW) D: Franz Antel. C: Johanna Matz, Karl Schonbock, Hannelore Bollmann, Jester Naefe, Marte Harell.

Savo Raskovitch. *War and Peace* (US-Italy/1956/208m/C) D: King Vidor. B/on the novel by Leo Tolstoy. C: Audrey Hepburn, Henry Fonda, Mel Ferrer, Vittorio Gassman, John Mills, Herbert Lom, Oscar Homolka, Anita Ekberg, Helmut Dantin.

Bernhard Wicki. *Queen Luise* (aka *Königin Luise*) (Germany/1957/102m/C) D: Wolfgang Liebeneiner. C: Ruth Leuwerik, Rene Deltgen, Dieter Borsche, Charles Regnier.

Curt Jurgens. *Der Kongress Amüsiert Sich* (Germany-Austria/1966/98m/C) D: Geza von Radvanvi. C: Lilli Palmer, Paul Meurisse, Hannes Messemer, Wolfgang Kieling, Brett Halsey.

V. Murganov. *War and Peace* (USSR/1966/373m/C) D: Sergei Bondarchuk. B/on the novel by Leo Tolstoy. C: Lyudmila Savelyeva, Sergei Bondarchuk, Viktor Stanitsin, Vyacheslav Tihonov, Hira Ivanov-Gubanova, Boris Zakhava, Vladislav Strzhelchik.

638 Nicholas I (1796–1855, r. 1825–1855)

Bos Ranevsky. *Balaclava* (aka *Jaws of Hell*) (GB/1930/94m/BW) D: Maurice Elvey & Milton Rosmer. B/on *The Charge of the Light Brigade* by Alfred Lord Tennyson. Made as a silent in 1928, with sound added in 1930. C: Benita Hume, Cyril McLaglen, J. Fisher White, Wallace Bosco, Marian Drada, Eugene Leahy.

N. Viteftof. *House of Death* (aka *The House of the Dead*) (USSR/1932/73m/BW) D: V. Fyodorov. B/on the novel by Fyodor Dostoyevsky. C: Nikolai Khmelyov, N. Podgorn.

Boris Livanov. *The Great Glinka* (aka *Glinka*) (USSR/1946/100m/BW) D: Leo Arnstam. C: Boris Chorkov, Sasha Sobolyev, Valentina Serova, Peter Aleynikov.

Mikhail Nazvanov. *Man of Music* (aka *Glinka*) (USSR/1952/100m/C) D: Grigori Alexandrov. C: Boris Smirnov, Lubov Orlova, L. Durasov, Svyatoslav Richter, B. Vinogradova.

639 Alexander II (1818–1881, r. 1855–1881)

Fritz Albertl. *Ein Liebesroman Im Hause Habsburg* (aka *Das Geheimnis Um Johannes Orth*) (Germany/1936/81m/BW) D: Willi Wolff. C: Paul Otto, Paul Richter, Karl Ludwig Diehl, Paul Wegener.

John Hamilton. *Song of My Heart* (US/1947/85m/BW) D: Benjamin Glazer. C: Frank Sundstrom, Audrey Lang, Cedric Hardwicke, David Leonard, Lewis Howard, Robert Barron.

Rudolf Lenz. *The Story of Vickie* (aka *Young Victoria.* (aka *Dover Interlude*) (aka *Girl Days of a Queen*) (aka *Mädchenjahre Einer Königin*) (Austria/1955/108–90m/C) D: Ernst Marischka. B/on the diaries of Queen Victoria. C: Romy Schneider, Adrian Hoven, Magda Schneider, Karl Ludwig Diehl, Christl Mardayn, Paul Horbiger, Alfred Neugebauer, Otto Tressler, Fred Liewehr, Eduard Strauss, Peter Weck.

Massimo Girotti. *The Cossacks* (Italy/1959/113m/C) D: Georgio Rivalta. C: John Drew Barrymore, Edmund Purdom, Georgia Moll.

Curt Jurgens. *The Magnificent Sinner* (France/1959/97m/C) D: Robert Siodmak. C: Romy Schneider, Pierre Blanchar, Monique Melinand.

Hans Unterkirchner. *Song Without End* (US/1960/145m/C) D: George Cukor & Charles Vidor. C: Dirk Bogarde, Capucine, Genevieve Page, Patricia Morison, Ivan Desny, Martita Hunt, Lou Jacobi, Lyndon Brook, E. Erlandsen, Alex Davion, Katherine Squire.

Appendix E:
Germany's Last Monarch,
Kaiser Wilhelm II

Listed below are film portrayals of Germany's last monarch, who was also the cousin of King George V of England and **Czar Nicholas II** of Russia.

640 Wilhelm II (1859–1941, r. 1888–1918)

Werner Hinz. *Die Entlassung* (aka *The Dismissal*) (Germany/1942/BW) D: Wolfgang Liebeneiner. C: Emil Jannings, Karl Diehl, Otto Hasse, Fritz Kampers, Werner Krauss, Theodor Loos.

John Mylong. *Annie Get Your Gun* (US/1950/107m/C) D: George Sidney. B/on the musical play, book by Herbert and Dorothy Fields. C: Betty Hutton, Howard Keel, Louis Calhern, J. Carrol Naish, Chief Yowlachie, Evelyn Beresford, Nino Pipitone.

O.E. Hasse. *Adventures of Arsene Lupin* (France-Italy-USA/1956/103m/C) D: Jacques Becker. C: Robert Lamoureaux, Lilo (Liselotte) Pulver, Henri Rollan.

Kenneth More. *Oh! What a Lovely War* (GB/1969/144m/C) D: Richard Attenborough. B/on the musical play by Joan Littlewood and the play *The Long, Long Trail* by Charles Chilton. Best English Language Foreign Film (GG), and the United Nations Award (BFA). C: Pamela Abbott, Jack Hawkins, Laurence Olivier, Ralph Richardson, John Mills, John Gabriel, Paul Daneman, Dirk Bogarde, Vanessa Redgrave, Michael Redgrave, Ian Holm, Wensley Pithey, Frank Forsyth, John Gielgud, Maggie Smith, Guy Middleton.

Wolf Kahler. *The Riddle of the Sands* (GB/1979/102m/C) D: Tony Maylam. B/on the novel by Erskine Childers. C: Michael York, Jenny Agutter, Simon MacCorkindale, Alan Badel.

Appendix F: Western Series (Fictional)

There were two budget Western film series in the 1940s which used the names of actual figures for the main characters but which bore no relationship to historical occurrences: PRC's *Billy the Kid* series and Columbia's *Wild Bill Hickok* series.

Bob Steele starred in six of the *Billy the Kid* films before being replaced by Buster Crabbe in 1941. The series name was changed to "*Billy Carson*" when parental groups complained that the films were portraying an outlaw-murderer as a hero.

Bill Elliott (formerly Gordon Elliott) played the lead in all of Columbia's "*Wild Bill Hickok*" films. He later billed himself as "Wild Bill" Elliott.

For historic films (as opposed to the fictional below), see the Portrayals section under **Billy the Kid** and **Hickok, Wild Bill**.

Billy the Kid
Bob Steele. *Billy the Kid in Texas* (1940)
Bob Steele. *Billy the Kid Outlawed* (1940)
Bob Steele. *Billy the Kid's Gun Justice* (1940)
Bob Steele. *Billy the Kid in Santa Fe* (1941)
Bob Steele. *Billy the Kid's Fighting Pals* (1941)
Bob Steele. *Billy the Kid's Range War* (1941)
Buster Crabbe. *Billy the Kid Wanted* (1941)
Buster Crabbe. *Billy the Kid's Roundup* (1941)
Buster Crabbe. *Billy the Kid Trapped* (1942)
Buster Crabbe. *Billy the Kid's Smoking Guns* (aka *Smoking Guns*) (1942)
Buster Crabbe. *Law and Order* (1942)
Buster Crabbe. *Sheriff of Sage Valley* (1942)
Buster Crabbe. *The Mysterious Rider* (aka *Panhandle Trail*) (1942)
Buster Crabbe. *Cattle Stampede* (1943)

Buster Crabbe. *Fugitive of the Plains* (aka *Raiders of Red Rock*) (1943)
Buster Crabbe. *The Kid Rides Again* (1943)
Buster Crabbe. *The Renegade* (aka *Code of the Plains*) (1943)
Buster Crabbe. *Western Cyclone* (aka *Frontier Fighters*) (1943)
Buster Crabbe. *Blazing Frontier* 1944)

Hickok, Wild Bill

Bill Elliott. *Prairie Schooners* (1940)
Bill Elliott. *Across the Sierras* (1941)
Bill Elliott. *Beyond the Sacramento* (1941)
Bill Elliott. *King of Dodge City* (1941)
Bill Elliott. *North from Lone Star* (1941)
Bill Elliott. *Wildcat of Tucson* (1941)
Bill Elliott. *Bullets for Bandits* (1942)
Bill Elliott. *The Devil's Trail* (1942)
Bill Elliott. *The Lone Star Vigilantes* (1942)

Bibliography

Amberg, George. *New York Times Film Reviews: A One Volume Selection*. New York: Arno Press, Quadrangle Books, 1971.

Bergan, Ronald, and Robyn Karney. *The Holt Foreign Film Guide*. New York: Henry Holt & Company, 1988.

Blum, Daniel. *Screen World*. 17 vols. New York: Bilbo and Tannen, 1949–1965.

Brown, Gene, ed. *New York Times Encyclopedia of Film*. 12 vols. New York: Garland Publishing, Times Books, 1984.

Bucher, Felix. *Screen Series. Germany: An Illustrated Guide*. New York: A. S. Barnes, 1970.

Corey, Melinda, and George Ocha, comps. *A Cast of Thousands: A Compendium of Who Played What in Film*. 3 vols. New York: Stone Song Press, Facts on File, 1992.

Fetrow, Alan G. *Sound Films 1927–1939: A United States Filmography*. Jefferson, NC: McFarland & Company, 1992.

Garfield, Brian. *Western Films: A Complete Guide*. N.p.: Da Capo Press, 1982.

Hammer, Tad Bentley. *International Film Prizes: An Encyclopedia*. New York: Garland, 1991.

Hanson, Patricia King, ed. *The American Film Institute Catalog of Motion Pictures Produced in the United States 1931–1940*. 2 vols. Berkeley and Los Angeles: University of California Press, 1993.

Hibben, Nina. *Screen Series. Eastern Europe: An Illustrated Guide*. New York: A. S. Barnes, 1969.

Katz, Ephram. *The Film Encyclopedia*. 3rd ed. Revised by Fred Klein and Ronald Dean Nolan. New York: HarperCollins, Harper Perennial, 1998.

Nash, Jay Robert, and Stanley Ralph Ross. *The Motion Picture Guide 1927–1984*. Chicago: Cinebooks, 1987.

New York Times Film Reviews. 13 vols. (1913–1986). New York: Garland Publishing, Times Books.

Pitts, Michael R. *Hollywood and American History: A Filmography of Over 250*

Motion Pictures Depicting U.S. History. Jefferson, NC: McFarland & Company, 1984.

Pitts, Michael R. *Western Movies: A TV & Video Guide to 4200 Genre Films.* Jefferson, NC: McFarland & Company, 1986.

Quinlan, David. *British Sound Films: The Studio Years 1928–1959.* Totowa, New Jersey: Barnes and Noble, 1984.

Ringgold, Gene, and DeWitt Bodeen. *The Complete Films of Cecil B. De Mille.* Secaucus, NJ: The Citadel Press, 1969.

Walker, John, ed. *Halliwell's Film Guide 1994.* 9th ed. New York: HarperCollins, Harper Perennial, 1994.

Willis, John. *Screen World.* 7 vols. New York: Bilbo and Tannen, 1966–1972.

Willis, John. *Screen World.* 18 vols. New York: Crown, 1973–1990.

Willis, John. *Screen World.* 11 vols. Edited by Barry Monash. New York: Applause, 1991–2001.

Variety Film Reviews 1930–1984. 20 vols. New York: R.R. Bowker, Garland, 1984.

Index

References are to entry numbers.

414